T0332748

Multicore and GPU Programming
An Integrated Approach

Multicore and GPU Programming
An Integrated Approach

Gerassimos Barlas

AMSTERDAM • BOSTON • HEIDELBERG • LONDON
NEW YORK • OXFORD • PARIS • SAN DIEGO
SAN FRANCISCO • SINGAPORE • SYDNEY • TOKYO

Morgan Kaufmann is an imprint of Elsevier

Acquiring Editor: Todd Green
Developmental Editor: Nate McFadden
Project Manager: Punithavathy Govindaradjane
Designer: Mark Rogers

Morgan Kaufmann is an imprint of Elsevier
225 Wyman Street, Waltham, MA 02451, USA

ISBN: 978-0-12-417137-4

British Library Cataloguing in Publication Data
A catalogue record for this book is available from the British Library

Library of Congress Cataloging-in-Publication Data
A catalog record for this book is available from the Library of Congress

For information on all MK publications
visit our website at www.mkp.com

*Dedicated to my late parents for making it possible,
and my loving wife and children for making it worthwhile.*

Contents

List of Tables

Preface

Parallel computing has been given a fresh breath of life since the emergence of multicore architectures in the first decade of the new century. The new platforms demand a new approach to software development; one that blends the tools and established practices of the network-of-workstations era with emerging software platforms such as CUDA.

This book tries to address this need by covering the dominant contemporary tools and techniques, both in isolation and also most importantly in combination with each other. We strive to provide examples where multiple platforms and programming paradigms (e.g., message passing & threads) are effectively combined. "Hybrid" computation, as it is usually called, is a new trend in high-performance computing, one that could possibly allow software to scale to the "millions of threads" required for exascale performance.

All chapters are accompanied by extensive examples and practice problems with an emphasis on putting them to work, while comparing alternative design scenarios. All the little details, which can make the difference between a productive software development and a stressed exercise in futility, are presented in a orderly fashion.

The book covers the latest advances in tools that have been inherited from the 1990s (e.g., the OpenMP and MPI standards), but also more cutting-edge platforms, such as the Qt library with its sophisticated thread management and the Thrust template library with its capability to deploy the same software over diverse multicore architectures, including both CPUs and Graphical Processing Units (GPUs).

We could never accomplish the feat of covering all the tools available for multicore development today. Even some of the industry-standard ones, like POSIX threads, are omitted.

Our goal is to both sample the dominant paradigms (ranging from OpenMP's semi-automatic parallelization of sequential code to the explicit communication "plumbing" that underpins MPI), while at the same time explaining the rationale and how-to, behind efficient multicore program development.

WHAT IS IN THIS BOOK

This book can be separated in the following logical units, although no such distinction is made in the text:

- *Introduction, designing multicore software*: Chapter 1 introduces multicore hardware and examines influential instances of this architectural paradigm. Chapter 1 also introduces speedup and efficiency, which are essential metrics used in the evaluation of multicore and parallel software. Amdahl's law and Gustafson-Barsis's rebuttal cap-up the chapter, providing estimates of what can be expected from the exciting new developments in multicore and many-core hardware.

Chapter 2 is all about the methodology and the design patterns that can be employed in the development of parallel and multicore software. Both work decomposition patterns and program structure patterns are examined.

- *Shared-memory programming*: Two different approaches for shared-memory parallel programming are examined: explicit and implicit parallelization. On the explicit side, Chapter 3 covers threads and two of the most commonly used synchronization mechanisms, semaphores and monitors. Frequently encountered design patterns, such as producers-consumers and readers-writers, are explained thoroughly and applied in a range of examples.

  On the implicit side, Chapter 4 covers the OpenMP standard that has been specifically designed for parallelizing existing sequential code with minimum effort. Development time is significantly reduced as a result. There are still complications, such as loop-carried dependencies, which are also addressed.

- *Distributed memory programming*: Chapter 5 introduces the *de facto* standard for distributed memory parallel programming, i.e., the Message Passing Interface (MPI). MPI is relevant to multicore programming as it is designed to scale from a shared-memory multicore machine to a million-node supercomputer. As such, MPI provides the foundation for utilizing multiple disjoint multicore machines, as a single virtual platform.

  The features that are covered include both point-to-point and collective communication, as well as one-sided communication. A section is dedicated to the Boost.MPI library, as it does simplify the proceedings of using MPI, although it is not yet feature-complete.

- *GPU programming*: GPUs are one of the primary reasons why this book was put together. In a similar fashion to shared-memory programming, we examine the problem of developing GPU-specific software from two perspectives: on one hand we have the "nuts-and-bolts" approach of Nvidia's CUDA, where memory transfers, data placement, and thread execution configuration have to be carefully planned. CUDA is examined in Chapter 6.

  On the other hand, we have the high-level, algorithmic approach of the Thrust template library, which is covered in Chapter 7. The STL-like approach to program design affords Thrust the ability to target both CPUs and GPU platforms, a unique feature among the tools we cover.

- *Load balancing* : Chapter 8 is dedicated to an often under-estimated aspect of multicore development. In general, load balancing has to be seriously considered once heterogeneous computing resources come into play. For example, a CPU and a GPU constitute such a set of resources, so we should not think only of clusters of dissimilar machines as fitting this requirement. Chapter 8 briefly discusses the Linda coordination language, which can be considered a high-level abstraction of dynamic load balancing.

  The main focus is on static load balancing and the mathematical models that can be used to drive load partitioning and data communication sequences.

A well-established methodology known as Divisible Load Theory (DLT) is explained and applied in a number of scenarios. A simple C++ library that implements parts of the DLT research results, which have been published over the past two decades, is also presented.

USING THIS BOOK AS A TEXTBOOK

The material covered in this book is appropriate for senior undergraduate or postgraduate course work. The required student background includes programming in C, C++ (both languages are used throughout this book), basic operating system concepts, and at least elementary knowledge of computer architecture.

Depending on the desired focus, an instructor may choose to follow one of the suggested paths listed below. The first two chapters lay the foundations for the other chapters, so they are included in all sequences:

- *Emphasis on parallel programming* (undergraduate):
  - Chapter 1: Flynn's taxonomy, contemporary multicore machines, performance metrics. Sections: 1.1–1.5.
  - Chapter 2: Design, PCAM methodology, decomposition patterns, program structure patterns. Sections 2.1–2.5.
  - Chapter 3: Threads, semaphores, monitors. Sections 3.1–3.7.
  - Chapter 4: OpenMP basics, work-sharing constructs. Sections 4.1–4.4.
  - Chapter 5: MPI, point-to-point communications, collective operations, object/structure communications, debugging and profiling. Sections 5.1–5.12, 5.15–5.18, 5.20.
  - Chapter 6: CUDA programming model, memory hierarchy, GPU-specific optimizations. Sections 6.1–6.6, 6.7.1, 6.7.3, 6.7.6, 6.9–6.11, 6.12.1.
  - Chapter 7: Thrust basics. Sections 7.1–7.4.
  - Chapter 8: Load balancing. Sections 8.1–8.3.
- *Emphasis on multicore programming* (undergraduate):
  - Chapter 1: Flynn's taxonomy, contemporary multicore machines, performance metrics. Sections 1.1–1.5.
  - Chapter 2: Design, PCAM methodology, decomposition patterns, program structure patterns. Sections 2.1–2.5.
  - Chapter 3: Threads, semaphores, monitors. Sections 3.1–3.10.
  - Chapter 4: OpenMP basics, work-sharing constructs, correctness and performance issues. Sections 4.1–4.8.
  - Chapter 5: MPI, point-to-point communications, collective operations, debugging and profiling. Sections 5.1–5.12, 5.16–5.18, 5.21.
  - Chapter 6: CUDA programming model, memory hierarchy, GPU-specific optimizations. Sections 6.1–6.10, 6.12.1.
  - Chapter 7: Thrust basics. Sections 7.1–7.4.
  - Chapter 8: Load balancing. Sections 8.1–8.3.

- *Advanced multicore programming*:
  - Chapter 1: Flynn's taxonomy, contemporary multicore machines, performance metrics. Sections 1.1–1.5.
  - Chapter 2: Design, PCAM methodology, decomposition patterns, program structure patterns. Sections: 2.1–2.5.
  - Chapter 3: Threads, semaphores, monitors, advanced thread management. Sections 3.1–3.10.
  - Chapter 4: OpenMP basics, work-sharing constructs, correctness, and performance issues. Sections 4.1–4.8.
  - Chapter 5: MPI, point-to-point communications, collective operations, object/structure communications, debugging and profiling. Sections 5.1–5.12, 5.15–5.18, 5.21–5.22.
  - Chapter 6: CUDA programming model, memory hierarchy, GPU-specific optimizations. Sections 6.1–6.12.
  - Chapter 7: Thrust datatypes and algorithms. Sections 7.1–7.7.
  - Chapter 8: Load balancing, "DLT" based partitioning. Sections 8.1–8.5.

SOFTWARE AND HARDWARE REQUIREMENTS

The book examples have been developed and tested on Ubuntu Linux. All the software used throughout this book are available in free or Open-Source form. These include:

- GNU C/C++ Compiler Suite 4.8.x (for CUDA compatibility) and 4.9.x (for OpenMP 4.0 compatibility)
- Digia's Qt 4.x or 5.x library
- OpenMPI 1.6
- MPE
- Nvidia's CUDA SDK 6.5
- Thrust library 1.7

A reasonably recent Linux installation, with the above or newer versions of the listed software, should have no problem running the sample code provided. Although, we do not provide makefiles or instructions for compiling and executing them using Visual Studio on a Windows platform, users without access to a Linux installation[1] should be able to port the examples with minimum changes. Given that we use standard C/C++ libraries, the changes—if any—should affect only header files, i.e., which ones to include.

In terms of hardware, the only real restriction is the need to have a Compute Capability 2.x or newer Nvidia GPU. Earlier generation chips maybe used, but their

---

[1]Linux can be easily installed without even modifying the configuration of a machine, via virtualization technology. The freely available Virtualbox software from Oracle can handle running Linux on a host Windows system, with minimal resource consumption.

peculiarities, especially regarding global memory access, are not explained in the text. Users without a Nvidia GPU may have some success in running CUDA programs, via the workarounds explained in Appendix E.

SAMPLE CODE

The programs presented in the pages of this book are made available in a compressed archive form, from the publisher's Web site (http://store.elsevier.com/9780124171374).

The programs are organized in dedicated folders, identified by the chapter name, as shown in Figure 1.

Each listing in the book, is headed by the location of the corresponding file, *relative* to the chapter's directory.

Single-file programs contain the command that compiles and links them, in their first-line comments. Multifile projects reside in their own directories, which also contain a makefile, or a project (.pro) file. Sample input data are also provided wherever needed.

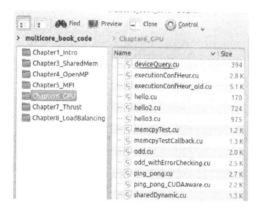

FIGURE 1

Screenshot showing how sample code is organized in chapter-specific folders.

Introduction

1

IN THIS CHAPTER YOU WILL

- Understand the current trends in computing machine design and how these trends influence software development.
- Learn how to categorize computing machines based on Flynn's taxonomy.
- Learn the essential tools used to evaluate multicore/parallel performance, i.e., speedup and efficiency.
- Learn the proper experimental procedure for measuring and reporting performance.
- Learn Amdahl's and Gustafson-Barsis's laws and apply them in order to predict the performance of parallel programs.

1.1 THE ERA OF MULTICORE MACHINES

Digital computers have been the cornerstone of much of the technological and scientific advancements that we have experienced over the past 40 years. The speed with which computers can process information has been increasing exponentially, as originally observed by Gordon E. Moore in the 1970s and expressed by the the now famous but mistakenly termed "law," allowing us to tackle ever more complex problems.

It is surprising that Moore's law is describing the industry trends even today but for a small clarification that is easily overlooked by popular science: It's the transistor count that grows exponentially and not the operational speed! A depiction of Moore's "law" is shown in Figure 1.1.[1]

It was an easy mistake to make since the increase in transistor count was accompanied by leaps in operating frequency (also known as the *clock*) that circuit miniaturization accommodated. However, increased clock frequencies resulted in elevated heat generation. Chip designers responded by lowering the operating voltages of the electronic circuits (currently running with as low as 1.29 V!), but this is not enough to counter the problem. This situation inevitably stalled the increase in clock frequencies that have remained for the better part of the past decade in the 2–4 GHz range.

So, the only route left for facilitating the demand for more computational power was to squeeze more computational logic and more computing cores inside a chip. Since the first dual-core, single-die chip introduced by AMD in 2005 (AMD 64 X2),

---

[1] The plot is an edited version of the one published under the Wikipedia Commons License at http://commons.wikimedia.org/wiki/File:Transistor_Count_and_Moore's_Law_-_2011.svg.

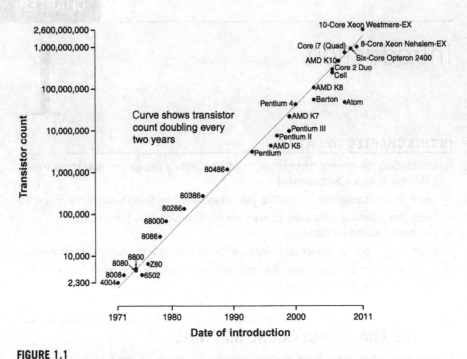

FIGURE 1.1

A logarithmic plot of CPU transistor count versus year of introduction.

a large variety of multicore chips have been released, including both *homogeneous* chips with a large number of cores, such as the 64-core Tilera TILE64,[2] and *heterogeneous* chips such as the Cell BE, which is powering, among other things, the Sony Playstation 3.

These chips were a natural evolution of the multisocket platforms, i.e., machines that could host several CPUs each on a separate chip, of the mid- to late 1990s. What was unexpected, however, was the emergence of GPGPU computing—the paradigm of doing General Purpose computing using a Graphical Processing Unit (GPU). Although a single GPU core compared with a contemporary CPU core is underpowered, GPUs boast massively parallel architectures with hundreds or thousands of cores, connected with high-bandwidth, high-speed RAM. The outcome is orders of magnitude faster computational speeds!

GPGPU offers an additional distinct advantage in a world where energy resources are dwindling: It provides superior GFlop/Watt performance. In other words, you can get more computation done per energy unit spent. This is especially critical in the server and cloud infrastructure domain, where the energy consumed by a CPU over its operational lifetime, can be much higher than its actual price.

---

[2]http://www.tilera.com/products/processors/TILE64.

The GPGPU technology is considered a *disruptive* one, and this is true in many levels: It enables the pursuit of solutions to problems that are out of reach with contemporary single or even multicore CPU technology, but it also demands new software design and development tools and techniques. It is projected that in the near future, millions of threads will be required to master the computing power of the next-generation high-performance computing hardware that will become available!

All this performance that multicore chips give us does not come for free: It requires an explicit redesign of algorithms that traditionally have been operating on a deterministic sequence of steps.

1.2 A TAXONOMY OF PARALLEL MACHINES

The quest for squeezing more performance out of contemporary computing technology by utilizing multiple resources is not a new one. It began as early as the 1960s, so finding a way of describing the architectural characteristics of parallel machines became essential. In 1966, Michael Flynn introduced a taxonomy of computer architectures whereby machines are classified based on how many data items they can process concurrently and how many different instructions they can execute at the same time. The answer to both of these criteria can be either single or multiple, which means that their combination can produce four possible outcomes:

- **Single Instruction, Single Data (SISD):** A simple sequential machine that executes one instruction at a time, operating on a single data item. Surprisingly, the vast majority of contemporary CPUs do not belong to this category. Even microcontrollers nowadays are offered in multicore configurations. Each of their cores can be considered a SISD machine.
- **Single Instruction, Multiple Data (SIMD):** A machine in which each instruction is applied on a collection of items. Vector processors were the very first machines that followed this paradigm. GPUs also follow this design at the level of the Streaming Multiprocessor[3] (SM; for Nvidia) or the SIMD unit (for AMD).
- **Multiple Instructions, Single Data (MISD):** This configuration seems like an oddity. How can multiple instruction be applied to the same data item? Under normal circumstances it does not make sense. However, when fault tolerance is required in a system (military or aerospace applications fit this description), data can be processed by multiple machines and decisions can be made on a majority principle.
- **Multiple Instructions, Multiple Data (MIMD):** The most versatile machine category. Multicore machines, including GPUs, follow this paradigm. GPUs are made from a collection of SM/SIMD units, whereby each can execute its own program. So, although each SM is a SIMD machine, collectively they behave as a MIMD one.

---

[3] For more information, see Section 6.3.

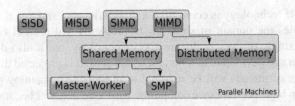

FIGURE 1.2

Flynn's extended taxonomy of computing systems.

This taxonomy has been refined over the years with the addition of subcategories, especially under the MIMD slot, as presented in Figure 1.2.

MIMD can be separated into two broad subcategories:

- Shared-memory MIMD: Machine architecture having a universally accessible shared memory space. The shared memory simplifies all transactions that need to take place between the CPUs with a minimum amount of overhead, but it also constitutes a bottleneck that limits the scalability of the system. One solution to this problem is to partition memory between the CPUs so that each CPU "owns" a part of the memory. Thus a CPU gets faster access to its local memory, but it can still access, albeit more slowly, nonlocal memory belonging to other CPUs. The partitioning does not affect the addressing scheme, which is universal. This design is known as Non-Uniform Memory Access, or NUMA, and it permits shared-memory machines to scale up to a few tens of CPUs.
- Distributed memory or shared-nothing MIMD: A machine that is made up of processors that communicate by exchanging messages. The communication cost is high, but since there is no single medium to be contested, such machines can scale without any practical limit apart from space and energy bounds.

Shared-memory machines can be further subdivided into master-worker and symmetric multiprocessing platforms. In the latter, all the participating CPUs are equivalent and capable of executing any program in the system, including system and application software. In a master-worker setup, some of the processors are dedicated for the execution of specialized software, i.e., we can treat them as coprocessors. GPU-equipped systems can be considered as belonging to this category, although the majority of high-performance GPU platforms have distinct memory spaces for the CPU and GPU. As such, they are not shared-memory platforms, despite recent driver software advances that hide much of the complexity involved in moving data between the two memories.

The same arrangement exists in machines equipped with the Intel Xeon Phi coprocessor. The Intel Xeon Phi coprocessor contains 61 Pentium cores operating as a shared-memory MIMD platform. It is installed on a PCIe card, and although it resides on the same enclosure/chassis as the host CPU, the most appropriate classification of the combined CPU/coprocessor system is the distributed-memory MIMD one.

1.3 A GLIMPSE OF CONTEMPORARY COMPUTING MACHINES

Contemporary machines blur the lines between the categories laid out by Flynn. The drive for more performance has led to machines that are both MIMD and SIMD, depending on the level at which they are examined.

There are currently two trends in utilizing the increased transistor count afforded by miniaturization and advancements in semiconductor materials:

1. Increase the on-chip core count, combined with augmented specialized SIMD instruction sets (e.g., SSE and its subsequent versions, MMX, AESNI, etc.) and larger caches. This is best exemplified by Intel's x86 line of CPUs and the Intel Xeon Phi coprocessor.
2. Combine heterogeneous cores in the same package, typically CPU and GPU ones, each optimized for a different type of task. This is best exemplified by AMD's line of Accelerated Processing Unit (APU) chips. Intel is also offering OpenCL-based computing on its line of CPUs with integrated graphics chips.

But why is the pairing of CPU and GPU cores on the same die an important feature? Before we answer this question, let's discuss what exactly GPUs bring to the game.

Graphics Processing Units (GPUs), also known as graphics accelerator cards, have been developed as a means of processing massive amount of graphics data very quickly, before they are placed in the card's display buffer. Their design envelope dictated a layout that departed from the one traditionally used by conventional CPUs. CPUs employ large on-chip (and sometimes multiple) memory caches, few complex (e.g., pipelined) arithmetic and logical processing units (ALUs), and complex instruction decoding and prediction hardware to avoid stalling while waiting for data to arrive from the main memory.

Instead, GPU designers chose a different path: small on-chip caches with a big collection of simple ALUs capable of parallel operation, since data reuse is typically small for graphics processing and programs are relatively simple. In order to feed the multiple cores on a GPU, designers also dedicated very wide, fast memory buses for fetching data from the GPU's main memory.

The contrast between the two worlds is evident in Figure 1.3. Although the block diagrams are not scaled properly relative to each other, it is clear that while memory cache dominates the die in the CPU case, compute logic dominates in the case of the GPU.

GPUs have been proven to offer unprecedented computing power. However, their use in a system in the form of a dedicated graphics card communicating with the main CPU over a slow bus such as PCIe compromises their effectiveness. The reason is that data have to be transferred to (and from) the main computer memory to the GPU's memory before the GPU can process them. This effectively creates a data size threshold, below which GPUs are not an effective tool. The case study of Section 8.5.2 highlights this problem (see Figure 8.16 for execution times versus data size on sample CPU and GPU cores).

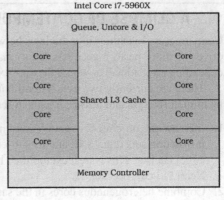

FIGURE 1.3

Block diagrams of the Nvidia Titan GPU and the Intel i7-5960X octa-core CPU, derived from silicon die photographs. The diagrams are not scaled relative to each other. They are only supposed to show the relative real-estate devoted to compute logic. Each SMX SIMD block contains 64 KB of cache/shared memory. Each i7 core also contains its own private 32 KB data and 32 KB instruction L1 caches, and 256 KB L2 cache. The shared L3 cache in i7-5960X is 20 MB.

Now it becomes obvious why having CPU and GPU cores share and access the same memory space is an important feature. On principle, this arrangement promises better integration of computing resources and potentially greater performance, but only time will tell.

In the following sections we review some of the most influential contemporary designs in multicore computing. It is certain that they will not be cutting-edge for a long time, but they provide insights into the direction in which processor designs are moving.

1.3.1 THE CELL BE PROCESSOR

The Cell BE (Broadband Engine) processor, famous for powering Sony's PS3 gaming console, was introduced in 2007, the outcome of a joint venture among Sony, Toshiba, and IBM. Cell features a design well ahead of its time: a master-worker, *heterogeneous*, MIMD machine on a chip. The chip variant that equips the PS3 console contains the following:

- The master is a 64-bit PowerPC core (called the Power Processing Element, or PPE), capable of running two threads. It is responsible for running the operating system and managing the workers.
- The workers are eight 128-bit vector processors (called the Synergistic Processing Elements, or SPEs). Each SPE has its own dedicated on-chip local (not cache) memory (256 KB) called the *local store*, used to hold the data and code it is running.

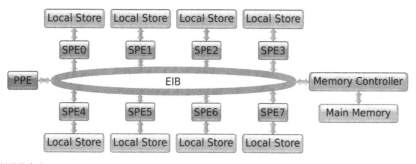

FIGURE 1.4

Block diagram of the Cell BE processor.

The SPE cores are not binary compatible with PPE: They have their own instruction set designed for SIMD operation. The PPE is responsible for initializing them and starting jobs on them. SPEs communicate via a high-speed ring interconnect called the Element Interconnect Bus (EIB), shown in Figure 1.4. SPEs do not have direct access to the main memory, but they can perform DMA transfers between the main memory and their local store.

The hardware was designed for maximum computing efficiency but at the expense of programming ease. The Cell is notorious for being one of the most difficult platforms to program on.

At the time of its introduction, the Cell was one of the most powerful processors available on the market, with a peak performance in double-precision arithmetic, of 102.4 GFlops for the combined total of eight SPEs. It very quickly became a component for building "budget supercomputers" in the form of PS3 clusters. Applications that run on these machines included astrophysics simulations, satellite imaging, and biomedical applications. It should be noted that the IBM Roadrunner supercomputer, which was the world's fastest during 2008–2009, contained 12,240 PowerXCell 8i and 6,562 AMD Opteron processors. PowerXCell 8i is an enhanced version of the original Cell with improved double-precision, floating-point performance.

The Cell processor is no longer been developed, probably a victim of its programming complexity and the advances in GPU computing.

1.3.2 Nvidia's KEPLER

Kepler is the third GPU architecture Nvidia has designed specifically for compute applications. The new architecture is as surprising to the uninitiated as the previous ones. The departure from the "traditional" SMP chips becomes obvious only when one tries to program an incarnation of such a design. In this section we look at architectural features that make this and other GPUs formidable computing machines.

The cores in a Kepler GPU are arranged in groups called **Streaming Multiprocessors** (abbreviated to **SMX** in Kepler, **SM** in previous architectures, and **SMM** in the upcoming Maxwell). Each Kepler SMX contains 192 cores that execute in a SIMD fashion, i.e., they run the same sequence of instructions but on different data.

Each SMX can run its own program, though. The total number of SMX blocks is the *primary* differentiating factor between different chips of the same family. The most powerful chip in the Kepler family is the GTX Titan, with a total of 15 SMXs. One of the SMXs is disabled in order to improve production yields, resulting in a total of $14 \cdot 192 = 2688$ cores! The extra SMX is enabled in the version of the chip used in the dual-GPU, GTX Titan Z card, resulting in an astonishing package of 5760 cores! AMD's dual-GPU offering in the form of the Radeon R9 295X2 card is also brandishing 5632 cores in a shootout that is delighting all high-performance enthusiasts.

The 2688 cores of the plain-vanilla Titan are rated for a peak performance of 4.5 TFlops for single-precision arithmetic. When double precision is required, the performance drops to 1.5 TFlops because each SMX has "only" 64 double-precision compute units (one third of the single-precision ones). Figure 1.5 shows a block diagram of a Kepler SMX.

The details of how such a "beast" can be programmed are covered in Chapter 5. As a short introduction to the topic, a GPU is used as a coprocessor, assigned work items from the main CPU. The CPU is referred to as the host. It would be awkward to have code spawning a separate thread for each of those 2688 cores. Instead, the GPU programming environment allows the launch of special functions called *kernels* that run with distinct, intrinsic/built-in variables. In fact, the number of threads that can be generated with a single statement/kernel launch comes to tens of thousands or even millions. Each thread will take its turn running on a GPU core.

The sequence can be summarized to the host (a) sending data to the GPU, (b) launching a kernel, and (c) waiting to collect the results.

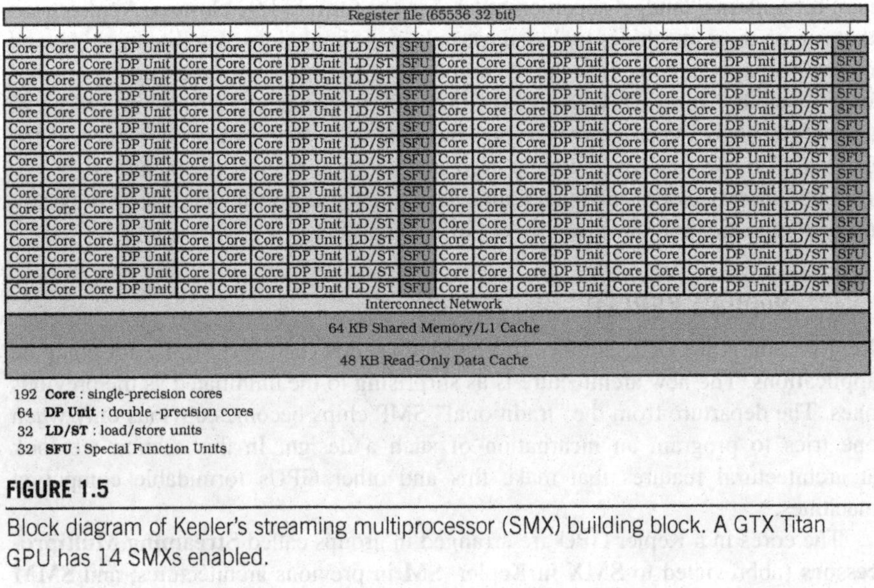

FIGURE 1.5

Block diagram of Kepler's streaming multiprocessor (SMX) building block. A GTX Titan GPU has 14 SMXs enabled.

To assist in the speedy execution of threads, on-chip memory configuration is designed for keeping data "close" to the cores (255 32-bit registers per core). Kepler adds a L2 cache to reduce latency, but the combined L1 cache/shared memory is pretty small compared to per-core caches on typical CPUs, which is usually on the order of MB. Shared memory is not transparent to the applications the way cache memory is. It is addressable memory, and it can be considered a form of user-managed cache.

These additions do indicate a move to incorporate traditional CPU design features. Earlier GPU designs had no cache, for example, whereas shared memory was limited to 16 KB per SM.

Another feature that is moving in that direction is the introduction of what Nvidia calls *dynamic parallelism*, which is the ability of a kernel to generate additional work. In simplistic terms, one can think of this ability as enabling recursion, but it is clearly more profound than this since the complexity of the code that can run on a GPU grows substantially.

Nvidia claims that the new architecture offers a threefold improvement in the GFlop/Watt ratio relative to its previous offerings, which is just the icing on the cake. What we have in Kepler is a very powerful class of machines that adopt CPU design features and push the performance boundaries by incorporating more and better cores.

The power and energy efficiency of the Kepler design is also evident in Table 1.1, where the top-performing machine in terms of measured TFlop/KW is Piz Daint, a Nvidia K20x (a GK110 implementation) GPU-equipped machine.

But could a GPU ever be on equal terms to a CPU as far as work generation and sharing are concerned? The next design on our list answers this question.

Table 1.1 The Top Nine Most Powerful Supercomputers as of June 2014, Sorted in Descending Order of their TFlop/KW Ratio

Rank	Site	System	Cores	Rpeak (TFlops)	Power (kW)	Tflop/KW
6	Swiss National Supercomputing Centre (CSCS), Switzerland	Piz Daint - Cray XC30, Xeon E5-2670 8C 2.600GHz, Aries interconnect, **NVIDIA K20x** - Cray Inc.	115984	6271	2325	2.697204
9	DOE/NNSA/LLNL, United States	Vulcan - BlueGene/Q, Power BQC 16C 1.600GHz, Custom Interconnect - IBM	393216	4293.3	1972	2.17713
8	Forschungszentrum Juelich (FZJ), Germany	JUQUEEN - BlueGene/Q, Power BQC 16C 1.600GHz, Custom Interconnect - IBM	458752	5008.9	2301	2.176836
3	DOE/NNSA/LLNL, United States	Sequoia - BlueGene/Q, Power BQC 16C 1.60 GHz, Custom - IBM	1572864	17173.2	7890	2.176578
5	DOE/SC/Argonne National Laboratory, United States	Mira - BlueGene/Q, Power BQC 16C 1.60GHz, Custom - IBM	786432	8586.6	3945	2.176578
2	DOE/SC/Oak Ridge National Laboratory, United States	Titan - Cray XK7 , Opteron 6274 16C 2.200GHz, Cray Gemini interconnect, **NVIDIA K20x** - Cray Inc.	560640	17590	8209	2.14277
1	National Super Computer Center in Guangzhou, China	Tianhe-2 (MilkyWay-2) - TH-IVB-FEP Cluster, Intel Xeon E5-2692 12C 2.200GHz, TH Express-2, Intel Xeon Phi 31S1P - NUDT	3120000	33862.7	17808	1.901544
7	Texas Advanced Computing Center/Univ. of Texas, United States	Stampede - PowerEdge C8220, Xeon E5-2680 8C 2.700GHz, Infiniband FDR, Intel Xeon Phi SE10P - Dell	462462	5168.1	4510	1.14592
4	RIKEN Advanced Institute for Computational Science (AICS), Japan	K computer, SPARC64 VIIIfx 2.0GHz, Tofu interconnect - Fujitsu	705024	10510	12660	0.830174

1.3.3 AMD's APUs

The third processor on our list also made its way to the internals of a gaming console: Sony's PS4. AMD's line of APU processors combine CPU and GPU cores on the same die. These are not the big news, though. What is significant is the unification of the memory spaces of the CPU and GPU cores. This means that there is no communication overhead associated with assigning workload to the GPU cores, nor any delay in getting the results back. This also removes one of the major hassles in GPU programming, which is the explicit (or implicit, based on the middleware available) data transfers that need to take place.

AMD's APU chips implement the *Heterogeneous System Architecture* (HSA), developed by the HSA Foundation (HSAF), which was formed as an open industry standards body by AMD, ARM, Imagination Technologies, MediaTek, Texas Instruments, Samsung Electronics, and Qualcomm.

The HSA architecture identifies two core types [31]:

- The **L**atency **C**ompute **U**nit (LCU), which is a generalization of a CPU. A LCU supports both its native CPU instruction set and the HSA intermediate language (HSAIL) instruction set.
- The **T**hroughput **C**ompute **U**nit (TCU), which is a generalization of a GPU. A TCU supports only the HSAIL instruction set. TCUs target efficient parallel execution.

Code written in HSAIL is translated to a compute unit's native instruction set before execution. Because of this compatibility arrangement, that is, CPU cores can run GPU code, an HSA application can run on any platform regardless of the composition of LCU and TCU cores. HSA also caters for the following:

- Shared virtual memory: The same page-table is shared between LCUs and TCUs, simplifying operating system memory maintenance and allowing the use of virtual memory by the TCUs. Contemporary graphics cards do not support virtual memory and are limited by the physical memory available on the card. Page faults can be also generated by TCUs.
- Coherent memory: A memory heap can be set up to maintain full coherency. This is done by default and enables developers to apply well-known software patterns for coupling LCUs and TCUs, such as the producer-consumer.
- User-level job queuing: Each application gets a dispatch queue that can be used to enter job requests from user space. The operating system kernel does not need to intervene. What is more important, though, is that *both LCU and TCU cores can enqueue work requests to other compute units, including themselves*. CPUs and GPUs can be on equal terms!
- Hardware scheduling: A mechanism is available so that the TCU engine hardware can switch between application dispatch queues automatically. This can be done without the intervention of the operating system, maximizing TCUs utilization.

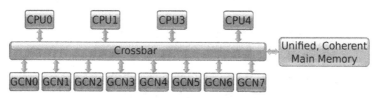

FIGURE 1.6

Block diagram of AMD's Kaveri architecture. GCN stands for Graphics Core Next, the designated name for AMD's next generation GPU core.

Tests also suggest that the core integration results in more energy-efficient computing, a feature critical for both the embedded and the server domains.

Figure 1.6 shows a block diagram of AMD's Kaveri chip generation. HSA is arguably the way forward, having the capability to assign each task to the computing node most suitable for it, without the penalty of traversing a slow peripheral bus. Sequential tasks are more suitable for the LCU/CPU cores, while data-parallel tasks can take advantage of the high-bandwidth, high-computational throughput of the TCU/GPU cores.

AMD's Kaveri generation, A10 7850k APU, is rated at a peak 856 GFlops. However, at the point of this writing, legacy software that is not specifically optimized for such an architecture cannot deliver on the true potential of the chip.

1.3.4 MULTICORE TO MANY-CORE: TILERA'S TILE-GX8072 AND INTEL'S XEON PHI

GPUs have been hosting hundreds of admittedly simple computing cores for almost a decade. But they can do so while being effective under special circumstances, which is typical of graphics workloads. Achieving the same feat for a general-purpose CPU capable of running operating system tasks and application software is a different ball game. The two designs that have managed to accomplish this feat are putting in silicon, well-known network configurations, that have been used to build parallel machines in past decades. It's a miniaturization success story!

The first manifestation of the many-core paradigm came in the form of Tilera's TILE64 coprocessor, released in August 2007. TILE64 offered 64 cores arranged in a 2-D grid. Later designs Tilera offered, came in different configurations, including 9, 16, 36, and 72 cores. The block diagram of the 72-core variant, TILE-Gx8072,[4] is shown in Figure 1.7. The 2-D grid of communication channels called the iMesh Interconnect comes with five independent mesh networks that offer an aggregate bandwidth exceeding 110 Tbps. The communication is done via nonblocking, cut-through switching with one clock cycle per hop. Each core has 32 KB data and 32 KB

---

[4]http://www.tilera.com/sites/default/files/productbriefs/TILE-Gx8072_PB041-03_WEB.pdf last accessed in July 2014.

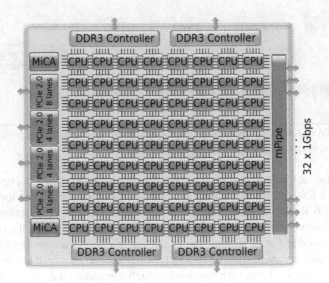

FIGURE 1.7

Simplified block diagram of Tilera's TILE-Gx8072 chip.

instruction L1 caches and a 256 KB L2 cache. An 18 MB L3 coherent cache is shared between the cores. Access to the main RAM is done via four DDR3 controllers.

The TILE-Gx8072 CPU is targeting networking (e.g., filtering, throttling), multimedia (e.g., transcoding), and cloud applications. Networking receives a lot of attention, as attested to by the 32 1 Gbps ports, the eight 10 Gbps XAUI ports, and the two dedicated compression and encryption acceleration engines (MiCA).

As with a GPU, Tilera's chip can be used as a coprocessor to offload heavy computational tasks from the main CPU/host. Four multilane PCIe interfaces are available to accelerate the transfer of data from/to the host. It can also be used as a standalone platform because it runs a Linux kernel. Tilera offers its Multicore Development Environment (MDE) as a software development platform for its chips. MDE is built upon OSS tools, such as the GNU C/C++ compiler, the Eclipse IDE, Boost, Thread Building Blocks (TBB), and other libraries. Hence, it leverages existing tools for multicore development, keeping compatibility with a wealth of languages, compilers, and libraries. Chapters 3 and 4 cover tools and techniques that are suitable for developing software for Tilera's chips.

Intel's entry in the many-core arena came at a much later date (2012), but it was no less spectacular. It is a telling fact that the Intel Xeon Phi coprocessor is a building block of two of the 10 supercomputers topping the June 2014 Top 500 list. One of them, China's Tianhe-2, is holding the top spot.

Xeon Phi comes equipped with 61 x86 cores that are heavily customized Pentium cores. The customizations include the ability to handle four threads at the same time in order to hide pipeline stalls or memory access delays, and a special 512-bit wide,

Vector Processing Unit (VPU) that operates in SIMD mode to process 16 single-precision or 8 double-precision floating-point numbers per clock cycle. The VPU also has an Extended Math Unit (EMU) to handle transcendental functions such as reciprocal, square root, and exponent on vectors. Each core comes equipped with 32 KB data and 32 KB instruction L1 caches and 512 KB L2 coherent cache.

The cores are connected with another well-known communication architecture, which also has been used in the Cell BE chip: the ring (see Figure 1.8).

The ring is bidirectional and it is actually made of six individual rings, three in each direction. Each direction has one 64-bytes-wide (!) data ring and two narrower rings, an address ring (AD) and an acknowledgment ring (AK). The AD ring is used to send read/write commands and memory addresses. The AK ring is used for L2 cache coherence.

The coherency is managed by distributed tag directories (TDs) that contain information about every L2 cache line on the chip.

When a core gets a L2 cache miss, it sends an address request on the AD ring to the tag directories. If the requested data block is found in another core's L2 cache, a forwarding request is sent to that core's L2 cache over the AD ring and the requested block is subsequently forwarded over the data ring. If the requested data is not on the chip, the memory address is sent from the tag directory to the memory controllers.

The redundancy, that is, having two from each type of ring, ensures scalability, since testing has shown that using only one of the AK and AD type rings causes performance to level off at around 30 to 35 cores.

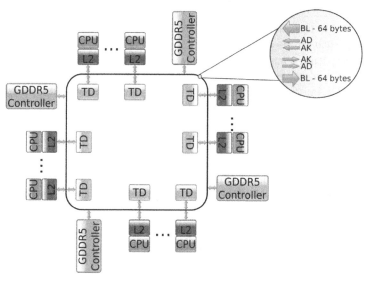

FIGURE 1.8

Block diagram of Intel Xeon Phi coprocessor.

The GDDR5 memory controllers are interleaved across the cores and accessed through these rings. Memory addresses are equally distributed between the controllers to avoid making any one of them a bottleneck.

The hardware is impressive. But how is it to program 61 cores? The Xeon Phi coprocessor is available as a PCIe card that runs Linux. A special device driver makes the PCIe bus appear as a network interface, which means that the coprocessor appears to the host machine as another machine to which it is connected over the network. A user can use SSH to log in the Xeon Phi machine!

Applications can be either run on the host machine and parts of them off-loaded to the Xeon Phi card, or they can run entirely on the coprocessor, in which case they are referred to as running in *native mode*. Xeon Phi leverages all the existing shared- and distributed-memory tools infrastructure. One can use threads, OpenMP, Intel TBB, MPI, and the like to build applications for it. This also constitutes a major advantage of the many core architectures compared with GPUs, since the latter require the mastering of new tools and techniques.

As a last word, it is worth noting one characteristic that is common to all architectures that host many cores: relatively low clock frequencies. This feature is shared by GPUs (0.8–1.5 GHz), TILE-Gx8072 (1.2 GHz) and Intel Xeon Phi (1.2–1.3 GHz). It is the price one has to pay for cramming billions of transistors on the same die, as the signal propagation delays increase.

1.4 PERFORMANCE METRICS

The motivation driving the multicore hardware and software efforts is the extraction of more performance: shorter execution time, bigger problems and data sets, etc. It is clear that an objective criterion or criteria are needed to be able to assess how effective or beneficial such efforts are.

At the very least, a parallel program should be able to beat in terms of execution time its sequential counterpart (but this is not something you can take to the bank every time). The improvement in execution time is typically expressed as the *speedup*, which is formally defined as the ratio:

$$speedup = \frac{t_{seq}}{t_{par}} \tag{1.1}$$

where t_{seq} is the execution time of the sequential program, and t_{par} is the execution time of the parallel program for solving the same instance of a problem.

Both t_{seq} and t_{par} are wall-clock times, and as such they are not objective. They can be influenced by:

- The skill of the programmer who wrote the implementations
- The choice of compiler (e.g., GNU C++ versus Intel C++)
- The compiler switches (e.g., turning optimization on/off)
- The operating system
- The type of filesystem holding the input data (e.g., EXT4, NTFS, etc.)
- The time of day (different workloads, network traffic, etc.)

In order to have some level of confidence on reported speedup figures, one should abide by the following rules:

1. Both the sequential and the parallel programs should be tested on identical software and hardware platforms and under similar conditions.
2. The sequential program should be the fastest known solution to the problem at hand.

The second one is the least obvious of the two, but it is a crucial requirement: Parallel algorithms are completely different beasts than their sequential counterparts. In fact, a sequential algorithm may not have a parallel derivative. It is even possible that a parallel derivative is infeasible to create.

The reason behind the second requirement is a fundamental one: The elevated (and expensive in terms of development cost) effort required to implement a parallel program is justified only if it yields tangible benefits.

The speedup offered by a parallel algorithm for a given number of processors can still vary based on the input data (an example illustrates this point later in this section). For this reason, it is customary to report average figures for the speedup after testing the two programs on a wide collection of inputs of the same size, or even average, maximum, and minimum observed.

Speedup tells only part of the story: It can tell us if it is feasible to accelerate the solution of a problem, e.g., if *speedup* > 1. It cannot tell us if this can be done efficiently, i.e., with a modest amount of resources. The second metric employed for this purpose is efficiency. *Efficiency* is formally defined as the ratio:

$$efficiency = \frac{speedup}{N} = \frac{t_{seq}}{N \cdot t_{par}} \tag{1.2}$$

where N is the number of CPUs/cores employed for the execution of the parallel program. One can interpret the efficiency as the average percent of time that a node is utilized during the parallel execution. If efficiency is equal to 100% this means that the speedup is N, and the workload is equally divided between the N processors, which are utilized 100% of the time (they are never idle during execution). When $speedup = N$, the corresponding parallel program exhibits what is called a *linear speedup*.

This, unfortunately, is an ideal scenario. When multiple processors work toward the accomplishment of a goal, they spend time coordinating with each other, either by exchanging messages or by handling shared resources. The activity related to coordination robs CPU time that ultimately reduces speedup below N.

Figure 1.9 shows speedup and efficiency curves for a sample program that calculates the definite integral of a function by applying the trapezoidal rule algorithm. The computational load is controlled by the number of trapezoids used for the calculation. The results plotted in Figure 1.9 were obtained on a i7 950 quad-core CPU and averaged over 10 runs.

There is a discrepancy here for the cautious reader: If we only have a quad-core CPU, how can we test and report speedup for eight threads?

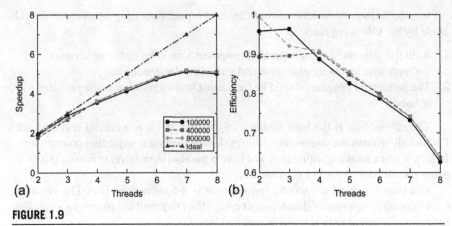

FIGURE 1.9

(a) Speedup and (b) efficiency curves for the execution of a parallel integral calculation by a variable number of threads on a multicore CPU. Each curve corresponds to a different number of divisions of the x-range (as shown in the legend). The ideal speedup line in (a) provides a measure of the performance deterioration, which is a common problem with increased coordination costs.

The i7 950 quad-core CPU supports a technique called *hyperthreading*, which allows a CPU core to run two software threads by duplicating parts of the CPU hardware. A CPU that has this feature enabled appears as having twice the number of physical cores it actually has. Unfortunately, the performance is increased on average by only 30%, which is very different from the two-fold increase suggested. In that regard, the results reported in Figure 1.9 are skewed, since on the given platform we do not have eight distinct physical CPUs on which to run eight threads.

However, the deterioration observed in efficiency with an increased number of threads is not bogus: It is typical behavior for parallel applications, although the degree of deterioration is application specific. It all comes down to what we can generally call the coordination cost, and this can increase only when more parties/CPUs talk to each other.

In that regard, Figure 1.9 serves two purposes: (a) it illustrates what typical speedup and efficiency curves look like, and (b) it raises awareness about proper experimentation techniques. Measuring performance should involve real hardware resources and not virtual ones in the way provided by hyperthreading.

The ideal speedup curve in Figure 1.9(a) acts as a measure of how successful our parallel program is. As we mentioned, this is the upper bound of performance. But not always!

There are situations where *speedup* > *N* and *efficiency* > 1 in what is known as a *superlinear speedup* scenario. According to the interpretation we gave to efficiency, this seems like an impossible case. However, we should keep in mind that sequential and parallel programs process their input data in different ways, following different execution paths. So, if the aim of a program is the acquisition of an item in a search space, a parallel program may reach this point far sooner than the number of computing resources utilized would suggest, just by following a different route to reach it.

This is, of course, not a typical case that can materialize under application and input data-specific circumstances. As an example, let's consider the problem of acquiring the encryption key of a ciphertext. In the DES encryption standard, a secret number in the range $[0, 2^{56} - 1]$ is used as the key to convert a message (plaintext) to a scrambled, unreadable mess (ciphertext). A brute-force attack on a ciphertext would involve trying out all the keys until the decoded message could be identified as a readable text. If we assume that each attempt to decipher the message costs time T on a single CPU, if the key was the number 2^{55}, then a sequential program would take $t_{seq} = (2^{55} + 1)T$ time to solve the problem.

If we were to employ two CPUs to solve the same problem, and if we partitioned the search space of 2^{56} keys equally among the two CPUs, i.e., range $[0, 2^{55} - 1]$ to the first one and range $[2^{55}, 2^{56} - 1]$ to the second one, then the key would be found by the second CPU after only one attempt! We would then have $speedup_{2p} = \frac{(2^{55}+1)T}{T} = 2^{55} + 1$ and $efficiency_{2p} = \frac{2^{55}+1}{2} \approx 2^{54}$!

It would seem quite natural to expect that throwing more computing resources at a problem, i.e., increasing N, would reduce the execution time. This is a fallacy! And our simple example can prove it: What happens if three CPUs are utilized? The first CPU would be assigned the range $\left[0, \lfloor \frac{2^{56}}{3} \rfloor - 1\right]$, the second one the range $\left[\lfloor \frac{2^{56}}{3} \rfloor, \lfloor 2\frac{2^{56}}{3} \rfloor - 1\right]$, and the third the range $\left[\lfloor 2\frac{2^{56}}{3} \rfloor, 2^{56} - 1\right]$. So, the second processor will find the solution after $2^{55} - \lfloor \frac{2^{56}}{3} \rfloor$ tries, resulting in a speedup of $speedup_{3p} = \frac{(2^{55}+1)T}{(2^{55}-\lfloor \frac{2^{56}}{3} \rfloor)T} = 3\frac{2^{55}+1}{3\cdot2^{55}-2^{56}} = 3\frac{2^{55}+1}{2^{55}+2\cdot2^{55}-2^{56}} = 3\frac{2^{55}+1}{2^{55}} \approx 3$, which is substantially inferior to $speedup_{2p}$.

Speedup covers the efficacy of a parallel solution—is it beneficial or not? *Efficiency* is a measure of resource utilization—how much of the potential afforded by the computing resources we commit is actually used? A low efficiency indicates a poor design, or at least one that should be further improved.

Finally, we would like to know how a parallel algorithm behaves with increased computational resources and/or problem sizes: *Does it scale?*

In general, *scalability* is the ability of a (software or hardware) system to handle a growing amount of work efficiently. In the context of a parallel algorithm and/or platform, scalability translates to being able to (a) solve bigger problems and/or (b) to incorporate more computing resources.

There are two metrics used to quantify scalability: strong scaling efficiency (related to (b)) and weak scaling efficiency (related to (a)).

Strong scaling efficiency is defined by the same equation as the generic efficiency defined in Equation 1.2:

$$strongScalingEfficiency(N) = \frac{t_{seq}}{N \cdot t_{par}} \tag{1.3}$$

It is a function of the number N of processors employed to solve the same problem as a single processor.

Weak scaling efficiency is again a function of the number N of processors employed, defined by:

$$weakScalingEfficiency(N) = \frac{t_{seq}}{t'_{par}} \qquad (1.4)$$

where t'_{par} is the time to solve a problem that is N times bigger than the one the single machine is solving in time t_{seq}.

There are a number of issues with calculating scaling efficiency when GPU computing resources are involved: What is the value of N that should be used? GPUs typically have hundreds or thousands of cores, but it would be awkward or just bad science to report as t_{seq} the time of executing on a single GPU core. If we choose to report as t_{seq} the time of execution of a single CPU core, are we justified to use the total number of GPU cores as N when calculating efficiency? Also, a GPU is a hosted device, i.e., it needs a CPU to perform I/O on its behalf. Does that CPU count?

It is clear that efficiency can be calculated in many different ways in such circumstances. To avoid the controversy, we report only speedup figures in the case studies covered in later chapters, that involve heterogeneous platforms.

1.5 PREDICTING AND MEASURING PARALLEL PROGRAM PERFORMANCE

Building a parallel application is substantially more challenging than its sequential equivalent. A programmer has to tackle coordination problems such as proper access to shared resources, load balancing issues (i.e., dividing the workload among the available computing resources so as to minimize execution time), termination problems (i.e., halting the program in a coordinated fashion), and others.

Embarking on such an endeavor should be attempted only when the application can actually benefit from it, by providing accelerated problem solution. Development costs dictate that one cannot simply implement multiple alternative designs and test them in order to select the best one, or worse, evaluate the feasibility of the project. This might be possible for the simplest of problems, but even then it would be preferable if we could determine *a priori* the best development route to follow.

The development of a parallel solution to a problem starts with the development of its sequential variant! This seems like an oxymoron, but just try to answer these questions: How can we know how much faster a parallel solution to a problem is if we do not have a sequential solution to compare against? We need a baseline, and this can only be obtained from a sequential solution. Also, how can we check to see whether the solution produced by the parallel program is correct? Not that the output of a sequential program is guaranteed to be correct, but it is much easier to get it to be correct.

The development of the sequential algorithm and associated program can also provide essential insights about the design that should be pursued for parallelization.

The issue is a practical one, since we need to answer the following questions related to the feasibility and cost-effectiveness of the parallel program:

- *Which are the most time-consuming parts of the program?* These should be the prime candidates for parallel execution.
- Once these parts are identified and assuming that they can be parallelized, *how much performance gain can be expected?*

A clarification is needed here: The sequential program that is required is not just any sequential program that solves the same problem. It has to be the sequential implementation of the same algorithm that is being parallelized.[5] For example, if we need to sort data in parallel, an algorithm that is suited for a parallel implementation is bucket sort. A sequential implementation of bucket sort can help us predict the parallel performance and also pinpoint the most time-consuming parts of the algorithm. A sequential implementation of quicksort can provide baseline performance information, but it cannot contribute to any of the two questions posed above.

Once the sequential version is implemented, we can use a *profiler* to answer these questions. A profiler is a tool that collects information about how frequently parts of a program are called, how long their duration is, and how much memory is used. Profilers use a number of different techniques to perform their task. The most commonly used techniques are:

- Instrumentation: Modifies the code of the program that is being profiled so that information can be collected, e.g., incrementing a special counter before every instruction to be executed. This results in very accurate information but at the same time increases the execution time substantially. This technique requires recompilation of the target program.
- Sampling: The execution of the target program is interrupted periodically in order to query which function is being executed. Obviously, this is not as accurate as instrumentation, but the program does not require recompilation and the execution time is only slightly disturbed.

The `valgrind` analysis tool collection contains an instrumentation-based profiler. The instrumentation is performed right before the profiling takes place, which means there is no need for user intervention. This is an example of how it can be called:

```
$ valgrind —— tool=callgrind ./bucketsort 1000000
```

where `./bucketsort 1000000` are the program to be profiled and its arguments.

The outcome is a file called `callgrind.out` that holds the results of the analysis. This can be visualized by a front-end program like `kcachegrind`. A sample screenshot is shown in Figure 1.10.

Experience or intimate knowledge of the problem domain are skills that can allow someone to pinpoint the hotspots that need to be parallelized, without profiling a sequential program.

---

[5]We still need the best sequential solution for proper speedup calculations.

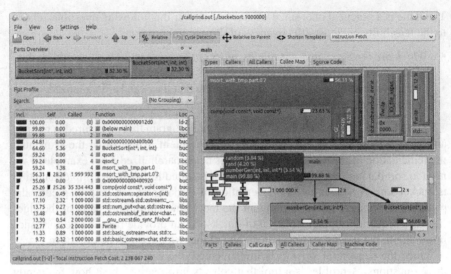

FIGURE 1.10

A sample screenshot of `kcachegrind`, showing the results of the profiling of a sequential bucket sort implementation that switches to quicksort for smaller buckets.

However, the profiler can help us answer the second question posed above, about the potential performance we can extract from a parallel solution. Traditionally, this is done by approximate mathematical models that allow us to capture the essence of the computation that is to be carried out. The parameters of these models can be estimated via profiling the sequential application. In the following section, we describe Amdahl's law, which is based on such a simple model.

Regardless of the mathematical model performance predictions, real-life testing of the implemented parallel design must be conducted for two reasons: correctness and performance. The correctness of the parallel implementation must be verified. Parallel programs can behave in a nondeterministic manner, as time may influence the outcome of the computation. This is typically an undesirable characteristic that must be rooted out if it exists. Furthermore, testing can reveal weaknesses with the original design or performance problems that need to be addressed.

The following list contains guidelines for conducting a proper experimental procedure:

- The duration of the whole execution should be measured unless specifically stated otherwise. For example, if only a part of a program is to be parallelized, speedup and efficiency could be calculated only for that particular part of the execution timeline. However, overall times could serve to put into perspective the impact of the parallel solution and whether it is cost effective or not. For example, a program that needs 100 seconds for solving a problem would still require 90+ seconds if a 10% part of it was executed with a speedup of 100x.

- Results should be reported in the form of averages over multiple runs, possibly including standard deviations. The number of runs is application specific; for example, repeating an experiment that lasts for three days 100 times and for many different scenarios would be totally unrealistic. However, to counter this, averaging over three runs can only produce unreliable statistical figures. So, a careful balance must be struck.
- Outliers, i.e., results that are too big or too small, should be excluded from the calculation of the averages because they typically are expressions of an anomaly (e.g., running out of main memory, or changes in the workload of the machines). However, care should be taken so that unfavorable results are not brushed away instead of being explained.
- Scalability is paramount, so results should be reported for a variety of input sizes (ideally covering the size and/or quality of real-life data) and a variety of parallel platform sizes.
- Test inputs should vary from very small to very big, but they should always include problem sizes that would be typical of a production environment, if these can be identified.
- When multicore machines are employed, the number of threads and/or processes should not exceed the number of available *hardware* cores. Hyperthreading is a special case, since this technology makes a CPU appear to the operating system as having twice the number of cores it actually has. However, these *logical* cores do not match the capabilities of full-blown cores. So, although the operating system may report the availability of, for example, eight cores, the corresponding hardware resources are just not there, in effect compromising any scalability analysis. Ideally, hyperthreading should be disabled for measuring scalability, or the number of threads limited to the number of hardware cores.

Out of the desire to predict parallel performance without going through the expensive step of implementing and testing a parallel program came the two laws described in the sections that follow. Amdahl's law especially remains still influential, although it has been shown to be flawed.

1.5.1 AMDAHL'S LAW

In 1967 Gene Amdahl formulated a simple thought experiment for deriving the performance benefits one could expect from a parallel program. Amdahl assumed the following:

- We have a sequential application that requires T time to execute of a single CPU.
- The application consists of a $0 \le \alpha \le 1$ part that can be parallelized. The remaining $1 - \alpha$ has to be done sequentially.
- Parallel execution incurs no communication overhead, and the parallelizable part can be divided evenly among any chosen number of CPUs. This assumption suits particularly well multicore architectures, where cores have access to the same shared memory.

Given these assumptions, the speedup obtained by N nodes should be upper-bounded by:

$$speedup = \frac{t_{seq}}{t_{par}} = \frac{T}{(1-\alpha)T + \frac{\alpha \cdot T}{N}} = \frac{1}{1-\alpha + \frac{\alpha}{N}} \qquad (1.5)$$

since we are ignoring any partitioning/communication/coordination costs. Equation 1.5 can give us the maximum possible speedup as well if we obtain the limit for $N \to \infty$:

$$lim_{N \to \infty}(speedup) = \frac{1}{1-\alpha} \qquad (1.6)$$

Equation 1.6 is a rare gem. In a simple, easy-to-remember form, it solves a difficult question: How much faster can a problem be solved by a parallel program? And it does so in a completely abstract manner, without consideration for the computing platform idiosyncrasies. It relies only on the characteristics of the problem, i.e., α.

Figure 1.11 visualizes the predictions of Amdahl's law for different values of α. It is immediately striking that the predicted speedup is severely restricted. Even for modest values of α, the maximum speedup is low. For example, if $\alpha = 0.9$, $speedup < 10$, regardless of the number of processors thrown at the problem.

The miserable predictions are also reflected in the efficiency curves of Figure 1.12, where efficiency drops rapidly, even for $\alpha = 95\%$.

Amdahl's law has an interesting consequence, which might have been the motivation behind its creation. Amdahl's law was formulated during an era that saw

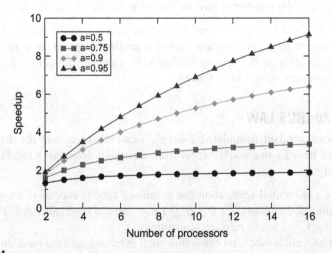

FIGURE 1.11

Speedup curves for different values of α, i.e., the part of an application that can be parallelized, as predicted by Ahdahl's law.

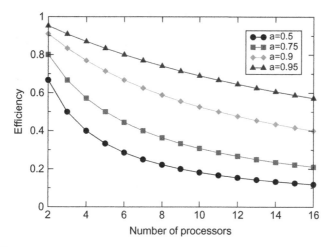

FIGURE 1.12

Efficiency curves for different values of α, as predicted by Ahdahl's law.

the introduction of the minicomputer. Minicomputers were much cheaper than the then-dominant mainframes, but they were also less powerful. A natural question popped-up: Which is the best investment for speeding up the solution of a problem? A few powerful but expensive machines or many more less powerful but inexpensive ones?

The metaphor used to describe this dilemma predicated the outcome without much doubt: "An army of ants versus a herd of elephants"! The mathematical proof based on the same assumptions as above is as follows: assuming that we have a program that can execute in time T_A on a single powerful CPU and time T_B on a less powerful, inexpensive CPU, we can declare, based on the execution time, that CPU A is $r = \frac{T_B}{T_A}$ times faster than B. If we can afford to buy N_B CPUs of the inexpensive type, the best speedup we can get relative to the execution on a single CPU of type A is:

$$speedup = \frac{T_A}{(1 - \alpha)T_B + \frac{\alpha T_B}{N_B}} = \frac{1}{(1 - \alpha)r + \frac{\alpha \cdot r}{N_B}} \tag{1.7}$$

For infinite N_B, we can get the absolute upper bound on the speedup:

$$lim_{N_B \to \infty}(speedup) = \frac{1}{(1 - \alpha)r} \tag{1.8}$$

which means that the speedup will never be above 1, no matter how many "ants" you use, if:

$$\frac{1}{(1 - \alpha)r} \leq 1 \Rightarrow r \geq \frac{1}{1 - \alpha} \tag{1.9}$$

So, if $\alpha = 90\%$ and $r = 10$, we are better off using a single expensive CPU than going the parallel route with inexpensive components.

The problem is that this conclusion does not reconcile with the reality of high-performance computing. The list of the Top 500 most powerful supercomputers in existence worldwide, as compiled in June 2014,[6] is populated exclusively by machines that have tens of thousands to millions of CPU cores (3,120,000 for the machine holding the top spot, Tianhe-2), built from off-the-shelf components that you can find in desktop machines. If the army of ants won, there must be a flaw in our approach. This is revealed in the following section.

1.5.2 GUSTAFSON-BARSIS'S REBUTTAL

Amdahl's law is fundamentally flawed as it has been repeatedly shown failing to explain empirical data: Parallel programs routinely exceed the predicted speedup limits.

Finally, two decades after Amdahl's law was published, Gustafson and Barsis managed to examine the problem from the proper point of view.

A parallel platform does more than just speed up the execution of a sequential program. It can accommodate bigger problem instances. So, instead of examining what a parallel program could do relative to a sequential one, we should examine how a sequential machine would perform if it were required to solve the same problem that a parallel one can solve.

Assuming:

- We have a parallel application that requires T time to execute of N CPUs.
- The application spends $0 \leq \alpha \leq 1$ percent of the total time running on all machines. The remaining $1 - \alpha$ has to be done sequentially.

Solving the same problem on a sequential machine would require a total time:

$$t_{seq} = (1 - \alpha)T + N \cdot \alpha \cdot T \tag{1.10}$$

as the parallel parts now have to be done sequentially.

The speedup would then be:

$$speedup = \frac{t_{seq}}{t_{par}} = \frac{(1 - \alpha)T + N \cdot \alpha \cdot T}{T} = (1 - \alpha) + N \cdot \alpha \tag{1.11}$$

and the corresponding efficiency:

$$efficiency = \frac{speedup}{N} = \frac{1 - \alpha}{N} + \alpha \tag{1.12}$$

The efficiency has a lower bound of α, as N goes to infinity.

The resulting speedup curves, as sampled in Figure 1.13, are worlds apart from the ones in Figure 1.11. Given the total disregard for the communication costs, the results are obviously overambitious, but the potential truly exists.

---

[6] Available at http://www.top500.org/lists/2014/06/.

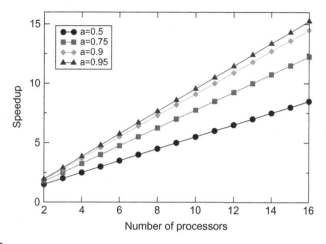

FIGURE 1.13

Speedup curves for different values of α as predicted by Gustafson-Barsis' law.

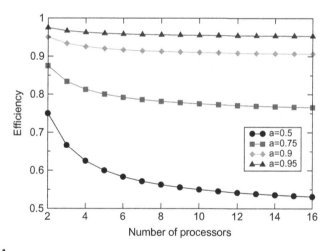

FIGURE 1.14

Efficiency curves for different values of α as predicted by Gustafson-Barsis' law.

In the efficiency curves of Figure 1.14 the picture remains a rosy one. Even for $\alpha = 50\%$, efficiency does not drop below 50% for up to 16 CPUs. This is just too good to be true. Even for the so-called embarrassingly parallel problems, communication overheads become a defining factor when N increases, diminishing speedup gains and plummeting efficiency. In general, obtaining efficiency above 90% in practice is considered a worthwhile achievement.

EXERCISES

1. Study one of the top 10 most powerful supercomputers in the world. Discover:
   - What kind of operating system does it run?
   - How many CPUs/GPUs is it made of?
   - What is its total memory capacity?
   - What kind of software tools can be used to program it?
2. How many cores are inside the top GPU offerings from Nvidia and AMD? What is the GFlop rating of these chips?
3. The performance of the most powerful supercomputers in the world is usually reported as two numbers *Rpeak* and *Rmax*, both in TFlops (tera floating point operations per second) units. Why is this done? What are the factors reducing performance from *Rpeak* to *Rmax*? Would it be possible to ever achieve *Rpeak*?
4. A sequential application with a 20% part that must be executed sequentially, is required to be accelerated three-fold. How many CPUs are required for this task?
   If the required speedup was 5, what would be the number of CPUs required?
5. A parallel application running on 5 identical machines, has a 10% sequential part. What is the speedup relative to a sequential execution on one of the machines? If we would like to double that speedup, how many CPU would be required?
6. An application with a 5% non-parallelizable part, is to be modified for parallel execution. Currently on the market there are two parallel machines available: machine X with 4 CPUs, each CPU capable of executing the application in 1 hour on its own, and, machine Y with 16 CPUs, with each CPU capable of executing the application in 2 hours on its own. Which is the machine you should buy, if the minimum execution time is required?
7. Create a simple sorting application that uses the mergesort algorithm to sort a large collection (e.g., 10^7) of 32-bit integers. The input data and output results should be stored in files, and the I/O operations should be considered a sequential part of the application. Mergesort is an algorithm that is considered appropriate for parallel execution, although it cannot be equally divided between an arbitrary number of processors, as Amdahl's and Gustafson-Barsis' laws require.
   Assuming that this equal division is possible, estimate α, i.e., the part of the program that can be parallelized, by using a profiler like `gprof` or `valgrind` to measure the duration of mergesort's execution relative to the overall execution time. Use this number to estimate the predicted speedup for your program.
   Does α depend on the size of the input? If it does, how should you modify your predictions and their graphical illustration?
8. A parallel application running on 10 CPUs, spends 15% of its total time, in sequential execution. What kind of CPU (how much faster) would we need to run this application completely sequentially, while keeping the same total time?

Multicore and parallel program design

IN THIS CHAPTER YOU WILL

- Learn the PCAM methodology for designing parallel programs.
- Use task graphs and data dependency graphs to identify parts of a computation that can execute in parallel.
- Learn popular decomposition patterns for breaking down the solution of a problem into parts that can execute concurrently.
- Learn major program structure patterns for writing parallel software, such as master-worker and fork/join.
- Understand the performance characteristics of decomposition patterns, such as pipelining.
- Learn how to combine a decomposition pattern with an appropriate program structure pattern.

2.1 INTRODUCTION

The transition to multicore programming is never an easy one, even for seasoned professional programmers. Multicore and parallel programming in general break the legacy of the sequential program that executes its statements in a strict order. When many things happen at the same time, as is the case for parallel programs, the possible ordering of statements is far from unique. Unless the program is carefully designed, problems such as erroneous updates to data or out-of-sync communications that block programs, can creep in.

In this chapter we delve into the development of multicore software by addressing the most fundamental aspect of the problem: *the design*.

Our objectives are two:

- Correctness
- Performance

Turning a sequential program into a parallel one is not necessarily the way to go. Parallel execution may require a completely new algorithm. In fact, GPUs impose so many restrictions on the program structure so that we can squeeze out their potential that a complete redesign is typically necessary.

2.2 THE PCAM METHODOLOGY

PCAM stands for **P**artitioning, **C**ommunication, **A**gglomeration, and **M**apping, and it is a four-step process for the design of parallel programs that was popularized by Ian Foster in his 1995 book [34].[1] Foster's book remains the definitive resource for understanding and properly applying PCAM. The core ideas of PCAM are still relevant today, even for multicore platforms.

The PCAM steps are as follows:

1. **Partitioning**: The first step involves the breakup of the computation into as many individual pieces as possible. This step brings out the parallelism (if it exists) in the algorithm. The granularity of the pieces is application specific. The breakup can be function-oriented, i.e., by separating the different steps that take place (called *functional decomposition*), or data-oriented, i.e., splitting the data that are to be processed (called *domain* or *data decomposition*). A rule of thumb is that the number of pieces should be one to two orders of magnitude bigger than the number of compute nodes available. This allows more flexibility in the steps that follow.

2. **Communication**: Ideally, the tasks that result from the breakup of the previous step are totally independent. However, it is usually the case that the tasks have interdependencies: For one to start, another one has to complete, and so on. This dependence may include the passing of data: *communication*. In this step, the *volume of data* that needs to be communicated between the tasks is determined. The combination of the first two steps results in the creation of the *task dependency graph*, with nodes representing tasks and edges representing communication volume.

3. **Agglomeration**: Communication is hampering parallel computation. One way to eliminate it is to group together tasks. Each group will be ultimately assigned to a single computational node, which means communication within the group is eliminated. The number of groups produced at this stage should be, as a rule of thumb, one order of magnitude bigger than the number of compute nodes available.

4. **Mapping**: For the application to execute, the task groups produced by the third step must be assigned/mapped to the available nodes. The objectives that need to be achieved at this stage are to (a) load balance the nodes, i.e., they should all have more or less the same amount of work to do as measured by execution time, and (b) reduce communication overhead even further by mapping groups with expensive data exchange between them, to the same nodes: Communication over shared-memory is virtually free.

How each of the steps can be performed is application dependent. Furthermore, it is known that the mapping step is a NP-complete problem, which means that in its general form it cannot be optimally solved for nontrivial graphs. A number of heuristics can be employed instead.

---

[1] Available online at http://www.mcs.anl.gov/~itf/dbpp/text/book.html.

Additionally, performance can be improved by duplicating computations, thus eliminating the need to communicate their results [9].

As an example of how PCAM can be applied, let's consider the problem of parallelizing a low-level image-processing algorithm such as image convolution, which can be used for noise filtering, edge detection, or other applications, based on the kernel used. The kernel is a square matrix with weights that are used in the calculation of the new pixel data. An illustration for a blur effect kernel is shown in Figure 2.1.

Convolution between a kernel K of odd size n and an image f is defined by the formula:

$$g(x,y) = \sum_{i=-n2}^{n2} \sum_{j=-n2}^{n2} k(n2+i, n2+j) f(x-i, y-j) \tag{2.1}$$

where $n2 = \lfloor \frac{n}{2} \rfloor$. If, for example, a 3x3 kernel is used:

$$K = \begin{vmatrix} k_{0,0} & k_{0,1} & k_{0,2} \\ k_{1,0} & k_{1,1} & k_{1,2} \\ k_{2,0} & k_{2,1} & k_{2,2} \end{vmatrix} \tag{2.2}$$

then for each pixel at row i and column j, the new pixel value $v'_{i,j}$ resulting from the convolution is determined by the values of the pixel and its eight neighbors according to the formula:

$$\begin{aligned} v'_{i,j} = & v_{i-1,j-1} \cdot k_{2,2} + v_{i-1,j} \cdot k_{2,1} + v_{i-1,j+1} \cdot k_{2,0} \\ & + v_{i,j-1} \cdot k_{1,2} + v_{i,j} \cdot k_{1,1} + v_{i,j+1} \cdot k_{1,0} \\ & + v_{i+1,j-1} k_{0,2} \cdot + v_{i+1,j} \cdot k_{0,1} + v_{i+1,j+1} \cdot k_{0,0} \end{aligned} \tag{2.3}$$

where v are original pixel values.

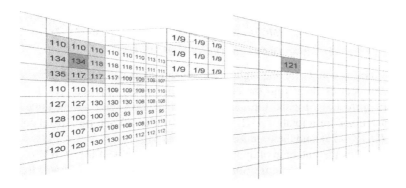

FIGURE 2.1

An illustation of how a 3x3 kernel is applied to the pixel values of an image to produce a desired effect. The shown 3x3 matrix produces a blurring effect. The new pixel values for the image on the right are produced by accummulating the products of the kernel weights and the pixel values of the area surrounding the pixel's location.

The pseudocode for a program applying a convolution-based filter is shown in Listing 2.1. To avoid handling boundary pixels (i.e., pixels on the four edges of the image) as special cases, the array holding the image data is enlarged by two rows and two columns. How these extra pixels are initialized is determined by how convolution is set to be calculated for the boundaries. For example, they can be initialized either to zero or to the value of the image pixel closest to them.

```
1   int img[IMGY+2][IMGX+2];
2   int filt[IMGY][IMGX];
3   int n2 = n/2;
4   for(int x=1;x <= IMGX; x++) {
5     for(int y=1; y <= IMGY ; y++)  {
6       int newV=0;
7       for(int i= -n2; i<= n2; i++)
8         for(int j= -n2; j<= n2; j++)
9           newV += img[ y - j][ x - i ] * k[n2 + j][n2 + i];
10      filt[y-1][x-1] = newV;
11      }
12    }
```

LISTING 2.1

Pseudocode for image filtering using convolution. The image is assume to be of size IMGX x IMGY and the kernel of size n x n.

Unrolling the first two for loops in Listing 2.1 and treating their body as a single task provides us with a task graph of size IMGX x IMGY. This is an example of domain decomposition, as each task is responsible for calculating the value of a single pixel. However, only the original value of the pixel is not sufficient for the calculation. The values of the neighboring pixels are also required, producing the graph that is shown in Figure 2.2.

The total communication operations required for the computations in Figure 2.2 to proceed are equal to:

$$totalComm = 8 \cdot IMGX \cdot IMGY - 3 \cdot 2 \cdot (IMGX - 2) - 3 \cdot 2 \cdot (IMGY - 2) - 4 \cdot 5$$

$$= 8 \cdot IMGX \cdot IMGY - 6 \cdot (IMGX + IMGY) + 14 \tag{2.4}$$

The first term accounts for the eight communications per pixel (dark gray task in Figure 2.2 receives data from the eight light gray tasks) required. The last three terms are corrections for the top and bottom pixel rows (each doing three fewer communications, for a total of $3 \cdot 2 \cdot (IMGX - 2)$), the left and right pixel columns ($3 \cdot 2 \cdot (IMGY - 2)$), and the four corner pixels ($4 \cdot 5$).

Figure 2.2 is the outcome of applying the first two steps of the PCAM methodology. The number of communication operations is obviously quite large. Grouping together tasks, as per the third phase of PCAM, aims to reduce this overhead by making required data local to a task. There are many ways that tasks can be grouped:

- 1-D: Group together tasks along the *x* or *y* axis.
- 2-D: Group together neighboring tasks to form rectangular groups of fixed size.

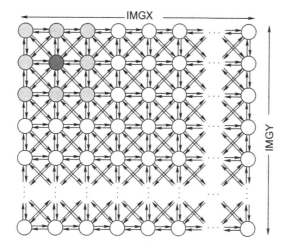

FIGURE 2.2

Task graph resulting from performing domain decomposition of the image convolution algorithm.

The sides of each group should evenly divide, if possible, the corresponding image dimension. Otherwise, the resulting groups will be unequal in terms of workload. This can in turn cause nodes to become idle while others keep computing when the mapping phase is done.

If the agglomeration is done across the x-axis, assuming that the number of groups M divides evenly the number of image columns, we get the task graph of Figure 2.3.

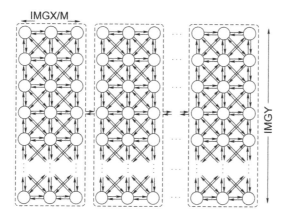

FIGURE 2.3

Task graph resulting from performing agglomeration on the graph of Figure 2.2 by grouping together columns of tasks into M groups.

Here the communication operations are reduced to just $2(M - 1)$, but each operation now carries *IMGY* pixel values. The number of groups for our simple example can match the number of available compute nodes, making the mapping stage trivial. It is also a possibility that the agglomeration is not uniform, i.e., the groups are not identical in size, if the execution platform is not homogeneous. The possibilities are endless and are obviously driven by the problem, the data representation as well as the execution platform.

2.3 DECOMPOSITION PATTERNS

The most challenging and at the same time critical part of the design process is arguably the decomposition phase, i.e., determining the parts of the computation that can proceed concurrently. Although the task graph approach is the most generic, it does not let developers gain from previous experience. This is where patterns come in. Mattson et al. [33] list a number of decomposition patterns (identified in their book as "algorithm structure design space patterns") that can cover the basic ways a workload can be decomposed for eventual distribution to the nodes of a parallel/multicore platform. Figure 2.4 shows the decision tree that leads to one of the six possible patterns.

The two categories of decomposition identified in the previous section, i.e., functional and domain decomposition, are joined by an additional one: Data flow decomposition. This category of patterns is applicable when the application is supposed to process a *stream of data* that pass through a number of processing stages. In that sense, it can be regarded as an extension of functional decomposition. The data may follow a predetermined sequence of steps leading to the use of the pipeline pattern, or they may follow irregular patterns, as

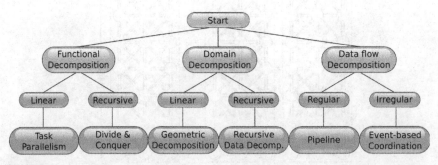

FIGURE 2.4

Decision tree for the decomposition of an algorithm. The bottom layer lists the possible decomposition patterns.

in the case of discrete event simulations, leading to the use of the event-flow decomposition.

The next decision step has to do with the *a priori* knowledge (or absence of knowledge) of the tasks that need to be executed toward the solution of a problem. *A priori* knowledge implies the ability to statically partition the jobs at the data or functional level (linear decomposition). In the opposite situation, run-time partitioning has to be utilized.

The following sections describe each of the six patterns in detail. It should be noted that there is no strict separation between the different decomposition patterns. A problem can in general be decomposed in several different ways. The variety of patterns allows us to think about the parallelization problem from different perspectives.

2.3.1 TASK PARALLELISM

Many sequential codes are structured in modules that interoperate toward the solution of a problem. As an example, let's consider the main loop of a game:

```
while(true) {
    readUserInput();
    drawScreen();
    playSounds();
    strategize();
    }
```

An easy approach to parallelism would be to assign each of the individual modules to a different compute node:

```
Task1 {
    while(true) {
        readUserInput();
        barrier();
        }
Task2 {
    while(true) {
        drawScreen();
        barrier();
        }
Task3 {
    while(true) {
        playSounds();
        barrier();
        }
Task4 {
    while(true) {
        strategize();
        barrier();
    }
```

The `barrier` synchronization primitive is supposed to ensure that all tasks coordinate together, by forcing them to wait until all complete a loop before the next iteration begins.

As long as complex dependencies do not exist between the tasks, concurrent execution is possible. This is, however, a scheme that does not scale well with the number of compute nodes, since the maximum number of nodes cannot exceed the usually limited number of tasks.

2.3.2 DIVIDE-AND-CONQUER DECOMPOSITION

A large collection of sequential algorithms are elegantly expressed recursively, i.e., the solution is expressed as the combination to the solutions of smaller disjoint subproblems.

The sequence of steps for a typical divide-and-conquer algorithm is shown below:

```
// Input: A
DnD(A) {
   if(A is a base case)
      return solution(A);
   else {
      split A into N subproblems B[N];
      for(int i=0;i<N;i++)
         sol[i] = DnD( B[i] );      // solve each subproblem
      return mergeSolution(sol);
   }
}
```

A simple example is the top-down mergesort algorithm, -partially- shown in pseudocode below:

```
// Input: array A and endpoints st, end
mergeSort(A, st, end) {
   if(end > st) {
      middle = (st+end) / 2;
      mergeSort(A, st, middle);
      mergeSort(A, middle+1, end);
      mergeLists(A, st, middle, end);
   }
}
```

The `mergeLists` call is the one that is actually doing the sorting, but the preceding listing reveals how the algorithm breaks up the input into pieces of ever-decreasing size that it subsequently joins together once they are sorted.

It should be stressed that the dependency graph, which allows us to explore the concurrency potential, does not coincide with the function call graph, so care should be exercised when such a graph is generated. Figure 2.5 shows the sequence of calls

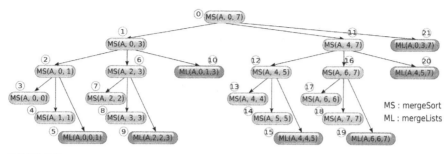

FIGURE 2.5

Call graph for a sequential execution of the top-down mergesoft algorithm for an input of eight items. The circled numbers next to each node represent the call order.

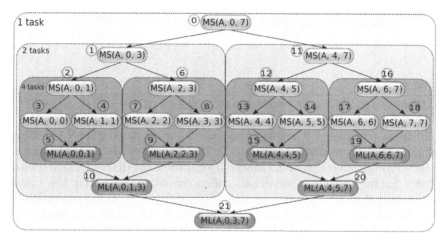

FIGURE 2.6

Dependency graph for the function calls made by the top-down mergesoft algorithm for an input of eight items. The dashed gray boxes represent possible task assignments. In our example, the maximum level of concurrency is four tasks, as the mergeSort calls for an array of size 1, return immediately, and do not represent any actual workload.

made by a sequential program for sorting an array of eight items. The parallelism is revealed when the dependency graph between those function calls is drawn as shown in Figure 2.6.

In general, the divide-and-conquer pattern is governed by the dynamic generation of tasks at run-time. The generation is performed until either we reach down to a specific problem size or the number of tasks that can run concurrently reaches the number of available compute nodes. This approach can be summarized in the form of pseudocode as shown in Listing 2.2.

```
1   // Input: A
2   DnD(A){
3     if(isBaseCase( A ))
4       return solution(A);
5     else {
6       if( bigEnoughForSplit( A ) ) { // if problem is big enough
7         split A into N subproblems B[N];
8         for(int i=0;i<N;i++)
9           task[i] = newTask( DnD( B[i] ) );   // non-blocking
10
11        for(int i=0;i<N;i++)
12          sol[i] = getTaskResult( task[i] );  // blocking results ↩
              wait
13
14        return mergeSolution( sol );
15      }
16      else {                          // else solve sequentially
17        return solution( A );
18      }
19    }
20  }
```

LISTING 2.2

Pseudocode for parallelizing a generic divide-and-conquer algorithm.

In the loop of lines 8-9, non-blocking calls are made to generate N tasks that will solve the subproblems created in line 7. The execution will only block when it is time to collect the results of the children-tasks executions (lines 11-12). It is also possible that the parent task, solves one of the subproblems, generating $N - 1$ new tasks, instead of idling. The actual scheduling or mapping of the tasks to the available compute nodes is another problem, that is largely platform specific as it depends on the associated costs of migrating tasks and communicating data. Therefore, it will be examined in later chapters.

2.3.3 GEOMETRIC DECOMPOSITION

Many algorithms involve the repetition of a sequence of steps on a collection of data. If the data are organized in linear structures such as arrays, 2D matrices, or the like, the data can be split along one or more dimensions and assigned to different tasks. Hence the name "geometric" decomposition.

If there are no dependencies between the data, we have an *embarrassingly parallel* problem, since all the resulting tasks can be executed in parallel, maximizing the potential speedup.

For example, let's consider the problem of simulating heat diffusion on a 2D surface. The equation that governs the temperature change of an isotropic and homogeneous medium is:

$$\frac{\partial u}{\partial t} = \alpha \nabla^2 u = \alpha \left(\frac{\partial^2 u}{\partial x^2} + \frac{\partial^2 u}{\partial y^2} \right) \tag{2.5}$$

where $u = u(x, y, t)$ is the temperature as a function of space and time, and α is a constant related to the material's thermal conductivity.

A simulation can be performed by dividing the surface into a discrete mesh of cells, each of size $h \cdot h$. Each cell's temperature can be updated over a number of time steps by using the following approximation to the Laplacian operator of Equation 2.5:

$$u'[i,j] = u[i,j] + \delta t \cdot \frac{u[i-1,j] + u[i+1,j] + u[i,j-1] + u[i,j+1] - 4u[i,j]}{h^2} \qquad (2.6)$$

where $u'[i,j]$ is the new temperature and $u[i,j]$ the old one at grid location $[i,j]$. δt is the time step.

Equation 2.6 means that in order to calculate the temperature at every time step, four neighboring values must be collected, as shown in Figure 2.7.

The geometric decomposition of this problem's data can proceed in one or two dimensions, as shown in Figure 2.8. But which one is preferable?

This is a question that can be answered only by taking into consideration the target execution platform. Fortunately, this can be accomplished without having to build and test multiple versions of the parallel program.

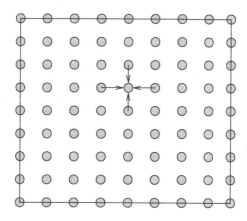

FIGURE 2.7

Data dependencies for the calculation of a cell's new temperature value in the simulation of heat transfer.

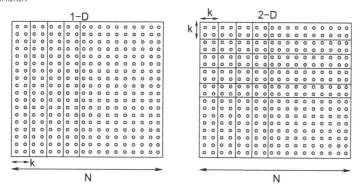

FIGURE 2.8

Geometric decomposition of the data in the simulation of heat transfer.

Let's assume that the execution platform is homogeneous, with single-port, full-duplex communication links, and that the following parameters describe the problem:

- N is the number of cells per dimension.
- k is number of cells per division along the dimension of decomposition.
- P is the number of compute nodes.
- t_{comp} represents processing cost per single update for a single cell.
- t_{comm} represents communication cost per data item sent between two compute nodes.
- t_{start} represents communication startup latency.

Then if 1D decomposition is used, we end up with $P = \lceil \frac{N}{k} \rceil$ groups that are supposed to be mapped to individual nodes. For the sake of simplicity we will assume that k divides N evenly. For each time step, each node will have to spend for execution and communication:

$$comp_{1D} = \frac{N}{k} \cdot N \cdot t_{comp} = \frac{N^2}{P} \cdot t_{comp} \tag{2.7}$$

$$comm_{1D} = 2 \cdot (t_{start} + t_{comm}N) \tag{2.8}$$

The communication time is calculated based on the need to send and receive a total of four batches of N values. The full-duplex links allow for simultaneous send and receive operations to take place; hence the 2 constant in Equation 2.8. Boundary nodes are an exception that can be ignored, since the other nodes dominate the overall execution time. The exception becomes the rule if we only have two nodes! Then, the coefficient in Equation 2.8 is reduced from 2 to 1.

If a 2D decomposition were used, each node would be responsible for k^2 cells, with $P = \frac{N^2}{k^2}$, and it would have to spend for execution and communication per time step:

$$comp_{2D} = k^2 t_{comp} = \frac{N^2}{P} t_{comp} \tag{2.9}$$

$$comm_{2D} = 4(t_{start} + t_{comm} \cdot k) = 4\left(t_{start} + t_{comm} \cdot \frac{N}{\sqrt{P}}\right) \tag{2.10}$$

As in the 1D case, boundary nodes are an exception that can be ignored unless we have only four nodes. In that case, each node performs two concurrent receive and send operations (for a total of four), reducing the coefficient in Equation 2.10 to 2.

So, if we have more than four nodes to utilize, the 1D decomposition is superior to the 2D one because of the communication overhead when:

$$comm_{1D} + comp_{1D} < comm_{2D} + comp_{2D}$$

$$\Rightarrow 2 \cdot (t_{start} + t_{comm}N) + \frac{N^2}{P} \cdot t_{comp} < 4\left(t_{start} + t_{comm} \cdot \frac{N}{\sqrt{P}}\right) + \frac{N^2}{P} t_{comp}$$

$$\Rightarrow t_{comm}N < t_{start} + 2t_{comm}\frac{N}{\sqrt{P}}$$

$$\Rightarrow t_{start} > t_{comm}N\left(1 - \frac{2}{\sqrt{P}}\right) \tag{2.11}$$

So, as long as the communication startup delay exceeds the threshold of Equation 2.11, 1D decomposition is preferable, given the communication setup described above.

It should be noted that Equation 2.6 can be also modeled as a convolution of an image with pixels representing the temperature of the cells and a 3x3 kernel:

$$K = \begin{vmatrix} 0 & 1 & 0 \\ 1 & -4 & 1 \\ 0 & 1 & 0 \end{vmatrix} \qquad (2.12)$$

The discussion of Section 2.2 would apply in this case, giving us the same results.

2.3.4 RECURSIVE DATA DECOMPOSITION

Recursive data structures such as trees, lists, or graphs cannot be partitioned in the straightforward manner of the previous section. In recursive data decomposition, the data structure is decomposed into individual elements. Each element (or group of elements) is then assigned to a separate compute node.

The process may involve a modification of the original algorithm so that concurrent operations can take place. The way of operation mimics *dynamic programming*, where bigger problems are solved based on the stored solutions of smaller problems.

For example, let's consider the problem of calculating the partial sums of an array: Given an input array A with N elements, calculate the partial sums $S_i = \sum_{j=0}^{i} A_j$. The linear complexity sequential algorithm is shown in Listing 2.3.

```
S[0] = A[0];
for(int i=1; i< N; i++)
    S[i] += S[i-1] + A[i];
```

LISTING 2.3

Sequential pseudocode for the calculation of partial sums of an array.

A variation to this algorithm would be to calculate partial sums of ever-increasing groups of numbers: first of groups of size 2, then of groups of size 4, then of groups of size 8, and so on, as shown in Listing 2.4.

```
1   // Input array A of size N
2   // Uses two arrays for calculating the sum, each of size N
3   int S[2][N];
4
5   S[1][0] = A[0];
6   S[0][0] = A[0];
7
8   int *Snew, *Sold, *aux;
9   Snew = S[0];
10  Sold = A;
11  aux = S[1];
12
13  int step=1;
14  while(step < N) {
15      int pos=0;
```

```
16
17      while (pos + step < N) {
18          Snew[pos + step] = Sold[ pos ] + Sold[pos + step];
19          pos ++;
20      }
21
22      Sold = Snew;
23      Snew = aux;
24      aux = Sold;
25      step *= 2;
26   }
27
28   // result is in array Sold
29 }
```

LISTING 2.4

Alternative sequential pseudocode for the calculation of partial sums of an array of integers.

A tracing of the code in Listing 2.4 for an array of size $N = 9$ is illustrated in Figure 2.9. The use of two arrays for holding the values of the result array as it is being computed is mandated by the fact that each iteration of the `while` loop of line 14 must be done without touching the old S values.

The swapping code of lines 22-24 ensures that the newly calculated values of S will be used for the next calculations. For the very first iteration of the loop (for `step=1`), the input array A is used instead of `Sold`, eliminating the need to initially copy A into `Sold`.

Listing 2.4 does not improve on the time complexity of Listing 2.3. On the contrary, actually: its time complexity is $O(NlgN)$,[2] a substantial increase over $N - 1$. However, it lends itself to parallel execution! Each of the maximum N steps of each iteration of the `while` loop of line 14 can be done in parallel. Before the next iteration

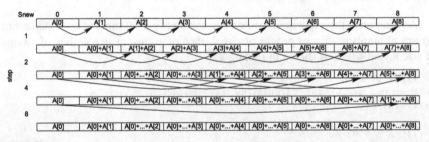

FIGURE 2.9

An illustration of the steps involved in the execution of the code in Listing 2.4 for an array of size $N = 9$. The `step` variable marks the sets of additions conducted. Each edge represents the accummulation of cell values, the arrow pointing at the destination cell.

---

[2]Number of steps is $\sum_{i=0}^{\lfloor lgN \rfloor}(N - 2^i) \approx \sum_{i=0}^{lgN}(N - 2^i) = N(lgN + 1) - \sum_{i=0}^{lgN} 2^i = N(lgN + 1)$
$- (2^{lgN+1} - 1) = N(lgN + 1) - 2N + 1 = NlgN - N + 1.$

starts, all nodes should synchronize (via a barrier) so that the updated values of the S array can be used in the next iteration.

If $N - 1$ processors were available, they could run the algorithm of Listing 2.4 in $O(lgN)$, yielding a potential speedup of:

$$speedup = \frac{N - 1}{\lceil lgN \rceil} \qquad (2.13)$$

Of course, having that many processors is an unrealistic proposition for any real-life problem, which in turn means that each of the P available nodes should be assigned a group of the updates done in each iteration. The parallel pseudocode is shown below in Listing 2.5.

```
1   // Input array A of size N
2   // Uses two arrays for calculating the sum, each of size N
3     int S[2][N];
4
5     S[1][0] = A[0];
6     S[0][0] = A[0];
7
8     int *Snew, *Sold, *aux;
9     Snew = S[0];
10    Sold = A;
11    aux = S[1];
12
13    int step=1;
14    while(step < N) {
15
16       parallel do {
17          int pos=ID;
18
19          while(pos + step < N) {
20             Snew[pos + step] = Sold[ pos ] + Sold[pos + step];
21             pos += P;
22          }
23       }
24       barrier();
25
26       Sold = Snew;
27       Snew = aux;
28       aux = Sold;
29       step *= 2;
30    }
31
32    // result is in array Sold
33  }
```

LISTING 2.5

Pseudocode of a parallel program for partial sums calculation of an array of integers, by P nodes. It is assumed that the individual nodes are identified by a unique ID that starts from 0.

In the parallel loop of lines 16-23 in Listing 2.5, each compute node identified by ID updates the partial sum of elements S[ID+step], S[ID+P+step], S[ID+2*P+step], etc. As long as N is a power of 2 and evenly divided by P, each node is assigned the same workload.

The barrier call of line 24 ensures that all nodes will proceed to the next iteration only when everyone has finished with the parallel do loop.

However, a question that naturally arises, given the increased complexity of the parallel algorithm, is whether the parallel code can deliver a speedup larger than 1.

The while loop of lines 14-30 in Listing 2.5 is executed $\lceil logN \rceil$ times. In each iteration, the total number of elements of the Snew array that are updated are equal to $N - step$. If we assume that the cost t_c of line 20 in the above listing dominates the execution time and that N is a power of 2, we can estimate the total execution time as being equal to:

$$
\begin{aligned}
t_{par} &= t_c \left(\lceil \frac{N-1}{P} \rceil + \lceil \frac{N-2}{P} \rceil + \cdots + \lceil \frac{N - 2^{lgN-1}}{P} \rceil \right) \\
&= t_c \sum_{i=0}^{lgN-1} \lceil \frac{N - 2^i}{P} \rceil \approx t_c \sum_{i=0}^{lgN-1} \frac{N - 2^i}{P} \\
&= t_c \left(\frac{N}{P} \sum_{i=0}^{lgN-1} 1 - \frac{1}{P} \sum_{i=0}^{lgN-1} 2^i \right) = t_c \left(\frac{N}{P} lgN - \frac{1}{P} \left(2^{lgN} - 1 \right) \right) \\
&= t_c \left(\frac{N}{P} lgN - \frac{N}{P} + \frac{1}{P} \right) = t_c \left(\frac{N}{P} (lgN - 1) + \frac{1}{P} \right)
\end{aligned} \tag{2.14}
$$

So, a speedup greater than one would require:

$$
speedup = \frac{t_{seq}}{t_{par}} = \frac{t_c (N - 1)}{t_c \left(\frac{N}{P} (lgN - 1) + \frac{1}{P} \right)} > 1
$$

$$
\Rightarrow (N - 1) > \frac{N}{P} (lgN - 1) + \frac{1}{P} \Rightarrow \text{(multipling both sides by } P)
$$

$$
P > \frac{N}{N-1} (lgN - 1) + \frac{1}{N-1} \tag{2.15}
$$

For large problem sizes, the above threshold can be approximated by $lgN - 1$; e.g., for 2^{20} items, the number of nodes should exceed 19.

2.3.5 PIPELINE DECOMPOSITION

A pipeline is the software/hardware equivalent of an assembly line. An item can pass through a pipeline made up of several *stages*, each stage applying a particular operation on it.

The pipeline is a popular pattern, encountered in many domains:

- **CPU architectures**: Machine instructions in modern CPUs are executed in stages that form a pipeline. This allows the concurrent execution of many instructions, each running in a different stage of the pipeline.

- **Signal processing**: Many signal-processing algorithms are formulated as pipelines. For example, an FFT-based filter may be designed around three stages executed in sequence: FFT transform, FFT coefficient manipulation, and inverse FFT transform.
- **Graphics rendering**: Contemporary GPUs have graphics or rendering pipelines that receive as input 3D vertices and produce as output 2D raster images. The pipeline stages include lighting and shading, clipping, projection transformation, and texturing.
- **Shell programming**: *nix provides the capability to feed the console *output* of one command at the console *input* of another, thus forming a command pipeline. This seemingly unsophisticated technique can make the simple *nix command-line tools perform highly complex tasks. For example, the following three-stage pipeline lists the commands executed by user guest with superuser privileges. This technique could be used by system administrators to detect hacking attempts:

```
$ sudo grep sudo /var/log/auth.log | grep guest | gawk -F ";" '{↩
    print $4}'
```

The first stage in the pipeline filters lines containing the word sudo in the /var/log/auth.log log file. The next stage limits the output of the first stage to the lines containing the word guest. Finally, the third stage parses the lines output from the second stage to produce the commands used by user guest.

Pipeline stages perform a variation of the following pseudocode, where sending and receiving operations are usually *synchronous* and concurrent in order to reduce any CPU idle times:

```
initialize();
while( moreData ) {
    readDataFromPreviousStage();
    process();
    sendDataToNextStage();
}
```

But what exactly is the benefit of arranging for a computation to take place as a sequence of communicating discrete stages? It turns out there is no benefit unless the stages can run concurrently, operating on different data items at a time. But even then, care must be taken to ensure that the stages' durations are very close or identical: The slowest (longest duration) stage dictates the speed of the pipeline.

A simple example followed by its analysis can shed light into pipeline behavior. Let's assume that we have five stages, arranged in a linear pipeline. Each stage gets its next input as soon as it has sent its output to the next stage. For simplicity we will assume that the *communication costs are negligible*. Then the processing of four data items might resemble the Gantt chart of Figure 2.10.

It is immediately obvious from Figure 2.10 that the longest-lasting stage (stage 3) dictates the rate at which the pipeline can process data.

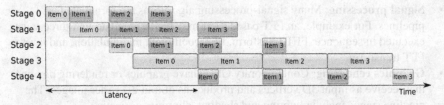

FIGURE 2.10

A Gantt chart of a five-stage pipeline with unequal stage durations processing a collection of four data items. The highlighted sequence of stage executions dictates the total execution time.

In general, if we have N data items to be processed by a M-stage pipeline, with each stage S_i taking t_i time to process its input, and S_l being the slowest stage, then the total execution time (see highlighted group of stage executions in Figure 2.10) is:

$$t_{total} = \sum_{j=0}^{l-1} t_j + N \cdot t_l + \sum_{j=l+1}^{M-1} t_j \qquad (2.16)$$

The processing rate of the pipeline (i.e., data items processed per time unit) is:

$$rate = \frac{N}{\sum_{j=0}^{l-1} t_j + N \cdot t_l + \sum_{j=l+1}^{M-1} t_j} \qquad (2.17)$$

The latency of the pipeline is defined as the time required until all stages are having some input to process:

$$latency = \sum_{j=0}^{M-2} t_j \qquad (2.18)$$

If all the pipeline stages are identical in duration, each lasting time t, then the previous equations can be simplified:

$$t_{total} = \sum_{j=0}^{M-2} t + N \cdot t = (N + M - 1)t \qquad (2.19)$$

$$rate = \frac{N}{(N + M - 1)t} \qquad (2.20)$$

$$latency = (M - 1)t \qquad (2.21)$$

If N is much larger relative to M, the pipeline can acheive an almost perfect speedup[3] score of:

$$speedup = \frac{N \cdot M \cdot t}{(N + M - 1)t} \approx M \qquad (2.22)$$

---

[3]Assuming that communication costs are negligible makes this possible.

An example of a linear pipeline is the pipeline sort[4]: For sorting N data items, create N stages that read an item from the previous stage, compare it with their current holding (if any), and send the biggest of the two items to the next stage. Each i-numbered stage (for $i \in [0, N-1]$) runs for a total of $N - i - 1$ iterations. The pseudocode describing the behavior of each stage is shown in Listing 2.6.

```
1   void stage(int sID)                // sID is the stage ID
2     T item = readFromStage(sID-1);   // for sID equal to 0 this reads ↩
           from the input
3     for(int j=0; j< N - sID -1 ; j++ ) {
4       T newItem = readFromStage(sID-1);
5       if(newItem < item)             // decide which should be send ↩
             forth
6         swap(item, newItem);
7       sendToStage(sID+1, newItem);
8     }
9     result[sID] = item;              // deposit result in destination ↩
           array
10  }
```

LISTING 2.6

Pseudocode of a single stage of a pipeline sort algorithm.

If we were able to execute all the stages in parallel, the total execution time would be equal to $2N - 1$ times the duration of the loop's body in Listing 2.6. Because the loop body has a constant duration, the time complexity of pipeline sort would be linear $O(N)$. However, having N stages is impractical. An alternative would be to have fewer stages that process batches of data items instead of comparing just two of them.

This formulation leads to the following adaptation of Listing 2.6, where we have K stages, each receiving batches of $\frac{N}{K}$ data, assuming that N is divided evenly by K, from its previous stage, as shown in Listing 2.7.

```
1   void stage(int sID)                   // sID is the stage ID
2     T part1[] = readFromStage(sID-1);  // reads an array of data
3     if(sID == 0) MergeSort(part1);     // a typical sequential sort
4     for(int j=0; j< K - sID -1 ; j++ ) {
5       T part2[] = readFromStage(sID-1);
6       if(sID == 0) MergeSort(part2);
7       MergeLists(part1, part2);         // merge part2 into part1
8       sendToStage(sID+1, secondHalf(part1));
9     }
10    store(result , part1, sID);         // deposit partial result
11  }
```

LISTING 2.7

Pseudocode of a single stage of a pipeline sort algorithm that processes batches of data items.

---

[4]There are many algorithms that can be designated as "pipeline sort." This is just one of the available variants.

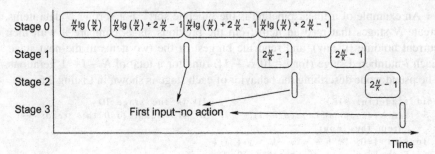

FIGURE 2.11

A Gantt chart of a four-stage sorting pipeline, as described in Listing 2.7. The worst-case numbers of key comparisons per stage are shown.

The time complexity of the mergesort algorithm in lines 3 and 6 is $O\left(\frac{N}{K}lg\frac{N}{K}\right)$. The merging of the two subarrays at line 7 has a worst-case complexity of $O\left(2\frac{N}{K}-1\right)=O\left(\frac{N}{K}\right)$. A parallel execution of all the K stages would result in a timing similar to the one shown in Figure 2.11 as the duration of the first stage would dominate the proceedings. The total execution would be proportional to the number of key comparisons performed in the parts that dominate the total time:

$$K\frac{N}{K}lg\left(\frac{N}{K}\right)+(K-1)\left(2\frac{N}{K}-1\right)+(K-2)\left(2\frac{N}{K}-1\right)$$

$$=Nlg\left(\frac{N}{K}\right)+(2K-3)\left(2\frac{N}{K}-1\right)\approx N\cdot lg\left(\frac{N}{K}\right) \quad (2.23)$$

This is admittedly a poor result as the speedup would be upper bounded by:

$$speedup_{max}=\frac{Nlg(N)}{Nlg\left(\frac{N}{K}\right)}=log_{\frac{N}{K}}(N) \quad (2.24)$$

However, this is an example that is counter to a pipeline's best practices: processing long streams of data (much longer that the pipeline's length) and keeping the stages equal in duration.

2.3.6 EVENT-BASED COORDINATION DECOMPOSITION

The previously examined decomposition patterns share an implicit common trait: Communication flow is fixed and can be taken into consideration in the design and performance evaluation of a parallel algorithm. In a number of applications, though, this is not true.

It is possible that we can identify a number of tasks or groups of tasks that interact dynamically by making decisions during run-time. In such cases, communication patterns are not fixed, and neither can the execution profile (frequency, duration, and idle times) of tasks be known *a priori*.

A typical example of such a scenario is a discrete-event simulation of a system. Discrete-event simulations are based on the modeling of system components or agents by objects or software modules that interact by generating events. An *event* is a *time-stamped message* that can represent a status change in the state of a module, a trigger to change the state, a request to perform an action, a response to a previously generated request, or the like.

2.4 PROGRAM STRUCTURE PATTERNS

Patterns can assist not only in the selection of an appropriate workload decomposition approach but also in the program development. This is the purpose of the program structure patterns. In the following sections we examine and analyze a few of the most prominent ones.

We can distinguish the parallel program structure patterns into two major categories:

- **Globally Parallel, Locally Sequential** (GPLS): GPLS means that the application is able to perform multiple tasks concurrently, with each task running sequentially. Patterns that fall in to this category include:
  - Single program, multiple data
  - Multiple program, multiple data
  - Master-worker
  - Map-reduce
- **Globally Sequential, Locally Parallel** (GSLP): GSLP means that the application executes as a sequential program, with individual parts of it running in parallel when requested. Patterns that fall in to this category include:
  - Fork/join
  - Loop parallelism

The distinction between the two categories is made more clear by the depiction of Figure 2.12. The GPLS patterns tend to offer greater scalability and are particularly

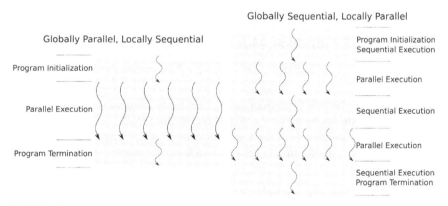

FIGURE 2.12

An illustration of how GPLS and GSLP paradigms work.

suited for shared-nothing architectures. On the other hand, GSLP tends to be employed for converting sequential programs into parallel ones by parallelizing the parts of the program that mostly affect performance.

2.4.1 SINGLE-PROGRAM, MULTIPLE-DATA

In the Single-Program, Multiple-Data (SPMD) pattern, all the nodes of the execution platform run the same program, but they either apply the same operations on different data and/or they follow different execution paths within the program.

Keeping all the application logic in a single program promotes easier and bug-free development, which makes SPMD a popular choice among programmers. The typical program structure involves the following steps:

- **Program initialization**: This step usually involves deploying the program to the parallel platform and initializing the run-time system responsible for allowing the multiple threads or processes to communicate and synchronize.
- **Obtaining a unique identifier**: Identifiers are typically numbered starting from 0, enumerating the threads or processes used. In certain cases, the identifier can be a vector and not just a scalar (e.g., CUDA). Identifier lifetime follows the thread or process lifetime it corresponds to. Identifiers can be also persistent, i.e., exist for the duration of the program, or they can be generated dynamically whenever they are needed.
- **Running the program**: Following the execution path corresponding to the unique ID. This could involve workload or data distribution, diversification of roles, etc.
- **Shutting down the program**: Shutting down the threads or processes, possibly combining the partial results generated into the final answer.

The SPMD approach is convenient, but it has a weakness: All the application's code and static (i.e., global) data are replicated in all the nodes. This can be an advantage, but it can also be a drawback, when said items are not required.

2.4.2 MULTIPLE-PROGRAM, MULTIPLE-DATA

The SPMD approach is flexible enough to cover most scenarios. It comes up short only when:

- The execution platform is heterogeneous, mandating the need to deploy different executables based on the nodes' architecture.
- The memory requirements of the application are so severe that memory space economy dictates a reduction of the program logic uploaded to each node to the bare essentials.

The Multiple-Program, Multiple-Data (MPMD) pattern covers these cases by allowing different executables, possibly generated from different tool chains, to be assembled into one application. Each compute node is free to run its own program logic and process its own data set. However, the sequence of steps identified in the previous section may still be followed.

Most major parallel platforms support the MPMD pattern. A special case is CUDA, where the program is compiled into a single file, but it actually contains two different binaries: one for the CPU host and one for the GPU coprocessor.

In most cases, a configuration file mapping the different executables to the appropriate compute nodes is all that is needed. Such an example is shown in Section 5.5.2.

2.4.3 MASTER-WORKER

The master-worker paradigm (also referred to as *master-slave*) separates the roles of the computational nodes into two distinct ones. The responsibilities of the master node(s) can involve:

- Handing out pieces of work to workers
- Collecting the results of the computations from the workers
- Performing I/O duties on behalf of the workers, i.e., sending them the data that they are supposed to process, or accessing a file
- Interacting with the user

In each simplest form, an implementation of the master-worker pattern involves a single master node and multiple worker nodes. However, this arrangement does not scale with the number of nodes, since the master can become the bottleneck. In that case we can have hierarchical schemes that incorporate a number of master modes, each commanding a part of the available machines and being accountable to a higher-authority master. Such an arrangement is shown in Figure 2.13(b).

The master-worker setup is very simple in its conception and can be naturally applied to a number of problems if the overall computation can be broken up into disjoint independent pieces that don't require internode communication. An added benefit is that this setup can provide implicit load balancing, i.e., it feeds workloads

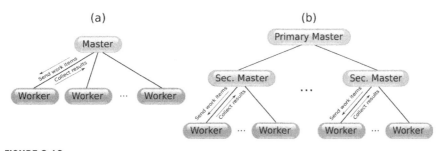

FIGURE 2.13

(a) A simple master-worker architecture. (b) A hierarchical master-worker setup with two types of master nodes: primary and secondary.

to the idle nodes, ensuring that overall there is little or no imbalance as far as work assignments are concerned.

The workloads can be described in a variety of ways, from the most *specific*, e.g., providing parameters for the execution of a known function, to the most *generic*, e.g., providing instances of classes with any kind of computation portfolio.

2.4.4 MAP-REDUCE

Map-reduce is a popular derivative of the master-worker pattern. It was made popular by Google's implementation for running its search engine. The context for the application of the map-reduce pattern is having to process a large collection of independent data (embarrassingly parallel) by applying ("mapping") a function on them. The collective results of all the partial computations have to be "reduced" by the application of a second function.

The map-reduce pattern, as evangelized by Google's tutorial [48], works in its generic form, as shown in Figure 2.14. A user program spawns a master process that oversees that whole procedure. A number of workers are also spawned; they are responsible for (a) processing the input data and producing intermediate results and (b) combining the results to produce the final answer.

In practice, the workers applying the map and the reduce stages don't have to be different. Also, the data storage between the two types of workers can be persistent (e.g., a file) or transient (e.g., a memory buffer).

The main difference between the map-reduce pattern and a typical master-worker setup is that the formulation allows for the use of automated tools that take care of

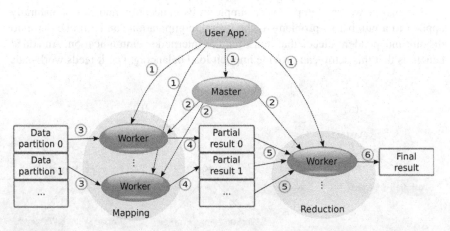

FIGURE 2.14

Generic form of the map-reduce pattern. The steps involve (1) spawning of the master and worker threads, (2) task assignments by the master, (3) data input by the workers performing the mapping, (4) saving of the partial results, (5) reading of the partial results from the "reducing" workers, and (6) saving the final result.

the deployment and load balancing of the application. The *Apache Hadoop*[5] project is an example of a framework employing a map-reduce engine. The Hadoop map-reduce engine provides two types of processes: *JobTracker*, which is equivalent to the master in Figure 2.14, and *TaskTracker*, which is equivalent to the worker type in Figure 2.14. These processes are spawned as system services (daemons). The JobTracker is responsible for assigning work to TaskTracker nodes, keeping track of their progress and state (e.g., if they die, the work is scheduled elsewhere). Each TaskTracker maintains a simple first-in, first-out (FIFO) queue of assigned tasks and executes them as separate processes (i.e., in separate Java Virtual Machines).

2.4.5 FORK/JOIN

The fork/join pattern is employed when the parallel algorithm calls for the dynamic creation (forking) of tasks at run-time. These children tasks (processes or threads) typically have to terminate (join) before the parent process/thread can resume execution.

The generated tasks can run by either spawning new threads or processes or by using an existing pool of threads to handle them. The latter is an approach that minimizes the overhead associated with the creation of threads and can potentially manage the processing resources of a machine optimally manage the processing resources of a machine (by matching the number of threads to the number of available cores).

An example of the fork/join pattern in action, is shown below, in the form of a parallel quicksort implementation[6]:

```
1   template <typename T>
2   void QuickSort<T>(T [] inp, int N) {
3     if(N <= THRES)  // for small input sort sequentially
4         sequentialQuickSort(inp, N);
5     else {
6         int pos = PartitionData(inp, N);        // split data into two ←
                parts
7         Task t = new Task( QuickSort(inp, pos)); // create new task to ←
                sort one of the parts
8         t.run();
9         QuickSort(inp + pos+ 1, N−pos−1);        // keep sorting the ←
                second part
10        waitUntilDone(t);                        // the sort is complete ←
                only if the child task is finished
11    }
12  }
```

LISTING 2.8

Pseudocode outline of a parallel version of the quicksort algorithm. The fork/join pattern is being used to spawn new sorting tasks for different pieces of the input data.

---

[5] http://hadoop.apache.org/.
[6] The details of how partitioning works in the context of quicksort can be found in most algorithm design textbooks.

The `PartitionData` call of line 6 separates the input data into two regions, one containing elements smaller or equal to a chosen element called the *pivot*, and one containing elements bigger or equal to the pivot. The `pos` index points to the position where the pivot element is placed, effectively separating the two regions, which span the ranges $[0, pos)$ and $[pos + 1, N)$. The two regions are subsequently sorted in parallel, one by spawning a new task (lines 7 and 8) and the other by the original thread/process (line 9). As long as the size of the array to be sorted exceeds the `THRES`, a new task will be generated for the task.

Reiterating a point made earlier, the generation of a new task does not necessarily mean that a new thread or process is created to handle it. This would be a recipe for disaster if a very large array were to be sorted, because that would very likely overwhelm the operating system. To illustrate how big an issue this can be, let's consider how many tasks are generated during the execution of the parallel quicksort of Listing 2.8.

If we represent as $T(N)$ the total number of tasks generated for an input of size N (*excluding the first, "parent" one*), and if we assume that the `PartitionData` function manages to separate the input data into two equal-size parts (a best-case scenario), then we have:

$$T(N) = \begin{cases} 0 & \text{if } N \leq THRES \\ 1 + 2T\left(\frac{N-1}{2}\right) \approx 1 + 2T\left(\frac{N}{2}\right) & \text{if } N > THRES \end{cases} \quad (2.25)$$

Backward substitution can solve this recurrence relation. If we assume the N and $THRES$ are powers of 2, then the expansion:

$$T(N) = 1 + 2T\left(\frac{N}{2}\right) = 1 + 2 + 2^2 T\left(\frac{N}{2^2}\right)$$

$$= \sum_{i=0}^{k-1} 2^i + 2^k T\left(\frac{N}{2^k}\right) = 2^k - 1 + 2^k T\left(\frac{N}{2^k}\right) \quad (2.26)$$

will stop when $\frac{N}{2^k} = THRES \Rightarrow k = lg\left(\frac{N}{THRES}\right)$. Substituting this value of k in Equation 2.26 yields:

$$T(N) = 2^k - 1 + 2^k \cdot T(THRES) = 2^{lg\left(\frac{N}{THRES}\right)} - 1 = \frac{N}{THRES} - 1 \quad (2.27)$$

as $T(THRES) = 0$. If, for example, we have $N = 2^{20}$ and $THRES = 2^{10}$, we will need $2^{10} - 1 = 1023$ tasks. A better approach would be to use a pool of threads to execute the tasks generated. This approach is explored thoroughly in Section 3.8.

2.4.6 LOOP PARALLELISM

The migration of software to multicore architectures is a monumental task. The loop parallelism pattern addresses this problem by allowing the developer to port existing sequential code by parallelizing the loops that dominate the execution time.

This pattern is particularly important for the OpenMP platform, where the loops are semiautomatically parallelized with the assistance of the programmer. The programmer has to provide hints in the form of directives to assist with this task.

Loop parallelism is a pattern with limited usability in the sense that it does not promote the design of a ground-up new parallel solution to a problem, but instead it focuses on the evolution of a sequential solution into a parallel one. This is also a reason that the performance benefits are usually small, but at least the development effort involved is equally minimal.

2.5 MATCHING DECOMPOSITION PATTERNS WITH PROGRAM STRUCTURE PATTERNS

A question that naturally arises is, given a decomposition pattern, which is the best way to structure the program? The answer is highly dependent on the application. Additionally, a number of platforms impose a particular program structure pattern on developers. For example, MPI uses the SPMD/MPMD pattern, whereas OpenMP promotes the loop parallelism pattern.

Still, given a specific decomposition pattern, certain program structure patterns are better suited for implementation purposes. Table 2.1 summarizes these pairings.

Table 2.1 Decomposition Patterns and the Most Suitable Program Structure Patterns for Implementing Them

| | Decomposition Patterns | | | | | |
	Task Parallelism	Divide and Conquer	Geometric Data	Recursive Data	Pipeline	Event-based Coordination
Single-Program Multiple Data	√	√	√	√	√	√
Multiple-Program Multiple Data	√	√	√	√	√	√
Master-Worker	√	√	√	√		
Map-Reduce		√	√	√		
Fork/Join	√	√	√	√	√	√
Loop Parallelism		√	√			

Program Structure Patterns

EXERCISES

1. Perform a 2D agglomeration step for the image convolution problem of Section 2.2. What is the resulting number of communication operations?
2. Perform the comparison between the 1D and 2D decompositions of the heat diffusion example in Section 2.3.3 by assuming that (a) half-duplex communication links are available and (b) n-port communications are possible, i.e., all communications can take place at the same time over all the links.
3. How would communication costs affect the pipeline performance? Derive variations of Equations 2.16 to 2.18 that take into account a constant communication overhead between the pipeline stages.
4. The total number of tasks calculated in Section 2.4.5 for the parallel quicksort of Listing 2.8 is based on the best-case assumption that the input is split in equal halves by every call to the `PartitionData` function. What would be the result if the worst case (i.e., one part gets $N - 1$ elements and the other part 0) were considered?
5. Use a simple problem instance (e.g., a small array of integers) to trace the execution of the parallel quicksort of Listing 2.8. Create a Gantt graph for the tasks generated, assuming an infinite number of compute nodes available for executing them. Can you calculate an upper bound for the speedup that can be achieved?

Shared-memory programming: threads

3

IN THIS CHAPTER YOU WILL

- Learn what threads are and how you can create them.
- Learn how to initialize threads in order to perform a desired task.
- Learn how to terminate a multithreaded program using different techniques.
- Understand problems associated with having threads access shared resources, such as race conditions and deadlocks.
- Learn what semaphores and monitors are and how you can use them in your programs.
- Become familiar with classical synchronization problems and their solutions.
- Learn how threads can be dynamically managed at run-time.
- Learn effective debugging techniques for multithreaded programs.

3.1 INTRODUCTION

The concurrent execution of multiple programs has been commonplace since the 1960s, when the Massachusetts Institute of Technology (MIT) introduced the Compatible Time Sharing System (CTSS) operating system (OS). Operating systems achieve this feat by interrupting the currently executing program and giving the control of the central processing unit (CPU) to another one. The switch, which effectively "shares" the CPU time (hence the term *time sharing*), can be triggered by:

- Regular hardware interrupts generated by a clock/timer
- Irregular hardware interrupts, e.g., those coming from a device requesting attention
- A call to the OS itself, e.g., a request to perform input/output (I/O)

Each running program constitutes a process, i.e., an OS entity that encapsulates the code, data, resources, and execution state required by the OS for managing the program.

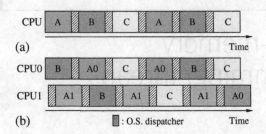

FIGURE 3.1

An example of the concurrent execution of multiple processes by (a) a single CPU and (b) multiple CPUs. (b) depicts a program running as two processes, A0 and A1.

Thus, each process takes control of the CPU for a "time slice" before surrendering it to the OS, which then hands over the CPU to another process, and so on. The timing for a single-CPU machine would be similar to that shown in Figure 3.1(a).

Time-sharing allows the efficient use of computational resources, but it cannot speed things up for each individual process. On the contrary, time sharing can slow the execution of a process by directly reducing the CPU time given to it and by indirectly diluting the available CPU time with the frequent execution of the OS/task switcher (also known as the *dispatcher*).

For a program to get a bigger share of computational time (bar scheduling directives that affect a program's priority), it has to be broken up into multiple processes. The same is true if the execution platform has more than one core. Such an example is shown in Figure 3.1(b). The mechanism that was originally used for creating, or *spawning*, multiple processes was the `fork` call. An example is shown in Listing 3.1.

```cpp
1   // File: fork.cpp
2   #include <cstdlib>
3   #include <iostream>
4   #include <unistd.h>
5
6   using namespace std;
7
8   int main (int argc, char **argv)
9   {
10      pid_t childID;
11
12      childID = fork ();
13      if (childID == 0)
14        {
15          cout << "This is the child process\n";
16        }
17      else
18        {
```

```
19          cout << "This is the parent process\n";
20      }
21    return 0;
22  }
```

LISTING 3.1

Skeleton for "forking" a process.

Forking a process results in the creation of a verbatim copy of the process's memory, including all code and data, as it was at the moment of the call (see Figure 3.2). The only thing that differs between the original (*parent*) and copy (*child*) is that the child process, which continues execution from the line following the call to fork, does not receive the return value from it (the pid_t is just an alias for). Hence, the childID for the child process in line 13 of Listing 3.1 is 0. This allows the creation of logic similar to the one starting at that line, to differentiate the actions of the two processes (it would not make sense to have them do the same thing).

Some obvious questions pop up in observing how the fork mechanism works:

- Why should we copy the code? Isn't this part of the memory immutable?
- The child process has private copies of all the parent's data. How can the two exchange information?

The answer to the first question is that there are instances of programs that modify their code at run-time. This feature is most prominent among viruses, but it cannot be excluded as a valid program behavior. For the latter question, system designers have provided mechanisms that solve this problem, but none is as easy or convenient as simply assessing a common set of variables.

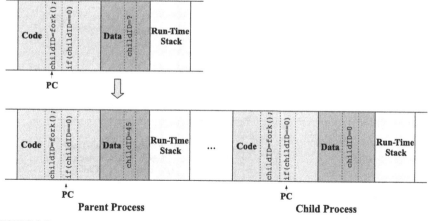

FIGURE 3.2

Memory layout that results from "forking" a process. *PC* stands for Program Counter.

The overhead associated with reserving and copying a process's image makes the fork call an expensive approach to achieving concurrency. Fortunately, an alternative exists in the form of threads, as explained in the following section.

3.2 THREADS

3.2.1 WHAT IS A THREAD?

A thread can be considered to be a lightweight process. A more precise definition is that it is an execution path, a sequence of instructions, that is managed separately by the operating system scheduler as a unit. There can be multiple threads per process.

Threads alleviate the overhead associated with the fork mechanism by copying only the bare essentials needed: the run-time stack. The run-time stack cannot be shared between two threads since it contains the *activation frames* (or *activation records*) for the functions or methods being called. A shared stack would mean, -among other things, that upon returning from a function, control could return to a point different than the one who called it.

When the *main* (or initial) thread of a process spawns a new thread, the resulting arrangement would be similar to the one shown in Figure 3.3. The parent and child relationships apply here also.

The additional overhead associated with reserving and copying a process's image makes the fork call an expensive approach to achieving concurrency. Having separate processes can be beneficial, like e.g., in providing enhanced memory protection, or more flexible scheduling, but for the most part the drawbacks outweigh the benefits.

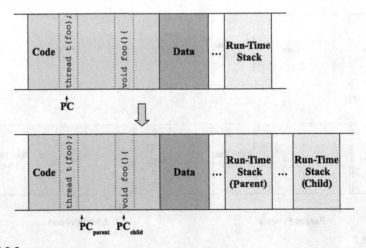

FIGURE 3.3

Memory layout that results from spawning a new thread from the main thread of a process.

3.2.2 WHAT ARE THREADS GOOD FOR?

Threads are usually associated with graphical user interface (GUI) programming. One cannot maintain a responsive user interface (UI) while performing a task initiated by the user without having a UI-dedicated thread. However, the gamut of their uses is much richer. Threads can be used for the following:

- **Improving performance**: By breaking up an application's load into multiple threads, we can get to utilize multiple cores in a system, boosting performance substantially.
- **Background tasks**: Interactive applications can use threads to perform background tasks, i.e., tasks that do not require user interaction while at the same time continuing to respond to user requests.
- **Asynchronous processing**: Sending a request to a server over a network involves substantial latency. By spawning a thread to handle the transaction with the server asynchronously (i.e., without waiting for the response), an application can continue doing useful work, improving performance and resource (e.g., CPU time) utilization.
- **Improving program structure**: A typical attribute of games is the need to perform concurrently a large collection of periodic tasks. Such tasks include screen redraw, sound playback, user input detection, and strategy making. These tasks don't have to run with the same frequency as the rest (e.g., strategy), and putting them inside the same loop and ensuring that they can run at the screen refresh rate is an extreme requirement that can only be satisfied with increased program complexity. Assigning the various tasks to different threads allows for much better structured code that is also more maintainable.

3.2.3 THREAD CREATION AND INITIALIZATION

Threads have been a neglected part of the C++ ecosystem for a long time, in the sense that thread creation and management were not part of the standard C++ library. A rich collection of third-party libraries filled this void, with notable members being:

- **pThreads**: A C-based library that is considered the common denominator for threading support.
- **winThreads**: A Windows-only C++-based library.
- **Qt threads**: A part of the Qt (pronounced "cute") cross-platform C++ based libraries and tools. It is characterized by ease of use and a rich application programming interface (API).

This problem was finally addressed in the C++ 11 standard, with the introduction of a thread class as part of the standard library. The threading equivalent to the example in Listing 3.1 is shown in Listing 3.2.

```
1  // File: cpp11Thread.cpp
2  #include <thread>
3  #include <iostream>
4
```

```
5   using namespace std;
6
7   void hello()
8   {
9       cout << "Hello from the child thread\n";
10  }
11
12  int main()
13  {
14      thread t(hello);
15      cout << "Hello from the parent thread\n";
16      t.join();
17      return 0;
18  }
```

LISTING 3.2

Skeleton for creating a thread in C++ 11.

Apart from line 2 that loads the appropriate class definition(s), there are two critical lines in Listing 3.2:

- Line 14 creates (and launches) a thread instance by providing a void-returning function with no parameters as the entry point for the execution of the child thread.
- It is recommended practice to have the parent thread wait for its children threads to finish execution (or forcefully terminate them), before terminating itself. The reason is to guarantee release of resources, closing of files, and so on. This is accomplished by line 16, which is a call to the blocking method join.

The problem is that currently, most compilers have partial support of the threading features of C++ 11. For this reason, in this chapter we explore threads and the mechanisms used to make them coordinate appropriately toward a common goal, with the assistance of the Qt library. The Qt library is a cross-platform dual-license library that offers support for UI development, database (DB) connectivity, networking, Extended Markup Language (XML) processing, and other things besides providing a very simple-to-use set of classes for managing threads. Qt is made available[1] as both an open-source library and a commercial product for developers that require close-source development. Currently Qt runs on top of Windows, MacOS X, Linux, and a small collection of embedded operating systems, offering a remarkable flexibility in program deployment.

Qt's paradigm for thread management resembles the one used by Java: Threads are created as instances of a subclass of the QThread class. The run method provides the thread's entry point. For example:

```
#include <QThread>

class MyThread: public QThread
```

---

[1] www.digia.com.

```
{
  public:
    void run() {}
};
```

Following the preceding class definition, a new thread can be started with the following statements:

```
MyThread thr;
thr.start();
```

Note that the `run` method is not invoked directly. Instead, the inherited `start` method will first create an OS thread[2] that will subsequently call the `run` method. This is contrary to the way the thread class operates in C++ 11, since the construction of an `QThread` object does not mean that a thread is spawned. The `start` method must be explicitly called for this to happen.

Making the main program thread wait for a child thread to terminate before ending execution, is a matter of calling the `wait` method:

```
thr.wait();
```

In order to direct a thread in performing a specific task, especially if more than one children threads are created, there are three choices:

- **Using global variables**: Violates the encapsulation principle, making the program prone to software errors.
- **Creating multiple QThread derivative classes**: Impractical if a large number of threads is required.
- **Using the thread object's data members**: This is the recommended approach. The thread object must be initialized prior to calling the `start` method, typically via an appropriate constructor. For example[3]:

```
1   // File: qtThreadsSimple.cpp
2   #include <QThread>
3   #include <iostream>
4
5   using namespace std;
6
7   class MyThread:public QThread
8   {
9   private:
10     int ID;
11   public:
12     MyThread(int id): ID(id) {};
13     void run () {
14       cout << "Hello from the child thread " << ID << "\n";
15     }
16   };
```

---

[2]The OS thread is what the scheduler manages. Whatever the `QThread` object contains is used for directing the execution path of the OS thread.

[3]Detailed instructions about how to compile a Qt program are found in Appendix A.

```
17
18  int main (int argc, char *argv[])
19  {
20    MyThread t(0);
21    t.start();
22    cout << "Hello from the main thread\n";
23    t.wait();
24    return 0;
25  }
```

LISTING 3.3

A simple multithreaded program with a single child thread.

Completing our simple introduction to thread creation and initialization in Qt, the following listing is a program that generates a variable number of threads, each sequentially numbered starting from zero. The number of threads is controlled from the command line. Each thread prints out a short message and exits.

```
1   // File: qtThreads.cpp
2   #include <QThread>
3   #include <iostream>
4
5   using namespace std;
6
7   class MyThread:public QThread
8   {
9   private:
10    int ID;
11  public:
12    MyThread (int i):ID (i) {}
13    void run () {
14      cout << "Thread " << ID << " is running\n";
15    }
16  };
17
18  int main (int argc, char *argv[])
19  {
20    int N = atoi (argv[1]);
21    MyThread *x[N];
22    for (int i = 0; i < N; i++)
23      {
24        x[i] = new MyThread (i);
25        x[i]->start ();
26      }
27
28    for (int i = 0; i < N; i++)
29      x[i]->wait ();
30    return 0;
31  }
```

LISTING 3.4

A Qt-based multithreaded program with a variable number of threads, as specified in the command line. Each thread prints out a short message containing its unique ID.

The main difference between the programs in Listings 3.3 and 3.4 is how the thread objects are created and initialized. In the latter, an array of MyThread object pointers is used to individually allocate and initialize the necessary threads, one by one (line 24). The use of the pointers mandates the "arrow" notation in lines 25 and 29.

3.2.3.1 Implicit thread creation

It is occasionally the case that a side task needs to be executed without the formality of creating a QThread object, starting it, and then waiting for it to finish. Qt supports this scenario with a set of functions in the QtConcurrent namespace. The syntax is as follows:

```
#include <QtConcurrent>

extern void foo();
...
QtConcurrent::run(foo);
```

When the static QtConcurrent::run function is called, a separate thread is used to run the supplied function. The thread is taken from a pool of Qt-managed threads that are preallocated to eliminate the OS overhead associated with starting a thread during program execution. The QThreadPool class is responsible for this task. This class is examined in more detail in Section 3.8.

There are three issues with the use of QtConcurrent::run:

- **How to pass parameters**: Since there is no object that can be initialized before the thread is called, the technique used to pass parameters is to list them as parameters to the QtConcurrent::run method after the reference to the function. These are copied and passed in turn to the function when the thread runs. This also prevents the function from modifying the original parameters, unless they are pass-by-reference.
- **How to detect when the thread is done**: The QtConcurrent::run function return a reference to a QFuture object that can be used to check the status of the execution and even block until the thread is done, so both polling and blocking checks can be conducted. Some of the most useful methods supported by QFuture are:
    - isStarted(): Returns true if the thread has started execution. The execution maybe delayed if there is no available thread in QThreadPool.
    - isRunning(): Returns true if the thread is currently running.
    - isFinished(): Returns true if the thread has competed execution of the provided function.
- **How to collect the result of the function**: QFuture is a template class that allows the retrieval of the function return value. The example that follows illustrates how.

Let's consider a MD5-hash calculating program, that is supposed to print-out the 16-byte checksum for every file specified as a parameter. The twist in Listing 3.5 is that each MD5 calculation is run concurrently.[4]

```cpp
1   // File : md5Ex/md5Ex.cpp
2   #include <cstdio>
3   #include <string>
4   #include <unistd.h>
5   #include "md5.h"
6   #include <QtConcurrentRun>
7   #include <QFuture>
8
9   using namespace std;
10
11  int main (int argc, char *argv[])
12  {
13    int N = argc - 1;
14    QFuture < string > f[N];
15    char *buffers[N];
16
17    // scan all the filenames supplied
18    for (int i = 0; i < N; i++)
19      {
20        buffers[i] = 0;
21        FILE *fin;
22        fin = fopen (argv[i + 1], "r");
23        if (fin != 0)          // if the file exists
24          {
25            fseek (fin, 0, SEEK_END);
26            int fileSize = ftell (fin);   // find out the size
27            fseek (fin, 0, SEEK_SET);
28
29            buffers[i] = new char[fileSize + 1];  // allocate enough ↩
                    memory
30            fread (buffers[i], fileSize, 1, fin); // read all of it in ↩
                    memory
31            buffers[i][fileSize + 1] = 0;          // terminate by 0 as ↩
                    md5() expects a string
32            fclose (fin);
33            string s (buffers[i]);
34            f[i] = QtConcurrent::run (md5, s);   // calculate the MD5 ↩
                    hash in another thread
35          }
36      }
37
38
39    for (int i = 0; i < N; i++)
40      if (buffers[i] != 0)              // if file existed
```

---

[4]Depending on the version of Qt used, lines similar to the following may be required in the .pro file, for a program using QtConcurrent facilities to compile successfully:

```
INCLUDEPATH += /usr/include/qt5/QtConcurrent
LIBS += -lQt5Concurrent
```

```
41          {
42              f[i].waitForFinished (); // wait for the calculation to ↵
                    complete
43              cout << argv[i + 1] << " : " << f[i].result () << endl;
44              delete [] buffers[i];      // cleanup the buffer
45          }
46      return 0;
47  }
```

LISTING 3.5

A program that invokes a Qt-managed thread for calculating the MD5 hash for each of the files passed as parameters to it.

The key points of the example in Listing 3.5 are:

- **Line 5**: Required include directive for using the md5 function.[5]
- **Lines 6,7**: Required include directives for using the Qt classes.
- **Line 13**: N equals the number of filenames supplied.
- **Line 14**: Array of QFuture<string> objects for accessing the results of each individual thread run.
- **Line 15**: Each file is loaded into memory before being processed. These pointers point to the individual blocks used.
- **Lines 25-27**: Discover the size of the file before allocating a buffer for it (line 29).
- **Line 31**: 0-terminate the buffer. The program does not produce correct output for binary files because the md5 function is coded to work on data of type string.
- **Line 34**: Request that the md5 function be run by a separate thread. The exact time that this will happen is unknown, depending on the availability of free threads.
- **Line 43**: Use the QFuture objects returned by QtConcurrent::run to print out the 16-character string returned by the md5 function.

3.2.4 SHARING DATA BETWEEN THREADS

Sharing of global data, as shown in Figure 3.3, simplifies a thread's access to common data repositories. However, there is a *precondition*: Access must be read-only. Otherwise, special mechanisms must be employed to ensure that when a thread is writing to a shared variable, it does so in isolation, i.e., no other thread should be allowed to do this at the same time. When modification are being made reading operation should be also blocked, as an inconsistent state could be retrieved otherwise. It is often the case that making write operations "atomic" (i.e., indivisible, uninterruptable) is not sufficient. It may be required that an object or data structure become locked (i.e., completely inaccessible) for the duration of a state-modifying operation.

As an example, consider two threads that operate on a bank account object. One is trying to withdraw funds and pay a utility bill, and the other is trying to deposit a

---

[5]The full code is provided in the book's supplementary material.

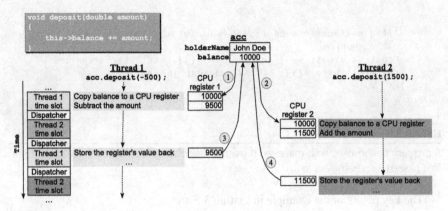

FIGURE 3.4

One of the possible outcomes resulting from having two threads modify a bank account object, without any means of coordination. The read and write operations to the `balance` field are numbered in the sequence in which they occur. The value stored back by operation #4 eliminates the change done by #3, placing the object in a wrong state (it should be 11000, not 11500).

monthly salary. Assuming that the account is represented by a simple data structure consisting of a string (for the holder's name) and a double (for the balance); then one of the possible outcomes of having the two threads run at the same time is shown in Figure 3.4. It is important to stress that this is one possible outcome, with the account being updated correctly being another. The problem is that there is no way to predict the outcome of maintaining an account in this fashion.

This is a simple instance of the readers-writers problem that is explored further in Section 3.5.4.

Another coded example that illustrates the side effects of unrestricted read-write access to shared data is shown in Listing 3.6. The phenomenon illustrated is called a *race condition*, the race being the contention between threads for access to the same data. A more formal definition of the term is that it is *an abnormal program behavior caused by dependence of the result on the relative timing of events in the program.* In other words, if race conditions exist, a program's output will not be always the same for the same input.

```
1   // File: raceCond.cpp
2   #include <QThread>
3   #include <iostream>
4   #include <unistd.h>
5
6   using namespace std;
7
8   int counter = 0;
9
10  class MyThread:public QThread {
```

```
11   private:
12     int ID;
13     int runs;
14   public:
15     MyThread (int i, int r):ID(i), runs(r) {}
16     void run () {
17       cout << "Thread " << ID << " is running\n";
18       for (int j = 0; j < runs; j++)
19         {
20             usleep (rand () % 3);
21             counter++;
22         }
23     }
24   };
25
26   int main (int argc, char *argv[])
27   {
28     srand (time (0));
29     int N = atoi(argv[1]);
30     int runs = atoi(argv[2]);
31     MyThread *t[N];
32     for (int i = 0; i < N; i++)
33       {
34           t[i] = new MyThread (i, runs);
35           t[i]->start ();
36       }
37
38
39     for (int i = 0; i < N; i++)
40       t[i]->wait ();
41
42     cout << counter << endl;
43     return 0;
44   }
```

LISTING 3.6

A multithreaded program that showcases a race condition. Each of the user-specified numbers of threads increments a global variable a constant number of times.

The program in Listing 3.6 accepts as parameters the number of children threads (*N*) and the number of increments (*runs*) that each thread is to perform on a global counter. When all threads are done (checked via the loop in lines 39 and 40), the main thread prints out the final value of the counter (line 42), which is expected to be $N \cdot runs$. This is a sample from one run:

```
$ ./raceCond 10 100
Thread Thread Thread Thread Thread Thread 0 is running
2 is running
Thread 37Thread 6 is running
Thread 8 is running
 is running
```

```
is running
1 is running
5 is running
Thread 9 is running
4 is running
985
```

Amazingly, the outcome is not the one expected, in more ways than one! First, the messages are all mixed up, since all threads compete for sending output to the console. Second, the result in the last line is not 1000, as expected. This is a result of having threads update the value of the counter out of sync, incrementing and storing a non-up-to-date value (Listing 3.6, line 21).

Unfortunately, in practice, race conditions are hard to detect and fix, since a multithreaded program's outcome can be heavily influenced by timing considerations and not just by the supplied input. In the example of Listing 3.6, the timing influence is exaggerated by forcing threads to go to sleep between increments (line 20). Otherwise it would be possible to fit each thread's run within the time slot assigned by the scheduler, effectively hiding the problem.

In the following sections we cover the most commonly used locking mechanisms in shared-memory programming. It is also possible to eliminate race conditions without blocking or locking a data item or structure, but this is not a trivial exercise, as we will see later.

3.3 DESIGN CONCERNS

The problem can be boiled down to the following: *How can you make a multi-threaded program behave in the same manner as a sequential one?*

This is where different *consistency models* come into play. A consistency model is a set of rules that, when followed, causes the system to behave in a specific way. A number of consistency models have been proposed, each offering a different trade-off between efficiency and strictness. One of the many models that have been proposed is the *sequential consistency model.*

In the sequential consistency model, all the events that operate on shared memory objects should appear to happen in a one-at-a-time order. Also, these events should appear to take effect in program order as far as each thread is concerned. The events that take place in different threads can be shifted so that the overall history (sequence of events/method invocations) of an object satisfies its sequential specification (i.e., how it behaves when run by a single thread). An example of this reordering is shown in Figure 3.5.

The sequential consistency model is problematic in the sense that it is not compositional: Combining two software modules that observe sequential consistency does not guarantee the production of a composite that is sequentially consistent. An example of how sequential consistency fails is shown in Figure 3.6, where the

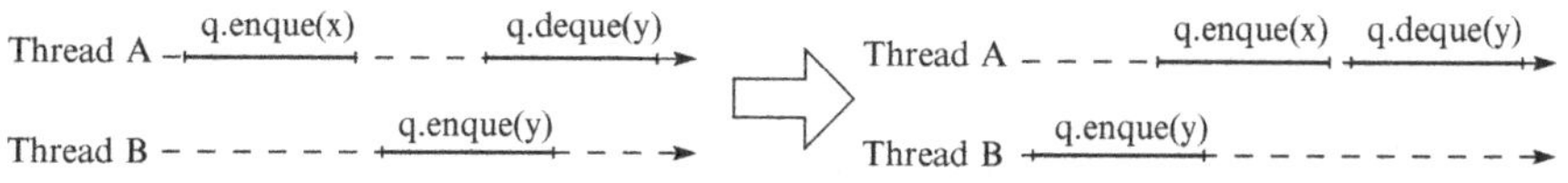

FIGURE 3.5

An example of reordering the timelines of two threads operating on a first-in, first-out (FIFO) queue without changing the program order, which makes the sequence of events (shown on the left) equivalent to using a sequential queue.

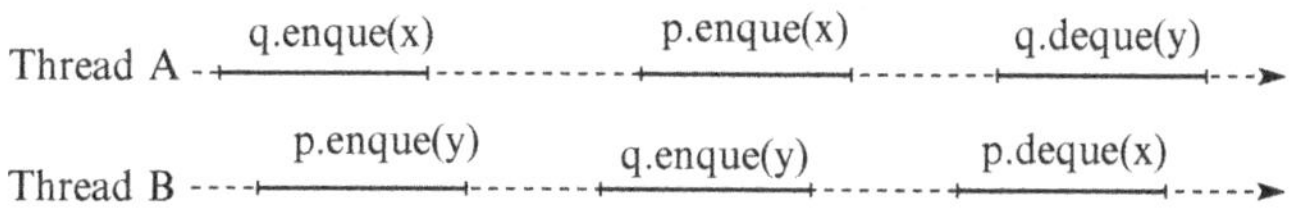

FIGURE 3.6

An example showing that the composition of two sequentially consistent objects (p and q FIFO queues) is not sequentially consistent.

sequence shown in Figure 3.5 is duplicated for a second queue, q. Although each individual queue is sequentially consistent, there is no way that the two timelines shown in Figure 3.6 can satisfy sequential consistency.

A more strict consistency model is that of *linearizability* [45]: Events should appear to happen in one-at-a-time order and should appear to take place *instantaneously*. The last requirement is modeled by the introduction of so-called *linearization points*. A linearization point is a time instance within the duration of a method call whereby the call is considered to take effect. The introduction of the linearization points has two implications:

1. The methods can be *totally ordered* according to their linearization points. A linearization point can be arbitrarily chosen within the timeframe between a method call invocation and its return. The resulting ordering must be equivalent to a sequential execution for the concurrent execution to be considered linearizable.
2. Although locking is not mandated (and actually it should be avoided, for performance reasons), locking down an object while a method is performed is the equivalent of having its effect take place instantaneously as far as everyone else is concerned. The simplest thing is to use locking mechanisms, and for this reason we explore these mechanisms in the following sections.

Every linearizable execution is sequentially consistent, but the reverse is not true. An example of a linearizable execution is shown in Figure 3.7.

In the following sections we explore two locking mechanisms that, although equivalent in functionality, promote dramatically different paradigms for synchronizing threads.

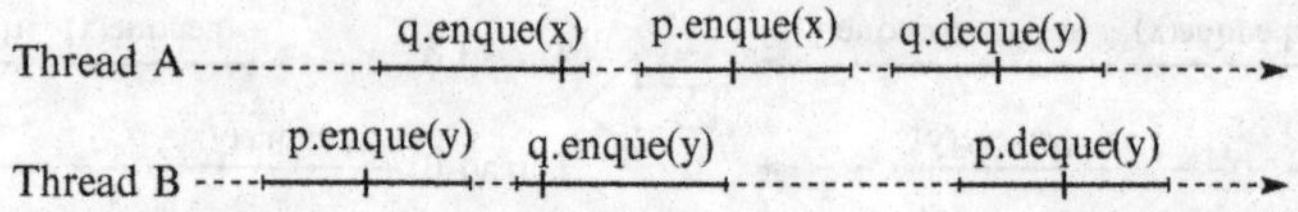

Thread A `- - - - - - - -` q.enque(x)   p.enque(x)   q.deque(y) `- - - - - - - ->`

Thread B `- - - -` p.enque(y)   q.enque(y) `- - - - - - - -` p.deque(y) `- - - - - ->`

FIGURE 3.7

An example of a linearizable execution by two threads operating on two FIFO queues.

3.4 SEMAPHORES

A *semaphore* is a software abstraction, proposed by the late Dutch computer scientist Edsger Dijkstra, that supports two *atomic* operations:

- P,[6] or lock
- V, or unlock

Various semaphore implementations use different naming conventions for replacing the cryptic P and V (e.g., Qt uses `lock - unlock` and `acquire - release`), but the semantics remain the same according to the type of semaphore implemented: *binary* or *counting*.

A *binary semaphore* or *mutex* (*MUTual EXclusion*) has a state indicating whether it is locked or unlocked. Here is what happens when a thread calls P or V:

- **P**: If the semaphore is unlocked, it becomes locked and the call returns, allowing the thread to continue. If the semaphore is locked, the thread is blocked and placed in a queue Q of waiting threads.
- **V**: If the semaphore's queue is empty, the semaphore becomes unlocked. Otherwise, a thread T is dequeued from Q and allowed to continue execution. Effectively, this is the time instance thread T's P call returns. Can you guess when the state of the semaphore will switch back to the unlocked state?

If the queue employed by a semaphore is a FIFO queue, the semaphore is called *strong*. Otherwise, it is called *weak*. In this case, there is no priority maintained between blocked threads, which could potentially lead to an indefinite block of a thread (a phenomenon called **starvation**, discussed later in this section).

A *counting semaphore* (also known as a *general semaphore*) has a counter C as a state, indicating how many resources of some type are available (e.g., messages, file handles, buffers, etc.). Here is what happens when a thread calls P or V on a counting semaphore:

- **P**: C is decremented.[7] If its new value is negative, the thread is blocked and placed in the waiting-threads queue Q.

---

[6]P and V names come from the Dutch language phrases *Probeer te verlagen* (try to decrease) and *Verhogen* (to increment), respectively.

[7]It is possible to have only nonnegative values for a counting semaphore. The implementation gets a bit more complex, and that is why it is not considered further.

- **V**: C is incremented. If the new value is zero or negative, a thread T is dequeued from Q and allowed to continue execution.

Whereas the P and V notations are handy for writing pseudocode, in the rest of this section we refer to the Qt implementation classes and their methods, summarized in Table 3.1. One notable addition to the repertoire of semaphores in Qt but also in other threading libraries are the `tryAcquire`/`tryLock` methods. These allow the calling thread to try to change the state of a semaphore, without blocking. These methods return TRUE if the change was successful or FALSE otherwise.

The example in Figure 3.8 shows the changes in the state of a counting semaphore being shared by three threads.

Table 3.1 Qt classes for implementing binary and counting semaphores and their most important methods. The `acquire(n)`, `release(n)`, and `tryAcquire(n)` are convenience methods that increment or decrement a general semaphore n times, without the need for a loop

	Binary	**General**
Class	QMutex	QSemaphore
P	lock()	acquire()
		acquire(n)
V	unlock()	release()
		release(n)
Nonblocking P	tryLock()	tryAcquire()
		tryAcquire(n)
Status query	N/A	available()

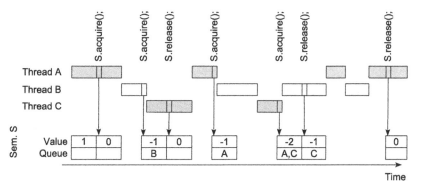

FIGURE 3.8

An example that shows the changes in the state of a general semaphore in response to acquire/release calls by three threads.

Armed with Qt's classes, we can solve the race condition that plagues the program of Listing 3.6 by introducing a mutex. The mutex must be shared by all the participating threads, which means that it has to:

- Be defined as a global variable, or
- Be passed as a constructor parameter to all

The latter choice is a better design approach, leading to the code of Listing 3.7. The introduction of the lock-unlock pair of methods in Listing 3.7 creates a critical section. A *critical section* is a part of the program in which access to different threads is mutually exclusive, i.e., only one thread at any time can be inside it. Critical sections allow us to safely access shared resources, without the risk of putting them in an inconsistent state when writing, or getting wrong data when reading. In principle, critical sections have to remain small in length or time duration because they defeat the purpose of introducing concurrency by forcing threads to execute them sequentially!

```
1   // File: raceCondSol.cpp
2   #include <QThread>
3   . . .
4   class MyThread:public QThread {
5   private:
6     . . .
7     QMutex *l;
8   public:
9     MyThread (int i, int r, QMutex *m):ID(i), runs(r), l(m) {}
10    void run () {
11      cout << "Thread " << ID << " is running\n";
12      for (int j = 0; j < runs; j++)
13        {
14          usleep (rand () % 3);
15          l->lock();
16          counter++;
17          l->unlock();
18        }
19    . . .
20  int main (int argc, char *argv[])
21  {
22    . . .
23    QMutex lock;
24    for (int i = 0; i < N; i++)
25      {
26        t[i] = new MyThread (i, runs, &lock);
27        t[i]->start ();
28      }
29    . . .
30  }
```

LISTING 3.7

A solution to the race-condition problem of Listing 3.6 that utilizes a mutex. (For brevity, only the changes from the original code are shown.)

Because mutices serve as locks, they are by default initialized as open. For general semaphores the initial counter value is 0 unless explicitly specified otherwise in the constructor.

The introduction of the semaphore in our previous example is rather straight-forward. However, the use of semaphores is a challenge not to be underestimated. Semaphores are a *fine-grained* mechanism for controlling concurrency, and as such they offer the potential of great performance at the expense of difficult use. Not only are race conditions difficult to detect, but also the mutual exclusion required to eliminate them can produce deadlocks or starvation.

A *deadlock* is a phenomenon involving multiple threads (two or more), whereby threads wait indefinitely to get access to resources while holding and not releasing other resources. An example is shown in Figure 3.9 in the form of a resource allocation graph.

Starvation, on the other hand, can affect individual threads. Starvation happens when the execution of a thread or a process is suspended or disallowed for an indefinite amount of time, although it is capable of continuing execution. Starvation is typically associated with enforcing of priorities or the lack of fairness in scheduling or access to resources.

An example of things that can go wrong are:

- Acquiring (locking up) a resource and forgetting to release it
- Releasing a resource that was never acquired
- Using a resource without locking it up; even read-only access can require a lock-up

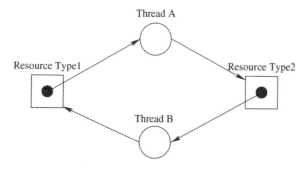

FIGURE 3.9

A resource allocation graph that shows a deadlock between two threads. Rectangles represent resource types; the dots inside them represent available resources of that type. Edges going from threads to rectangles represent pending requests; edges going from resources to threads indicate resource ownership.

Unfortunately, there is no magic bullet for learning how to properly use semaphores. We start by distinguishing the roles a semaphore can play and identifying the software patterns involved in each of the roles. We then proceed to apply these to a number of classical problems that have wide applicability in software design.

A semaphore can be utilized in three distinct ways:

1. As a **lock**. Suitable semaphore type: **binary**.
2. As a **resource counter**. Suitable semaphore type: **general**.
3. As a **signaling mechanism**. Suitable semaphore type: **binary** or **general** depending on the application.

As will be demonstrated, a semaphore can serve multiple of the above roles at one time.

For each of the preceding uses, there is a pattern as to how they can be deployed. These patterns are shown for the case of two threads in Table 3.2.

Table 3.2 will serve as a guideline as we explore how semaphores can be properly used via the study of a number of classical problems.

Table 3.2 Software patterns employed for using a semaphore in each of its three distinct roles.

Use	Semaphore Initialization	Thread1	Thread2	Thread Relationship

S1	Lock	QMutex l;	void run() {
			...
			l.lock();
			...
			l.unlock();
			...
			}
				void run() {
				...
				l.lock();
				...
				l.unlock();
				...
				}
					Threads compete to acquire the lock to a shared resource.

S2	Resource Counter Scenario 1	QSemaphore s;	void run() {
			...
			s.release();
			...
			}
				void run() {
				...
				s.acquire();
				...
				}
					One thread produces resources (Thread1) and another consumes them (Thread2). Initially there are no available ones.

S3	Resource Counter Scenario 2	QSemaphore s(N);	void run() {
			...
			s.acquire();
			...
			s.release();
			...
			}
				void run() {
				...
				s.acquire();
				...
				s.release();
				...
				}
					Threads compete to acquire resources from a pool of N available ones.

S4	Signaling Mechanism	QSemaphore s;	void run() {
			...
			s.release();
			...
			}
				void run() {
				...
				s.acquire();
				...
				}
					One thread (Thread2) waits for a signal from the other (Thread1).

RECURSIVE SEMAPHORES

Qt (in suit with other semaphore libraries) allows what could be regarded as a programming error: The same thread can be allowed to lock a mutex multiple times. Such a mutex is called *recursive* and for the lock to become open, the thread has to unlock it the same number of times. By default, binary semaphores are initialized to be nonrecursive. The alternative requires a constructor parameter:

```
QMutex l(QMutex::Recursive);
```

Although this may seem like an odd behavior, it can simplify a program's code in certain scenarios, such as recursive functions that call themselves multiple times.

3.5 APPLYING SEMAPHORES IN CLASSICAL PROBLEMS

In the following sections we explore a set of problems that serve two purposes:

- They represent scenarios that are widely encountered in practice.
- They introduce special conditions that can be observed or anticipated in reallife.

3.5.1 PRODUCERS-CONSUMERS

The producers-consumers problem concerns the synchronization of two types of threads via a shared buffer. The buffer is used for holding resources made by the producer threads until they are requested by the consumer threads. In its most generic form the problem involves n-producers and m-consumers.

The pseudocode showing how the two types of threads operate is shown in Listing 3.8.

```
1  const int BUFFSIZE=100;
2  class Resource {...};
3
4  Resource buffer[BUFFSIZE];
5  int in=0, out=0, resCount=0;
6
7  class Producer:public QThread {
8  public:
9    void run ()  {
10     while(1) {
11       Resource item = produce();
12       while(resCount == BUFFSIZE) ;  // wait for an empty slot in ↩
                  the buffer
13       buffer[in] = item;              // store the item
14       in = (in+1) % BUFFSIZE;         // update the in index
15       resCount++;                     // increment the resource ↩
                  counter
16     }
```

```
17      }
18    };
19
20    class Consumer:public QThread {
21    public:
22      void run () {
23        while(1) {
24          while(resCount == 0) ;      // wait for an available item
25          Resource item = buffer[out];// take the item out
26          out = (out+1) % BUFFSIZE;   // update the out index
27          resCount--;                 // decrement the resource counter
28          consume(item);
29        }
30      }
31    };
```

LISTING 3.8

Pseudocode for producer-consumer threads, without any synchronization logic. The buffer is a circular one, which means that producers and consumers operate on different positions in the buffer's space.

We begin by laying out the requirements that the two types of threads must satisfy, given the bounded nature of the buffer and the need to safely access shared variables:

- When a producer stores an item in the buffer, it must lock down the in parameter. Related pattern in Table 3.2: S1.
- When a consumer removes an item from the buffer, it must lock down the out parameter. Related pattern in Table 3.2: S1.
- If the buffer is empty, consumers must wait for resources to be generated by the producers. Related pattern in Table 3.2: S2.
- If the buffer is full, producers must wait for resources to be removed by the consumers. Related pattern in Table 3.2: S2.

The above discussion can be summarized to needing *two binary semaphores* for locking down in and out and *two counting semaphores* for alerting the threads when it is appropriate to operate on the buffer. The suggested solution, illustrated in Listing 3.9, overcomes one particularly inefficient aspect of Listing 3.8: the idle loops of lines 13 and 25. Because a semaphore can block a thread until a resource is made available, the while loops can be discarded.

```
1   const int BUFFSIZE=100;
2   class Resource {...};
3
4   Resource buffer[BUFFSIZE];
5   int in=0, out=0;
6
7   QSemaphore slotsAvail(BUFFSIZE);    // counts how many buffer slots are ↵
                                            free
8   QSemaphore resAvail(0);             // counts how many buffer slots are ↵
                                            taken
9   QMutex l1, l2;                      // by default initialized open
```

```
10
11   class Producer:public QThread {
12   public:
13     void run () {
14       while(1) {
15         Resource item = produce();
16         slotsAvail.acquire() ;    // wait for an empty slot in the ←
                 buffer
17         l1.lock();
18         int tmpIn = in;
19         in = (in+1) % BUFFSIZE;  // update the in index safely
20         l1.unlock();
21         buffer[tmpIn] = item;     // store the item
22         resAvail.release();       // signal resource availability
23       }
24     }
25   };
26
27   class Consumer:public QThread {
28   public:
29     void run () {
30       while(1) {
31         resAvail.acquire() ;      // wait for an available item
32         l2.lock();
33         int tmpOut = out;
34         out = (out+1) % BUFFSIZE;// update the out index
35         l2.unlock();
36         Resource item = buffer[tmpOut];// take the item out
37         slotsAvail.release();     // signal for a new empty slot
38         consume(item);
39       }
40     }
41   };
```

LISTING 3.9

Pseudocode for properly synchronizing *n*-producers and *m*-consumer threads using semaphores.

Comparing Listings 3.8 and 3.9 side by side raises some questions:

- **Q.**: What about the resCount counter? It is a shared variable, yet it is not protected by a mutex. Instead it is completely removed!
  A.: It's removed because the idle loops where it served are no longer needed. If the counter were to be kept in the code, it would require a mutex.
- **Q.**: Is it possible to replace the resAvail and slotsAvail counting semaphores with a single one? It should be that resAvail + slotsAvail = BUFFSIZE.
  A.: In a sequential program it would be always true that resAvail + slotsAvail = BUFFSIZE. However, while a thread or two (one of each type) are interacting with the buffer, it may actually be the case that

Table 3.3 A summary of the required number and type of semaphores needed to solve the producers-consumers problem

		Producers	
		1	N
Consumers	1	2 counting semaphores for signaling	2 counting semaphores and 1 binary semaphore for the producers
	M	2 counting semaphores and 1 binary semaphore for the consumers	2 counting semaphores and 2 binary semaphores

$$resAvail + slotsAvail = BUFFSIZE-1$$

or even

$$resAvail + slotsAvail = BUFFSIZE-2.$$

The additional reason that prevents the elimination of these semaphores is that they serve a signaling purpose, waking up threads waiting for a slot or a resource.[8]

- **Q.:** Can we replace the two mutices with one? They only thing they seem to do is lock the buffer.
  A.: This is possible but inefficient, since it will force a producer to wait on a consumer to update the out index and vice versa. However, it is possible to eliminate one or both of the mutices if there is only one of a type of thread. So, if there is only one producer, l1 (and the related logic) can be eliminated, and if there is only one consumer, l2 can be eliminated. Table 3.3 summarizes this discussion.
- **Q.:** The locks for in and out are released before an item is stored or taken out of the buffer. Doesn't this create a race-condition?
  A.: The corresponding buffer positions that in and out point to (before being updated) can never be accessed by another thread (regardless of the type) before the resAvail and slotsAvail semaphores are accordingly increased. The temporary pointers of lines 18 and 33 also ensure that the duration of the critical sections and the impact on concurrency are minimized.

One might argue about Listing 3.8 that further gains in code simplicity can be made by making the buffer a proper class, with methods protected by mutices. This would relegate the synchronization problem to the buffer itself, making the threads completely unaware of any concurrency issues. This is a fair comment that will be explored further in Section 3.6.

---

[8]The slotAvail semaphore and the associated statements can be eliminated only if the buffer is always big enough to hold the resources deposited. This is the equivalent of having an infinite buffer. See Exercise 11 for an example.

3.5.2 DEALING WITH TERMINATION

A significant problem in shared-memory and distributed applications is program termination. It is often the case that a complex condition needs to be evaluated that renders the continuation of execution unnecessary. This condition is usually evaluated locally (e.g., finding a matching hash value in a password-cracking program, or a GUI thread reacting to a press of the Exit button) and it is propagated to the other threads. In this section we present two methods that can be used to facilitate proper multithreaded program termination.

There are two key elements in both of the suggested solutions:

- The termination signal, in whatever form, should reach all threads.
- The threads should be able to detect the signal within a reasonable amount of time.

The two solutions are presented in the context of the producers-consumers problem, but they can be adjusted to fit other situations. The only real restriction is that each thread should periodically check to see whether the termination condition has been met or not.

3.5.2.1 Termination using a shared data item

Using a shared data item for termination seems like a trivial approach, but there are a few caveats! Contemporary CPU designs use multilevel caches for speeding up access to main memory. The consistency models employed in these caches may not be strict, i.e., cached copies of a shared variable may not be invalidated and updated immediately after one of the copies is modified. Most *cache coherence* implementations follow the *weak consistency*, which means that synchronization variables (e.g., semaphores) have a globally consistent state, but read/write operations on ordinary data may appear in any order to the threads of a program.

So, to be able to properly support termination based on a flag, we must use either an atomic data type (such as a semaphore or Qt's QAtomicInt) or force the compiler to avoid caching copies of the flag by using the volatile keyword.[9]

In the context of the producers-consumers problem, there are two design alternatives, based on whether the threads need to perform a fixed or variable number of iterations. We distinguish two cases:

1. *The number of iterations is known a priori.* In that case, a counting semaphore can be used for each type of thread, replacing their infinite while(1) loops with a while(sem.tryAcquire()) statement. The tryAcquire method is a nonblocking version of the acquire one that returns true if decrementing the semaphore was successful and false otherwise. The resulting code is shown in Listing 3.10, which contains working code incorporating template classes for the producer and consumer threads.

---

[9]The volatile keyword deserves a word of caution: Though it works as expected with primitive data types (e.g., bool or int), with structures or classes it does not prevent race conditions. If multiple threads access a shared structure or class, they must do so inside a critical section.

```
1   // File: terminProdCons.cpp
2   . . .
3   const int BUFFSIZE = 100;
4
5   template <typename T>
6   class Producer: public QThread {
7   private:
8       int ID;
9       static QSemaphore *slotsAvail;
10      static QSemaphore *resAvail;
11      static QMutex l1;
12      static QSemaphore numProducts;
13      static T *buffer;
14      static int in;
15  public:
16      static T(*produce)();
17      static void initClass(int numP, QSemaphore *s, QSemaphore *a, T *b↩
        , T(*prod)());
18      Producer<T>(int i): ID(i) {};
19      void run();
20  };
21  //────────────────────────────────────────
22  . . .
23  template <typename T> void Producer<T>::initClass(int numP, QSemaphore ↩
        *s, QSemaphore *a, T *b, T(*prod)()) {
24      numProducts.release(numP);
25      slotsAvail = s;
26      resAvail = a;
27
28      buffer = b;
29      produce = prod;
30  }
31  //────────────────────────────────────────
32
33  template <typename T>
34  void Producer<T>::run() {
35      while (numProducts.tryAcquire()) {
36          T item = (*produce)();
37          slotsAvail->acquire(); // wait for an empty slot in the buffer
38          l1.lock();
39          int tmpIn = in;
40          in = (in + 1) % BUFFSIZE; // update the in index safely
41          l1.unlock();
42          buffer[tmpIn] = item; // store the item
43          resAvail->release(); // signal resource availability
44      }
45  }
46  //────────────────────────────────────────
47
48  template <typename T>
49  class Consumer: public QThread {
50  private:
```

```
51        int ID;
52        static QSemaphore *slotsAvail;
53        static QSemaphore *resAvail;
54        static QMutex l2;
55        static T *buffer;
56        static int out;
57        static QSemaphore numProducts;
58   public:
59        static void (*consume)(T i);
60        static void initClass(int numP, QSemaphore *s, QSemaphore *a,T *b,↩
               void (*cons)(T));
61        Consumer<T>(int i): ID(i) {};
62        void run();
63   };
64   //────────────────────────────────────────
65   . . .
66   template<typename T> void Consumer<T>::initClass(int numP, QSemaphore ↩
        *s, QSemaphore *a, T *b, void (*cons)(T)) {
67        numProducts.release(numP);
68        slotsAvail = s;
69        resAvail = a;
70
71        buffer = b;
72        consume = cons;
73   }
74   //────────────────────────────────────────
75
76   template<typename T> void Consumer<T>::run() {
77        while (numProducts.tryAcquire()) {
78            resAvail->acquire(); // wait for an available item
79            l2.lock();
80            int tmpOut = out;
81            out = (out + 1) % BUFFSIZE; // update the out index
82            l2.unlock();
83            T item = buffer[tmpOut]; // take the item out
84            slotsAvail->release(); // signal for a new empty slot
85            (*consume)(item);
86        }
87   }
88   //────────────────────────────────────────
89   template<> int (*Producer<int>::produce)() = NULL;
90   template<> void (*Consumer<int>::consume)(int) = NULL;
91   . . .
92
93   int produce() {
94        // to be implemented
95        return 1;
96   }
97   //────────────────────────────────────────
98
99   void consume(int i) {
100       // to be implemented
```

```
101    }
102    //───────────────────────────────────────────

103
104    int main(int argc, char *argv[]) {
105        . . .
106        int N = atoi(argv[1]);
107        int M = atoi(argv[2]);
108        int numP = atoi(argv[3]);
109        int *buffer = new int[BUFFSIZE];
110        QSemaphore avail, buffSlots(BUFFSIZE);

111
112        Producer<int>::initClass(numP, &buffSlots, &avail, buffer, &↵
               produce);
113        Consumer<int>::initClass(numP, &buffSlots, &avail, buffer, &↵
               consume);

114
115        Producer<int> *p[N];
116        Consumer<int> *c[M];
117        for (int i = 0; i < N; i++) {
118            p[i] = new Producer<int>(i);
119            p[i]->start();
120        }
121        . . .
122    }
```

LISTING 3.10

Generic solution to the *n*-producers and *m*-consumers problem with a fixed number of iterations. For the sake of brevity, the more significant parts are shown.

The program in Listing 3.10 is run by providing the number of producers, consumers, and iterations, as in the following example:

```
$ ./terminProdCons
Usage ./terminProdCons #producers #consumers #iterations

$ ./terminProdCons 3 4 1000
```

Its key points are the following:

- Both the Producer and Consumer classes are defined as generic types (templates), capable of handling any class of resource.
- Class invariants such as the semaphores, buffer reference, and the in/out indices are stored as static members of each class (lines 9-14 and 52-56) and are initialized by the initClass static methods. The latter are called before any thread can be spawned (lines 112 and 113) and once the main function allocates all the necessary data.
- The resource-specific parts, i.e., the creation and consumption of the handled items, is done by two functions, pointers to which are passed as parameters to the initClass methods. The actual functions used in the code are just stubs.
- The avail and buffSlots semaphores are shared between both classes, and that is why they have to be declared outside of them. In contrast, the l1 and l2 mutices are class specific, declared in lines 11 and 54 respectively.

- Static template function pointer syntax in C++ forces the specialization of lines 89 and 90. For use with another *concrete* data type T, the int specifier in these lines must be replaced by T.

2. *The number of iterations is determined at run-time.*

In this case we can have an arrangement similar to:

```
. . .
static volatile bool *exitFlag; //declared as a pointer to allow ←
    sharing between classes
. . .
void Producer<T>::run() {
    while (*exitFlag == false) {
. . .
```

But another issue comes up: threads cannot terminate unless they are able to check the status of the shared exitFlag. How can we wake-up threads which *may be* blocked in a semaphore's queue, when termination is detected? Unblocking threads requires that the corresponding semaphores are increased, permitting threads to resume execution.

An obvious choice for this task is to assign it to the first thread that detects the end of the execution. In the implementation (only partly shown for brevity) in Listing 3.11, the termination is triggered by the consume function and detected by one of the Consumer threads that proceeds to set the termination flag to true (line 66).

```
1   // File: terminProdCons2.cpp
2   . . .
3
4   template <typename T>
5   class Producer: public QThread {
6   private:
7       . . .
8       static volatile bool *exitFlag;
9   public:
10      static T(*produce)();
11      static void initClass(QSemaphore *s, QSemaphore *a, T *b,         T←
            (*prod)(), bool *e);
12      Producer<T>(int i): ID(i) {}
13      void run();
14  };
15  //————————————————————————————————
16  . . .
17
18  template <typename T>
19  void Producer<T>::run() {
20      while (*exitFlag == false) {
21          T item = (*produce)();
22          slotsAvail->acquire(); // wait for an empty slot in the buffer
23
24          if (*exitFlag) return; // stop immediately on termination
25
26          l1.lock();
27          int tmpIn = in;
28          in = (in + 1) % BUFFSIZE; // update the in index safely
```

```
29          l1.unlock();
30          buffer[tmpIn] = item; // store the item
31          resAvail->release(); // signal resource availability
32      }
33  }
34  //————————————————————————————————
35
36  template<typename T>
37  class Consumer: public QThread {
38  private:
39      . . .
40      static volatile bool *exitFlag;
41  public:
42      static bool (*consume)(T i);
43      static void initClass(QSemaphore *s, QSemaphore *a, T* b, bool (*↵
                cons)(T), int N, int M, bool *e);
44      Consumer<T>(int i): ID(i) {}
45      void run();
46  };
47  //————————————————————————————————
48      . . .
49  template<typename T> void Consumer<T>::run() {
50      while (*exitFlag == false) {
51          resAvail->acquire(); // wait for an available item
52
53          if (*exitFlag) return; // stop immediately on termination
54
55          l2.lock();
56          int tmpOut = out;
57          out = (out + 1) % BUFFSIZE; // update the out index
58          l2.unlock();
59          T item = buffer[tmpOut]; // take the item out
60          slotsAvail->release(); // signal for a new empty slot
61
62          if ((*consume)(item)) break; // time to stop?
63      }
64
65      // only the thread initially detecting termination reaches here
66      *exitFlag = true;
67      resAvail->release(numConsumers - 1);
68      slotsAvail->release(numProducers);
69  }
70  //————————————————————————————————
71      . . .
72  bool consume(int i) {
73      // to be implemented
74      cout << "@"; // just to show something is happening
75      if (i % 10 == 0) return true;
76      else return false;
77  }
78  //————————————————————————————————
79
```

```
80   int main(int argc, char *argv[]) {
81       . . .
82
83       bool exitFlag = false;
84
85       Producer<int>::initClass(&buffSlots, &avail, buffer, &produce, &↵
             exitFlag);
86       Consumer<int>::initClass(&buffSlots, &avail, buffer, &consume, N, ↵
             M, &exitFlag);
87
88       . . .
89   }
```

LISTING 3.11

Generic solution to the *n*-producers and *m*-consumers problem, when the number of iterations is unknown. For the sake of brevity, only the parts different from Listing 3.10 are shown.

Other key differences between Listings 3.10 and 3.11 are:

- The thread that detects the end of execution (line 62) makes sure that all the other threads of both types are able to terminate by increasing appropriately both resAvail and slotsAvail (lines 67 and 68).
- Because the termination is carried out by a Consumer thread, the class is initialized to contain the number of both Consumer and Producer threads (line 86).
- The declared-as-volatile *exitFlag boolean is shared between both types of threads, allowing them to terminate with a simple while(*exitFlag == false) loop control statement (lines 20 and 50).
- The threads that are woken up check the termination condition immediately before proceeding to interact with the buffer (lines 24 and 53). This prevents any undesirable side effects or overhead.

3.5.2.2 Termination using messages

A very elegant approach that can be also extended to distributed-memory applications is the delivery of termination messages. In our consumers-producers setup, we can treat the items that are exchanged via the shared buffer as implicit messages. A special (i.e., invalid in the application context) item (such as a negative number in an application that expects only positive ones) can be used to indicate the end of the program. For example, let's assume that the producer threads generate and deposit in the buffer instances of the class:

```
class Triangle3D{
  public:
      float point1[3];
      float point2[3];
      float point3[3];
};
```

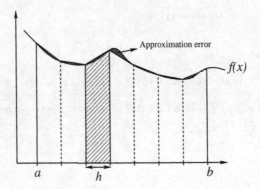

FIGURE 3.10

An illustration of the trapezoidal rule application to the calculation of a function's integral. The red area represents the approximation error, which can be substantially reduced by shrinking the size of h.

Then a `Triangle3D` instance with two equal points could be considered by the consumer threads as a termination signal.

The only restriction we have is that termination has to be handled by the producers, since the flow of resources is unidirectional. If the consumer threads were to be used for this purpose, a technique from the ones described in the previous section should be applied.

To illustrate this concept, in the example shown in Listing 3.12, a multi-threaded integration of a function is performed. The producer thread deposits in the shared buffer the specifications that should be followed by the consumer threads in calculating the result for a particular part of the range, i.e., the range boundaries and the number of divisions. The program loosely follows the map-reduce pattern described in Section 2.4.4.

The integration is performed using the trapezoidal rule: The integration region $[a, b]$ is split into n equal-width slices of length h, as shown in Figure 3.10. The area for each slice between points x_i and x_{i+1} is approximated by $h \cdot \frac{f(x_i) + f(x_{i+1})}{2}$. The whole area between $[a, b]$ is then:

$$\sum_{i=0}^{n-1} h \cdot \frac{f(x_i) + f(x_{i+1})}{2} = h \left(\frac{f(a) + f(b)}{2} + \sum_{i=1}^{n-1} f(x_i) \right)$$

where $x_0 = a$, $x_n = b$, $x_i = a + i \cdot h$, and $h = \frac{b-a}{n}$.

```
1  // File: terminProdConsMess.cpp
2  . . .
3  const int BUFFSIZE = 10;
4  const double LOWERLIMIT = 0;
5  const double UPPERLIMIT = 10;
6  //----------------------------------------------
7  typedef struct Slice {    // structure used for specifying
8      double start;          // which part to integrate over
```

```
9        double end;
10       int divisions;
11   } Slice;
12   //────────────────────────────────────────────
13   double func(double x) {   // function to be integrated
14       return fabs(sin(x));
15   }
16   //────────────────────────────────────────────
17   // acts as a consumer
18   class IntegrCalc: public QThread {
19   private:
20       int ID;
21       static QSemaphore *slotsAvail;
22       static QSemaphore *resAvail;
23       static QMutex l2;
24       static QMutex resLock;
25       static Slice *buffer;
26       static int out;
27       static double *result;
28       static QSemaphore numProducts;
29   public:
30       static void initClass(QSemaphore *s, QSemaphore *a, Slice *b, ↩
             double *r);
31
32       IntegrCalc(int i): ID(i) {}
33       void run();
34   };
35   //────────────────────────────────────────────
36   . . .
37   void IntegrCalc::initClass(QSemaphore *s, QSemaphore *a, Slice *b, ↩
         double *res) {
38       slotsAvail = s;
39       resAvail = a;
40       buffer = b;
41       result = res;
42       *result = 0;
43   }
44   //────────────────────────────────────────────
45
46   void IntegrCalc::run() {
47       while (1) {
48           resAvail->acquire(); // wait for an available item
49           l2.lock();
50           int tmpOut = out;
51           out = (out + 1) % BUFFSIZE; // update the out index
52           l2.unlock();
53
54           // take the item out
55           double st = buffer[tmpOut].start;
56           double en = buffer[tmpOut].end;
57           double div = buffer[tmpOut].divisions;
58
```

```
59          slotsAvail->release(); // signal for a new empty slot
60
61          if (div == 0) break; // exit
62
63          // calculate area using trapezoidal rule
64          double localRes = 0;
65          double step = (en - st) / div;
66          double x;
67          x = st;
68          localRes = func(st) + func(en);
69          localRes /= 2;
70          for(int i=1; i< div; i++)    {
71              x += step;
72              localRes += func(x);
73            }
74          localRes *= step;
75
76
77          // add it to result
78          resLock.lock();
79          *result += localRes;
80          resLock.unlock();
81      }
82 }
83 //————————————————————————————————————————
84
85 int main(int argc, char *argv[]) {
86      . . .
87      int N = atoi(argv[1]);
88      int J = atoi(argv[2]);
89      Slice *buffer = new Slice[BUFFSIZE];
90      QSemaphore avail, buffSlots(BUFFSIZE);
91      int in = 0;
92      double result;
93
94      IntegrCalc::initClass(&buffSlots, &avail, buffer, &result);
95
96      IntegrCalc * t[N];
97      for (int i = 0; i < N; i++) {
98          t[i] = new IntegrCalc(i);
99          t[i]->start();
100     }
101
102     // main thread is responsible for handing out 'jobs'
103     // It acts as the producer in this setup
104     double divLen = (UPPERLIMIT - LOWERLIMIT) / J;
105     double st, end = LOWERLIMIT;
106     for (int i = 0; i < J; i++) {
107         st = end;
108         end += divLen;
109         if (i == J - 1) end = UPPERLIMIT;
110
```

```
111            buffSlots.acquire();
112            buffer[in].start = st;
113            buffer[in].end = end;
114            buffer[in].divisions = 1000;
115            in = (in + 1) % BUFFSIZE;
116            avail.release();
117        }
118
119        // put termination 'sentinels' in buffer
120        for (int i = 0; i < N; i++) {
121            buffSlots.acquire();
122            buffer[in].divisions = 0;
123            in = (in + 1) % BUFFSIZE;
124            avail.release();
125        }
126
127    . . .
128    }
```

LISTING 3.12

Multithreaded integration of a function, with message termination of worker/consumer threads.

The key points of the above program are the following:

- The IntegrCalc class defined at lines 18-34 acts as a consumer, receiving Slice structures (defined between lines 7-11) from the program's main thread as assignments for calculation.
- The main thread assumes the responsibility of the producer, preparing Slice structures and flagging their availability (lines 111-116).
- The class invariants are initialized by the initClass method, which also is passed as parameters, references to the semaphores shared between the main and consumer threads (line 94).
- The run method sports an infinite loop (line 47), that is terminated when a Slice structure with div equal to zero is received (line 61).
- The termination of the program is the responsibility of the main thread. After all slices have been deposited in the shared buffer, the main thread deposits as many "sentinel" structures as the number of spawned threads (lines 120-125). Note that the termination loop is structured in the exact same fashion as the one producing slice assignments above it. It could not be otherwise, given the nature of the shared buffer.
- The IntegrCalc threads extract the calculation parameters from the Slice structure they acquire and proceed to calculate the area using the trapezoidal method. The partial result calculated is accumulated in the *result. The latter being shared between all the IntegrCalc threads sits inside a critical section (lines 78-80).

3.5.3 THE BARBERSHOP PROBLEM: INTRODUCING FAIRNESS

The barbershop problem is a thread/process synchronization problem that has been described in various forms in the literature. In its simplest incarnation, the problem is the following:

We have a hypothetical barbershop with one barber. The shop has one barber chair and a waiting room with a fixed number of chairs in it. A customer entering the barbershop would sit in a chair in the waiting room and proceed to sit in the barber's chair when called by the barber. When the barber completes a customer's haircut, he lets the customer go and gets the next customer from the waiting room.

Based on the specifics of how the customers and barber behave and the number of corresponding threads, there can be many possible solutions. We will explore one particular problem setting that brings out the issue of *fairness*. Fairness is usually used in the context of a scheduler, e.g., a scheduler is fair if all ready-to-run processes of the same priority get the same allocation of CPU time. In this context, fairness means that signals meant for a particular thread should be delivered to it.

To illustrate the problem, we assume that we have two barbers in the shop, each using one of two available barber chairs. The pseudocode of the solution is shown below in Listing 3.13:

```
1   QSemaphore waitChair(NUMCHAIRS);
2   QSemaphore barberChair(2);
3   QSemaphore barberReady;
4   QSemaphore barberDone;
5   QSemaphore customerReady;
6
7   class Customer: public QThread {
8    public:
9      void run() {
10       waitChair.aquire();    // wait for a chair
11       barberReady.acquire(); // wait for a barber to be ready
12       waitChair.release();   // get up from the chair
13       barberChair.acquire(); // wait for an available barber chair
14       customerReady.release();// signal that customer is ready
15       barberDone.aquire();   // wait for barber to finish haircut
16       barberChair.release(); // get up from barber's chair
17     }
18   };
19
20   class Barber : public QThread {
21    public:
22      void run() {
23        while(1){
24          barberReady.release();    // signal availability
25          customerReady.acquire();  // wait for customer to be sitted
26          barberDone.release();     // signal that hair is done
```

```
27        }
28      }
29    };
```

LISTING 3.13

Pseudocode for solving the barbershop problem with two barber threads.

The solution in Listing 3.13 works but has a fatal flaw. The timing diagram in Figure 3.11 illustrates a scenario in which a barber cutting a customer's hair signals that he is done and the customer in the other chair gets up. This sequence can be produced by having a difference in the speed between the two barber threads. Once Cust1 increases `customerReady` and releases Barb1 from the corresponding queue, the two threads become implicitly associated. Barb1 is too slow to finish the job, so when Barb2 increases `barberDone`, Cust1 leaves his chair. This is clearly an unfair solution.

The only way this problem can be addressed is to establish an association between a customer and the barber serving him. There are two alternatives that can create this connection:

1. A customer has to acquire the ID of the barber thread that will serve him.
2. A barber has to acquire the ID of the customer he is to serve.

Both solutions require that some of the semaphores in the original solution are replaced by arrays of semaphores, with as many elements as the number of threads that need to be identified. Obviously, the more economical solution is to use the first approach, where we have arrays of two elements, one element for each barber.

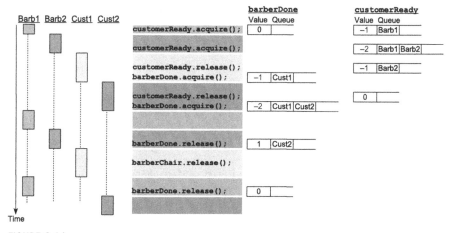

FIGURE 3.11

Sequence diagram of a possible interaction between two barber and two customer threads. The right side of the figure shows the value and queues of two of the semaphores employed after each of the shown statements is executed.

For a customer to be able to acquire the ID of a barber, we must establish a buffer in which the IDs of the available barbers are deposited. In that respect, this part of the solution has to follow the producers-consumers pattern. There is a twist to the circumstances surrounding how this pattern is applied: If the buffer holding the IDs is as big as the number of IDs, the barbers (producers) don't have to wait until there is an available slot in the buffer. From the barber's perspective, the buffer is infinite, and so the associated counting semaphore can be eliminated! The essential parts of the solution are shown in Listing 3.14.

```cpp
1   // File: fairBarber.cpp
2   . . .
3   void concurPrint(int cID, int bID) {
4       static QMutex l;
5       l.lock();
6       cout << "Customer " << cID << " is being serviced by barber " << ←
            bID << endl;
7       l.unlock();
8   }
9   //————————————————————————————
10
11  class Barber: public QThread {
12  private:
13      int ID;
14      static QSemaphore *barberReady;    // allocated in main and passed ←
                to initClass
15      static QSemaphore *customerReady;
16      static QSemaphore *barberDone;
17
18      static QMutex ll;
19      static QSemaphore customersLeft;
20      static int *buffer;
21      static int in;
22      static int numBarbers;
23  public:
24      static void initClass(int numB, int numC, QSemaphore *r, ←
                QSemaphore *c, QSemaphore *d, int *b);
25
26      Barber(int i): ID(i) {}
27      void run();
28  };
29  //————————————————————————————
30  . . .
31  void Barber::initClass(int numB, int numC, QSemaphore *r, QSemaphore *←
            c, QSemaphore *d, int *b) {
32      customersLeft.release(numC);
33      barberReady = r;
34      customerReady = c;
35      barberDone = d;
36      buffer = b;
37      numBarbers = numB;
38  }
```

```
39  //─────────────────────────────────────────
40
41  void Barber::run() {
42      while (customersLeft.tryAcquire()) {
43          l1.lock();
44          buffer[in] = ID;                // deposit ID in buffer for
45          in = (in + 1) % numBarbers;     // customer to pick-up
46          l1.unlock();
47          barberReady->release();         // signal availability
48          customerReady[ID].acquire();    // wait for customer to be sitted
49          barberDone[ID].release();       // signal that hair is done
50      }
51  }
52  //─────────────────────────────────────────
53
54  class Customer: public QThread {
55  private:
56      int ID;
57      static QSemaphore *barberReady;
58      static QSemaphore *customerReady;
59      static QSemaphore *barberDone;
60      static QSemaphore waitChair;
61      static QSemaphore barberChair;
62      static QMutex l2;
63      static int *buffer;
64      static int out;
65      static int numBarbers;
66      static QSemaphore numProducts;
67  public:
68      static void initClass(int numB, QSemaphore *r, QSemaphore *c, ↩
                QSemaphore *d, int *b);
69
70      Customer(int i): ID(i) {}
71      void run();
72  };
73  //─────────────────────────────────────────
74  . . .
75  QSemaphore Customer::waitChair(NUMCHAIRS);
76  . . .
77  //─────────────────────────────────────────
78  void Customer::run() {
79      waitChair.acquire();      // wait for a chair
80      barberReady->acquire();   // wait for a barber to be ready
81      l2.lock();
82      int bID = buffer[out];    // extract barber ID from buffer
83      out = (out + 1) % numBarbers;
84      l2.unlock();
85      waitChair.release();      // get up from the chair
86      barberChair.acquire();    // wait for an available barber chair
87      customerReady[bID].release(); // signal to barber that customer is ↩
                ready
88      concurPrint(ID, bID);
```

```
89        barberDone[bID].acquire(); // wait for barber to finish haircut
90        barberChair.release();      // get up from barber's chair
91    }
92    //─────────────────────────────────────────────
93
94    int main(int argc, char *argv[]) {
95    . . .
96        int N = atoi(argv[1]);
97        int M = atoi(argv[2]);
98        int *buffer = new int[N];
99
100       QSemaphore barberReady;
101       QSemaphore *customerReady = new QSemaphore[N];
102       QSemaphore *barberDone = new QSemaphore[N];
103
104       Barber::initClass(N, M, &barberReady, customerReady, barberDone, ↩
                buffer);
105       Customer::initClass(N, &barberReady, customerReady, barberDone, ↩
                buffer);
106   . . .
107   }
```

LISTING 3.14

A fair solution to the barbershop problem. Each customer collects the ID of the barber that will serve him and through it uses a set of semaphores specific to that barber.

The key points of Listing 3.14 solution are:

- Each barber is associated with an element in two semaphores arrays, customerReady and barberDone, defined in lines 101,102 respectively.
- As with previous solutions in this chapter, the data shared between the two types of threads are allocated in main() and passed as parameters to methods initializing the two classes' data members (lines 98-105).
- A buffer is set up to hold the available barber IDs. The customer threads extract the IDs in a setup reminiscent of producers-consumers. The only thing missing is the equivalent of the slotsAvail semaphore, since the buffer is as big as the number of barbers; hence, there is always going to be a slot available. The producers part is in lines 43-47, and the consumers part is in lines 81-84.
- The Customer threads do not perform any looping, so the termination responsibility lies with the Barber threads. To facilitate this functionality, the customersLeft semaphore is initialized to the number of customers in line 32 and decremented/tested at line 42 if the Barber::run method.
- Last but not least, lines 3-7 define the concurPrint function that is used to generate non-mangled console output, by restricting the use of the cout object only inside a critical section.

3.5.4 **READERS-WRITERS**

The readers-writers problem manifests itself whenever a shared resource is accessed by threads trying to modify it alongside threads trying to read it. In its simplest form, the problem is governed by the following two conditions:

- Each writer must have exclusive access to the resource while it is modifying it. All other threads, including readers, are blocked.
- If a reader is accessing the resource, other readers may do so as well. Obviously, adhering to the previous condition, writer threads cannot access the resource while a reader is doing so.

These two rules allow us to preserve the resource in a consistent state, avoiding race conditions and erroneous changes. What they don't specify, though, is the *order* in which the threads are allowed to access the resource.

Should there be a priority given to one or the other kind of thread? Priorities entail the danger of *starvation*, but under certain circumstances priorities can be an application requirement. The key to solving this problem is the management of the queue of threads that try to access the resource.

The three distinct possibilities in terms of how the threads' ordering problem can be solved are analyzed in the sections that follow.

3.5.4.1 *A solution favoring the readers*

Favoring the readers means that when a reader tries to access the resource and the resource is currently being read by other readers, the reader is allowed to proceed regardless of any writer threads waiting.

Listing 3.15 shows the core of the solution in pseudocode.

```
1   QMutex writerLock;
2   QMutex countLock;
3   int numReaders=0;
4
5   void Reader::run()
6   {
7     countLock.lock();
8     numReaders++;
9     if(numReaders == 1)
10       writerLock.lock();
11    countLock.unlock();
12
13    // reader critical section
14
15    countLock.lock();
16    numReaders--;
17    if(numReaders == 0)
18      writerLock.unlock();
19    countLock.unlock();
20  }
21
```

```
22  void Writer::run()
23  {
24    writerLock.lock();
25    // writer critical section
26    writerLock.unlock();
27  }
```

LISTING 3.15

A solution to the readers-writers problem favoring the readers.

The design of the preceding solution is fairly simple:

- The writer threads share a mutex (`writerLock`) that controls entry to their critical section.
- The readers also share a mutex (`countLock`) that controls access to a shared counter (`numReaders`). Before the counter is modified in lines 8 and 16, the mutex must be locked.
- The first reader to acquire the `countLock` tries to also acquire the `writerLock` mutex. If there is a writer inside its critical section, the reader thread will wait (any other incoming reader threads will also block on trying to acquire the `countLock`). Otherwise, the reader thread will continue, effectively blocking any writer threads from entry.
- After the last reader thread exits its critical section, the writers' mutex is released (line 18).

The solution favors the readers because once a reader enters its critical section, any other incoming readers can join in, bypassing waiting writers.

3.5.4.2 Giving priority to the writers

Favoring the writers means that any writer in the queue of threads waiting to access their critical section, will bypass any waiting readers. The solution is very similar to the previous one despite the more complex appearance! Listing 3.16 shows the core of the solution in pseudocode.

```
1   QMutex writerLock;
2   QMutex readerLock;
3   QMutex countLock;
4   QMutex writerCountLock;
5   int numReaders=0;
6   int numWriters=0;
7
8   void Reader::run()
9   {
10    readerLock.lock();
11    countLock.lock();
12    numReaders++;
13    if(numReaders == 1)
14      writerLock.lock();
```

```
15      countLock.unlock();
16      readerLock.unlock();
17
18      // reader critical section
19
20      countLock.lock();
21      numReaders--;
22      if(numReaders == 0)
23        writerLock.unlock();
24      countLock.unlock();
25    }
26
27    void Writer::run()
28    {
29      writerCountLock.lock();
30      numWriters++;
31      if(numWriters==1)
32        readersLock.lock();
33      writerCountLock.unlock();
34
35      writerLock.lock();
36      // writer critical section
37      writerLock.unlock();
38
39      writerCountLock.lock();
40      numWriters--;
41      if(numWriters==0)
42        readersLock.unlock();
43      writerCountLock.unlock();
44    }
```

LISTING 3.16

A solution to the readers-writers problem favoring the writers.

At first glance, the readers part is identical to the one shown in Listing 3.15, with the sole addition of a seemingly inconsequential lock-unlock pair on a readersLock mutex. It's actually this mutex that allows the writers to exercise control over readers entry. Going into more detail:

- The readerLock has no other purpose than to inhibit reader threads from entering their critical section. That is why readers release it almost immediately (line 16). Writers exercise this control when they first start running (line 32).
- Only the first writer needs to block the readers; hence the line 31 condition. The last of the writers to leave unblocks the readers (lines 41 and 42).
- The need to enumerate the waiting writers via the numWriters variable also necessitates the use of a mutex (writerCountLock) to prevent race conditions.
- The readers that start execution before the arrival of the first writer operate in the same fashion as in the previous solution.

3.5.4.3 A fair solution

A fair solution dictates the application of a strict FIFO policy on the queue of waiting threads. This means that threads are allowed in their critical section in the order in which they request entry, always abiding by the two rules set in Section 3.5.4.

The trick that we can use to solve the problem fairly is to use one more semaphore that all the threads will have to acquire once they start running. Both types of threads should release this semaphore once they are allowed to enter their critical section. As long we use a strong semaphore, the order is FIFO and there is no danger of starvation.

The pseudocode of the fair solution is shown in Listing 3.17.

```
1   QMutex writerLock;
2   QMutex fairLock;
3   QMutex countLock;
4   int numReaders=0;
5   int numWriters=0;
6
7   void Reader::run()
8   {
9     fairLock.lock();
10     countLock.lock();
11     numReaders++;
12     if(numReaders == 1)
13       writerLock.lock();
14     countLock.unlock();
15     fairLock.unlock();
16
17     // reader critical section
18
19     countLock.lock();
20     numReaders--;
21     if(numReaders == 0)
22       writerLock.unlock();
23     countLock.unlock();
24   }
25
26   void Writer::run()
27   {
28     fairLock.lock();
29     writerLock.lock();
30     fairLock.unlock();
31
32     // writer critical section
33
34     writerLock.unlock();
35   }
```

LISTING 3.17

A fair solution to the readers-writers problem.

Some key observations about the solution:

- The code for the readers is identical to the one used to give priority to them. However, the introduction of the fairLock mutex forces all types of threads in the same queue.
- When a reader acquires fairLock, it proceeds to increment the numReaders counter and possibly acquire the writerLock mutex. It releases fairLock immediately before entering its critical section, allowing other readers to also proceed.
- If a writer follows a reader in the fairLock queue, it will block at line 29 and prevent any other thread from acquiring fairLock.

Qt provides a convenient class called QReadWriteLock for solving the readers-writers problem. The class supports the following methods:

- lockForRead: The lock is acquired for read-only access to a resource. Other reader threads are also allowed to join if a writer is not ahead of them in the waiting queue.
- lockForWrite: The lock is acquired for modifying a resource. All other threads are excluded.
- unlock: The lock is released

An assortment of nonblocking try* methods (e.g., tryLockForRead) is also supported. QReadWriteLock solves the problem in a way that favors the writers. Therefore, it is better suited for applications that feature infrequent writes.

3.6 MONITORS

Semaphores offer a great deal of flexibility and *if* they are properly used, one can extract the maximum amount of parallelism from a multithreaded application. However, this is a big "if"! Semaphores are notoriously difficult to use properly, since they offer very fine-grained concurrency control with program logic that can be spread across multiple threads. In the era of object-oriented (OO) programming, semaphores seem out of place.

Fortunately, an alternative solution exists in the form of a monitor. A *monitor* is an object or module that is designed to be accessed safely from multiple threads. To accomplish this feat, only one thread at a time may be executing any of the public methods of a monitor. In order to be able to block a thread or signal a thread to continue, both essential functionalities for establishing critical sections, monitors provide a mechanism called a *condition variable*.

A condition variable, which is typically accessed only inside a monitor, has a queue and supports two operations:

- A wait **operation**: If a thread executes the wait operation of a condition variable, it is blocked and placed in the condition variable's queue.

- A signal **operation**: If a thread executes the signal operation of a condition variable, a thread from the condition variable's queue is released (i.e., it becomes ready). If the queue is empty, the signal is ignored.

The wait and signal operations resemble the semaphore ones. However, there are distinct differences: A wait operation on a condition variable results in the *unconditional* blocking of the thread, whereas for a semaphore the block depends on its value. Also, a condition variable signal may be ignored, whereas in the case of a semaphore a release always increments it.

A condition variable is always associated with a condition, i.e., a set of rules that dictate when a thread will block or continue execution. This is actually one of the biggest advantages of monitors over semaphores, since any complex condition can be easily handled without an interwoven sequence of semaphore acquisitions, like the ones we saw in the readers-writers problem.

As a simple example, consider a monitor class for performing transactions to a bank account. The pseudocode of the withdraw and deposit methods would be similar to this:

```
1   class AccountMonitor
2   {
3     private:
4       Condition insufficientFunds;
5       Mutex m;
6       double balance;
7     public:
8       void withdraw(double s) {
9         m.lock();
10        if(balance < s)
11          {
12            m.unlock();
13            insufficientFunds.wait();
14            m.lock();
15          }
16
17        balance -= s;
18
19        m.unlock();
20      }
21
22      void deposit(double s) {
23        m.lock();
24        balance += s;
25        insufficientFunds.signal();
26        m.unlock();
27      }
28  };
```

To ensure that only one thread will be running inside an AccountMonitor instance, a mutex is locked on entry on both methods. This mutex is released upon exit (line 19) or when a thread is about to be blocked (upon finding insufficient funds to withdraw) and placed in the condition variable's queue (line 12). A blocked thread wakes up when funds are deposited in the account (line 25).

What if the deposited funds are still insufficient when a thread wakes up? What if there are multiple pending withdraw operations and it's possible that at least one could be completed, but not necessarily the one released by the `signal` statement?

Obviously, the program logic shown above does not cover these circumstances. The answers will come as a direct consequence of the following discussion.

The exact moment when a woken-up thread will run depends on the monitor's implementation. Two possibilities exist:

1. The thread runs immediately. Because a monitor cannot have two active threads running its methods, this automatically leads to the suspension of the thread that issued the signal. This thread will run as soon as the woken-up one exits the monitor. This approach follows the *Hoare* monitor specification, named after the scientist who originally suggested the monitor concept in the early 1970s.
2. The woken-up thread waits until the signal-issuing thread exits the monitor. Because of the delay until the thread is handed control of the monitor, the condition on which it was waiting originally may have been modified again. This necessitates a recheck, replacing the `if` statement controlling the wait with a `while` statement. This approach follows the *Lampson-Redell* monitor specification, and it offers some distinct advantages over the Hoare one. These include the ability to have timed-out waits and the ability to wake all the threads that are waiting on a condition variable. Both of these are enabled by having the condition a thread is waiting for, reevaluated whenever it starts running again.

   To indicate the difference in behavior, the signal method is called *notify*, and the signal to all waiting threads of a condition variable is called *notify all*.

The majority of monitor implementations, including the ones available in Qt and Java, follow the Lampson-Redell specification, since the extra functionality is coupled by an intrinsically simpler implementation. Equipped with such a monitor, we can complete the bank account monitor example so that we also cover the two questions posed above. We will rewrite the code after exploring the monitor facilities provided by Qt.

Qt provides a condition variable implementation in the form of the `QWaitCondition` class, which supports the following set of methods:

- `wait`: Forces a thread to block. To eliminate the need for the programmer to separately unlock or lock the mutex controlling entry to the monitor, a reference to this mutex is passed to the method for performing these operations automatically.
- `wakeOne`: Notifies one thread.
- `wakeAll`: Notifies all blocked threads. They will all run, one by one, inside the monitor.

Qt provides one more convenience class that simplifies the management of the entry-controlling mutex: `QMutexLocker`. An instance of this class should be created at the very first line of each monitor method. Its responsibility is to lock the entry-controlling mutex, and that is why its constructor is passed a reference to it. The benefit of this seemingly redundant act is that a monitor method can terminate at multiple program positions without requiring an explicit mutex unlock. When the destructor of the QMutexLocker class is called (upon method termination), the mutex is unlocked, saving effort and eliminating potential programming errors.

We are now ready to rewrite the bank account monitor class, as shown in Listing 3.18.

```
1   class AccountMonitor
2   {
3     private:
4       QWaitCondition insufficientFunds;
5       QMutex m;
6       double balance;
7     public:
8       void withdraw(double s) {
9         QMutexLocker ml(&m);
10        while(balance < s)
11          insufficientFunds.wait(&m);
12
13        balance -= s;
14      }
15
16      void deposit(double s) {
17        QMutexLocker ml(&m);
18        balance += s;
19        insufficientFunds.wakeAll();
20      }
21  };
```

LISTING 3.18

A monitor-based bank account class.

One can easily distinguish three parts in a monitor's method, with two of them being optional:

1. **Entry** (optional): Checking if the conditions are right for a thread to proceed.
2. **Midsection**: Manipulating the state of the monitor to the desired effect, plus performing any operations that require mutual exclusion.
3. **Exit** (optional): Signaling to other threads that it is their turn to enter or continue execution in the monitor.

Can you identify these parts in the methods of Listing 3.18?

The mutual exclusion offered by a monitor simplifies the design of multi-threaded applications to a large extent, since it encapsulates the corresponding program logic in a central location, making it easier to understand and modify.

Monitors and semaphores have been proven to be equivalent in the sense that any program using semaphores can be transformed into one using monitors, and vice versa. Alas, the complexity of the solutions is a different aspect of the problem.

A monitor-based solution can follow two possible paradigms based on where the critical sections are maintained. One option is to keep the critical sections inside the monitor. The second option is to use the monitor for gaining and releasing entry to the critical sections. Each of these design approaches has its set of advantages and disadvantages. We set out to explore them in the following sections.

3.6.1 DESIGN APPROACH 1: CRITICAL SECTION INSIDE THE MONITOR

Putting a critical section inside a monitor makes perfect sense because threads are forced to execute one at a time. However, this is a strategy that works only if the critical section is relatively short. Otherwise, efficiency is sacrificed and in extreme cases it may very well turn a multithreaded program into a sequential one. The bank account example presented above follows this design approach and justifiably so, since the duration of both `deposit` and `withdraw` methods is negligible.

Another scenario where this design would be suitable is the use of a monitor for serializing output to a console or a file:

```
1   class ConsoleMonitor
2   {
3     private:
4       QMutex m;
5     public:
6       void printOut(string s) {
7         QMutexLocker ml(&m);
8         cout << s;
9       }
10  };
```

A twist to this example brings up the Achilles heel of this approach: What if the output were destined to a collection of different files? Would the following solution still work if only one instance of the class were employed?

```
1   class FileOutputMonitor
2   {
3     private:
4       QMutex m;
5     public:
6       void writeOut(string s, ofstream &out) {
7         QMutexLocker ml(&m);
8         out << s;
9       }
10  };
```

The answer depends on the frequency of the `writeOut` calls and the number of output streams being used. In principle, though, this is a suboptimal solution. A better solution would be to have a different monitor object for each output stream or to design a monitor in the fashion described in the next section.

3.6.2 DESIGN APPROACH 2: MONITOR CONTROLS ENTRY TO CRITICAL SECTION

In this approach, a monitor is used as a mutex, i.e., is designed with a pair of methods, one for allowing entry to the critical section (getting a permit) and one for signaling exit from the critical section (releasing the permit). Although this may seem like an overcomplicated approach that mimics the lock-unlock sequence of a simple mutex, the reality is that a monitor is able to exercise much finer control over critical section entry than a simple mutex can.

For example, let's consider the "cigarette smokers' problem": The problem consists of three smoker and one agent threads. Each smoker continuously makes a cigarette and smokes it. But to make a cigarette, a smoker needs three ingredients: tobacco, paper, and a match. Each of the three smokers has an infinite supply of only one of the ingredients: one has only paper, another has only tobacco, and the third has only matches. The agent thread has an infinite supply of everything and places two randomly selected ingredients on the table. Then it signals the availability of the two ingredients and blocks. The smoker who misses the two ingredients on the table takes them, makes a cigarette, and smokes it for a random amount of time. Upon finishing his cigarette, he signals the agent, who then repeats the cycle.

It should be stressed that the problem definition used here is far more challenging than the typical setup described in the literature. In the literature, the agent signals the appropriate smoker to start making a cigarette. Here it is the smokers who must decide who should continue.

The solution is shown in Listing 3.19.

```
1   // File: smokers.cpp
2   . . .
3   #define TOBACCO_PAPER 0
4   #define TOBACCO_MATHCES 1
5   #define PAPER_MATHCES 2
6   #define MAXSLEEP 1000
7   const char *msg[]={"having matches", "having paper", "having tobacco"↩
        };
8   //****************************************************
9   class Monitor
10  {
11    private:
12        QMutex l;
13        QWaitCondition w, finish;
14        int newingred;
15        int exitf;
16    public:
17        Monitor();
18        // return 0 if OK. Otherwise it means termination
19        int canSmoke(int);
20        void newIngredient(int );
21        void finishedSmoking();
22        void finishSim();
23  };
```

```
24   //----------------------------------------------------
25   Monitor::Monitor(): newingred(-1), exitf(0) {}
26   //----------------------------------------------------
27   void Monitor::newIngredient(int newi)
28   {
29     QMutexLocker ml(&l);
30     newingred = newi;
31     w.wakeAll();
32     finish.wait(&l);
33   }
34   //----------------------------------------------------
35   int Monitor::canSmoke(int missing)
36   {
37     QMutexLocker ml(&l);
38     while(newingred != missing && ! exitf)
39       w.wait(&l);
40     return exitf;
41   }
42   //----------------------------------------------------
43   void Monitor::finishedSmoking()
44   {
45     newingred = -1;
46     QMutexLocker ml(&l);
47     finish.wakeOne();
48   }
49   //----------------------------------------------------
50   void Monitor::finishSim()
51   {
52     exitf=1;
53     w.wakeAll();
54   }
55   //****************************************************
56   class Smoker: public QThread
57   {
58     private:
59       int missing_ingred;
60       Monitor *m;
61       int total;
62     public:
63       Smoker(int, Monitor *);
64       void run();
65   };
66   //----------------------------------------------------
67   Smoker::Smoker(int missing, Monitor *mon): missing_ingred(missing), m(←
         mon), total(0){}
68   //----------------------------------------------------
69   void Smoker::run()
70   {
71     while((m->canSmoke(missing_ingred)) ==0)
72     {
73       total++;
74       cout << "Smoker " << msg[missing_ingred] << " is smoking\n";
```

```
75        msleep(rand() % MAXSLEEP);
76        m->finishedSmoking();
77    }
78  }
79  // **************************************************
80  class Agent: public QThread
81  {
82    private:
83      int runs;
84      Monitor *m;
85    public:
86      Agent(int, Monitor *);
87      void run();
88  };
89  //————————————————————————————————
90  Agent::Agent(int r, Monitor *mon): runs(r), m(mon){}
91  //————————————————————————————————
92  void Agent::run()
93  {
94      for(int i=0;i<runs; i++)
95      {
96          int ingreds = rand() % 3;
97          m->newIngredient(ingreds);
98      }
99    m->finishSim();
100 }
101 // **************************************************
102 int main(int argc, char **argv)
103 {
104     Monitor m;
105     Smoker *s[3];
106     for(int i=0;i<3;i++)
107     {
108       s[i] = new Smoker(i, &m);
109       s[i]->start();
110     }
111     Agent a(atoi(argv[1]), &m);
112     a.start();
113
114     a.wait();
115     for(int i=0;i<3;i++)
116       s[i]->wait();
117
118     return EXIT_SUCCESS;
119 }
```

LISTING 3.19

A monitor-based solution to the cigarette smokers' problem.

The solution is made up of three classes: a `Smoker` class, the instances of which are identified by the type of resources they require (resources are enumerated in lines 3-5); an `Agent` class that runs for a predetermined number of iterations (defined in the constructor); and a `Monitor` class that is used for letting the other two classes communicate. The key points of the solution are:

- The Monitor provides two sets of public methods:
    - A `canSmoke` and `finishedSmoking` pair employed by the Smoker threads. They correspond to a `get` and `release permit` type of methods.
    - The `newIngredient` and `finishSim` methods used by the Agent thread.
- The `Agent` calls the `Monitor`'s `newIngredient` method by passing the type of resources that become available. The `Monitor` proceeds to wake up any waiting threads (line 31) and then forces the `Agent` thread to block until a Smoker is done (line 32).
- The `Agent` thread is given responsibility for program termination. After the specified number of runs is completed, the `finishSim` method of the monitor is called. This in turn switches on a boolean flag (`exitf`, line 52) inside the monitor and wakes up all threads waiting on the condition variable `w`.
- Each `Smoker` thread runs a loop that terminates when the value returned by the `Monitor`'s `canSmoke` method is nonzero. The latter method returns the value of the `exitf` flag.

This is what a sample run of this program looks like:

```
$ ./smokers 3
Smoker having paper is smoking
Smoker having matches is smoking
Smoker having tobacco is smoking
```

3.7 APPLYING MONITORS IN CLASSICAL PROBLEMS
3.7.1 PRODUCERS-CONSUMERS REVISITED

The manipulation of the buffer in the producers-consumers context is a typically lightweight affair. However, for the sake of completeness, we explore monitor-based solutions sporting both aforementioned designs.

3.7.1.1 Producers-consumers: buffer manipulation within the monitor
In this case, the monitor just needs to publish `put` and `get` methods for the producers and consumers to use. The expressive power of the monitor construct, especially in comparison to the simplicity of semaphores, becomes apparent from the solution described in Lising 3.20.

```
1   // File: monitor1ProdCons.cpp
2   . . .
3   template <typename T>
4   class Monitor {
5   private:
```

```
6       QMutex l;
7       QWaitCondition full, empty;
8       int in, out;
9       int N;
10      int count;
11      T *buffer;
12   public:
13      void put(T);
14      T get();
15      Monitor(int n = BUFFSIZE);
16      ~Monitor();
17   };
18   //————————————————————————————————————
19   . . .
20   template <typename T>
21   void Monitor<T>::put(T i) {
22      QMutexLocker ml(&l);
23      while (count == N)
24          full.wait(&l);
25      buffer[in] = i;
26      in = (in + 1) % N;
27      count++;
28      empty.wakeOne();
29   }
30   //————————————————————————————————————
31
32   template <typename T>
33   T Monitor<T>::get() {
34      QMutexLocker ml(&l);
35      while (count == 0)
36          empty.wait(&l);
37      T temp = buffer[out];
38      out = (out + 1) % N;
39      count--;
40      full.wakeOne();
41      return temp;
42   }
43   //*************************************************************
44
45   template <typename T>
46   class Producer: public QThread {
47   private:
48      static QSemaphore numProducts;
49      int ID;
50      static Monitor<T> *mon;
51   public:
52      static T(*produce)();
53      static void initClass(int numP, Monitor<T> *m, T(*prod)());
54
55      Producer<T>(int i): ID(i) {}
56      void run();
57   };
```

```
58   //————————————————————————
59   . . .
60   template<typename T> void Producer<T>::initClass(int numP, Monitor<T> ↵
         *m, T(*prod)()) {
61       mon = m;
62       numProducts.release(numP);
63       produce = prod;
64   }
65   //————————————————————————
66
67   template<typename T>
68   void Producer<T>::run() {
69       while (numProducts.tryAcquire()) {
70           T item = (*produce)();
71           mon->put(item);
72       }
73   }
74   //————————————————————————
75
76   template<typename T>
77   class Consumer: public QThread {
78   private:
79       int ID;
80       static Monitor<T> *mon;
81       static QSemaphore numProducts;
82   public:
83       static void (*consume)(T i);
84       static void initClass(int numP, Monitor<T> *m, void (*cons)(T));
85
86       Consumer<T>(int i): ID(i) {}
87       void run();
88   };
89   //————————————————————————
90   . . .
91   template<typename T> void Consumer<T>::initClass(int numP, Monitor<T> ↵
         *m, void (*cons)(T)) {
92       numProducts.release(numP);
93       mon = m;
94       consume = cons;
95   }
96   //————————————————————————
97
98   template<typename T> void Consumer<T>::run() {
99       while (numProducts.tryAcquire()) {
100          T item = mon->get(); // take the item out
101          (*consume)(item);
102      }
103  }
104  //————————————————————————
105  . . .
106  int main(int argc, char *argv[]) {
107      . . .
```

```
108        int N = atoi(argv[1]);
109        int M = atoi(argv[2]);
110        int numP = atoi(argv[3]);
111        Monitor<int> m;
112
113        Producer<int>::initClass(numP, &m, &produce);
114        Consumer<int>::initClass(numP, &m, &consume);
115        . . .
116    }
```

LISTING 3.20

A monitor-based solution to the producers-consumers problem, where the buffer is encapsulated within the monitor.

The producers and consumers code is reduced to the bare minimum (lines 67-72 and 98-102), while all the intricate details of buffer manipulation are encapsulated inside the put (lines 20-29) and get (lines 32-43) Monitor methods. Listing 3.20 has many features in common with Listing 3.10 in the way producers and consumers terminate (i.e., by giving them the total number of resources to operate upon) and the use of template classes to facilitate a generic solution.

In contrast to Listing 3.10, though, the producers and consumers are not aware of the inner workings of the shared buffer, nor are they signaling each other via semaphores. All the communication is done implicitly through the Monitor class.

The Monitor class uses two wait conditions, full and empty, to block producers when the queue is full (lines 23 and 24) and to block consumers when the queue is empty (lines 35-36), respectively. Note that the Monitor class uses a large collection of variables that used to be shared between threads in Listing 3.10, without the need to protect them against race conditions. Now the only thing shared by the two types of threads is a Monitor instance, to which they become aware via the initClass methods of their respective classes.

3.7.1.2 Producers-consumers: buffer insertion/extraction exterior to the monitor

If the addition or removal of resources from the shared buffer takes a considerable amount of time (e.g., requires copying objects instead of references), using the second design approach can improve performance. Getting and releasing a permit from the monitor means that the run methods will be a bit longer than the miniscule ones of the previous design.

The idea is that producers and consumers will use a pair of functions to first acquire exclusive access to a buffer's location and second to release the location back to the monitor to utilize.

```
1    // File: monitor2ProdCons.cpp
2    . . .
3    template<typename T>
4    class Monitor {
5    private:
```

```
6        QMutex l;
7        QWaitCondition full, empty;
8        int in, out;
9        int N;
10       int count;
11       T *buffer;
12   public:
13       T* canPut();
14       T *canGet();
15       void donePutting();
16       void doneGetting();
17       Monitor(int n = BUFFSIZE);
18       ~Monitor();
19   };
20   //————————————————————————
21   . . .
22   template<typename T>
23   T* Monitor<T>::canPut() {
24       QMutexLocker ml(&l);
25       while (count == N)
26           full.wait(&l);
27       T *aux = &(buffer[in]);
28       in = (in + 1) % N;
29       return aux;
30   }
31   //————————————————————————
32
33   template<typename T>
34   T* Monitor<T>::canGet() {
35       QMutexLocker ml(&l);
36       while (count == 0)
37           empty.wait(&l);
38       T* temp = &(buffer[out]);
39       out = (out + 1) % N;
40       return temp;
41   }
42   //————————————————————————
43
44   template<typename T>
45   void Monitor<T>::donePutting() {
46       QMutexLocker ml(&l);
47       count++;
48       empty.wakeOne();
49   }
50   //————————————————————————
51
52   template<typename T>
53   void Monitor<T>::doneGetting() {
54       QMutexLocker ml(&l);
55       count--;
56       full.wakeOne();
57   }
```

```
58   // ***************************************************************
59   . . .
60   template<typename T>
61   void Producer<T>::run() {
62       while (numProducts.tryAcquire()) {
63           T item = (*produce)();
64           T* aux = mon->canPut();
65           *aux = item;
66           mon->donePutting();
67       }
68   }
69   //─────────────────────────────────────────────────
70   . . .
71   template<typename T> void Consumer<T>::run() {
72       while (numProducts.tryAcquire()) {
73           T*aux = mon->canGet();
74           T item = *aux; // take the item out
75           mon->doneGetting();
76           (*consume)(item);
77       }
78   }
```

LISTING 3.21

A monitor-based solution to the producers-consumers problem, where the buffer elements are directly manipulated by the producer and consumer threads under the supervision of the monitor. For the sake of brevity, only the differences with Listing 3.20 are shown.

The key points of the solution in Listing 3.21 are:

- The Monitor class provides two pairs of methods:
  - canPut and donePutting for Producer threads
  - canGet and doneGetting for Consumer threads

  The bodies of these methods essentially contain the two halves (unevenly divided) of the put and get methods, respectively, of Listing 3.20.
- The canPut and canGet methods return pointers to buffer locations that can be used for storage or retrieval of resources. By incrementing the in and out pointers but not the count counter, the location returned is effectively locked from any further manipulation by the Monitor.
- The Producer and Consumer threads can take their time to store or extract a resource after the canPut and canGet methods return. The Monitor is able to serve other threads at that time.
- Once the donePutting/doneGetting methods are called, the count is incremented/decremented and a waiting Consumer/Producer is alerted via the empty/full wait conditions.

3.7.2 READERS-WRITERS

Monitor-based solutions also shine in the context of the readers-writers problem. Assigning priority to one or the other type of thread is much, much simpler using a monitor than using semaphores. The nature of the problem mandates the use of the second design approach, i.e., each thread will have to acquire a permit to access the resource and then release this permit when all is done.

The threads do not have to be concerned with priorities or about the existence of other threads running in their critical sections. This functionality is embedded in the monitor's methods.

In all three solutions described in the following sections, the Reader and Writer threads execute a fixed number of operations, as shown here:

```
void Reader::run() {
    for(int i=0;i<NUMOPER;i++)
    {
        mon->canRead();
        // critical section
        coord->finishedReading();
    }
}
void Writer::run() {
    for(int i=0;i<NUMOPER;i++)
    {
        mon->canWrite();
        // critical section
        coord->finishedWriting();
    }
}
```

In the next sections we analyze the details of the monitor's implementations.

3.7.2.1 A solution favoring the readers

In order to assign priority to the reader threads, one has to just keep track of the waiting reader threads readersWaiting and prevent a writer from entering its critical section if readersWaiting > 0.

```
1   // File: readersFav.cpp
2   class Monitor
3   {
4    private:
5       QMutex l;
6       QWaitCondition wq;  // for blocking writers
7       QWaitCondition rq;  // for blocking readers
8       int readersIn;  // how many readers in their critical section
9       bool writerIn;  // set if a write is in its critical section
10      int readersWaiting;
```

```
11   public:
12     Monitor(): readersIn(0), writerIn(0), readersWaiting(0) {}
13     void canRead();
14     void finishedReading();
15     void canWrite();
16     void finishedWriting();
17   };
18   // ***********************************
19   void Monitor::canRead()
20   {
21     QMutexLocker ml(&l);
22     while(writerIn==true)
23     {
24       readersWaiting++;
25       rq.wait(&l);
26       readersWaiting--;
27     }
28
29     readersIn++;
30   }
31   // ***********************************
32   void Monitor::canWrite()
33   {
34     QMutexLocker ml(&l);
35     while(writerIn==true || readersWaiting >0 || readersIn>0)
36       wq.wait(&l);
37
38     writerIn=true;
39   }
40   // ***********************************
41   void Monitor::finishedReading()
42   {
43     QMutexLocker ml(&l);
44     readersIn--;
45     if(readersIn==0)
46       wq.wakeOne();
47   }
48   // ***********************************
49   void Monitor::finishedWriting()
50   {
51     QMutexLocker ml(&l);
52     writerIn=false;
53     if(readersWaiting>0)
54       rq.wakeAll();
55     else
56       wq.wakeOne();
57   }
```

LISTING 3.22

A monitor implementation favoring the Reader threads.

The important points of the solution shown in Listing 3.22 are:

- The monitor maintains two wait conditions: wq for queuing up waiting writers and rq for waiting readers.
- A running count of the readers inside their critical sections is maintained. It is incremented at line 29 and decremented at line 44 once a reader leaves. If the count reaches 0, a signal is sent to any waiting writers (line 46).
- A writer thread blocks if readers are inside their critical section or they are waiting to enter it (line 35).
- The last part, which completes the shift in priority to readers, is the management of the wait condition queues in the finishedWriting method: A writer is woken up only if there are no readers waiting (lines 53-56).

3.7.2.2 Giving priority to the writers

In order to assign priority to the writer threads, one has to simply keep track of the waiting writer threads writersWaiting and prevent a reader from entering its critical section if writersWaiting > 0.

The two classes in Listing 3.22 and 3.23 are nearly identical. Their differences are concentrated at the lines that control entry to the critical section and queue management upon exit from the critical section. On the former listing, line 22 forces readers to block if there are writers waiting to enter their critical section. Handing priority over to writers is completed by lines 52-55 in Listing 3.23, where a writer leaving its critical section picks a waiting writer, if there is one over the readers. However, if there are no waiting writers, all readers are woken up (line 55).

```cpp
1   // File: writersFav.cpp
2   class Monitor
3   {
4     private:
5         QMutex l;
6         QWaitCondition wq;   // for blocking writers
7         QWaitCondition rq;   // for blocking readers
8         int readersIn;   // how many readers in their critical section
9         bool writerIn;   // set if a write is in its critical section
10        int writersWaiting; // how many writers are waiting to enter
11    public:
12        Monitor(): readersIn(0), writerIn(0), writersWaiting(0) {}
13        void canRead();
14        void finishedReading();
15        void canWrite();
16        void finishedWriting();
17   };
18   // **************************************
19   void Monitor::canRead()
20   {
21     QMutexLocker ml(&l);
22     while(writerIn==true || writersWaiting>0)
23         rq.wait(&l);
```

```
24
25      readersIn++;
26   }
27   // *************************************
28   void Monitor::canWrite()
29   {
30      QMutexLocker ml(&l);
31      while(writerIn==true || readersIn>0)
32      {
33          writersWaiting++;
34          wq.wait(&l);
35          writersWaiting--;
36      }
37      writerIn=true;
38   }
39   // *************************************
40   void Monitor::finishedReading()
41   {
42      QMutexLocker ml(&l);
43      readersIn--;
44      if(readersIn == 0)
45          wq.wakeOne();
46   }
47   // *************************************
48   void Monitor::finishedWriting()
49   {
50      QMutexLocker ml(&l);
51      writerIn=false;
52      if(writersWaiting>0)
53          wq.wakeOne();
54      else
55          rq.wakeAll();
56   }
```

LISTING 3.23

A monitor implementation favoring the `Writer` threads.

3.7.2.3 A fair solution

Creating a fair solution to the readers-writers problem is a challenge. Although it has never been a consideration in our previous examples, the order in which threads are released from the queue of a wait condition is crucial for achieving a FIFO order in serving critical section entry requests.

The Qt documentation on the `wakeOne` and `wakeAll` methods reads: "The order in which the threads are woken up depends on the operating system's scheduling policies and cannot be controlled or predicted."

It should be noted that it is not Qt's implementation that is at fault here. Once a group of threads becomes ready again, the order of their execution is the responsibility of the operating system and cannot be influenced directly. An identical problem would plague any monitor implementation.

Qt's documentation provides a hint as to how one can address this shortcoming: "If you want to wake up a specific thread, the solution is typically to use different wait conditions and have different threads wait on different conditions."

The solution shown in Listing 3.24 exhibits this feature exactly: Threads that are forced to block do so on different wait conditions, allowing us precise control over which will be woken up and in what order. A fixed array of wait conditions is allocated and managed as a circular queue (with `in` and `out` indices and a `counter` of how many are used). It is accompanied by a boolean array (`writeflag`) that helps us distinguish what type of thread is blocked in each wait condition. If all the wait conditions are used, threads are forced to queue up in a generic wait condition (`quefull`). This is actually the only departure from a completely fair solution (because threads leaving this queue don't do so in a FIFO manner), but it is a small compromise.

```cpp
// File: readWriteFair.cpp
const int QUESIZE = 100;
//**************************************
class Monitor
{
private:
  QMutex l;
  QWaitCondition c[QUESIZE];      // a different condition for each ↵
        waiting thread
  bool writeflag[QUESIZE];        // what kind of threads wait?
  QWaitCondition quefull;         // used when queue of waiting threads ↵
        becomes full
  int in, out, counter;
  int readersIn;                  // how many readers in their critical ↵
        section
  int writersIn;                  // how many writers in their critical ↵
        section (0 or 1)
public:

  Monitor ():in (0), out (0), counter (0), readersIn (0), writersIn ↵
        (0) {}
  void canRead ();
  void finishedReading ();
  void canWrite ();
  void finishedWriting ();
};
//**************************************

void Monitor::canRead ()
{
  QMutexLocker ml (&l);
  while (counter == QUESIZE)
    quefull.wait (&l);

  if (counter > 0 || writersIn)
    {
      int temp = in;
      writeflag[in] = false;
```

```
34          in = (in + 1) % QUESIZE;
35          counter++;
36          c[temp].wait (&l);
37        }
38      readersIn++;
39  }
40  // ************************************
41
42  void Monitor::canWrite ()
43  {
44      QMutexLocker ml (&l);
45      while (counter == QUESIZE)
46        quefull.wait (&l);
47
48      if (counter > 0 || writersIn > 0 || readersIn > 0)
49        {
50          int temp = in;
51          writeflag[in] = true;
52          in = (in + 1) % QUESIZE;
53          counter++;
54          c[temp].wait (&l);
55        }
56      writersIn++;
57  }
58  // ************************************
59
60  void Monitor::finishedReading ()
61  {
62      QMutexLocker ml (&l);
63      readersIn--;
64      if (readersIn == 0 && counter > 0)
65        {
66          c[out].wakeOne ();   // must be a writer that is being woken up
67          out = (out + 1) % QUESIZE;
68          counter--;
69          quefull.wakeOne ();
70        }
71  }
72  // ************************************
73
74  void Monitor::finishedWriting ()
75  {
76      QMutexLocker ml (&l);
77      writersIn--;
78      if (counter > 0)
79        {
80          if (!writeflag[out])
81            {
82              while (counter > 0 && !writeflag[out]) // start next readers
83                {
84                  c[out].wakeOne ();
85                  out = (out + 1) % QUESIZE;
```

```
86                 counter--;
87             }
88         }
89     else                    // next writer
90         {
91             c[out].wakeOne ();
92             out = (out + 1) % QUESIZE;
93             counter--;
94         }
95     quefull.wakeAll ();
96     }
97 }
```

LISTING 3.24

A fair monitor implementation for the readers-writers problem.

Other major points in the monitor of Listing 3.24 are the following:

- All threads requesting entry into their critical section first inspect the status of the queue of wait conditions and the type of threads currently in their critical section.
- Reader threads are allowed to proceed in canRead only if there is no writer inside and the queue of wait conditions is empty[10] (counter == 0). If the latter is false (line 30), this means that at least one writer is ahead of this thread in the service order.
- A writer thread is allowed to proceed in canWrite if the queue of wait conditions is empty and there are no writers or readers inside (line 48).
- If the conditions in lines 30 and 48 are true, a thread is blocked using an element of the c array, and the corresponding element in writeflag is set/reset to indicate a writer/reader is blocked.
- When finishWriting is called and the queue of wait conditions is not empty (counter >0), the type of thread at the head of the queue (pointed by out) is examined (line 80). If the first element is a reader, all the readers up to the end of the queue or the encounter of the first writer are signaled (lines 82-86). Otherwise a writer is woken up (lines 91-93).

The ability to manage the threads requesting entry into their critical section with such a fine-grained approach opens up a number of possibilities that go beyond the simple readers-writers scenario. For example, arbitrary objective functions can be used to evaluate which thread will proceed next (e.g., based on priority, monetary considerations, etc.). A fitting example would be the case of a multithreaded DBMS system, serving incoming client requests. These could be ranked based on client rank, request urgency, or any other set of criteria.

---

[10]The term "empty queue" is used loosely here. Literally, the queue is "empty" if none of the wait conditions has a non-empty queue of threads.

3.8 DYNAMIC VS. STATIC THREAD MANAGEMENT

As mentioned in Section 3.2.3.1, Qt maintains a pool of threads that are ready to go, without the need for the OS to allocate and initialize a new thread entity. Although the overhead of thread creation compared to forking a new process is orders of magnitude smaller, it can still be significant, especially if threads need to be dynamically spawned at run-time. A classic example is that of a *concurrent* web or database server[11] that listens to incoming requests and dedicates a thread to servicing each one. Instead of creating a new thread for every request, the thread could be reused, taken from a repository of idle threads. This repository is exactly the kind of functionality the QThreadPool class provides.

In this section we explore both how QThreadPool can be utilized and how we can create our own thread repository, even if the threading library used does not support a built-in one.

3.8.1 QT'S THREAD POOL

The QThreadPool class and QtConcurrent namespace functions provide the means for an efficient and easy transition to multithreaded applications, especially when the threads do not have to share common resources. The only problem is that the functions that are designated to be run by separate threads will run only if there is a free thread available.

As an example of how these can be utilized, the Listing 3.25 program is a rewrite of the producers-consumers code of Listing 3.10.

```
1   // File: qtconcurProdCons.cpp
2   . . .
3       if(N + M > QThreadPool::globalInstance() -> maxThreadCount())
4           QThreadPool::globalInstance() -> setMaxThreadCount (N+M);
5
6       QFuture<void> prodF[N];
7       QFuture<void> consF[M];
8       Producer<int> *p[N];
9       Consumer<int> *c[M];
10
11      for (int i = 0; i < N; i++)    {
12          p[i] = new Producer<int >(i);
13          prodF[i] = QtConcurrent::run(*p[i], &Producer<int >::run);
14      }
15
16      for (int i = 0; i < M; i++)    {
17          c[i] = new Consumer<int >(i);
18          consF[i] = QtConcurrent::run(*c[i], &Consumer<int >::run);
19      }
20
21      for (int i = 0; i < N; i++)
22          prodF[i].waitForFinished();
```

---

[11] An alternative is to have **iterative** servers that serve only one request at a time. Unless the server is very simple, for example, a time server like the one listening to port 13 in Unix systems, this design cannot scale to handle increased loads.

```
23
24      for (int i = 0; i < M; i++)
25          consF[i].waitForFinished();
26      . . .
```

LISTING 3.25

Generic solution to the *n*-producers and *m*-consumers problem with a fixed number of iterations, using the `QThreadPool` class and `QtConcurrent::run` function. Only the differences from Listing 3.10 are shown.

As can be easily deduced from the length of the Listing 3.25, only minimal changes are required in order to introduce the new functionality. The `QtConcurrent::run` function can also work on an object's method if an object reference is provided first, followed by the address of the method to call. Because threads are unnamed, the main thread has to use the `QFuture` objects returned by `QtConcurrent::run`, to wait for them to complete (lines 22 and 25).

The object references used in lines 13 and 18 (`*p[i]` and `*c[i]`) imply that the methods called are `const`, i.e., they do not modify the objects. If we did not have `const` methods, object pointers should have been used instead:

```
prodF[i] = QtConcurrent::run(p[i], &Producer<int>::run);
. . .
consF[i] = QtConcurrent::run(c[i], &Consumer<int>::run);
```

A final clarification about the syntax in lines 13 and 18, is that the address-of (&) operator is required because non-static methods cannot be referenced otherwise, in the absense of a class instance.

Lines 3 and 4 ensure that all the requested threads will start running, even if this number is suboptimal according to Qt's criteria. The ideal number of threads is estimated and made available by the `QThread::idealThreadCount()` method, and this is the default setting for the active number of threads. By getting a reference to the intrinsic `QThreadPool` instance via the `QThreadPool::globalInstance()` static method, the available number of threads can be modified (line 4).

3.8.2 CREATING AND MANAGING A POOL OF THREADS

Applications that require the frequent spawning of threads can gain in performance by reusing threads, i.e., using the same threads to perform *different tasks*. The gains come from reduced demands on the memory management subsystem because the operating system does not have to allocate and initialize all the components necessary for a thread to run (run-time stack, thread control block, etc.).

Creating a pool of threads for that purpose requires that one is able to:

1. Describe computational tasks.
2. Communicate computational tasks.
3. Identify threads that are executing a task.
4. Signal the termination of a task's execution.

The way threads are initialized in Qt is an inspiration regarding how the first of the above requirements can be fulfilled: Describe a computational task as a class with a single point of entry for a thread to execute. An abstract class can be defined to establish what the interface should be like.

Communicating instances of concrete, derivative classes of `Computation-alTask` between one or more task-generating (*producing*) threads and the pool threads that are supposed to execute (*consume*) them is a perfect example of the producers-consumers pattern. The problem is reminiscent of the setup we used in Section 3.5.2 to perform numerical integration, with the key difference being that the goal is to be able to execute any task and not just a single type of task.

The third and fourth requirements can be satisfied by uniquely branding the tasks (e.g., via a task ID) and forcing the threads that execute them to use the associated identifier for indicating the status of their execution (i.e., termination). Based on the preceding discussion, we can write an abstract class to be used as the base class for any task to be submitted to the thread pool, as in Listing 3.26.

```
// File: customThreadPool.h
class ComputationalTask {
   private:
      unsigned int taskID;
   public:
      virtual void compute() = 0;
      void setTaskID(int id) { taskID = id;}
      unsigned int getTaskID() {return taskID;}
};
```

LISTING 3.26

Abstract class to be used as a base class for creating task objects.

The `taskID` data member serves to uniquely identify a task, regardless of which thread it is running on. This seemingly contradicts the setting used in previous sections, where the main thread stored references to children threads. A reference to a pool thread has no meaning now to our main thread, since what is of real concern are the submitted tasks. A pool thread may be running any task (or be idle) at a given time.

The following listings show a monitor-based custom thread-pool class and its corresponding thread class. For clarity, each listing shows the code of a single class. The actual code is distributed over two files: a header file and an implementation file.

```
1    // File(s): customThreadPool.h and customThreadPool.cpp
2    class CustomThread: public QThread
3    {
4       public:
5          static CustomThreadPool *tp;
6          void run();
7    };
8    //──────────────────────────────────────
9    CustomThreadPool *CustomThread::tp;
10   //──────────────────────────────────────
11   void CustomThread::run()
12   {
13      ComputationalTask *task = tp->get();
14      while(task != NULL)
```

```
15        {
16            task->compute();
17            tp->complete(task->getTaskID());
18            task = tp->get();
19        }
20   }
```

LISTING 3.27

A custom thread class used for populating a pool of threads.

The CustomThread class is the workhorse of our code. It maintains a class-wide reference to a CustomThreadPool singleton object, and each of its instances uses it to get a new task (lines 13 and 18), execute it (line 16), and flag its completion (line 17). The CustomThread instances run until a null task reference is returned to them. This serves as an indication of the program's termination.

The CustomThreadPool class in Listing 3.28 is a *monitor* offering two sets of methods: one set for task-producers to use and one set for the pool threads to use. All the public methods, bar the constructor and destructor, start by locking down the object. Also, a set of wait conditions ensure that task-producer threads will block when the task buffer is full, and pool threads will block when the task buffer is empty.

```
1    // File(s): customThreadPool.h and customThreadPool.cpp
2
3    class CustomThreadPool
4    {
5    private:
6        static const int BUFFERSIZE;
7        static const int NUMTHREADS;
8        QWaitCondition notDone;   // for blocking while a thread is not ↵
                finished
9        QWaitCondition empty;     // for blocking pool-threads if buffer ↵
                is empty
10       QWaitCondition full;
11       QMutex l;
12       ComputationalTask **buffer;  // pointer to array of pointers
13       int in, out, count, N, maxThreads;
14       unsigned int nextTaskID;     // used to enumerate the assigned ↵
                tasks
15       set<unsigned int> finished;  // keeps the task IDs of finished ↵
                tasks.
16                               // IDs are removed from the set, once
17                               // the isDone method is called for them
18       CustomThread **t;
19   public:
20       CustomThreadPool(int n = BUFFERSIZE, int nt = NUMTHREADS);
21       ~CustomThreadPool();
22
23       ComputationalTask *get();   // to be called by the pool-threads
24       void complete(unsigned int); // to be called by the pool-threads
25
26       unsigned int schedule(ComputationalTask *);
```

```
27      void waitTillDone(unsigned int); // to be called by the task ↩
            generator
28    };
29    //————————————————————————————————————————
30
31    CustomThreadPool::CustomThreadPool(int n, int numThr)
32    {
33      N = n;
34      buffer = new ComputationalTask*[n];
35      in=out=count=0;
36      nextTaskID=0;
37      maxThreads = numThr;
38      t = new CustomThread*[maxThreads];
39      CustomThread::tp = this;
40      for(int i=0;i<maxThreads;i++)
41      {
42          t[i] = new CustomThread();
43          t[i]->start();
44      }
45    }
46    //————————————————————————————————————————
47
48    CustomThreadPool::~CustomThreadPool()
49    {
50        for(int i=0;i<maxThreads;i++)
51            this->schedule(NULL);
52
53        for (int i = 0; i < maxThreads; i++) {
54            this->t[i]->wait();
55            delete t[i];
56        }
57        delete []t;
58        delete []buffer;
59    }
60    //————————————————————————————————————————
61
62    unsigned int CustomThreadPool::schedule(ComputationalTask *ct)
63    {
64        QMutexLocker ml(&l);
65        while(count == N)
66            full.wait(&l);
67        buffer[in] = ct;
68        in =(in+1) % N;
69        count++;
70
71        if(ct != NULL)  // check it is not the termination task
72        {
73            ct->setTaskID(nextTaskID);
74            nextTaskID++;
75        }
76
77        empty.wakeOne();
```

```
78
79        return (nextTaskID-1);
80    }
81    //—————————————————————————————
82
83    ComputationalTask *CustomThreadPool::get()
84    {
85        QMutexLocker ml(&l);
86        while(count == 0)
87            empty.wait(&l);
88
89        ComputationalTask *temp = buffer[out];
90        out =(out+1) % N;
91        count--;
92
93        full.wakeOne();
94        return temp;
95    }
96    //—————————————————————————————
97
98    void CustomThreadPool::complete(unsigned int id)
99    {
100       QMutexLocker ml(&l);
101       finished.insert(id);
102       notDone.wakeAll();
103   }
104   //—————————————————————————————
105
106   void CustomThreadPool::waitTillDone(unsigned int id)
107   {
108       QMutexLocker ml(&l);
109       while(finished.find(id) == finished.end())
110           notDone.wait(&l);
111       finished.erase(id);
112   }
```

LISTING 3.28

A custom thread-pool class.

A set of CustomThread objects is created and the associated threads spawned (lines 40-44) once an instance of the CustomThreadPool is created. The number of threads defaults to 16, but the actual number can be specified in the class constructor. References to these threads are maintained in the t array so that the destructor of CustomThreadPool can block while all the submitted tasks are completed (lines 53-55).

The CustomThreadPool object maintains a circular queue of references to ComputationalTask objects. The queue is modified by methods:

- schedule: Deposits a task reference in the queue. If the reference is not null, the task is also assigned a unique ID by incrementing the static nextTaskID variable (lines 73 and 74). This ID is also returned to the "producer" thread as a handle.
- get: Dequeues and returns a task reference from the queue.

Both of these methods contain the typical queue manipulation statements that we examined in Section 3.7.1.

Once a pool thread finishes a task (i.e., its `compute` method returns), it informs the monitor by calling the `complete` method. This in turn inserts the task's ID in a set of finished tasks (line 101), and any "producer" thread waiting for a submitted task to finish is woken up (line 102). This set maintains (for efficiency purposes) only the IDs of the completed tasks that have not been *reported* as completed back to the thread that generated them. The task-generating threads can check to see whether a task is complete by calling the `waitTillDone` method with the task's ID as a parameter. A failed search through the `finished` set (line 109) leads to the blocking of the calling thread.

Only when the condition of line 109 fails, i.e., the ID is found, does the thread proceed to clear the ID from the set (line 111) and return.

As an example on the use of the `CustomThreadPool` class, the following program generates a number of independent tasks for calculating the Mandelbrot fractal set. Admittedly, this is not the most appropriate example, because the load can be partitioned and assigned to a fixed number of threads *a priori*, which is not a recipe for a problem requiring dynamic thread spawning.

The Mandelbrot set[12] is a set of points $c = x + i \cdot y$ on the complex plane that produce a bounded sequence of numbers $z_0, z_1, z_2, \ldots$ when the recursive formula:

$$z_{n+1} = z_n^2 + c \tag{3.1}$$

with $z_0 = c$ is applied, i.e., $z_n = \sqrt{x_n^2 + y_n^2} < \infty \forall n$.

The famous Mandelbrot fractal image is produced by calculating, for each point c on the complex plane, the number of iterations n at which the sequence diverges: $|z_n| > 2$, as if the magnitude goes above 2 the sequence is known to diverge. The number n is used to pseudo-color the point. Obviously, for the Mandelbrot set of points the number of iterations must be bounded as they never diverge.

The following program breaks-up the area of the complex plane specified in the command-line into a set of disjoint parts, and assigns the calculation of each part to a different task. Each part is identified by its upper left and lower right corners. Figure 3.12 shows how the tasks are initialized. The required parameters include (a) the upper-left and lower-right corners of the part of the complex plane to examine, and (b) the top-left corner coordinates, the height and the width in pixels of the part of the image to be generated.

```
1    // File(s): mandelbrot_threadPool/main.cpp
2    . . .
3    #include "customThreadPool.h"
4
5    //************************************************************
6
7    class MandelCompute : public ComputationalTask {
8    private:
9        static const int MAXITER;
```

---

[12]http://en.wikipedia.org/wiki/Mandelbrot_set.

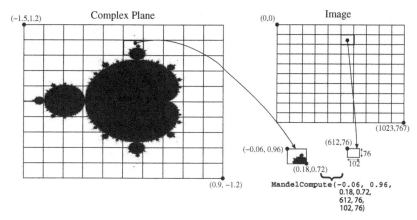

FIGURE 3.12

An illustration of the parameters required to generate an instance of the `MandelCompute` class in Listing 3.29. The parameters include a description of both the "source" area in the complex plane and the "destination" part of the image to be computed. The actual code also includes a reference to a `QImage` object.

```
10        int diverge(double cx, double cy);
11
12        double upperX, upperY, lowerX, lowerY;
13        int imageX, imageY, pixelsX, pixelsY;
14        QImage *img;
15
16  public:
17        MandelCompute(double, double, double, double, QImage *, int, int, ↵
              int, int);
18        virtual void compute();
19  };
20  const int MandelCompute::MAXITER = 255;
21
22  //————————————————————————————————————
23
24  int MandelCompute::diverge(double cx, double cy) {
25        int iter = 0;
26        double vx = cx, vy = cy, tx, ty;
27        while (iter < MAXITER && (vx * vx + vy * vy) < 4) {
28            tx = vx * vx − vy * vy + cx;
29            ty = 2 * vx * vy + cy;
30            vx = tx;
31            vy = ty;
32            iter++;
33        }
34        return iter;
35  }
```

```
36   //————————————————————————————
37
38   MandelCompute::MandelCompute(double uX, double uY, double lX, double ↵
         lY, QImage *im, int iX, int iY, int pX, int pY) {
39       upperX = uX;
40       upperY = uY;
41       lowerX = lX;
42       lowerY = lY;
43       img = im;
44       imageX = iX;
45       imageY = iY;
46       pixelsX = pX;
47       pixelsY = pY;
48   }
49
50   //————————————————————————————
51
52   void MandelCompute::compute() {
53       double stepx = (lowerX − upperX) / pixelsX;
54       double stepy = (upperY − lowerY) / pixelsY;
55
56       for (int i = 0; i < pixelsX; i++)
57           for (int j = 0; j < pixelsY; j++) {
58               double tempx, tempy;
59               tempx = upperX + i * stepx;
60               tempy = upperY − j * stepy;
61               int color = diverge(tempx, tempy);    // find when ↵
                       divergence happens
62               img−>setPixel(imageX + i, imageY + j, qRgb(256 − color, ↵
                       256 − color, 256 − color)); // pseudocolor pixel
63           }
64   }
65   //*************************************************************
66
67   int main(int argc, char *argv[]) {
68       double upperCornerX, upperCornerY;
69       double lowerCornerX, lowerCornerY;
70
71       upperCornerX = atof(argv[1]);
72       upperCornerY = atof(argv[2]);
73       lowerCornerX = atof(argv[3]);
74       lowerCornerY = atof(argv[4]);
75       double partXSpan, partYSpan;
76
77
78       int Xparts = 10, Yparts = 10;
79       int imgX = 1024, imgY = 768;
80       int pxlX, pxlY;
81
82       partXSpan = (lowerCornerX − upperCornerX) / Xparts;
83       partYSpan = (upperCornerY − lowerCornerY) / Yparts;
84       pxlX = imgX / Xparts;
```

```
85        pxlY = imgY / Yparts;
86        QImage *img = new QImage(imgX, imgY, QImage::Format_RGB32);
87        CustomThreadPool tp;
88        unsigned thIDs[Xparts][Yparts];
89
90
91
92        for (int i = 0; i < Xparts; i++)
93            for (int j = 0; j < Yparts; j++) {
94                double x1, y1, x2, y2;
95                int ix, iy, pX, pY; //image coords. and pixel spans
96
97                x1 = upperCornerX + i * partXSpan;
98                y1 = upperCornerY - j * partYSpan;
99                x2 = upperCornerX + (i + 1) * partXSpan;
100               y2 = upperCornerY - (j + 1) * partYSpan;
101
102               ix = i*pxlX;
103               iy = j*pxlY;
104               pX = (i == Xparts - 1) ? imgX - ix: pxlX;
105               pY = (j == Yparts - 1) ? imgY - iy: pxlY;
106
107               MandelCompute *t = new MandelCompute(x1, y1, x2, y2, img, ←┘
                      ix, iy, pX, pY);
108               thIDs[i][j] = tp.schedule(t);
109           }
110
111
112       // now wait for all threads to stop
113       for (int i = 0; i < Xparts; i++)
114           for (int j = 0; j < Yparts; j++) {
115               tp.waitTillDone(thIDs[i][j]);
116           }
117
118       img->save("mandel.png", "PNG", 0);
119       return 0;
120   }
```

LISTING 3.29

A Mandelbrot fractal set calculator that generates a task for each part of the image to be computed.

The main points of the program in Listing 3.29 are:

- The part of the complex plane to be examined (as specified by command-line parameters that are extracted at lines 71-74), is split into Xparts * Yparts disjoint pieces. For each piece, a separate task is generated (line 107) and deposited in the CustomThreadPool object's queue (line 108).
- The tasks are instances of the MandelCompute class, which is declared as a subclass of ComputationalTask. The calculations take place inside the compute and diverge methods.

- The main thread, after creating the `CustomThreadPool` singleton `tp` (line 87), deposits the generated tasks in `tp`'s queue and keeps the returned task ID in an array (line 108). These IDs are subsequently used to check that the tasks are completed (lines 113-115) before the generated image is saved to a file.
- A `QImage` instance is used for handling the generated image data and finally storing the complete image in a file (line 118). All the methods in class `QImage` are *reentrant*, which means it is safe to call them from multiple threads. Because each of the threads is instructed to operate on a different part of the `QImage` object, there are no race conditions to worry about.

3.9 DEBUGGING MULTITHREADED APPLICATIONS

Debugging of multithreaded applications goes way beyond merely having a debugger capable of managing multiple threads. Most contemporary debuggers support the execution and individual debugging of threads, with thread-specific breakpoints, watch windows, etc. In this section, we are not concerned primarily with how a debugger can be utilized. For example, Figure 3.13 shows the DDD, GNU DeBugger (GDB) front end executing the fair readers-writers solution of Listing 3.24. The only requirement for being able to use DDD and GDB (for the CLI affictionatos) in Unix/Linux is to compile your program with debugging information support, i.e., use the -g switch of the compiler.

Bugs in multithreaded programs typically manifest sporadically only under special circumstances that have to do with the precise timing of events. A debugger disrupts timings by pausing or slowing down the execution of threads, making bug reproduction and discovery a challenge. Ultimately, finding the bugs becomes a matter of experience and intuition, but appropriately instrumented program code can be of great help.

In the following list, we enumerate a number of steps a developer can take to ensure a bug-free multithreaded application:

- The first step in eliminating bugs in multithreaded applications is, of course, to not introduce them in the first place! A sound software design that precedes the writing of the code is critical in this regard.
- The classical problems studied in this chapter are not merely of educational value. The majority of the concurrency problems one can encounter in real life are either instances of these problems or can be reduced to them with a few simple steps. Utilizing the solutions presented in this chapter can eliminate problems that stem from trying to reinvent the wheel.
- The application should be modified to produce some type of log or trace history that can be examined off-line. This would permit the collection of information about the run-time behavior of the application.
- Having too many threads in an application can complicate the interpretation of the logs produced. It is a generally good design to have the application

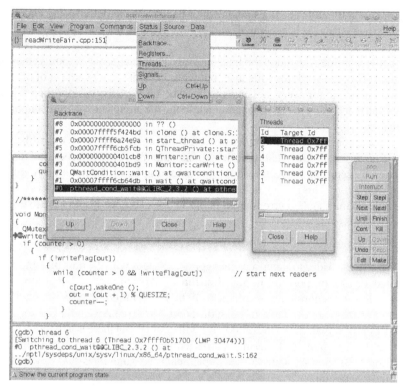

FIGURE 3.13

A screenshot of the DDD debugger, which is a GDB front-end, running an instance of the fair solution to the readers-writers problem of Listing 3.24. The program is running six threads, as shown in the dialog window: the main thread, two readers, and three writers. A breakpoint has stopped the writer threads at line 115 in the code. The backtrace of a selected thread is also shown, indicating that it is blocked on a wait condition.

parameterized as far as the number of threads is concerned. By limiting the threads to 1, bugs not specific to timings can be discovered. Also, by limiting them to 2 or 3, we can reduce the overhead of extracting information from the logs substantially.

Peppering your code with `printf` or `cout` statements to keep track of the execution path and state of the program is not sufficient. Having multiple threads produce console (or file) output at the same time typically results in mangled messages that cannot be deciphered. The solution is to treat the console (or the file stream) as a shared resource and place the output statements inside a critical section.

Some authors advocate keeping the debugging/tracing information in a memory buffer (called a *trace buffer*) to be saved upon the termination of the program. This is a questionable approach for misbehaving programs. It requires that the program

(a) terminate normally (i.e., does not crash or hang), (b) the buffer is big enough to accommodate whatever is generated, and (c) the buffer is not corrupted by memory errors.

A better solution is to dump the trace messages to the console as soon as they are generated. This can work for a file also, but with the additional overhead of opening and closing the file for every message that is to be saved. Otherwise, if the program crashes one risks losing the last changes made to the file along with possibly important information.

To differentiate normal program output from trace messages, we can utilize the standard error stream. But what if the debugging output needs to be processed further, e.g., filtered according to the thread that generated it, etc.? The solution is simple: *stream redirection*. This is a capability common to both the *nix and Windows worlds. So, to redirect the standard error output to file `trace.log`, we would have to use the following syntax:

```
$ myprog 2> trace.log
```

It is also a good idea to stamp any debugging messages with the time that they were generated. For this purpose, the normal time functions (such as `clock`) that come with 1msec or lower resolution are insufficient. A high-resolution timer is required, and a number of them are available through different APIs (see Appendix C.2 for more details). For the remainder of the section we will assume that there is a function called `hrclock` (high-resolution clock) that returns a timestamp in seconds of type `double`.

Listing 3.30 shows a sample that implements the guidelines laid down in the preceding discussion.

```
1   // File: debugSample.cpp
2   . . .
3   #define DEBUG
4
5   // *************************************************
6   double time0 = 0;
7   QMutex l;
8
9   // *************************************************
10  double hrclock ()
11  {
12    timespec ts;
13    clock_gettime (CLOCK_REALTIME, &ts);
14    double aux = ts.tv_sec + ts.tv_nsec / 1000000000.0;
15    return aux - time0;
16  }
17
18  // *************************************************
19  void debugMsg (string msg, double timestamp)
20  {
21    l.lock ();
```

```
22        cerr << timestamp << " " << msg << endl;
23        l.unlock ();
24      }
25

26   // ***********************************************
27      . . .
28   void MyThread::run ()
29      {
30        cout << "Thread " << ID << " is running\n";
31        for (int j = 0; j < runs; j++)
32          {
33   #ifdef DEBUG
34            ostringstream ss;
35            ss << "Thread " << ID << " counter=" << counter;
36            debugMsg (ss.str (), hrclock ());
37   #endif
38            usleep (rand () % 3);
39            counter++;
40          }
41      }
42   };
43   // ***********************************************
44

45   int main (int argc, char *argv[])
46   {
47   #ifdef DEBUG
48     time0 = hrclock ();
49   #endif
50      . . .
51   }
```

LISTING 3.30

A sample of how a multithreaded application can be set up for debugging. The code is a modified version of the program in Listing 3.6.

The key points of the sample program are:

- The additional code segments are inside C++ preprocessor conditional blocks (lines 33-37 and 47-49). One just has to comment-out line 3, to get a production-ready version of the program.
- A global-scope mutex is used to ensure that the body of the debugMsg function is a critical section.
- Time is measured from the moment the program starts execution. The timestamp of that instance is stored in the time0 variable, which is subsequently subtracted from every timestamp calculated (line 15).

A sample run of this program and a close inspection of the debugging output reveal the race condition at work:

```
$ ./debugSample 10 100 2> log
Thread Thread Thread Thread Thread Thread Thread 6419 is running
Thread 8 is running
Thread 3 is running
 is running
7 is running
5 is running
Thread 2 is running
0 is running
 is running
 is running
994
$ sort log
. . .
0.0033443 Thread 5 counter=216
0.00335193 Thread 7 counter=218
0.00335193 Thread 8 counter=217    <————
0.00335503 Thread 3 counter=219
. . .
```

Finally, a word of caution regarding properly debugging a program: You should *disable compiler optimizations.* An optimizing compiler can change the execution order of statements, or even discard variables that you declare in your program, in its effort to streamline execution. As a result, debugging an optimized executable can produce surprising results, such as jumps between statements, which can strain the programmer. In rare cases, it can be the compiler optimizations that cause a bug to appear. Although this is an extraordinary event, there are a number of compiler optimizations that are characterized as "unsafe." Developers that desire to push a compiler to its limits should ensure that the resulting executable behaves in the same way as an unoptimized one.

For example, the `-ftree-loop-if-convert-stores` GCC compiler switch converts conditional memory writes into unconditional memory writes. Here is a sample taken from the manual page of the compiler:

```
for (i = 0; i < N; i++)
    if (cond)
        A[i] = expr;
```

which would be transformed to

```
for (i = 0; i < N; i++)
    A[i] = cond ? expr: A[i];
```

Both the original and the transformed code provide opportunity for a race condition if the A array is a shared resource. In the transformed version, though, the problem is exaggerated.

3.10 HIGHER-LEVEL CONSTRUCTS: MULTITHREADED PROGRAMMING WITHOUT THREADS

Qt goes beyond the elementary provisions of the QThread, QMutex, and associated classes by providing support for automatic thread creation, job distribution, and result collection. The QThreadPool class and QtConcurrent functions provide the underpinning for creating multithreaded programs without ever subclassing the QThread class or explicitly managing the execution and termination of threads. Furthermore, a program that uses QtConcurrent's high-level functionality will automatically adjust to the available cores in the execution platform, without any programmer consideration.

The provisions of the **QtConcurrent** namespace functions address embarrassingly parallel problems, i.e., problems that require computations on data items that have no interdependencies. Surprisingly, there are many problems that satisfy this requirement. Qt provides two versions for each of the functions described below: a *blocking/synchronous* and a *nonblocking/asynchronous* variant. The nonblocking version allows the calling thread to continue execution until it needs to check for the termination of the assigned tasks. In that case, a QFuture instance is returned and used to handle the check and subsequent result collection.

Table 3.4 lists the available functions. Because the functions discussed in this section are overloaded, for the sake of brevity their signatures are not reported in

Table 3.4 A list of the functions provided by the QtConcurrent namespace. T represents the type of element to which the map/filter/reduce functions apply

Function	Result	Modifies Original Data	Header
blockingFilter	void	✓	QtConcurrentFilter
blockingFiltered	QList(T)		QtConcurrentFilter
blockingFilteredReduced	T		QtConcurrentFilter
blockingMap	void	✓	QtConcurrentMap
blockingMapped	QList(T)		QtConcurrentMap
blockingMappedReduced	T		QtConcurrentMap
filter	QFuture(void)	✓	QtConcurrentFilter
filtered	QFuture(T)		QtConcurrentFilter
filteredReduced	QFuture(T)		QtConcurrentFilter
map	QFuture(void)	✓	QtConcurrentMap
mapped	QFuture(T)		QtConcurrentMap
mappedReduced	QFuture(T)		QtConcurrentMap

this book. The reader should consult the Qt documentation utility, assistant, for complete and up-to-date (e.g., upgrades) information.

3.10.1 CONCURRENT MAP

The QtConcurrent::map function applies a supplied function to all the members of a sequence (e.g., vector, list) in parallel. The following example is illustrative:

```
1   // File: concurrentmap/map.cpp
2   #include <QtConcurrentMap>
3   #include <QFuture>
4   . . .
5   const double a = 2.0;
6   const double b = -1.0;
7   void func(double &x)
8   {
9       x = a*x + b;
10  }
11  //————————————————————————————————————————
12  int main(int argc, char *argv[])
13  {
14      int N = atoi(argv[1]);
15      vector<double> data;
16      // populate the input data
17      . . .
18      QFuture<void> res = QtConcurrent::map(data.begin(),
19                                            data.end(),
20                                            func);
21
22      res.waitForFinished();
23  . . .
```

LISTING 3.31

An example of the application of QtConcurrent::map() for calculating the value of a function y over all the points x in an array.

The QtConcurrent::map function operates in place, i.e., the calculated values are stored in the input container, overwriting the corresponding input data. This has two consequences: (1) the signature of the function to be applied should be:

```
void mapFuncName(T &);
```

where *T* is the input datatype, i.e., the input should be passed by reference, and (2) a QFuture<void> reference is returned, as in line 18, since no results can be retrieved explicitly. The QFuture<void> reference can be used to check the termination of the "mapping" (as in line 22) or to cancel or pause the task (with methods cancel() and pause(), respectively).

QtConcurrent can work with both STL containers such as vector<> and Qt containers such as QVector<> and QList<>. Performance is better, though, if a container that provides random-access iterators is used, such as the ones listed as examples in the previous sentence. QtConcurrent can operate on a range of input (as specified by the begin() and end() iterators in lines 18 and 19, for example), or a whole container.

In order for a Makefile to be generated properly, the following two lines that point to the QtConcurrent header files and library should be added to the project file[13]:

```
INCLUDEPATH += /usr/include/qt5/QtConcurrent
LIBS += -lQt5Concurrent
```

If the input data are to be preserved, the QtConcurrent::mapped() function can be used instead as shown in Listing 3.32, creating a new container with the results.

```
24  // File: concurrentmapped/mapped.cpp
25  . . .
26  double func(const double x)
27  {
28      return a*x + b;
29  }
30  //————————————————————————————————————————
31  int main(int argc, char *argv[])
32  {
33      int N = atoi(argv[1]);
34      vector<double> data;
35      // populate the input data
36      for(int i=0;i<N;i++)
37          data.push_back(i);
38
39      QFuture<double> res = QtConcurrent::mapped(data,
40                                                 func);
41
42      res.waitForFinished();
43      QList<double> y = res.results();
44      cout << "Calculated " << y.size() << " results\n";
45      cout << "Results:\n";
46      for(QFuture<double>::const_iterator iter = res.begin(); iter != ↩
            res.end() ; iter++)
47          cout << *iter << endl;
48  . . .
```

LISTING 3.32

An example of QtConcurrent::mapped() application. Only the differences with Listing 3.31 are shown.

The differences from QtConcurrent::map() are limited to mapping function signature and the treatment of the QFuture<> object returned. The signature has to be as shown in Listing 3.33.

---

[13]These lines are obviously installation and distribution specific. We can locate the header and library files and adjust the project file accordingly by executing: $ locate QtConcurrent.

```
T mappedFuncName(const T );
// or
T mappedFuncName(const T &);
```

LISTING 3.33

Signature of the mapping function used by QtConcurrent::mapped() and QtConcurrent::blockingMapped().

The results can be retrieved in the form of a QList<> collection, as done in line 43 from the QFuture<> object. Alternatively, the QFuture<> object can be queried (e.g., with methods resultAt(), resultCount()) or traversed with the use of iterators, as shown in line 46.

The blocking variants QtConcurrent::blockingMap() and QtConcurrent::blockingMapped() do not return a QFuture<> object reference. Instead, one gets nothing/void for the former and a QList<T> for the latter function, where T is the input datatype. For example, the code of Listing 3.32, modified to work with the blocking function, would be:

```
49      . . .
50      QList<double> data;
51      // populate the input data
52      for(int i=0;i<N;i++)
53          data.append(i);
54
55      QList<double> res = QtConcurrent::blockingMapped(data,
56                                              func);
57
58      cout << "Calculated " << res.size() << " results\n";
59      cout << "Results:\n";
60      for(int i=0;i<res.size(); i++)
61          cout << res.at(i) << endl;
62      . . .
```

3.10.2 MAP-REDUCE

Qt provides a convenient implementation of the map-reduce pattern presented in Section 2.4.4. Reiterating the discussion of that section, map-reduce is a pattern made up of two stages: a mapping stage that applies a function to/transforms the supplied input data and a reduction stage that performs a summary-type operation on the "transformed" data.

Qt's implementation in the form of the QtConcurrent::mappedReduced() and QtConcurrent::blockingMappedReduced() functions requires two functions to be passed as input, one for performing the mapping and one for performing the reduction. Following the same naming convention as in the previous section, the "mapped" function name prefix implies that a new container is created to hold the results of the mapping procedure.

The signature for the mapping function is the same as the one shown in Listing 3.33. The reduction function should have the signature shown in Listing 3.34, i.e., accepting two parameters and using the first one to return the result of the reduction.

```
void reductionFuncName(T & , const T&);
```

LISTING 3.34

Signature of the reduction function used by `QtConcurrent::mappedReduced()` and `QtConcurrent::blockingMappedReduced()`.

For example, let's consider the problem of finding the variance of a random variable x using a sample x_i for $i = 0, \ldots, N - 1$, as given by the formula:

$$\sigma^2 = \overline{(x - \mu)^2} = \overline{x^2} - \mu^2 = \frac{\sum_{i=0}^{N-1} x_i^2}{N} - \mu^2 \tag{3.2}$$

where $\mu = \overline{x}$.

The code shown in Listing 3.35 uses map-reduce to calculate the $\overline{x^2}$ term:

```
1  #include <QtConcurrentMap>
2  #include <QList>
3  . . .
4  // ******************************************
5  long powX2 (const long &x)
6  {
7    return x * x;
8  }
9
10 // ******************************************
11 void sumFunc (long &x, const long &y)
12 {
13   x += y;
14 }
15
16 // ******************************************
17 int main (int argc, char *argv[])
18 {
19   // initialize the random-number generator seed
20   srand (time (0));
21
22   // get how big the sample will be
23   int N = atoi (argv[1]);
24
25   // and populate a QList<> with the data
26   QList < long >data;
27   for (int i = 0; i < N; i++)
28     data.append ((rand () % 2000000) - 1000000);
29
30   // calculate the average
31   long sum = 0;
32   for (int i = 0; i < N; i++)
33     sum += data[i];
```

```
34    double mean = sum * 1.0 / N;
35
36    // map-reduce to find the sum of x_i^2
37    long res = QtConcurrent::blockingMappedReduced (data, powX2, sumFunc↩
          );
38
39    // calculate variance, not forgetting to multiple res by 1.0 to ↩
          avoid truncation when dividing by N
40    double var = res * 1.0 / N - mean * mean;
41    cout << "Average: " << mean << " Variance " << var << endl;
42
43    return 0;
44  }
```

LISTING 3.35

A map-reduce Qt implementation of the variance calculation for a set of samples.

Line 37 is used to compute the term $\sum_{i=0}^{N-1} x_i^2$ by mapping the data collection to data * data, via function powX2() (lines 5-8) and summing up the results with the reduction sumFunc() (lines 11-14).

There is just one shortcoming to Qt's implementation: Reduction is performed sequentially, since only one reduction operation is allowed to be carried out at any point in time. This is mandated by thread-safety considerations, since the reduction function is called in a mutual exclusion fashion. As a result, if the reduction stage constitutes a substantial part of the overall execution time, one should aim at a separate implementation. A user-supplied reduction implementation can still use QThreadPool::start() to carry out the reduction in parallel.

3.10.3 CONCURRENT FILTER

Along the lines of the "mapping" functionality, Qt also offers filtering capabilities, i.e., concurrently selecting a subset of items from a collection. The selection/rejection is based on the result of applying a predicate function on each item. Four function variants are provided, following the conventions observed in the previous sections:

- QtConcurrent::filter: Modifies the original collection. Returns a QFuture<void> reference for checking completion of operation.
- QtConcurrent::filtered: Generates a new sequence with the filtered items. Returns a QFuture<T> reference for checking completion of operation and for retrieving the results.

The above are augmented with their blocking variants QtConcurrent:: blockingFilter and QtConcurrent::blockingFiltered. The signature of the predicate function required by all the filtering functions is shown in Listing 3.36.

```
bool filterPredFuncName(const T&);
```

LISTING 3.36

Signature of the predicate function used by QtConcurrent::filter() and its variants. T is the type of items being filtered.

As an example, let's consider the problem of eliminating the outliers from a sample of data. Several methods exist for establishing the criteria on which such a decision can be made, although it is a process that remains controversial. In the Listing 3.37 code, we simply filter out all data that lie outside a supplied range of values [*lower*, *upper*].

```
1   // File: outliers.cpp
2   #include <QtConcurrentFilter>
3   #include <QList>
4   #include <boost/bind.hpp>
5   ...
6   bool filterFunc (const int &x, const int &lower, const int &upper)
7   {
8     if(x>upper)
9       return false;
10    if(x<lower)
11      return false;
12    return true;
13  }
14
15  //*****************************************
16  int main (int argc, char *argv[])
17  {
18    srand (time (0));
19    int N = atoi (argv[1]);
20    int l = atoi (argv[2]);
21    int u = atoi (argv[3]);
22    QList < int >data;
23    for (int i = 0; i < N; i++)
24      data.append ((rand () % 2000000) - 1000000);
25
26    QList<int> out = QtConcurrent::blockingFiltered (data, boost::bind(↩
          filterFunc, _1, l, u));
27
28    cout << "Filtered array is " << out.size() << " long\n";
29  ...
```

LISTING 3.37

An example of how QtConcurrent's filtering capabilities can be used to remove samples that lie outside a given range.

The predicate function in lines 6-13 requires three parameters, which is in disagreement with the signature of Listing 3.36. One solution would be to replace the second and third parameters with global variables, but this is a bad design choice. Instead we use the boost::bind() function to generate the function required by QtConcurrent::blockingFiltered by binding the second and third parameters to the values passed as command-line parameters. The boost::bind(filterFunc, _1, l, u) call in line 26 generates a unary function that is equivalent to calling filterFunc(*, 1, u). The _1 acts as a placeholder, replaced by an actual parameter upon a call to the generated function.

3.10.4 FILTER-REDUCE

Similarly to the map-reduce functionality, QtConcurrent offers a pair of filter-reduce methods that first filter elements in a collection before reducing them to a single result.

Qt's implementation in the form of the QtConcurrent::filteredReduced() and QtConcurrent::blockingFilteredReduced() functions requires two functions to be passed as input: one for performing the filtering and one for performing the reduction. The "filtered" function name prefix implies that a new container is created to hold the subset of items generated.

The required signature for the filtering function is the same as the one shown in Listing 3.36, whereas the reduction step requires a function with the signature shown in Listing 3.34.

The example we examine here is from the realm of statistics: Observatories around the world have been trying to discover and track near-earth objects (NEOs), such as asteroids and comets, in an attempt to predict and possibly avert a catastrophic collision. If a collection of such objects were available, one could answer the question of which is the average mass of the ones having a radius above 10 meters using the code in Listing 3.38.

```
1   #include <QtConcurrentFilter>
2   ...
3   struct NEO
4   {
5       double radius;
6       double mass;
7       int groupNum;
8       ...
9   };
10  //─────────────────────────────────────────────
11  bool filtFunc(const NEO &x)
12  {
13      return  x.radius >= 10;
14  }
15  //─────────────────────────────────────────────
16  void reduFunc(NEO  &x, const NEO  &y)
17  {
18      x.mass += y.mass;
19      x.groupNum += y.groupNum;
20  }
21  //─────────────────────────────────────────────
22  int main (int argc, char *argv[])
23  {
24      QVector<NEO> data;
```

```
25    ...
26    NEO average = QtConcurrent::blockingFilteredReduced(data, filtFunc, ↵
          reduFunc);
27    cout << "Average " << average.mass / average.groupNum << endl;
28    ...
```

LISTING 3.38

An example of how Qt's filter-reduce can be applied to a collection of data.

The application filter function `filtFunc()` guides `QtConcurrent::blocking-FilteredReduced()` into the creation of a container with the NEO instances that satisfy the condition of line 13. Subsequently, the `reduFunc()` function accumulates the mass of the two NEO instances passed to it and stores it in the first one. The `groupNum` field maintains the number of objects reduced (line 19). The accumulated values are returned as a NEO instance and copied to the `average` structure in line 26.

As mentioned in Section 3.10.2, Qt's reduction implementation suffers from being performed in a sequential manner. The programmer can control the order in which the individual operations are performed, but performance-wise this is clearly a problematic approach. In the following sections, we show how to work around this problem via two cases studies.

3.10.5 A CASE STUDY: MULTITHREADED SORTING

Searching and sorting are the most commonly used components for algorithm design. In this section we explore how concurrency can significantly speed up data sorting by using the high-level constructs of the `QtConcurrent` namespace.

Mergesort is an algorithm that can be easily extended to support concurrency, given that the algorithm examines disjoint parts of the input at different stages on its execution. Figure 3.14 illustrates how the bottom-up, nonrecursive version of merge-sort sorts N data items by merging disjoint neighboring blocks in $\Theta(\lceil lg(N) \rceil)$ phases.

Each of the merging operations during a phase of mergesort is independent of the others, making them candidates for concurrent execution. However, using a thread to only merge two items, as is done during the first phase, would produce an extraordinary amount of housekeeping overhead. An easy adaptation that would eliminate this problem would be to start using threads for merging once the size of the blocks exceeds a certain threshold. An equivalent approach that would allow us to escape the obligation to come up with such a threshold would be to break the input into a predetermined number of blocks and merge these concurrently, after they are individually sorted.

Conceptually, *parallel mergesort can be implemented as a map-reduce operation*: Mapping would sort each block individually, and reduction would merge the blocks in a pairwise fashion until the whole input is sorted.

Figure 3.15 shows the concept that can be described by the Algorithm 3.1:

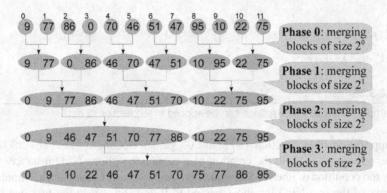

FIGURE 3.14

An illustration of how mergesort operates in a bottom-up fashion, merging ever-increasing adjacent blocks of data. Each new phase doubles the size of the blocks merged relative to the previous one.

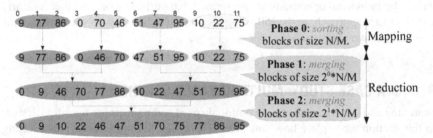

FIGURE 3.15

An example of how mergesort can be run in parallel with an initial phase where *M* disjoint blocks are sorting individually, followed by merging phases with exponentially increasing sizes. Colors in each phase indicate the maximum number of threads that can be utilized.

ALGORITHM 3.1 PARALLEL MERGESORT: SORTING *N* DATA ITEMS BY *M* THREADS

1. Break the input into *M* blocks of size $\frac{N}{M}$
2. Sort each of the *M* blocks by a separate thread using any sequential sorting algorithm
3. *blockSize* $\leftarrow \frac{N}{M}$
4. **while** *blockSize* < *N* **do**
5.   Use multiple threads to merge adjacent blocks of size *blockSize*
6.   *blockSize* $\leftarrow$ *blockSize* · 2

Ideally, *M* should be twice the number of available cores in the execution platform so that maximum CPU utilization can be achieved during the first merging phase, where $\frac{M}{2}$ merge operations occur. It should be noted that there is no design characteristic that would prevent any number of blocks from being used.

The implementation of the above algorithm is given below, broken-up in separate listings to allow for easier exploration of the code. The main component of the shown solution is the ArrayRange template class that allows the description, sorting and merging of data blocks (lines 10-122). Each instance of this class carries the starting and ending index of the block it represents (line 15), plus a pointer to the array containing the data (store, line 13) to be sorted. As the merging operation requires the transfer of the data to a temporart array, each ArrayRange also has a pointer to such a repository (temp, line 14).

In an attempt to minimize the copy operations mandated by merging, the ArrayRange<>::merge() method (lines 63-108) does not copy the sorted data from *temp back to the *store array. Instead, a switch of the pointers is performed (method ArrayRange<>::switchPointers() called at line 107, defined at lines 45-51), so that this->store always points to the array that contains the valid data of the block with indices [this->start, this->end).

The only side effect of this optimization strategy is that we may reach a point where blocks residing in different arrays need to be merged (check of line 66). In that case, the smaller of the blocks is moved prior to the merging operation (lines 69-75) by utilizing the ArrayRange<>::switchStore() method.

When the merging is complete, the first of the two ArrayRange objects passed as parameters assumes responsibility for the merged data (lines 103, 104). In every other way, the merging operation in ArrayRange<>::merge() is a textbook implementation.

```cpp
1   // File: concurrent_mergesort.cpp
2   . . .
3   #include <QRunnable>
4   #include <QThreadPool>
5   #include <QtConcurrentMap>
6   #include <QVector>
7
8
9   // **************************************************
10  template < class T > class ArrayRange
11  {
12  private :
13    T * store;        // where data reside
14    T *temp;          // where they can be shifted for sorting
15    int start, end;   // end points 1 spot further than the last item.
16  public :
17    ArrayRange (T * x, T * y, int s, int e);
18    static void merge (ArrayRange * x, ArrayRange * y);
19    static void sort (ArrayRange * x);
20    int size ();
21    T *getStore ()
22    {
23      return store;
24    }
25    void switchStore ();
26    void switchPointers ();
27  };
```

```
28
29  //————————————————————————————————————————
30  template < class T > int ArrayRange < T >::size ()
31  {
32    return end - start;
33  }
34
35  //————————————————————————————————————————
36  template < class T > void ArrayRange < T >::switchStore ()
37  {
38    for (int i = start; i < end; i++)
39      temp[i] = store[i];
40    switchPointers ();
41  }
42
43  //————————————————————————————————————————
44  // Only swaps the pointers
45  template < class T > void ArrayRange < T >::switchPointers ()
46  {
47    T *aux;
48    aux = temp;
49    temp = store;
50    store = aux;
51  }
52
53  //————————————————————————————————————————
54  template < class T > ArrayRange < T >::ArrayRange (T * x, T * y, int s↵
        , int e)
55  {
56    store = x;
57    temp = y;
58    start = s;
59    end = e;
60  }
61
62  //————————————————————————————————————————
63  template < class T > void ArrayRange < T >::merge (ArrayRange * x, ↵
        ArrayRange * y)
64  {
65    // check if a copy is needed for input data to be in the same array
66    if (x->store != y->store)
67      {
68        // determine which is smaller
69        int xlen = x->end - x->start;
70        int ylen = y->end - y->start;
71
72        if (xlen > ylen)
73          y->switchStore ();
74        else
75          x->switchStore ();
76      }
77
```

```
78    // now perform merge-list
79    int idx1 = x->start, idx2 = y->start;
80    int loc = min (idx1, idx2);    // starting point in temp array
81    while (idx1 != x->end && idx2 != y->end)
82      {
83        if (x->store[idx1] <= y->store[idx2])
84          {
85            x->temp[loc] = x->store[idx1];
86            idx1++;
87          }
88        else
89          {
90            x->temp[loc] = x->store[idx2];  // same as y->store[idx2]
91            idx2++;
92          }
93        loc++;
94      }
95
96    // copy the rest
97    for (int i = idx1; i < x->end; i++)
98      x->temp[loc++] = x->store[i];
99
100   for (int i = idx2; i < y->end; i++)
101     x->temp[loc++] = x->store[i];
102
103   x->start = min (x->start, y->start);
104   x->end = max (x->end, y->end);
105
106   // the sorted "stuff" are in temp now, so swap store and temp
107   x->switchPointers ();
108 }
109
110 //————————————————————————————
111 int comp (const void *a, const void *b)
112 {
113   int x = *((int *) a);
114   int y = *((int *) b);
115   return x - y;
116 }
117
118 //————————————————————————————
119 template < class T > void ArrayRange < T >::sort (ArrayRange * x)
120 {
121   qsort (x->store + x->start, x->end - x->start, sizeof (int), comp);
122 }
```

LISTING 3.39

A parallel mergesort implementation based on the functionalities offered by QThreadPool and QtConcurrent: block management code.

The standalone sorting of a block is supported by the `ArrayRange<>::sort()` method, which in turn calls the standard C library `qsort()` function (line 121). Thus, in the event that someone would like to adapt the code for sorting items of a different datatype T, the only changes/additions that would be required are:

- A function similar to `comp()` (lines 111-116), capable of comparing instances of T
- Type T should support `operator<=()` so that a comparison during merging (line 83) is possible

`QtConcurrent::mappedReduced()` is poised to be the vehicle of choice for "gluing" together our map-reduce formulation of parallel mergesort. Alas, the reduction phase in `QtConcurrent::mappedReduced()` is done sequentially, which would translate to a big performance hit. Instead, our implementation separates the two stages, using the `QThreadPool::start()` method to direct the reduction/merging stages through its $\lceil lg(M) \rceil$ phases, as shown in Listing 3.40.

```
123  //——————————————————————————————————————————————
124  template < class T >
125  void concurrentMergesort (T * data, int N, int numBlocks = −1)
126  {
127    if (numBlocks < 0)
128      numBlocks = 2 * sysconf (_SC_NPROCESSORS_ONLN);
129
130    T *temp = new T[N];
131
132    // 1st step: block setup
133    QVector < ArrayRange < T > *>b;
134    int pos = 0;
135    int len = ceil (N * 1.0 / numBlocks);
136    for (int i = 0; i < numBlocks − 1; i++)
137      {
138        b.append (new ArrayRange < T > (data, temp, pos, pos + len));
139        pos += len;
140      }
141    // setup last block
142    b.append (new ArrayRange < T > (data, temp, pos, N));
143
144    // 2nd step: sort the individual blocks concurrently
145    QtConcurrent::blockingMap (b, ArrayRange < T >::sort);
146
147    //3rd step: "mergelisting" the pieces
148    // merging is done in lg(numBlocks) phases in a bottom−up fashion
149    for (int blockDistance = 1; blockDistance < numBlocks; blockDistance↩
           *= 2)
150      {
151        for (int startBlock = 0; startBlock < numBlocks − blockDistance;↩
               startBlock += 2 * blockDistance)
152          {
153            QThreadPool::globalInstance ()−>start (new MergeTask < T > (↩
                   b[startBlock], b[startBlock + blockDistance]));
```

```
154          }
155        // barrier
156        QThreadPool::globalInstance ()->waitForDone ();
157      }
158
159    // b[0]->store points to the sorted data
160    if (b[0]->getStore () != data)          // need to copy data from temp↩
                                              -> data array
161      b[0]->switchStore ();
162    delete [] temp;
163  }
164
165  //—————————————————————————————————————————
166  void numberGen (int N, int max, int *store)
167  {
168    int i;
169    srand (time (0));
170    for (i = 0; i < N; i++)
171      store[i] = rand () % max;
172  }
173
174  //—————————————————————————————————————————
175  int main (int argc, char *argv[])
176  {
177    if (argc < 3)
178      {
179        cout << "Use: " << argv[0] << " numData numBlocks\n";
180        exit (1);
181      }
182
183    int N = atoi (argv[1]);
184    int *data = new int[N];
185    numberGen (N, MAXVALUE, data);
186
187    QTime t;
188    t.start();
189    concurrentMergesort (data, N, numBlocks);
190    // print-out sorting time in msec
191    cout << t.elapsed() << endl;
192    ...
```

LISTING 3.40

A parallel mergesort implementation: data block "mapping" and "reduction."

The key points of the `concurrentMergesort()` function (lines 124-163) are:

- The temporary array needed by the merge operations, equal in size to the input array, is allocated at the beginning (line 130).
- Pointers to the input data and the temporary arrays are passed as parameters to the constructor of the `ArrayRange` class, along with the part of these arrays that each `ArrayRange` is responsible for, as delimited by the range [*start, end*). So, although each `ArrayRange` manages its own disjoint part of the data, these

collectively reside in the same two arrays (`data` or `temp`). This approach eliminates the need for any additional, costly memory management operations that would result in performance degradation.

- An instance of type `QVector < ArrayRange < T > *>` is used to collectively manage the block representations. The required `ArrayRange` objects are generated with the loop of lines 136-140. The last `ArrayRange` in the sequence is created separately (line 142) to incorporate the last block in its entirety, without requiring special logic to handle the case where N is not evenly divided by M.

- The "mapping" phase is accomplished in line 145. The $\lceil lg(M) \rceil$ phases of the reduction, are controlled by the loop of lines 149-157. Each i reduction phase, for $i = 1, \ldots, \lceil lg(M) \rceil$ initiates $min(1, \lfloor \frac{M}{2^i} \rfloor)$ merging jobs in the form of instances of the `MergeTask<>` template class (explained below). These are submitted as requests for multithreaded execution in line 153. The parent thread is blocked until each merging phase is complete (line 156).

Figure 3.16 traces the execution of the `concurrentMergesort()` function through the data structures it sets up and maintains.

The final component of our implementation is the `MergeTask<>` template class shown in Listing 3.41. Its instances act as stubs for the execution of the `ArrayRange<T>::merge()` method (line 210). This class is so simple that one could wonder why the `ArrayRange` class is not derived from `QRunnable` to reduce the length of the code.

Actually, its existence is mandated by the fact that `QThreadPool` deletes the `QRunnable` objects passed to the `start()` method upon execution completion. This would make the reuse of `ArrayRange` objects impossible if they were used instead of a `MergeTask<>` instance.

```
193  // ************************************************
194  template < class T > class MergeTask: public QRunnable
195  {
196  private:
197    ArrayRange < T > *part1;
198    ArrayRange < T > *part2;
199
200  public:
201  MergeTask (ArrayRange < T > *p1, ArrayRange < T > *p2):part1 (p1), ↩
        part2 (p2)
202    {
203    }
204    void run ();
205  };
206
207  //─────────────────────────────────────────────────
208  template < class T > void MergeTask < T >::run ()
209  {
210    ArrayRange < T >::merge (part1, part2);
211  }
```

LISTING 3.41

A parallel mergesort implementation: task management code.

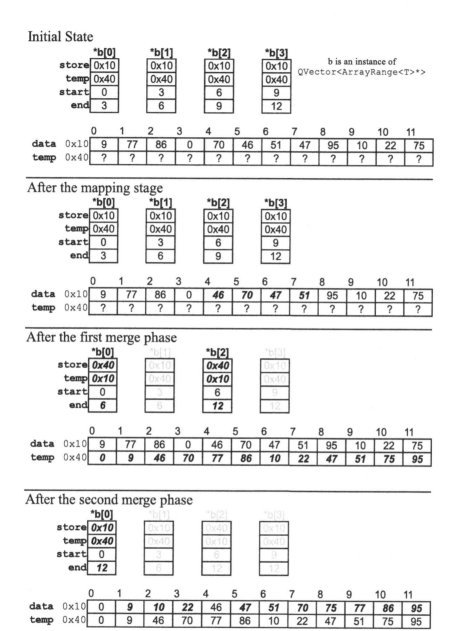

FIGURE 3.16

An example of how the ArrayRange instances generated by the concurrentMergesort() function of Listing 3.40 are initialized to manage the different data blocks and how they evolve over the function's execution. It is assumed that the data array starts at address 0x10 and the temp array at address 0x40. The changes that occur in memory between successive phases are in bold-italics font, while the ArrayRange instances that become irrelevant for subsequent steps are greyed-out.

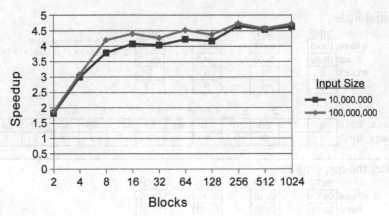

FIGURE 3.17

Speedup of the multithreaded mergesort of Listing 3.39 over quicksort. Data consisted of type int arrays sized at 10^7 and 10^8 elements. Displayed data points were averaged over 10 runs.

The performance of our implementation in terms of speedup and efficiency is shown in Figure 3.17. The execution platform used to generate these graphs was a third-generation i7 CPU, clocked at 4.2 GHz, with hyperthreading enabled. The baseline sequential times were calculated by using only one block for the initial data partitioning, resulting in the use of quicksort only.

As can be clearly observed in Figure 3.17, the speedup reaches a plateau of ∼4.5 at 256 blocks. Beyond this point speed gains are trivial. This is a good result given that the CPU is a four-core machine, despite appearing to the operating system as an eight-core one. Intel claims that hyperthreading can increase performance up to 30%, which means that a four-core machine would perform on par with one that has 5.2 cores.

An important observation is that our parallel mergesort does not differ in the total number of comparisons performed from a plain-vanilla mergesort. The first phase where quicksort is used requires $M\frac{N}{M}lg\left(\frac{N}{M}\right) = Nlg\left(\frac{N}{M}\right)$ comparisons, whereas the reduction phase requires $\sum_{i=1}^{lg(M)} \frac{2^i N}{M} \frac{M}{2^i} = Nlg(M)$ comparisons in the worst case. The two combined account for a total of $Nlg\left(\frac{N}{M}\right) + Nlg(M) = Nlg(N)$ comparisons. This means that the performance gain observed is the result of the parallel execution and does not stem from a fundamental change in the algorithmic approach. Naturally, linear complexity sorting algorithms such as bucket-sort could form the basis for extracting much better performance if they are properly formulated for parallel execution.

3.10.6 A CASE STUDY: MULTITHREADED IMAGE MATCHING

The problem of finding, among a set of images, a subset that best matches a target image is a typically computationally expensive problem that would benefit from multicore execution. In this section, it serves to exemplify the expressive power of the map/reduce/filter formulation.

Establishing whether a match between two images is positive or not depends on the operator used to compare them. A large collection of such operators has been established in the literature, such as the absolute and squared differences, the correlation coefficient, the mutual information, and others [36, 9]. In this section we use the mutual information of two images I and J, defined as:

$$MI(I,J) = \sum_{\forall x} \sum_{\forall y} p_{xy} log_2 \left(\frac{p_{xy}}{p_x p_y} \right) \tag{3.3}$$

where x represents a gray level in I and y a gray level in J. p_x is the probability of having a pixel in I with a gray level of x (similarly for p_y for J). p_{xy} is the joint probability defined by $p_{xy} = \frac{n_{xy}}{n}$, where n is the total number of pixels in I, J, and $n_x y$ is the number of pixels that have a gray level of x in I and y in J.

Selecting a single image would require a straightforward application of the filter-reduce pattern. In this section we solve a more generic problem that involves the selection of the best candidate images. The selection process could be materialized in a variety of ways: It could be based on meeting certain criteria, e.g., having $MI(I,J)$ exceed an *a priori* specified threshold, or on sorting the images according to their performance and picking a fixed number of them. In this section, we use the latter approach.

The solution shown in Listing 3.42 is built around an `Image` class that provides functionality for reading PGM formatted images and for calculating the probabilities required for the calculation of the mutual information.

```
1   // File: image_matching / main . cpp
2   ...
3   #include <boost/bind.hpp>
4   #include <QtConcurrentMap >
5   #include <QThreadStorage >
6   #include <QVector >
7
8   using namespace std;
9
10  #define MAXLEVELS 2048
11  // **********************************************************
12  class Image
13  {
14  private:
15    int width;
16    int height;
17    int levels;
18    unsigned int *pixel;
19    double *p;  // probabilities
20    double MI;  // mutual information with a target image
21    char filename[20];
22
23    // joint probs. This is a per-thread value
```

```
24    static QThreadStorage < double *>jointProb;
25    void calcJointProb (Image * x);
26
27  public:
28      Image (char *);
29    ~Image ();
30    static double mutualInformation (Image *, Image *);
31    static void calcProb (Image *);
32    double getMI () {return MI;}
33    char *getFilename () {return filename;}
34  };
35
36  QThreadStorage < double *>Image::jointProb;
37  //————————————————————————————————————————————
38  // Used to compare and sort images in descending order of
39  // the mutual information calculated
40  bool comp (Image * x, Image * y)
41  {
42    return x->getMI () > y->getMI ();
43  }
44
45  //————————————————————————————————————————————
46  // Assumes that the file does not contain any comment lines
47  // starting with #. Allocates the memory for the pixel values
48  // and the value probabilities
49  Image::Image (char *fname)
50  {
51    FILE *fin;
52    strncpy (filename, fname, 20);
53    filename[19] = 0;
54    fin = fopen (fname, "rb");
55    fscanf (fin, "%*s%i%i%i", &(width), &(height), &(levels));
56
57    pixel = new unsigned int[width * height];
58    // first set all values to 0. This is needed as in 2 of the 3 cases
59    // only a part of each pixel value is read from the file
60    memset ((void *)pixel, 0,width * height * sizeof (unsigned int));
61    if (levels < 256)  // each pixel is 1 byte
62      for (int i = 0; i < width * height; i++)
63        fread ((void *) &(pixel[i]), sizeof (unsigned char), 1, fin);
64    else if (levels < 65536) // each pixel is 2 bytes
65      for (int i = 0; i < width * height; i++)
66        fread ((void *) &(pixel[i]), sizeof(unsigned short), 1, fin);
67    else // each pixel is 4 bytes
68      fread (pixel, sizeof (unsigned int), width * height, fin);
69
70    levels++;
71    fclose (fin);
72    p = new double[levels];
73  }
74
75  //————————————————————————————————————————————
```

```
76   // Releases memory
77   Image::~Image ()
78   {
79     if (pixel != NULL)
80       {
81         delete []pixel;
82         delete []p;
83         pixel = NULL;
84         p = NULL;
85       }
86   }
87
88   //————————————————————————————————————————————
89   void Image::calcProb (Image * x)
90   {
91     int numPixels = x->width * x->height;
92
93     // first set all values to 0
94     memset ((void *)x->p, 0, x->levels * sizeof(double));
95     for (int i = 0; i < numPixels; i++)
96       x->p[x->pixel[i]]++;
97
98     for (int i = 0; i < x->levels; i++)
99       x->p[i] /= numPixels;
100  }
101
102  //————————————————————————————————————————————
103  // Precondition: images must have the same spatial resolution and ↵
         number of grayscale levels
104  void Image::calcJointProb (Image * x)
105  {
106    double *pij;
107    if (jointProb.hasLocalData ()) // joint probabilities storage exist ↵
             , retrieve its location
108      {
109        pij = jointProb.localData ();
110      }
111    else                            // otherwise allocate it and store ↵
             its address
112      {
113        pij = new double[MAXLEVELS * MAXLEVELS];
114        jointProb.setLocalData (pij);
115      }
116
117    int numPixels = width * height;
118
119    // first set all values to 0
120    memset ((void *) pij, 0, x->levels * x->levels * sizeof (double));
121    for (int i = 0; i < numPixels; i++)
122      pij[pixel[i] * x->levels + x->pixel[i]]++;
123
124    for (int i = 0; i < x->levels * x->levels; i++)
```

```
125        pij[i] /= numPixels;
126    }
127
128    //----------------------------------------------------------
129    // The probabilities must be calculated before hand
130    double Image::mutualInformation (Image * x, Image * y)
131    {
132      x->calcJointProb (y);
133      double *pij = jointProb.localData (); // the array has been created ↵
             already by the previous statement
134      double mutual = 0;
135      for (int i = 0; i < x->levels; i++)
136        for (int j = 0; j < y->levels; j++)
137          {
138            int idx = i * y->levels + j;
139            if (x->p[i] != 0 && y->p[j] != 0 && pij[idx] != 0)
140              mutual += pij[idx] * log (pij[idx] / (x->p[i] * y->p[j]));
141          }
142      x->MI = mutual / log (2);
143      return x->MI;
144    }
145
146    // *********************************************************
147    int main (int argc, char *argv[])
148    {
149      int numImages = atoi (argv[1]);
150      QTime t;
151      t.start ();
152
153      // read the target and all other images
154      Image target ("images/main.pgm");      // target image
155      QVector < Image * >pool;
156      for (int picNum = 0; picNum < numImages; picNum++)
157        {
158          char buff[100];
159          sprintf (buff, "images/(%i).pgm", picNum);
160          pool.append (new Image (buff));
161        }
162      int iodone = t.elapsed ();
163
164      // pixel value probabilities calculation
165      Image::calcProb (&target);
166
167      QtConcurrent::blockingMap (pool, Image::calcProb);
168
169      // mutual information (MI) calculation
170      QtConcurrent::blockingMap (pool, boost::bind (Image:: ↵
             mutualInformation, _1, &target));
171
172      // sorting of the images according to MI findings
173      qSort (pool.begin (), pool.end (), comp);
174      printf ("%i %i\n", iodone, t.elapsed () - iodone);
```

```
175
176    return 0;
177  }
```

LISTING 3.42

Mutual information-based image-matching implementation that uses QtConcurrent namespace functions.

The program in Listing 3.42 can be executed by supplying the number of images to compare the target image with:

```
$ ./imageMatch 100
```

The images are stored in PGM format, in the image_matching/images directory. The same directory holds the target image in a file named main.pgm. All the images have been resized to the same spatial (1024 x 768 pixels) and color resolutions (256 shades of gray).

The key points of the code in Listing 3.42 are:

- The program has been designed so that small modifications would permit the execution in sequence of multiple match operations for different target images, instead of the "one-shot" operation used here. As such, the pixel value probabilities for each image are stored within each Image instance.
- The calculation of the joint probabilities p_{xy} for a pair of images I and J requires a matrix with $Levels_I$, $Levels_J$ elements, where $Levels_I$ and $Levels_J$ are the maximum gray-scale pixel values of I and J, respectively. This is a matrix that can be reused for every image pair requested, making it a candidate for becoming a static data member of the Image class. However, because multiple threads need to use this storage, a single copy is out of the question. A separate instance of this matrix is required for each thread using it. The solution to this problem is to use a QThreadStorage<double *> reference as part of the Image class. The template class QThreadStorage<> will store a separate instance of its data[14] for every thread accessing it. The three essential methods of the QThreadStorage<> class are:

```
bool hasLocalData () // returns true if a data item has been stored↩
     on behalf of the current thread
T localData ():      // retrieves the data item corresponding to the↩
     currently running thread
void setLocalData ( T ): // associates a data item with the ↩
     currently running thread
```

The pointer to the joint probability matrix is managed in lines 107-115. If the current thread has executed the Image::calcJointProb() function before,

---

[14]**Caution:** A QThreadStorage<> instance takes ownership of the data held within, and it will delete them upon termination of the threads that use them.

the pointer is retrieved (line 109). Otherwise, the necessary memory is allocated and its address stored in the `jointProb` variable (lines 113 and 114).

- The `QtConcurrent::blockingMap()` function is used twice in lines 167 and 170 in order to calculate the pixel probabilities for each individual image and subsequently their mutual information with the target image. The only particular thing about line 170 is that the `boost::bind()` function (see also Section 3.10.3) is utilized to allow a binary function (`Image::mutualInformation()`) to be used in the place of a unary one, as dictated by `QtConcurrent::blockingMap()`.

The performance of the multithreaded solution, as far as the mutual information computation is concerned, is shown in Figure 3.18. The execution platform was a third-generation i7 CPU, clocked at 4.2 GHz, with hyperthreading enabled. Speedup increases as more images are used, reaching the modest figure of 4.87 for 256 images, despite the penalty of the sequential execution of lines 165 and 173.

The biggest issue is that the mutual information calculation is dwarfed by the I/O and memory allocation costs of lines 154-161. The overall execution speedup is around 1.3, i.e., only roughly 24% reduction over the sequential time is witnessed. However, looking at the bigger picture, this is something that could be expected, given the simple nature of the chosen matching operator. In practice, I/O is only a fraction of the overall execution time as more computationally expensive algorithms, and typically multiple ones, are employed.

Finally, it is worth clarifying why the `Image::mutualInformation` and `Image::calcProb` methods are declared as static: Normal methods would require

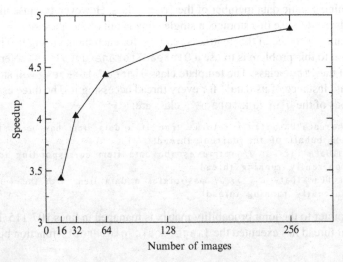

FIGURE 3.18

Speedup achieved by the multithreaded image matching program of Listing 3.42 for the mutual information computation. Displayed data points were averaged over 100 runs.

the use of a wrapper object for the application of the mapping process in lines 167 and 170. An example of how this could be achieved for the calcProb() invocation in line 167 of Listing 3.42, is shown in Listing 3.43.

```cpp
1    // File: image_matching/main_wrapper.cpp
2    ...
3    class Image
4    {
5        ...
6
7    public:
8        void calcProb();
9        ...
10   };
11   ...
12
13   //************************************************************
14   struct Wrapper
15   {
16       void operator()(Image *x)
17       {
18           x->calcProb();
19       }
20   };
21
22   //************************************************************
23   int main (int argc, char *argv[])
24   {
25       ...
26
27       // pixel value probabilities calculation
28       target.calcProb ();
29
30       Wrapper w;
31       QtConcurrent::blockingMap (pool, w);
32       ...
```

LISTING 3.43

An example of how a nonstatic method can be used with the QtConcurrent namespace functions. Only the differences to Listing 3.42 are shown.

As can be observed, we just need to create an instance of a *wrapper* class or structure that overloads the parentheses operator (lines 16-19) and pass it as a parameter to QtConccurrent function being used (line 31). The wrapper's operator() method should have a parameter of the type that is managed by the container used in the mapping/reduction/filtering operation. The same trick could be also used in place of the boost::bind function, in case a method with a different signature than the one mandated needs to be used.

EXERCISES

1. Enumerate and create the other timing diagrams that show the alternatives of Figure 3.4 when it comes to the final balance of the bank account.
2. Research the term "fork bomb" and write a program that performs as such.
3. Modify the producer-consumer example shown in Listing 3.11 so that the threads terminate after the number 100 is generated.
4. Suggest a modification to the program of Listing 3.12 so that the `IntegrCalc` threads can use any function that returns a double and takes a double as a parameter.
5. In a remote region of Siberia there are single tracks joining railroad stations. Obviously only one train can use a piece of track between two stations. The other trains can wait at the stations before they do their crossings. The following graph indicates the track and station layout:

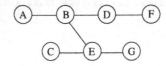

   Write a Qt program that simulates the journey of three trains with the following schedules:
   - $A \rightarrow B \rightarrow E \rightarrow C$
   - $D \rightarrow B \rightarrow E \rightarrow G$
   - $C \rightarrow E \rightarrow B \rightarrow D \rightarrow F$

   As each trains arrives at a station, display a relative message. You can assume that a station can hold any number of trains waiting.
6. Modify the program of the previous exercise so that each station can hold only 2 trains. Can this lead to deadlocks?

   If you have not done so already, make sure that your program uses only one thread class.
7. A desktop publishing application such as PageMaker has two threads running: one for running the GUI and one for doing background work. Simulate this application in Qt. Your implementation should have the thread corresponding to the GUI send requests to the other thread to run tasks on its behalf. The tasks should be (obviously just printing a message is enough for the simulation):
   - Printing
   - Mail merging
   - PDF generation

   After performing each requested task, the second thread should wait for a new request to be sent to it. Make sure that the first thread does not have to wait for the second thread to finish before making new requests.
8. A popular bakery has a baker that cooks a loaf of bread at a time and deposits it on a counter. Incoming customers pick up a loaf from the counter and exit the bakery. The counter can hold 20 loaves. If the counter is full, the baker stops

baking bread. If it is empty, a customer waits. Use semaphores to solve the coordination problem between the baker and the customers.

9. Because of customer demand, the bakery owner is considering the following enhancements to his shop:

   a. Increase the capacity of the counter to 1000

   b. Hire three more bakers

   Modify the solution of the previous exercise to accommodate these changes. Which is the easiest option to implement?

10. A bank account class is defined as follows:

```
class BankAccount {
  protected:
      double balance;
      string holderName;
  public:
      double getBalance();
      void deposit(double);
      void withdraw(double, int); // the highest the second ↩
          argument, the higher the priority of the request
};
```

Write the implementation of the three methods given above so that withdraw operations are prioritized: If there are not enough funds in the account for all, the withdrawals must be done in order of priority, regardless of whether there are some that can be performed with the available funds. You can assume that the priority level in the withdraw method is by default equal to 0, and that it is upper bounded by a fixed constant MAXPRIORITY.

11. The IT department of a big corporation is equipped with five high-speed printers that are used by a multitude of threads. The threads are part of the same accounting process. Each of the threads is supposed to perform the following (pseudocode) sequence in order to print any material:

```
...
printerID = get_available_printer();
// print to printerID printer
releasePrinter(printerID);
...
```

Write an appropriate implementation for the two functions listed above using semaphores. You can assume that the available printer IDs are stored in a shared buffer.

12. Create three threads, each printing out the letters A, B, and C. The printing must adhere to these rules:

   • The total number of Bs and Cs that have been output at any point in the output string cannot exceed the total number of As that have been output at that point.

   • After a C has been output, another C cannot be output until one or more Bs have been output.

   Use semaphores to solve the problem.

13. Modify the previous exercise so that the printing is governed by this set of rules:
    - One C must be output after two As and three Bs are output.
    - Although there is no restriction on the order of printing A and B, the corresponding threads must wait for a C to be printed when the previous condition is met.

    Use a monitor to solve the problem.
14. Address the termination problem in the previous exercise. How can the three threads terminate after, for example, a fixed number of As have been output? Or when a fixed total number of characters have been output?
15. Create four threads, each printing out the letters A, B, C, and D. The printing must adhere to these rules:
    - The total number of As and Bs that have been output at any point in the output string cannot exceed the total number of Cs and Ds that have been output at that point.
    - The total number of As that have been output at any point in the output string cannot exceed twice the number of Bs that have been output at that point.
    - After a C has been output, another C cannot be output until one or more D have been output.

    Solve the problem using (a) semaphores and (b) a monitor.
16. Use semaphores to solve the typical cigarette smokers' problem, where the agent directly signals the smoker missing the two ingredients placed on the table.
17. Solve the cigarette smokers' problem as described in Section 3.6.2 using semaphores.
18. Model the movie-going process at a multiplex cinema using a monitor. Assume the following conditions:
    - There are three different movies playing at the same time in three theaters. The capacities of each theater are 4, 5, and 7, respectively.
    - One hundred customers are waiting to see a randomly chosen movie.
    - A cashier issues the tickets.
    - If a theater is full, a movie begins to play.
    - A customer cannot enter a theater while a movie is playing or while the previous viewers are exiting the theater.
    - A movie will play for the last customers, even if the corresponding theater is not full.
19. Write a multithreaded password cracker based on the producer-consumer paradigm. The producer should generate plaintext passwords according to a set of rules, and the consumers should be hashing each password and checking whether it matches a target signature. All the threads should terminate upon the discovery of a matching password. You can use the MD5 cryptographic hash function for this exercise.

20. Write a multithreaded program for finding the prime numbers in a user-supplied range of numbers. Compare the following design approaches:

   a. Split the range in equal pieces and assign each one to a thread.

   b. Have a shared QAtomicInt variable that holds the next number to be checked. Threads should read and increment this number before testing it.

   c. Have a shared "monitor" object that returns, upon request, a range of numbers to be tested. This can be considered a generalization of the previous design.

   Which of the designs is more efficient? Explain your findings.

21. Use the QtConcurrent functionality to implement a prime number checker. Compare it in terms of speed, efficiency, and programming effort to your QThread-based attempt of the previous exercise.

22. Create a big array of randomly generated 2D coordinates (x, y). Each of the coordinates should be a number in the range [-1000, 1000]. Use appropriate QtConcurrent functions to find the points that are in a ring of distances between 100 and 200 from the point of origin. Compare the performance of your solution against a sequential implementation.

23. Use the QtConcurrent functionality to implement a parallel bucketsort. Does the number of buckets play a significant role in your implementation's performance?

Shared-memory programming: OpenMP

4

IN THIS CHAPTER YOU WILL

- Learn how to use OpenMP compiler directives to introduce concurrency in a sequential program.
- Learn the most important OpenMP #pragma directives and associated clauses for controlling the concurrent constructs generated by the compiler.
- Understand which loops can be parallelized with OpenMP directives.
- Use synchronization constructs to address the dependency issues that OpenMP-generated threads face.
- Learn how to use OpenMP to create function-parallel programs.
- Learn how to write thread-safe functions.
- Understand the issue of cache-false sharing and learn how to eliminate it.

4.1 INTRODUCTION

Parallel program development is a tedious endeavor, even when it targets shared-memory machines. It requires careful planning and is full of caveats. The use of patterns such as the ones covered in Chapter 3 (e.g., producers-consumers) can help to a certain degree, but it is still an exercise outside the comfort zone of most programmers, who are usually accustomed to sequential programs only.

There is also the issue of the extensive library of existing sequential programs that drive the world's economic, industrial, and scientific institutions. How can this software take advantage of multicore hardware without the need to rewrite it completely? A rewrite would face several hurdles in terms of both cost and correctness. A parallel version of a sequential program not only must run faster but also must produce identical results as its sequential counterpart.

OpenMP is the answer to this problem. It is a technology capable of allowing the *incremental* conversion of sequential programs to parallel ones. OpenMP's support for C/C++ and Fortran is also evidence to its target audience. OpenMP, which stands for Open Multi-Processing, is an industry standard controlled by the OpenMP Architecture Review Board (ARB), which is a nonprofit corporation. The latest version of the OpenMP standard[1] is 4.0, published in July 2013. As far as the GNU C++ compiler support is concerned, given that this is the platform used by our examples, as of GCC 4.7 the compiler supports the OpenMP 3.1 specification, whereas GCC 4.9 supports OpenMP 4.0.

In OpenMP, the compiler is responsible for handling all the "ugly" implementation details associated with spawning, initiating, and terminating threads. The trade-off (typical of similar approaches) is that programmer control is sacrificed for convenience. The OpenMP Application Program Interface (API) consists of compiler directives, library routines, and environmental variables. OpenMP uses what it calls *work-sharing constructs* to direct the compiler to start threads and have them perform a specific task. The work-sharing constructs range from automated loop parallelization to explicit task description.

In an OpenMP program, the execution profile follows the Globally Sequential, Locally Parallel (GSLP) structure (see Section 2.4). In effect, we have a sequential program that (ideally) has its most time-consuming parts parallelized by the compiler, with the elementary assistance of the programmer. Obviously, this is not the most flexible model for introducing concurrency, but it works well with existing sequential programs and it is also faster to produce results in terms of development cost.

4.2 YOUR FIRST OpenMP PROGRAM

As mentioned in the introduction, OpenMP relies on the compiler to generate threads. Nowadays, most C/C++ compilers offer OpenMP support, often with the specification of an appropriate switch.

The instructions to the compiler come in the form of #pragma preprocessor directives. Pragma directives allow a programmer to access compiler-specific preprocessor extensions. For example, a common use of pragmas is in the management of include files. The following pragma directive:

```
#pragma once
```

will prevent the compiler from including the same file more than once. It is equivalent to having "include guards" in each file, as in:

```
#ifndef __FILE_H_
#define __FILE_H_

. . . // code

#endif
```

The following program illustrates some of the essential components that make up an OpenMP program, namely:

---

[1] See http://openmp.org/wp/openmp-specifications/.

- The inclusion of the header file that declares the OpenMP library functions (line 4).
- A #pragma omp directive (line 12). The #pragma omp parallel line launches multiple threads, each executing the *block of statements* that follows. Pragma directives typically have a number of optional clauses that modify their behavior. Clauses can be comma or white-space separated. In our example, the num_threads clause modifies the number of threads that will be spawned.
- OpenMP library function calls to inspect or modify the state of the OpenMP run-time. The omp_get_thread_num() function in line 13 returns the ID of the thread executing that statement. This tool can be used to diversify the action of each thread, in a similar fashion to the one examined in Chapter 3.

In OpenMP jargon, the parallel directive is called a **Single Program, Multiple Data** (SPMD) directive because we have the same program code run by multiple threads, each applying its logic on a separate data, as shown in Listing 4.1.

```cpp
1   // File : hello.cpp
2   #include <iostream>
3   #include <stdlib.h>
4   #include <omp.h>
5
6   using namespace std;
7
8   int main (int argc, char **argv)
9   {
10    int numThr = atoi (argv[1]);
11
12  #pragma omp parallel num_threads(numThr)
13    cout << "Hello from thread " << omp_get_thread_num () << endl;
14
15    return 0;
16  }
```

LISTING 4.1

"Hello World" in OpenMP.

The compilation of this sample program can be done with GNU C++:

```
$ g++ hello.cpp -fopenmp -o hello
```

with -fopenmp being the switch that activates the OpenMP extensions. If you are using a different compiler, you should check the corresponding documentation for the appropriate switch (e.g., the Intel Compiler requires an -openmp switch). The output of a run is similar to:

```
$ ./hello 4
Hello from thread Hello from thread Hello from thread 12

0
Hello from thread 3
```

with the output out of order and mangled, since there is no control over when each thread executes and there is no coordination for access to the console. As the "Hello from thread" string is output at a different instance than the value returned from the omp_get_thread_num() call, they can become separated. The only thing common between the output of multiple runs would be that there always are as many lines as the number of threads.

But how exactly does the program in Listing 4.1 execute? OpenMP programs have a Globally Sequential, Locally Parallel structure (see Section 2.4), which means that there is a main sequential flow of control that forks to multiple threads. These threads subsequently join back to the main thread, and this process can be repeated. This is also known as *fork-join parallelism*. The operating system, upon launching the hello program, starts a *master thread* that will, based on the pragma directives, spawn more threads to execute in parallel parts of the program. These parallel parts are called *parallel regions*, and these threads are called *child threads*. Collectively, the master and child threads constitute a *team of threads*. When the flow of execution transitions from a parallel region back to a sequential part of the program, the master thread waits for all the child threads to terminate in what is effectively an implicit *barrier*. Figure 4.1 visualizes this process in the form of a UML sequence diagram.

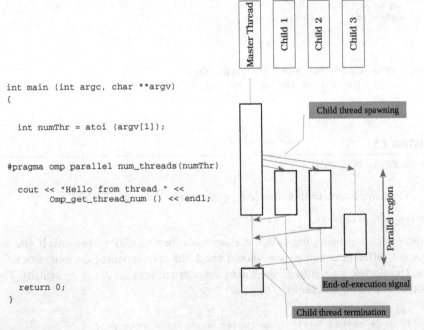

FIGURE 4.1

UML sequence diagram of a possible execution of our "Hello World" program with four threads.

OpenMP makes a distinction between *regions* and *constructs*: A parallel region is the *dynamic* sequence of statements produced during the execution of a parallel construct. A parallel construct is the combination of an OpenMP pragma directive and a structured block of statements that follows it.

Parallel constructs can be nested, i.e., we can have nested parallel pragmas, in which case a child thread can spawn more threads. This would result in a tree hierarchy of threads, with the master thread at the root of the tree. OpenMP uses tree terminology to describe the relationships between the threads, such as parent, child, ancestor, or descendant.

OpenMP will, by default, use as big a team of threads as the number of available cores in the system. The size of the team can be controlled in the following ways:

- **Universally**, i.e., for all OpenMP programs, via the `OMP_NUM_THREADS` environmental variable:

```
$ echo ${OMP_NUM_THREADS}  # to query the value
$ export OMP_NUM_THREADS=4 # to set it in BASH
```

- **At the program level**, via the `omp_set_number_threads` function:

```
void omp_set_num_threads(int n) // size of the team of threads (IN)
```

The `omp_get_num_threads` call returns the active threads in a parallel region. If it is called in a sequential part, it returns 1.
- **At the pragma level**, via the `num_threads` clause.

The lower an item is in this list, i.e., the more specific it is, the higher precedence it has.

Compilers that do not support particular pragmas ignore the corresponding statements. This means that it is possible for an OpenMP program to be compiled by a nonsupporting compiler, albeit without concurrency support. So, it is critical that one does not forget the compiler switches that activate OpenMP! The program in Listing 4.1 would fail to compile in that case, since the code in the `omp.h` header file does not allow the declaration of the OpenMP library functions if OpenMP is not enabled, causing in turn a compilation error (an undefined reference to `omp_get_thread_num`).

4.3 VARIABLE SCOPE

When a parallel region is executing, each of the threads in the team executes a copy of the designated block of statements. The question is, what kind of access do threads have to the variables declared outside the block? How about the variables that are declared inside the block? Are these variables shared or not? And if they are shared, how can we coordinate access to them so that there is no race condition?

Outside the parallel regions, normal scope rules apply. OpenMP specifies the following types of variables:

- **Shared**: All variables declared outside a parallel region are by default shared.
- **Private**: All variables declared inside a parallel region are allocated in the run-time stack of each thread. So, we have as many copies of these variables as the size of the thread team. Private variables are destroyed upon the termination of a parallel region.
- **Reduction**: A special type of shared variable that is actually a private one! The contradiction is not real; a reduction variable gets individual copies for each thread running the corresponding parallel region. Upon the termination of the parallel region, an operation is applied to the individual copies (e.g., summation) to produce the value that will be stored in the shared variable.

The default scope of variables can be modified by clauses in the pragma lines.

An example will help us illustrate the purpose of the preceding list. We start from a sequential program that calculates the definite integral of a given function, as shown in Listing 4.2.

```cpp
1   // File : integration_seq.cpp
2   . . .
3   //————————————————————————————————————
4   double testf (double x)
5   {
6     return x * x + 2 * sin (x);
7   }
8
9   //————————————————————————————————————
10  double integrate (double st, double en, int div, double (*f) (double))
11  {
12    double localRes = 0;
13    double step = (en - st) / div;
14    double x;
15    x = st;
16    localRes = f (st) + f (en);
17    localRes /= 2;
18    for (int i = 1; i < div; i++)
19      {
20        x += step;
21        localRes += f (x);
22      }
23    localRes *= step;
24
25    return localRes;
26  }
27
28  //————————————————————————————————————
29  int main (int argc, char *argv[])
30  {
31    if (argc == 1)
32      {
33        cerr << "Usage " << argv[0] << " start end divisions\n";
```

```
34              exit (1);
35          }
36      double start, end;
37      int divisions;
38      start = atof (argv[1]);
39      end = atof (argv[2]);
40      divisions = atoi (argv[3]);
41
42      double finalRes = integrate (start, end, divisions, testf);
43
44      cout << finalRes << endl;
45      return 0;
46  }
```

LISTING 4.2

Sequential program for calculating the integal of a function.

There is nothing special to mention about Listing 4.2 other than that it is a straight-forward implementation of the trapezoid rule. A few simple optimizations in the loop of lines 18-22 avoid repeated calculations. (See Section 3.5.2.2 for more information on the trapezoid rule.) The program reads three command-line parameters, two for the endpoints of the integration interval and one for the number of subdivisions to use in the calculation.

Any function can be used for testing. The one shown in Listing 4.2 has a known solution, $\int (x^2 + 2 \cdot sin(x)) = \frac{1}{3}(x^3 - 6 \cdot cos(x))$, which makes the verification of the computed results easier.

In the following section we examine three possible OpenMP derivatives of this program, progressing towards a version that better captures the ethos of OpenMP.

4.3.1 OpenMP INTEGRATION V.O: MANUAL PARTITIONING

Partitioning the work done by the `integrate()` function in Listing 4.2, line 10, could be done by calling the function multiple times from different threads, but with different parameters. Effectively it is like breaking up the integration interval into as many pieces as the number of threads N, as shown in Figure 4.2. We can use the thread ID returned from the `omp_get_thread_num()` library function to derive distinct parameters for each thread $i \in [0, N - 1]$ using the formulas:

$$localStart = start + ID \cdot localDiv \cdot step \qquad (4.1)$$

and

$$localEnd = localStart + localDiv \cdot step \qquad (4.2)$$

where *localDiv* is the number of divisions assigned to each thread: $localDiv = \frac{divisions}{N}$.

The resulting program is shown in Listing 4.3, with modifications pertaining only to the invocation of the `integrate()` function, which is now located inside a parallel region.

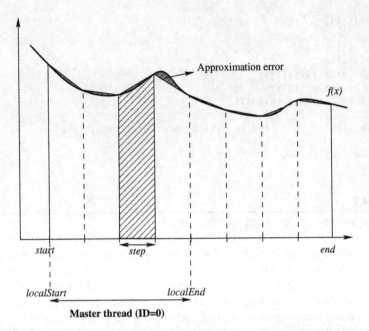

Master thread (ID=0)

FIGURE 4.2

An illustration of how the trapezoid rule can be applied in parallel by evenly breaking up the integration interval [*start*, *end*] among the team of threads (made up of two threads in our figure). The red/dark gray area represents the approximation error.

```
1    // File : integration_omp_V0.cpp
2    . . .
3    //——————————————————————————————————————————————
4    int main (int argc, char *argv[])
5    {
6      if (argc == 1)
7      {
8        cerr << "Usage " << argv[0] << " start end divisions\n";
9        exit (1);
10     }
11     double start, end;
12     int divisions;
13     start = atof (argv[1]);
14     end = atof (argv[2]);
15     divisions = atoi (argv[3]);
16
17     // get the number of threads for next parallel region
18     int N = omp_get_max_threads ();
19     divisions = (divisions / N) * N;    // make sure divisions is a ↩
             multiple of N
20     double step = (end — start) / divisions;
21
```

```
22      double finalRes = 0;
23   #pragma omp parallel
24      {
25        int localDiv = divisions / N;
26        int ID = omp_get_thread_num ();
27        double localStart = start + ID * localDiv * step;
28        double localEnd = localStart + localDiv * step;
29        finalRes += integrate (localStart, localEnd, localDiv, testf);
30      }
31
32      cout << finalRes << endl;
33
34      return 0;
35   }
```

LISTING 4.3

OpenMP-based program for calculating the integal of a function. This version suffers from a race condition. Only the changes from Listing 4.2 are shown.

The block between lines 24 and 30 is executed by multiple threads, all having (by default) shared access to the variables declared outside: start, end, step, finalRes, etc. Each thread retrieves its own ID (the master thread's ID is always 0) in line 26 and proceeds to calculate the limits of its own part of the integration interval (lines 27, 28).

The number of threads that will be used in a parallel region in the absence of a modifier (e.g., a num_threads clause) can be queried with the omp_get_max_threads() function, as shown in line 18. The reasoning behind lines 18 and 19 is that divisions must be a multiple of the number of threads. Otherwise the step variable will not match the localDiv subdivisions used by each thread to cover its part of the integration interval.

All the variables declared inside the parallel block are private, and they cease to exist once the parallel region terminates. For this reason, we need a shared scope variable(s) so that the calculated partial integrals from line 29 can be saved and made available beyond the block. For this purpose, we are using the finalRes variable, but there is a catch: There is no coordination between the threads. The resulting race condition makes our first attempt a failure! But there is an easy fix, as shown in the next section.

4.3.2 OpenMP INTEGRATION V.1: MANUAL PARTITIONING WITHOUT A RACE CONDITION

The race condition of Listing 4.3 can be fixed if each thread could store the results it calculates at a separate repository: The partial shared array defined in line 24 of Listing 4.4 holds as many elements as the size of the thread team. Line 31 uses a thread's ID to store its partial result to its "own" array element. Once the parallel block terminates, we only need to *reduce* the partial results to the final one, via the loop of lines 35-37.

```cpp
1    // File : integration_omp_V1 .cpp
2    . . .
3    //————————————————————————————
4    int main (int argc, char *argv[])
5    {
6
7      if (argc == 1)
8        {
9          cerr << "Usage " << argv[0] << " start end divisions\n";
10         exit (1);
11       }
12     double start, end;
13     int divisions;
14     start = atof (argv[1]);
15     end = atof (argv[2]);
16     divisions = atoi (argv[3]);
17
18     // get the number of threads for next parallel region
19     int N = omp_get_max_threads ();
20     divisions = (divisions / N) * N;      // make sure divisions is a ↵
            multiple of N
21     double step = (end − start) / divisions;
22
23     // allocate memory for the partial results
24     double *partial = new double[N];
25   #pragma omp parallel
26     {
27       int localDiv = divisions / N;
28       int ID = omp_get_thread_num ();
29       double localStart = start + ID * localDiv * step;
30       double localEnd = localStart + localDiv * step;
31       partial[ID] = integrate (localStart, localEnd, localDiv, testf);
32     }
33
34     // reduction step
35     double finalRes = partial [0];
36     for (int i = 1; i < N; i++)
37       finalRes += partial[i];
38
39     cout << finalRes << endl;
40
41     delete []partial;
42     return 0;
43   }
```

LISTING 4.4

OpenMP-based program for calculating the integal of a function with a shared array
holding per-thread partial results. Changes relative to Listing 4.2 are limited to the main
function of the program.

Listing 4.4 is a working program, but it does not really feel that this is the "easy way" to transform a sequential program into a multithreaded one, since it required extensive changes to the original source code. Fortunately, OpenMP provides an easier way, as shown next.

4.3.3 OpenMP INTEGRATION V.2: IMPLICIT PARTITIONING WITH LOCKING

Listing 4.4 constitutes a design approach that is familiar territory to programmers exposed to the traditional "manual" way of managing threads. But it is totally over the top for OpenMP! Because the bulk of the work is typically done in loops, OpenMP provides a parallel for construct for breaking up the iterations of a for loop and assigning them to different threads. There are a number of conditions on the form of the loop, but we leave this discussion for a later section.

The parallel for construct can only be applied on a for loop (including nested for loops) and not a block of statements like the omp parallel pragma. By heading the for loop of line 14 in Listing 4.5, with a parallel for pragma, OpenMP launches multiple threads that execute the loop's iterations in some system-specific fashion (more details are given in Section 4.4.3).

The accumulation of the results (something that was problematic in the previous versions of the program) is accomplished via a shared local variable, localRes. This avoids the necessity of having to keep a separate partial sum for each thread, but we need to make any changes to the localRes variable atomic (otherwise we end up with a race condition, as in Listing 4.3). A critical pragma is employed for this purpose, as shown in line 18 of Listing 4.5.

```
1   // File : integration_omp_V2.cpp
2   . . .
3   //──────────────────────────────────────────
4   double integrate (double st, double en, int div, double (*f) (double))
5   {
6      double localRes = 0;
7      double step = (en − st) / div;
8      double x;
9      x = st;
10     localRes = f (st) + f (en);
11     localRes /= 2;
12
13  #pragma omp parallel for private(x)
14     for (int i = 1; i < div; i++)
15        {
16           x = st + i * step;
17           double temp = f (x);
18  #pragma omp critical
19           localRes += temp;
20        }
21
```

```
22    localRes *= step;
23
24    return localRes;
25 }
26    . . .
```

LISTING 4.5

OpenMP-based program for calculating the integal of a function using a critical section. Only changes relative to Listing 4.2 are shown. The main function remains unchanged.

The `critical` construct restricts execution of the associated block to a single thread at a time.

The `private` clause in the `parallel for` construct of line 13 modifies the scope of variable x. x needs to be private because each thread must use it to obtain the value of the function to be integrated, at a different location. In fact, it could be also declared inside the `for` loop with less drama.

There is also a more subtle change from Listing 4.2 involving the calculation of x. The original statement:

```
x += step;
```

is completely inappropriate, since it requires a shared variable and a sequential execution of the loop: There are *loop-carried dependencies*. If child thread 1 was assigned the iterations from, for example, 100 to 200 during its first execution of the loop's body, it would not be able to get the proper value for x, nor for any subsequent iterations. The form used in line 16 eliminates any such dependencies, since the value of x depends only on the loop variable and not the execution sequence. The role of dependencies in `for` loop parallelism is examined in more detail in Section 4.4.1.

4.3.4 OpenMP INTEGRATION V.3: IMPLICIT PARTITIONING WITH REDUCTION

We can still improve on the version of the previous section: If each thread could calculate its own partial sum that we accumulate at the end of the loop, there would not be any reason to use the performance-sapping critical section. A `reduction` clause can help us achieve this, as shown in Listing 4.6.

```
1  // File : integration_omp_V3 .cpp
2  . . .
3  //————————————————————————————————————
4  double integrate (double st, double en, int div, double (*f) (double))
5  {
6     double localRes = 0;
7     double step = (en − st) / div;
8     double x;
9     x = st;
10    localRes = f (st) + f (en);
11    localRes /= 2;
12
```

```
13   #pragma omp parallel for private(x) reduction(+: localRes)
14     for (int i = 1; i < div; i++)
15     {
16       x = st + i * step;
17       localRes += f (x);
18     }
19
20     localRes *= step;
21
22     return localRes;
23   }
24   . . .
```

LISTING 4.6

OpenMP-based program for calculating the integal of a function using a *reduction variable*. Only changes relative to Listing 4.2 are shown. The main function remains unchanged.

localRes is defined outside the parallel region, so it would be normally shared. However, by introducing the reduction clause in line 13, each thread creates a local copy of localRes that is initialized to zero (the initial value depends on the reduction operation). Each thread accumulates its partial result in its local localRes copy. Upon termination of the parallel region, the operation specified in the reduction clause (addition in our example) is repeatedly applied to produce the final result, which is subsequently stored in the shared localRes.

The syntax of the reduction clause is:

```
reduction( reduction_identifier : variable_list)
```

where variable_list is a comma-separated list of variable identifiers, and reduction_identifier is one of the following binary arithmetic and boolean operators: $+$, $*$, $-$, $\&$, $\&\&$, $|$, $||$, $\wedge$, max, and min. The specified operator is applied between the private copies of the threads and the shared variable declared outside the parallel block until a single value is obtained. The initial value of the private copies depends on the chosen operator, as shown in Table 4.1.

Table 4.1 List of the available operators for the reduction clause, along with the initial value of the reduction variable's private copies [37].

Operator	Private Copy Initial Value
$+$, $-$, $|$, $||$, $\wedge$	0
$*$, $\&\&$	1
$\&$	0xFFFF...FFF, i.e., all bits set to 1
max	Smallest possible number that can be represented by the type of the reduction variable
min	Largest possible number that can be represented by the type of the reduction variable

As an example of a different reduction operator, the parallel `for` loop shown in Listing 4.7 can be used to determine the maximum of an array of elements in parallel.

```
int maxElem = data[0];
#pragma omp parallel for reduction(max : maxElem)
  for (int i = 1; i < sizeof (data) / sizeof (int); i++)
    if (maxElem < data[i])
      maxElem = data[i];

  cout << "Maximum is : " << maxElem << endl;
```

LISTING 4.7

Calculating the maximum of an array in parallel via reduction.

The reduction operation is a really significant asset in a parallel program designer's toolbox. The mechanisms through which it can be implemented in parallel, plus more elaborate uses of it, are examined in Sections 5.11.3 and 7.4.3.

4.3.5 FINAL WORDS ON VARIABLE SCOPE

Variable scope rules for parallel regions are rather simple. The problem is that race conditions can arise without careful consideration from the programmer. Read-only variables pose no threat, but variables that need to be modified must do so in an orderly fashion. OpenMP does not warn of such potential problems, so it is prudent to act proactively. What this translates to is that we should explicitly declare the desired type of access to all shared variables (i.e., variables declared outside the parallel block) inside a parallel construct.

The `default(none)` clause causes OpenMP to ignore all symbols declared outside of a parallel construct that are missing explicit access declarations. Using this clause in the code of Listing 4.6 would mandate the following additional changes[2]:

```
#pragma omp parallel for default(none) \
            shared(step, div, st, f) \
            private(x)  \
            reduction(+: localRes)
  for (int i = 1; i < div; i++)
    {
      x = st + i * step;
      localRes += f (x);
    }
```

The following list summarizes the OpenMP clauses (a.k.a. *data-sharing* clauses) that modify the scope of a variable or variables, since they can take as parameters

---

[2] Pragmas, like all other preprocessor directives, are supposed to occupy a single line only. Long lines, like the one used in this example, can be split into several lines by "escaping" the change of line with a \.

a comma-delimited list of identifiers. These clauses are common (with a few exceptions) to most OpenMP parallel constructs:

- `shared`: The default behavior for variables declared outside a parallel block. It needs to be used only if `default(none)` is also specified.
- `reduction`: A reduction operation is performed between the private copies and the "outside" object. The final value is stored in the "outside" object.
- `private`: Creates a separate copy of a variable for each thread in the team. Private variables are not initialized, so we should not expect to get the value of the variable declared outside the parallel construct.
- `firstprivate`: Behaves the same way as the `private` clause, but the private variable copies are initialized to the value of the "outside" object.
- `lastprivate`: Behaves the same way as the `private` clause, but the thread finishing the last iteration of the sequential block (for the final value of the loop control variable that produces an iteration) copies the value of its object to the "outside" object.
- `threadprivate`: Creates thread-specific, *persistent* storage (i.e., for the duration of the program) for *global* data. In contrast, a `private` clause only creates parallel-block storage that is automatic, i.e., data are destroyed upon block termination. The `threadprivate` clause is used outside a parallel construct, typically immediately after the declaration of the corresponding variables.
  A `private` clause only masks or hides global data, whereas a `threadprivate` creates a private-per-thread copy for each thread in a team.
- `copyin`: Used in conjunction with the `threadprivate` clause to initialize the threadprivate copies of a team of threads from the master thread's variables.

Examples for the clauses we have not covered so far are reserved for subsequent sections.

4.4 LOOP-LEVEL PARALLELISM

In the examples of the previous section, we sampled the `parallel for` construct to derive a multithreaded version of a sequential program with a handful of changes. But can we use the same approach on any `for` loop? The answer is, unfortunately, no. The `for` loop has to satisfy certain conditions, which in OpenMP jargon are called the *canonical form*.

These are the restrictions of the canonical form:

- The loop control variable must be an integer type (signed or unsigned), a pointer type (e.g., base address of an array), or a random access iterator (for C++). The loop control variable is made `private` by default, even if it is declared outside the loop.
- The loop control variable must not be modified in the body of the loop.

• The limit against which the loop control variable is compared to determine the truth of the termination condition must be loop invariant, i.e., it cannot change during the loop's execution. The following loop, which eliminates the even numbers from a data array of size M, violates both this and the previous rule:

```
for (int i = 0; i < M; i++)
{
    if(data[i] % 2 == 0)
    {
        data[i] = data[M-1]; // copy over
        M--;  // limit modified
        i--;  // loop control var change
    }
}
```

• The increment/decrement step of the loop control variable must be loop invariant.
• The logical and arithmetic operators allowed in the for statement are limited to the ones shown in Figure 4.3.
• No program logic that transfers control outside the loop body is allowed. This includes break, goto, and throw statements. One can use goto and throw only if the destination address and the exception handling, respectively, take place within the loop body.
• The program is allowed to terminate from within the loop body via an exit call.

The last two requirements are common to all blocks handled by OpenMP constructs. The transition to the code outside a parallel region can only take place after all the team threads are synchronized. This extends to code entry (which is more or less obvious for loops), i.e., you cannot jump inside a parallel block. OpenMP calls these blocks *structured*. A structured block has a single point of entry and a single point of exit.

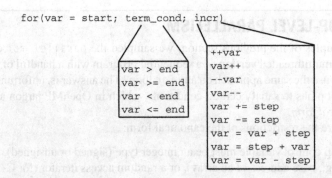

FIGURE 4.3

Canonical loop form. Expressions/variables start, end, and step must be loop invariant and of a compatible type to var.

The purpose of the canonical form is to ensure that the number of iterations can be computed *a priori*, i.e., before the loop executes. This way, OpenMP can distribute the iterations to the team of threads and produce a result consistent with the corresponding sequential for loop.

As a final word, the parallel for directive is actually a shortcut for the following *nested* directives:

```
#pragma omp parallel
#pragma omp for
for (...
```

The significance of this shortcut is not in having a separate for directive but in being able to place in the block managed by the parallel directive all sorts of work-sharing constructs, as in:

```
#pragma omp parallel
{
#pragma omp for
    for (. . .
#pragma omp sections
. . .
}
```

We discuss this possibility in more depth later in the chapter.

4.4.1 DATA DEPENDENCIES

A loop being in canonical form is the first step in making it available for parallelization. The next step is making sure that the loop body permits "out-of-order" execution of the iterations. The loop-carried dependency we treated in Listing 4.5 is just a hint of the bigger problem.

Let's assume that we have a loop body with two statements S1 and S2 that operate on a common memory location:

```
for(i =...
{
  S1 : operate on a memory location x
  ...
  S2 : operate on a memory location x
}
```

The kind of operations performed, e.g., read or write, determines the kind of dependency formed between the two statements. When such dependencies are limited within the execution of the same iteration, there are no problems in the parallel execution of the loop by a parallel for directive.[3]

---

[3]Dependencies in general cause problems for vectorizing compilers, i.e., compilers that attempt to concurrently execute the dependent statements within an iteration. However, this is a topic for a compiler book [5].

The four kind of dependencies are [26]:

- **Flow dependence**: When S1 writes x and S2 reads x (Read After Write, or RAW), denoted by $S1 \, \delta^f \, S2$. The name stems from the notion that the value produced by S1 is transmitted or flows to S2. For example:

```
x = 10;          // S1
y = 2 * x + 5;   // S2
```

- **Antidependence**: When S1 reads x and S2 writes x (Write After Read, or WAR), denoted by $S1 \, \delta^a \, S2$. This is the antithesis of the flow dependence. For example:

```
y = x + 3;    // S1
x ++ ;        // S2
```

- **Output dependence**: When S1 writes x and S2 writes x (Write After Write, or WAW), denoted by $S1 \, \delta^o \, S2$. For example:

```
x = 10;        // S1
x = x + c ;    // S2
```

- **Input dependence**: When S1 reads x and S2 reads x (Read After Read, or RAR), denoted by $S1 \, \delta^i \, S2$. For example:

```
y = x + c;        // S1
z = 2 * x + 1;    // S2
```

This is not considered a real dependence, so it is not examined further here.

These dependencies are transformed into loop-carried dependencies if S1 and S2 depend explicitly (using an expression of the loop control variable i) or implicitly (via iteration sequence or a condition on i) on different values of the loop control variable. For example, S1 could write a location during iteration i that is read by S2 during iteration j.[4] It should be noted that in loop-carried dependencies, the relationship between S1 and S2 is characterized based on the sequential *execution* order and not only on their sequence in the code. This is a critical point when arrays are involved.

Each dependency type requires a different elimination approach, so it is essential that we recognize its type. In the following sections we provide examples of how we treat each dependence type. However, in the case of flow dependencies, a successful elimination is far from guaranteed. Often an algorithmic change is necessary to ensure that parallel execution is possible.

When a dependency cannot be eliminated, our only course of action is to try to rewrite the code so that at least some part of the code can be parallelized while at the same time *honoring* the dependencies that exist. Dependence violation is not an option, since it leads to an incorrect program [6].

---

[4]In principle, we could have nested loops, in which case i and j are vectors representing the values of the control variables going from the outer to the inner loop. In this section we keep things simple by working mostly with single-level loops.

4.4.1.1 Flow Dependencies

Flow dependencies are the most difficult to remove, if even possible. In this section we progress from simple to more challenging cases of flow dependencies.

Case 1: **Reduction, Induction Variables**

The Listing 4.8 code is a snippet from a integration program, similar to the example we used in Section 4.3.

```
double v = start;
double sum=0;
for(int i = 0; i < N; i++)
{
    sum = sum + f(v);    // S1
    v = v + step;        // S2
}
```

LISTING 4.8

Sequential loop with flow dependencies.

We have three flow dependencies:

- *S1 δ^f S1* is caused by a *reduction variable*, sum. The value of sum is read in each iteration, and it is updated with the use of the same operator and an iteration-specific value. Because the initial value is produced from the previous iteration, we have a read after a write, which is the definition of flow dependence.
- *S2 δ^f S2* is caused by an *induction variable*, v. An induction variable is a variable for which the value is an affine function of the loop control variable, e.g.:

```
var = a * i + b;
```

where a and b are loop invariant expressions. In our example, we have b = start and a = step.
- *S2 δ^f S1* is also caused by the v induction variable.

A reduction-variable-caused dependence is easily treated by the use of the reduction clause, which does not actually break the dependence but instead localizes it to each thread.

An induction-variable-caused dependence, on the other hand, can be completely removed if we use the affine formula to update the value of the variable in a loop-independent way.

The resulting code is shown in Listing 4.9.

```
double v = start; // now irrelevant. v can be an automatic ↵
        variable declared inside the loop
double sum=0;

#pragma omp parallel for reduction(+ : sum) private(v) shared(↵
        step)
```

```
for(int i = 0; i < N; i++)
{
    v = i * step + start;
    sum = sum + f(v);
}
```

LISTING 4.9

OpenMP version of Listing 4.8, with loop-carried flow dependencies treated.

Case 2: Loop skewing

Another technique for removing flow dependencies is *loop-skewing*, i.e., rearrangement of the loop body's statements. In the Listing 4.10 example, we have $S2 \, \delta^f \, S1$, since the values of the x array produced during iteration i are consumed during iteration $i + 1$.

```
for(int i = 1; i < N; i++)
{
    y[ i ] = f( x[ i-1 ] );      // S1
    x[ i ] = x[ i ] + c[ i ];    // S2
}
```

LISTING 4.10

Sequential program with a flow dependence.

By taking the calculation of a single y element outside of the loop, we can eliminate the dependence. The modification aims at having the statement that consumes the x[i] value be executed at the same iteration that computes x[i], as shown in Listing 4.11.

```
y[ 1 ] = f( x[ 0 ] );
for(int i = 1; i < N - 1; i++)
{
    x[ i ] = x[ i ] + c[ i ];
    y[ i + 1 ] = f( x[ i ] );
}
```

LISTING 4.11

OpenMP version of Listing 4.10, that removes the loop-carried flow dependence via loop skewing.

Case 3: Partial Parallelization

There may be cases in which dependencies cannot be removed. In Listing 4.12 we have two flow dependencies in the body of two nested for-loops.

```
for (int i = 1; i < N; i++)
    for (int j = 1; j < M; j++)
        data[i][j] = data[i - 1][j] + data[i - 1][j - 1];
```

LISTING 4.12

Sequential code with two flow dependencies in the body of a nested loop.

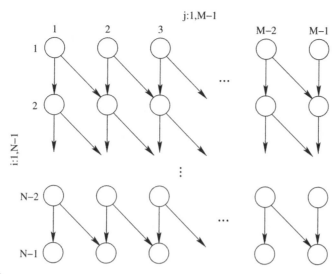

FIGURE 4.4

Iteration space dependency graph for Listing 4.12.

To better appreciate the nature of these dependencies and how they could be dealt with, we can draw a iteration space dependency graph (ISDG). This graph has nodes that represent iterations and edges that represent data flow. The source of an edge is the iteration that produces a value or changes a location in memory, and the sink of the edge is the iteration where this value is utilized.

The ISDG of Listing 4.12 is shown in Figure 4.4, and, as can be observed, there are no edges between the nodes of the same row. This means that the j-loop can be parallelized, in contrast to the i-loop that cannot. For a given value of i, we can execute the iterations of the j loop in parallel as shown in Listing 4.13.

```
for (int i = 1; i < N; i++)
#pragma omp parallel for
    for (int j = 1; j < M; j++)
        data[i][j] = data[i - 1][j] + data[i - 1][j - 1];
```

LISTING 4.13

Partial OpenMP parallelization of Listing 4.12, affecting only the inner loop.

Case 4: Refactoring

In Listing 4.14, we have two nested for loops with three flow dependencies, all involving S1:

```
// File : nested_flowDep.cpp
. . .
  int N = atoi(argv[1]), M = atoi(argv[2]);
  double **data = new double *[N];
  for (int i = 0; i < M; i++)
    data[i] = new double[M];

  // init data array with sample values
  . . .
  // compute
  for (int i = 1; i < N; i++)
    for (int j = 1; j < M; j++)
      data[i][j] = data[i − 1][j] + data[i][j − 1] + data[i − ↵
        1][j − 1];   // S1
```

LISTING 4.14

Sequential code with multiple flow dependencies in the body of a nested loop.

The ISDG of Listing 4.14 is shown in Figure 4.5.

At first glance, it does not seem possible that we could ever run the iterations of these nested loops concurrently. But close examination of the graph reveals that there are groups of iterations that are independent of each other, and they could execute in parallel without violating the dependencies of the graph. These groups, highlighted in Figure 4.6, can be executed in a "wavelike" fashion. The waves have to be executed in sequence, but the iterations of each group or wave can be executed in parallel.

The resulting code is shown in Listing 4.15. As can be observed, only the inner loop can be parallelized to ensure correct execution.

```
1    // File : nested_flowDepFixed.cpp
2    . . .
3      int smallDim;
```

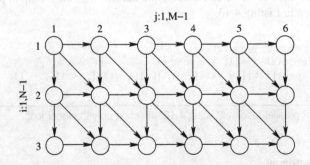

FIGURE 4.5

Iteration space dependency graph for Listing 4.14 for N=4 and M=7.

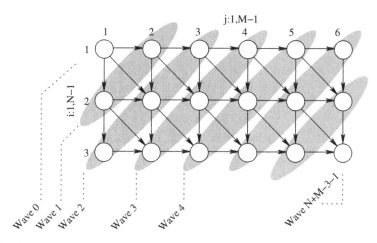

FIGURE 4.6

The iteration space dependency graph of Figure 4.5, with highlighted groups of iterations that can be executed concurrently. The groups have to be executed in sequence.

```
4      int largeDim;
5      if (N > M)
6        {
7          smallDim = M;
8          largeDim = N;
9        }
10     else
11       {
12         smallDim = N;
13         largeDim = M;
14       }
15
16     // compute
17     for (int diag = 1; diag <= N + M - 3; diag++)
18       {
19         int diagLength = diag;
20         if (diag + 1 >= smallDim)
21           diagLength = smallDim - 1;
22         if (diag + 1 >= largeDim)
23           diagLength = (smallDim - 1) - (diag - largeDim) - 1;
24
25   #pragma omp parallel for default(none) shared(data, diag, ↩
         diagLength, N, M)
26         for (int k = 0; k < diagLength; k++)
27           {
28             int i = diag - k;
29             int j = k + 1;
30             if (diag > N - 1)
```

```
31                      {
32                          i = N - 1 - k;
33                          j = diag - (N - 1) + k + 1;
34                      }
35                      data[i][j] = data[i - 1][j] + data[i][j - 1] + data[↩
                        i - 1][j - 1];
36                  }
37              }
```

LISTING 4.15

Parallelized version of Listing 4.14, with groups of iterations executed in parallel.

The important points of the Listing 4.15 code are as follows

- The execution in waves requires a change of loop variables from the original i and j. The new loop control variables represent the wave index (diag in the for statement of line 17) and the member of the wave or group, scanning from bottom left to top right, respectively (k in the for statement of line 26).
- There are exactly $N + M - 3$ waves, but the exact size of each one has to be calculated based on the number or rows (N) and columns (M) of our data table. The size is calculated in lines 19-23 by comparing the wave index with the smaller and bigger of the two dimensions N, M.
- The parallel loop of lines 25-36 transforms the two new loop control variables to the original i and j indices so that the statement of line 35 can be executed.

Case 5: Fissioning

The last technique we could employ before a full-blown change of the underlying algorithm is *fissioning*, which is splitting the loop body into two loops, a parallelizable one and a sequential one. The latter is obviously the holding place of the computations whose dependencies force a sequential computation.

An example that requires this treatment is shown in Listing 4.16.

```
s = b[ 0 ];
for (int i = 1; i < N; i++)
{
    a[ i ] = a [ i ] + a[ i - 1 ];  // S1
    s = s + b[ i ];
}
```

LISTING 4.16

Sequential code with a flow dependence that requires fissioning.

S1 introduces a loop-carried flow dependence that can be partially treated by splitting the loop in two, as shown in Listing 4.17.

```
// sequential part
for (int i = 1; i < N; i++)
```

```
        a[ i ] = a [ i ] + a[ i - 1 ];

// parallel part
s = b[ 0 ];
#pragma omp parallel for reduction( + : s)
for (int i = 1; i < N; i++)
    s = s + b[ i ];
```

LISTING 4.17

Split-up version of Listing 4.16 that can be partially parallelized.

Actually, in the preceding code, the first loop constitutes a *prefix-sum* or *scan* calculation that can be also parallelized, but not using just an OpenMP parallel for directive! A reduction is a special case of a prefix-sum operation. More details are presented in Section 7.4.4.

Case 6: **Algorithm Change**

It is an oddity that a simple example that is usually reserved as an introduction to recursion can also serve as an example of a code that cannot be parallelized. The following code, which computes all the Fibonacci terms up to N, contains two loop-carried flow dependencies:

```
for(int i = 2; i < N; i++)
{
    F[i] = F[i-1] + F[i-2];
}
```

We could rewrite the code as:

```
for(int i = 2 ; i < N; i++)
{
    int x =  F[i-2]; // S1
    int y =  F[i-1]; // S2
    F[i] =  x + y;   // S3
}
```

with $S1 \; \delta^f \; S3$ and $S2 \; \delta^f \; S3$, as, for example, F[i-2] is being read during iteration i, but it was computed during a previous iteration $i - 2$, which makes it contribute to a flow dependence.

Dependencies in this code cannot be eliminated without modifying the algorithm that computes the term. Instead of using the recursive definition, we could use a closed-form solution based on Binet's formula:

$$F_n = \frac{\varphi^n - (1 - \varphi)^n}{\sqrt{5}} \tag{4.3}$$

where $\varphi = \frac{1+\sqrt{5}}{2} \approx 1.161803$ is the golden ratio. This allows parallel computation of all terms without requiring a sequence to be followed.

4.4.1.2 Antidependencies

The following sample code contains a loop-carried antidependence:

```
for(int i = 0; i < N-1; i++)
{
  a[ i ] = a[ i + 1 ] + c;
}
```

We can rewrite the code as:

```
for(int i = 0; i < N-1; i++)
{
  x = a[ i + 1 ];   // S1
  a[ i ] = x + c;   // S2
}
```

The location read by S1 is written to by S2 in the next iteration; thus $S1 \; \delta^a \; S2$.

Antidependencies can be eliminated by providing a copy of the data that need to be read prior to their modification. The outcome for our example is as follows, with the a2 array serving as the repository for the "saved" values of the original:

```
for(int i = 0; i < N-1; i++)
{
  a2[ i ] = a[ i + 1 ];
}

#pragma omp parallel for
for(int i = 0; i < N-1; i++)
{
  a[ i ] = a2[ i ] + c;
}
```

The separate loop that copies the data has no loop-carried dependencies, since the a array is not modified during its execution.

This technique of course entails an additional time and space overhead that needs to be evaluated carefully. The objective is to gauge whether the overhead is justified or offset by the speed-up offered by the parallel execution.

4.4.1.3 Output Dependencies

The following code contains a loop-carried output dependence:

```
for(int i = 0; i < N; i++)
{
  y[i] = a * x[i] + c; // S1
  d = fabs( y[i] );    // S2
}
```

There is also a flow dependence ($S1 \; \delta^f \; S2$), but it is not loop-carried.

Output dependencies can be resolved easily, even if the value that is modified is required after the termination of the parallel for block by making it lastprivate:

```
#pragma omp parallel for shared( a, c ) lastprivate( d )
for(int i = 0; i < N; i++)
{
    y[i] = a * x[i] + c;
    d = fabs( y[i] );
}
```

The lastprivate clause will make the thread executing the last (in sequential order) iteration, to store its private value of d into the location of the external-to-block d.

Listing 4.7 also shows how the output dependence of the following sequential program that calculates the maximum of an array of values can be removed by using a reduction variable:

```
int maxElem = data[0];
for (int i = 1; i < sizeof (data) / sizeof (int); i++)
  if (maxElem < data[i])
    maxElem = data[i];

cout << "Maximum is : " << maxElem << endl;
```

4.4.2 NESTED LOOPS

As of OpenMP 3.0, perfectly nested loops (i.e., with no statement between the successive for) can be parallelized in unison. OpenMP can "collapse" multiple nested loops into a single one and then proceed to partition this derivative loop between the team of threads. The following matrix multiplication sample has two perfectly nested loops:

```
double A[K][L];
double B[L][M];
double C[K][M];
. . .
#pragma omp parallel for collapse(2)
  for (int i = 0; i < K; i++)
    for (int j = 0; j < M; j++)
      {
        C[i][j] = 0;
        for (int k = 0; k < L; k++)
          C[i][j] += A[i][k] * B[k][j];
      }
```

where the collapse clause instructs OpenMP how many of the nested loops should be converted into a single one.

The question is, why would we want to do the collapse in the first place? Multiple reasons can justify such an action:

• The outer loop has too few iterations to balance the workload properly. Imagine if in our matrix multiplication code we had $K = 5, L = 1000$, and $M = 3000$. Parallelizing the outer loop only would translate to having just five work items to give to our threads. How could we evenly distribute these to the eight threads that are the typical team size for quad core hyperthreaded CPUs? The 15,000 work items that would be produced by the collapse are a different story, though.

- It is possible that the execution cost of each loop iteration is different. Collapsed loops are easier to balance in that regard, especially with the clause that we examine in the next section.

4.4.3 SCHEDULING

OpenMP can use a variety of ways to assign iterations to a team of threads in a parallel loop, the motivation being that an ad hoc, even split can yield poor performance if the execution cost of each iteration is not, more or less, the same.

In this section we explain how the available partitioning and scheduling schemes work. To assist in this effort, we assume that the team is made up of p threads and that the total number of iterations, collapsed or otherwise, to be assigned is N. All schemes can have a parameter called chunk_size that determines how the partitioning is done:

- static: In this scheme, the loop is broken into groups of chunk_size iterations. If chunk_size is unspecified, it defaults to $\lceil \frac{N}{p} \rceil$, with the last group possibly being a bit smaller if N is not a multiple of p. The groups are assigned to the threads in a round-robin fashion in the order of the thread number.
- dynamic: This scheme mimics the operation of a dynamic load balancer, where groups of size chunk_size are assigned to the threads on a first-come, first-served basis. A thread executes a group, then requests another, and so on. If chunk_size is unspecified, it defaults to 1.
- guided: The dynamic scheme offers flexibility, but the coordination overhead associated with requesting a new group can deteriorate performance. The guided scheme tries to offset this overhead by using variable-sized groups that shrink over time to allow for load balancing. The group size given out at each new request is equal to the number of *unassigned* iterations divided by p. The chunk_size specifies a lower bound for the size of a group (the very last being an exception, obviously). If chunk_size is unspecified, it defaults to 1. The groups sizes can be determined by the formula:

$$groupSize = min(remainingIter, max(chunk\_size, \lceil \frac{remainingIter}{p} \rceil))$$

Figure 4.7 shows how these schemes work for a few example cases. The dynamic and guided schemes cannot be traced exactly, since the group assignment is taking place during run-time. The group sizes in the guided scheme are of particular interest because they shrink exponentially until the chunk_size limit is reached. The gradually smaller groups serve to fill in gaps in thread utilization.

Upon specifying the scheduling scheme to OpenMP, a programmer has the additional option of setting it to auto, in which case the compiler and/or the OpenMP run-time decide on the best partitioning scheme from the preceding list.

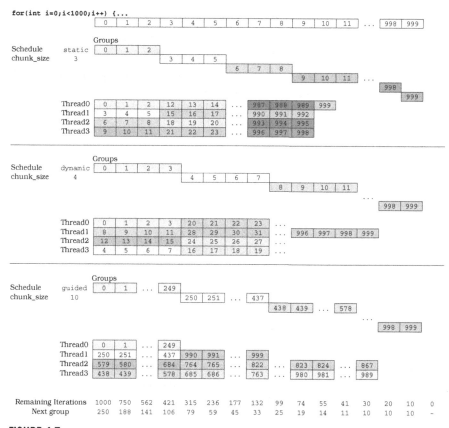

FIGURE 4.7

Examples of resulting iteration partitioning and assignment based on the scheduling scheme for a 1000-iteration `for` loop. We end up with 334 groups for `static`, 250 groups for `dynamic`, and 15 groups for `guided` scheduling for the given `chunk_size` parameters. Only for the `static` scheme do we have *a priori* knowledge of the iteration group assignment to threads.

The programmer can specify the desired scheduling using any of the following methods, going from the most generic to the most specific, the latter always having precedence over the former:

- **The `OMP_SCHEDULE` environmental variable**: This should be set to a string adhering to the form `static | dynamic | guided | auto [, chunk_size ]`. Such a setting potentially affects the execution of all OpenMP programs. Examples:

```
export OMP_SCHEDULE="static,1"      # in BASH
export OMP_SCHEDULE="guided"        # in BASH
setenv OMP_SCHEDULE "dynamic,5"     # in TCSH/CSH
```

- **The** `omp_set_schedule` **function:** The syntax is:

```
void omp_set_schedule(omp_sched_t kind, // Scheduling scheme (IN)
                      int chunk_size);  // (IN)
```

The `omp_sched_t` is just an enumerated type, and the available symbolic constants for the first parameter are `omp_sched_static`, `omp_sched_dynamic`, `omp_sched_guided`, and `omp_sched_auto`. Example:

```
omp_set_schedule(omp_sched_guided, 10);
#pragma omp parallel for
for(...
```

In the absence of a `schedule` clause, this function sets the scheduling for all parallel loops that follow in a program.
- **The** `schedule` **clause:** This `parallel for` exclusive clause accepts parameters in the form `schedule(static | dynamic | guided | auto | runtime [, chunk_size ])`. The `runtime` option delegates the scheduling decision for the execution of the program, where a previous setting (e.g., via `OMP_SCHEDULE`) can be inspected for suggestions. This is exclusive to the `schedule` clause only. Example:

```
#pragma omp parallel for schedule( dynamic )
for(...
```

How can we use these options in a parallel loop? Which is the best schedule option? As long as the iterations do not differ substantially or *unpredictably* in execution cost, the `static` scheme is a safe option. For example, in the following code, the cost increases linearly as *i* increases:

```
#pragma omp parallel for schedule( static , 1 )
for(int i = 1; i <= N; i++)
{
    long sum = 0;
    for(int j = 1; j <= i; j++)
        sum += j;
}
```

but a cyclic distribution of iterations, as dictated by the `chunk_size = 1` option, would assign to each thread the same workload, more or less.[5] If, on the other hand, there is no way to predict the cost of each iteration, a `dynamic` or `guided` option would be more suitable, with the `guided` option being preferable if the resulting number of groups is very high.

Finally, if in doubt, a set of simple tests can reveal the ideal strategy. All we have to do is set:

---

[5]If N is evenly divided by the number of threads p, then the master thread would perform $\frac{N}{p} + N\frac{(\frac{N}{p}-1)}{2}$ additions, and the $(p-1)$-th child thread would perform $N + N\frac{(\frac{N}{p}-1)}{2}$ additions. Thus the maximum imbalance would be $N - \frac{N}{p}$ additions. So, this clearly depends on the values of N and p.

```
#pragma omp parallel for schedule( runtime )
for(. . .
```

and time multiple executions of the program, each with a different OMP_SCHEDULE setting. A recompilation would not be required. The following BASH script could automate the whole process:

```
#!/bin/bash
# File : schedule_script.sh

for scheme in static dynamic guided
do
    for chunk in 1 2 4 8 16 32
        do
            export OMP_SCHEDULE="${scheme},${chunk}"
            echo $OMP_SCHEDULE '/usr/bin/time -o tmp.log -p $1 >/dev/null;↵
                head -n 1 tmp.log | gawk '{print $2}' ' >> $2
        done
done
```

The script uses the time command to measure the overall execution time of the target program. Subsequently, the head and gawk filters extract the measurement in seconds from the output of the time command.

All that is required is that the user passes the name of the executable, and the name of the file for storing the results, as parameters to the script, as in:

```
$ ./schedule_script.sh ./myProg timingResults.csv
```

Each scheduling option can be tested multiple times if required by nesting a third loop in the script for this purpose.

4.5 TASK PARALLELISM

The parallel for directive can assist in the parallelization of a data parallel program, i.e., a program where concurrency is derived from processing disjoint subsets of data in parallel. Any data dependencies can spoil this recipe, and that is why we addressed this issue exclusively in Section 4.4.1. On the other hand, we have instances of programs whereby multiple actions can potentially take place at the same time, not necessarily involving a particular dataset. We call these programs function or task parallel (see Section 2.3.1).

OpenMP can support this functionality via the parallel directive, but dedicated directives also exist, to avoid having to introduce control logic similar to the following:

```
#pragma omp parallel
switch( omp_get_thread_num() )
{
  case 0:
    ...
}
```

into a program.

There is nothing particularly wrong about this logic. It is perfectly legal, and we have already employed something similar in our first two versions of the integration program in Section 4.3. The additional feature that the dedicated "tasking" work-sharing constructs offer, apart from a cleaner code structure, is that they decouple the task description from the task execution. OpenMP may execute the different tasks at different points in time, based on the availability of cores and their execution cost.

4.5.1 THE sections DIRECTIVE

The sections directive is a means for specifying to OpenMP, a list of code blocks that are to be executed in parallel. The sections directive (like the for one) can appear as an element of a parallel region or in combination with a parallel pragma as a shortcut:

```
#pragma omp parallel
{
...
#pragma omp sections
    ...
}

// OR

#pragma omp parallel sections
{
    ...
}
```

The individual blocks that make up a sections directive are defined by embedding one or more section directives:

```
#pragma omp parallel sections
{
#pragma omp section
    {
        // concurrent block 0
    }
...
#pragma omp section
    {
        // concurrent block M-1
    }
}
```

The sections directive can have the same optional clauses as the parallel directive, e.g., shared, private, num_threads, etc. The included section directives cannot have any clauses, so any required clause additions should be done at the sections level.

When OpenMP processes a `sections` directive, it starts a number of threads that execute the section blocks concurrently. The assignment of sections to threads is implementation-specific. There is no restriction between the team size and the number of sections. If the team is bigger than the number of sections, some threads will remain idle, whereas if the the number of sections exceeds the size of the team, there will be an OpenMP implementation-specific[6] mapping of sections to threads. There is an implicit barrier at the end of a `sections` block, which means that the statements following it will execute only when all the individual `section` blocks are complete.

In the following section we solve the producers-consumers problem, as an application of the `sections` directive.

4.5.1.1 Producers-Consumers in OpenMP

The problem setting is thoroughly established in Section 3.5.1, where we also summarize the semaphore-based solution guidelines (see Table 3.3). OpenMP provides its own implementations of a binary semaphore in the form of the `omp_lock_t` and `omp_nest_lock_t` datatypes. The two types of locks provided are: simple and nestable. The latter is the same as a recursive lock, i.e., a lock that can be locked multiple times by the same thread. (For more details, see Section 3.4.)

A lock can be in one of three states: uninitialized, locked, and unlocked. OpenMP includes functions for initializing, setting (locking), unsetting (unlocking), testing, and destroying locks[7]:

```
// Initializes an instance of the omp_lock_t structure. It should be
// called prior to any operations with a lock.
void omp_init_lock(omp_lock_t *lock);

// Destroys a lock. Clean-up call at the end of a lock's use.
void omp_destroy_lock(omp_lock_t *lock);

// Acquires a lock. This is a blocking call.
void omp_set_lock(omp_lock_t *lock);

// Releases a lock. This is a non-blocking call.
void omp_unset_lock(omp_lock_t *lock);

// Acquires the lock and returns true if the lock is unlocked.
// Otherwise, false is returned. This is a non-blocking call.
int omp_test_lock(omp_lock_t *lock);
```

However, the omission of a general or counting semaphore implementation is a weak point of the standard. The creation of one is not a big challenge, since all that are required are two binary semaphores and a counter, but it is a hassle we can do without. Fortunately, we can combine OpenMP and Qt without any problem.

---

[6]This means that the standard does not specify or enforce a specific behavior in that regard.
[7]There is a matching set of functions for nestable locks.

The only requirement is the inclusion of the `-fopenmp` flag in the compiler switches, as specified in the Qt's project file. The following example, with the addition of the `QMAKE_CXXFLAGS` and `QMAKE_LFLAGS` lines, accomplishes just that:

```
SOURCES += prodCons.cpp
TARGET = prodCons
CONFIG += qt
QMAKE_CXXFLAGS += -fopenmp
QMAKE_LFLAGS += -fopenmp
```

The combination of OpenMP and Qt allows us to use the former for thread management while taking advantage of the rich library of classes provided by the latter. The use of the "native" OpenMP locks can be a fall back for platforms where Qt is not available.

Listing 4.18 presents a single-producer, multiple-consumers-based program for integrating a function. As discussed in Section 3.5.1, a semaphore-based solution requires two counting semaphores for safely counting space and available items in the shared buffer and one binary semaphore for coordinating consumer access to the "output" index (variable `out`).

```
1   // File : prod_cons/prodCons.cpp
2   . . .
3   #include <omp.h>
4   #include <QSemaphore>
5   #include <QMutex>
6
7   using namespace std;
8
9   const int BUFFSIZE = 10;
10  const double LOWERLIMIT = 0;
11  const double UPPERLIMIT = 10;
12
13  const int NUMCONSUMERS = 2;
14  //————————————————————————————————————
15  typedef struct Slice
16  {
17    double start;
18    double end;
19    int divisions;
20  } Slice;
21  //————————————————————————————————————
22  double func (double x)
23  {
24    return fabs (sin (x));
25  }
26
27  //————————————————————————————————————
28  void integrCalc (Slice * buffer, QSemaphore &buffSlots, QSemaphore &↵
        avail, QMutex &l, int &out, QMutex &resLock, double &res)
29  {
```

```
30     while (1)
31       {
32         avail.acquire ();          // wait for an available item
33         l.lock ();
34         int tmpOut = out;
35         out = (out + 1) % BUFFSIZE;          // update the out index
36         l.unlock ();
37
38         // take the item out
39         double st = buffer[tmpOut].start;
40         double en = buffer[tmpOut].end;
41         double div = buffer[tmpOut].divisions;
42
43         buffSlots.release ();      // signal for a new empty slot
44
45         if (div == 0)
46           break;                        // exit
47
48         //calculate area
49         double localRes = 0;
50         double step = (en - st) / div;
51         double x;
52         x = st;
53         localRes = func (st) + func (en);
54         localRes /= 2;
55         for (int i = 1; i < div; i++)
56           {
57             x += step;
58             localRes += func (x);
59           }
60         localRes *= step;
61
62         // add it to result
63         resLock.lock ();
64         res += localRes;
65         resLock.unlock ();
66       }
67   }
68
69   //────────────────────────────────────────
70   int main (int argc, char **argv)
71   {
72     if (argc == 1)
73       {
74         cerr << "Usage " << argv[0] << " #jobs\n";
75         exit (1);
76       }
77     int J = atoi (argv[1]);
78     Slice *buffer = new Slice[BUFFSIZE];
79     int in = 0, out = 0;
80     QSemaphore avail, buffSlots (BUFFSIZE);
81     QMutex l, integLock;
```

```
82     double integral = 0;
83  #pragma omp parallel sections default(none) \
84                    shared(buffer, in, out, \
85                    avail, buffSlots, 1, \
86                    integLock, integral, J)
87     {
88  // producer part
89  #pragma omp section
90      {
91        // producer thread, responsible for handing out 'jobs'
92        double divLen = (UPPERLIMIT - LOWERLIMIT) / J;
93        double st, end = LOWERLIMIT;
94        for (int i = 0; i < J; i++)
95          {
96            st = end;
97            end += divLen;
98            if (i == J - 1)
99              end = UPPERLIMIT;
100
101            buffSlots.acquire ();
102            buffer[in].start = st;
103            buffer[in].end = end;
104            buffer[in].divisions = 1000;
105            in = (in + 1) % BUFFSIZE;
106            avail.release ();
107          }
108
109        // put termination sentinels in buffer
110        for (int i = 0; i < NUMCONSUMERS; i++)
111          {
112            buffSlots.acquire ();
113            buffer[in].divisions = 0;
114            in = (in + 1) % BUFFSIZE;
115            avail.release ();
116          }
117      }
118
119  // 1st consumer part
120  #pragma omp section
121      {
122        integrCalc (buffer, buffSlots, avail, 1, out, integLock, ↵
               integral);
123      }
124
125
126  // 2nd consumer part
127  #pragma omp section
128      {
129        integrCalc (buffer, buffSlots, avail, 1, out, integLock, ↵
               integral);
130      }
131    }
```

```
132
133      cout << "Result is : " << integral << endl;
134      delete [] buffer;
135
136      return 0;
137    }
```

LISTING 4.18

Multithreaded integration of a function using the sections directive. The producer thread uses "messages" to terminate the consumer threads. Each of the "parties" (producer or consumer) to the program has its own dedicated section.

This program follows the same guidelines for load assignment/balancing and termination as Listing 3.12, allowing direct comparison between the Qt and the OpenMP solutions. The key points of this program are as follows:

- The parallel region is enclosed in the block between lines 87 and 131, headed by the sections directive. The items to be shared between the producer and consumer threads are explicitly listed in the shared clause of line 84. This would include even std:cout, if it were to be used.
- As in Listing 3.12, we have a producer thread that generates a sequence of Slice structure instances, each representing a part of the integration range. These are deposited in a shared buffer. The producer thread runs the block between lines 89 and 117. The producer thread also flags the end of the computation to the consumer threads by enqueuing Slice instances with the number of divisions set to 0.
- In the Qt program of Listing 3.12, the main thread also serves as a producer. In the preceding program, the OpenMP run-time selects the team thread that will execute the producer section.
- The consumer threads have to be explicitly listed as separate section-headed blocks. For the reason, we do not have the flexibility of dynamically specifying the number of consumer threads, as we did in Listing 3.12.
- To shorten the consumer section parts, the consumer code is delegated to the integrCalc() function of lines 28-67. All the data items that need to be shared between the threads (e.g., semaphores, indices, the data buffer, etc.) are passed by reference to the function.
- The code in function integrCalc() is an almost verbatim copy of the consumer thread code of Listing 3.12. The consumer threads keep retrieving Slice instances from the shared buffer, calculating the corresponding area (lines 49-60) and accumulating the results in a shared variable that is accessed inside a critical section (lines 63-65). The function terminates upon retrieving a Slice structure with the number of divisions set to zero (lines 45-46).
- The critical section of lines 63-65 could be also established with a critical directive, as:

```
#pragma omp critical
        res += localRes;
```

The need to have multiple `section` blocks, even if the desired threads are supposed to execute the same code, is a shortcoming of the `sections` work-sharing construct. A solution to this problem exists, and it is described in the next section.

4.5.2 THE `task` DIRECTIVE

The `task` directive was originally introduced as part of the OpenMP 3.0 standard. OpenMP has been always working internally with "tasks," the term referring to entities consisting of:

- **Code**: A block of statements designated to be executed concurrently.
- **Data**: A set of variables or data owned by the task (e.g., local variables).
- **Thread Reference**: References the thread (if any) executing the task.

OpenMP performs two activities related to tasks:

- **Packaging**: Creating a structure to describe a task entity.
- **Execution**: Assigning a task to a thread.

The `task` directive allows the decoupling of these two activities, which means that *tasks can be dynamically created and queued for later execution*. This not only solves the problem of creating a variable number of concurrent blocks, as expressed in the previous section; it also opens up a rich set of additional possibilities.

The syntax of the `task` directive is:

```
#pragma omp task [clause *]
{
    // Block of code to be assigned to a thread
}
```

where the clauses (apart from the scope clauses listed in Section 4.3) of the optional list are examined later in this section.

As an example, we examine the problem of traversing a linked list of data and applying an operation on each item. An array could be easily handled by a `parallel for` construct, but a linked list demands a sequential traversal. What the `task` construct allows us to do is to conform to a sequential traversal while spinning off threads to process concurrently the items that are discovered, as shown in Listing 4.19.

```
1  // File : linked_list.cpp
2  . . .
3  // template structure for a list's node
4  template <class T>
5  struct Node
```

```
6   {
7     T info;
8     Node *next;
9   };
10  //——————————————————————————————
11  // Appends a value at the end of a list pointed by the head *h
12  template <class T>
13  void append (int v, Node<T> ** h)
14  {
15    Node<T> *tmp = new Node<T> ();
16    tmp->info = v;
17    tmp->next = NULL;
18
19    Node<T> *aux = *h;
20    if (aux == NULL)                // first node in list
21      *h = tmp;
22    else
23      {
24        while (aux->next != NULL)
25          aux = aux->next;
26        aux->next = tmp;
27      }
28  }
29
30  //——————————————————————————————
31  // function stub for processing a node's data
32  template <class T>
33  void process (Node<T> * p)
34  {
35  #pragma omp critical
36    cout << p->info << " by thread " << omp_get_thread_num () << endl;
37  }
38
39  //——————————————————————————————
40  int main (int argc, char *argv[])
41  {
42    // build a sample list
43    Node<int> *head = NULL;
44    append (1, &head);
45    append (2, &head);
46    append (3, &head);
47    append (4, &head);
48    append (5, &head);
49
50  #pragma omp parallel
51    {
52  #pragma omp single
53      {
54        Node<int> *tmp = head;
55        while (tmp != NULL)
56          {
57  #pragma omp task
```

```
58              process (tmp);
59              tmp = tmp->next;
60          }
61      }
62  }
63
64  return 0;
65  }
```

LISTING 4.19

Multithreaded processing of a linked list's elements, using the task directive.

A task directive should normally reside inside a parallel directive. Otherwise, the generated task is undeferred, i.e., it is executed sequentially by the master thread. This is the justification for nesting the task directive inside a parallel construct on the listing.

A new pragma is used in line 52: the single directive. The single directive is typically used in combination with a parallel directive to limit a block of code to single-threaded execution. So, while the outer parallel directive of line 50 sets up the multithreaded execution of the whole block, the single directive forces a sequential traversal of the linked list with the while loop of lines 55-60.

The traversal is done in sequence, but the processing of the data items is performed in parallel via the task directive of line 57. We cannot be certain about when, or by which thread, the actual processing of a node will take place. But we do know that when the parallel region finishes, all the generated tasks would have completed as well due to the implicit barrier at the end of the parallel block.

However, there is an issue that we bypassed: How many tasks are we allowed to generate? If the linked list had one million elements, would it make sense to generate one million tasks in one go? Does OpenMP have the appropriate structures for accommodating such a scenario? Would it even be sensible to have something like this, even if it were possible?

OpenMP addresses this issue in two ways: First, the OpenMP run-time may suspend the generating task and execute one or more of the generated tasks if the task "pool" grows too big. Second, the programmer may direct OpenMP to suspend the current task and execute the generated task. A number of clauses that can accompany the task-directive, can control this behavior.

The clauses that affect the scheduling of tasks are:

- if(scalar-expression): If the expression evaluates to 0, the generated task becomes *undeferred*, i.e., the current task is suspended, until the generated task completes execution. The generated task may be executed by a different thread.

An undeferred task that is executed *immediately* by the thread that generated it is called an *included task*.

- `final(scalar-expression)`: When the expression evaluates to true, the task and all its child tasks (i.e., other tasks that can be generated by its execution) become *final* and *included*. This means that a task and all its descendants will be executed by a single thread.
- `untied`: A task is by default tied to a thread. If it gets suspended, it will wait for the particular thread to run it again, even if there are other idle threads. This, in principle, creates better CPU cache utilization. If the `untied` clause is given, a task may resume execution on any free thread.
- `mergeable`: A *merged task* is a task that shares the data environment of the task that generated it. If the `mergeable` clause is present and an undeferred task is generated (via an `if` or `final` clause), then OpenMP may generate a merged task.

All types of undeferred tasks can suppress runaway programs from generating an extraordinary number of *pending* tasks. Listing 4.20 calculates a term of the Fibonacci sequence using the recursive definition. To spice things up, each recursive call constitutes a task.

```
1   // File : fibo.cpp
2   . . .
3   int fib (int i)
4   {
5     int t1, t2;
6     if (i == 0 || i == 1)
7       return 1;
8     else
9       {
10  #pragma omp task shared(t1) if(i>25) mergeable
11          t1 = fib (i - 1);
12  #pragma omp task shared(t2) if(i>25) mergeable
13          t2 = fib (i - 2);
14  #pragma omp taskwait
15          return t1 + t2;
16      }
17  }
18
19  //————————————————————————
20  int main (int argc, char *argv[])
21  {
22    // build a sample list
23    int N = atoi (argv[1]);
24
25  #pragma omp parallel
26    {
27  #pragma omp single
```

```
28      {
29          cout << fib (N) << endl;
30      }
31  }
32
33      return 0;
34  }
```

LISTING 4.20

OpenMP-based calculation of the N-th term of the Fibonacci sequence using a task work-sharing construct.

As in our linked-list example, the main function sets up a parallel region with the pragma of line 25 and starts a single thread (with the `single` directive of line 27) to call the recursive function and print the result. The `fib` function generates two new tasks for calculating the two previous terms `t1` and `t2`, with the `task` constructs of lines 10 and 12. Summing up these two terms in line 15 requires that the corresponding tasks are complete. There is an implicit barrier at the end of the parallel region, but this is obviously not sufficient. The `taskwait` directive of line 14 is a barrier for the child tasks of the current task, so it just ensures that `t1` and `t2` have been computed regardless of what is taking place in other tasks.

The `if` clauses of lines 10 and 12 produce undeferred tasks if the `i` parameter goes below 26, which limits the size of the task pool (the 25 threshold is arbitrary, just for our tests). The `mergeable` clause potentially reduces the memory management overhead associated with the child tasks, since it permits them to use the data environment of the current task.

An extra optimization to Listing 4.20 would be the elimination of line 12 (the pragma, not the block it controls). Because the thread generating the child tasks will become idle until the barrier of line 14 is reached, it makes sense to simply let it compute the second term `t2`.

Of course, the optimality of this program is not in question; it is desperately inefficient! If we did eliminate the pragma of line 12, we would have, for the calculation of the N-th Fibonacci term, the generation of $t(N)$ child tasks, with:

$$t(N) = 1 + t(N-1) + t(N-2) \tag{4.4}$$

with $t(0) = 0$ and $t(1) = 0$. The 1 term is contributed by the task directive of line 10, and $t(N-1)$ and $t(N-2)$ by the recursion.

This recurrence relation produces the sequence 0,0,1,2,4,7,12,..., which is just the Fibonacci sequence with terms reduced by 1:

$$t(N) = F(N) - 1 \tag{4.5}$$

As an illustration of how significant the `if` clause can be in our extreme example, calculating $F(40)$ can take less than 1 sec with the `if(i>25)` and `mergeable` clauses and around 108 sec without them,[8] the result of having to schedule a total of 165,580,140 child tasks!

This extreme example serves just one purpose: to raise awareness that dynamic generation of tasks does not come free. It is justified as long as we can create enough tasks to keep the cores of the execution platform busy.

Naturally, the task construct is the primary tool for modeling function-parallel programs in OpenMP. Such programs, though, typically have dependencies between the different tasks and functions that can be expressed in the form of a dependency graph. Such dependencies, which essentially translate into an execution precedence, can be enforced through the use of binary semaphores.

Alternatively, since OpenMP 4.0, the standard supports the capability to declare and enforce such dependencies with the depend clause. Dependencies can only be established between sibling tasks, i.e., tasks generated by the same parent task. The syntax of the depend clause is:

```
#pragma omp task [ depend( dependence-type : list ) ]
{
   ...
}
```

where the list contains one or more variable identifiers and/or array sections. The list should contains data items that are either input to the task or the result of the task computation. The dependence-type describes the nature of these data items by being one of the following:

- in: The task is dependent on all *previously generated sibling* tasks that reference at least one of the list items in an out or inout dependency type.
- out, inout: The task is dependent on all *previously generated sibling* tasks that reference at least one of the list items in an in, out, or inout dependency type.

Listing 4.21 shows the use of a loop to generate multiple tasks, with T2 and T3 dependent on T1.

```
1   // File : depend_test.cpp
2   . . .
3   #pragma omp parallel
4   #pragma omp single
5      {
6        for (int i = 0; i < 3; ++i)
7           {
8   #pragma omp task shared(x) depend(out: x)
9             // T1
10            printf ("T1 %i\n", i);
11  #pragma omp task shared(x) depend(in: x)
12            // T2
13            printf ("T2 %i\n", i);
```

[8] As tested on a i7-4700HQ, 2.40 GHz CPU with the GNU C++ 4.9.1 compiler and the -02 compiler switch.

```
14  #pragma omp task shared(x) depend(in: x)
15          // T3
16          printf ("T3 %i\n", i);
17      }
18  }
19  . . .
```

LISTING 4.21

An example of establishing dependent tasks using the `depend` clause. This program requires a compiler implementing OpenMP 4.0 to compile successfully.

It is worthwhile to note that the variable x used in the `depend` clauses does not appear in the tasks' blocks. The `for` loop is executed by a single thread, and while the order of T2 and T3 may be switched (T3 may output before T2), T1 has to be complete before any of them can begin execution. Additionally, there is an inter-iteration dependence among T1, T2, and T3: T1 during the second iteration cannot begin before the T2 and T3 tasks generated during the first iteration finish. The same is true for the third iteration because T1 then has to wait for the T2 and T3 that were generated during the second iteration. A sample output of this program is shown here. The clustering of the tasks generated during an iteration verifies our discussion:

```
$ ./depend_test
T1  0
T3  0
T2  0
T1  1
T2  1
T3  1
T1  2
T3  2
T2  2
```

4.6 SYNCHRONIZATION CONSTRUCTS

Shared-memory, parallel-program correctness hinges on the ability to perform changes to shared data items in a coordinated fashion. OpenMP provides a number of synchronization directives that serve two purposes: mutual exclusion and event synchronization.

The mutual exclusion directives ensure that certain blocks of code will be executed as critical sections. This category of directives includes:

- `critical`: Allows only one thread at a time to enter the structured block that follows. The syntax involves an optional identifier:

```
#pragma omp critical [ ( identifier ) ]
{
    // structured block
}
```

The identifier allows the establishment of *named critical sections*. The identifier serves to group critical sections together. Using the same identifier in different critical directives means that there can be only one thread at any time executing any of the corresponding blocks. All critical directives without an identifier are assumed to have the same name. We can think of grouped critical constructs as using the same mutex.

Obviously, explicitly naming the critical constructs can provide better performance, since it allows threads executing disjoint critical sections to do so concurrently.

- atomic: This is a lightweight version of the critical construct that uses platform-specific atomic machine instructions (such as the Intel x86 CMPXCHG Compare and Exchange) to accelerate the execution of single-statement critical sections. Given that the statement should correlate closely with an atomic CPU instruction, the operations that can be "decorated" by an atomic directive are very limited.[9] These operations are:

```
x++;
x--;
++x;
--x;
x binop= expr;
x = x binop expr;
x = expr binop x;
```

where x has to be a variable of scalar type; binop can be one of these:

```
+, *, -, /, &, ^, |, << , or >>
```

and expr is a scalar expression.

Caution should be used in the calculation of the expr. In the following example:

```
#pragma omp atomic
    x += y++;
```

although the update to the x variable is atomic, the update to the y variable is not, and thus it could be the possible cause of a race condition. In that case a critical directive should be used instead.

- master: Forces only the master thread in a parallel region to execute a block of code. The master directive has no associated clauses and no implied barrier on entry to or on exit from the corresponding block. This means that when a thread other than the master reaches this construct, it just skips over it.

The master directive can be reserved for I/O operations, such as updating the program status on the console, as in the following example:

```
int examined = 0;
int prevReported = 0;
#pragma omp for shared( examined, prevReported )
    for( int i = 0 ; i < N ; i++ )
```

---

[9]The atomic directive has a number of optional clauses that extend the types of statements that it can pair with. The OpenMP specification contains more details [37].

```
    {
        // some processing

        // update the counter
#pragma omp atomic
        examined++;

        // use the master to output an update every 1000 newly ↩
            finished iterations
#pragma omp master
        {
            int temp = examined;
            if( temp − prevReported >= 1000)
            {
                prevReported = temp;
                printf("Examined %.2lf%%\n", temp * 1.0 / N );
            }
        }
    }
```

- single: Forces the execution of a block by one thread only. It is similar to the master directive, but for the implicit barrier at the end of the single block, which means that the two constructs are not interchangeable in general. The barrier can be eliminated by adding the nowait clause to the single directive. We have seen multiple examples of the single directive in the previous sections, so we are repeating our discussion here for completeness. The single directive is typically paired with a parallel construct to limit the execution of certain parts of the code to one thread only. Notably, this problem does not exist with the sections or task constructs, since each thread is assigned specific work in these cases.

  In Listing 4.22, the processing of some arbitrary data can start only after they are read from a file. The single directive assigns this task to one of the team threads.

```
double data[ N ];
#pragma omp parallel shared( data, N )
{

#pragma omp single
    {
        // read data from a file
    }

#pragma omp for
    for(int i = 0; i < N; i++)
        {
            // process the data
        }
}
```

LISTING 4.22

An example of using the single directive to perform I/O prior to the processing of some data.

Could we possibly do the same with a `master` directive? The answer is given in the following discussion of the `barrier` directive.

The second category of synchronization directives deals with events that include coordination, data consistency, and operation ordering:

- `barrier`: Explicit barrier directive that ensures threads begin or continue work after some point in time where certain conditions are met. All threads in a team must reach the `barrier` directive before execution can continue beyond that point. The `barrier` directive has no associated block. It is just placed inside an OpenMP work-sharing construct.

  The code in Listing 4.22 could be modified to use the `master` directive if an explicit barrier forced all team threads to wait until the data have been read:

```
double data[ N ];
#pragma omp parallel shared( data , N )
{

#pragma omp master
   {
      // read data from a file
   }

#pragma omp barrier

#pragma omp for
   for(int i = 0; i < N; i++)
      {
         // process the data
      }
}
```

- `taskwait`: This is the `barrier` equivalent for tasks generated from a particular parent task. Although the `barrier` directive applies to a team of *threads*, the `taskwait` directive applies to a group of *tasks*.

  Listing 4.23 shows how we can utilize `taskwait` for the post-order traversal of a binary tree. In a post-order traversal, a node is processed only after all its children have been processed.

```
1   // File : tree_postOrder.cpp
2   . . .
3   // template structure for a tree node
4   template < class T > struct Node
5   {
6     T info;
7     Node *left, *right;
8
9       Node (int i, Node < T > *l, Node < T > *r) :
10                 info (i), left (l), right (r) { }
11  };
12
13  //─────────────────────────────────
```

```
14   // function stub for processing a node's data
15   template < class T > void process (T item)
16   {
17   #pragma omp critical
18     cout << "Processing " << item << " by thread " << ↵
               omp_get_thread_num () << endl;
19   }
20
21   //————————————————————————————————
22   template < class T > void postOrder (Node < T > *n)
23   {
24     if (n == NULL)
25       return;
26
27   #pragma omp task
28     postOrder (n->left);
29   #pragma omp task
30     postOrder (n->right);
31   #pragma omp taskwait
32
33     process (n->info);
34   }
35
36   //————————————————————————————————
37   int main (int argc, char *argv[])
38   {
39     // build a sample tree
40     Node < int >*head =
41     . . .
42
43   #pragma omp parallel
44     {
45   #pragma omp single
46       {
47         postOrder (head);
48       }
49     }
50
51     return 0;
52   }
```

LISTING 4.23

A post-order traversal of a binary tree.

The `parallel` pragma of line 43 sets up the multithreaded execution of the structured block that follows. Although the `single` directive limits to one the calls to the `postOrder()` function, this in turn creates two new tasks to handle the two children of a node (via the `task` directives in lines 27 and 29). The recursive nature of the postOrder() function means that we eventually get one task for every node in the tree. As discussed earlier, we can limit the "explosion" of task creation by using the if or final clauses in the task directives, but this is not the essence of our example.

In order to force a post-order traversal, the tasks associated with the children of a node must be complete prior to processing the node itself via the call of line 33. The taskwait directive of line 31 ensures just that by blocking the execution of the current task running the postOrder() function until all the child tasks it spawned are complete.

- ordered: Used inside a parallel for region to enforce the sequential execution of the structured block it heads. So, although the iterations of a for loop maybe partitioned according to the schedule clause and assigned to different threads to execute out of order, the ordered block has to execute as though it were done sequentially. This also means that threads executing iterations that follow in order have to block until the ordered block of the previous iterations are complete.

Any type of schedule can be used in a parallel for that contains an ordered directive. The only restriction is that the parallel for must have an ordered clause specified. However, if the ordered block is executed in every iteration, a static or dynamic schedule with a chunk size of 1 should maximize the concurrency potential. On the other hand, a guided schedule will result in a mostly sequential execution.

It should be noted that the ordered directive does not have to be *lexically* included in a parallel for. It can just as well be in a function that is called by the loop. The ordered clause should still be included in the for pragma. A for directive with an ordered clause suffers no consequence if it does not encounter an ordered block during the execution of its body.

In the following example, we use the ordered directive to ensure that the program's output matches the one produced by the corresponding sequential program:

```
double data[ N ];
#pragma omp parallel shared( data , N )
{

#pragma omp for ordered schedule( static , 1 )
  for( int i = 0; i < N; i++)
    {
        // process the data

        // print the results in order
#pragma omp ordered
        cout << data[i];
    }
}
```

- flush: Used to make a thread's view of *shared data*[10] *consistent* with main memory. This is an odd statement that requires clarification. Shared data are stored in main memory locations that are supposed to be accessible by all threads. One would expect that reading or writing to these variables involves data transfer from or modification of the corresponding memory locations. Alas, CPU caches and/or compiler optimizations cause deviations from these expectations: Shared data may be held in disjoint, CPU-specific cache memories or even CPU registers for faster access.

So, when a shared variable is modified, this modification may not propagate to the appropriate main memory location immediately. A thread running on another core may get "stale" data if it tries to access this variable before the other CPU's cache and the main memory become consistent again.

The flush directive is like a *memory fence*: All memory operations initiated before the flush, must complete before the flush can complete, i.e., the modifications have to propagate from the cache or registers to main memory. All operations that follow the flush directive cannot commence until the flush is complete.

The flush is a standalone directive that affects only the thread that executes it. It is only accompanied by an optional list of variables that will be restored to a consistent state:

```
#pragma omp flush [ ( list_of_variables ) ]
```

If the list is missing, *all* thread-visible data return to a consistent state. Both the modified and the unchanged data by a thread are affected; the modified data have to be stored to the main memory *before* the flush can complete, and the unchanged data have to be read again from the main memory (refreshed) *after* the flush is complete.

An implicit flush operation takes place when one of the following occurs:
- A barrier directive
- Upon entry to and exit from a parallel, critical and ordered regions
- Upon exit from a worksharing region unless a nowait clause is specified
- Upon entry to and exit from an atomic operation
- During any OpenMP lock operation that causes the lock to be set or unset (e.g., omp_set_lock, omp_test_lock, etc.)
- Immediately before and immediately after every task-scheduling point

The extent of this list means that under normal circumstances, an explicit flush directive is not necessary. The flush directive is a low-level synchronization directive because it affects one thread only. This is both an asset, since it can be

---

[10]It actually involves all thread-visible data, but it is only the shared ones that are of any consequence. It makes absolutely no difference to a thread, what is the state of automatic, private, or threadprivate variables of other threads : it cannot "see" them. That is why we limit our discussion on shared variables.

used to optimize coordination between subsets of threads, and a drawback, since it demands careful design in order to avoid logical programming errors. In Listing 4.24, we use the `flush` directive to send a signal between two threads.

```
1    // File : flush_test.cpp
2    . . .
3      bool flag = false;
4    #pragma omp parallel sections default( none ) shared( flag , cout )
5      {
6
7    #pragma omp section
8        {
9            // wait for signal
10           while (flag == false)
11           {
12   #pragma omp flush ( flag )
13           }
14           // do something
15           cout << "First section\n";
16       }
17
18   #pragma omp section
19       {
20           // do something first
21           cout << "Second section\n";
22           sleep (1);
23           // signal other section
24           flag = true;
25
26   #pragma omp flush ( flag )
27
28       }
29     }
```

LISTING 4.24

Using the `flush` directive to propagate a signal in the form of a shared boolean between two threads.

The first `flush` directive in line 12 ensures that an updated value for `flag` is fetched every time from the main memory. The second directive in line 26 makes the main memory consistent with the updated state of the `flag` boolean. Wouldn't this work without the `flush` directives? This is a question that cannot be answered outside the context of a particular execution platform. We have to know how the target platform treats cache updates. The `flush` directive allows us to keep memory consistent, in a cross-platform way, without considering the restrictions of the underlying machine.

4.7 CORRECTNESS AND OPTIMIZATION ISSUES

The issues addressed in this section are not unique to OpenMP. In fact, they are generic concerns for all shared-memory parallel programs. They are especially relevant to OpenMP, because in OpenMP, the development process frequently starts from a sequential program, not from a design specifically targeting parallel execution. These issues are thread safety and false sharing.

4.7.1 THREAD SAFETY

A function or method (or even a block of code in general) is called *thread-safe* if it can be executed concurrently by several threads without any problems.

Thread-safe functions are also mistakenly called reentrant, although these are two different qualities. A *reentrant* function can be interrupted while being executed and then safely called again (reentered) before the previous call or calls are complete. Reentrancy is a concept usually associated with operating system code (like interrupt handlers) and does not deal with concurrency. A function can be thread-safe or reentrant, or both, or neither of the two.

Although being reentrant does not a thread-safe function make, a reentrant function does a good job of isolating its inner workings from the outside world. This is a desirable feature for multithreaded programs. Usually, making a function reentrant is a step toward making it thread-safe also.

An analogy that allows us to capture the essence of these two properties is the baking recipe one: Imagine that a function is a cake recipe, and several chefs are using it (our threads). A reentrant function would allow the chefs to go about their business as long as they use their own materials and cooking utensils (input data). A chef may interrupt his or her preparation and come back to it at a later time without any issue. On the other hand, a thread-safe recipe would allow the chefs to work concurrently while sharing the oven or other resources (shared data). If a chef can lock the common oven and leave, thread safety is preserved, but the recipe is not reentrant. Unless the chef using the oven returns, the other chefs cannot bake a cake.

The conditions that need to be met by a **reentrant** function are [2]:

- The function should not use `static` or global data, i.e., data that are persistent between calls. Global data may be accessed (e.g., hardware status registers), but they should not be modified unless atomic operations are used.
- In the case of an object method, either the method is an accessor method (does not change the state of the object, also known as a *getter*), or it is a mutator (or *setter*) method, in which case the object should be modified inside a critical section.
- All data required by the function should be provided by the caller. If a program calls a function multiple times with the same arguments, it is the responsibility of the caller to ensure that the calls are properly done. For example, the `qsort_r` C-library function is a reentrant implementation of the quicksort algorithm, which allows additional information to be passed in the form of a pointer to the

comparison function without having to use global data. If two threads call this function with the same input array, the results cannot be predicted:

```cpp
// File : reentrant_test.cpp
// Comparison function for int. The extra argument is unused
int comp(const void *x, const void *y, void *extra)
{
  int a = *(int *)x;
  int b = *(int *)y;
  return a-b;
}
. . .

  int *data = new int[N];

  // populate the array

#pragma omp parallel num_threads(2)
  {
    qsort_r(data, N, sizeof(int), comp, NULL);
  }

// data may not be sorted!
. . .
```

- The function does not return pointers to static data. If an array needs to be returned, it can be either dynamically allocated or provided by the caller.
- The function does not call any non-reentrant functions.
- The function does not modify its code unless private copies of the code are used in each invocation.

The requirement for making a function thread-safe is rather simple: Provide *linearizable* access (see Section 3.3) to shared data. Whenever a function modifies a shared resource (e.g., a file pointer, a global object, etc.), changes need to be performed in a way that would be consistent with a sequential program. This can be accomplished using a critical section. Critical sections can be built via an OpenMP lock, a `critical` construct, condition variables, or the like.

The `qsort_r` function is just one of many reentrant alternatives to standard C-library functions that are not safe to use in multithreaded programs. A programmer should be aware of the availability of these functions and switch the program code to using them instead. Front-end functions with locks can be used in the case where reentrant variants are not available, although this comes at a significant performance penalty.

For example, Listing 4.25 using the non-reentrant `strtok`[11] parsing function achieves thread safety by blocking access to `strtok` while it is being used, effectively making the program sequential.

---

[11] `strtok` is not reentrant because it stores a reference to the string being tokenized between successive calls.

```cpp
1   // File : thrsafe_strtok.cpp
2   . . .
3   omp_lock_t l;
4   //————————————————————————————————
5   void threadSafeParse (char *s, const char *delim)
6   {
7     omp_set_lock (&l);  // acquire the lock
8     char *tok;
9     tok = strtok (s, delim);
10    while (tok)
11      {
12        printf ("Thread %i : %s\n", omp_get_thread_num (), tok);
13        tok = strtok (NULL, delim);
14      }
15
16    omp_unset_lock (&l); // release the lock
17  }
18
19  //————————————————————————————————
20  int main (int argc, char *argv[])
21  {
22    if (argc != 4)
23      {
24        fprintf (stderr, "Usage: %s string1 string2 delim\n", argv[0]);
25        exit (EXIT_FAILURE);
26      }
27    char *str1 = argv[1], *str2 = argv[2], *delim = argv[3];
28
29  #pragma omp parallel
30    {
31  #pragma omp single
32      {
33  // one task per input string
34  #pragma omp task
35        threadSafeParse (str1, delim);
36
37  #pragma omp task
38        threadSafeParse (str2, delim);
39      }
40    }
41
42    exit (EXIT_SUCCESS);
43  }
```

LISTING 4.25

A multithreaded program that uses tasks to parse two strings concurrently. A lock makes sure that only one of the two threads gets to use the strtok function each time.

Our example is a bit mundane, since we do have a reentrant variant in the form of the strtok_r function. But we will stick with it in order to answer an interesting question: Do we *need* locks to have a thread-safe function?

The reentrant and thread-safe, string-parsing function in Listing 4.26 answers this question in a definitive manner.

```
1   // File : thrsafe_strtokV2.cpp
2   . . .
3   char *strtokV2 (char *s, const char *delim, char **aux)
4   {
5     int idx1 = 0, idx2 = -1;
6     char needle[2] = { 0 };
7     int i;
8     char *temp = s;
9     if (s == NULL) // not the first call?
10      temp = *aux;
11
12    // iterate over all characters of the input string
13    for (i = 0; temp[i]; i++)
14      {
15        needle[0] = temp[i];
16        // check if a character matches a delimiter
17        if (strstr (delim, needle) != NULL)         // strstr is reentrant
18          {
19            idx1 = idx2 + 1;    // get the index boundaries of the token
20            idx2 = i;
21            if (idx1 != idx2)  // is it a token or a delimiter following↩
                   another?
22              {
23                temp[i] = 0;
24                *aux = temp + i + 1; // skip to next char. for next call
25                return temp+idx1;
26              }
27          }
28      }
29
30    // repeat checks for the token preceding the end of the string
31    idx1 = idx2 + 1;
32    idx2 = i;
33    if (idx1 != idx2)
34      {
35        *aux = temp + i; // point to \0
36        return temp+idx1;
37      }
38    else
39      return NULL;
40  }
41
42  //————————————————————————————————
43  void threadSafeParse (char *s, const char *delim)
44  {
45    char *state;
46    char *tok;
47
48    tok = strtokV2 (s, delim, &state);
```

```
49    while (tok)
50    {
51      printf ("Thread %i : %s\n", omp_get_thread_num (), tok);
52      tok = strtokV2 (NULL, delim, &state);
53    }
54  }
```

LISTING 4.26

A reentrant, thread-safe string tokenizer function (strtokV2) and a thread-safe function (threadSafeParse) that uses it to parse a string. The main function part of the program is identical to the one shown in Listing 4.25.

This strtokV2 function is a straightforward replacement for strtok or strtok_r. Its exclusive reliance on automatic and caller-provided variables means that it is reentrant. Furthermore, because it is not using any shared resources, it is thread-safe without requiring locks or atomic operations. The code in the threadSafeParse function (lines 43-54) is identical to a sequential counterpart using the C-library's strtok_r function. The operation of strtokV2 can be distilled to the following points:

- The s (or *aux if s is NULL) pointer is used to initialize a temporary pointer (temp) and iterate over the characters of the input until a zero value is encountered (for loop of line 13).
- The strstr reentrant function is used to check whether the examined character (temp[i]) matches any of the specified in the set of delimiters (line 17). The idx1 and idx2 indices point to the beginning and end of a detected token. Obviously, if they coincide, we have an empty string that is bypassed (check of line 21).
- If we have a nonzero length token, we mark its end by inserting the end-of-string at the position of the delimiter (line 23) and return the beginning of the search string for the next call to the caller (line 24). The function then ends by returning the address of the token.
- Lines 30-39 share the logic of lines 19-26 to treat the case of the very last token in the input string.

4.7.2 FALSE SHARING

Cache memory speeds up access to main memory contents by holding copies of the most frequently used data. Cache memory takes advantage of both *temporal* and *spatial* locality in data access patterns; a data item that has been referenced in the past is likely to be referenced again in the near future, along with other items in neighboring locations.

Cache memory tries to exploit spatial redundancy by fetching data from main memory in fixed-sized blocks called *cache lines*. The size of the cache line is architecture-specific, but a commonly used value is 64 bytes. Caches hold data aligned at addresses that are integer multiples of the cache line size.

To explain what kind of problem the presence of the extra data in a cache line creates, we will use an example of a dual-core system running the following `parallel for` loop for calculating the values of a `double` array:

```
double x[N];
#pragma omp parallel for schedule(static, 1)
  for( int i = 0; i < N; i++ )
    x[ i ] = someFunc( x [ i ] );
```

Given the `schedule` clause, the L1 caches of the two cores[12] might at some point in time be in the state shown in Figure 4.8. Because the cache can contain data from every available memory location, a cache line consists of the actual data, their addresses (so the CPU knows where they came from), and a state.

The state is used to implement a *coherency protocol*, i.e., a mechanism that allows data stored in multiple disjoint caches to be kept in a consistent state [34]. For example, if core 0 changes the value of x[10], core 1 should be able to read the updated value and not keep using an outdated one.

A simple state model is MESI, an acronym standing for the four possible cache line states covered by the model: **M**odified, **E**xclusive, **S**hared, and **I**nvalid. An excellent source of information for MESI, is the online article by Paul E. McKenney [34]. This is the meaning of these states:

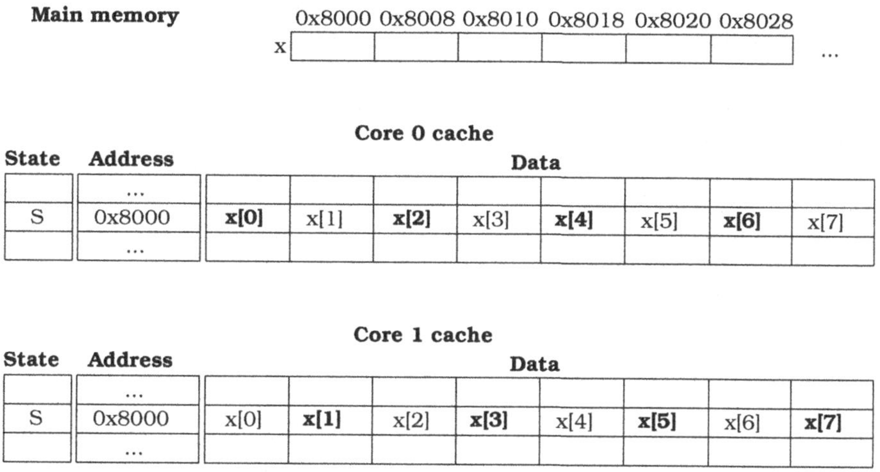

FIGURE 4.8

A possible L1 cache state for two cores processing alternating array elements of type `int`. We assume that the cache line size is 64 bytes. The elements accessed by each core are highlighted. The state of the cache lines is "shared."

---

[12]Complexity and efficiency reasons dictate separate L1 caches in multicore CPUs. Most CPUs employ multiple cache hierarchies, but for our purposes we can limit our discussion to L1 cache only.

- **Modified**: The CPU has recently changed part of the cache line, and the cache line holds the only up-to-date value of the corresponding item. No other CPU can hold copies of these data, so the CPU can be considered the owner of the data. The pending changes are supposed to be written back to the main memory according to the rules of the CPU architecture.
- **Exclusive**: Similar to the modified state in that the CPU is considered the owner of the data. No change has been applied, however. The main memory and the cache hold identical values.
- **Shared**: At least one more cache holds a copy of the data. Changes to the data can only be performed after coordination with the other CPUs that are holding copies.
- **Invalid**: Represents an empty cache line. It can be used to hold new data from the main memory.

What is of interest to us is what happens when a *shared* cache line is modified by one of the CPUs using it. The CPU applying the change sends "invalidate" messages to the CPUs that have copies of the cache line and awaits "acknowledge" responses from them before changing the state from *shared* to *modified*. The CPUs that receive an "invalidate" message clear the corresponding cache line by changing its state to "invalid" and send back an "acknowledge" message. This means that if they want to access the data that got cleared, they have to either fetch it from the "owning" cache or *read it again from memory*.

Now that we have covered the basic mechanisms of cache management, let's return to our example: What happens to the state of Figure 4.8 if core 0 modifies the value of x[0]? Although core 1 does not actually access this item, it shares the cache line that holds it. The resulting "invalidate" message will cause core 1 to dump the cache line and reread from the main memory the items it needs, at a substantial time overhead. This is exactly the definition of *false sharing*, i.e., sharing cache lines without actually sharing data.

The resulting performance degradation can be very significant [40]. There are three ways to eliminate false sharing:

- *Pad the data* with extra bytes so that distinct elements map to distinct cache lines. This is a viable option for data structures in which the extra padding will not cause an extreme memory space overhead. For an array and scheduling arrangement like the one in our example, this would cause a seven fold increase in the memory footprint of array x, which by itself would defeat the benefits of cache memory, if not starve the application from memory. The padding in our example would have to take the form of:

```
double x[N][8];
#pragma omp parallel for schedule(static , 1)
  for( int i = 0; i < N; i++ )
    x[ i ][ 0 ] = someFunc( x [ i ][ 0 ] );
```

so that each array row would occupy a complete cache line.

- The second alternative is to change the *mapping of data* to threads or cores. This is a far simpler and more economical proposition:

```
double x[N];
#pragma omp parallel for schedule(static, 8)
  for( int i = 0; i < N; i++ )
    x[ i ] = someFunc( x [ i ] );
```

- The third alternative is to reduce the sharing by *using private or local variables*. In our example, we can intermediately store a bunch of the results locally before sending them back to main memory.[13]

```
// assuming that N is a multiple of 8
double x[N];
#pragma omp parallel for schedule(static, 1)
  for( int i = 0; i < N; i += 8 )
  {
    double temp[ 8 ];
    for(int j = 0; j < 8; j++)
      temp[ j ] = someFunc( x [ i + j] );
    memcpy( x + i, temp, 8 * sizeof( double ));
  }
```

This can be combined with a partial loop unrolling:

```
// assuming that N is a multiple of 8
double x[N];
#pragma omp parallel for schedule(static, 1)
  for( int i = 0; i < N; i += 8 )
  {
    double temp[ 8 ];
    temp[ 0 ] = someFunc( x [ i ] );
    temp[ 1 ] = someFunc( x [ i + 1 ] );
    temp[ 2 ] = someFunc( x [ i + 2 ] );
    temp[ 3 ] = someFunc( x [ i + 3 ] );
    temp[ 4 ] = someFunc( x [ i + 4 ] );
    temp[ 5 ] = someFunc( x [ i + 5 ] );
    temp[ 6 ] = someFunc( x [ i + 6 ] );
    temp[ 7 ] = someFunc( x [ i + 7 ] );
    memcpy( x + i, temp, 8 * sizeof( double ));
  }
```

In order to test the severity of the problem false sharing constitutes, and also apply the three elimination techniques shown above, we study the problem of matrix multiplication. Listing 4.27 shows an initial solution that follows the discussion of Section 4.4.2, where it is explained that collapsing the two outer loops is a good choice for load balancing.

---

[13]The example is not very good because it is equivalent to a change in the data mapping. For a better example, continue reading!

```
void mmult (double *A, double *B, double *C, int N, int K, int M)
{
#pragma omp parallel for collapse(2) schedule(static, 1)
  for (int i = 0; i < N; i++)
    for (int j = 0; j < M; j++)
      {
        int idx = i * M + j;
        C[idx] = 0;
        for (int l = 0; l < K; l++)
          C[idx] += A[i * K + l] * B[l * M + j];
      }
}
```

LISTING 4.27

A simple OpenMP adaptation of a matrix multiplication function. Matrix A is assumed to be NxK, and B is assumed to be KxM in size.

But this is clearly not the end of the story, since false sharing affects the updates to the product matrix C.

Padding the matrix so that there is only one element of C per cache line results in the following code (assuming that the cache line is 64 bytes long), as shown in Listing 4.28.

```
//————————————————————————————————————
void mmult (double *A, double *B, double *C, int N, int K, int M)
{
#pragma omp parallel for collapse(2) schedule(static, 1)
  for (int i = 0; i < N; i++)
    for (int j = 0; j < M; j++)
      {
        int idx = (i * M + j) * 8; // using 1 element from each group ↩
            of 8
        C[idx] = 0;
        for (int l = 0; l < K; l++)
          C[idx] += A[i * K + l] * B[l * M + j];
      }
}
//————————————————————————————————————
int main (int argc, char *argv[])
{
  . . .
  double *A = new double[N * K];
  double *B = new double[K * M];
  double *C = new double[N * M * 8]; // 8x the original space
  . . .
```

LISTING 4.28

OpenMP matrix multiplication, with padding of the result matrix C, so that each cache line can hold only a single element of C.

Changing the data mapping can be accomplished by modifying the `schedule` clause, as shown in Listing 4.29.

```
void mmult (double *A, double *B, double *C, int N, int K, int M)
{
#pragma omp parallel for collapse(2) schedule(static, 8)
  for (int i = 0; i < N; i++)
    for (int j = 0; j < M; j++)
      {
        int idx = i * M + j;
        C[idx] = 0;
        for (int l = 0; l < K; l++)
          C[idx] += A[i * K + l] * B[l * M + j];
      }
}
```

LISTING 4.29

OpenMP matrix multiplication with a schedule having a chunk size of 8 so that each cache line holding C elements is exclusive to a core. This is a modification of the data elements mapping to threads or cores.

Finally, a temporary, automatic variable can be used for accumulating the result in the inner loop, leaving only a single reference to each element of the resulting matrix, as shown in Listing 4.30.[14]

```
void mmult (double *A, double *B, double *C, int N, int K, int M)
{
#pragma omp parallel for collapse(2)
  for (int i = 0; i < N; i++)
    for (int j = 0; j < M; j++)
      {
        double temp = 0;
        for (int l = 0; l < K; l++)
          temp += A[i * K + l] * B[l * M + j];
        C[i * M + j] = temp;
      }
}
```

LISTING 4.30

OpenMP matrix multiplication with a temporary variable for the element of C being calculated that eliminates false sharing.

The measured speed-up, averaged over 10 runs, is reported in Figure 4.9. The test platform was a i7-4700HQ, 2.40 GHz quad core CPU, with hyperthreading enabled (so OpenMP used eight threads by default) and all programs were compiled with the GNU C++ 4.9.1 compiler and the `-O2` compiler switch.

Figure 4.9 results are astonishing. The plain-vanilla OpenMP version of Listing 4.27 offers hardly any speed-up over the sequential version, despite employing four

---

[14]To be exact, Listing 4.30 combines both a temporary variable and a mapping modification, because OpenMP defaults to a chunk size of $\left\lceil \frac{N\,M}{p} \right\rceil$ for p threads.

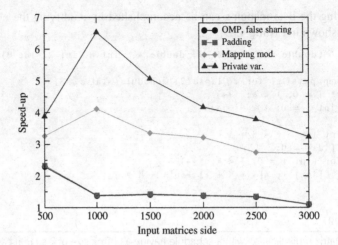

FIGURE 4.9

Matrix multiplication average speed-up versus different sides of the square input matrices. Tested programs include the false-sharing OpenMP program and the three variants that eliminate cache false sharing. Mean values were obtained by running each test 10 times.

hyperthreaded cores on a problem that is essentially embarrassingly parallel. The padding approach also falters miserably by reducing the effectiveness of the cache as it is filled up with useless data. Both the mapping alteration and the use of a private variable fare much better than the other two methods. Especially the use of private variables proves to be the best of all.

The difference between the "mapping change" and "use of private variables" methods can be explained by how they utilize the cache: The former keeps updating `C[idx]` in the inner loop, which means that writes have to propagate to the main memory at a significant overhead. The former uses an automatic variable that the compiler can place in a register without needing to send writes to the main memory, but at the end of the inner loop.

4.8 A CASE STUDY: SORTING IN OpenMP

Searching and sorting are quintessential operations in algorithm design. In this section we explore how mergesort, a well-known sorting algorithm, can be amended for multithreaded execution by the OpenMP run-time. Mergesort, in its bottom-up form, is explored in great detail in Section 3.10.5. In the following paragraphs we also examine the case of the top-down mergesort, as OpenMP provides the mechanisms that allow both formulations of the algorithm to be parallelized. These also provide a good opportunity for applying the worksharing constructs listed in this chapter.

4.8.1 BOTTOM-UP MERGESORT IN OpenMP

Figure 3.14 illustrates how the bottom-up, nonrecursive version of mergesort can sort N data items by merging disjoint neighboring blocks in $\Theta(\lceil lg(N) \rceil)$ phases. We can summarize the overall operation as a merging of ever-increasing neighboring array parts, starting from a size 1 (i.e., individual array items) and doubling in size after each phase.

Algorithm 4.1 shows a more concise description of the bottom-up mergesort in pseudocode. In order to keep things short, we assume that N is a power of 2 so that every array part has another part with which it can merge. Obviously, a special case needs to be treated inside the loop of lines 3-5 to allow the use of arbitrary N.

ALGORITHM 4.1 BOTTOM-UP MERGESORT: SORTING N DATA ITEMS, WHERE N IS A POWER OF 2.

1. *grpSize* ← 1
2. **while** *grpSize* < N **do**
3.   **for** *stIdx* ← 0 to N − 1 step 2 · *grpSize* **do**
4.   *nextIdx* ← *stIdx* + *grpSize*
5.   Merge array parts of size *grpSize*, starting at indices *stIdx* and *nextIdx*
6.   *grpSize* ← *grpSize* · 2

The *stIdx* and *nextIdx* indices point to the start of the array parts that need to be merged. The actual sorting takes place during the merging operation of line 5, where the resulting conglomeration of items forms an ascending (or descending, based on the comparison operator used) sequence.

A sequential implementation of the bottom-up mergesort, with the addition of the special case code for arbitrary N and a further optimization concerning the moving of data between the data array and the temporary storage, is shown in Listing 4.31.

```
1   template < class T > void mergeList (T * src1, T * src2, int len1, int↩
        len2, T * dest)
2   {
3     int idx1 = 0, idx2 = 0;
4     int loc = 0;                    // starting point in dest array
5     while (idx1 < len1 && idx2 < len2)
6       {
7         if (src1[idx1] <= src2[idx2])
8           {
9             dest[loc] = src1[idx1];
10            idx1++;
11          }
12        else
13          {
14            dest[loc] = src2[idx2];
15            idx2++;
16          }
17        loc++;
18      }
```

```
19
20      // copy the rest
21      for (int i = idx1; i < len1; i++)
22        dest[loc++] = src1[i];
23
24      for (int i = idx2; i < len2; i++)
25        dest[loc++] = src2[i];
26    }
27
28    //——————————————————————————————————————
29    template < class T > void mergesort (T * data, int N)
30    {
31      // allocate temporary array
32      T *temp = new T[N];
33      // pointers to easily switch between the two arrays
34      T *repo1, *repo2, *aux;
35
36      repo1 = data;
37      repo2 = temp;
38
39      // loop for group size growing exponentially from 1 element to floor↵
            (lgN)
40      for (int grpSize = 1; grpSize < N; grpSize <<= 1)
41        {
42          for (int stIdx = 0; stIdx < N; stIdx += 2 * grpSize)
43            {
44              int nextIdx = stIdx + grpSize;
45              int secondGrpSize = min (max (0, N - nextIdx), grpSize);
46
47              // check to see if there are enough data for a second group ↵
                    to merge with
48              if (secondGrpSize == 0)
49                {
50                  // if there is no second part, just copy the first part ↵
                        to repo2 for use in the next iteration
51                  for (int i = 0; i < N - stIdx; i++)
52                    repo2[stIdx + i] = repo1[stIdx + i];
53                }
54              else
55                {
56                  mergeList (repo1 + stIdx, repo1 + nextIdx, grpSize, ↵
                        secondGrpSize, repo2 + stIdx);
57                }
58            }
59
60          // switch pointers
61          aux = repo1;
62          repo1 = repo2;
63          repo2 = aux;
64        }
65
66
```

```
67      // move data back to the original array
68      if (repo1 != data)
69        memcpy (data, temp, sizeof (T) * N);
70
71      delete [] temp;
72    }
```

LISTING 4.31

A sequential implementation of the bottom-up mergesort algorithm.

The key points of this implementation are:

- The mergeList() template function of lines 1-26 is a typical implementation of an array merging operation. It receives the addresses of two array segments (src1 and src2) and their lengths (len1 and len2) and deposits the sorted result in the destination array (dest). The loop of lines 5-18 compares the smaller elements of the two segments before moving the smaller of the two to the destination array. This process continues until either of the two parts is exhausted.
  The two for loops that follow simply copy whatever elements remain in one of the two subarrays to dest. What is different in our implementation from what is discussed in most algorithm books is that the data are not moved back to the source array. The motivation is the minimization of the data movement overhead. The mergesort() template function anticipates this "bouncing" of data between repositories and adjusts accordingly.
- The mergesort() template function contains two nested for loops: The outer one controls the array segment sizes that get merged, and the inner one iterates over the starting index of the first array part to be merged. The starting index of the second part (nextIdx) is just grpSize distance from the first one.
- The mergesort() template function maintains two pointers, repo1 and repo2, that reference the holding place of the input data and the temporary storage used during the merging operation, respectively. These pointers get switched at the end of each merging phase (lines 61-63).
- The only major problem caused by *N* not being a power of 2 is that there can be array parts with no counterpart with which to merge. In order to maintain the data in either of the two repositories as a whole, these "orphaned" parts are just copied to the temporary storage pointed to by repo2 (lines 51-52).
  A minor issue is also that the very last part to be merged in every phase might not be of grpSize length. The adjustment of the second group size takes place in line 45.
- If at the end on the sorting procedure the data reside at the temporary storage, they are copied back to the original array (lines 68, 69).

Our sequential implementation seems ripe for parallelization with a parallel for construct, given the two nested loops in the mergesort() template function. However, only the inner loop can be parallelized in this fashion, since there a loop-carried flow dependency affecting the outer loop: The array referenced by repo2 is written during iteration grpSize before being used as an input in iteration grpSize*2. Since we cannot eliminate this RAW dependency, we have to settle for the inner loop.

Amazingly, the only thing we need to do to turn Listing 4.31 into a multi-threaded implementation is to insert a pragma line between lines 41 and 42, as shown in Listing 4.32.

```
// File : mergesort_omp_bottomup .cpp
. . .
  for (int grpSize = 1; grpSize < N; grpSize <<= 1)
    {
#pragma omp parallel for
      for (int stIdx = 0; stIdx < N; stIdx += 2 * grpSize)
        {
. . .
```

LISTING 4.32

The OpenMP-based multi-threaded version of Listing 4.31 requires only a single additional line.

For clarity, we omit in this pragma line the recommended default(none) and shared(...) clauses.

In Section 4.8.3 we compare the performance of our OpenMP-based implementation against the Qt-based one that is described in Section 3.10.5.

4.8.2 TOP-DOWN MERGESORT IN OpenMP

Arguably, the most studied version of mergesort is the recursive, top-down one. It does have a number of features in its favor, such as a shorter and easier-to-describe structure and no need for special N-case treatment. Although relying on the same merging process as the bottom-up algorithm, it partitions the input in a different way. The bottom-up mergesort merges subarrays in a carefully orchestrated manner so that the subarrays are already sorted when the merging commences. On the other hand, the top-down variant calls itself in order to sort the two halves of the input array before the merging can be done.

A sequential implementation is shown in Listing 4.33.

```
1  template < class T > void mergeList (T * src1, T * src2, int len1, int↩
       len2, T * dest)
2  {
3    int idx1 = 0, idx2 = 0;
4    int loc = 0;                    // starting point in dest array
5    while (idx1 < len1 && idx2 < len2)
6      {
7        if (src1[idx1] <= src2[idx2])
8          {
9            dest[loc] = src1[idx1];
10           idx1++;
```

```
11            }
12          else
13            {
14              dest[loc] = src2[idx2];
15              idx2++;
16            }
17          loc++;
18        }
19
20    // copy the rest
21    for (int i = idx1; i < len1; i++)
22      dest[loc++] = src1[i];
23
24    for (int i = idx2; i < len2; i++)
25      dest[loc++] = src2[i];
26
27    memcpy(src1, dest, sizeof(T)*(len1+len2));
28  }
29
30  //————————————————————————————————————————————
31  // sort data array of N elements, using the temp array as temporary ↩
          storage
32  template < class T > void mergesortRec (T * data, T * temp, int N)
33  {
34    // base case
35    if(N < 2)
36      return;
37    else
38      {
39        int middle = N/2;
40        mergesortRec(data, temp, middle);
41        mergesortRec(data+middle, temp+middle, N - middle);
42        mergeList(data, data+middle, middle, N—middle, temp);
43      }
44  }
45  //————————————————————————————————————————————
46  template < class T > void mergesort (T * data, int N)
47  {
48    // allocate temporary array
49    T *temp = new T[N];
50    int middle = N/2;
51
52    mergesortRec(data, temp, middle);
53    mergesortRec(data+middle, temp+middle, N - middle);
54    mergeList(data, data+middle, middle, N—middle, temp);
55
56    delete []temp;
57  }
```

LISTING 4.33

A sequential implementation of the top-down mergesort algorithm.

The only difference between the mergeList() template function of Listing 4.31 and the one shown previously is the inclusion of line 27, which ensures that the input data always stay in their original array. The mergesort() front-end function allocates the temporary memory needed for the merging operation and calls the recursive mergesortRec() function to sort the two halves of the input before subsequently merging them in line 54.

The recursive function checks for the base cases of no data or one data item only (line 35) so that the recursion can be terminated before following the same routine as mergesort(), i.e., calling itself to sort the two halves of the input before subsequently merging them in line 42.

As the calls to mergesortRec() in lines 40, 41, 52, and 53 deal with disjoint parts of the input array, we can use sections or task directives to allow them to execute concurrently. The only restriction is that the mergeList() calls in lines 42 and 54 can be issued only after the preceding sorting operations are complete.

The required modifications, albeit way more extensive that in the bottom-up algorithm, are still straight forward, as shown in Listing 4.34.

```
1   // File : mergesort_omp_topdown.cpp
2   . . .
3   template < class T > void mergesortRec (T * data, T * temp, int N)
4   {
5     if (N < 2)
6       return;
7     else
8       {
9         int middle = N / 2;
10  #pragma omp task if(N>10000) mergeable
11        {
12          mergesortRec (data, temp, middle);
13        }
14  #pragma omp task if(N>10000) mergeable
15        {
16          mergesortRec (data + middle, temp + middle, N − middle);
17        }
18
19  #pragma omp taskwait
20
21          mergeList (data, data + middle, middle, N − middle, temp);
22      }
23  }
24
25  //───────────────────────────────────────────────────────────
26  template < class T > void mergesort (T * data, int N)
27  {
28    // allocate temporary array
29    T *temp = new T[N];
30
31  #pragma omp parallel
32    {
33
```

```
34   #pragma omp single
35       {
36           int middle = N / 2;
37   #pragma omp task
38           {
39               mergesortRec (data, temp, middle);
40           }
41   #pragma omp task
42           {
43               mergesortRec (data + middle, temp + middle, N - middle);
44           }
45
46   #pragma omp taskwait
47
48           mergeList (data, data + middle, middle, N - middle, temp);
49       }
50   }
51
52   delete [] temp;
53   }
```

LISTING 4.34

OpenMP, multithreaded implementation of the top-down mergesort algorithm.

The `parallel` directive in line 31 of the front-end function sets up the parallel execution of the algorithm. The `task` directives in lines 10, 14, 37, and 41 enable the concurrent sorting of disjoint parts of the array. The `taskwait` directives in lines 19 and 46, guarantee that the parts to be merged have been sorted already.

If left unchecked, lines 10 and 14 would produce a task for every item in the input array! The `if` clauses limit the generation of new tasks to inputs that exceed 10,000 items. The 10,000 threshold is arbitrary and is a weak point of our implementation.

Could it be possible that we always roughly get an *a priori* specified number of tasks, regardless of the size of the input?

Let's assume that we target an implementation that will generate a maximum of T tasks. The tasks that are generated by the implementation in Listing 4.34 form a binary tree like the one shown in Figure 4.10.

We could propose the following formulation in order to limit the number of tasks:

```
. . .
// A global numTasks counter is used to enumerate the number of tasks
// generated and limit the generation of new ones
#pragma omp task if(numTasks < maxTasks) mergeable
        {
#pragma omp atomic
            numTasks++;

            mergesortRec (data, temp, middle);
        }
. . .
```

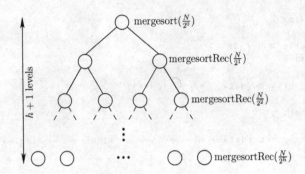

FIGURE 4.10

A binary tree of tasks is formed during the execution of the top-down mergesort function in Listing 4.34. The tree nodes are decorated by the name of the function executed by the corresponding task and the size of the array part to be sorted (assuming N is a power of 2). In this figure we assume that the generation of new tasks stops when the size of the array parts to be sorted falls below $\frac{N}{2^h}$.

However, this is a bad idea, since the task tree is not necessarily generated in a breadth-first manner. This way, we could end up with tasks that are very big or very small and just plain inappropriate for properly load balancing the computation.

A better approach would be to have a variable size threshold associated with the overall array size.

If N is a power of 2, then the binary tree of tasks is perfect, and the total number of tasks for a tree of height h is $2^{h+1} - 1$. If h is the maximum height that the tree can grow to, before we exceed our maximum number of tasks T, then we have:

$$2^{h+1} - 1 \le T < 2^{h+2} - 1 \qquad (4.6)$$

and we can express h as a function of T:

$$2^{h+1} - 1 \le T \Rightarrow h \le lg(T+1) - 1 \qquad (4.7)$$

Since h has to be an integer, its maximum value has to be:

$$h = \lfloor lg(T+1) \rfloor - 1 \qquad (4.8)$$

The smallest size of a subarray to be sorted in such a tree is:

$$\frac{N}{2^h} = \frac{N}{2^{\lfloor lg(T+1) \rfloor - 1}} \approx \frac{2 \cdot N}{T+1} \qquad (4.9)$$

Equation 4.9 requires no complex computations and can be used conveniently to limit the generation of tasks in our implementation, as shown in Listing 4.35.

```
1  // File : mergesort_omp_topdown_v2.cpp
2  . . .
3  const int maxTasks=4096;
4  int _thresh_; // used for the if clauses
```

```
5      . . .
6    //—————————————————————————————————
7    // sort data array of N elements, using the aux array as temporary ↵
         storage
8    template < class T > void mergesortRec (T * data, T * temp, int N)
9    {
10     if (N < 2)
11         return;
12     else
13         {
14             int middle = N / 2;
15   #pragma omp task if(N > _thresh_ ) mergeable
16         {
17             mergesortRec (data, temp, middle);
18         }
19   #pragma omp task if(N > _thresh_ ) mergeable
20         {
21             mergesortRec (data + middle, temp + middle, N — middle);
22         }
23
24   #pragma omp taskwait
25
26         mergeList (data, data + middle, middle, N — middle, temp);
27         }
28   }
29
30   //—————————————————————————————————
31   template < class T > void mergesort (T * data, int N)
32   {
33     // allocate temporary array
34     T *temp = new T[N];
35     _thresh_ = 2.0 * N / (maxTasks + 1);
36
37   #pragma omp parallel
38     {
39     . . .
```

LISTING 4.35

Modifications to the OpenMP, multithreaded implementation of the top-down mergesort algorithm in order to limit the number of generated tasks in an input size-agnostic manner.

The only changes required in this updated version of Listing 4.34 is the calculation of the size threshold once, in the front-end function (line 35), and the expression of the if clauses in lines 15 and 19.

4.8.3 PERFORMANCE COMPARISON

The bottom-up, nonrecursive sequential version of mergesort is considered more efficient than the corresponding top-down one. But is this performance benefit carried over to the OpenMP implementations?

Another interesting question is, how does OpenMP fare against the map-reduce, "hybrid,"[15] mergesort implementation of Section 3.10.5? In terms of development effort, there is no question about the superiority of the single-pragma-turns-multithreaded of Listing 4.32! OpenMP is instrumental in that regard. But does it deliver in terms of performance?

For this battery of tests we used a fourth-generation i7-4700HQ CPU, clocked at 2.4 GHz, with hyper threading enabled. Our platform run 64-bit Kubuntu Linux 14.04 and all programs were compiled by GCC 4.9.1 with the `-O2` switch. For the map-reduce mergesort we used $M = 256$ blocks, since that was found to be a good choice in the tests conducted in Section 3.10.5. The sequential sorting times were obtained by using the map-reduce version with a single block, which means that only a sequential quicksort was executed (details are available in Section 3.10.5). The measured speed-up curves are shown in Figure 4.11.

The results are surprising, both in terms of the margin by which the bottom-up approach wins over the top-down one, and in terms of the ability of the bottom-up algorithm to edge-out the map-reduce mergesort. The top-down algorithm is penalized by recursion and the explicit generation and management of tasks.

A similar reason, i.e., the book keeping overhead associated with map-reduce, is also the shortcoming of the the hybrid algorithm. Although our results take nothing away from the elegance and power of the map-reduce design, they do show that keeping things simple can also be very beneficial in terms of performance.

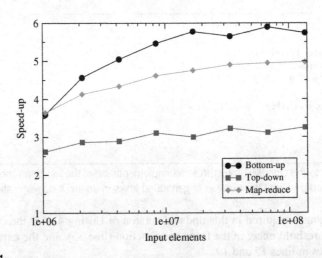

FIGURE 4.11

Average speed-up of three parallel mergesort implementations for different input sizes. Mean values were obtained by running each test 10 times.

---

[15] We call it hybrid because it employs a combination of quicksort and mergesort.

EXERCISES

1. Modify the program in Listing 4.1 so that `printf` is used instead of `cout`. Do you see any difference in the output compared to the one reported in Section 4.2? Can you explain it?

2. In the matrix multiplication example of Section 4.4.2, we could get three perfectly nested loops if we initialize the C matrix outside:

```
double A[K][L];
double B[L][M];
double C[K][M];
. . .
#pragma omp parallel for collapse(3)
  for (int i = 0; i < K; i++)
    for (int j = 0; j < M; j++)
      for (int k = 0; k < L; k++)
        C[i][j] += A[i][k] * B[k][j];
```

   Is this code correct? If not, what kind of modification is required to fix it?

3. Draw the iteration space dependency graph for the following program:

```
for (int i = 0; i < K; i++)
  for (int j = 0; j < M; j++)
    a[i][j] = a[i-1][j] + a[i+1][j];
```

   What kind of dependencies exist? How can you eliminate them?

4. Create a C++ program for visualizing the thread iteration assignment performed by a `parallel for` directive for different `schedule` schemes. Your program should have a per-thread vector that accumulates the loop control variable values assigned to each thread. Use this program and appropriate `schedule` settings to experiment with multiple schemes without recompiling your program. This is a sample of the output you should be able to get for a loop of 100 iterations:

```
$ export OMP_SCHEDULE="static ,5"
$ ./solution
Thread 0 : 0 1 2 3 4 40 41 42 43 44 80 81 82 83 84
Thread 1 : 5 6 7 8 9 45 46 47 48 49 85 86 87 88 89
Thread 2 : 10 11 12 13 14 50 51 52 53 54 90 91 92 93 94
Thread 3 : 15 16 17 18 19 55 56 57 58 59 95 96 97 98 99
Thread 4 : 20 21 22 23 24 60 61 62 63 64
Thread 5 : 25 26 27 28 29 65 66 67 68 69
Thread 6 : 30 31 32 33 34 70 71 72 73 74
Thread 7 : 35 36 37 38 39 75 76 77 78 79
```

5. In Listing 4.19 we examined the issue of processing a linked-list concurrently. Is there a way to improve this program for a doubly linked list? Write the corresponding program.

6. Write a program for traversing and processing the elements of a binary tree in parallel using a pre-order, in-order, or post-order traversal. Use the `task` construct to that effect.

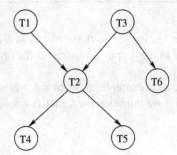

FIGURE 4.12

A dependency graph consisting of six tasks.

7. Modify the program of the previous exercise so that *undeferred tasks* are generated after the traversal has moved beyond the fifth level of the tree. (Assume that the root sits at level 0.)
8. Modify the Fibonacci sequence-calculating program of Listing 4.20 so that it counts the number of child tasks generated.
9. Use the `task` directive to create a solution to the single-producer, multiple-consumers problem with a variable number of consumers, as specified in the command line.
10. Use the `task` directive and its `depend` clause to model the dependency graph of Figure 4.12. You can use stub functions to represent each of the tasks in the figure.
11. Finding the odd integers in an array can be accomplished by the following OpenMP code:

```
int data[N];
int oddCount=0;
#pragma omp parallel for
  for (int i = 0; i < N; i++)
      if( data[i] % 2 )
#pragma omp atomic
          oddCount ++;
```

Modify this code so that there is no need for a `critical` or `atomic` directive by introducing a counter array with one element per thread. Compare the performance of your version with and without cache false sharing. If we were to use a reduction variable, to what false-sharing elimination technique does this correspond?
12. Quicksort rightfully holds the place of the top performer among generic sorting algorithms. Its design can be considered a reflection of mergesort, although both algorithms employ a divide-and-conquer design. Write a sequential implementation of quicksort and proceed to parallelize it using OpenMP constructs. Measure the speed-up that can be achieved, and compare it to the performance that can be obtained from the bottom-up mergesort of Section 4.8.1.

Distributed memory programming

5

IN THIS CHAPTER YOU WILL

- Learn what the Message Passing Interface is and how you can use it to create applications that run on distributed-memory platforms.
- Understand how an MPI program can be deployed for execution.
- Learn how to perform point-to-point communications using MPI.
- Learn how to perform collective communications using MPI.
- Utilize non blocking and/or buffered communication primitives to increase the performance of your application.
- Learn to use Remote Memory Access (RMA) functions to implement one-sided communications.
- Learn how to use C and C++ MPI bindings via the Boost.MPI library.
- Combine threads and MPI processes to maximize the performance of distributed platforms with multicore nodes.

5.1 COMMUNICATING PROCESSES

The emergence of the workstation platform and networking capabilities in the 1980s prompted the creation of libraries that could be used to deploy and manage programs over intranets. The core concept was to run multiple processes that could communicate by exchanging messages. The libraries alleviated the troubles of node discovery, message routing, and process identification with which plain-vanilla, socket-based approaches had to contend. One of the first popular examples was the Parallel Virtual Machine (PVM) library that was developed during the summer of 1989 at Oak Ridge National Laboratory and was released to the public in early 1991.

However, more often than not those early attempts duplicated each other and led to the construction of software that was pretty much non portable. This prompted a common initiative by academia and industry partners that resulted in the creation of the first Message-Passing Interface standard (MPI-1) in 1994.

5.2 MPI

The Message-Passing Interface (MPI) is considered the de facto standard for distributed-memory or shared-nothing programming. MPI is not a programming language but a set of functions (i.e., an API) that can be used from a variety of languages. It should also be stressed that MPI is not a specific library but a standardized specification for one. The latest MPI version is 3.0 (aka MPI-3), published in Fall 2012. The standard defines the syntax and semantics of a core of library routines.

A number of vendors, both government institutions and private corporations, have developed MPI implementations that adhere to a lesser or greater degree to one or more MPI specifications. The reason for partial compliance is the size and complexity of the complete standard, which also entails some infrequently used features (such as dynamic process management). A sample list of MPI implementations follows:

- LAM/MPI: OSS developed by the Indiana University. Currently it is no longer being developed.
- OpenMPI: MPI-2 fully compliant OSS implementation. It is hosted by the Indiana University but a number of academia and industry contributors are involved in its development.
- MPICH2: OSS implementation of MPI-1 and MPI-2 standards. It is supported by the Mathematics and Computer Science Division of the Argonne National Laboratory. MPICH-2 also runs on Windows platforms.
- MPICH: OSS implementation of MPI-1, MPI-2, and MPI-3 standards. MPICH uses the same name as the project that resulted in the creation of MPICH2, but it is a renewed effort that started in 2012. A number of industry (e.g., IBM, Intel, Microsoft) and academic partners work with MPICH on derivative implementations.

Many Linux distributions (Ubuntu being one of them) offer installation packages for OpenMPI and MPICH2/MPICH. Installation in Ubuntu Linux can be as simple as that shown in Listing 5.1.

```
$ sudo apt-get install openmpi*
```

LISTING 5.1

Installing OpenMPI in Ubuntu.

Differences between the libraries lay not only in the degree of compliance to the standard but also in the level of optimization, the architectures supported (custom or otherwise, as in, for example, support of Infiniband), and the toolsets used for program development, deployment, management, and instrumentation.

MPI uses a language-independent specification to describe the semantics of the supported calls. These are made available to programmers via specific language bindings or APIs. MPI-1 implementations typically offered bindings for C and Fortran. Later, C++ bindings also became available. In the sections that follow we offer examples that use the C and the C++ bindings as implemented by the Boost.MPI wrapper library wherever possible. The Boost set of libraries is considered the breeding ground for libraries that could later become part of the C++ Standard Library. The Boost.MPI library offers a welcome level of abstraction in comparison to the C bindings.[1]

Although it is possible to learn to use MPI only via the Boost.MPI classes, the study of the C bindings reveals certain aspects of the MPI operations that are critical for a thorough understanding of the standard. It is therefore recommended that the reader does not skip over the C-only sections of the text. Additionally, Boost.MPI currently covers only a subset of the full MPI standard.

MPI remains relevant even today in the era of multiple cores due to its flexible design. The primary concern of a software engineer is to decompose the target application into parts that can be executed as separate processes. The MPI run-time environment will take care of the actual mapping (guided or otherwise) of processes to physical nodes/CPUs. The underlying machine can be easily switched between a multicore PC and an intranet of homogeneous or even heterogeneous machines.

It is indicative of the importance of MPI that Nvidia's CUDA toolkit supports (since version 4.1) MPI communication primitive inside CUDA kernels! This opens up a whole new world of possibilities for GPU programming, as we explore in Chapter 6.

5.3 CORE CONCEPTS

The abstraction MPI presents, is one of processes that can exchange messages with each other just by specifying the other end of the communication operation. The processes could be just as easily deployed over a single machine or a network of *heterogeneous* machines without needing to modify or recompile the code. A configuration file and/or command-line parameters allow control of the deployment at launch time. The MPI library and run-time environment are responsible for:

- **Process identification**: A unique non negative number per process, also known as a *rank* in MPI nomenclature, is used for this purpose. This identification number is defined within the context of a group of processes, known as a *communicator*. By default, all processes in an MPI program belong to the global communicator identified by the symbolic constant MPI_COMM_WORLD. In the following sections we also use the term *node* to refer to an MPI process.
- **Message routing**: MPI takes care of efficiently delivering the messages to their destinations by using either sockets (for inter-machine communications) or shared buffers (for intra-machine communications).

---

[1]Boost.MPI offers a different set of C++ bindings than have been originally developed. The latter are considered deprecated as of MPI-2.2 and they have been completely removed from MPI-3.0. The rationale is that they barely offer anything different from their C counterparts.

- **Message buffering**: Once a message has been dispatched by its sender, it is typically buffered by MPI on its way to its destination. Multiple messages can await collection in a receiver's MPI buffer space. MPI provides mechanisms for delegating buffering duties to the application. This can be useful for managing very long messages.
- **Data marshaling**: MPI accommodates the construction of parallel machines from heterogeneous architectures (e.g., big-indian and small-indian) by converting data representations to suit the message's destination. This is the reason why MPI calls require the explicit declaration of the data types being communicated.

In the following sections we use the C-language bindings exclusively, to present and explain the different functions offered by MPI. Fortran bindings are almost identical to the C ones (the naming is different in the sense that all function names are uppercase). C++ bindings have been deprecated in MPI-2.2 and completely removed in MPI-3. C++ users can either use the C bindings or resort to the excellent Boost.MPI library, which is presented in Section 5.19.

5.4 YOUR FIRST MPI PROGRAM

The typical structure of a C MPI program is shown in Listing 5.2.

```
#include <mpi.h>
...
int main(int argc, char **argv)
{
    . . .
    // No MPI calls prior to this point
    MPI_Init(&argc, &argv);

    // MPI statements

    MPI_Finalize();
    // No MPI calls beyond this point
    . . .
}
```

LISTING 5.2

Skeleton of a C MPI program.

The MPI_Init function initializes the MPI execution environment, by for example, allocating the memory space necessary for message buffering. Command-line parameters are also parsed in order to extract any directives to MPI, hence the parameter list of MPI_Init. MPI_Finalize terminates the MPI execution environment and frees up any resources taken up by MPI.

The naming convention used by MPI for C is that functions start with the MPI_ prefix and only the first letter of the remaining function name is capitalized. If the name is made of multiple components, they are separated by an underscore, e.g., MPI_Comm_size. Constants follow the same rule, with the exception that all characters are upper case.

Along the lines of the traditional "Hello World" programs, the "mpihello.c" program in Listing 5.3 prints a greeting from every MPI process spawned.

```
1   #include <mpi.h>
2   #include <stdio.h>
3   int main (int argc, char **argv)
4   {
5     int rank, num, i;
6     MPI_Init (&argc, &argv);
7     MPI_Comm_rank (MPI_COMM_WORLD, &rank);
8     MPI_Comm_size (MPI_COMM_WORLD, &num);
9     printf ("Hello from process %i of %i\n", rank, num);
10    MPI_Finalize ();
11    return 0;
12  }
```

LISTING 5.3

MPI's "Hello World" in C.

Line 7 in Listing 5.3 is where each MPI process requests to find out its ID/rank in the global communicator MPI_COMM_WORLD. The communicator's size, i.e., the total number of processes, is determined in line 8. Processes are numbered from 0 to $N - 1$, where N is the communicator size. To compile the above program, the mpicc command can be used to automate the process[2]:

```
$ mpicc mpihello.c -o mpihello
```

where the -o flag determines the filename of the executable generated.

The same can be accomplished by calling the GNU C compiler (gcc) directly:

```
$ gcc hello.c -o hello2 -I /usr/include/mpi -lmpi
```

The benefit of using mpicc is that we avoid the hassle of having to specify where the header files are located (with the -I switch) and which libraries to link with (the -lmpi switch).

The execution environment is determined during program launch via the mpirun command.[3] In order to explore both intra- (i.e., single) and inter-node (i.e., over multiple machines) deployment, we assume that we have at our disposal the heterogeneous network shown in Figure 5.1. Assuming that the user is running the program from

---

[2]Please note that in all the examples of this chapter, the files (source code, binary, or otherwise) are assumed to be in the current directory and that the current directory is in the ${PATH} environmental variable. If this is not the case, a relative or an absolute pathname has to be used.

[3]mpiexec and orterun are synonyms of mpirun in OpenMPI.

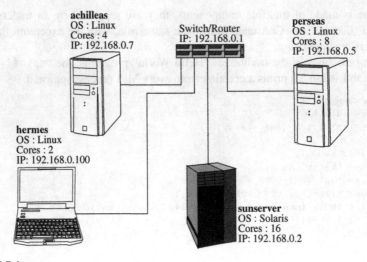

FIGURE 5.1

Intranet example used for explaining MPI execution configurations.

a console window in the **hermes** laptop, spawning a group of four processes is as simple as entering:

```
$ mpirun —np 4 mpihello
```

This will in turn produce an output that may or may not resemble the ones shown in Table 5.1, since there is no guarantee on the relative timing of the different processes. The third column in Table 5.1 clearly reveals the problems that uncoordinated console output can cause in this case. The solution to this problem would be to designate only one of the processes to output to the console (for more, see Section 5.15).

This simple execution command that uses only the -np switch is sufficient for debugging programs on a standalone machine. Under normal circumstances, we would not expect a speedup from such an execution unless the machine used was a multicore one!

Table 5.1 A sample of the possible outputs that can be generated from a run of the program in Listing 5.3 using four processes

Output #1	Output #2	Output #3
Hello from process 1 of 4	Hello from process 3 of 4	Helfrom Hello from process 2 of 4
Hello from process 2 of 4	Hello from process 2 of 4	lo process 1 of 4
Hello from process 0 of 4	Hello from process 0 of 4	Hello from process 0 of 4
Hello from process 3 of 4	Hello from process 1 of 4	Hello from process 3 of 4

An important issue that has to be addressed is how the different nodes in your intranet access the needed code and data. The simplest approach is to have all the machines mount a shared NFS or CIFS volume that contains the required files. If your Linux home directory is handled by a NFS server and the accounts are handled by NIS or LDAP, there is nothing more to be done. If a shared volume is not used, the files will have to be transferred with FTP or SSH protocols to all the nodes.

Running a program on a remote host requires a particular security setup that is outlined step by step in Appendix B.1. Failure to do so will result in a sequence of credential (login) requests for each of the processes that are to be executed.

To deploy the program over multiple machines, a "hostfile" has to be specified. The hostfile is a text file containing a list (one per line) of the IPs (or DNS names) of the machines that will host the executing processes. For the network of Figure 5.1, the hostfile would contain the following (note the absence of sunserver's IP):

```
192.168.0.5
192.168.0.7
192.168.0.100
```

or a permutation of the above. If these lines are saved in file hosts, distributing four processes over the three available nodes would require:

```
$ mpirun —hostfile hosts —np 4 mpihello
```

The processes would be distributed in a round-robin fashion starting from the first entry in the hostfile and the process with rank 0. Thus, the perseas machine would end up with two processes, ranked 0 and 3.[4] The optional "**slots**" modifier for each node in the hostfile can allow us to run one process per available core.

```
192.168.0.5 slots=8
192.168.0.7 slots=4
192.168.0.100 slots=2
```

Then we would get all four processes processes running on perseas.[5]

The slots modifiers can be used in conjunction with the -loadbalance switch, which tries to distribute the processes evenly across nodes.

The construction and maintenance of the hostfile is a simple matter when static IPs are used. Dynamic IPs present a challenge, that is actually trivial if a sequence of simple steps is employed. These steps, which can also be automated with the use of a script, are described in detail in Appendix B.2.

---

[4] A *rankfile* can be used to fine-tune the mapping of processes to available nodes. The interested reader should consult the mpirun's manual page for more information.

[5] Actually, this would cause the generation of an error, i.e., the program would not start, since the machine from which the program is launched, in our case, the hermes laptop, must participate in the execution.

5.5 PROGRAM ARCHITECTURE

5.5.1 SPMD

MPI software can be constructed according to the Single-Program, Multiple-Data (SPMD) paradigm or the Multiple-Program, Multiple-Data (MPMD) one discussed in the next section. The former one facilitates easy source code management and dictates that the nodes query their rank and adjust their behavior accordingly. Consequently, the `main` function is made up of a switch or if-else statements that navigate the nodes to their workloads. The node with rank 0 (typically representing the node that controls the terminal managing the standard I/O streams) is usually reserved to play the role of the work coordinator or *master*. SPMD is the typical approach used by MPI programs.

An example along the guidelines set above is shown in Figure 5.2. Code sections ③ and ④ in Figure 5.2 serve to differentiate node behavior. The syntax and semantics of the communication calls in ⑤ and ⑥ are explained in Section 5.6.

5.5.2 MPMD

Multiple-Program Multiple-Data (MPMD) programs are appropriate when, either heterogeneous machines make up the execution platform (hence the need for different executable binaries), or the code and static data are just too large to be forcefully propagated to all nodes/processes. MPMD programs require more housekeeping than the SPMD ones, but because they do not need to incorporate code and data that will not be used, the memory footprint of each process can be minimized. Another way to look at it is that available memory is maximized.

One can specify different executables to use for groups of processes in two ways, which are pretty similar:

1. **Using command-line parameters:** In this approach, the `mpirun` should be accompanied by two or more `-np #` exec specifications separated by a semicolon (;), each specifying how many copies of the `exec` binary to run. Example:

   ```
   $ mpirun —np 2 pr1 : —np 5 pr2
   ```

   will run two processes with the `pr1` and five processes with the `pr2` executable, all part of the same global communicator.

2. **Using an *appfile* (application file):** An *appfile* is a text file containing all the parameters required by `mpirun`. If an appfile is specified, all other command-line parameters are ignored. Hence, an appfile needs to also contain the IPs or DNS names of the hosts because a `-hostfile` parameter will be ignored.
   Assuming that we would like to use the `sunserver` of Figure. 5.1 in our execution platform, we should prepare two executables: one for `sunserver` and one for the other nodes. This can be done by using a cross-compiler on one machine or by running the native compiler on each platform. If the binaries

```
①  #include<mpi.h>
    #include<string.h>
    #include<stdio.h>
    #define MESSTAG 0
    #define MAXLEN 100


    int main (int argc, char **argv) {
②      MPI_Init (&argc, &argv);
③      int rank, num, i;
        MPI_Comm_rank (MPI_COMM_WORLD, &rank);
        MPI_Comm_size (MPI_COMM_WORLD, &num);
④      if (rank == 0) {
            char mess[] = "Hello World";
            int len = strlen(mess)+1;
            for (i = 1; i < num; i++)
⑤              MPI_Send (mess, len, MPI_CHAR, i, MESSTAG, MPI_COMM_WORLD);
        } else {
            char mess[MAXLEN];
            MPI_Status status;
⑥          MPI_Recv (mess, MAXLEN, MPI_CHAR, 0, MESSTAG, MPI_COMM_WORLD, &status);
            printf ("%i received %s\n", rank, mess);
        }
⑦      MPI_Finalize ();
        return 0;
    }
```

Key:

①	MPI-related header files
②	MPI initialization. Any command-line parameters destined for the MPI runtime are passed on.
③	Rank query.
④	Code branching based on process identity/rank
⑤	Basic send operation.
⑥	Basic MPI receiving operation. The *MPI_Status* structure holds information about the message.
⑦	MPI termination and cleanup.

FIGURE 5.2

A SPMD "Hello World" MPI program using the C bindings.

produced are named `myapp.linux` and `myapp.solaris`, the following appfile would suffice for running eight copies of `myapp.solaris` on sunserver and two copies of `myapp.linux` on each of the other three nodes.

```
-host 192.168.0.2   -np 8 myapp.solaris
-host 192.168.0.5   -np 2 myapp.linux
-host 192.168.0.7   -np 2 myapp.linux
-host 192.168.0.100 -np 2 myapp.linux
```

LISTING 5.4

A sample appfile for executing an MPI program on a heterogeneous platform.

As can be observed in the preceding example, the contents of the appfile are just normal parameters that could have been given directly to mpirun (although it would be a very long line!). If the name of the appfile is appconf, the execution could be initiated by:

```
$ mpirun —app appconf
```

A MPMD example is given in Listing 5.5 in the following section. A more extensive example that combines computations on CPU and GPU nodes is given in Section 6.12.2.3.

5.6 POINT-TO-POINT COMMUNICATION

Figure 5.2, and the ⑤ and ⑥ statements in particular, are examples of the functionality for which MPI is most famous, i.e., the easy exchange of information between processes or nodes. MPI provides a diverse variety of send and receive primitives that allow programmers to select the ones that are most suitable in every imaginable scenario. The simplest are the ones used in Figure 5.2. The syntax of MPI_Send is

```
int MPI_Send(void         *buf,       // Address of the send buffer (IN)
             int          count,      // Number of items in message (IN)
             MPI_Datatype datatype,   // MPI—based symbolic constant
                                      //    representing the type of data
                                      //    being communicated (IN)
             int          dest,       // Destination process rank (IN)
             int          tag,        // Label identifying the type
                                      //    of message (IN)
             MPI_Comm     comm        // Identifies the communicator
                                      //    context of 'dest' (IN)
    )
```

MPI_Send (as most of MPI calls) returns an error value. If this value is 0 (or the symbolic constant MPI_SUCCESS), no error has occurred.

The first half of the parameters serve to describe the message and the second half to describe the destination process. MPI_Send follows the footsteps of other standard C library functions that operate of arrays of arbitrary data, such as qsort, which implements the quicksort algorithm. The syntax of qsort is:

```
void qsort(void       *base,         // Address of data buffer to sort
           size_t     nmemb,         // Number of items in buffer
           size_t     size,          // Size of each item in buffer
           int(*comp)(const void *,  // Pointer to a function that can
                      const void *)  //    compare the items pairwise
      )
```

The similarities are many, but so are the differences. Why is MPI_Send requiring the specification of the datatype, whereas qsort is happy with the size of each item? The answer can be given through another question: If a big-indian machine, such as an i7 processor, were sending data to a little-indian machine, such as a PowerPC processor, how would the latter be able to read the data? One would need to go over the buffer and change the byte ordering. But what if a 32-bit machine were sending data to a 64-bit one? Clearly, this is a burden that should not be left to the application programmer.[6]

MPI can do the job automatically if we explicitly specify the datatypes in a machine-agnostic (i.e., MPI-based) fashion. Such translations do not take place for homogeneous platforms, but forcing the source code to be written in such a manner means that it will never need to be modified, regardless of the target execution platform. Table 5.2 lists some of the MPI datatypes.

The second half of MPI_Send parameters relate to the routing of the message as the destination process is identified through the pair of (communicator, rank) values. The tag parameter (which should be a non negative number[7]) is used so that two processes can identify and filter the different messages that are exchanged between them. The filtering takes place on the receiving side that should obviously execute an MPI_Recv call. The syntax is:

```
int MPI_Recv(void        *buf,    // Address of receive buffer (OUT)
             int          count,  // Buffer capacity in items (IN)
             MPI_Datatype datatype,// Same as in MPI_Send (IN)
             int          source, // Rank of sending process (IN)
             int          tag,    // Label identifying the type
                                  //   of message expected (IN)
             MPI_Comm     comm,   // Identifies the communicator
                                  //   context of 'source' (IN)
             MPI_Status   *status // Pointer to structure holding
                                  //   message parameters (OUT)
            )
```

The syntax of MPI_Recv mirrors the one by MPI_Send with the exclusion of the MPI_Status structure pointer. Its purpose will be explained shortly. The buffer used by the receiving process must be big enough to accommodate the data sent.

Table 5.2 A partial list of MPI datatypes

MPI Datatypes	C Datatypes
MPI_CHAR	signed char
MPI_UNSIGNED_CHAR	unsigned char
MPI_INT	signed int
MPI_LONG	signed long int
MPI_FLOAT	float
MPI_DOUBLE	double
MPI_LONG_DOUBLE	long double

---

[6]Data representation and type size are some of the nastiest sources of bugs in computer software. The Y2K bug is such an example.

[7]MPI-1 specifies that it should be between 0 and MPI_TAG_UB.

Obviously, the datatype should match the actual type of items being communicated. The source parameter can be either a non negative integer, in which case it identifies the (comm, source) process, or set to the symbolic constant MPI_ANY_SOURCE (a quick search in the mpi.h header file reveals this to be equal to -1). In the latter case any process from the specified communicator can be the source of the message. The communicator identifier must match the one used by the sender process.

The tag can be set to a non negative number to select a particular type of message, or it can be set to MPI_ANY_TAG (again representing -1) to just get any incoming message from the source, regardless of its tag.

The above points mean that there is a bit of flexibility to how a process receives messages. So, after a successful message acquisition, how can the process know where the message came from? What is its exact length? And what is the tag that the sender attached?

Fortunately, all this information is stored in the MPI_Status structure that the receiver provides. Its declaration is:

```
typedef struct ompi_status_public_t MPI_Status;
struct ompi_status_public_t {
   int MPI_SOURCE;    // The rank of the source
   int MPI_TAG;       // The tag set by the source
   int MPI_ERROR;     // If not 0, it indicates an error
   int _count;        // Size of message in bytes
   int _cancelled;
};
```

The last two data members of the MPI_Status structure are not meant to be directly accessible. Instead, the MPI_Get_count function can be used to return the length of the message in data items:

```
int MPI_Get_count(MPI_Status    *status,   // Address of a structure
                                           //    set by MPI_Recv (IN)
                  MPI_Datatype datatype,   // MPI datatype expected (IN)
                  int *count               // Number of items read (OUT)
                 )
```

If a developer chooses to ignore this information, the MPI_Status reference can be replaced with the MPI_STATUS_IGNORE symbolic constant.

Having become acquainted with the intricacies of the basic communication primitives in MPI, we can put them to work in the MPMD program of Listing 5.5, where the rank-0 process receives and prints out messages from the other running processes.

```
1   //————— master.c —————
2   #include <mpi.h>
3   #include <stdio.h>
4   #include <string.h>
5
6   #define MAXLEN 100
7   char buff[MAXLEN];
8
```

```
 9   int main (int argc, char **argv)
10   {
11     MPI_Status st;
12     int procNum;
13
14     MPI_Init (&argc, &argv);
15     MPI_Comm_size (MPI_COMM_WORLD, &procNum);
16     while (--procNum)
17       {
18         MPI_Recv (buff, MAXLEN, MPI_CHAR, MPI_ANY_SOURCE, MPI_ANY_TAG,
19                   MPI_COMM_WORLD, &st);
20         int aux;
21         MPI_Get_count (&st, MPI_CHAR, &aux);
22         buff[aux] = 0;
23         printf ("%s\n", buff);
24       }
25     MPI_Finalize ();
26   }
27
28
29   //————— worker.c —————
30   #include <mpi.h>
31   #include <stdio.h>
32   #include <string.h>
33   #include <stdlib.h>
34   #define MAXLEN 100
35   char *greetings[] = { "Hello", "Hi", "Awaiting your command" };
36   char buff[MAXLEN];
37
38   int main (int argc, char **argv)
39   {
40     int grID, rank;
41     srand (time (0));
42     MPI_Init (&argc, &argv);
43     grID = rand () % 3;
44     MPI_Comm_rank (MPI_COMM_WORLD, &rank);
45     sprintf (buff, "Node %i says %s", rank, greetings[grID]);
46     MPI_Send (buff, strlen (buff), MPI_CHAR, 0, 0, MPI_COMM_WORLD);
47     MPI_Finalize ();
48   }
```

LISTING 5.5

A MPMD example made up of two files: master.c and worker.c, which make use of
MPI_Send, MPI_Recv, and MPI_Status.

The worker processes initialize the pseudo-random number generator in line 41
before randomly selecting one of the three greeting messages in line 43. The node
rank (retrieved in line 44) and the selected message are printed to a character array
in line 45 before being sent to process 0 in line 46.

The master process, on the other hand, waits for as many incoming messages as
the communicator size minus 1, via the line 16 loop. The messages are read in the

random order in which they arrive, and are subsequently printed out (line 23) after a zero termination character is appended at the end of the received string (line 22). The actual size of the message is needed for this purpose, and that is why it is calculated in line 21.

The Listing 5.5 program can compile and execute with the following sequence of commands:

```
$ mpicc master.c -o master
$ mpicc worker.c -o worker
$ mpirun -np 1 master : -np 3 worker
```

Because the execution will be done on the same machine (a `-hostfile` parameter is absent above), one can expect to get the same greeting (most of the time) from all workers, since the pseudo-random number generator is initialized with the same value (current time in seconds in line 41), e.g.:

```
Node 2 says Hi
Node 3 says Hi
Node 1 says Hi
```

When two processes exchange messages back and forth, the ordering (blocking) of send and receive operations is critical.

5.7 ALTERNATIVE POINT-TO-POINT COMMUNICATION MODES

As reported in the previous section, `MPI_Send` returns `MPI_SUCCESS` if no error has occurred. Is this an indication that the message was delivered successfully to its destination? In MPI nomenclature, `MPI_Send` is called a *blocking send* operation, implying that the sender blocks until the message is delivered. However, this term is misleading because the function may return before the message is delivered!

`MPI_Send` uses the so called *standard communication mode*. What really happens is that MPI decides, based on the size of the message, whether to block the call until the destination process collects it or to return before a matching receive is issued. The latter is chosen if the message is small enough, making `MPI_Send` **locally blocking**, i.e., the function returns as soon as the message is copied to a local MPI buffer, boosting CPU utilization. The copy is necessary so as to release the buffer used by the source process for subsequent operations, because with this form of send, there is no way for the sender process to know when the message has been delivered.

There are three additional communication modes:

- **Buffered**: In buffered mode, the sending operation is always locally blocking, i.e., it will return as soon as the message is copied to a buffer. The second difference with the standard communication mode is that the buffer is user-provided.
- **Synchronous**: In synchronous mode, the sending operation will return only after the destination process has initiated and started the retrieval of the message

(the receiving may not be complete, though). This is a proper *globally blocking* operation.

- **Ready**: The send operation will succeed only if a matching receive operation has been initiated already. Otherwise, the function returns with an error code. The purpose of this mode is to reduce the overhead of handshaking operations.

To distinguish the different communication modes, a single letter is prefixed before Send: **B** for buffered, **S** for synchronous, and **R** for ready. All the additional functions share the same signature with the standard MPI_Send:

```
int [ MPI_Bsend | MPI_Ssend | MPI_Rsend ] (void *buf, int count, ↩
    MPI_Datatype datatype, int dest, int tag, MPI_Comm comm);
```

Buffered and synchronous modes constitute the two opposite ends of what a send operation could do. The first one mandates the use of a buffer (a user-supplied one so that it is always sufficiently large), whereas the latter forgoes the need of a buffer by forcing the sender to wait for the message to reach the destination.

The buffered mode requires a bit of setup work in order to be deployed. The details are supplied in the following section.

5.7.1 BUFFERED COMMUNICATIONS

The buffered communication mode requires that the user allocate a dedicated buffer for MPI to hold the messages that are sent via *buffered* send calls. Each process can specify only one buffer, and thus it is important that this buffer is big enough to accommodate all the communication needs of the buffered communication calls. If the specified buffer overflows, MPI will signal an error. Non buffered send calls are handled natively by MPI, i.e., by using MPI's own buffers if it is deemed to be necessary. A typical sequence is:

```
MPI_Buffer_attach (...);
...
MPI_Bsend (...);
...
MPI_Buffer_detach (...);
```

MPI_Bsend has the same signature as MPI_Send and there is no modification required to the receiving end of the communication, i.e., MPI_Recv is used as normal.

The MPI_Buffer_attach function informs MPI of the location and size of the user-provided buffer space. This memory can be reclaimed and either used for another purpose or freed by calling the MPI_Buffer_detach function. Care should be used when passing parameters to the latter. Although in MPI_Buffer_attach the pointer is an input parameter, in MPI_Buffer_detach the double pointer is an output parameter, i.e., the address of a pointer variable is expected.

An example along the lines of the "Hello World" program explained previously is given in Listing 5.6.

```
#include <mpi.h>
#include <stdio.h>
#include <stdlib.h>
#include <string.h>

#define COMMBUFFSIZE 1024    /* This would be too small under most ←
        circumstances */
#define MAXMSGSIZE 10
#define MSGTAG 0

int main (int argc, char **argv)
{
  int rank, num, i;
  MPI_Init (&argc, &argv);
  MPI_Comm_rank (MPI_COMM_WORLD, &rank);
  MPI_Comm_size (MPI_COMM_WORLD, &num);

  if (rank == 0)
    {
      // allocate buffer space and designate it for MPI use
      unsigned char *buff = (unsigned char *) malloc (sizeof (unsigned ←
            char) * COMMBUFFSIZE);
      MPI_Buffer_attach (buff, COMMBUFFSIZE);
      char *msg = "Test msg";
      for (i = 1; i < num; i++)
          MPI_Bsend (msg, strlen (msg) + 1, MPI_CHAR, i, MSGTAG, ←
              MPI_COMM_WORLD);

      // detach and release buffer space
      unsigned char *bptr;
      int bsize;
      MPI_Buffer_detach (&bptr, &bsize);
      free (bptr);
    }
  else
    {
      MPI_Status status;
      char msg[MAXMSGSIZE];
      MPI_Recv (msg, MAXMSGSIZE, MPI_CHAR, 0, MSGTAG, MPI_COMM_WORLD, ←
          &status);          // no change at receiving end
      printf ("%s\n", msg);
    }

  MPI_Finalize ();
  return 0;
}
```

LISTING 5.6

A variation to the "Hello World" program that uses buffered communications on node 0.

5.8 **NON BLOCKING COMMUNICATIONS**

In general, buffered sends are considered a bad practice because of the explicit need to perform a memory copy, which is an operation that is not mandated by the normal send primitive. Performance can be enhanced if no copy ever takes place, and this is the domain of the "immediate" non blocking functions. One just has to use the MPI_Isend function in place of MPI_Send.

On the receiving side, concurrency can be improved if the MPI_Recv function is replaced by the MPI_Irecv one, which does not block. However, this is no free lunch! Both immediate functions initiate the communication, but upon their return to the caller, the status of the message is unknown. This is a problem for both parties, since the sender would not know when it is possible to reuse or modify the area holding the data being sent, and the receiver would not know when it can use the buffer designated for holding the message.

To overcome this problem, polling has to be used, i.e., both parties have to query the MPI environment on the status of the initiated action. For this purpose, a special handle is returned to the two processes upon completion of the corresponding functions in the form of an MPI_Request structure. The signatures of the two aforementioned functions are:

```
typedef int MPI_Request;

int MPI_Isend(void        *buf,      // Address of data buffer (OUT)
              int          count,    // Number of data items (IN)
              MPI_Datatype datatype, // Same as in MPI_Send (IN)
              int          source,   // Rank of destination proc. (IN)
              int          tag,      // Label identifying the type
                                     //    of message (IN)
              MPI_Comm     comm,     // Identifies the communicator
                                     //    context of 'source' (IN)
              MPI_Request *req       // Used to return a handle for
                                     //    checking status (OUT)
             )

int MPI_Irecv(void        *buf,      // Address of receive buff. (OUT)
              int          count,    // Buffer capacity in items (IN)
              MPI_Datatype datatype, // Same as in MPI_Send (IN)
              int          source,   // Rank of sending process (IN)
              int          tag,      // Label identifying the type
                                     //    of message expected (IN)
              MPI_Comm     comm,     // Identifies the communicator
                                     //    context of 'source' (IN)
              MPI_Request *req       // Used to return a handle for
                                     //    checking status (OUT)
             )
```

Polling can be performed via the `MPI_Wait` and `MPI_Test` functions, which are blocking and non blocking, respectively. Both can set an `MPI_Status` structure, which, for the receiver, holds crucial message information:

```
int MPI_Wait(MPI_Request *req, // Address of the handle identifying
                               //    the operation queried (IN/OUT)
                               //    The call invalidates *req by
                               //    setting it to MPI_REQUEST_NULL.
             MPI_Status *st    // Address of the structure that will
                               //    hold the comm. information   (OUT)
            )

int MPI_Test(MPI_Request *req, // Address of the handle identifying
                               //    the operation queried (IN)
             int       *flag,  // Set to true if operation is
                               //    complete (OUT).
             MPI_Status *st    // Address of the structure that will
                               //    hold the comm. information   (OUT)
            )
```

A side effect of `MPI_Wait` (and `MPI_Test`, upon a successful return) is that the `MPI_Request` handle is destroyed and the corresponding pointer is set to the symbolic constant `MPI_REQUEST_NULL`.

The proper use of the immediate communication primitives is illustrated through the example shown in Listing 5.7. It is assumed that a range of numbers is to be to partitioned and assigned to the participating nodes by the master node. In the code that follows, we assume that the partitioning is homogeneous, i.e., everyone gets an equal share of the work (including the master), but in practice this can be easily changed. An illustration of the communication involved for a total of three nodes is shown in Figure 5.3.

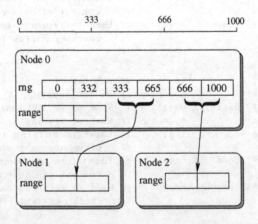

FIGURE 5.3

An illustration of the distribution taking place in Listing 5.7 for three nodes.

```
 1   // File : isend_example.c
 2   #include <mpi.h>
 3   #include <stdio.h>
 4   #include <stdlib.h>
 5   #include <string.h>
 6
 7   #define RANGEMIN 0
 8   #define RANGEMAX 1000
 9   #define MSGTAG 0
10
11   int main (int argc, char **argv)
12   {
13     int rank, num, i;
14     int range[2];
15     MPI_Init (&argc, &argv);
16     MPI_Comm_rank (MPI_COMM_WORLD, &rank);
17     MPI_Comm_size (MPI_COMM_WORLD, &num);
18     MPI_Status status;
19
20     if (rank == 0)
21       {
22           MPI_Request rq[num-1];
23           int rng[2*num];
24           int width = (RANGEMAX - RANGEMIN) / num;
25           rng[0] = RANGEMIN;                // left limit
26           rng[1] = rng[0] + width - 1;      // right limit
27           for(i=1;i<num;i++)
28              {
29                 rng[i*2] = rng[i*2-1] + 1;       // message preparation
30                 rng[i*2+1] = (i==num-1) ? RANGEMAX : rng[i*2] + width - 1;
31              }
32
33           for(i=1;i<num;i++)             // initiate all send operations
34                MPI_Isend(rng+i*2, 2, MPI_INT, i, MSGTAG, MPI_COMM_WORLD,
35                      &(rq[i-1]));
36
37           for(i=1;i<num;i++)             // block unti all are complete
38                MPI_Wait(&(rq[i-1]), &status);
39
40       range[0] = rng[0];                 // master's limits
41       range[1] = rng[1];
42       }
43     else
44       {
45         MPI_Request rq;
46         MPI_Irecv (range, 2, MPI_INT, 0, MSGTAG, MPI_COMM_WORLD,&rq);
47         MPI_Wait(&rq, &status);
48       }
```

```
49
50    printf ("Node %i's range : ( %i, %i )\n", rank, range[0], range[1]);
51
52    MPI_Finalize ();
53    return 0;
54 }
```

LISTING 5.7

A immediate communications example, where a range of numbers is evenly split among the nodes. The master sends the range for which each node is responsible.

Key points of this program are:

- Multiple send operations can be initiated at the same time (lines 33 and 34). However, each can be tracked only by maintaining a separate handle for it. Hence, the need to have an array of type `MPI_Request` (line 22).
- If multiple operations are initiated, their associated data buffers are free for modification only after `MPI_Wait` returns. In order to allow multiple concurrent communications to take place, each message is designated its own buffer (line 23).
- If an `MPI_Irecv` is immediately followed by a call to `MPI_Wait` (lines 46 and 47), the two calls can be replaced by a normal `MPI_Recv` call.

The preceding program is in no way optimal. MPI provides very powerful *collective* (i.e., involving more than two nodes) communication operations that could reduce the loops of lines 33-38 to a single line (see Section 5.11). Not to mention that for static partitionings like the one shown, no communication is really necessary as each node can calculate its own range, replacing lines 20-48 with:

```
int width = (RANGEMAX − RANGEMIN) / num;
range[0] = RANGEMIN + rank * width;
range[1] = (rank == num−1) ? RANGEMAX : range[0] + width − 1;
```

The same could apply if the range limits were given as command-line parameters (e.g., via the `argv` array), as these become available to all MPI processes.

Immediate communications can also employ one of the three alternative modes explained in Section 5.7. So, we have, buffered, synchronous, and ready modes. To distinguishing them, a single letter is sandwiched between I and s in Isend: **b** for buffered, **s** for synchronous, and **r** for ready. All the additional functions share the same signature with the standard `MPI_Isend`:

```
int [ MPI_Ibsend I MPI_Issend I MPI_Irsend ] (void *buf, int count, ↵
     MPI_Datatype datatype, int dest, int tag, MPI_Comm comm, ↵
     MPI_Request &req);
```

Their semantics are identical to the alternative calls discussed in Section 5.7.

It should be noted that blocking sends can be matched with non blocking receives, and vice versa. The crucial parts that need to match are the endpoints, as identified by the (communicator, rank, message tag) tuple.

5.9 POINT-TO-POINT COMMUNICATIONS: SUMMARY

Under normal circumstances the wealth of all these different communication modes is redundant. But in the case where MPI_Send is not good enough for your purposes, the decision comes down to one of the following choices:

A sending process ...	Function
... must block until the message is delivered	MPI_Ssend
... should wait only until the message is buffered	MPI_Bsend
... should return immediately without ever blocking	MPI_Isend

5.10 ERROR REPORTING AND HANDLING

MPI provides rudimentary error reporting facilities, especially in comparison with the exception hierarchy that platforms such as Java provide. MPI is designed to offer reliable communications, so developers do not have to check to see whether errors happened during data transmissions. However, if MPI functions are called with the wrong parameters, they can still malfunction.

All MPI calls (except MPI_Wtime and MPI_Wtick, which are explained in Appendix F.2, Section C.5) return an integer value that represents an error condition. If the returned value is equal to MPI_SUCCESS (0), no error was detected, at least locally. An example of what this means is that we can have an MPI_Send call returning successfully after copying the message to a local MPI buffer, but the message may never be delivered to a destination, for a number of reasons. Such reasons include the use of a mismatched tag, wrong destination rank, or the like.

By default, MPI calls that detect an error fail catastrophically, i.e., they abort the application.

MPI-2 provides the capability to change this behavior by calling the MPI_Comm_set _errhandler function[8]:

```
int MPI_Comm_set_errhandler(MPI_Comm comm,          // Communicator (IN)
                    MPI_Errhandler errhandler) // structure identi-
                                               // fying the error
                                               // handler (IN)
```

We can either switch to one of the predefined handlers or define our own error handler. The predefined handlers that can be passed as parameters to MPI_Comm_set_errhandler are:

- MPI_ERRORS_ARE_FATAL: The default, terminate-upon-error handler.

---

[8]MPI-1 provides an alternative in the form of the MPI_Errhandler_set function. This function is considered deprecated in MPI-2 and it should not be used. Most deprecated functions in MPI-2 have been completely removed from MPI-3.

- `MPI_ERRORS_RETURN`: MPI calls return with an error code, but the program is not aborted. MPI will try, but it is not guaranteed to be able, to recover from the error condition.

A custom error handler can be registered with MPI to handle errors in a different manner. The error-handling function must be defined as a variadic function (i.e., allowing a variable number of parameters) with the following signature:

```
void my_handler(MPI_Comm *comm, int *errcode, ...);
```

The parameters beyond the second one can be accessed with the stdarg standard C library. However, MPI does not specify what is supposed to come after the second parameter, so any attempt to access them results in code that is non portable across different MPI implementations.

The custom handler must be registered with MPI with the following function:

```
int MPI_Comm_create_errhandler (
        MPI_Comm_errhandler_fn *function,   // Pointer to a handler
                                            // function (IN)
        MPI_Errhandler          *errhandler)// Pointer to a
                                            // MPI_Errhandler
                                            // structure , to be used
                                            // for registration (OUT)
```

Listing 4.8 provides an example.

```
1   // File : errorHandling .c
2   . . .
3   void customErrHandler(MPI_Comm *comm, int *errcode, ...) {
4     printf("Error %i\n", *errcode);
5   }
6
7   int main (int argc, char **argv) {
8     MPI_Init (&argc, &argv);
9     MPI_Errhandler eh;
10
11    MPI_Comm_create_errhandler (customErrHandler, &eh);
12    MPI_Comm_set_errhandler (MPI_COMM_WORLD, eh);
13    MPI_Comm c;
14
15    int rank, num, i;
16    MPI_Comm_rank (MPI_COMM_WORLD, &rank);
17    MPI_Comm_size (MPI_COMM_WORLD, &num);
18    if (rank == 0) {
19        char mess[] = "Hello World";
20        for (i = 1; i < num; i++)
21          MPI_Send (mess, strlen (mess) + 1, MPI_CHAR, i, MESSTAG, c);
22    }
23    else {
24        char mess[MAXLEN];
```

```
25        MPI_Status status;
26        MPI_Recv (mess, MAXLEN, MPI_DOUBLE, 0, MESSTAG, MPI_COMM_WORLD, ↵
              &status);
27        printf ("%i received %s\n", rank, mess);
28      }
29    . . .
```

LISTING 5.8

A variation of the "Hello World" example with a custom error handler. The MPI_Send call in line 21 will cause the customErrHandler function to execute in response to using an invalid/uninitialized communicator.

MPI-2 provides three different types of error handlers: for communicators, for windows (used in remote memory access), and for files (for parallel I/O). In this section we discussed explicitly only communicator-specific error handling. However, the functions we discussed have direct equivalents in the other two cases. The only thing that changes is that the Comm part of the function name is replaced by Win and File, respectively: MPI_Win_set_errhandler, MPI_File_create_errhandler, and so on.

5.11 COLLECTIVE COMMUNICATIONS

The term *collective communications* refers to operations that involve more than two nodes. Communication time is idle time for compute nodes and so it is of critical importance to minimize it. The non blocking variants of our point-to-point primitives allow for overlap between computation and communication. Collective primitives go one step further by also allowing *communications that involve multiple parties to take place concurrently.*

Here is an example that illustrates the necessity of having such operations: The 0-ranked process in MPI has exclusive access to the standard input stream. So, if the user enters a parameter required by all the nodes of an application, the only way it can be made accessible to the other MPI nodes is if process 0 sends/**broadcasts** it to them:

```
. . .
MPI_Comm_rank (MPI_COMM_WORLD, &rank);
MPI_Comm_size (MPI_COMM_WORLD, &num);
MPI_Status status;

if (rank == 0)
  {
     int param;
     cin >> param;
     for(i=1;i<num;i++)
         MPI_Send(&param, 1, MPI_INT, i, MSGTAG, MPI_COMM_WORLD);

  }
```

```
    else
    {
        int param;
        MPI_Recv (&param, 1, MPI_INT, 0, MSGTAG, MPI_COMM_WORLD, &status↩
            );
        . . .
    }
```

The communication cost of the preceding code snippet is proportional to the number of processes involved, since it requires $\Theta(N)$ individual communication operations conducted in sequence. This is obviously an expensive approach. Using MPI_Isend would not solve this problem, because what matters is the completion of the communication, not just the availability of node 0.

If, however, we make the nodes that have already received the data act as repeaters, we could reduce the overall cost, as shown in Listing 5.9.

```
1   // File : broadcast.c
2   . . .
3   // Returns the position of the most significant set bit of its ↩
        argument
4   int MSB(int i) {
5       int pos = 0;
6       int bitMask = 0xFFFFFFFE;
7       while (i != 0) {
8           i = i & bitMask;
9           pos++;
10          bitMask <<= 1;
11      }
12      return pos - 1;
13  }
14  //*****************************************
15
16  int main(int argc, char **argv) {
17      MPI_Init(&argc, &argv);
18
19      int rank, num, i;
20      MPI_Comm_rank(MPI_COMM_WORLD, &rank);
21      MPI_Comm_size(MPI_COMM_WORLD, &num);
22      MPI_Status status;
23
24      if (rank == 0) {
25          int destID = 1;
26          double data;
27          scanf("%lf", &data);
28          while (destID < num) {     // a subset of nodes gets a message
29              MPI_Send(&data, 1, MPI_DOUBLE, destID, MESSTAG, ↩
                    MPI_COMM_WORLD);
30              destID <<= 1;
31          }
32      } else {
33          int msbPos = MSB(rank);
```

```
34        int srcID = rank ^ (1 << msbPos);    // the message is not ←
              coming from 0 for all
35        printf("#%i has source %i\n", rank, srcID);
36
37        // receive the message
38        double data;
39        MPI_Recv(&data, 1, MPI_DOUBLE, srcID, MESSTAG, MPI_COMM_WORLD, ←
              &status);
40        printf("Node #%i received %lf\n", rank, data);
41
42        // calculate the ID of the node that will receive a copy of ←
              the message
43        int destID = rank | (1 << (msbPos + 1));
44        while (destID < num) {
45            MPI_Send(&data, 1, MPI_DOUBLE, destID, MESSTAG, ←
                  MPI_COMM_WORLD);
46            msbPos++;
47            destID = rank | (1 << (msbPos + 1));
48        }
49    }
50    . . .
```

LISTING 5.9

An efficient broadcasting approach that takes $\Theta(\lceil lgN \rceil)$ steps to complete.

The program of Listing 5.9 works by treating the nodes of the MPI program as being arranged in a hypercube. Every node sends a message to one of its neighbors using a dimension that has not yet been used to carry a message. To accomplish this feat, the destination's rank is calculated by switching one of the zero bits of the source's rank that are above its most significant set bit. The same is true for the 0-ranked node. The source ID for a node that is expecting a message (line 39) is calculated by resetting the most significant bit of its own rank.

For example, if a node's rank is 7 (111 in binary), it will receive its message from node 3 (011 in binary), and it will proceed to send this message to nodes 15 (1111 in binary), 23 (10111 in binary), 39 (100111 in binary), etc. These calculations can be clearly observed in Figure 5.4, which traces an execution of the preceding code.

The second broadcast variation performs better, needing only a cost proportional to $\Theta(\lceil lgN \rceil)$ to complete, as long as there is a direct communication link between all nodes. The proof is easy: At the end of every iteration of the preceding algorithm, the number of nodes that have received the message doubles.

After k iterations we would be able to reach the following number of nodes:

$$1 + 2 + 4 + \cdots + 2^{k-1} = 2^k - 1 \tag{5.1}$$

Starting with node 0, reaching the remaining $N - 1$ nodes would require:

$$N - 1 = 2^k - 1 \Rightarrow k = lg(N) \tag{5.2}$$

steps to complete. Obviously, because k needs to be an integer, we have to round up to $k = \lceil lg(N) \rceil$.

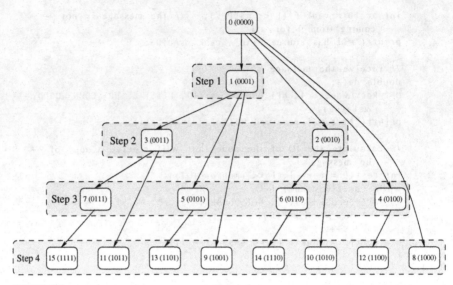

FIGURE 5.4

An illustration of how a message is broadcast, according to the program in Listing 5.9, to 15 nodes in four steps. The nodes are decorated by their ranks, with their binary representation in parentheses.

However, this is a complex solution! Additionally, there is a problem with architectures for which the communication links don't form a complete graph but rather a subset of it, like e.g., a 2D or a 3D mesh, a cylinder, or even have an irregular communication network, such as a Network of Workstations (NoW). The preceding program would still work, but it would no longer be optimized, and our analysis would be flawed as far as the total cost is concerned.

Fortunately, MPI collectives solve this problem also: MPI implementations can provide *optimized* collective operations specifically tuned to perform as efficiently as possible, given the execution platform's communication infrastructure.

MPI provides its own optimized implementation of a broadcast operation via the `MPI_Bcast` function:

```
int MPI_Bcast( void        *buffer,    // address of the buffer that
                                       // either holds or receives
                                       // the data (IN/OUT)
               int          count,     // size of buffer (IN)
               MPI_Datatype dtype,     // MPI type of the elements
                                       //     in the buffer (IN)
               int          root,      // rank of source process (IN)
               MPI_Comm     comm       // communicator (IN)
             )
```

Equipped with the `MPI_Bcast`, we can provide the same functionality as Listing 5.9, with the code shown in Listing 5.10.

```
1   // File : broadcast2.c
2   . . .
3   if (rank == 0) {
4       double data;
5       scanf("%lf", &data);
6       MPI_Bcast( &data, 1, MPI_DOUBLE, 0, MPI_COMM_WORLD );
7   } else {
8       double data;
9       MPI_Bcast( &data, 1, MPI_DOUBLE, 0, MPI_COMM_WORLD );
10      printf("Node #%i received %lf\n", rank, data);
11  }
12  . . .
```

LISTING 5.10

Broadcasting using the MPI_Bcast function.

Lines 6 and 9 in Listing 5.10 are identical, since this is a requirement for the use of MPI_Bcast. Having common or compatible parameters is actually a requirement for using any of the collective MPI operations.

MPI collective operations have distinct traits in comparison to regular point-to-point operations. These are:

- Operations are not distinguished by a tag. They apply *universally* to all the nodes of a *communicator*. If multiple operations are used, they will be executed in the order in which they are called.
- The calls must be identical for all participating processes, regardless of whether they are sources or sinks.
  The parameters used must be identical or at least "compatible." Compatibility has a different meaning for input and output message-related parameters, depending on whether they are used in the source or the destination nodes. The typical rules, unless stated otherwise in the MPI documentation, are:
  - **Input parameters, source nodes:** The type and number of items (if arrays are used), must be identical.
  - **Input parameters, destination nodes:** These are ignored. If pointers are expected, a null reference can be used instead.
  - **Output parameters, source nodes:** These are ignored. If pointers are expected, a null reference can be used instead.
  - **Output parameters, destination nodes:** The type and number of items (if arrays are used), must be identical.

A deviation from these points may cause a call to fail (best case) or produce erroneous results (worst case).

MPI_Bcast can also be used to provide *multicasting* functionality, i.e., sending a message to a subset of the available processes. This can be achieved by creating a custom communicator. This option is explored further in Section 5.13.

MPI provides a large variety of collective operations that we explore in the following sections. They can be divided into the following groups:

- **One-to-all**: MPI_Bcast, MPI_Scatter, MPI_Scatterv
- **All-to-one**: MPI_Gather, MPI_Gatherv, MPI_Reduce
- **All-to-all**: MPI_Alltoall, MPI_Alltoallv, MPI_Allreduce, MPI_Allgather, MPI_Barrier

MPI-3 adds immediate versions of these functions to the standard. The naming convention follows the one used for MPI_Isend, so the function names are produced by replacing MPI_ with MPI_I and making the rest of the name lowercase. The parameters and their order are identical, with the exception of the addition of an extra argument of type MPI_Request* at the end. The request parameter allows the caller process to check to see whether the call is complete or not via the functions MPI_Test and MPI_Wait (see Section 5.8).

In the following sections we explore these operations, going beyond the mere syntax of the commands. The study of the inner workings of the collective operations constitutes a valuable educational tool because it exposes a number of important techniques about managing processes and orchestrating communications between them.

5.11.1 SCATTERING

Scattering refers to the distribution of a dataset to the processes of a communicator. The MPI function is:

```
int MPI_Scatter(void        *sendbuf,   // address of the buffer to be
                                        // sent (IN)
                int         sendcnt,    // number of sendbuf items to
                                        // send per process(IN)
                MPI_Datatype sendtype,  // MPI type of sendbuf
                                        // elements (IN)
                void        *recvbuf,   // address of receiving
                                        // buffer (OUT)
                int         recvcnt,    // size of recvbuf (IN)
                MPI_Datatype recvtype,  // MPI type of recvbuf
                                        // elements (IN)
                int         root,       // rank of source process (IN)
                MPI_Comm    comm)       // communicator (IN)
```

Two buffers are designated: a send buffer that contains the data to be evenly distributed among the processes, including the root, and a receive buffer, where the data will be deposited. The sendcnt parameter specifies how many elements will be sent to each process. As a consequence, sendcnt is a lower bound for the size of the recvbuf, and sendbuf should contain at least $N \cdot recvcnt$ elements, where N is the size of the communicator.

Two datatypes need to be specified, one for the sending and one for the receiving buffer. Typically, these should be identical. However, there are a number of cases in which they can be different, but only if they are derived types based on the same type of primitive type. Such a scenario is examined in Section 5.12, where derived datatypes are examined.

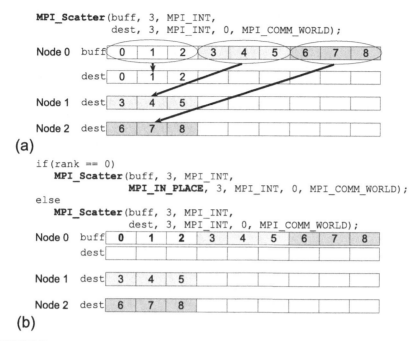

(a)

(b)

FIGURE 5.5

An illustration of how scattering an array works when (a) the root has a destination buffer and (b) the scatter is in place for the root.

The scatter operation has a memory copy overhead for the root process. This can be avoided by specifying as *recvbuf* the symbolic constant MPI_IN_PLACE for the call made by the root. This option does not move the part assigned to the root process. An illustration of MPI_Scatter in action is shown in Figure 5.5.

As an example of the use of MPI_Scatter, let's consider the problem of matrix-vector multiplication, i.e., multiplying a *MxM* matrix A by a *M* element vector B. A parallel solution can be easily designed by applying the geometric data decomposition pattern (see Section 2.3.3). We can split matrix A row-wise into blocks and assign each of the blocks to one MPI node. This decomposition pattern is also favored by the fact that C/C++ uses a row-major memory allocation for 2D arrays.

The calculations taking place in a matrix-vector multiplication are illustrated in Figure 5.6.

If *M* is not evenly divided by the number of MPI processes, a memory violation fault is likely to be produced when MPI_Scatter tries to access the data destined for the last process. In that case, we can still use MPI_Scatter to perform the data distribution if we make sure that the input buffer holding A is padded with enough extra rows to avoid this error. MPI_Bcast can be used for sending the vector B as shown in Listing 5.11.

$$
\begin{pmatrix}
A_{0,0} & A_{0,1} & \dots & A_{0,M-1} \\
A_{1,0} & A_{1,1} & \dots & A_{1,M-1} \\
\vdots & \vdots & & \vdots \\
A_{M-1,0} & A_{M-1,1} & \dots & A_{M-1,M-1}
\end{pmatrix}
\cdot
\begin{pmatrix}
B_0 \\
B_1 \\
\vdots \\
B_{M-1}
\end{pmatrix}
=
$$

$$
\begin{pmatrix}
A_{0,0} \cdot B_0 + A_{0,1} \cdot B_1 + \dots + A_{0,M-1} \cdot B_{M-1} \\
A_{1,0} \cdot B_0 + A_{1,1} \cdot B_1 + \dots + A_{1,M-1} \cdot B_{M-1} \\
\vdots \\
A_{M-1,0} \cdot B_0 + A_{M-1,1} \cdot B_1 + \dots + A_{M-1,M-1} \cdot B_{M-1}
\end{pmatrix}
$$

FIGURE 5.6

An illustration of how a matrix-vector multiplication is performed.

```
1   // File : matrix_vector.cpp
2   . . .
3   const int M = 100;
4
5   //*******************************************
6   // Performs C=A*B with A a matrix "rows X columns", and B a vector ↩
        with "columns" elements
7   void MV (double *A, double *B, double *C, int columns, int rows)
8   {
9     for (int i = 0; i < rows; i++)
10      {
11        double temp = 0;
12        for (int j = 0; j < columns; j++)
13          temp += A[i * columns + j] * B[j];
14
15        C[i] = temp;
16      }
17  }
18
19  //*******************************************
20  int main (int argc, char **argv)
21  {
22    MPI_Init (&argc, &argv);
23
24    int rank, N;
25    MPI_Comm_rank (MPI_COMM_WORLD, &rank);
26    MPI_Comm_size (MPI_COMM_WORLD, &N);
27    MPI_Status status;
28
29
30    int rowsPerProcess;              // size of block per MPI process
31    int rowsAlloc = M;
32    if (M % N != 0)
33      rowsAlloc = (M / N + 1) * N;
34    rowsPerProcess = rowsAlloc / N;
35
36    if (rank == 0)
```

```
37      {
38        double *A = new double[M * rowsAlloc];
39        double *B = new double[M];
40        double *C = new double[M];          // result vector
41
42        for (int i = 0; i < M * M; i++)  A[i] = i; // initialize A and B
43        for (int i = 0; i < M; i++)        B[i] = 1;
44
45        MPI_Scatter (A, M * rowsPerProcess, MPI_DOUBLE, MPI_IN_PLACE, 0,↩
                     MPI_DOUBLE, 0, MPI_COMM_WORLD);
46        MPI_Bcast (B, M, MPI_DOUBLE, 0, MPI_COMM_WORLD);
47        MV (A, B, C, M, rowsPerProcess);          // root does its ↩
               share of the computation
48
49        // collect results now
50        for (int i = 1; i < N - 1; i++)
51          MPI_Recv (C + rowsPerProcess * i, rowsPerProcess, MPI_DOUBLE, ↩
                   i, RESTAG, MPI_COMM_WORLD, &status);
52
53        // last process treated differently
54        MPI_Recv (C + rowsPerProcess * (N - 1), M - (N - 1) * ↩
                 rowsPerProcess, MPI_DOUBLE, N - 1, RESTAG, MPI_COMM_WORLD, &↩
                 status);
55
56        for (int i = 0; i < M; i++)
57          cout << C[i] << " ";
58        cout << endl;
59      }
60    else
61      {
62        double *locA = new double[M * rowsPerProcess];
63        double *B = new double[M];
64        double *partC = new double[rowsPerProcess];          // partial ↩
               result vector
65
66        MPI_Scatter (NULL, M * rowsPerProcess, MPI_DOUBLE, locA, M * ↩
                   rowsPerProcess, MPI_DOUBLE, 0, MPI_COMM_WORLD);
67        MPI_Bcast (B, M, MPI_DOUBLE, 0, MPI_COMM_WORLD);
68
69        if (rank == N - 1)
70          rowsPerProcess = M - (N - 1) * rowsPerProcess; // strip ↩
                 padded rows for the last process
71
72        MV (locA, B, partC, M, rowsPerProcess);
73        MPI_Send (partC, rowsPerProcess, MPI_DOUBLE, 0, RESTAG, ↩
                 MPI_COMM_WORLD);
74      }
75    . . .
```

LISTING 5.11

Matrix-vector multiplication that uses MPI_Scatter and MPI_Bcast for data distribution.

In detail, the fine points of Listing 5.11 are the following:

- The program is calculating the product of a 100x100 matrix with a 100-element vector. The sizes are controlled by line 3, which defines the symbolic constant M. In a real-life situation, one would expect that the problem data would be read from a file instead of having them initialized to dummy values in lines 42 and 43. However, there is a substantial benefit to using properly manipulated dummy data at the testing phase of an application: You can easily verify the correctness of your parallel algorithm implementation. Given the values used in lines 42 and 43, the preceding program should output a sequence of numbers that represent the sum of the rows of the A matrix: $\frac{(M-1)M}{2} + i \cdot M^2$ for each of the i-th elements, with $i \in [0, M)$. For $M = 100$ we should get "4950 14950 24950 34950 44950 54950 64950 74950 ...."
- The MV function in lines 7-17 calculates a matrix-vector product, given the addresses and sizes of the matrix and vectors involved. Each process calls it once the input data are collected from the root process (line 72).
- The 0-rank process (root) uses in-place scatter to distribute matrix A to all the processes (line 45). The vector is sent via MPI_Bcast (lines 46, 67).
- The (partial) results are collected via point-to-point communications (lines 50-54 and 73).
- The scenario of having M not evenly divided by the number of processes N, is addressed by padding the A matrix with extra rows (lines 32 and 33). Thus, every process gets the same number of matrix rows (rowsPerProcess). During product calculation and result collection, the last process adjusts the rows according to the true size of A and the actual rows that can be used (lines 69-70).
- In order to pass references to multidimensional arrays to functions, C/C++ requires that all but one of the dimension sizes (the higher one) are fixed and declared in the function header. To overcome this limitation and pass arbitrarily sized matrices to the MV function, the A matrix is defined as a 1D array (lines 38, 62). To access the x-column and y-row element (numbering starting from 0) of A, one has to use the index $y \cdot numColumns + x$, since the elements are stored row after row consecutively in memory and the beginning of row y starts at index $y \cdot numColumns$.

One thing that can be considered as a potential pitfall of MPI_Scatter is the need to send the same volume of data to all the members of a communicator. But what if the execution platform is not homogeneous? Faster CPUs should be assigned a larger portion of the workload if execution time is to be minimized. This need is addressed by MPI_Scatterv, where the v suffix stands for vector. MPI_Scatterv syntax requires two additional arrays as input so that the precise amount of data each process will get can be specified. The exact syntax is:

```
int MPI_Scatterv(void      *sendbuf, // Address of the buffer to be
                                     // sent (IN)
                 int       *sendcnts,// Array with as many elements
```

```
                                    // as the communicator size.
                                    // Contains the number of items
                                    // to send to each process (IN)
                                    // Significant only at the root
              int        *displs,   // Same array size as sendcnts
                                    // Contains the offsets in
                                    // sendbuf where each of the
                                    // parts resides (IN)
                                    // Significant only at the root
              MPI_Datatype sendtype, // MPI type of sendbuf
                                    // elements (IN)
              void       *recvbuf,  // Address of receiving
                                    // buffer (OUT)
              int        recvcnt,   // Size of recvbuf (IN)
              MPI_Datatype recvtype, // MPI type of recvbuf
                                    // elements (IN)
              int        root,      // Rank of source process (IN)
              MPI_Comm   comm)      // Communicator (IN)
```

Equipped with MPI_Scatterv, we can avoid having to pad the matrix A. Instead, the code in Listing 5.12 would have to be used.

```
1   // File : matrix_vector2.cpp
2   . . .
3   int rowsPerProcess;            // size of block per MPI process
4   rowsPerProcess = M/N;
5
6   if (rank == 0) {
7       double *A = new double[M * M];
8       double *B = new double[M];
9       double *C = new double[M];        // result vector
10      . . .
11      int displs[N];
12      int sendcnts[N];
13      for(int i=0;i<N;i++) {
14          sendcnts[i] = rowsPerProcess*M;
15          displs[i] = i*rowsPerProcess*M;
16          if(i==N-1)
17              sendcnts[i] = (M - (N-1)*rowsPerProcess)*M;
18      }
19
20      MPI_Scatterv (A, sendcnts,displs, MPI_DOUBLE, MPI_IN_PLACE, 0, ↩
            MPI_DOUBLE, 0, MPI_COMM_WORLD);
21      MPI_Bcast (B, M, MPI_DOUBLE, 0, MPI_COMM_WORLD);
22      MV (A, B, C, M, rowsPerProcess);
23      . . .
24  }
25  else
26  {
27      if (rank == N - 1)
28          rowsPerProcess = M - (N - 1) * rowsPerProcess;
```

```
29        . . .
30        MPI_Scatterv (NULL, NULL, NULL, MPI_DOUBLE, locA, M * ↵
              rowsPerProcess, MPI_DOUBLE, 0, MPI_COMM_WORLD);
31        . . .
32      }
33    . . .
```

LISTING 5.12

A variation of Listing 5.11 that uses MPI_Scatterv. Only the major differences with the original code are shown.

The major addition to Listing 5.11 is the calculation of the send counts and displacement arrays in lines 13-18. These parameters are not required in any other process but the root, and so in line 30 all the corresponding arguments used by the receiving processes are NULL.

Finally, Listing 5.11 has one flaw: Result collection is effectively a collective all-to-one operation. The details of how this can be accomplished with a single statement are discussed in the following section.

Gathering is the exact operation of scattering: It collects data

5.11.2 GATHERING

Gathering is the exact anti-symmetric operation of scattering: It collects data from all the processes of a communicator into the destination process's repository. Similarly to scattering, MPI provides two functions accommodating uniform and variable data collection: MPI_Gather and MPI_Gatherv. Their syntax is:

```
int MPI_Gather(void      *sendbuf,  // Address of the buffer to be
                                    // sent. Separate in each
                                    // source process. (IN)
                                    // Ignored at the destination.
               int        sendcnt,  // Contains the number of items
                                    // to be sent from each process
                                    // Ignored at the destin.(IN)
               MPI_Datatype sendtype, // MPI type of sendbuf
                                    // elements (IN)
               void       *recvbuf,  // Address of receiving
                                    // buffer (OUT)
                                    // Ignored at the sources.
               int        recvcnt,  // Reserved space in recvbuf per
                                    // sending process (IN).
                                    // Ignored at the sources.
               MPI_Datatype recvtype, // MPI type of recvbuf
                                    // elements (IN)
               int        root,     // Rank of destination (IN)
               MPI_Comm   comm)     // Communicator (IN)

int MPI_Gatherv(void      *sendbuf,  // Address of the buffer to be
                                    // sent. Separate in each
                                    // source process. (IN)
```

```
                            // Ignored at the destination.
        int         sendcnt,    // Contains the number of items
                            // to be sent from each process
                            // Ignored at the destin.(IN)
        MPI_Datatype sendtype,  // MPI type of sendbuf
                            // elements (IN)
        void        *recvbuf,   // Address of receiving
                            // buffer (OUT)
                            // Ignored at the sources.
        int         *recvcnts,  // How many items to get from
                            // each source. (IN)
                            // Ignored at the sources.
        int         *displs,    // Location offsets in recvbuf
                            // for each of the sources (IN)
                            // Ignored at the sources.
        MPI_Datatype recvtype,  // MPI type of recvbuf
                            // elements (IN)
        int         root,       // Rank of destination (IN)
        MPI_Comm    comm)       // Communicator (IN)
```

Adopting Listing 5.12 to use gathering instead of point-to-point communications is straightforward. Given the need to treat the last process in the communicator differently, even during the result collection phase, MPI_Gatherv is deemed more suitable for the circumstances.

In Listing 5.13, we are reusing the sending counts (sendcnts) and displacements arrays (displs) for specifying how MPI_Gatherv will collect data from the processes.

```
1   // File : matrix_vector3.cpp
2   . . .
3   int rowsPerProcess;              // size of block per MPI process
4   rowsPerProcess = M/N;
5
6   if (rank == 0)  {
7       . . .
8       MV (A, B, C, M, rowsPerProcess);
9
10      for(int i=0;i<N;i++)
11      {
12          sendcnts[i] = rowsPerProcess;
13          displs[i] = i*rowsPerProcess;
14          if(i==N-1)
15              sendcnts[i] = M - (N-1)*rowsPerProcess;
16      }
17
18      MPI_Gatherv(C, rowsPerProcess, MPI_DOUBLE, C, sendcnts, displs, ↩
            MPI_DOUBLE, 0, MPI_COMM_WORLD);
19      // print out C
20      . . .
21  }
22  else
23      {
```

```
24      . . .
25      MPI_Scatterv (NULL, NULL, NULL, MPI_DOUBLE, locA, M * ↵
            rowsPerProcess, MPI_DOUBLE, 0, MPI_COMM_WORLD);
26      MPI_Bcast (B, M, MPI_DOUBLE, 0, MPI_COMM_WORLD);
27      MV (locA, B, partC, M, rowsPerProcess);
28
29      MPI_Gatherv(partC, rowsPerProcess, MPI_DOUBLE, NULL, NULL, NULL, ↵
            MPI_DOUBLE, 0, MPI_COMM_WORLD);
30      }
31      . . .
```

LISTING 5.13

Modifications to Listing 5.12 so that MPI_Gatherv can be used to collect the matrix-vector product.

5.11.3 REDUCTION

An operation that is frequently taking place in the processing of large collections of data is *reduction*: selecting, extracting, or deriving one or a subset of data items. Some of the simplest examples include summation and finding the minimum or maximum of a set of items.

As an example of reduction, let's consider an MPI version of the multithreaded function integration program presented in Section 3.5.2. Instead of dynamically assigning parts of the input range and focusing on how to terminate the program, we can do a static uniform partitioning and assign $\frac{1}{N}$ of the input range to each process, where N is the number of processes. We effectively switch our focus from problem data distribution to result collection. The shared static variable *result of the IntegrCalc class of Listing 3.12 is no longer available in our distributed memory platform.

In order to be able to accumulate the final result, the root could use point-to-point communication to collect the individual partial results and add them up, in an $\Theta(N)$ time complexity operation. However, this process can be sped up considerably by having pairs of processes sum up their results in successive steps, as shown in Figure 5.7. As illustrated, N does not have to be a power of 2 to be able to use this tournament tree pattern to solve the problem in $\Theta(\lceil lgN \rceil)$.

The mechanics of how the tree in Figure 5.7 is constructed are revealed if the binary representation of the process ranks are taken into consideration. The communications taking place in Figure 5.7 are depicted using a different visualization technique in Figure 5.8.

The reduction operation is taking place over $\lceil lgN \rceil$ steps, one step for each of the bits required to represent the process ranks. During step i, the $i - th$ bit of a process is examined. If it is 1, it sends its partial sum to the process with the same ID as itself but with the i-th bit reset. Subsequently, it takes no action. These steps can be more concisely expressed as the code shown in Listing 5.14.

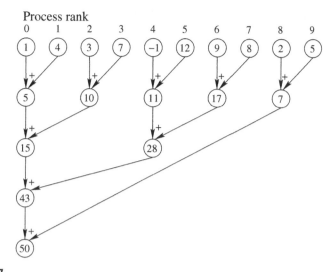

FIGURE 5.7

Calculating a summation using a tournament tree pattern.

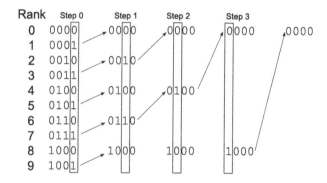

FIGURE 5.8

Graph illustrating the pairings of processes that take place in the tournament tree of Figure 5.7. Edges represent data communications, and the frames highlight the bits considered during each step of the reduction.

```
// File : manual_reduction.cpp
. . .
  int rank, N;
  MPI_Comm_rank (MPI_COMM_WORLD, &rank);
  MPI_Comm_size (MPI_COMM_WORLD, &N);
  MPI_Status status;

  int partialSum = rank;   // just a sample value
  int bitMask = 1;
```

```
10    bool doneFlag = false;    // set when a process sends its partial sum
11    while (bitMask < N && !doneFlag) {
12        int otherPartyID;      // process rank of communication endpoint
13        if ((rank & bitMask) == 0) { // destination process
14            otherPartyID = rank | bitMask;
15            if (otherPartyID >= N) { // invalid otherPartyID indicates
16                bitMask <<= 1;        // that process is not involved
17                continue;             // in current step
18            }
19            int temp;
20            MPI_Recv (&temp, 1, MPI_INT, otherPartyID, MPI_ANY_TAG, ←
                 MPI_COMM_WORLD, &status);
21            partialSum += temp;
22        }
23        else {                        // source process
24            otherPartyID = rank ^ bitMask;
25            doneFlag = true;
26            MPI_Send (&partialSum, 1, MPI_INT, otherPartyID, 0, ←
                 MPI_COMM_WORLD);
27        }
28        bitMask <<= 1;
29    }
30
31    if (rank == 0)
32        cout << partialSum << endl;
33    . . .
```

LISTING 5.14

Summing up the partial results in MPI processes by performing reduction.

MPI provides a built-in reduction function that allows us to perform the magic of Listing 5.14 in a single statement. The syntax of MPI_Reduce, which reduces the values in all the provided buffers to a single value stored at the specified root, is the following:

```
int MPI_Reduce(void       *sendbuf,  // Address of the buffer to be
                                     // sent. Separate in each
                                     // source process. (IN)
               void       *recvbuf,  // Address of receiving
                                     // buffer (OUT)
                                     // Significant only at the root.
               int         count,    // Number of elements to send
               MPI_Datatype datatype, // MPI type of sendbuf and
                                     // recvbuf elements (IN)
               MPI_Op      op,       // symbolic constant identifying
                                     // the type of reduction to be
                                     // performed (IN)
               int         root,     // Rank of destination (IN)
               MPI_Comm    comm)     // Communicator (IN)
```

Table 5.3 List of predefined reduction operators in MPI

Symbolic Name	Description
MPI_SUM	Summation
MPI_MIN	Minimum
MPI_MAX	Maximum
MPI_PROD	Product
MPI_LAND	Logican AND
MPI_BAND	Bitwise AND
MPI_LOR	Logican OR
MPI_BOR	Bitwise OR
MPI_LXOR	Logican exclusive OR
MPI_BXOR	Bitwise exclusive OR
MPI_MAXLOC	Maximum and its location
MPI_MINLOC	Minimum and its location

The fifth parameter specifies the operator to be applied during the reduction. The list of predefined reduction operators is given in Table 5.3.

Equipped with MPI_Reduce, we can complete the distributed memory function integration example, as shown in Listing 5.15.

```cpp
1   // File : integration_reduction.cpp
2   . . .
3   double testf (double x) {
4     return x * x + 2 * sin (x);
5   }
6
7   //————————————————————————————————
8   //calculate and return area
9   double integrate (double st, double en, int div, double (*f) (double))↩
          {
10    double localRes = 0;
11    double step = (en − st) / div;
12    double x;
13    x = st;
14    localRes = f (st) + f (en);
15    localRes /= 2;
16    for (int i = 1; i < div; i++) {
17        x += step;
18        localRes += f (x);
19      }
20    localRes *= step;
21
22    return localRes;
23  }
24
25  //————————————————————————————————
```

```
26   int main (int argc, char *argv[]) {
27
28     MPI_Init (&argc, &argv);
29
30     int rank, N;
31     MPI_Comm_rank (MPI_COMM_WORLD, &rank);
32     MPI_Comm_size (MPI_COMM_WORLD, &N);
33     MPI_Status status;
34
35     if (argc == 1) {
36       if (rank == 0)
37         cerr << "Usage " << argv[0] << " start end divisions\n";
38       exit (1);
39     }
40     double start, end;
41     int divisions;
42     start = atof (argv[1]);
43     end = atof (argv[2]);
44     divisions = atoi (argv[3]);
45
46     double locSt, locEnd, rangePerProc;
47     int locDiv;
48     locDiv = (divisions > N) ? ceil (1.0 * divisions / N) : N;
49     rangePerProc = (end - start) / N;    // range part per process
50     locSt = start + rangePerProc * rank; // local range start
51     locEnd = (rank == N - 1) ? end
52                   : start + rangePerProc * (rank + 1); // local range end
53     double partialResult = integrate (locSt, locEnd, locDiv, testf);
54     double finalRes;
55     MPI_Reduce (&partialResult, &finalRes, 1, MPI_DOUBLE, MPI_SUM, 0, ↩
56         MPI_COMM_WORLD);
57     if (rank == 0)
58       cout << finalRes << endl;
59   . . .
```

LISTING 5.15

Function integration example that uses `MPI_Reduce` to accumulate the partial results of the MPI processes.

Listing 5.15 has a peculiarity in that the computations can start and complete in all the processes without the root needing to send any kind of initializing messages. Because all processes have access to the command-line parameters, lines 42-44 can extract all the information required for the computation to commence. Processes then proceed to calculate the subrange of the desired [*start, end*] that they will operate upon by splitting the range evenly between them (lines 48-51). The partial integrals are subsequently calculated by calling the `integrate` function with the process-local range and a pointer to the function that is to be integrated. `MPI_Reduce` in line 55 accumulates the final result by using the `MPI_SUM` reduction operator. The only special duties assigned to the root process are error (lines 36 and 37) and final result reporting (lines 57 and 58).

5.11.4 ALL-TO-ALL GATHERING

In Section 5.11.2, we used the matrix-vector multiplication as an example of the need to gather results efficiently. A number of applications require that the result of the gathering operation is propagated back to the MPI processes for subsequent steps. For example, we could be applying a sequence of transformations to a vector $\vec{x}$:

$$\vec{y} = A_{k-1} \cdot A_{k-2} \ldots A_0 \cdot \vec{x} = A_{k-1}(A_{k-2}(\ldots(A_0 \cdot \vec{x}))) \tag{5.3}$$

In order to calculate $\vec{y}$, each new vector that is produced by one multiplication must be made available to all the processes. One solution would be to have one gathering step followed by a broadcasting step, as in the following code (with N representing the number of processes and M the size of the vector):

```
double *y = new double[M];
double *newY = new double[M];
. . .
MPI_Gather(y, M/N, MPI_DOUBLE, newY, M/N,  MPI_DOUBLE, 0, ↩
    MPI_COMM_WORLD);
MPI_Bcast(newY, M, MPI_DOUBLE, 0, MPI_COMM_WORLD);
```

This sequence of statements would amount to a total of $2\lceil lgN \rceil$ steps, each step involving a number of concurrent message exchanges. An alternative communication scheme can be employed to effectively cut this cost in half (as far as the number of steps is concerned), as long as duplex communications are supported, i.e., it is possible for two processes to send and receive messages between them concurrently. The only restriction to the *butterfly* communication pattern, as it is known due to its appearance (see Figure 5.9), is that the number of processes must be a power of 2.

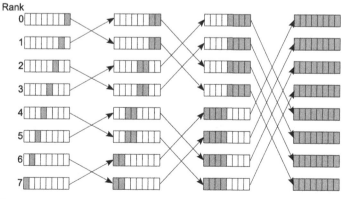

FIGURE 5.9

Implementation of a all-to-all gathering operation using a "butterfly" communication scheme. The gray boxes represent parts of the data present at a node.

The pattern illustrated in Figure 5.9 is performed over $\lceil lgN \rceil$ steps. During each i-th step, the processes that have their ranks different in the i-th bit only, exchange the *data they have collected so far*. Eventually, all the processes end up having a complete copy of the data to be gathered. The operation is reminiscent of the way the tournament tree is built in the reduction implementation of Listing 5.14, with the difference that in our all-to-all gathering, the data communicated double in volume with every step.

The code snippet shown in Listing 5.16 implements the butterfly communication pattern using point-to-point communications to gather K-sized arrays from all the processes.

```cpp
1   // File : allgather.cpp
2   const int K = 10;
3   const int ALLGATHERTAG = 0;
4   . . .
5     double *localPart = new double[K];
6     double *allParts = new double[K * N];
7
8     // test data init.
9     for (int i = 0; i < K; i++)
10      localPart[i] = rank;
11    int bitMask = 1;
12    int acquiredCount = K;
13    int acquiredStart = rank * K;
14
15    // copy local data to array that will hold the complete data
16    memcpy (allParts + rank * K, localPart, sizeof (double) * K);
17    while (bitMask < N)
18      {
19        int otherPartyID = rank ^ bitMask;
20        if ((rank & bitMask) == 0)  {
21          MPI_Send (allParts + acquiredStart, acquiredCount, ←
                MPI_DOUBLE, otherPartyID, ALLGATHERTAG, MPI_COMM_WORLD);
22          MPI_Recv (allParts + acquiredStart + acquiredCount, ←
                acquiredCount, MPI_DOUBLE, otherPartyID, ALLGATHERTAG, ←
                MPI_COMM_WORLD, &status);
23        }
24        else {
25          MPI_Recv (allParts + acquiredStart - acquiredCount, ←
                acquiredCount, MPI_DOUBLE, otherPartyID, ALLGATHERTAG, ←
                MPI_COMM_WORLD, &status);
26          MPI_Send (allParts + acquiredStart, acquiredCount, ←
                MPI_DOUBLE, otherPartyID, ALLGATHERTAG, MPI_COMM_WORLD);
27          acquiredStart -= acquiredCount;
28        }
29        acquiredCount *= 2;
30        bitMask <<= 1;
31      }
32
33    // printout / verification step
```

```
34    if (rank == 0) {
35        for (int i = 0; i < K * N; i++)
36            cout << allParts[i] << " ";
37        cout << endl;
38    }
39    . . .
```

LISTING 5.16

MPI implementation of the butterfly pattern using point-to-point communication for achieving an all-to-all gathering operation.

The key variables in Listing 5.16 are:

- localPart: Array that is contributed in the gathering by all processes. Each localPart contains K elements for a total of $K \cdot N$ items that have to be gathered. localPart is initialized to the rank of the process in order to produce an output in lines 35-37 that is easily checked for correctness.
- allParts: Placeholder for the gathered data. Initially each process places in the appropriate offset in allParts its own data parts, which are originally in array localPart. At the end of the procedure, all processes will hold a verbatim copy of allParts.
- acquiredCount: Counts how many of the desired data are already resident in a process. Initialized to K.
- acquiredStart: Index in the allParts array, where a process's resident data are.
- bitMask: Serves as a loop control variable and as a bit mask for determining the rank of the process to pair with during each communication step, given one's own rank (line 19).

The allParts array fills up in the fashion observed in the boxes of Figure 5.9 (memory addresses growing from right to left). During each iteration of the loop in lines 17-31, a process determines the rank of the other process that it should exchange data with (line 19), performs the exchange (lines 21-22, 25-26), updates the offset of the resident data (if need be, line 27), and increases the number of items currently resident (line 29).

One noteworthy feature of Listing 5.16 is that the two parties exchanging messages follow a different send/receive sequence: One is sending and then receiving, whereas the other is following the opposite order. This arrangement would guarantee that our processes would not face a deadlock, even if the sending call would block. Of course, as explained in Section 5.7, MPI_Send is locally blocking, but even if we were to use MPI_Ssend, our program would still function properly.

A sample run of the program in Listing 5.16 is shown below:

```
$ mpirun −np 8 ./allgather
0 0 0 0 0 0 0 0 0 0 1 1 1 1 1 1 1 1 1 1 2 2 2 2 2 2 2 2 2 2 3 3 3 3 3 ↵
    3 3 3 3 3 4 4 4 4 4 4 4 4 4 4 5 5 5 5 5 5 5 5 5 5 6 6 6 6 6 6 6 6 ↵
    6 6 7 7 7 7 7 7 7 7 7 7
```

MPI provides two all-to-all gathering functions for uniform and variable data collection: MPI_Allgather and MPI_Allgatherv, respectively. Their syntax is:

```
int MPI_Allgather(void         *sendbuf,  // Address of the buffer to be
                                          // sent. (IN)
                  int          sendcount, // Number of elements to send
                                          // per process. Should be
                                          // identical in all. (IN)
                  MPI_Datatype sendtype,  // MPI type of sendbuf
                                          // elements. (IN)
                  void         *recvbuf,  // Address of receiving
                                          // buffer (OUT)
                  int          recvcount, // Space available in
                                          // recvbuf per process. (IN)
                  MPI_Datatype recvtype,  // MPI type of recvbuf. (IN)
                  MPI_Comm     comm)      // Communicator (IN)
```

and

```
int MPI_Allgatherv(void         *sendbuf,  // Address of the buffer to
                                           // be sent. (IN)
                   int          sendcount, // Count of items to
                                           // send (IN)
                   MPI_Datatype sendtype,  // MPI type of sendbuf
                                           // elements. (IN)
                   void         *recvbuf,  // Address of receiving
                                           // buffer (OUT)
                   int          *recvcnts, // Array of counters. They
                                           // indicate the available
                                           // space in recvbuf, per
                                           // sending process. Array is
                                           // as big as the communica-
                                           // tor size. (IN)
                   int          *displs,   // Array of indices, marking
                                           // the beginning in recvbuf,
                                           // of the dest. blocks. (IN)
                   MPI_Datatype recvtype,  // MPI type of recvdbuf
                                           // elements. (IN)
                   MPI_Comm     comm)      // Communicator (IN)
```

Naturally, in both functions the recvcnt (or the contents of recvcnts) should be at least equal to sendcnt (sendcnts). The MPI_Allgather function would reduce much of the code in Listing 5.16 to a single line, also alleviating the restriction on the number of processes, as shown in Listing 5.17.

```
1  // File : allgatherMPI.cpp
2  const int K = 10;
3  . . .
4     double *localPart = new double[K];
5     double *allParts = new double[K * N];
6
7     // test data init.
```

```
8     for (int i = 0; i < K; i++)
9        localPart[i] = rank;
10
11    MPI_Allgather(localPart, K, MPI_DOUBLE, allParts, K, MPI_DOUBLE, ↩
          MPI_COMM_WORLD);
12
13    // printout/verification step
14    if (rank == 0) {
15       for (int i = 0; i < K * N; i++)
16          cout << allParts[i] << " ";
17       cout << endl;
18    }
19    . . .
```

LISTING 5.17

An alternative implementation of the example of Listing 5.16 using the MPI_Allgather function.

5.11.5 ALL-TO-ALL SCATTERING

Occasionally, the need arises to collect and distribute data to and from all the processes. This would be the equivalent of using *N* distinct MPI_Scatter operations, one from each of our processes. Figure 5.10 shows the outcome of an all-to-all scattering when it involves four processes.

MPI provides two functions catering to the uniform and variable block distribution, respectively:

```
int MPI_Alltoall(void      *sendbuf, // Address of the buffer to be
                            //  sent. (IN)
                 int       sendcount,// Number of elements to send
```

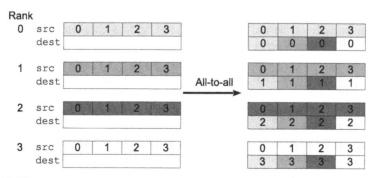

FIGURE 5.10

Outcome (on the right side) of an all-to-all scattering operation involving four processes. Data blocks are numbered to indicate their order in their source array and colored to indicate their origin.

```
                                      // per process. Should be
                                      // identical in all. (IN)
              MPI_Datatype sendtype,  // MPI type of sendbuf
                                      // elements. (IN)
              void         *recvbuf,  // Address of receiving
                                      // buffer (OUT)
              int          recvcount, // Number of elements available
                                      // in recvbuf per process. (IN)
              MPI_Datatype recvtype,  // MPI type of recvbuf. (IN)
              MPI_Comm     comm)      // Communicator (IN)
```

and

```
int MPI_Alltoallv(void    *sendbuf,  // Address of the buffer to be
                                     // sent. (IN)
              int        *sendcnts,// Array holding the number of
                                     // items to send to each
                                     // process. (IN)
              int         *sdispls, // Array of indices, marking
                                     // the beginning in sendbuf,
                                     // of the data blocks. (IN)
              MPI_Datatype sendtype, // MPI type of sendbuf
                                     // elements. (IN)
              void         *recvbuf, // Address of receiving
                                     // buffer (OUT)
              int         *recvcnts,// Array of counters. Indicate
                                     // the available space in
                                     // recvbuf, per sending
                                     // process (IN)
              int          *rdispls, // Array of indices, marking
                                     // the beginning in recvbuf,
                                     // of the dest. blocks. (IN)
              MPI_Datatype recvtype, // MPI type of recvdbuf
                                     // elements. (IN)
              MPI_Comm     comm)     // Communicator (IN)
```

As an example of the use of MPI_Alltoallv, let's consider parallelizing the *bucket sort* algorithm. Bucket sort works by scanning the input data and placing the items to be sorted in separate bins or buckets based on the range they fall into. A fixed number of bins is used, implying that the data input range must be known *a priori*. Each individual bucket can be subsequently sorted by recursively calling bucket sort or another nonrecursive algorithm if the contents of the bucket fall below a predetermined threshold.

If we assume that we have M items to be sorted, B buckets are used, and the items are uniformly distributed over their input range, then the time complexity of bucket sort is governed by the recurrence relation:

$$C(M) = \begin{cases} M + B \cdot C\left(\frac{M}{B}\right) & \text{if } N > 1 \\ 0 & \text{if } N = 1 \end{cases} \tag{5.4}$$

because each bucket is expected to get the same number of items $\frac{M}{B}$ and each bucket is to be subsequently recursively sorted. We can easily show that $C(M) = M \cdot log_B(M)$, making the complexity approach a linear one as the number of buckets increases.

What makes bucket sort particularly interesting among sorting algorithms is that it can be easily parallelized,[9] by applying the geometric data decomposition pattern (see Section 2.3.3). The required steps that amount to assigning one bucket per process are:[10]

1. Split the input data into N groups and distribute (*scatter*) them to the processes.
2. Each process scans and separates the $\frac{M}{N}$ data into N buckets.
3. Processes exchange the data that are supposed to be handled by other processes (*all-to-all scatter*).
4. Each process sorts its part of the data using any sorting algorithm.
5. Sorted data are collected using a *gather* operation.

A sample implementation of this algorithm is shown in Listing 5.18.

```
1   // File : bucketsort.cpp
2   . . .
3     int rank, N;
4     MPI_Comm_rank (MPI_COMM_WORLD, &rank);
5     MPI_Comm_size (MPI_COMM_WORLD, &N);
6     MPI_Status status;
7
8     if (argc == 1)
9       {
10        if (rank == 0)
11          cerr << "Usage " << argv[0] << " number_of_items\n";
12        exit (1);
13      }
14
15    int M = atoi (argv[1]);
16    int maxItemsPerBucket = ceil (1.0 * M / N); // used in case M is not
17                                                // evenly divided by N
18    int deliveredItems;
19    int bucketRange = ceil (1.0 * (MAX - MIN) / N);
20    int *data = new int[N * maxItemsPerBucket]; // array allocation
21                                                // exceeds M to allow
22                                                // easy scattering
23    int *buckets = new int[N * maxItemsPerBucket];
24    int *bucketOffset = new int[N];   // where do buckets begin?
25    int *inBucket = new int[N];       // how many items in each one?
26
27    int *toRecv = new int[N];         // counts how many items will be
```

---

[9]The communication overhead involved in parallelizing a sorting algorithm makes the latter a dubious endeavor, especially if the algorithm is a linear complexity one. However, there are cases where it is a worthwhile consideration, such as when practicing collective communications in MPI!

[10]This is not the only way parallelization can be accomplished. An alternative is considered in the Exercises section at the end of the chapter.

```
28                                      // received from each process
29    int *recvOff = new int[N];         // offsets for received data
30
31    if (rank == 0)
32      initData (MIN, MAX, data, M);
33
34    // initialize bucket counters and offsets
35    for (int i = 0; i < N; i++) {
36        inBucket[i] = 0;
37        bucketOffset[i] = i * maxItemsPerBucket;
38      }
39
40    // step 1
41    MPI_Scatter (data, maxItemsPerBucket, MPI_INT, data, ←
              maxItemsPerBucket, MPI_INT, 0, MPI_COMM_WORLD);
42    deliveredItems = (rank == N - 1) ? (M - (N - 1) * maxItemsPerBucket)←
              : maxItemsPerBucket;
43
44    // step 2
45    // split into buckets
46    for (int i = 0; i < deliveredItems; i++) {
47        int idx = (data[i] - MIN) / bucketRange;
48        int off = bucketOffset[idx] + inBucket[idx];
49        buckets[off] = data[i];
50        inBucket[idx]++;
51      }
52
53    // step 3
54    // start by gathering the volume of data the other processes will ←
              send
55    MPI_Alltoall (inBucket, 1, MPI_INT, toRecv, 1, MPI_INT, ←
              MPI_COMM_WORLD);
56    recvOff[0] = 0;
57    for (int i = 1; i < N; i++)
58      recvOff[i] = recvOff[i - 1] + toRecv[i - 1];
59
60    MPI_Alltoallv (buckets, inBucket, bucketOffset, MPI_INT, data, ←
              toRecv, recvOff, MPI_INT, MPI_COMM_WORLD);
61
62    // step 4
63    // apply quicksort to the local bucket
64    int localBucketSize = recvOff[N - 1] + toRecv[N - 1];
65    qsort (data, localBucketSize, sizeof (int), comp);
66
67    // step 5
68    MPI_Gather (&localBucketSize, 1, MPI_INT, toRecv, 1, MPI_INT, 0, ←
              MPI_COMM_WORLD);
69    if (rank == 0) {
70        recvOff[0] = 0;
71        for (int i = 1; i < N; i++)
72          recvOff[i] = recvOff[i - 1] + toRecv[i - 1];
73      }
```

```
74
75    MPI_Gatherv (data, localBucketSize, MPI_INT, data, toRecv, recvOff, ↵
          MPI_INT, 0, MPI_COMM_WORLD);
76
77    // print results
78    if (rank == 0) {
79        for (int i = 0; i < M; i++)
80            cout << data[i] << " ";
81        cout << endl;
82    }
83    . . .
```

LISTING 5.18

A parallel implementation of bucket sort in MPI using collective communications. Once the buckets are split, they are sorted using quicksort.

The five steps identified above for our parallel bucket sort are clearly marked in the code. The following discussion fills in the implementation details:

- Bucket sort is not an in-place algorithm. A separate buffer is required for holding the data while they are being distributed to buckets. Each bucket should have enough space allocated to it to be able to hold the complete input data. Because the M data are uniformly scattered to our N processes (line 41), each process must allocate $N \cdot \frac{M}{N} = M$ bucket space. Buckets are allocated as a single array (buckets). The beginning of each individual bucket within the single array, as well as the number of items it contains, are the job of arrays bucketOffset and inBucket, respectively. The former may seem redundant, since a bucket's offset is a matter of a simple calculation (line 37), but it is actually required for calling MPI_Alltoallv (line 60).
- Processes exchange the data that belong to other buckets with their respective "owner" processes. In this case, an all-to-all scatter would be the ideal candidate for minimizing the communication overhead. Because there is typically a nonuniform distribution of the data in the buckets, using MPI_Alltoall would require the transmission of dummy data, and it would result in a noncontiguous storage of data in each process.
  To overcome this problem, the processes initially exchange the number of data that they intend to send to the other ones (line 55). With this information, each process calculates the offsets where the incoming data will be stored (lines 56-58) and proceeds to use MPI_Alltoallv for the exchange (line 60). This results in contiguous data storage in the data array that can be then sorted (line 65).
- A similar problem with the data exchange of step 3, exists for the gathering of the data to the root process. The root initially collects the amount of data each process will submit using MPI_Gather (line 68). Appropriate receive offsets can then be calculated (lines 69-73), prior to using MPI_Gatherv (line 75) to complete the parallel sorting operation.

Step	PC	Variable	Process 0	Process 1	Process 2
	35	data	2 7 3 8 7 6 9 1 4		
1	42	data	2 7 3 8 7 6 9 1 4	8 7 6	9 1 4
2	55	buckets	2 3 _ _ 7	_ _ 6 _ 8 7	1 _ 4 _ 9
		inBucket	2 0 1	0 1 2	1 1 1
3	56	toRecv	2 0 1	0 1 1	1 2 1
	60	recvOff	0 2 2	0 0 1	0 1 3
	64	data	2 3 1	6 4	7 8 7 9
4	68	data	1 2 3	4 6	7 7 8 9
	69	toRecv	3 2 4		
5	75	recvOff	0 3 5		
	78	data	1 2 3 4 6 7 7 8 9		

FIGURE 5.11

A trace of the parallel bucket sort of Listing 5.18 upon sorting nine integers using three processes. PC, which stands for Program Counter, represents the next line of code in Listing 5.18 to be executed. Time runs from top to bottom. The corresponding steps and the variables that are affected by them in each process are shown.

The inner workings of Listing 5.18 can be more easily comprehended via the simple tracing example shown in Figure 5.11, where nine integers in the range [1, 9] are sorted.

5.11.6 ALL-TO-ALL REDUCTION

The all-to-all reduction operation has no difference from the reduction discussed in Section 5.11.3 other than the fact that all participating processes get a copy of the reduction result and not just the root. The syntax of the MPI_Allreduce function reflects this feature by the removal of the "root" parameter:

```
int MPI_Allreduce(void      *sendbuf,// Address of the buffer to be
                                     // sent. Separate in each
                                     // source process. (IN)
                  void      *recvbuf,// Address of receiving
                                     // buffer (OUT)
                                     // Significant in all proc.
                  int        count,  // Number of elements to send
                  MPI_Datatype datatype,// MPI type of sendbuf and
                                     // recvbuf elements (IN)
                  MPI_Op     op,     // Symbolic const. identifying
                                     // the type of reduction to be
                                     // performed (IN)
                  MPI_Comm   comm )  // Communicator (IN)
```

Similarly to the all-to-all gathering operation, an all-to-all reduction can be accomplished by using the butterfly communication pattern. The only difference with the scheme discussed in Section 5.11.3 is that between steps/stages of the algorithm, reduction is performed on the data received thus far. In that respect, butterfly-based, all-to-all reduction requires a much smaller amount of data to be communicated overall.

An example for the use of the all-to-all reduction operation would be a parallel genetic algorithm. Genetic algorithms are heuristic optimization techniques that describe possible solutions to an optimization problem as a population of "individuals," each solution modeled as an individual. This population "evolves" over several iterations (called *generations*) by applying changes to the individuals inspired by biology: crossover and mutation. The best individuals of a population are selected to survive into the next iteration/generation of the algorithm.

A parallel genetic algorithm could be designed around the partitioning of the population (data decomposition), whereas each node/process evolves a subset of the individuals. The best individuals can be selected and used for the next generation by employing an all-to-all reduction.

5.11.7 GLOBAL SYNCHRONIZATION

Some algorithms, such as Jacobi's method for solving a system of linear equations, require that data are collected and updated prior to continuing with the next iteration. This data collection and synchronization step can be done via the `MPI_Alltoall` function or some other form of collective operation. If no data need to be exchanged, though, synchronization can be accomplished by the `MPI_Barrier` function.

`MPI_Barrier` receives as a parameter a communicator:

```
int MPI_Barrier( MPI_Comm comm )
```

All processes of that communicator must call the function, and the function returns only when it has been called by all of them.

5.12 COMMUNICATING OBJECTS

MPI communication functions cater for the communication of arrays of primitive datatypes via their second parameter. However, it is frequently desirable to be able to communicate structures or objects. One can, of course, break up the structures that need to be communicated into individual elements or arrays of elements and then proceed to perform a series of send operations. This is a viable but costly and counter productive approach. From a software engineering perspective, breaking data encapsulation, among other things, complicates the code, and thus it does not constitute a recommended solution.

From a cost perspective, it is well known that multiple communication operations result in a higher overall communication cost than if one operation had been used to carry the same amount of data. The culprit lies in what is sometimes referred to as the *start-up latency*. This more or less fixed cost incorporates the activation of multiple OS layers, the network interface, and so on. So, although the actual over-the-wire times may be identical, the accumulation of the extra start-up latencies penalizes this approach.

A quick hack could be something like this:

```
const int N = ...;

typedef struct Point
  {
    int x;
    int y;
    int color;
  };

Point image[N];
. . .
MPI_Send(image, N*sizeof(Point), MPI_BYTE, dest, tag, MPI_COMM_WORLD);
```

But this solution would not work all the time. It's a viable option only if the execution platform is homogeneous i.e., all the machines use the same data representation. This requirement extends to the compiler optimizations used to compile the executables in case an MPMD approach is employed.

MPI provides two mechanisms that can be used to communicate structure between heterogeneous machines:

- Creating MPI derived datatypes
- Packing/unpacking data

Both are preferable to the hack presented previously in that they ensure the validity of the program, even if it were to run on a different platform. Anticipating change is always a prudent thing to do.

5.12.1 DERIVED DATATYPES

Figure 5.12 displays the memory layouts of the same data structure used in a 32-bit program and a 64-bit program. There are differences in the size of the individual data members of the structure and, naturally, their relative location in regard to the beginning of the structure (different offsets). Consequently, if MPI were to be able to transfer and translate an instance of a structure from one machine to another, it would need all the information listed below:

- The number and types of all the data members/fields.
- The relative offset of the fields from the beginning of the structure (where to deposit data).
- The total memory occupied by a structure, including any padding necessary to align it to specific boundaries. This is needed so that arrays of structures can be communicated.

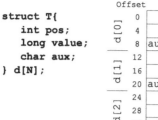

FIGURE 5.12

Two possible memory layouts for the array of structures shown on the left: one for a 32-bit architecture (where type `long int` is 4 bytes long) and one for a 64-bit architecture (where type `long int` is 8 bytes long). By default, the Gnu C compiler uses padding to ensure that all access to memory is aligned at 4-byte boundaries, for x86 binaries.

MPI provides a variety of functions for creating "derived" or general datatypes. A general datatype is an opaque object that is capable of describing all the above information. Once a derived datatype is defined, a reference to this object can be used in any communication function that requires a datatype specification parameter. Derived datatypes must be declared individually/locally in all the processes that will employ them.

Two of the most commonly used functions for creating derived datatypes are `MPI_Type_vector` and `MPI_Type_create_struct`. The first one comes handy for extracting blocks of data from single or multidimensional arrays of a single datatype in the form of a vector. The second one is the most generic of the available functions, allowing the use of blocks made of different datatypes. Their syntax is the following:

```
int MPI_Type_vector(int          count,      // Number of blocks
                                             // making up vector (IN)
                    int          blocklength,// Size of each block in
                                             // number of items (IN)
                    int          stride,     // Number of items
                                             // between the start of
                                             // successive blocks (IN)
                    MPI_Datatype old_type,   // MPI datatype of each
                                             // item (IN)
                    MPI_Datatype *newtype_p) // Reference to store
                                             // derived datatype (OUT)


int MPI_Type_create_struct(int          count,   // Number of blocks
                                                 // making up structure ↩

                                                 // It is also the size
                                                 // of the three array
                                                 // parameters that
                                                 // follow next. (IN)
```

```
int          blklen[],// Number of elements
                      // per block (IN)
MPI_Aint     displ[], // Offset of each
                      // block in bytes (IN)
MPI_Datatype types[], // Type of elements
                      // in each block (IN)
MPI_Datatype *newtype)// Reference to store
                      // derived type (OUT)
```

Each specification of a derived datatype must be followed by a call to the MPI_Type_commit function for having MPI store the specification internally. Once a datatype is committed, it can be used repeatedly in communication functions. MPI_Type_commit takes just a single parameter, which is a reference to the MPI_Datatype object:

```
int MPI_Type_commit(MPI_Datatype *datatype) // Reference to derived
                                            // datatype. (IN)
```

As an example for the use of MPI_Type_vector, let's now consider the problem of dense matrix-to-matrix multiplication, i.e., multiplying a *KxM* matrix A by a *MxL* matrix B. A parallel solution can be easily designed by applying the geometric data decomposition pattern (see Section 2.3.3). Among the variety of ways we can partition the data, in this example we use a 2D decomposition of the result matrix C as shown in Figure 5.13, which necessitates that a subset of A's rows and a subset of B's rows are communicated to the available processes.

The communication of A's rows is a simple matter, given the row-major memory allocation used for 2D arrays by C/C++. However, B's columns reside in noncontiguous memory locations. This can be dealt with by either transposing matrix B so that columns become rows or creating a derived datatype that can extract the columns

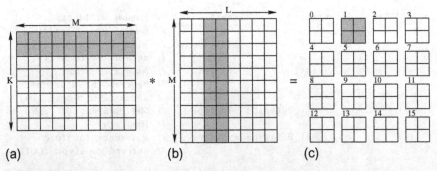

FIGURE 5.13

Illustration of a 2D partitioning of the result matrix C in a matrix A by matrix B multiplication. The highlighted cells indicate dependencies that must be resolved by communicating the corresponding rows of A and columns of B to the process calculating that part of C. Process ranks are shown next to C's blocks in the order in which they are assigned in the program of Listing 5.19.

from their existing memory location. The latter is the preferred approach, especially if very large matrices are involved.

The code shown in Listing 5.19 uses the exact same method as Listing 5.12 for propagating the rows of matrix A to the available processes. The only difference in the communication of A is that the move from 1D to 2D partitioning of the data necessitates the use of a nested loop for calculating the displacements and send counts (lines 34-45). Careful manipulation of these arrays allows us to send the same rows of A multiple times, as required. Each set of rowsPerProcess rows of A is sent procX times.

```cpp
1   // File : matrixMult.cpp
2   . . .
3     MPI_Datatype columnGroup;      // Datatype for B's columns
4     MPI_Datatype matrBlock;        // Datatype for C's blocks
5
6     int procX, procY;
7     procX = atoi (argv[1]);        // expects a X*Y grid of processes for
8     procY = atoi (argv[2]);        // calculating the product
9     if (procX * procY != N)        // It will abort if there are not ←
           enough processes to form the grid
10      MPI_Abort (MPI_COMM_WORLD, 0);
11
12    int rowsPerProcess;            // size of block related to A
13    int columnsPerProcess;         // size of block related to B
14    rowsPerProcess = K / procY;    // each process will calculate
15    columnsPerProcess = L / procX; // rowsPerProcess*columnsPerProcess ←
           elements of C
16
17    if (rank == 0)
18      {
19        MPI_Type_vector (M, columnsPerProcess, L, MPI_DOUBLE, &←
               columnGroup);
20        MPI_Type_commit (&columnGroup);
21        MPI_Type_vector (rowsPerProcess, columnsPerProcess, L, ←
               MPI_DOUBLE, &matrBlock);
22        MPI_Type_commit (&matrBlock);
23        double *A = new double[K * M];
24        double *B = new double[M * L];
25        double *C = new double[K * L];
26
27        // A and B are initialized to values that can be used to check
28        // the correctness of the result.
29        for (int i = 0; i < K * M; i++)  A[i] = i;
30        for (int i = 0; i < M * L; i++)  B[i] = 0;
31        for (int i = 0; i < M; i++)      B[i * L + i] = 1;  // B is the ←
               identity matrix
32
33        // distribute A first
34        int displs[N];
35        int sendcnts[N];
36        int cntr = 0;
```

```
37      for (int i = 0; i < procY; i++)
38        for (int j = 0; j < procX; j++)
39          {
40            sendcnts[cntr] = rowsPerProcess * M;
41            displs[cntr] = i * rowsPerProcess * M;
42            if (i == procY - 1)
43              sendcnts[cntr] = (M - (procY - 1) * rowsPerProcess) * M;
44            cntr++;
45          }
46
47      MPI_Scatterv (A, sendcnts, displs, MPI_DOUBLE, MPI_IN_PLACE, 0, ↩
              MPI_DOUBLE, 0, MPI_COMM_WORLD);
48
49      // now distribute B
50      cntr = 1;
51      for (int i = 0; i < procY; i++)
52        for (int j = 0; j < procX; j++)
53          if (i + j != 0)
54            {
55              MPI_Send (B + j * columnsPerProcess, 1, columnGroup, ↩
                  cntr, 0, MPI_COMM_WORLD);
56              cntr++;
57            }
58
59      // partial result calculation
60      MMpartial (A, B, C, rowsPerProcess, M, columnsPerProcess, L);
61
62
63      // now collect all the subblocks of C
64      cntr = 1;
65      for (int i = 0; i < procY; i++)
66        for (int j = 0; j < procX; j++)
67          if (i + j != 0)
68            {
69              MPI_Recv (C + i * L * rowsPerProcess + j * ↩
                  columnsPerProcess, 1, matrBlock, cntr, 0, ↩
                  MPI_COMM_WORLD, &status);
70              cntr++;
71            }
72
73      printMatrix (C, K, L);
74
75    }
76  else
77    {
78      if (rank == N - 1)
79        rowsPerProcess = M - (procY - 1) * rowsPerProcess;
80
81      MPI_Type_vector (M, columnsPerProcess, columnsPerProcess, ↩
              MPI_DOUBLE, &columnGroup);
82      MPI_Type_commit (&columnGroup);
```

```
83        MPI_Type_vector (rowsPerProcess, columnsPerProcess, ↵
              columnsPerProcess, MPI_DOUBLE, &matrBlock);
84        MPI_Type_commit (&matrBlock);
85
86        double *locA = new double[rowsPerProcess * M];
87        double *locB = new double[M * columnsPerProcess];
88        double *partC = new double[rowsPerProcess * columnsPerProcess]; ↵
              // partial result matrix
89
90        MPI_Scatterv (NULL, NULL, NULL, MPI_DOUBLE, locA, rowsPerProcess↵
              * M, MPI_DOUBLE, 0, MPI_COMM_WORLD);
91
92        MPI_Recv (locB, 1, columnGroup, 0, 0, MPI_COMM_WORLD, &status);
93
94        MMpartial (locA, locB, partC, rowsPerProcess, M, ↵
              columnsPerProcess, columnsPerProcess);
95
96        MPI_Send (partC, 1, matrBlock, 0, 0, MPI_COMM_WORLD);
97      }
98    . . .
```

LISTING 5.19

Part of an MPI program for multiplying a *KxM* matrix A with a *MxL* matrix B. The program uses derived datatypes to simplify the communication of blocks of data between the processes.

The key points of Listing 5.19 are as follows:

- The program requires that procX * procY processes are available for distributing the workload. Parameters procX and procY are supplied by the user in the command line.
- Each process receives rowsPerProcess rows of matrix A and columnsPerProcess columns of matrix B in order to calculate a rowsPerProcess x columnsPerProcess block of the result matrix C.
- Two derived datatypes are defined in lines 19-22 and 81-84. These must be declared in all the processes that use them. While each *must account for the same amount of data, the actual layout of a derived datatype can be different in each process.* In the root process, the layout has to account for the extra rows and columns of data present in B and C (lines 19-22), while in the worker processes there are no such extra items (lines 81-84). So, while in the root process, the "stride" parameter for the columnGroup derived datatype is L, in the worker processes it is equal to columnsPerProcess. This difference is also obvious if one compares the array memory layouts established in lines 23-25 with the local ones established in lines 86-88.
- The columnGroup derived datatype is used to extract columns of data from matrix B. The derived "vector" is made up of *M* individual blocks (as many as the rows of B), and each block consists of columnsPerProcess items of type MPI_DOUBLE. The blocks are *L* distance apart in process 0, i.e., as many items as the total number of columns. This distance is exactly columnsPerProcess in the other processes. Figure 5.14 illustrates this difference.

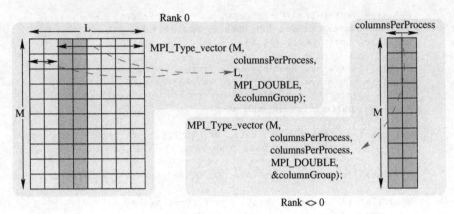

FIGURE 5.14

Illustration of how the derived datatype `columnGroup` is defined for the 0-ranked process and all other processes in the program of Listing 5.19, based on the memory layout of matrices B (left) and `locB` (right).

Once `columnGroup` is defined, the root process can send blocks of columns to the other processes by manipulating the starting offset in the B matrix (line 55). The processes that receive the data are waiting for just one element of type `columnGroup` (line 92).

- The `matrBlock` derived datatype is used for collecting the computed partial results. The derived "vector" is made up of `rowsPerProcess` blocks, each `columnsPerProcess` items of type `MPI_DOUBLE` wide. The distance between the blocks in the root process is L, the length of C's row.

As an example of the use of the `MPI_Type_create_struct` function, we will consider the problem of communicating the following data structure:

```
struct Pixel {
    int x;
    int y;
    unsigned char RGB[3];
};
```

`MPI_Type_create_struct` requires a much more explicit setup for the creation of a derived datatype than `MPI_Type_vector`. Each of the data members of a structure must be documented: their individual datatypes, their sizes, and their offset from the beginning of the structure must be declared. The length of the associated code means that it is a good idea to encapsulate the details in a separate function, as shown in Listing 5.20.

```
1  // File : derivedExample.cpp
2  void deriveType (MPI_Datatype * t)
3  {
```

```
4     struct Pixel sample;
5
6     int blklen[3];
7     MPI_Aint displ[3], off, base;
8     MPI_Datatype types[3];
9
10    blklen[0] = 1;
11    blklen[1] = 1;
12    blklen[2] = 3;
13
14    types[0] = MPI_INT;
15    types[1] = MPI_INT;
16    types[2] = MPI_UNSIGNED_CHAR;
17
18    displ[0] = 0;
19    MPI_Get_address (&(sample.x), &base);
20    MPI_Get_address (&(sample.y), &off);
21    displ[1] = off-base;
22    MPI_Get_address (&(sample.RGB[0]), &off);
23    displ[2] = off - base;
24
25    MPI_Type_create_struct (3, blklen, displ, types, t);
26    MPI_Type_commit (t);
27    }
```

LISTING 5.20

A function for defining a derived datatype for the communication of a `Pixel` structure.

`MPI_Aint` is an alias for a `signed int` or a `signed long` integer, depending on whether the system architecture is 32 or 64 bit. Variables of this type are typically used with the `MPI_Get_address` function to extract the address of a memory location. The results are usually the same as the outcome of the address-of (&) C operator, although this does not need to be true for systems with word-addressable (versus byte-addressable) memory. The syntax of `MPI_Get_address` is:

```
int MPI_Get_address(void    *location, // Address of a memory
                                        // location (IN)
                    MPI_Aint *address)  // Storage for the
                                        // address (OUT)
```

Lines 10-12 in Listing 5.20 document the length of each of the three components of the Pixel structure, i.e., the sizes of the corresponding arrays. Lines 14-16 document their type, and lines 18-23 calculate their offset from the beginning of the structure. For the offset calculations, a sample instance of the structure is allocated (line 4) and its base address calculated at line 19.

5.12.2 PACKING/UNPACKING

In the case of an unstructured message, e.g., a collection of data that are not part of the same structure or array, or a message that is communicated only once or very infrequently, we can skip the process of creating a derived datatype. A byte array can be prepared with all the data that need to be transmitted, somewhat similarly to a serialization buffer, and sent to its destination. The destination process will need to follow the same order of insertion to extract the data one by one from the byte array.

MPI provides two functions for inserting/packing and extracting/unpacking data from a byte array:

```
int MPI_Pack(void        *inbuf,    // Address of data to store in
                                    // byte array (IN)
             int         incount,   // Count of data in *inbuf (IN)
             MPI_Datatype datatype, // Datatype of *inbuf (IN)
             void        *outbuf,   // Address of byte array (IN)
             int         outcount,  // Size of outbuf in bytes (IN)
             int         *position, // Position of first available
                                    // free space in *outbuf.
                                    // Function reads and updates
                                    // it. (IN/OUT)
             MPI_Comm    comm)      // Communicator (IN)


int MPI_Unpack(void       *inbuf,   // Address of byte array to read
                                    // from (IN)
               int        insize,   // Size of *inbuf in bytes (IN)
               int        *position,// Position in *inbuf to read
                                    // from. Function updates
                                    // *position after extracting to
                                    // *outbuf (IN/OUT)
               void       *outbuf,  // Address of array to store
                                    // extracted data. (IN)
               int        outcount, // Nuber of items to extract (IN)
               MPI_Datatype datatype,// Datatype of *outbuf (IN)
               MPI_Comm   comm)     // Communicator (IN)
```

Apart from this being a rather code-intensive approach to communicating arbitrary data, the only real challenge in using this pair of functions is to correctly estimate the space necessary to hold the byte buffer. An underestimate, i.e., a too small buffer, would produce a crashing program in the best case and a misbehaving one in the worst.

If we were to communicate the Pixel structure used as an example in the previous section, the code sequence shown in Listing 5.21 would be required for packing/unpacking.

```
1   // File : packUnpack.cpp
2   . . .
3   unsigned char *buffer = new unsigned char[100];
4   if (rank == 0)
5     {
6       struct Pixel test; // followed by initialization code
7       . . .
8       // pack everything up
```

```
9          int position=0;
10         MPI_Pack(&(test.x), 1, MPI_INT, buffer, 100, &position, ↩
               MPI_COMM_WORLD);
11         MPI_Pack(&(test.y), 1, MPI_INT, buffer, 100, &position, ↩
               MPI_COMM_WORLD);
12         MPI_Pack(test.RGB, 3, MPI_UNSIGNED_CHAR, buffer, 100, &position,↩
               MPI_COMM_WORLD);
13         MPI_Send (buffer, position, MPI_UNSIGNED_CHAR, 1, 0, ↩
               MPI_COMM_WORLD);
14      }
15   else
16      {
17         struct Pixel test;
18         int position=0;
19         MPI_Recv (buffer, 100, MPI_UNSIGNED_CHAR, 0, 0, MPI_COMM_WORLD, ↩
               &status);
20
21         // now start unpacking
22         MPI_Unpack(buffer, 100, &position, &(test.x), 1, MPI_INT, ↩
               MPI_COMM_WORLD);
23         MPI_Unpack(buffer, 100, &position, &(test.y), 1, MPI_INT, ↩
               MPI_COMM_WORLD);
24         MPI_Unpack(buffer, 100, &position, test.RGB, 3, ↩
               MPI_UNSIGNED_CHAR, MPI_COMM_WORLD);
25         . . .
26      }
27   . . .
```

LISTING 5.21

Using `MPI_Pack`/`MPI_Unpack` to communicate an instance of a `Pixel` structure.

As can be observed in Listing 5.21, the sequences of packing and unpacking mirror each other completely. When the packing process is done, the value of the `position` variable reflects the total length of the assembled message. Hence, we can use it in place of the `count` parameter in `MPI_Send` (line 13).

On the receiving process, once the buffer is collected (line 19), a sequence of unpacking calls extracts the data in the same order in which they were inserted. The `position` variable is updated by each call to point to the next data item to be retrieved.

In summary, when we face the task of communicating collections of data in MPI, we should use:

- *count* **parameter**: If data are an array of primitive types.
- **Derived datatypes**: If data are heterogeneous and/or in noncontiguous memory locations, and are communicated often.
- **Packing/unpacking**: If data are heterogeneous and/or in noncontiguous memory locations, and are not communicated often.

5.13 NODE MANAGEMENT: COMMUNICATORS AND GROUPS

The *communicator* is the fundamental object that is used for communication in MPI. Upon initializing MPI with the `MPI_Init` call, the global communicator `MPI_COMM_WORLD` is created, encompassing all running processes. A communicator is a container for information concerning communication routing (virtual topologies), process identification, message caching, and differentiation based on tagging (called *contexts* in MPI terminology) as well as other information that might be used by the system.

`MPI_COMM_WORLD` is a predefined *intra-communicator*, i.e., it serves communications taking place between processes belonging to its own group of processes. MPI defines also another kind of communicator: an inter-communicator. An *inter-communicator* is used for sending messages between processes that belong to two separate logical groups. This functionality can come handy if in big application processes are split into separate, typically disjoint, groups, each responsible for a different part of the application. It is definitely easier to have processes in the same group communicate using ranks starting from 0 up to the size of the group minus 1. For this a new intra-communicator must be created.

Inter-communicators are then used to bridge processes belonging to two different intra-communicators or groups. In this section we focus only on the creation of intra-communicators and groups, because especially the latter are required for one-sided communications (see Section 5.14).

5.13.1 CREATING GROUPS

A *group* is an ordered set of process identifiers. Each process in a group is associated with an integer rank. Ranks are contiguous starting from zero, in the same fashion as communicator ranks. Ranks are not unique, but they are relative to a group or communicator. *One can think about ranks as though they were array indices used to access inside a group the process ID and host IP that uniquely identify a process.*

MPI uses the `MPI_Group` opaque object to represent this information. MPI defines two symbolic group constants: `MPI_GROUP_EMPTY`, which is used to represent an empty group, and `MPI_GROUP_NULL`, which is used to represent an invalid group. The latter is returned upon freeing up a group object with the `MPI_Group_free` function.

A group can be created in a variety of ways:

- **From a communicator**: We can extract all the process information of a communicator into a group for further manipulation:

```
int MPI_Comm_group(MPI_Comm  comm,   // Communic. to access (IN)
                   MPI_Group *group) // Reference to store comm's
                                     // group (OUT)
```

- **From an existing group**: We can start from an existing group and extract a new set by inclusion or exclusion. The corresponding functions are:

```
int MPI_Group_incl(MPI_Group group,    // Existing group (IN)
                   int       n,         // Size of *ranks (IN)
                   int       *ranks,    // Address or array with
                                        // ranks to include in
                                        // new group (IN)
                   MPI_Group *newgroup) // New group refer. (OUT)


int MPI_Group_excl(MPI_Group group,    // Existing group (IN)
                   int       n,         // Size of *ranks (IN)
                   int       *ranks,    // Address or array with
                                        // ranks to remove from
                                        // new group (IN)
                   MPI_Group *newgroup) // New group refer. (OUT)
```

- **From the union of two groups**:

```
int MPI_Group_union(MPI_Group group1,
                    MPI_Group group2,
                    MPI_Group *newgr) // New group
                                      // reference. (OUT)
```

- **From the intersection of two groups**: The syntax for the MPI_Group_intersection function is the same as the MPI_Group_union one.
- **From the difference of two groups**: The syntax for the MPI_Group_difference function is the same as the MPI_Group_union one.

As an example of the use of these functions, the program in Listing 5.22 separates the odd and even ranked processes into two groups. The program illustrates the use of two more accessor functions: MPI_Group_size, which returns the size of a group, and MPI_Group_rank, which returns the group rank of the calling process, or MPI_UNDEFINED if the process does not belong to the group. Their syntax is identical to the communicator-related ones:

```
int MPI_Group_size(MPI_Group group, // Group structure (IN)
                   int       *size) // Address to store size (OUT)


int MPI_Group_rank(MPI_Group group, // Group structure (IN)
                   int       *rank) // Address to store rank
                                    // or MPI_UNDEFINED (OUT)
```

```
1   // File : groupExample.cpp
2   . . .
3     int num, i, rank;
4     MPI_Group all, odd, even;
5
6     MPI_Init (&argc, &argv);
7     // copy all the processes in group "all"
8     MPI_Comm_group (MPI_COMM_WORLD, &all);
9     MPI_Comm_size (MPI_COMM_WORLD, &num);
10    MPI_Comm_rank (MPI_COMM_WORLD, &rank);
```

```
11
12    int grN = 0;
13    int ranks[num / 2];
14
15    for (i = 0; i < num; i += 2)
16      ranks[grN++] = i;
17
18    // extract from "all" only the odd ones
19    MPI_Group_excl (all, grN, ranks, &odd);
20    // sutract odd group from all to get the even ones
21    MPI_Group_difference (all, odd, &even);
22
23    // print group sizes
24    if (rank == 0)
25      {
26        MPI_Group_size (odd, &i);
27        printf ("Odd group has %i processes\n", i);
28        MPI_Group_size (even, &i);
29        printf ("Even group has %i processes\n", i);
30      }
31
32    // check group membership
33    MPI_Group_rank (odd, &i);
34    if (i == MPI_UNDEFINED)
35      printf ("Process %i belongs to even group\n", rank);
36    else
37      printf ("Process %i belongs to odd group\n", rank);
38
39    // free up memory
40    MPI_Group_free (&all);
41    MPI_Group_free (&odd);
42    MPI_Group_free (&even);
43    . . .
```

LISTING 5.22

A program that splits the processes into two groups, one for the even-ranked and one for the odd-ranked.

5.13.2 CREATING INTRA-COMMUNICATORS

An intra-communicator can be constructed from an existing intra-communicator, either through duplication or through selection of a subset of processes. The three functions that support these approaches are:

```
// Duplicates a communicator
int MPI_Comm_dup(MPI_Comm comm,        // Original communicator (IN)
                 MPI_Comm *newcomm),   // Pointer to copy storage (OUT)


// Creates a communicator according to the group membership
int MPI_Comm_create(MPI_Comm  comm,    // Original communicator (IN)
```

```
             MPI_Group group,   // Set of processes to include
                                // in new communicator (IN)
             MPI_Comm *newcomm) // Pointer to comm. storage (OUT↵
                  )
```

And finally, `MPI_Comm_split` creates an array of communicators according to how many different values the `color` parameter gets. Each process gets to participate in just one of them:

```
int MPI_Comm_split(MPI_Comm comm,    // Original communicator (IN)
                   int       color,  // Property of processes that
                                     // places in the same group
                                     // those that match (IN)
                   int       key,    // Rank of process in new
                                     // communicator (IN)
             MPI_Comm *newcomm) // Pointer to comm. storage. One
                                // new communicator per color
                                // is created. (OUT)
```

A simple example that extends the code in Listing 5.22 is shown in Listing 5.23.

```
1   // File : commExample.cpp
2   . . .
3     int num, i, rank, localRank;
4     MPI_Group all, odd, even;
5     MPI_Comm oddComm, evenComm;
6     char mess[11];
7
8     MPI_Init (&argc, &argv);
9     // copy all the processes in group "all"
10    MPI_Comm_group (MPI_COMM_WORLD, &all);
11    MPI_Comm_size (MPI_COMM_WORLD, &num);
12    MPI_Comm_rank (MPI_COMM_WORLD, &rank);
13
14    int grN = 0;
15    int ranks[num / 2];
16
17    for (i = 0; i < num; i += 2)
18      ranks[grN++] = i;
19
20    // extract from "all" only the odd ones
21    MPI_Group_excl (all, grN, ranks, &odd);
22    // sutract odd group from all to get the even ones
23    MPI_Group_difference (all, odd, &even);
24
25    MPI_Comm_create (MPI_COMM_WORLD, odd, &oddComm);
26    MPI_Comm_create (MPI_COMM_WORLD, even, &evenComm);
27
28    // check group membership
29    MPI_Group_rank (odd, &localRank);
30    if (localRank != MPI_UNDEFINED)
31      {
32        if (localRank == 0)       // local group root, sets-up message
```

```
33        strcpy (mess, "ODD GROUP");
34      MPI_Bcast (mess, 11, MPI_CHAR, 0, oddComm);
35      MPI_Comm_free (&oddComm);  // free communicator in processes ←
              where it is valid
36    }
37    else
38    {
39      MPI_Comm_rank (evenComm, &localRank);
40      if (localRank == 0)        // local group root, sets-up message
41        strcpy (mess, "EVEN GROUP");
42      MPI_Bcast (mess, 11, MPI_CHAR, 0, evenComm);
43      MPI_Comm_free (&evenComm);
44    }
45
46    printf ("Process %i with local rank %i received %s\n", rank, ←
            localRank, mess);
47
48    // free up memory
49    MPI_Group_free (&all);
50    MPI_Group_free (&odd);
51    MPI_Group_free (&even);
52    . . .
```

LISTING 5.23

A program that splits the processes into two groups, creates two communicators based on the groups, and performs broadcasting within each of the two groups.

The groups that are created in lines 21 and 23 are used to create two intra-communicators in lines 25 and 26. These communicators are valid only in the processes that are their members, and that is why their deallocation is inside the if-else structure of lines 30-44. The deallocation takes place via the MPI_Comm_free function (lines 35, 43), but the actual cleaning up of the memory takes place only after all pending communications are completed. In contrast, the deallocation of the groups takes place in all the nodes (lines 49-51).

The approach used in Listing 5.23 is the most generic in the sense that very complex criteria can be used to separate the processes into groups and communicators. In the case of simple rules, a shorter path to follow is to use MPI_Comm_split. With this function we can transform Listing 5.23 into the program shown in Listing 5.24.

```
1   // File : commExampleSplit.cpp
2   . . .
3    int num, i, rank, localRank;
4    MPI_Comm newComm;
5    char mess[11];
6
7    MPI_Init (&argc, &argv);
8    MPI_Comm_size (MPI_COMM_WORLD, &num);
9    MPI_Comm_rank (MPI_COMM_WORLD, &rank);
10
```

```
11    MPI_Comm_split(MPI_COMM_WORLD, rank%2, rank/2, &newComm);
12
13    if (rank == 0)        // root of even group
14        strcpy (mess, "EVEN GROUP");
15    else if(rank == 1)    // root of odd group
16        strcpy (mess, "ODD GROUP");
17
18
19    MPI_Bcast (mess, 11, MPI_CHAR, 0, newComm);
20    MPI_Comm_rank (newComm, &localRank);
21    MPI_Comm_free (&newComm);   // free communicator in processes where ↩
          it is valid
22
23    printf ("Process %i with local rank %i received %s\n", rank, ↩
          localRank, mess);
24    . . .
```

LISTING 5.24

A program that splits MPI_COMM_WORLD into two intra-communicators based on whether their rank is even or odd. Broadcasting is performed within each of the two communicators.

The color and key parameters to MPI_Comm_split in Listing 5.24 are as shown in Table 5.4.

Table 5.4 The color and key parameters to MPI_Comm_split as they are calculated in Listing 5.24

rank	0	1	2	3	4	5	6	7	8	9
color	0	1	0	1	0	1	0	1	0	1
key	0	0	1	1	2	2	3	3	4	4

5.14 ONE-SIDED COMMUNICATIONS

Two-sided communications, i.e., those that need explicitly designated source and destination processes, pose two challenges for developers:

- **Correctness**: Each send must be coupled with a receive operation with compatible parameters. Small deviations can be difficult to detect.
- **Performance**: It is difficult to overlap communication and computation, although the alternative forms of MPI_Send and MPI_Recv examined in Section 5.7 contribute to a solution.

Since MPI-2 (and with substantial extensions in MPI-3) an alternative communication paradigm is available that facilitates accessing a process's memory remotely. MPI's Remote Memory Access (RMA) mechanism allows the use of one-sided communication, whereas there can be only one process specifying all the transaction parameters that will affect a remote memory location.

RMA is an attractive alternative to two-sided communications, especially when the communication patterns vary during run-time and a two-sided communication could require polling or global operations before it could take place.

The procedure for conducting RMA operations is the following:

1. Create a window. *Window* is the term used to refer to a structure/object exposing a specified memory area for remote access.
2. Perform a sequence of communication operations. Communications are finished only when synchronization calls are made and completed.
3. Destroy the window.

The MPI_Win_create function is used for creating a window using pre-allocated memory:

```
int MPI_Win_create(void      *base,      // Address of the memory to be
                                         // remotely accessed. (IN)
                   MPI_Aint size,        // Memory size in bytes. (IN)
                   int      disp_unit, // Displacement between
                                         // successive elements of the
                                         // type of data stored in the
                                         // memory region. (IN)
                   MPI_Info info,        // Object used for optimization
                                         // parameters (IN)
                   MPI_Comm comm,        // Communicator (IN)
                   MPI_Win  *win)        // Address of the window object
                                         // to be initialized. (OUT)
```

MPI_Win_create is a collective call, so it must be called by all processes in a communicator. Each process may specify different parameters for its own local buffer that is exposed via the window object. One-sided communication calls require the specification of both the window reference and the target's rank. As long as remote memory accesses fit inside the prescribed buffer, there should be no problem.

The disp_unit parameter should be set to the size of the datatype of the buffer. Its purpose is to simplify access to individual array elements.

The MPI_Info parameter is an opaque pointer (pointer to an unspecified datatype) to a structure that serves as a placeholder for (key, value) pairs. MPI provides a set of functions for setting or querying the pairs in an MPI_Info object (MPI_Info_create, MPI_Info_get, etc.). For our purposes, we can simply use the MPI_INFO_NULL symbolic constant instead.

A window object is destroyed by the call:

```
int MPI_Win_free(MPI_Win  *win) // Address of the window object (IN/↩
   OUT)
```

Upon a successful execution, win is set to MPI_WIN_NULL.

RMA distinguishes between two types of functions: *communication* and *synchronization*. Remote memory access suffers from the same consistency problems that are examined in Section 3.3. MPI provides a set of synchronization functions that allow the developers to implement strict or loose consistency models as best suited for the application at hand.

5.14.1 RMA COMMUNICATION FUNCTIONS

RMA provides three communication functions:

* `MPI_Put`: Copies data from the caller memory to the target memory.
* `MPI_Get`: Copies data from the target memory to the caller memory.
* `MPI_Accumulate`: Adds local data to the target memory.

All these functions are non blocking; the call initiates the transfer, but there is no way to know when it will be complete other than to call the synchronization functions discussed in the next section. This behavior opens up an opportunity for optimizations, since MPI can choose to send aggregate access requests (i.e., a bunch of them together) instead of individual ones. It also opens the back door for programming errors due to memory corruption: A process should not access a buffer it has exported via a window until it is known that RMA calls have been completed.

The syntax of these functions and an explanation of their parameters follow:

```
int MPI_Get(void       *origin_addr,    // Address of buffer to store
                                        // retrieved data. (OUT)
            int        origin_count,    // Buffer size in number of
                                        // items. (IN)
            MPI_Datatype origin_datatype,// *origin_addr datatype.(IN)
            int        target_rank,     // Rank of process to read
                                        // from. (IN)
            MPI_Aint   target_disp,     // Displacement/array index
                                        // to start getting data
                                        // from. Displacement is in
                                        // datatype units. (IN)
            int        target_count,    // Number of items to
                                        // retrieve. (IN)
            MPI_Datatype target_datatype,// Source buffer datatype.
                                        // Actual address is infered
                                        // from the window.(IN)
            MPI_Win    win)             // Window object. (IN)
int MPI_Put(void       *origin_addr,    // Address of data to be
                                        // sent. (IN)
            int        origin_count,    // Buffer size in number of
                                        // items. (IN)
            MPI_Datatype origin_datatype,// *origin_addr datatype.(IN)
            int        target_rank,     // Rank of process to send
                                        // data. (IN)
            MPI_Aint   target_disp,     // Displacement/array index
                                        // to start putting data
                                        // in. (IN)
```

```
              int          target_count,   // Storage size in number
                                           // of items. (IN)
              MPI_Datatype target_datatype,// Target buffer datatype.
                                           // Actual address is infered
                                           // from the window.(IN)
              MPI_Win      win)            // Window object. (IN)

int MPI_Accumulate(void     *origin_addr,// Buffer address of data
                                         // to be sent. (IN)
              int          origin_count,// Buffer size in number
                                        // of items. (IN)
              MPI_Datatype orig_type,   // *origin_addr type.(IN)
              int          target_rank, // Rank of process to send
                                        // data to. (IN)
              MPI_Aint     target_disp, // Starting array index in
                                        // destin. process.(IN)
                                        // Actual target address
                                        // is infered from the
                                        // window.
              int          target_count,// Storage size in number
                                        // of items. (IN)
              MPI_Datatype target_type, // Target buffer datatype.
              MPI_Op       op,          // Reduction operation.
                                        // Symbolic constant , same
                                        // as in MPI_Reduce. (IN)
              MPI_Win      win)         // Window object. (IN)
```

MPI_Accumulate behaves in a similar manner to MPI_Reduce, taking local and remote data and storing their reduction in the remote process buffer. MPI_Accumulate allows the simple implementation of shared counters, among other things.

An example of the use of these functions is presented following the discussion of the synchronization functions.

MPI-3 has added request-based versions of these functions that return a reference to an MPI_Request structure that can be used to check when the operation is complete. These versions are only valid for use in passive target operations (see Section 5.14.2).

5.14.2 RMA SYNCHRONIZATION FUNCTIONS

MPI provides two different approaches to implementing RMA, each coming with its own set(s) of functions for synchronization:

- **Active target**: The process having its memory accessed is actively participating in the data exchange. The time span during which a process is allowed to perform RMA communications is called *exposure epoch*, and it is controlled by the *target* process, i.e., the owner of the memory exported through the window. Two sets of functions can be used in this case. Their difference lies in how the exposure epoch is set up.

- **Passive target**: Only the process performing the get, put, or accumulate operation(s) is controlling the proceedings. Similarly to the active target case, all RMA communications have to take place within a time span identified as an *access epoch*. This time period is controlled by the *origin* process, i.e., the one conducting the operations.

The epochs (exposure for the target, and access for the origin) essentially mark periods of time where changes are allowed in the shared memory of the target process, and any attempt to use the data by the target process may result in incoherent results. The end of an epoch marks the application of all the pending/requested changes and the implied permission to start using the data at the target process.

When exactly communications take place during an epoch is not specified by the MPI standard, leaving room for optimizations by the MPI implementations. The only certain thing is that when an epoch is closed, the corresponding calls (e.g., MPI_Win_complete, MPI_Win_fence, etc.) will return when any modifications made to the window data are committed, both at the target processes and at any local copies that may be privately kept by MPI at the origin processes.

The three sets of synchronization functions are:

1. MPI_Win_fence: This function is used for *active target* RMA. The access epoch in the origin process and the exposure epoch in the target process are started and completed by a call to MPI_Win_fence. MPI_Win_fence is similar to MPI_Barrier in the sense that all the processes in a communicator used to create a window must call it. The syntax is the following:

```
int MPI_Win_fence(int      assert,   // Assertion flags, used for
                                     // optimization (IN)
                  MPI_Win win)       // Window object. (IN)
```

The assert parameter, which is also found in other synchronization functions, is a bitwise OR of symbolic constants that represent conditions (assertions) that could be taken into consideration in streamlining the communications taking place during synchronization. A value of 0 can be safely used in place of the assert flag, which indicates that no condition is guaranteed.

During an access epoch, a process *P* may access any of the remote memory blocks exported via the window, and any other process may access *P*'s own local memory block. This kind of synchronization is best suited for application that sport interleaved periods of computation and global data exchange. An example of the interaction taking place in this case is shown in Figure 5.15. Because MPI_Win_fence is a collective operation, it suffers from high synchronization costs.

2. MPI_Win_start, MPI_Win_complete, MPI_Win_post, MPI_Win_wait: This set of functions was introduced to allow pair-wise synchronization between origin and target processes. This reduces the communication overhead involved, thus making it a far more scalable approach. An additional benefit is that fine-grained control over the ordering of local and remote accesses to a target's

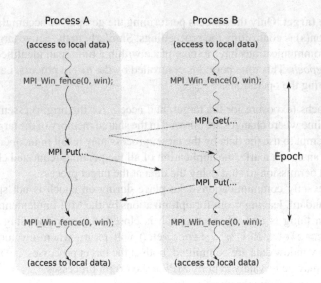

FIGURE 5.15

An example of the interaction between two processes when MPI_Win_fence is used to establish and terminate an epoch. The slanted dashed lines represent communications. The vertical dotted lines represent idle times.

memory is allowed, by forcing the declaration at the beginning of an exposure (access) epoch of the process ranks that will serve as origins (targets).

This active target approach requires that the origin calls MPI_Win_start and MPI_Win_complete, while the target calls MPI_Win_post and MPI_Win_wait, to start and end the access and exposure epochs, respectively. The MPI_Win_start call can be blocking until the target processes issue a corresponding MPI_Win_post call. Furthermore, the termination of the exposure epoch in a target process via MPI_Win_wait will block until all origin processes issue a matching MPI_Win_complete call.

Their syntax is as follows:

```
// to begin an exposure epoch
int MPI_Win_post(MPI_Group group, // Group of origin proc. (IN)
                 int        assert,// Flags that can be used for
                                   // optimization. Zero can be
                                   // used for default. (IN)
                 MPI_Win    win)   // Window object (IN)

// to terminate an exposure epoch
int MPI_Win_wait(MPI_Win win) // Window object. (IN)

// to begin an access epoch
int MPI_Win_start(MPI_Group group, // Group of target proc. (IN)
```

```
int        assert,// Flags that can be used for
                  // optimization. Zero can be
                  // used for default. (IN)
MPI_Win    win)   // Window object (IN)
```

```
// to terminate an access epoch
int MPI_Win_complete(MPI_Win win) // Window object (IN)
```

An example of the interaction taking place in this case is shown in Figure 5.16.

3. MPI_Win_lock, MPI_Win_unlock: These functions behave in a similar manner to the signal and wait methods of a semaphore. The origin process may use them to get exclusive access to the target's shared memory (at least as far as MPI-controlled access is concerned) without the explicit cooperation of the target (*passive target*). Unless access to the shared buffer is done through appropriate RMA calls, there is no guarantee that these calls will operate as specified.

Their syntax is as follows:

```
int MPI_Win_lock(int     lock_type,  // Lock type (IN). One of:
                                     // MPI_LOCK_EXCLUSIVE
                                     // MPI_LOCK_SHARED
                 int     rank,       // Rank of target. (IN)
                 int     assert,     // Assertion flag. (IN)
                 MPI_Win win)        // Window object (IN)
```

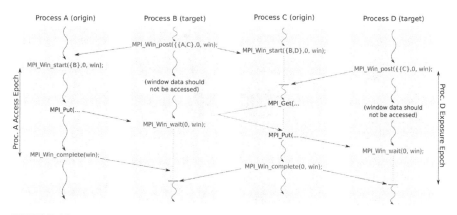

FIGURE 5.16

An example of the interaction between four processes when MPI_Win_post and MPI_Win_start are used to begin epochs. The slanted dashed lines represent communications. The {} notation is used to represent groups of processes without deviating too much from the C-language syntax. MPI_Win_start calls can block until the corresponding targets issue MPI_Win_post statements, as shown. However, this is not the default behavior. The exact action depends on the assert flags specified and the particular MPI implementation. The vertical dotted lines represent idle times.

```
int MPI_Win_unlock(int      rank,// Rank of target. (IN)
                   MPI_Win win) // Window object. (IN)
```

The MPI_LOCK_SHARED lock type can be used to implement "reader" functionality, i.e., allowing multiple processes to get data from the target while preventing any modifications from taking place.

On the other hand, the MPI_LOCK_EXCLUSIVE lock type can be used to implement "writer" functionality, preventing access to the window data from any other process while they are being modified.

As with previous synchronization functions, an assert flag of 0 can be used as a default.

Figure 5.17 shows a possible interaction scenario between three processes that utilize MPI_Win_lock to acquire exclusive access to a window's memory.

To demonstrate the use of the RMA functions, we show how the bucketsort implementation of Listing 5.18 can be converted to use remote memory access. For educational purposes, we use all three different methods of RMA synchronization.

The initial steps that follow entail the allocation of memory for the data array (line 23), the buckets (line 24), the bucket offsets (line 25), the bucket content counters (line 26), the receive counters (line 28), and offsets for data retrieval (line 29).

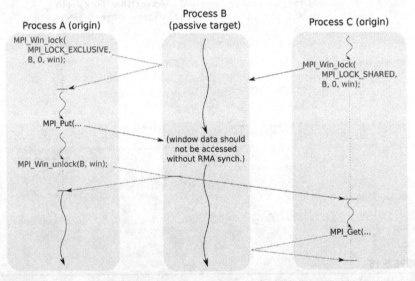

FIGURE 5.17

An example of the interaction between three processes when MPI_Win_lock and MPI_Win_unlock are used to establish passive target synchronization. Process A is trying to get an exclusive lock in order to modify the target's memory, whereas process C is trying to get a shared lock in order to read the target's memory. The slanted dashed lines represent communications; the vertical dotted lines represent idle times.

Lines 43 and 44 create two process groups: one containing all the processes (`all`) and one containing all the processes but the calling one (`allOtherGroup`). These two groups are used for commencing the exposure epochs.

In addition, three windows are created: one for accessing the buckets (`bucketWin`, line 46), one for the bucket counters (`cntWin`, line 47), and one for the unsorted, initial data arrays (`dataWin`, line 48).

```
1   // File : bucketsortRMA .cpp
2   . . .
3   int main (int argc, char **argv)
4   {
5     MPI_Init (&argc, &argv);
6
7     int rank, N;
8     MPI_Comm_rank (MPI_COMM_WORLD, &rank);
9     MPI_Comm_size (MPI_COMM_WORLD, &N);
10    MPI_Status status;
11
12    if (argc == 1)
13      {
14        if (rank == 0)
15          cerr << "Usage " << argv[0] << " number_of_items\n";
16        exit (1);
17      }
18
19    int M = atoi (argv[1]);
20    int maxItemsPerBucket = ceil (1.0 * M / N);
21    int deliveredItems;
22    int bucketRange = ceil (1.0 * (MAX - MIN) / N);
23    int *data = new int[N * maxItemsPerBucket];   // to allow easy ↵
               scattering
24    int *buckets = new int[N * maxItemsPerBucket];
25    int *bucketOffset = new int[N];        // where do buckets begin?
26    int *inBucket = new int[N];   // how many items in each one?
27
28    int *toRecv = new int[N];       // how many items to receive from each↵
               process
29    int *recvOff = new int[N];      // offsets for sent data
30
31    if (rank == 0)
32      initData (MIN, MAX, data, M);
33
34    // initialize bucket counters and offsets
35    for (int i = 0; i < N; i++)
36      {
37        inBucket[i] = 0;
38        bucketOffset[i] = i * maxItemsPerBucket;
39      }
40
41    // three windows created , one for the bucket counts, one for the ↵
               buckets themselves and one for the data
42    MPI_Group all, allOtherGroup;
```

```
43    MPI_Comm_group (MPI_COMM_WORLD, &all);
44    MPI_Group_excl (all, 1, &rank, &allOtherGroup);
45    MPI_Win cntWin, bucketWin, dataWin;
46    MPI_Win_create (buckets, N * maxItemsPerBucket * sizeof (int), ↵
          sizeof (int), MPI_INFO_NULL, MPI_COMM_WORLD, &bucketWin);
47    MPI_Win_create (inBucket, N * sizeof (int), sizeof (int), ↵
          MPI_INFO_NULL, MPI_COMM_WORLD, &cntWin);
48    MPI_Win_create (data, N * maxItemsPerBucket * sizeof (int), sizeof (↵
          int), MPI_INFO_NULL, MPI_COMM_WORLD, &dataWin);
```

LISTING 5.25

A parallel bucketsort implementation that uses RMA for data exchange between the processes.

The first step following the data allocation and initialization is to scatter the data that initially reside in process 0 to all the other processes. This is a step that uses the MPI_Put function to remotely access the remote data arrays (line 57). The remote access is enclosed in MPI_fence calls (executed by all processes in lines 51 and 60) that start and end the exposure/access epochs. Because these are collective calls, all the processes will have to wait for the root process to finish the data distribution before continuing.

```
49    // step 1
50    // replacing MPI_Scatter (data, maxItemsPerBucket, MPI_INT, data, ↵
          maxItemsPerBucket, MPI_INT, 0, MPI_COMM_WORLD);
51    MPI_Win_fence (0, dataWin);
52    if (rank == 0)
53      {
54        for (int i = 1; i < N; i++)
55          {
56            deliveredItems = (rank == N - 1) ? (M - (N - 1) * ↵
                  maxItemsPerBucket) : maxItemsPerBucket;
57            MPI_Put (&(data[bucketOffset[i]]), deliveredItems, MPI_INT, ↵
                  i, 0, N * maxItemsPerBucket, MPI_INT, dataWin);
58          }
59      }
60    MPI_Win_fence (0, dataWin);
61    deliveredItems = (rank == N - 1) ? (M - (N - 1) * maxItemsPerBucket)↵
          : maxItemsPerBucket;
```

In the next step, which does not involve any communication, the processes go over their local data items and sort them into N buckets, as many as the number of processes.

```
62    // step 2
63    // split into buckets
64    for (int i = 0; i < deliveredItems; i++)
65      {
66        int idx = (data[i] - MIN) / bucketRange;
67        int off = bucketOffset[idx] + inBucket[idx];
```

```
68        buckets[off] = data[i];
69        inBucket[idx]++;
70      }
```

At the next step, the buckets have to be redistributed so that they end up at their appropriate process. Mirroring the bucketsort implementation in Listing 5.18 that used collective operations, we start by having each process get from all the other processes the sizes of the buckets that it needs to retrieve. Each process starts an exposure epoch (line 75) so that its bucket counters can be accessed by all other processes, and then it starts an access epoch (line 76) in order to access the remote bucket counters. The allOtherGroup MPI_Group variable is used to control which processes are granted access rights in the exposure epoch or are to be accessed in the access epoch. These epochs end (lines 80 for access and line 81 for exposure) after all counters are retrieved by the loop of lines 77-79.

The loop of lines 83-85 is then used to calculate where each of the to-be-retrieved buckets should be stored in local memory.

```
71    // step 3
72    // start by gathering the counts of data the other processes will ↩
         send
73    // replacing MPI_Alltoall (inBucket, 1, MPI_INT, toRecv, 1, MPI_INT, ↩
         MPI_COMM_WORLD);
74    toRecv[rank] = inBucket[rank];
75    MPI_Win_post (allOtherGroup, 0, cntWin);
76    MPI_Win_start (allOtherGroup, 0, cntWin);
77    for (int i = 0; i < N; i++)
78      if (i != rank)
79        MPI_Get (&(toRecv[i]), 1, MPI_INT, i, rank, 1, MPI_INT, cntWin);
80    MPI_Win_complete (cntWin);
81    MPI_Win_wait (cntWin);
82
83    recvOff[0] = 0;
84    for (int i = 1; i < N; i++)
85      recvOff[i] = recvOff[i - 1] + toRecv[i - 1];
```

The remote buckets are then retrieved by starting a new exposure epoch for all the processes (line 87). The use of the all MPI_Group allows for simpler code in the loop of lines 89 and 90, since there is no need for a special check that distinguishes between local and remote bucket arrays. MPI_Get can be used even for copying the local bucket to the appropriate offset of the data array.

The last step before sorting the individual buckets in their respective processes is to lock the dataWin window (line 94) so that the root process will have to wait for the sorting to complete before starting to copy the buckets to its memory.

```
86    // replacing MPI_Alltoallv (buckets, inBucket, bucketOffset, MPI_INT ↩
         , data, toRecv, recvOff, MPI_INT, MPI_COMM_WORLD);
87    MPI_Win_post (all, 0, bucketWin);
88    MPI_Win_start (all, 0, bucketWin);
89    for (int i = 0; i < N; i++)
```

```
90      MPI_Get (&(data[recvOff[i]]), toRecv[i], MPI_INT, i, bucketOffset[↵
            rank], maxItemsPerBucket, MPI_INT, bucketWin);
91    MPI_Win_complete (bucketWin);
92    MPI_Win_wait (bucketWin);
93
94    MPI_Win_lock (MPI_LOCK_EXCLUSIVE, rank, 0, dataWin);   // limit ↵
            access to data array until it is sorted
```

The sorting can be done with the standard-C library qsort function (line 98) before unlocking the dataWin window (line 100).

```
95    // step 4
96    // apply quicksort to the local bucket
97    int localBucketSize = recvOff[N - 1] + toRecv[N - 1];
98    qsort (data, localBucketSize, sizeof (int), comp);
99
100   MPI_Win_unlock (rank, dataWin);       // data array is available again
```

Finally, the root process gathers the sizes of the individual buckets (line 102) and calculates the offsets where each one will have to be copied (lines 103-108). Line 102 holds the only collective function remnant of the original Listing 5.18. The reason is just simplicity. Replacing collective communication functions with RMA operations tends to enlarge the code, as a direct comparison to Listing 5.18 can reveal.

Once the bucket sizes are known to the root process, it can start to lock each individual bucket (line 115) before copying the remote, sorted, subarray to its proper place in its local memory (line 116). The passive target RMA is terminated by line 117.

```
101   // step 5
102   MPI_Gather (&localBucketSize, 1, MPI_INT, toRecv, 1, MPI_INT, 0, ↵
            MPI_COMM_WORLD);
103   if (rank == 0)
104     {
105       recvOff[0] = 0;
106       for (int i = 1; i < N; i++)
107         recvOff[i] = recvOff[i - 1] + toRecv[i - 1];
108     }
109
110   // replacing MPI_Gatherv (data, localBucketSize, MPI_INT, data, ↵
            toRecv, recvOff, MPI_INT, 0, MPI_COMM_WORLD);
111   if (rank == 0)
112     {
113       for (int i = 1; i < N; i++)
114         {
115           MPI_Win_lock (MPI_LOCK_EXCLUSIVE, i, 0, dataWin);       // ↵
                gain access to remote data array
116           MPI_Get (&(data[recvOff[i]]), toRecv[i], MPI_INT, i, 0, ↵
                toRecv[i], MPI_INT, dataWin);
117           MPI_Win_unlock (i, dataWin);  // release lock to remote data↵
                array
118         }
119     }
```

```
120
121    // print results
122    if (rank == 0)
123      {
124        for (int i = 0; i < M; i++)
125          cout << data[i] << " ";
126        cout << endl;
127      }
```

The window and group memory clean-up (lines 128-132) is the last operation preceding MPI_Finalize. If we neglect to clean up, MPI can produce run-time errors informing of this fact.

```
128    MPI_Group_free (&all);
129    MPI_Group_free (&allOtherGroup);
130    MPI_Win_free (&cntWin);
131    MPI_Win_free (&bucketWin);
132    MPI_Win_free (&dataWin);
133    MPI_Finalize ();
134    delete [] buckets;
135    delete [] inBucket;
136    delete [] bucketOffset;
137    delete [] toRecv;
138    delete [] recvOff;
139    delete [] data;
140    return 0;
```

The comparison of the RMA-based bucketsort implementation with Listing 5.18 is not a flattering one as far as complexity and the length of the code are concerned. This is a natural consequence of replacing collective operations with individual memory accesses. RMA-based implementations are not much different in that respect with point-to-point communication based ones, i.e., they lack expressiveness. The choice of tool is ultimately the prerogative of the programmer, given performance and other application-specific restrictions.

5.15 I/O CONSIDERATIONS

In MPI the root process has the special privilege of exclusive use of the standard input, i.e., it is the only one that can read user input from the keyboard. However, all processes have access to the standard output and the command-line parameters used to launch the application. So, if the command line contains a set of parameters critical to the execution of the program, these can be accessed and parsed directly instead of having the root process parse them and broadcast them.

The real issue lays elsewhere: How can we maximize the I/O speed from secondary storage to MPI processes? Keeping the processes busy means that they must have easy and fast access to the problem's data. The least common denominator is to have universal access to a common filesystem, such as an NFS volume. This would guarantee that all processes can access the problem's data without requiring special action from the root process, e.g., reading and scattering of file data. Additionally, a parallel filesystem such as IBM's Elastic Storage [1] or the Parallel Virtual File System (PVFS) [3] can be used to maximize the I/O data rates that can be achieved.

A parallel filesystem can improve I/O performance at the system level. However, there is one more facet of the problem that needs to be addressed: *parallel access to data at the application or process level*. Figure 5.18 illustrates the issue at hand by showing three different I/O configurations. Clearly, Figure 5.18(b) provides the greatest performance potential, but it might also make it necessary to post-process the program's output (e.g., joining the files into one). Figure 5.18(c) would then seem to be the best compromise, although special support needs to be provided to avoid having processes step on each others' toes!

MPI provides a set of parallel I/O functions aimed at solving this problem. These functions should be used instead of the typical POSIX file library to open, close, read, and write to a file or files from multiple processes. MPI uses a special nomenclature to describe its I/O functions:

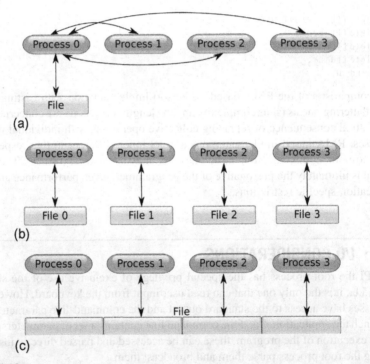

FIGURE 5.18

MPI applications with different I/O configurations: (a) root process controls access to the data file, (b) each process has access to a separate file, and (c) all processes have access to the same file concurrently. Configurations (b) and (c) qualify as parallel I/O.

- **etype**: This is the elementary datatype, i.e., the fundamental data unit that a file is made of. All I/O is performed in etype units. Also, when MPI accesses a file, the size of the declared etype is used for calculating offsets and file pointers. Any primitive or derived datatype can be used as the etype of a file.
- **filetype**: A filetype is a single etype or a collection of etypes in the form of a derived datatype. A filetype forms the basis for partitioning a file among processes.
- **view**: A view defines what is currently accessible in a file from a process. A view consists of a displacement or offset from the beginning of file, an etype, and a filetype. The pattern defined by the filetype is repeated, starting at the declared offset, to define the view. Figure 5.19(a) shows the relationship among the etype, the filetype, and the view.

A group of processes that access a file can have the same etype but different filetypes and views so that each one gets a distinct part of the file, as shown in Figure 5.19(b). The files to be accessed by MPI I/O must be binary ones, with fixed lengths per etype. Text files, generally, do not satisfy this requirement.

The most commonly used MPI I/O functions are as follows:

```
int MPI_File_open(MPI_Comm comm,     // Communicator (IN)
                  char      *filename,// Path to file (IN)
```

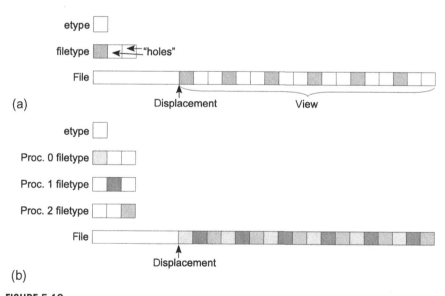

(a)

(b)

FIGURE 5.19

(a) Relationship among etype, filetype, and view for MPI I/O functions. (b) Each MPI process can have a different filetype associated with a file in order to be able to partition the file into disjoint sets.

```
          int       amode,    // Mode of operation (IN)
          MPI_Info info,      // Info object for
                              // optimizations (IN)
          MPI_File *fh)       // File handle (OUT)
```

`MPI_File_open` is a *collective* function, so it has to be called by all the processes in the declared intra-communicator. The `amode` parameter can be a bitwise OR of different constants (some are mutually exclusive) that direct MPI on how the file will be opened. A list of these constants is shown in Table 5.5.

All files opened by MPI must be closed before `MPI_Finalize` is called:

```
int MPI_File_close(MPI_File *mpi_fh) // File handle (IN)
```

For reading and writing collections of etypes, we can use:

```
int MPI_File_read(MPI_File    mpi_fh,   // File handle (IN)
             void        *buf,     // Address of data buffer (OUT)
             int         count,    // Number of elements in
                                   // *buf (IN)
             MPI_Datatype datatype,// Etype (IN)
             MPI_Status  *status)  // Status object (OUT)


int MPI_File_write(MPI_File   mpi_fh,   // File handle (IN)
             void        *buf,     // Address of data buffer (IN)
             int         count,    // Number of elements in
                                   // *buf (IN)
             MPI_Datatype datatype,// Etype (IN)
             MPI_Status  *status)  // Status object (OUT)
```

Finally, a view can be specified for a file via the following function:

```
int MPI_File_set_view(MPI_File    mpi_fh,   // File handle (IN)
                 MPI_Offset  disp,     // File offset in etype
                                       // units (IN)
```

Table 5.5 A list of file opening modes that can be used in `MPI_File_open`

Mode	Description
MPI_MODE_RDONLY	read only
MPI_MODE_RDWR	read and write
MPI_MODE_WRONLY	write only
MPI_MODE_CREATE	create the file if it does not exist
MPI_MODE_EXCL	error will be flagged if file exists when trying to create it
MPI_MODE_DELETE_ON_CLOSE	delete file upon closing it
MPI_MODE_UNIQUE_OPEN	file will be exclusively accessed
MPI_MODE_APPEND	file pointer set at end of file
MPI_MODE_SEQUENTIAL	file will be accessed sequentially

```
                    MPI_Datatype etype,      // Etype handle (IN)
                    MPI_Datatype filetype,   // Filetype handle (IN)
                    char         *datarep,   // Data represent−
                                             // ation (IN)
                    MPI_Info     info)       // Info object for
                                             // optimizations (IN)
```

The *datarep string can have one of these values:

- **"native":** Data are stored as if they were dumped from memory. This is appropriate only for homogeneous environments. Since no data conversion is performed, a change from big-to little-indian or a change in the length of the representation (32 to 64 bit) would render the data unreadable.
- **"external32":** Data on the file are stored in a canonical representation, which allows them to be converted appropriately for I/O in a heterogeneous environment. The compromise for ensuring the cross-platform readability of the data is that I/O performance deteriorates. In addition, a loss of precision is possible.

As a simple example of the use of MPI I/O, let's consider the distribution of data to processes for sorting. In our bucketsort example of Listing 5.25, the sample data are generated at the root process. One would normally expect that the data reside in a file. Breaking up the file into roughly equal parts can be accomplished with the code in Listing 5.26. For this simple example, the structure of the code mimics closely what would be required if POSIX calls were used.

```
1   // File : fileIO.cpp
2   . . .
3     MPI_Init (&argc, &argv);
4
5     int rank, N;
6     MPI_Comm_rank (MPI_COMM_WORLD, &rank);
7     MPI_Comm_size (MPI_COMM_WORLD, &N);
8     MPI_Status status;
9
10    if (argc == 1)
11      {
12        if (rank == 0)
13          cerr << "Usage " << argv[0] << " filetoload\n";
14        exit (1);
15      }
16
17    MPI_File f;
18    MPI_File_open (MPI_COMM_WORLD, argv[1], MPI_MODE_RDONLY, ↵
          MPI_INFO_NULL, &f);
19
20    int *data;
21    int blockSize;
22
23    MPI_Offset filesize;
24    MPI_File_get_size (f, &filesize); // get file size in bytes
```

```
25    filesize /= sizeof(int);          // convert to number of items
26    blockSize = filesize / N;         // calculate size of block to read↩
         per process
27    int pos = rank * blockSize;       // initial file position per ↩
         process
28    if(rank == N-1)
29       blockSize = filesize - pos;    // get all remaining in last ↩
            process
30
31    data = new int[blockSize];
32    MPI_File_seek(f, pos*sizeof(int), MPI_SEEK_SET);
33    MPI_File_read (f, data, blockSize, MPI_INT, &status);
34    MPI_File_close (&f);
35
36    sleep (rank);
37    cout << rank << " read " << blockSize << " numbers." << endl;
38    for (int i = 0; i < 30; i++)
39       cout << data[i] << " ";
40    cout << ".... Last one is : " << data[blockSize - 1];
41    cout << endl;
42
43    delete [] data;
44    MPI_Finalize ();
45    return 0;
46 }
```

LISTING 5.26

An example of a roughly equal block distribution of int type data via MPI I/O.

Line 18 opens the file provided as a command-line parameter in read-only mode. The size of the file in bytes is queried in line 24, with the result stored in variable filesize. The MPI_Offset type is just a typedef for type long long. The actual number of integers in the file is calculated in line 25 so that the size of the blocks that will be assigned to each process and the initial position to read from can be calculated (lines 26 and 27, respectively). The last ($N - 1$ -ranked) process is treated separately (lines 28 and 29) in order to be able to get all the data in the file, regardless of whether the file size is evenly divided by the size of the communicator or not.

The data are read in line 33 after the local file pointer is moved to the appropriate offset in the file with the MPI_File_seek function (line 32). MPI_File_seek and the respective constants used for placing the file pointer (MPI_SEEK_SET, MPI_SEEK_CUR, and MPI_SEEK_END) mirror the corresponding C99 function fseek and its constants (SEEK_SET, SEEK_CUR, and SEEK_END), resulting in a fairly familiar setup.

Finally, Line 36 delays each process for a sufficient amount of time to allow for a tidy output to the console of some debugging information (lines 37-41). Running the program of Listing 5.26 on a file containing a sequence of 10,000 integers from 0 to 9999 would produce the following output:

```
$ mpirun —np 3 ./fileIO  data
0 read 3333 numbers.
0 1 2 3 4 5 6 7 8 9 10 11 12 13 14 15 16 17 18 19 20 21 22 23 24 25 26↩
      27 28 29 .... Last one is : 3332
1 read 3333 numbers.
3333 3334 3335 3336 3337 3338 3339 3340 3341 3342 3343 3344 3345 3346 ↩
      3347 3348 3349 3350 3351 3352 3353 3354 3355 3356 3357 3358 3359 ↩
      3360 3361 3362 .... Last one is : 6665
2 read 3334 numbers.
6666 6667 6668 6669 6670 6671 6672 6673 6674 6675 6676 6677 6678 6679 ↩
      6680 6681 6682 6683 6684 6685 6686 6687 6688 6689 6690 6691 6692 ↩
      6693 6694 6695 .... Last one is : 9999
```

A *cyclic, block distribution* of the file's contents to the available processes can be accomplished by declaring a filetype and view for a file, as shown in Listing 5.27. In a cyclic, block distribution, fixed-sized blocks of the data are assigned to the processes in a round-robin fashion.

```
1  // File : viewExample.cpp
2  . . .
3  const int BLOCKSIZE = 10;
4
5  //*****************************************
6  int main (int argc, char **argv)
7  {
8    MPI_Init (&argc, &argv);
9
10   int rank, N;
11   MPI_Comm_rank (MPI_COMM_WORLD, &rank);
12   MPI_Comm_size (MPI_COMM_WORLD, &N);
13   MPI_Status status;
14
15   if (argc == 1)
16     {
17       if (rank == 0)
18         cerr << "Usage " << argv[0] << " filetoload\n";
19       exit (1);
20     }
21
22   MPI_File f;
23   MPI_File_open (MPI_COMM_WORLD, argv[1], MPI_MODE_RDONLY, ↩
         MPI_INFO_NULL, &f);
24
25   MPI_Datatype filetype;
26   int sizes = N * BLOCKSIZE, subsizes = BLOCKSIZE, starts = 0;
27   MPI_Type_create_subarray (1, &sizes, &subsizes, &starts, MPI_ORDRE_C↩
         , MPI_INT, &filetype);
28   MPI_Type_commit (&filetype);
29   MPI_File_set_view (f, rank * BLOCKSIZE * sizeof (int), MPI_INT, ↩
         filetype, "native", MPI_INFO_NULL);
```

LISTING 5.27

An example of a cyclic, block distribution of data via MPI I/O.

Lines 25-29 of Listing 5.27 constitute the first major difference with Listing 5.26. A derived datatype is created for establishing a filetype for the opened file. The `MPI_Type_create_sub-array` function is useful for extracting a portion of a multidimensional array. Its syntax is:

```
int MPI_Type_create_subarray(
        int            ndims,      // Number of array dimensions (IN)
        int            sizes[],    // Size of each dimension (IN)
        int            subsizes[], // Number of elements to extract from ↩
            each dimension (IN)
        int            starts[],   // Starting offsets in each dimension ↩
            (IN)
        int            order,      // Array storage order (IN)
        MPI_Datatype oldtype,      // Array element datatype (IN)
        MPI_Datatype *newtype)     // Derived datatype (OUT)
```

The array storage order can be set to one of `MPI_ORDER_C` or `MPI_ORDER_FORTRAN`.

By creating a subarray type of `BLOCKSIZE` elements from a 1D array N times as big as that (line 27), and by setting the byte offset to start reading from the file to `rank*BLOCKSIZE*sizeof(int)` (line 29), each process is made to read a different block of data. Figure 5.20 illustrates the resulting effect.

Although the amount of data each process will read can be computed *a priori*, in the remainder of the code we use a type `vector<int>` object for having a dynamically grown data repository, since the data are read one block at a time.

```
30   vector < int >data;
31   int temp[BLOCKSIZE];
32
33   MPI_Offset filesize;
34   MPI_File_get_size (f, &filesize); // get size in bytes
35   filesize /= sizeof (int);         // convert size in number of items
36   int pos = rank * BLOCKSIZE;       // initial file position per ↩
         process
37   while (pos < filesize)
```

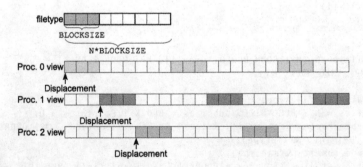

FIGURE 5.20

An illustration of the filetype and views associated with three processes, as used in Listing 5.27 to achieve a cyclic, block distribution of a file's data.

```
38        {
39          MPI_File_read (f, temp, 1, filetype, &status);
40          int cnt;
41          MPI_Get_count (&status, filetype, &cnt);
42
43          pos += BLOCKSIZE * N;
44          for (int i = 0; i < cnt * BLOCKSIZE; i++)
45            data.push_back (temp[i]);
46        }
47
48      MPI_File_close (&f);
49
50      sleep (rank);
51      cout << rank << " read " << data.size () << " numbers." << endl;
52      for (int i = 0; i < 30; i++)
53        cout << data[i] << " ";
54      cout << ".... Last one is : " << data[data.size () - 1];
55      cout << endl;
56
57      MPI_Finalize ();
```

The pos variable, which is defined in line 36 and updated in line 43, keeps track of the file pointer so that the loop of lines 37-46 can terminate when all the data have been read. The data are read temporarily in the temp array before being appended at the end of the data vector. The status variable allows us to know the exact number of items read (line 41), which should be normally equal to one.

Running the program of Listing 5.27 on a file containing a sequence of 10,000 integers from 0 to 9999 would produce the following output:

```
$ mpirun −np 3 ./viewExample  data
0 read 3340 numbers.
0 1 2 3 4 5 6 7 8 9 30 31 32 33 34 35 36 37 38 39 60 61 62 63 64 65 66↩
    67 68 69 .... Last one is : 9999
1 read 3330 numbers.
10 11 12 13 14 15 16 17 18 19 40 41 42 43 44 45 46 47 48 49 70 71 72 ↩
    73 74 75 76 77 78 79 .... Last one is : 9979
2 read 3330 numbers.
20 21 22 23 24 25 26 27 28 29 50 51 52 53 54 55 56 57 58 59 80 81 82 ↩
    83 84 85 86 87 88 89 .... Last one is : 9989
```

5.16 COMBINING MPI PROCESSES WITH THREADS

MPI is primarily concerned with communication, although it does provide the means for dynamic process creation. However, it is arguably preferable to spawn multiple threads on multicore systems than to spawn individual MPI processes with all the additional memory and management overhead. The only downside we might consider when using threads in MPI programs is that only one of the threads may have access to MPI for communications. This has nothing to do with function thread safety but rather with the fact that MPI identifies or ranks processes, and thus it cannot address individual threads.

In this section we discuss the setup required for deploying multiple threads from each MPI process. The spawning mechanism is nothing special. A variety of libraries can be used, including the Qt one covered in Chapter 3. The challenge is to properly compile and link the executable, a process that is somewhat complicated by the fact that `mpicc/mpiCC/mpic++/mpicxx` are actually compiler front ends that hide much of the compilation inner workings from the developers.

Ultimately, `mpicc/mpiCC/mpic++/mpicxx` just call the C/C++ compiler with the appropriate switches for locating the header files during compilation, and locating and linking-in the MPI library. A simple way to integrate MPI and Qt is to modify the project (.pro) file so that all compiler and linker invocations are handled via the `mpicc/mpiCC/mpic++/mpicxx` scripts. In this way, a developer does not have to worry about MPI-specific include and library file locations and/or switches.[11]

A simple program that demonstrates the use of Qt threads and MPI processes is given in Listing 5.28, where each process spawns as many threads as the number of available cores minus 1. A process can query the number of available cores via the POSIX function `sysconf`, which returns a number of run-time system configuration information based on the parameter passed to it. In our case the parameter is `_SC_NPROCESSORS_ONLN`.

```
1   // File : mpiAndQt.cpp
2   . . .
3   class MyThread:public QThread
4   {
5   private :
6     int ID, rank;
7   public :
8       MyThread (int i, int r):ID (i), rank (r) {}
9     void run ()
10    {
11        cout << "Thread " << ID << " is running on process " << rank << "\↩
          n";
12    }
13  };
14
15  //────────────────────────────────────────
16  int main (int argc, char **argv)
17  {
18    MPI_Init (&argc, &argv);
19
20    int rank, N;
21    MPI_Comm_rank (MPI_COMM_WORLD, &rank);
22    MPI_Comm_size (MPI_COMM_WORLD, &N);
```

---

[11] This setup has been tested with OpenMPI 1.6.5 and Qt 5.2.1, on Ubuntu Linux 14.04. However, it should work with other configurations as well.

```
23
24    int numThreads = sysconf (_SC_NPROCESSORS_ONLN);
25    MyThread *x[numThreads];
26    for (int i = 0; i < numThreads; i++)
27      {
28        x[i] = new MyThread (i, rank);
29        x[i]->start ();
30      }
31
32    for (int i = 0; i < numThreads; i++)
33      x[i]->wait ();
34
35    MPI_Finalize ();
36    return 0;
37  }
```

LISTING 5.28

An example of an MPI program spawning threads using the Qt library.

This program can be compiled and subsequently executed using mpirun by providing a project file similar to the one shown here:

```
#File : mpiAndQt.pro
SOURCES+=mpiAndQt.cpp
CONFIG+=qt
TARGET=mpiAndQt
QMAKE_CXX=mpiCC
QMAKE_CC=mpicc
QMAKE_LINK=mpiCC
```

The last three lines are the key to successfully making qmake and the Qt toolchain use the MPI compiler front-end for compilation and linking. These lines effectively force qmake to generate a Makefile that uses mpiCC for compiling C++ programs (by setting QMAKE_CXX), mpicc for compiling C programs (by setting QMAKE_CC), and mpiCC for linking object and library files into the target executable (by setting QMAKE_LINK). In the case of MPICH, mpic++ should be used in the place of mpiCC.

Compiling and running the program is then as simple as (see Appendix A for more details on the use of qmake):

```
$ qmake mpiAndQt.pro
$ make
$ mpirun -np 2 ./mpiAndQt
```

If only the main thread of an MPI process will perform MPI calls, then the above discussion is the end of the story. However, MPI can be configured to allow multiple threads from an MPI process to perform MPI calls. Enabling threading support takes place during the compilation phase of an MPI library. For example, if OpenMPI is being built from the source code, the configuration script should be given the following parameter:

```
$ ./configure --enable-mpi-thread-multiple
```

Similarly, for MPICH, the configuration command is[12]:

```
$ ./configure —enable-threads=multiple —with-thread-package=posix
```

The level of threading support can be one of the following:

- MPI_THREAD_SINGLE: Only one thread per process is allowed.
- MPI_THREAD_FUNNELED: Multiple threads are allowed, but only one is supposed to make MPI calls (all MPI calls are "funneled" to the main thread).
- MPI_THREAD_SERIALIZED: Multiple threads making MPI calls are allowed, but only one of them can do so at any given time.
- MPI_THREAD_MULTIPLE: Multiple threads are allowed, all of them making concurrent MPI calls.

The thread-level support that an MPI implementation provides can be queried by the MPI_Query_thread function or by the MPI_Init_thread function that should be used instead of the typical MPI_Init to initialize MPI in a multithreaded software system. The syntax of MPI_Init_thread is the following:

```
int MPI_Init_thread(int  *argc,     // Pointer to the number of
                                    // program arguments (IN)
                    char ***argv,   // Pointer to the argument
                                    // pointer vector (IN)
                    int  required,  // Required thread-level support.
                                    // One of the above listed cons-
                                    // tants should be specified.(IN)
                    int  *provided ) // Level of provided threading
                                    // support (OUT).
```

MPI_Init_thread should be called once by the main thread of an MPI process as a replacement to MPI_Init. The threads spawned by an MPI process still share a single identifier (the process rank) through which they can communicate with the other nodes.

An extensive example of the use of MPI and threads is provided in Section 5.22.2.

5.17 TIMING AND PERFORMANCE MEASUREMENTS

In terms of timing, MPI provides two functions: MPI_Wtime (wall time) and MPI_Wticks. The first reads the system clock; the second returns the clock's resolution in seconds per tick. Their syntax is the following:

```
double MPI_Wtime( void );
double MPI_Wtick( void );
```

[12]Different MPI implementations or more recent versions of these libraries may require other options. It is always a good idea to check the installation instructions.

MPI_Wtime returns the time since an unspecified time in the past. Therefore, a single returned value has no meaning, but by subtracting two readings of the function, we can measure a time span:

```
double timeStart, timeEnd;
timeStart = MPI_Wtime();
. . . // do something
timeEnd = MPI_Wtime();
cout << "Total time spent : " << timeEnd - timeStart << endl;
```

In retrospect, there is no practical reason to prefer these functions over any others provided natively by C/C++ or external libraries, as long as CPU-specific mechanisms (such as the RDTSC x86 command) are not employed. Ultimately, it all comes down to the system clock and its resolution that these libraries are reading.

5.18 DEBUGGING AND PROFILING MPI PROGRAMS

Debugging MPI programs presents the same challenges as the debugging of multithreaded applications. Using console output is still a developer's primary weapon for detecting bugs and fixing them. A useful trick that can be used to distinguish the output of the different processes on the console is to have them generated at staggered intervals by making them sleep for an amount of time proportional to their rank:

```
MPI_Comm_rank (MPI_COMM_WORLD, &rank);
do_some_work();
sleep(rank);       // puts the process to sleep for "rank" seconds
outputDebugInfo();
```

A convenient approach that can be used to check each and every error code returned by MPI functions is to define the following preprocessor macro:

```
#define MEC(call) {int res; \
                   res = call; \
                   if(res != MPI_SUCCESS) { \
                       fprintf(stderr, "Call "#call" return error code ↩
                       %i\n", res); \
                       MPI_Abort(MPI_COMM_WORLD, res);}   }
```

and use the MEC (**MPI E**rror **C**heck) macro to encapsulate all MPI function calls. The #call expression expands to a string containing the macro argument, without trying to execute the command. Example:

```
MEC(MPI_Send(&data, k, dest, tag, MPI_COMM_WORLD));
```

MPI errors are by default fatal. The MEC macro can only be useful if the default behavior is changed to MPI_ERRORS_RETURN, as explained in Section 5.10.

The Multi-Processing Environment (MPE) [13] is a set of tools for debugging and profiling MPI applications. MPE used to be a part of a typical MPICH installation,

---

[13] Available for download at http://www.mcs.anl.gov/research/projects/perfvis/download/index.htm.

but it can be also compiled and installed alongside any standard-compliant MPI implementation. In the case of OpenMPI, the following command sequence is adequate for installing MPE from a source code archive, if mpicc is installed in /usr/local/bin and the Fortran functionality is disabled:

```
$ tar -tzf mpe2.tar.gz
$ cd mpe2-1.3.0
$ ./configure MPI_CC=/usr/local/bin/mpicc \
         CC=gcc \
         --prefix=/usr/local \
         --disable-f77
$ make
$ make install
```

MPE can record events in an MPI program, either automatically, i.e., via MPI function calls, or programmatically, i.e., as explicitly directed by the programmer. The events are recorded in a log file allowing for a post-execution analysis of the behavior, performance, and potential bottlenecks of the program. Of particular interest are extensive idle periods in the execution trace of a program. These can be identified by visualizing the trace with MPE's jumpshot program.

In order to compile an MPI program so that MPI function calls automatically register in a log file, the following command has to be issued, where the mpecc is effectively a replacement for mpicc[14]:

```
$ mpecc -mpilog -lmpi_cxx source.c -o target
```

The mpecc script inserts the log-generating statements in the program before compilation takes place, without affecting the original source code. The executable program can then be run normally. The last message output to the console informs the user of the generation (and filename) of the logfile. For example:

```
$ mpirun -np 2 ./sampleApp
. . .
Writing logfile....
Enabling the Default clock synchronization...
Finished writing logfile ./sampleApp.clog2.
```

The execution's timeline can then be visualized by invoking:

```
$ jumpshot ./sampleApp.clog2
```

The jumpshot program operates natively on slog2-formatted logs, and it will prompt the user for a conversion of the clog2-formatted log. An explicit conversion can also take place before jumpshot is called:

```
$ clog2TOslog2 ./sampleApp.clog2
```

Figure 5.21 shows a sample output of the jumpshot program.

---

[14]This has been tested with OpenMPI 1.6.3 and MPE2 1.3.0.

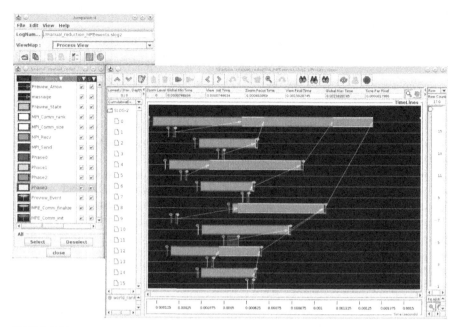

FIGURE 5.21

A screenshot of jumpshot in action. The trace displayed corresponds to a run of the program of Listing 5.29 for 16 processes. It should be noted that the trace displays nested events, with the outer ones forming boxes surrounding the inner ones (colors have been manipulated from the default used in Listing 5.29).

In order for user-defined events to be logged and displayed by MPE tools, the following sequence is typically required:

1. Get a unique number/ID to be associated with the event. For events that cover a time span, two IDs are needed: one marking the start and one marking the end of the event. For this purpose the MPE_Log_get_state_eventIDs function can be used:

```
int MPE_Log_get_state_eventIDs(int *startID,   // ID for event
                                              // beginning (OUT)
                               int *finalID )  // ID for event
                                              // end (OUT)
```

2. The jumpshot program displays each event using a string and a color that helps the event stand out. Similarly, user-defined events need to have a string and a color attached to them, something that can be accomplished by MPE_Describe_state:

```
int MPE_Describe_state(int         startID, // Beginning ID (IN)
                       int         finalID, // Ending ID (IN)
                       const char *name,   // Event name (IN)
                       const char *color ) // Event color (IN)
```

3. Finally, a log entry can be generated via MPE_log_event:

```
int MPE_Log_event(int event,          // Event ID (IN)
                  int data,           // Unused, set to 0
                  const char *bytebuf ) // Optional information.
                                      // Set to NULL if
                                      // unused (IN)
```

The following listing, which is a derivative of the reduction code of Listing 5.14, illustrates how these functions can be utilized. The program logs the beginning and end of each phase of the reduction process.

After the total number of phases are calculated between lines 16 and 20, three arrays are set up for holding the unique starting and ending IDs and description strings of the reduction phases events: startID, finalID, and eventNames. These arrays are initialized with calls to MPE_Log_get_state_eventIDs and MPE_Describe_state in the loop of lines 24-30.

```
1   // File : manual_reduction_MPEevents.cpp
2   #include <mpe.h>
3   . . .
4   int main (int argc, char **argv)
5   {
6     MPI_Init (&argc, &argv);
7
8     int rank, N;
9     MPI_Comm_rank (MPI_COMM_WORLD, &rank);
10    MPI_Comm_size (MPI_COMM_WORLD, &N);
11    MPI_Status status;
12
13    // calculate how many events will be monitored
14    int numEvents = 0;
15    int bitMask = 1;
16    while (bitMask < N)
17      {
18        numEvents++;
19        bitMask <<= 1;
20      }
21    int startID[numEvents];
22    int finalID[numEvents];
23    char *eventNames[numEvents];
24    for (int i = 0; i < numEvents; i++)
25      {
26        MPE_Log_get_state_eventIDs (&(startID[i]), &(finalID[i]));
27        eventNames[i] = new char[10];
28        sprintf (eventNames[i], "Phase%i\0", i);
29        MPE_Describe_state (startID[i], finalID[i], eventNames[i], "red"↩
            );
30      }
```

LISTING 5.29

A version of the "manual" reduction program of Listing 5.14, instumented with MPE functions.

Subsequently, the `phase` variable is used to keep track of the progress of the reduction, and `MPE_Log_event` calls are issued before and after every communication function involved in the reduction: lines 46 and 51 for a receiving process, and lines 55 and 59 for a sending process.

```
31    int partialSum = rank;
32    bitMask = 1;
33    bool doneFlag = false;
34    int phase = 0;
35    while (bitMask < N && !doneFlag)
36      {
37        int otherPartyID;
38        if ((rank & bitMask) == 0)
39          {
40            otherPartyID = rank | bitMask;
41            if (otherPartyID >= N)
42              {
43                bitMask <<= 1;
44                continue;
45              }
46            MPE_Log_event (startID[phase], 0, NULL);
47
48            int temp;
49            MPI_Recv (&temp, 1, MPI_INT, otherPartyID, MPI_ANY_TAG, ←
                  MPI_COMM_WORLD, &status);
50            partialSum += temp;
51            MPE_Log_event (finalID[phase], 0, NULL);
52          }
53        else
54          {
55            MPE_Log_event (startID[phase], 0, NULL);
56            otherPartyID = rank ^ bitMask;
57            doneFlag = true;
58            MPI_Send (&partialSum, 1, MPI_INT, otherPartyID, 0, ←
                  MPI_COMM_WORLD);
59            MPE_Log_event (finalID[phase], 0, NULL);
60          }
61        bitMask <<= 1;
62        phase++;
63      }
64    . . .
```

5.19 THE BOOST.MPI LIBRARY

The Boost.MPI wrapper library constitutes a major departure from the C/Fortran idiosyncrasies of MPI and toward simplicity and elegance. The only problem is that at the time of this writing, Boost.MPI does not support or provide abstractions for the full spectrum of communication primitives made available by MPI. Additionally, only the MPI 1.1 standard is supported. This means that the C bindings are still the best vehicle to extract the maximum of performance from your parallel platform, but it is also arguably true that Boost.MPI is the best way of extracting the maximum performance from your programming effort!

Boost.MPI is a small part of the Boost library that is primarily made of template classes but also some binary library files. Apart from abstracting and encapsulating MPI functionality, it offers a rich variety of classes for serialization, regular expression evaluation, threading, image processing, and so on. Compared with MPI, the available documentation covering Boost.MPI is relatively scant. Fortunately, the source code of the library itself is handsomely commented.

The typical structure of a Boost.MPI program is shown in Listing 5.30.

```
1  #include <boost/mpi.hpp>
2  . . .
3  int main (int argc, char **argv)
4  {
5    // No MPI calls prior to this point
6    boost::mpi::environment env (argc, argv);
7    boost::mpi::communicator world;
8
9    // MPI statements
10   . . .
11   return 0;
12 }
```

LISTING 5.30

Skeleton of a Boost.MPI program.

The MPI library is initialized with the construction of the `boost::mpi::environment` object. In contrast to the C bindings case, the MPI environment is terminated implicitly with the destruction of the `boost::mpi::environment` object. In addition, there is no symbolic constant representing the global communicator, but the default constructor of the `boost::mpi::communicator` class returns an object that in turn can be queried for rank information.

The Boost.MPI program that would correspond to the one shown in Listing 5.3 is shown in Listing 5.31.

```
1  // File : mpihello.cpp
2  #include <boost/mpi.hpp>
3  #include <iostream>
4
5  using namespace std;
6
7  int main (int argc, char **argv)
8  {
9    boost::mpi::environment env (argc, argv);
```

```
10    boost::mpi::communicator world;
11    cout << "Hello from process " << world.rank() << " of " << world.↩
          size() << endl;
12    return 0;
13  }
```

LISTING 5.31

"Hello World" in Boost.MPI.

The mpi.hpp header file includes all the Boost.MPI header files. Individual header files can also be used if the compilation time is critical.

The program in Listing 5.31 can be compiled with OpenMPI:

```
$ mpiCC mpihello.cpp −o mpihello −lboost_mpi
```

The two differences from the C case are the need to specify the shared object files (.so) containing the Boost library[15] and the use of the C++ compiler (invoked by the mpiCC command).

Obviously, the appropriate compilation command depends on the MPI implementation used and the configuration of the Boost library. For example, if libboost_mpi was not compiled as a shared library, and MPICH was used, we would need (assuming Boost was installed under /usr/local/):

```
$ mpic++ mpihello.cpp −o mpihello /usr/local/lib/libboost_mpi.a
```

The procedure for execution is identical to the ones detailed in Sections 5.4 and 5.5.2.

In Figure 5.22, we compare side by side the program of Figure 5.2 with its Boost/MPI equivalent. What is immediately obvious is that the use of Boost.MPI reduces clutter substantially.

The capabilities offered by Boost.MPI include:

- Point-to-point communication abstractions
- Collective operations
- Communicator management
- Serializing structures for communication

A table detailing the mapping from MPI C bindings to Boost.MPI is included in Appendix D.

5.19.1 BLOCKING AND NON BLOCKING COMMUNICATIONS

Boost.MPI takes advantage of C++ OO capabilities to simplify MPI communication calls. For example, in place of the single MPI_Send function, Boost.MPI offers a set of overloaded template methods of the mpi::communicator class, allowing the

---

[15] -lboost_mpi refers to the libboost_mpi.so file, located in one of the system-declared library directories.

MPI C Bindings	Boost.MPI
① `#include<mpi.h>`	`#include<boost/mpi.hpp>`
`#include<string.h>`	`#include<iostream>`
`#include<stdio.h>`	`#include<string>`
`#define MESSTAG 0`	`using namespace std;`
`#define MAXLEN 100`	`using namespace boost;`
	`#define MESSTAG 0`
`int main (int argc, char **argv) {`	`int main (int argc, char **argv) {`
② `  MPI_Init (&argc, &argv);`	`  mpi::environment env (argc, argv);`
③ `  int rank, num, i;`	`  mpi::communicator world;`
`  MPI_Comm_rank (MPI_COMM_WORLD, &rank);`	`  int rank = world.rank ();`
`  MPI_Comm_size (MPI_COMM_WORLD, &num);`	
④ `  if (rank == 0) {`	`  if (rank == 0) {`
`      char mess[] = "Hello World";`	`      string mess ("Hello World");`
`      int len = strlen(mess)+1;`	
`      for (i = 1; i < num; i++)`	`      for (int i = 1; i < world.size (); i++)`
⑤ `        MPI_Send (mess, len, MPI_CHAR,`	`        world.send (i, MESSTAG, mess);`
`             I,MESSTAG, MPI_COMM_WORLD);`	
`  } else {`	`  } else {`
`      char mess[MAXLEN];`	`      string mess;`
`      MPI_Status status;`	
⑥ `      MPI_Recv (mess, MAXLEN, MPI_CHAR, 0,`	`      world.recv (0, MESSTAG, mess);`
`          MESSTAG, MPI_COMM_WORLD, &status);`	
`      printf ("%i received %s\n", rank,`	`      cout << rank << " received " << mess`
`          mess);`	`                      << endl;`
`  }`	`  }`
⑦ `  MPI_Finalize ();`	`  return 0;`
`  return 0;`	`}`
`}`	

⑧ `mpicc hello.c -o hello`	`mpic++ hello.cpp -lboost_mpi \` `              -lboost_serialization -o hello`

Key:	
①	MPI-related header files
②	MPI initialization. Any command-line parameters destined for the MPI runtime are passed on.
③	Rank query. The default constructor in Boost.MPI returns the *MPI_COMM_WORLD* equivalent.
④	Code branching based on process identity/rank
⑤	Basic send operation. In Boost, the data type is implicitly passed, via polymorphism.
⑥	Basic MPI receiving operation. The *MPI_Status* structure holds critical information about the message.
⑦	MPI termination. In Boost, the destruction of the *boost::mpi::environment* object does the same.
⑧	Compilation command

FIGURE 5.22

Comparison of a "Hello World" MPI program using the C bindings and the Boost.MPI wrapper classes. The side-by-side comparison clearly highlights the differences between the two platforms. Please note that both the `mpicc` and `mpic++` commands are symbolic links to `/usr/bin/opal_wrapper`.

programmer to skip the declaration of the type of data being communicated. Type declarations can be a source of programming errors, and MPE has a specific operation mode for detecting those.

Point-to-point communications are handled as methods of a mpi::communicator class instance. The send, recv, isend, and irecv methods provide a consistent interface as far as the order and semantics of their first parameters are concerned. The first one is always the rank of the destination/source process and the second, the message tag. The remaining parameters describe the data to be sent or the buffer to receive the message.

A sample of the available send methods is shown here:

```
void send(int dest, int tag) const;   // Sends an empty message

template<typename T>              // Sends a single data item
   void send(int dest, int tag, const T& value) const;

template<typename T>              // Sends an array of n elements
   void send(int dest, int tag, const T* values, int n) const;
```

The matching recv methods follow similar guidelines. The only difference is that they return a status object:

```
status recv(int source, int tag) const; // Receives an empty message

template<typename T>              // Receives a single item
   status recv(int source, int tag, T& value) const;

template<typename T>              // Receive an array of values.
                                  // Buffer *values size is n.
   status recv(int source, int tag, T* values, int n) const;
```

A receiving node can get any incoming message by using the constants mpi::any_source and mpi::any_tag in place of MPI_ANY_SOURCE and MPI_ANY_TAG used in C.

The status class offers a number of methods:

```
int source(); // Returns the message source
int tag();    // Returns the message tag
int error();  // Returns the error code, or 0
template<typename T> // Returns the number of items T transfered
   optional<int>     // if they can be determined, hence the
      count() const; // optional<int> return object
```

Immediate versions of the send and recv methods are provided, with almost identical signatures: the only difference is that they return a request object that can be queried about the progress of the communication. The request class provides wait and test methods, which are equivalent to MPI_Wait and MPI_Test. Method wait returns a status object upon completion. Method test returns an optional<status> object, which means that the status is returned only if the operation is complete. For example:

```
string message;
. . .
mpi::request r = world.irecv(0, MESSTAG, message);
```

```
mpi::status s = r.wait();              // block until ←
    communication is done
cout << s.count<int>() << " items received\n";   // Type of items must ←
    be supplied
```

Boost.MPI also provides a set of `wait*` and `test*` template functions, for performing blocking and non-blocking reporting of communication progress respectively, of collections of `request` objects. These methods can operate on ranges of `request` arrays or vectors, as specified by two delimiting references/iterators. They allow checking of all or any of the supplied request objects for completion. Their syntax is:

```
// Waits until all communication are complete
template<typename ForwardIterator>
    void wait_all(ForwardIterator first, ForwardIterator last)

// Waits until any communication is complete. Returns a pair ←
    containing the status object corresponding to the completed ←
    operation and an iterator pointing to the completed request.
template<typename ForwardIterator>
    std::pair<status, ForwardIterator>
        wait_any(ForwardIterator first, ForwardIterator last)

// Tests if any of the supplied requests are complete. Returns an ←
    optional pair type identical to the one described for wait_any()
template<typename ForwardIterator>
    optional< std::pair<status, ForwardIterator> >
        test_any(ForwardIterator first, ForwardIterator last)
```

Listing 5.32 contains a variation of the "Hello World" program explained earlier, with the master using non blocking communication and the `test_any` function to check the completion of the operations. The `optional` template class that is used as a type for the return value of `test_any` allows the return of an object that evaluates to a `std::pair<status, ForwardIterator>` object or a NULL reference if nothing is returned.

In the example of Listing 5.32, if any of the communications described by the `r` vector completed (check of line 30), then the position of that request object in the `r` vector (calculated in line 32) is used to get which node was the target of the operation and print an assorted message (line 33). The vectors are trimmed in lines 34 and 35 so that the completed operation's request object is not returned again.

The receiver processes use `irecv` and the simple `wait` method of the request class to block until the operation is complete (lines 42, 43). The `status` object returned by the `wait` method is used in line 44 to print the number of received data items of type `string`.

```
1   // File : boostnonblock.cpp
2   #include <boost/mpi.hpp>
3   #include <boost/optional.hpp>
4   . . .
5   using namespace boost;
6   #define MESSTAG 0
```

```
7   int main (int argc, char **argv)
8   {
9     mpi::environment env (argc, argv);
10    mpi::communicator world;
11
12    int rank = world.rank ();
13    int N = world.size ();
14
15    if (rank == 0)
16      {
17        string mess ("Hello World");
18        vector < mpi::request > r; // a vector for the request objects
19        vector < int >dest;        // a vector for the destination IDs
20        for (int i = 1; i < N; i++)    // initiate the sending and store ←
              the request objects
21          {
22            r.push_back (world.isend (i, MESSTAG, mess));
23            dest.push_back (i);
24          }
25
26        // loop until all communications are done
27        while (r.size() >0)
28          {
29            optional < pair < mpi::status, vector < mpi::request >::←
                iterator > > res = mpi::test_any < vector < mpi::request←
                >::iterator > (r.begin (), r.end ());
30            if (res)  // if return value is initialized
31              {
32                int idx = (res->second) − r.begin ();
33                cout << "Message delivered to " << dest[idx] << endl;
34                r.erase (res->second);   // remove completed operations ←
                  from the vector
35                dest.erase (dest.begin () + idx);
36              }
37          }
38      }
39    else    // receiver code
40      {
41        string mess;
42        mpi::request r = world.irecv (0, MESSTAG, mess);
43        mpi::status s = r.wait ();          // block until communication ←
              is done
44        cout << rank << " received " << mess << " − " << s.count < ←
              string >() << " item(s) received\n";
45      }
46
47    return 0;
48  }
```

LISTING 5.32

A Boost.MPI-based "Hello World" program, which uses non blocking communications.

5.19.2 DATA SERIALIZATION

Boost.MPI brings something new to MPI communications when we consider the exchange of nonprimitive datatypes. MPI's approach is lengthy and cumbersome, but Boost.MPI uses C++ features to hide most of the details involved from the user.

As with the plain-vanilla MPI, Boost effectively offers two methods for communicating objects and/or data structures. One method is based on *serialization*, which is equivalent to using `MPI_Pack/MPI_Unpack`, and one is based on the separation of structure (*skeleton*) and content, which is equivalent to the definition of derived datatypes.

Serialization is appropriate for data that are communicated infrequently or for which the structure is dynamic in nature. To turn a class into a serializable one, we must define a `serialize` method that sends an object's data members, one by one, to a stream (`Archive` in Boost's jargon). For example:

```
class MyData
{
  private:
    int num;
    string s;
  public:
    template<class Archive>
      void serialize(Archive & ar, const unsigned int version);
};

template<class Archive>
  void MyData::serialize(Archive & ar, const unsigned int version)
{
    ar & num;
    ar & s;
}
```

The reverse process of deserialization calls the same method, since the & operator behaves differently based on the type of `Archive` object used: as operator `>>` for input streams and as operator `<<` for output streams.

The (de)serialization of an object is called automatically by Boost.MPI's point-to-point and collective operations. So, in order for an instance of the above class to be communicated between two processes, we would just need to write:

```
. . .
MyData item;
int r = world.rank();
if(r==0)
  {
    // initialization code for item
    ...
    world.send(1, 0, item);  // send to process 1, with tag 0
  }
else
    world.recv(0, 0, item);  // receive from process 0
```

The separation of structure and content is suitable for data structures that keep a fixed memory layout (e.g., a fixed size array) throughout the program's execution. It is essentially the same restriction that permits the creation of MPI's derived datatypes. However, Boost.MPI greatly simplifies this approach, requiring just the use of two functions:

- `mpi::skeleton()`: For capturing and communicating the structure, memory layout, or skeleton of an object.
- `mpi::get_content()`: For communicating the actual data that populate the skeleton.

The user must still supply a `serialize` function along the lines described previously. Serializing an instance of a class allows Boost.MPI to extract all the necessary information about the location and size of its data members, which is mirroring the procedure followed for the definition of a derived datatype (see Section 5.12.1).

The example in Listing 5.33 serves as a guideline for the use of these two functions, and it is in no way complete or optimized. It shows the outline of a master-worker configuration where the master distributes work items to the worker processes in a round-robin fashion. Section 5.22 offers a more complete coverage of this scenario.

```cpp
// File : boostSkeleton.cpp
. . .
struct WorkItem
{
public:
  int param1;
  double param2;
  string param3;

  template < class Arch > void serialize (Arch & r, int version)
  {
    r & param1;
    r & param2;
    r & param3;
  }
};

//============================================================
int main (int argc, char **argv)
{
  mpi::environment env (argc, argv);
  mpi::communicator world;

  WorkItem item;
  item.param3 = "work";
  int rank = world.rank ();
  int N = world.size ();
```

```
28      int numWork = atoi (argv[1]);
29
30      if (rank == 0)
31        {
32          for (int i = 1; i < N; i++)
33            world.send (i, TAGSKELETON, mpi::skeleton (item));
34
35          int destID = 1;
36          for (int i = 0; i < numWork; i++)
37            {
38              item.param1 = i;
39              world.send (destID, TAGWORKITEM, mpi::get_content (item));
40              destID = (destID == N - 1) ? 1 : destID + 1;
41            }
42
43          // signal end of execution
44          item.param3 = "done";
45          for (int i = 1; i < N; i++)
46            world.send (i, 1, mpi::get_content (item));
47        }
48      else
49        {
50          world.recv (0, TAGSKELETON, mpi::skeleton (item));
51          world.recv (0, TAGWORKITEM, mpi::get_content (item));  // read ↩
                first work item
52          while (item.param3 != "done")
53            {
54              // process work item
55              cout << "Worker " << rank << " got " << item.param1 << endl;
56
57              // read next one
58              world.recv (0, TAGWORKITEM, mpi::get_content (item));
59            }
60        }
61
62      return 0;
63    }
```

LISTING 5.33

A Boost.MPI-based outline of a master-worker setup that uses skeleton communications
to speed up data exchange.

Lines 3-17 in Listing 5.33 define a structure with a variety of fields to represent a
work item. The serialize template function (lines 10-15) saves/reads these fields
in sequence to/from a supplied data stream. The layout of an instance of the class
WorkItem is communicated from the master process (lines 32, 33) to all the worker
processes (line 50).

Once the layout is known, it is repeatedly used to accelerate the communication
of the work items the master process generates (line 38) and sends (line 39). The

number of work items is determined by the command-line parameter supplied by the user (line 28). The termination of the worker processes is triggered by having the master process send work items with `param3` set to `done` (lines 44-46).

A sample output of the previous program would look like this:

```
$ mpirun —np 3 ./boostSkeleton 4
Worker 2 got 1
Worker 1 got 0
Worker 1 got 2
Worker 2 got 3
```

5.19.3 COLLECTIVE OPERATIONS

Broadcasting, reduction, scattering, and gathering are all implemented in Boost.MPI in the form of template functions. Overloading allows the handling of different scenarios, e.g., gathering of scalars and arrays, with the same function names.

Table 5.6 lists a sample of them so that the reader can become familiar with the syntax. The naming gives away their correspondence to MPI functions. The semantics of each function are discussed thoroughly in Section 5.11, which introduces the collective operations. In any case, the Boost.MPI collective functions are just wrappers of the corresponding MPI ones.

All the functions shown in Table 5.6 have overloaded versions where the `vector<>` parameters are replaced by pointers to arrays (`T*`). The use of `vector<>` types for out-parameters is preferred, since a vector will automatically be resized if its capacity is insufficient.

The `Op` parameter for the `reduce` functions can be any binary function. A collection of commonly used functions is defined within the `boost/mpi/operations.hpp` header file. These include:

- `maximum`
- `minimum`
- `bitwise_and, bitwise_or, bitwise_xor`
- `logical_and, logical_or, logical_xor`

A user-supplied function can be also used in a reduction operation. Functions used with `reduce` must be associative, i.e., $f(x, f(y, z)) = f(f(x, y), z)$; otherwise the results will be inconsistent, e.g., they will depend on the ordering of the partial reductions.

An example of how a custom reduction operation can be implemented is provided in Listing 5.34. The starting point of the procedure is the subclassing of the `std::binary_function` template class. The `std::binary_function` class serves as a base class for *function objects*, i.e., for objects that provide an `operator()` method.

The specialization of the template class `std::binary_function` requires the specification of three types: the type of the first and second arguments and the type of the result of the `operator()` method.

Table 5.6 A selection of collective operations supported by Boost.MPI

Broadcast	`template<typename T> void`
	`  broadcast(const communicator& comm, T& value, int root);`
	`template<typename T> void`
	`  broadcast(const communicator& comm, T* values, int n, int root);`

Gather	`template<typename T> void`
	`  gather(const communicator& comm, const T& in_value,`
	`  std::vector<T>& out_values, int root);`
	`template<typename T> void`
	`  gather(const communicator& comm, const T* in_values, int n,`
	`  std::vector<T>& out_values, int root);`

Scatter	`template<typename T> void`
	`  scatter(const communicator& comm, const std::vector<T>&`
	`  in_values, T& out_value, int root);`
	`template<typename T> void`
	`  scatter(const communicator& comm, const std::vector<T>&`
	`  in_values, T* out_values, int n, int root);`

All-Gather	`template<typename T> void`
	`  all_gather(const communicator& comm, const T& in_value,`
	`  std::vector<T>& out_values);`
	`template<typename T> void`
	`  all_gather(const communicator& comm, const T* in_values, int n,`
	`  std::vector<T>& out_values);`

All-to-all	`template<typename T> void`
	`  all_to_all(const communicator& comm, const std::vector<T>&`
	`  in_values, std::vector<T>& out_values);`
	`template<typename T> void`
	`  all_to_all(const communicator& comm, const std::vector<T>&`
	`  in_values, int n, std::vector<T>& out_values);`

Reduce	`template<typename T, typename Op> void`
	`  reduce(const communicator& comm, const T& in_value, T& out_value,`
	`  Op op, int root);`
	`template<typename T, typename Op> void`
	`  reduce(const communicator& comm, const T* in_values, int n, T*`
	`  out_values, Op op, int root);`

All-Reduce	`template<typename T, typename Op> void`
	`  all_reduce(const communicator& comm, const T& in_value, T&`
	`  out_value, Op op);`
	`template<typename T, typename Op> void`
	`  all_reduce(const communicator& comm, const T* in_values, int n,`
	`  T* out_values, Op op);`

Parameters index:

  comm : communicator to apply the operation on
  in_value : a single T item to be sent
  in_values : an array or vector of items to be sent
  n : number of items to be collected from each process
  op : binary function to be applied during the reduction operation
  out_value : buffer for a single T item
  out_values : array or vector buffer for collected items of type T
  root : source/destination process of broadcast/gather operation

For example:

```
struct LabelEnumClass : public binary_function<string, int, string> {
  string operator () (string a, int b) {return (a==b);}
}
. . .
LabelEnumClass o;  // creating a function object
string base;
int ID;
. . .
string label = o(base, ID); // calling operator()
```

In the case of a reduction operator, all the types passed to the `binary_function` template should be identical. In Listing 5.34, the `CenterOfMass::operator()` method is used to calculate the center of mass of two objects, each described by a vector (x, y, z) and a mass. If each process in the application computes the center of mass of a subset of objects, then the reduction operation can yield the center of mass of the whole set. The mass M and center of mass $\vec{R}$ of a set of objects described by the tuples $(m_i, \vec{r}_i)$, where $\vec{r}_i$ are their locations, are calculated as follows:

$$M = \sum_{\forall i} m_i \tag{5.5}$$

and

$$\vec{R} = \frac{\sum_{\forall i} m_i \vec{r}_i}{M} \tag{5.6}$$

It can be easily shown that these functions and the operator based on them are both commutative and associative.

As the `CenterOfMass::operator()` will use exclusively `CenterOfMass` instances, the `binary_function` class is specialized using the `CenterOfMass` type (line 3). Equations 5.5 and 5.6 are implemented by the code of lines 27-40, whereas the `serialize` method of lines 18-25 allows Boost.MPI to communicate `CenterOfMass` instances.

The `main` function serves only to initialize one `CenterOfMass` instance per process with dummy data (line 56), and perform the reduction (line 59). The fourth parameter of the `reduce` function is an unnamed or anonymous `CenterOfMass` instance. A process will use its instance to execute the `operator()` method and perform a phase of the reduction.

```
1  // File : boostReduction.cpp
2    . . .
3  class CenterOfMass:public std::binary_function < CenterOfMass, ↩
         CenterOfMass, CenterOfMass >
4  {
5  public:
6    double x, y, z, mass;
7
8    CenterOfMass (double a, double b, double c, double m):x (a), y (b), ↩
           z (c), mass (m) {}
```

```
9
10      CenterOfMass () {}
11
12      template < class Archive > void serialize (Archive & ar, const ←
            unsigned int version);
13
14      const CenterOfMass & operator () (const CenterOfMass & o1, const ←
            CenterOfMass & o2) const;
15  };
16
17  //————————————————————————————————————————————
18  template < class Archive > void CenterOfMass::serialize (Archive & ar, ←
            const unsigned int version)
19  {
20    ar & x;
21    ar & y;
22    ar & z;
23    ar & mass;
24  }
25
26  //————————————————————————————————————————————
27  const CenterOfMass & CenterOfMass::operator () (const CenterOfMass & ←
            o1, const CenterOfMass & o2)
28        const
29        {
30          CenterOfMass *res = new CenterOfMass ();
31          res->x = o1.x * o1.mass + o2.x * o2.mass;
32          res->y = o1.y * o1.mass + o2.y * o2.mass;
33          res->z = o1.z * o1.mass + o2.z * o2.mass;
34          double M = o1.mass + o2.mass;
35          res->x /= M;
36          res->y /= M;
37          res->z /= M;
38          res->mass = M;
39          return *res;
40        }
41
42  //============================================================
43  ostream & operator << (ostream & out, const CenterOfMass & obj)
44  {
45    out << obj.mass << " at (" << obj.x << ", " << obj.y << ", " << obj.←
          z << ") " << endl;;
46  }
47
48  //============================================================
49  int main (int argc, char **argv)
50  {
51    mpi::environment env (argc, argv);
52    mpi::communicator world;
53
54    int rank = world.rank ();
55
```

```
56    CenterOfMass m1(1.0 * rank, 1.0 * rank, 1.0 * rank, 1.0 * rank + 1);
57    CenterOfMass m2;
58
59    reduce (world, m1, m2, CenterOfMass (), 0);
60    if (world.rank () == 0)
61      cout << m2 << endl;
62    return 0;
63  }
```

LISTING 5.34

A reduction example in Boost.MPI using a user-supplied reduction operation. The reduction operation produces the center of gravity of two masses.

5.20 A CASE STUDY: DIFFUSION-LIMITED AGGREGATION

Diffusion-limited aggregation (DLA) is a crystal formation process whereby particles performing Brownian motion (i.e., random motion in all directions) are "glued" together to form aggregates. The formations that result from this process are also known as *Brownian trees*.

DLA can be simulated in two dimensions by having a 2D grid of cells populated by moving particles and crystal parts. In the simulation code described below, for simplicity we assume that each cell can be occupied by one or more free-moving particles. A particle becomes part of the crystal (and stops moving) when it moves into a cell that is in proximity to the already formed crystal. A visualization of the formed crystal over multiple iterations is shown in Figure 5.23.

The simulation's basic parameters are the size of the 2D grid, the initial number of particles, the number of iterations, and the initial crystal "seed," i.e., the fixed part to which particles will start attaching as the simulation progresses. In the following code, the seed is a cell fixed in the center of the 2D grid, whereas the remaining parameters can be provided as command-line parameters. The following structure definition is used to hold the positions of moving particles:

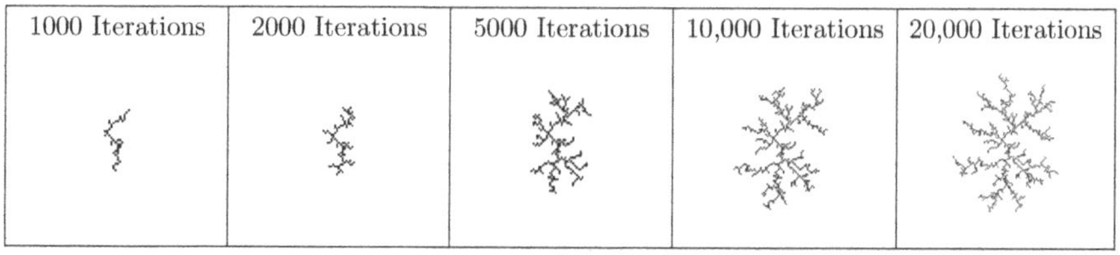

FIGURE 5.23

The output of a DLA simulation for a grid of 200x200 cells with an initial population of 1000 particles for different numbers of iterations.

```
1   typedef struct PartStr
2   {
3     int x;
4     int y;
5   } PartStr;
```

If the particles are maintained in an array of type PartStr, a single simulation step can be done with the following function, which is available as part of file dla_core.c:

```
1   /* Parameters:
2    *     pic : (in) pointer to a 2D array of type int
3    *     rows: (in) number of rows in array pic
4    *     cols: (in) number of columns in array pic
5    *     p   : (in/out) array holding particles
6    *     particles : (in/out) pointer to particle counter
7    *     changes   : (out) pointer to array holding pending changes
8    *                       to pic array
9    *     numChanges: (out) pointer to the counter of pending changes
10   */
11  void dla_evolve_plist (int *pic, int rows, int cols, PartStr *p, int *↵
         particles, PartStr *changes, int *numChanges)
12  {
13    int i;
14    *numChanges=0;
15
16    for (i = 0; i < *particles; i++)
17      {
18        int new_x = p[i].x + three_way ();
19        if (new_x == 0)  // bounce off boundaries
20          new_x = 1;
21        else if (new_x == cols − 1)
22          new_x = cols − 2;
23
24        int new_y = p[i].y + three_way ();
25        if (new_y == 0)  // bounce off boundaries
26          new_y = 1;
27        else if (new_y == rows − 1)
28          new_y = rows − 2;
29
30        if (pic[new_y * cols + new_x] == 0)   // steps into empty space
31          {
32            int turnCrystal = check_proxim (pic, cols, new_x, new_y);
33            if(turnCrystal <0)
34              {
35                // record crystal change
36                changes[*numChanges].x = new_x;
37                changes[*numChanges].y = new_y;
38                (*numChanges) ++;
39                // erase particle from list
40                p[i] = p[(*particles) − 1];
41                i−−;   // re−examine position i
```

```
42                 (*particles)--;
43               }
44             else  // change particle position
45               {
46                 p[i].x=new_x;
47                 p[i].y=new_y;
48               }
49           }
50       }
51   }
```

The function goes over all the available particles, updating their position (lines 18-28) and then checking their proximity to an aggregate formation as represented by the (rows x cols) 2D array pic. The position update is based on the three_way() function, which returns -1, 0, and 1 with equal probability:

```
inline int three_way ()
{
  return (random() % 3)-1;
}
```

The check_proxim() function returns -1 if the new position of a particle lies next to the crystal. By surrounding the grid with empty single-boundary rows and rows (keeping them empty is the task of lines 19-22 and 25-28 in the above code), check_proxim() can be simplified to:

```
// Checks the 3x3 cell neighborhood in 2D array pic,
// around coordinate (x,y)
int check_proxim (int *pic, int cols, int x, int y)
{
  int *row0, *row1, *row2;
  row0 = pic+(y - 1) * cols + x - 1;
  row1 = row0 + cols;
  row2 = row1 + cols;
  if (*row0 < 0 || *(row0+1) < 0 || *(row0+2) < 0 ||
      *row1 < 0 || *(row1+1) < 0 || *(row1+2) < 0 ||
      *row2 < 0 || *(row2+1) < 0 || *(row2+2) < 0   )
    return (-1);
  else
    return (1);
}
```

where *row0, *row1, and *row2 represent the leftmost cells of the three rows making up the neighborhood of a particle. Figure 5.24 serves to visualize these details.

The output of the dla_evolve_plist() function is stored in a pre-allocated array of type PartStr, which is passed via pointer changes (lines 36-42). The actual array part that is used is stored in the *numChanges counter; as a side effect, the array holding the particles and their number (*particles) is also updated.

A *sequential* program (provided as dla_sequential.c) can perform the simulation by running the following loop:

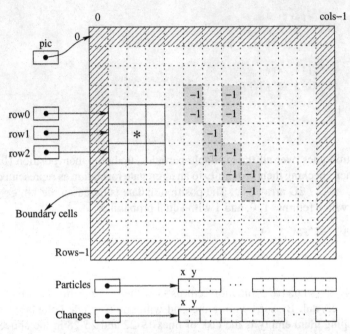

FIGURE 5.24

A visualization of the structures and variables used in functions `dla_evolve_plist()` and `check_proxim()`. A * represents a particle that is screened for proximity to the formed crystal (represented by the gray cells). Its proximity range is represented by the nine solid rectangles.

```
while (--iter)
{
  dla_evolve_plist (pic, rows, cols, p, &particles,
                    changes, &numChanges);
  apply_changes (pic, rows, cols, changes, numChanges);
}
```

where the `apply_changes()` function updates the state of the aggregate formation with the latest cells to become part of it:

```
void apply_changes(int *pic, int rows, int cols,
                   PartStr *changes, int numChanges)
{
  int i;
  for(i=0;i<numChanges;i++)
    pic[changes[i].y * cols + changes[i].x] = -1;
}
```

Parallelizing the sequential program comes down to figuring out how to partition the problem's data. These can be partitioned space-wise or particle-wise. In the former approach, each MPI process is responsible for a disjoint part of the 2D grid and whatever lies within it. The decomposition can be made in a regular and homogeneous way (i.e., all processes take an equal share of the rows[16] of the grid) if the participating nodes are homogeneous, but it is complicated by the need to exert special care on the particles "living" on boundary rows, e.g., right on the edge of the grid's division lines.

The alternative of splitting the particles produces a smaller challenge. In the case of a homogeneous platform, the particles can be evenly split among the available processes:

```
52    int rank, num;
53    MPI_Init (&argc, &argv);
54    MPI_Comm_rank (MPI_COMM_WORLD, &rank);
55    MPI_Comm_size (MPI_COMM_WORLD, &num);
56    ...
57    int particlesPerNode = particles / num;
58    if (rank == num - 1)      // assign remaining particles in
59                              // case they cannot be split evenly
60       particlesPerNode = particles - particlesPerNode * (num - 1);
```

Still, the processes have to maintain a copy of the state of the aggregate formation, implicitly mandating a barrier at the end of each iteration. During this synchronization phase, each process must communicate to all the others any changes it made to the aggregate. Using point-to-point communications in a N-process communicator would require each process to execute $2(N - 1)$ individual send and receive operations, for a grand total of $2N^2 - N$ operations per iteration!

A faster solution is to use collective communications. Because the changes need to propagate to all processes, a natural choice is the MPI_Allgather function, which can be completed in $\lceil log_2N \rceil$ steps. The only complication is that the number of changes is not the same in all processes, which prompts the use of the MPI_Allgatherv alternative. MPI_Allgatherv allows each process to contribute a different size part to the collection being assembled and communicated.

The last piece of the puzzle for making the communication of an array of PartStr structures possible, is the declaration of an MPI data type. This is accomplished with:

```
61    PartStr *p = (PartStr *) malloc (sizeof (PartStr) *
62                                particlesPerNode);
63    int lengths[2] = { 1, 1 };
64    MPI_Datatype types[2] = { MPI_INT, MPI_INT };
65    MPI_Aint add1, add2;
66    MPI_Aint displ[2];
67    MPI_Datatype Point;
68
69    MPI_Address (p, &add1);
70    MPI_Address (&(p[0].y), &add2);
71    displ[0] = 0;
72    displ[1] = add2 - add1;
```

---

[16] At first glance a column-wise partitioning seems equally plausible. Is it really? Does the way C/C++ allocates 2D arrays have any influence in this regard?

```
73
74    MPI_Type_struct (2, lengths, displ, types, &Point);
75    MPI_Type_commit (&Point);
```

The *universally* declared `Point` datatype can then be used inside our main loop:

```
76    while (--iter)
77      {
78        dla_evolve_plist (pic, rows, cols, p, &particlesPerNode,
79                          changes, &numChanges);
80
81        // exchange information with other nodes
82        MPI_Allgather (&numChanges, 1, MPI_INT, changesPerNode, 1,
83                       MPI_INT, MPI_COMM_WORLD);
84
85        // calculate offsets
86        numTotalChanges = 0;
87        for (i = 0; i < num; i++)
88          {
89            buffDispl[i] = numTotalChanges;
90            numTotalChanges += changesPerNode[i];
91          }
92
93        if(numTotalChanges >0)
94          {
95            MPI_Allgatherv (changes, numChanges, Point,
96                            totalChanges, changesPerNode, buffDispl,
97                            Point, MPI_COMM_WORLD);
98            apply_changes (pic, rows, cols, totalChanges, numTotalChanges);
99          }
100     }
```

Because the size of the data each process will contribute needs to be known ahead of time, a separate collective operation is required (line 82 above), where the number of changes per process is collected. Subsequently, the location where each set of changes will be deposited in array `totalChanges` can be calculated using the loop of lines 86-91 and stored in the integer array `buffDispl`. A side benefit of this additional communication step is that no changes need to be collected if the `numTotalChanges` counter is found to be zero (line 93).

5.21 A CASE STUDY: BRUTE-FORCE ENCRYPTION CRACKING
5.21.1 VERSION #1 : "PLAIN-VANILLA" MPI

Encryption (and how to crack it) has always been a fascinating subject among computer science scholars. Our study of the subject is admitedly rather superficial, and it is only performed as an example of how one can synchronize and load-balance MPI processes.

The Data Encryption Standard (DES) is a widely used encryption method that entails the use of a 56-bit secret key for encrypting and decrypting data. Although the length of the key allows for $2^{56} = 7.2 \cdot 10^{16}$ possible keys, DES is not considered safe enough for contemporary applications. In 1998, the Electronic Frontier Foundation (EFF) showed a custom-built machine called Deep Crack that was capable of going through all the DES keys in a matter of days. The idea was to show that the DES key length was not secure enough. Since then considerably cheaper and faster tools have been developed for the task. It is no wonder that the Advanced Encryption Standard (AES) has been gradually replacing DES since its ratification as a standard in 2001.

In this section we will see how a brute-force cracking of a DES-encrypted message can be performed using MPI.

DES is implemented in Unix/Linux by the `ecb_crypt()` function. The encryption/decryption process of a message requires the calculation of the key's parity, as in the function shown here:

```
1   // File : decrypt.cpp
2   #include <rpc/des_crypt.h>
3   ...
4   void decrypt(long key, char *ciph, int len)
5   {
6       // prepare key for the parity calculation. Least significant bit in↵
            all bytes should be empty
7       long k = 0;
8       for(int i=0;i<8;i++)
9       {
10          key <<= 1;
11          k += (key & (0xFE << i*8));
12      }
13
14      des_setparity((char *)&k);
15
16      // Decrypt ciphertext
17      ecb_crypt((char *)&k,(char *) ciph, 16, DES_DECRYPT);
18  }
```

The parameters of the `decrypt()` function are more or less self-explanatory. The `ciph` pointer points to the byte buffer containing the ciphertext of total length `len`. The length of the buffer should be a multiple of 8 bytes, although no check is performed to that effect.

Lines 7-12 prepare the key by shifting its contents to the left so that the low-order bit in every byte is left empty. These bits are filled up with the parity when the `des_setparity()` function is called in line 14. Figure 5.25 shows the outcome of these lines.

The decryption is performed in line 17. Encryption can be performed just by replacing the `DES_DECRYPT` constant with `DES_ENCRYPT`. The produced output overwrites the original input.

In order to decide whether the plaintext produced by trying out a key is the correct one, we will assume that part of the message is known, i.e., we will filter out keys that do not produce a plaintext that contains a given substring. In effect, we can utilize the

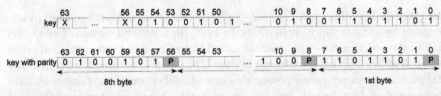

FIGURE 5.25

An example showing how the key must be preprocessed prior to DES encryption or decryption. *X* represents unused bits and *P* the parity bits calculated by the `des_setparity()` function.

`decrypt()` function to build a function that will return *true* when a key is a candidate for producing the correct plaintext:

```
19  char search[]=" the ";
20  //————————————————————————————————————————
21  // Returns true if the plaintext produced containes the "search" ↵
        string
22  bool tryKey(long key, char *ciph, int len)
23  {
24    char temp[len+1];
25    memcpy(temp, ciph, len);
26    temp[len]=0;
27    decrypt(key, temp, len);
28    return strstr((char *)temp, search)!=NULL;
29  }
30  ...
```

In line 25 the ciphertext is copied to a temporary buffer so that it can be decrypted (line 27). The produced string is null-terminated (line 26) so that it can be checked against the known substring (stored in the global array `search`) using the `strstr()` C-library string function. This function returns a pointer to the first occurrence of the substring or NULL if none is found.

In the worst-case scenario, one would have to try all the 2^{56} possible keys before finding the correct one. The problem is, how can we partition the key search space in a way that minimizes the overall execution time? There are two general possibilities, although many variations of each can be implemented:

- **Static partitioning**: The division of the workload is done *a priori*. We can have both equal and unequal partitioning based on the capabilities of the nodes that make up the execution platform.
- **Dynamic partitioning**: The division and assignment of the workload is done at run-time, permitting load balancing to be performed, albeit at the cost of a more complicated solution.

Dynamic partitioning is examined in far greater detail in Section 5.22. In this section we deal only with static partitioning.

The only lingering question that needs to be answered is what should happen once a candidate solution has been found. One could either continue until all the keys are exhausted or terminate the program. The early termination is a more challenging problem to tackle, and for this reason it is the approach chosen in the solutions discussed here.

An easy solution to the partitioning problem would be to have each MPI process calculate which part of the key search space it will be responsible for, as shown in Listing 5.35.

```cpp
31  // File : decrypt.cpp
32  ...
33  unsigned char cipher[]={108, 245, 65, 63, 125, 200, 150, 66, 17, 170, ↩
        207, 170, 34, 31, 70, 215, 0};
34
35  //————————————————————————————————————————
36  int main(int argc, char **argv)
37  {
38    int N, id;
39    long upper=(1L << 56); // upper bound for keys
40    long mylower, myupper;
41    MPI_Status st;
42    MPI_Request req;
43    int flag;
44    int ciphLen = strlen(cipher);
45
46     MPI_Init(&argc, &argv);
47
48     MPI_Comm_rank(MPI_COMM_WORLD, &id);
49     MPI_Comm_size(MPI_COMM_WORLD, &N);
50     int range_per_node = upper / N;
51
52     mylower = range_per_node * id;
53     myupper = range_per_node * (id + 1) - 1;
54     if(id == N-1)
55       myupper = upper;
56
57     long found = 0;
58     MPI_Irecv(&found, 1, MPI_LONG, MPI_ANY_SOURCE, MPI_ANY_TAG, ↩
          MPI_COMM_WORLD, &req);
59     for(int i=mylower; i<myupper && found==0;i++)
60     {
61       if(tryKey(i, (char *)cipher, ciphLen))
62       {
63         found=i;
64         for(int node=0; node<N; node++)
65           MPI_Send(&found, 1, MPI_LONG, node, 0, MPI_COMM_WORLD);
66         break;
67       }
68     }
69
70     if(id==0)
```

```
71    {
72       MPI_Wait (&req, &st);
73       decrypt(found, (char *)cipher,ciphLen);
74       printf("%li %s\n", found, cipher);
75    }
76
77    MPI_Finalize();
78  }
```

LISTING 5.35

A static key search-space partitioning solution for DES cracking.

The range of keys that each MPI process should test is calculated in lines 52-55. The if statement of lines 54-55 eliminates the possibility of missing keys at the end of the $[0, 2^{56})$ range, due to round-off errors.

Each process sets up an immediate receive operation in line 58 that targets the found flag. The found flag can be set by either discovering a key in line 61 or by receiving the "news" of the discovery by the process that accomplished this feat, via the loop of lines 64, 65. The solution is printed out by process 0 in lines 70-75. The MPI_Wait() call in line 72 ensures that the communication of the found key is complete before any attempt to use the corresponding variable is made.

The main problem with the solution of Listing 5.21.1 is that the speedup that can be achieved depends on the actual key used for the encryption. The following list of scenarios depicts the chaotic, seemingly unpredictable behavior that is to be expected:

- **Scenario 1**: For $key = 2^{20}$, a two-node MPI program will have an expected speedup of 1. The same would be true for any key in the range $[0, \frac{2^{56}}{N})$. If the program executed on N *homogeneous* nodes, this would hold for any key in the range $[0, \frac{2^{56}}{N})$.
- **Scenario 2**: For $key = 2^{55}$, a two-node MPI program will have an expected speedup $= \frac{2^{55}+1}{1} = 2^{55} + 1$! The second MPI process terminates after just one attempt, whereas the sequential program would have to perform a total of $2^{55} + 1$ attempts before reaching the same solution. Generalizing for N nodes (assuming N divides 2^{56} evenly), for $key = \frac{N-1}{N}2^{56}$ the expected speedup would be $\frac{\frac{N-1}{N}2^{56}+1}{1} = \frac{N-1}{N}2^{56} + 1$. This is clearly a *super-linear speedup*.
- **Scenario 3**: A two-node MPI program will have an expected speedup of 2 only for $key = 2^{56} - 1$. The same key is the only one that would yield a 100% efficiency for N homogeneous nodes (assuming N divides 2^{56} evenly).

An easy fix to this problem that also allows for a shorter and simpler program to be implemented, is to have each MPI process "stagger" through the range of keys as shown in Listing 5.36.

```
79  // File : decrypt2.cpp
80  ...
81  //————————————————————————————————————————
```

```
82   int main (int argc, char **argv)
83   {
84     int N, id;
85     long upper=(1L << 56);
86     long found = 0;
87     MPI_Status st;
88     MPI_Request req;
89     int flag;
90     int ciphLen = strlen((char *)cipher);
91
92     MPI_Init (&argc, &argv);
93     MPI_Comm_rank (MPI_COMM_WORLD, &id);
94     MPI_Comm_size (MPI_COMM_WORLD, &N);
95     MPI_Irecv ((void *)&found, 1, MPI_LONG, MPI_ANY_SOURCE, MPI_ANY_TAG, ↵
                 MPI_COMM_WORLD, &req);
96     int iterCount=0;
97     for (long i = id; i < upper; i += N)
98       {
99         if (tryKey (i, (char *) cipher, ciphLen))
100          {
101            found = i;
102            for (int node = 0; node < N; node++)
103              MPI_Send ((void *)&found, 1, MPI_LONG, node, 0, ↵
                    MPI_COMM_WORLD);
104            break;
105          }
106        if(++iterCount % 1000 == 0) // check the status of the pending ↵
               receive
107          {
108            MPI_Test(&req, &flag, &st);
109            if(flag) break;
110          }
111      }
112
113    if (id == 0)
114      {
115        MPI_Wait (&req, &st); // in case process 0 finishes before the ↵
               key is found
116        decrypt (found, (char *) cipher, ciphLen);
117        printf ("%li %s\n", found, cipher);
118      }
119    MPI_Finalize ();
120  }
```

LISTING 5.36

An alternative static key search-space partitioning solution for DES cracking.

The major differences with Listing 5.21.1 are two: the for-loop of line 97 and the regular check for the completion of the immediate receive operation in lines 106-110. The loop structure is very simple in its inception: Every process starts from a key equal to its rank and goes through the key range with a step equal to the total number of processes. This ensures that the whole range is covered in a wave-like fashion that makes the run-time behavior better match our performance expectations.

The regular test of lines 106-110 ensures that the communication completion will be acknowledged, even if a stale value of found is kept in the CPU's cache memory. The frequency of the test is a completely ad hoc choice, driven by the desire to not burden the overall execution with too frequent tests while at the same time permitting a timely termination of the program. Note that line 97 no longer contains a check on the value of found, since the mere completion of the communication is adequate for the loop's termination.

Testing of the program of Listing 5.36 with a message encrypted with the key 107481429 produced the results in Table 5.7 on a third-generation i7 CPU clocked at 4.2 GHz, with hyperthreading enabled. It is clear that the intended purpose of predictability as far as performance improvement is concerned is accomplished.

The Achilles' heel of our static partitioning solutions is that they fail to properly exploit heterogeneous execution platforms. Dynamic partitioning (examined in the next section) is the obvious answer to this problem, although as it is shown in Chapter 8, a more elaborate static partitioning technique would also fit the bill.

5.21.2 VERSION #2 : COMBINING MPI AND OPENMP

In the previous section we presented performance measurements on a single multicore machine. MPI is perfectly capable of utilizing the computational resources of such platforms, but to purists it may seem inappropriate. The reason is that MPI spawns processes, an action that is orders of magnitude slower than spawning threads. So, in principle, the following deployment scenario promises the best resource utilization: first start a single process for each *physical* node in the system, and then spawn as many threads as is necessary, to fully exploit the multiple cores in that system.

In that setting, we can have MPI implement the first phase and OpenMP take care of the second one. OpenMP is poised as a very good choice in that regard, especially

Table 5.7 Average encryption cracking time for the program of Listing 5.36 on a third-generation i7 CPU clocked at 4.2 GHz. The message was encrypted with the key 107481429. Reported numbers are averaged over 100 runs

Nodes	Exec. Time (sec)	Speedup	Efficiency
1	37.33	-	-
2	18.83	1.982	0.991
3	12.62	2.958	0.986
4	10.13	3.684	0.921

given that as we have shown in Chapter 4, the development effort associated with OpenMP parallel constructs is minimal. However, when combined with MPI this advantage is lost. OpenMP requires an additional effort over the already substantial one necessary for dividing the workload amongst distributed memory nodes. One would have to develop the MPI program first, and then insert the OpenMP pragmas that would automatically generate threads.

In general, a "hybrid" computation that combines MPI and OpenMP can be accomplished in a variety of ways. The most appropriate classification distinguishes two design approaches[38]:

- **Master-only** : only one MPI process per machine is launched. The communications are performed only by the master thread, either inside a master construct, or outside a parallel region. This design approach can hinder the utilization of cores, as while MPI is being *called*, there can be only one application thread active.
- **Overlapping communication/computation** : multiple OpenMP threads may make MPI calls. MPI must be specifically compiled to handle this functionality (see also Section 5.16). It is also possible that we can have multiple MPI processes per machine, each using its own team of threads [17].

The naming of the second design approach is a bit misleading though, as making an MPI call and returning from it, is not the same as starting and completing the actual communication. MPI provides immediate and locally blocking calls, that carry out the communication in the background. So, there can be an overlap between the computation and the communication, even if a "master-only" design is employed.

In the following code, we convert the program of Listing 5.36 into an MPI-OpenMP hybrid, using the "master-only" design. The changes are limited to the loop that processes the part of the key search-space assigned to a node:

```cpp
// File : decrypt2_omp.cpp
#include <omp.h>
...
const int BLOCK = 1000000;
//————————————————————————————————————————————
int main (int argc, char **argv)
{
  int N, id;
  long upper = (1L << 56);
  long found = -1;
  MPI_Status st;
  MPI_Request req;
  int flag = 0;
  int ciphLen = strlen ((char *) cipher);

  MPI_Init (&argc, &argv);
  double start = MPI_Wtime ();
  MPI_Comm_rank (MPI_COMM_WORLD, &id);
  MPI_Comm_size (MPI_COMM_WORLD, &N);
```

```
20      MPI_Irecv ((void *) &found, 1, MPI_LONG, MPI_ANY_SOURCE, MPI_ANY_TAG↵
          , MPI_COMM_WORLD, &req);
21      int iterCount = 0;
22
23      long idx = 0;
24      while (idx < upper && found < 0)
25      {
26  #pragma omp parallel for default(none) shared(cipher, ciphLen, found, ↵
          idx, id, N)
27        for (long i = idx + id; i < idx + N * BLOCK; i += N)
28        {
29            if (tryKey (i, (char *) cipher, ciphLen))
30            {
31  #pragma omp critical
32                found = i;
33            }
34        }
35
36        // communicate termination signal
37        if (found >= 0)
38          {
39            for (int node = 0; node < N; node++)
40              MPI_Send ((void *) &found, 1, MPI_LONG, node, 0, ↵
                  MPI_COMM_WORLD);
41          }
42
43        idx += N * BLOCK;
44      }
45
46      // print out the result from node 0
47      if (id == 0)
48      {
49        MPI_Wait (&req, &st);      // in case process 0 finishes before ↵
            the key is found
50        decrypt (found, (char *) cipher, ciphLen);
51        printf ("%i nodes in %lf sec : %li %s\n", N, MPI_Wtime () - ↵
            start, found, cipher);
52      }
53    MPI_Finalize ();
54  }
```

LISTING 5.37

OpenMP-based variation of the static, key search-space partitioning solution for DES cracking, of Listing 5.36. Changes are limited to the main() function.

There is a key difference between Listing 5.37 and 5.36, in that there is a split of the for-loop in Listing 5.36 into a pair of nested loops (lines 23, 26) in the above code. The reason for the split is the need to be able to detect the discovery of the secret key by another node (an early termination condition).

A parallel for loop must have a single point of entry and a single point of exit, which means that it is not possible to break out of the loop when the found variable is set, using a conditional statement. Additionally, we cannot add the check of the found variable in the `for` termination condition, as e.g.:

```
#pragma omp parallel for default(none) shared(cipher, ciphLen, ...
      for (long i = idx + id; i < idx + N*BLOCK && found < 0; i += N)
```

as this violates the canonical form dictated by OpenMP (see Section 4.4).

As it is impossible to cater for the detection of the key discovery in a `parallel for` loop, we are forced to break the loop into smaller fragments. Between the multi-threaded execution of these smaller loops, we can check the `found` flag (line 24) and/or propagate the discovery to other nodes using `MPI_Send` (lines 37-41). The granularity of the split is controlled by the `BLOCK` constant of line 4.

This program can be compiled and run (on a single node in our example) by the following lines:

```
$ mpic++ -fopenmp decrypt2_omp.cpp -o decrypt2_omp
$ mpirun -np 1 ./decrypt2_omp
```

Enabling OpenMP support is just a matter of including the `-fopenmp` switch for the GNU C/C++ compiler, as `mpicc/mpic++` are just compiler front-ends. In comparison, utilizing all the cores in a quad-core hyperthreaded CPU, using just MPI, would require the command:

```
$ mpirun -np 8 ./decrypt2
```

The selection of the `BLOCK` parameter is critical, and should not be glossed over, as it influences how frequently we check the termination condition (`BLOCK` should be made smaller for this), and how often we launch a team of threads to run the inner loop (`BLOCK` should be made bigger for this). For example, a setting of `BLOCK=1000` results in a running time of $\sim$ 23sec on a i7-4700HQ, 2.40GHz quad core CPU, with hyperthreading enabled, while a setting of `BLOCK=1,000,000` results in a running time of $\sim$ 10sec.

It is therefore obvious, that the need to start-stop the OpenMP threads in order to check the termination condition, acts against the efficiency of the program. Through experimentation we settled for `BLOCK=`10^7, but we still could not beat the running time of the plain-vanilla MPI program over the same platform. Averaged over 10 runs, we were able to get 9.24 ± 0.30sec for the MPI version and 9.72 ± 0.10sec for the MPI-OpenMP combination. The larger standard deviation of the MPI program is probably due to the inconsistent start-up times of the MPI processes.

We could solve the problem stemming from the split for-loop, by using `task` constructs instead of a `parallel for`. It is however highly unlikely that any significant performance gains over the plain-vanilla MPI could be materialized. What is certain though, is that the complexity of the code will increase.

As closing remarks, we can summarize the benefits and drawbacks of combining OpenMP and MPI as follows:

- Lowers the memory footprint, as OpenMP threads reuse the code and the global data of a single process.

- Simplifies program deployment as we do not need to know the number of cores in each machine. All we need is the machine's IP or DNS name.
- There is no need for intra-node communications. OpenMP code can use shared variables.
- Intra-node load balancing is easy to achieve, by using a "dynamic" of "guided" setting for the `schedule` clause of `parallel for` constructs.
- OpenMP threads do not have distinct ranks/IDs within an MPI communicator. As such, it is cumbersome to establish communication between specific threads running on different physical machines[17].
- Performance gains are dubious (more on this below). We can expect start-up costs to improve, but computationally-heavy applications do not really suffer from start-up times.
- Development effort is increased.

In terms of performance benefits, this is an issue that is application and machine architecture dependent. There have been many studies on the subject of MPI-OpenMP hybrid software, and the results are generally mixed. For example, in [17], the authors report that pure MPI is superior for small number of nodes, while the MPI-OpenMP combination delivers better performance for larger collections of machines.

5.22 A CASE STUDY: MPI IMPLEMENTATION OF THE MASTER-WORKER PATTERN

The master-worker pattern (see also Section 2.4.3) is a popular choice for laying out the structure of an MPI program. In general, there are two choices for the partitioning of the workload:

- **Static partitioning**: The master node calculates, *a priori*, the workload that will be assigned to each of the worker processes and possibly to itself. In order for the distribution to be balanced, relatively accurate cost models of the involved computation and communication must be employed to predict the total execution time of all the nodes. This also entails detailed knowledge about the performance characteristics of the execution platform. A balanced distribution is not necessarily one that assigns the same workload in terms of execution time to all the nodes, since communication overheads can be substantial. The ultimate purpose is to minimize the overall execution time of the program and as such a balanced distribution is typically skewed, varying the workload according to the characteristics of the execution platform and the communication overheads.

---

[17]It is cumbersome but not impossible, as message tags can be used to filter messages sent between nodes.

A static partitioning has the potential to minimize the communication costs, since master-worker communication is limited to the beginning and end of the computation.

- **Dynamic partitioning**: This means that the master node distributes workload in discrete pieces to the workers on a round-robin, or a first-come, first-served, or some other application-specific order until the work is complete. This approach is simpler than the static partitioning approach since there is no need for the derivation of cost models and an *a priori* partitioning of the load. This is a heuristic that can provide implicit workload balancing with, however, some performance penalty due to increased communication traffic between the master and worker nodes.

The Achilles, heel for static partitioning is the need to derive accurate cost models; for dynamic partitioning it is the choice of the *work item size*, i.e., how much workload will be assigned as a unit to a process. A too-small work item can produce extraordinary amounts of communication traffic, whereas a too-big work item can leave nodes idle or underutilized. Getting it right is the major challenge in the deployment of dynamic partitioning.

The workloads can be described in a variety of ways, from the most *specific*, e.g., providing parameters for the execution of a known function, to the most *generic*, e.g., providing instances of classes with any kind of computation portfolio. In the following sections we explore sample implementations of the master-worker pattern that use dynamic partitioning.

5.22.1 **A SIMPLE MASTER-WORKER SETUP**

In this section we show how a simple, dynamic partitioning, round-robin distribution, master-worker setup can be implemented in MPI. The target application is the calculation of the Mandelbrot fractal set, which is a problem that was previously examined in Section 3.8.2.

The work item for workload distribution is a rectangular portion of the desired fractal image. The sides of the work item are provided by the user in the command line that launches the program, allowing us to test the performance of the program as a parameter of the work item size.

The master and worker processes operate using a simple protocol:

1. The worker sends to the master the result of a computation. In the beginning, a special null result is used to commence the transaction by using an appropriate message tag.
2. The master responds by sending a work item to the worker. If there are no more work items available, a special null work item is sent by using an appropriate message tag.

An overview of the system architecture and the communication traffic involved is shown in Figure 5.26.

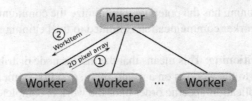

FIGURE 5.26

An overview of the software architecture and communication protocol used in Listing 5.38. Circled numbers indicate message order. The seemingly reverse order is essential for a proper hand-shake between the master and the workers.

A large portion of the code is carried over from Listing 3.29 with the necessary adaptations, because in a distributed memory setup there cannot be a shared QImage object, nor can object references be exchanged between the nodes. In order to preserve the cross-platform compatibility MPI offers, the essential information that defines a work item is encapsulated in a structure (struct WorkItem) and communicated using a derived datatype. If the execution platform was homogeneous, object serialization could be employed for communicating work items. However, it is quite doubtful that any performance gains could be had from such an approach, which essentially equates to using MPI_Pack/MPI_Unpack. Additionally, the code itself would not also gain anything in terms of length or complexity.

The code is shown over several parts in Listing 5.38. The program uses MPI and a couple of Qt classes for image manipulation. For this reason, the compilation process is accomplished with the techniques discussed in Section 5.16. The first part of the program is devoted to the definition of a set of symbolic constants to be used as communication tags (lines 10-13). Lines 17-21 define the structure that encapsulates the data that define a work item. These include the boundaries of the complex plane where calculation is to take place as well as the size of the image to be calculated (pixelsX x pixelsY) and its location in the "bigger" picture (imageX, imageY).

Lines 25-104, which are carried mostly unchanged from Listing 3.29, contain a class for calculating the pixel values that correspond to a work item. The only changes relate to the need to initialize the class from a work item structure (hence the change from a constructor to a method-based initialization in line 72) and perform some basic memory management.

```
1   // File : mandlebrot / mandlebrot .cpp
2   . . .
3   #include "mpi.h"
4   #include <QImage>
5   #include <QRgb>
6   using namespace std;
7
8   // *************************************************************
9   // Communication tags
10  #define NULLRESULTTAG 0
11  #define RESULTTAG       1
```

```
12  #define WORKITEMTAG     2
13  #define ENDTAG          3
14
15  // ************************************************************
16
17  typedef struct WorkItem
18  {
19    double upperX, upperY, lowerX, lowerY;
20    int pixelsX, pixelsY, imageX, imageY;
21  } WorkItem;
22
23  // ************************************************************
24  // Class for computing a fractal set part
25  class MandelCompute
26  {
27  private:
28    double upperX, upperY, lowerX, lowerY;
29    int pixelsX, pixelsY;
30    int *img;
31
32    static int MAXITER;
33    int diverge (double cx, double cy);
34
35  public:
36      MandelCompute ();
37    void init (WorkItem * wi);
38     ~MandelCompute ();
39    int *compute ();
40  };
41  int MandelCompute::MAXITER = 255;
42
43  //————————————————————————————
44  int MandelCompute::diverge (double cx, double cy)
45  {
46    int iter = 0;
47    double vx = cx, vy = cy, tx, ty;
48    while (iter < MAXITER && (vx * vx + vy * vy) < 4)
49      {
50        tx = vx * vx — vy * vy + cx;
51        ty = 2 * vx * vy + cy;
52        vx = tx;
53        vy = ty;
54        iter++;
55      }
56    return iter;
57  }
58  //————————————————————————————
59  MandelCompute::~MandelCompute ()
60  {
61    if (img != NULL)
62      delete[]img;
63  }
```

```
64
65   //————————————————————————————
66   MandelCompute :: MandelCompute ()
67   {
68     img = NULL;
69   }
70
71   //————————————————————————————
72   void MandelCompute :: init (WorkItem * wi)
73   {
74     upperX = wi->upperX;
75     upperY = wi->upperY;
76     lowerX = wi->lowerX;
77     lowerY = wi->lowerY;
78
79     if (img == NULL || pixelsX != wi->pixelsX || pixelsY != wi->pixelsY)
80       {
81         if (img != NULL)
82           delete [] img;
83         img = new int [(wi->pixelsX) * (wi->pixelsY)];
84       }
85     pixelsX = wi->pixelsX;
86     pixelsY = wi->pixelsY;
87   }
88
89   //————————————————————————————
90   int *MandelCompute :: compute ()
91   {
92     double stepx = (lowerX - upperX) / pixelsX;
93     double stepy = (upperY - lowerY) / pixelsY;
94
95     for (int i = 0; i < pixelsX; i++)
96       for (int j = 0; j < pixelsY; j++)
97         {
98           double tempx, tempy;
99           tempx = upperX + i * stepx;
100          tempy = upperY - j * stepy;
101          img[j * pixelsX + i] = diverge (tempx, tempy);
102        }
103    return img;
104  }
```

LISTING 5.38

A master-worker implementation of a Mandelbrot fractal set calculator.

To be able to communicate a `WorkItem` structure, a derived datatype is created and committed in lines 106-127. It should be noted that only part of the structure needs to be communicated, since a worker is not concerned with putting the image together. Since `imageX` and `imageY` do not need to be communicated, the size of the `int` block in line 115 is limited to 2.

This "stitching" of the individual images resulting from the processing of the work items is reserved for the master node. This task is done by the savePixels function in lines 131-140.

```
105   // *************************************************************
106   void registerWorkItem (MPI_Datatype * workItemType)
107   {
108     struct WorkItem sample;
109
110     int blklen[2];
111     MPI_Aint displ[2], off, base;
112     MPI_Datatype types[2];
113
114     blklen[0] = 4; // treating the 4 individual doubles as an array of 4
115     blklen[1] = 2; // the part's location in the final image is not ↩
            communicated
116
117     types[0] = MPI_DOUBLE;
118     types[1] = MPI_INT;
119
120     displ[0] = 0;
121     MPI_Get_address (&(sample.upperX), &base);
122     MPI_Get_address (&(sample.pixelsX), &off);
123     displ[1] = off − base;
124
125     MPI_Type_create_struct (2, blklen, displ, types, workItemType);
126     MPI_Type_commit (workItemType);
127   }
128
129   // *************************************************************
130   // Uses the divergence iterations to pseudocolor the fractal set
131   void savePixels (QImage * img, int *imgPart, int imageX, int imageY, ↩
          int height, int width)
132   {
133     for (int i = 0; i < width; i++)
134       for (int j = 0; j < height; j++)
135         {
136           int color = imgPart[j * width + i];
137           img−>setPixel (imageX + i, imageY + j, qRgb (256 − color, 256 ↩
              − color, 256 − color));
138         }
139   }
140
141   // *************************************************************
142   int main (int argc, char *argv[])
143   {
144     int N, rank;
145     double start_time, end_time;
146     MPI_Status status;
147     MPI_Request request;
148
```

```
149    start_time = MPI_Wtime ();
150
151    MPI_Init (&argc, &argv);
152    MPI_Comm_size (MPI_COMM_WORLD, &N);
153    MPI_Comm_rank (MPI_COMM_WORLD, &rank);
154
155    MPI_Datatype workItemType;
156    registerWorkItem (&workItemType);
```

The master node is responsible for retrieving the user-supplied parameters from the command line and customizing the resulting image size so that it is made up of an integer number of work items (lines 179-182). The structures representing work items are allocated and initialized before any communications take place in lines 189-204. The benefits of doing this are twofold:

- MPI_Isend can be used to communicate work items without worrying about the overhead of buffer copies or the overwriting of message memory before it is sent out.
- An association can be established and maintained between assigned work items and worker processes. This allows the master node to place incoming results in the appropriate place of the target image without requiring that placement information (i.e., imageX and imageY) is communicated back-and-forth between the master and the worker.

```
157    if (rank == 0)    // master code
158      {
159        if (argc < 6)
160          {
161            cerr << argv[0] << " upperCornerX upperCornerY lowerCornerX ↵
                   lowerCornerY workItemPixelsPerSide \n";
162            MPI_Abort (MPI_COMM_WORLD, 1);
163          }
164
165        double upperCornerX, upperCornerY;
166        double lowerCornerX, lowerCornerY;
167        double partXSpan, partYSpan;
168        int workItemPixelsPerSide;
169        int Xparts, Yparts;
170        int imgX = 1024, imgY = 768;
171
172        upperCornerX = atof (argv[1]);
173        upperCornerY = atof (argv[2]);
174        lowerCornerX = atof (argv[3]);
175        lowerCornerY = atof (argv[4]);
176        workItemPixelsPerSide = atoi (argv[5]);
177
178        // make sure that the image size is evenly divided in work items
179        Xparts = (int) ceil (imgX * 1.0 / workItemPixelsPerSide);
180        Yparts = (int) ceil (imgY * 1.0 / workItemPixelsPerSide);
181        imgX = Xparts * workItemPixelsPerSide;
```

```
182        imgY = Yparts * workItemPixelsPerSide;
183
184        partXSpan = (lowerCornerX − upperCornerX) / Xparts;
185        partYSpan = (upperCornerY − lowerCornerY) / Yparts;
186        QImage *img = new QImage (imgX, imgY, QImage::Format_RGB32);
187
188        // prepare the work items in individual structures
189        WorkItem *w = new WorkItem[Xparts * Yparts];
190        for (int i = 0; i < Xparts; i++)
191          for (int j = 0; j < Yparts; j++)
192            {
193              int idx = j * Xparts + i;
194
195              w[idx].upperX = upperCornerX + i * partXSpan;
196              w[idx].upperY = upperCornerY − j * partYSpan;
197              w[idx].lowerX = upperCornerX + (i + 1) * partXSpan;
198              w[idx].lowerY = upperCornerY − (j + 1) * partYSpan;
199
200              w[idx].imageX = i * workItemPixelsPerSide;
201              w[idx].imageY = j * workItemPixelsPerSide;
202              w[idx].pixelsX = workItemPixelsPerSide;
203              w[idx].pixelsY = workItemPixelsPerSide;
204            }
```

The `assignedPart` array has one element per process, and it is used for holding the index of the work item that has been assigned to a process. Once the master receives a result message from a worker, it sends the next available work item to that worker, and then saves the pixel values in the `QImage` object used for this purpose (lines 216-219). The worker's ID is retrieved from the `MPI_Status` structure set by the `MPI_Recv` function (line 211).

The placement of the returned image portion (`*imgPart`) is controlled by the `imageX` and `imageY` fields of the work item assigned to that worker (line 213).

Once all the work items have been distributed, the master waits for the last results and sends back to each worker a message with a tag that flags the termination of the program (lines 223-237).

```
205        // now distribute the work item to the worker nodes
206        int *assignedPart = new int[N];   // keep track of what its ↵
                 worker is assigned
207        int *imgPart = new int[workItemPixelsPerSide * ↵
                 workItemPixelsPerSide];
208        for (int i = 0; i < Xparts * Yparts; i++)
209          {
210            MPI_Recv (imgPart, workItemPixelsPerSide * ↵
                   workItemPixelsPerSide, MPI_INT, MPI_ANY_SOURCE, ↵
                   MPI_ANY_TAG, MPI_COMM_WORLD, &status);
211            int workerID = status.MPI_SOURCE;
212            int tag = status.MPI_TAG;
213            int widx = assignedPart[workerID];
214            assignedPart[workerID] = i;
```

```
215         MPI_Isend (&(w[i]), 1, workItemType, workerID, WORKITEMTAG, ←
                MPI_COMM_WORLD, &request);
216         if (tag == RESULTTAG)
217           {
218             savePixels (img, imgPart, w[widx].imageX, w[widx].imageY ←
                  , workItemPixelsPerSide, workItemPixelsPerSide);
219           }
220         }

221
222       // now send termination messages
223       for (int i = 1; i < N; i++)
224         {
225           MPI_Recv (imgPart, workItemPixelsPerSide * ←
                workItemPixelsPerSide, MPI_INT, MPI_ANY_SOURCE, ←
                MPI_ANY_TAG, MPI_COMM_WORLD, &status);

226
227           int workerID = status.MPI_SOURCE;
228           int tag = status.MPI_TAG;

229
230           if (tag == RESULTTAG)
231             {
232               int widx = assignedPart[workerID];
233               savePixels (img, imgPart, w[widx].imageX, w[widx].imageY ←
                    , workItemPixelsPerSide, workItemPixelsPerSide);
234             }
235           assignedPart[workerID] = -1;
236           MPI_Isend (NULL, 0, workItemType, workerID, ENDTAG, ←
                MPI_COMM_WORLD, &request);
237         }

238
239       img->save ("mandel.png", "PNG", 0); // save the resulting image

240
241       delete []w;
242       delete []assignedPart;
243       delete []imgPart;

244
245       end_time = MPI_Wtime ();
246       cout << "Total time : " << end_time - start_time << endl;
247     }
```

The worker nodes first establish communication with the master in line 251. This can be considered an implicit availability message: "We are here waiting for your commands!" This is preferable to having the master simply assign work items in order of rank, for the simple reason that during program initialization not all MPI processes start at the same time instance, since they are affected by network traffic and system loads. By having the "faster-starting" workers receive work earlier, performance can be boosted.

```
248   else        // worker code
249     {
250       MandelCompute c;
```

```
251        MPI_Send (NULL, 0, MPI_INT, 0, NULLRESULTTAG, MPI_COMM_WORLD); ←
                    // establish communication with master
252        while (1)
253          {
254            WorkItem w;
255            MPI_Recv (&w, 1, workItemType, 0, MPI_ANY_TAG, ←
                      MPI_COMM_WORLD, &status); // get a new work item
256            int tag = status.MPI_TAG;
257            if (tag == ENDTAG)    // check for termination
258              break ;
259
260            c.init (&w);   // initialize MandelCompute object from ←
                      WorkItem
261            int *res = c.compute ();
262            MPI_Send (res, w.pixelsX * w.pixelsY, MPI_INT, 0, RESULTTAG, ←
                      MPI_COMM_WORLD); // return the results
263          }
264        }
265
266    MPI_Finalize ();
267    return 0;
268  }
```

5.22.2 A MULTITHREADED MASTER-WORKER SETUP

In this section we improve on the master-worker code of Listing 5.38 in two major ways:

- Each worker spawns a number of threads with the aim to more effectively utilize multicore execution platforms.
- A separate thread (the main one) in each worker is responsible for communication with the master node, making sure that communication and computation overlap as much as possible.

In order for the code presented in this section to work properly, your MPI implementation must be compiled with threading support enabled (see Section 5.16). The overall architecture of the code that follows is shown in Figure 5.27. Two individual FIFO queues are used inside each worker process:

- *inque[18]: For holding work items arriving from the master nodes.
- *outque: For holding results that are produced from the threads and are waiting to be forwarded to the master.

The sequence of events that leads to the transformation of a work item into a partial result, as shown in Figure 5.27, is the following:

---

[18] inque and outque are actually pointers to QueueMonitor<> objects. The * notation is used to maintain consistency.

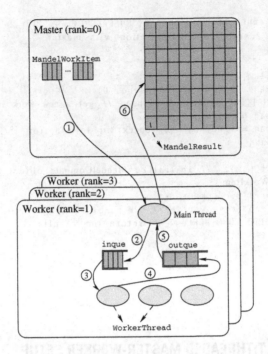

FIGURE 5.27

An overview of the software architecture used in Listing 5.40. Circled numbers indicate event order.

1. The master node distributes work items (represented by instances of class MandelWorkItem) to the worker processes.
2. The main thread in each worker process deposits the received work items in queue *inque.
3. When a worker thread is done with a work item, it collects the next available one from *inque.
4. When a work item is complete, the result (represented by an instance of class MandelResult) is deposited in queue *outque.
5. The main thread reads any available results from outque and sends them to the master process.
6. The master process consolidates the partial results as they arrive.

Due to the size of the code, we proceed to discussing the individual building blocks separately. The two queues are central to the proper coordination of the threads in a worker process, so we begin by discussing this component. Both queues are instances of the template class QueueMonitor shown in Listing 5.39. Because they are shared by the worker threads, QueueMonitor is a monitor-based class (see Section 3.6 for a discussion on monitors) with methods protected by a mutex.

QueueMonitor offers a FIFO interface with a twist: Both enqueue and dequeue operations are two-stage affairs.

This design was prompted by the need to eliminate memory allocation overhead. Work item and result structures are preallocated and managed by the queues, which maintain two lists: one for the structures currently being populated (queue, defined in line 8) and one for the structures being free (freeList, defined in line 7). A preallocated array of structures is passed as a parameter to the constructor of the class (lines 22-26) and its elements are used to populate the freeList.

```
1   // File : mandlebrot_mt/sharedQue .h
2   . . .
3   template<typename T>
4   class QueueMonitor
5   {
6   private:
7       list<T> freeList;
8       list<T> queue;
9
10      QMutex l;
11      QWaitCondition full, empty;
12
13  public:
14      QueueMonitor(int , T prealloc);
15      T reserve(); // reserve an item for management. reserve and enque ↩
              are supposed to be used in tandem
16      void enque(T);
17      T deque();        // deque and release are supposed to be used in ↩
              tandem
18      void release(T); // returns an item to the free list
19      int availItems ();
20  };
21  //————————————————————————————————————————
22  template<typename T> QueueMonitor<T>::QueueMonitor(int s, T prealloc)
23  {
24      for(int i=0;i<s;i++)
25          freeList.push_back(prealloc+i);
26  }
```

LISTING 5.39

A monitor-based template class that implements a FIFO interface, with two-stage enqueue and dequeue operations. A header file is used for this class, since C++ templates do not generate code unless they are instantiated.

When a thread needs to deposit an item in a QueueMonitor instance, it should (a) reserve one of the items managed by the object by calling the reserve method, (b) populate the item with the needed data, and (c) deposit the item by calling the enque method.

```
27   //─────────────────────────────────────────────────────────
28   // reserves an item so that its fields can be populated before it is ↵
         enqueued
29   template<typename T> T QueueMonitor<T>::reserve()
30   {
31       QMutexLocker ml(&l);
32       while(freeList.empty())  // block until a free item is available
33           full.wait(&l);
34       T tmp = freeList.front();
35       freeList.pop_front();
36       return tmp;
37   }
38   //─────────────────────────────────────────────────────────
39   // this is non-blocking because the item has been reserved before
40   template<typename T> void QueueMonitor<T>::enque(T item)
41   {
42       QMutexLocker ml(&l);
43       queue.push_back(item);
44       empty.wakeOne();
45   }
```

When a thread needs to withdraw an item from a QueueMonitor instance, it should (a) reserve one of the available items managed by the object by calling the deque method, (b) extract the information required from the item, and (c) release the acquired item back to the object by calling the release method.

```
46   //─────────────────────────────────────────────────────────
47   template<typename T> T QueueMonitor<T>::deque()
48   {
49       QMutexLocker ml(&l);
50       while(queue.empty())  // block until an item can be taken from the ↵
             queue
51           empty.wait(&l);
52       T tmp = queue.front();
53       queue.pop_front();
54       return tmp;
55   }
56   //─────────────────────────────────────────────────────────
57   template<typename T> void QueueMonitor<T>::release(T item)
58   {
59       QMutexLocker ml(&l);
60       freeList.push_back(item);
61       full.wakeOne();
62   }
63   //─────────────────────────────────────────────────────────
64   template<typename T> int QueueMonitor<T>::availItems()
65   {
66       QMutexLocker ml(&l);
67       return queue.size();
68   }
```

The main file of the program holds the classes that describe the work items and result sets. The MandelWorkItem class encapsulates the data describing a work item.

It also provides MPI registration for the successful communication of class instances between the master and worker processes. The static `init` method needs to be called for a derived datatype to be created and registered.

```cpp
// File : mandlebrot_mt/mandlebrot_mt.cpp
. . .
//*************************************************************
class MandelWorkItem
{
public:
    double upperX, upperY, lowerX, lowerY;
    int imageX, imageY, pixelsX, pixelsY;
    static MPI_Datatype type;

    static void init();
};
MPI_Datatype MandelWorkItem::type;

//*************************************************************
void MandelWorkItem::init()
{
    MandelWorkItem sample;

    int blklen[2];
    MPI_Aint displ[2], off, base;
    MPI_Datatype types[2];

    blklen[0] = 4;   // declare field sizes
    blklen[1] = 4;

    types[0] = MPI_DOUBLE; // declare field types
    types[1] = MPI_INT;

    displ[0] = 0;            // declare field displacements
    MPI_Get_address (&(sample.upperX), &base);
    MPI_Get_address (&(sample.imageX), &off);
    displ[1] = off - base;

    MPI_Type_create_struct (2, blklen, displ, types, &type);
    MPI_Type_commit (&type);
}
```

LISTING 5.40

A multithreaded, master-worker implementation of a Mandelbrot fractal set calculator.

The `MandelResult` class is responsible for representing the partial results that are generated from the worker threads. Similarly to the `MandelWorkItem` class, a static `init` method is provided for registering an MPI-derived datatype (lines 84-99) and for declaring the size, in pixels, of the subpicture each work item will generate (data member `numItems`).

A slight complication exists with the fact that MPI will not traverse pointers in communicating a data structure, i.e., it performs what is known as a *shallow copy*. In order to be able to communicate back to the master process, the pixel values (stored in a dynamically created array) of a subpicture, and the coordinates where it belongs, the following approach is used:

- The MandelResult class is equipped with a getResultAddress method for getting the address of the array holding the data. The getResultSize method, which currently returns one by default, could be used in a future extension of the code if variable-size work items were to be used, resulting in variable-size result sets.
- The derived datatype is basically a 1D array of integers. The getResultAddress method is used to get the proper location of the data to send, which is obviously not the address of the MandelResult object owning it.
- The *imgPart array is extended on allocation by two elements (lines 60 and 72). The extra space is used to hold the imageX and imageY subpicture coordinates (lines 61-62 and 73, 74). The init method of lines 70-75, which is separate from the constructor, allows the initialization of an object past its construction (e.g., after an array of MandelResult objects is created).

The alternative to the above would be to use MPI_Pack/MPI_Unpack, with all the additional overhead that is entailed.

```
38  // *****************************************************************
39  class MandelResult
40  {
41  public:   // public access is not recommended but it is used here to ↩
                shorten the code
42      int *imgPart;
43      // the needed imageX and imageY parameters, i.e. the location of ↩
                computed image in bigger picture, are placed at the end of the↩
                pixel buffer
44      static int numItems;         // not part of the communicated data
45      static MPI_Datatype type;
46
47      MandelResult();
48      MandelResult(int , int );
49      void init(int , int );
50      ~MandelResult();
51      void *getResultAddress() {return (void*)imgPart;}
52      int getResultSize() {return 1;}
53      static void init(int blkSize);
54  };
55  MPI_Datatype MandelResult::type;
56  int MandelResult::numItems;
57  //─────────────────────────────────────────────────────────────
58  MandelResult::MandelResult(int iX, int iY)
59  {
60      imgPart = new int[numItems+2]; // +2 to hold imageX and imageY
61      imgPart[numItems] = iX;
```

```
62          imgPart[numItems+1] = iY;
63      }
64      //——————————————————————————————————————————————————————————
65      MandelResult::MandelResult()
66      {
67          imgPart = NULL;
68      }
69      //——————————————————————————————————————————————————————————
70      void MandelResult::init(int iX, int iY)
71      {
72          imgPart = new int[numItems+2]; // +2 to hold imageX and imageY
73          imgPart[numItems] = iX;
74          imgPart[numItems+1] = iY;
75      }
76      //——————————————————————————————————————————————————————————
77      MandelResult::~MandelResult()
78      {
79          if(imgPart != NULL)
80              delete [] imgPart;
81          imgPart = NULL;
82      }
83      //——————————————————————————————————————————————————————————
84      void MandelResult::init(int s)
85      {
86          numItems = s;
87          int blklen;
88          MPI_Aint displ;
89          MPI_Datatype types;
90
91          blklen = numItems + 2;
92
93          types = MPI_INT;
94
95          displ = 0;
96
97          MPI_Type_create_struct (1, &blklen, &displ, &types, &type);
98          MPI_Type_commit (&type);
99      }
```

The MandelCompute class is fairly unchanged from the version used in Listing 5.38. The main difference is that it is now operating on a MandelWorkItem and a MandelResult objects, which are supplied before the computation takes place.

```
100     // ***************************************************************
101     // Class for computing a fractal set part
102     class MandelCompute
103     {
104     private:
105         double upperX, upperY, lowerX, lowerY;
106         int pixelsX, pixelsY, imageX, imageY;
107         MandelResult *res;
108
```

```
109      static int MAXITER;
110      int diverge (double cx, double cy);
111
112  public:
113      void compute();
114      void init(MandelWorkItem *, MandelResult *);
115      MandelResult* getResult();
116  };
117  int MandelCompute::MAXITER = 255;
118
119  //————————————————————————————————————
120
121  int MandelCompute::diverge (double cx, double cy)
122  {
123      int iter = 0;
124      double vx = cx, vy = cy, tx, ty;
125      while (iter < MAXITER && (vx * vx + vy * vy) < 4)
126      {
127          tx = vx * vx − vy * vy + cx;
128          ty = 2 * vx * vy + cy;
129          vx = tx;
130          vy = ty;
131          iter++;
132      }
133      return iter;
134  }
135
136  //————————————————————————————————————
137  void MandelCompute::init (MandelWorkItem* wi, MandelResult *r)
138  {
139      upperX = wi->upperX;    //local copies are used to speed up ↩
                 computation
140      upperY = wi->upperY;
141      lowerX = wi->lowerX;
142      lowerY = wi->lowerY;
143      imageX = wi->imageX;
144      imageY = wi->imageY;
145
146      res = r;
147
148      pixelsX = wi->pixelsX;
149      pixelsY = wi->pixelsY;
150  }
151
152  //————————————————————————————————————
153
154  void MandelCompute::compute ()
155  {
156      double stepx = (lowerX − upperX) / pixelsX;
157      double stepy = (upperY − lowerY) / pixelsY;
158
159      int *img = res->imgPart;  // shortcut
```

```
160          for (int i = 0; i < pixelsX; i++)
161              for (int j = 0; j < pixelsY; j++)
162              {
163                  double tempx, tempy;
164                  tempx = upperX + i * stepx;
165                  tempy = upperY - j * stepy;
166                  img[j * pixelsX + i] = diverge (tempx, tempy);
167              }
168          img[pixelsX * pixelsY] = imageX;
169          img[pixelsX * pixelsY + 1] = imageY;
170      }
171      //————————————————————————————————————
172      MandelResult* MandelCompute::getResult()
173      {
174          return this ->res;
175      }
```

Following Qt's guidelines for setting up threads (see Section 3.2.3), the QThread-derived class WorkerThread is used to start up a number of threads at each worker process. Each thread object is supplied references to the *inque and *outque objects (declared in lines 377 and 378, respectively), which are used in the worker process to traffic messages to and from the master process.

A thread runs for as long as a nonnull MandelWorkItem reference is withdrawn from the inque (check at line 205). Upon termination, a thread deposits a NULL reference in the outque to signal the end of its stream of results.

```
176      // **************************************************************
177      class WorkerThread : public QThread
178      {
179      private:
180          int ID;
181          int runs;
182          QueueMonitor<MandelWorkItem *> *in;
183          QueueMonitor<MandelResult *> *out;
184
185      public:
186          WorkerThread(int i, QueueMonitor<MandelWorkItem *> *, QueueMonitor↩
                 <MandelResult *>*);
187          void run();
188      };
189      //————————————————————————————————————
190      WorkerThread::WorkerThread(int id, QueueMonitor<MandelWorkItem *> *i, ↩
                 QueueMonitor<MandelResult *> *o)
191      {
192          ID = id;
193          in = i;
194          out = o;
195          runs=0;
196      }
197
198      //————————————————————————————————————
```

```
199   void WorkerThread::run()
200   {
201       MandelCompute *c = new MandelCompute();
202       while(1)
203       {
204           MandelWorkItem * work = in->deque();
205           if(work==NULL) break;
206
207           MandelResult *res = out->reserve();
208           c->init (work, res);
209           in->release(work);
210
211           c->compute ();
212
213           out->enque(res);
214       }
215       out->enque(NULL);
216       delete c;
217   }
218   // ************************************************************
219   // Uses the divergence iterations to pseudocolor the fractal set
220   void savePixels (QImage * img, int *imgPart, int imageX, int imageY, ↵
          int height, int width)
221   {
222       for (int i = 0; i < width; i++)
223           for (int j = 0; j < height; j++)
224           {
225               int color = imgPart[j * width + i];
226               img->setPixel (imageX + i, imageY + j, qRgb (256 − color, ↵
                      256 − color, 256 − color));
227           }
228   }
```

The most notable differences with the initial statements in the main function are that `MPI_Init_thread` is used to initialize the MPI run-time, and thread support is checked (rather forcefully by an assertion) in lines 242 and 243, respectively. In this version of the code, we use a single thread per process to conduct communications, thus requiring the `MPI_THREAD_FUNNELED` support. Using multiple threads for communication is left as an exercise.

The number of available cores is discovered via the call of line 238, and this is subsequently used to generate as many worker threads and size the FIFO structures `*inque` and `*outque` accordingly.

The class method calls of lines 259-260 ensure that derived datatypes are available for MPI communications.

```
229   // ************************************************************
230   int main (int argc, char *argv[])
231   {
232       int N, rank, numCores;
233       double start_time, end_time;
234       MPI_Status status;
```

```
235        MPI_Request request;
236
237
238        numCores = sysconf(_SC_NPROCESSORS_ONLN);
239
240        // init MPI and check thread support
241        int provided;
242        MPI_Init_thread (&argc, &argv, MPI_THREAD_FUNNELED, &provided);
243        assert(provided >= MPI_THREAD_FUNNELED);
244        start_time = MPI_Wtime ();
245
246        MPI_Comm_size (MPI_COMM_WORLD, &N);
247        MPI_Comm_rank (MPI_COMM_WORLD, &rank);
248
249        // check that all parameters are supplied
250        if (rank == 0 && (argc < 6))
251        {
252            cerr << argv[0] << " upperCornerX upperCornerY lowerCornerX ↵
                   lowerCornerY workItemPixelsPerSide \n";
253            MPI_Abort (MPI_COMM_WORLD, 1);
254        }
255
256        int workItemPixelsPerSide = atoi (argv[5]);
257
258        // create samples of the work item and result classes and register↵
                   their types with MPI
259        MandelWorkItem::init();
260        MandelResult::init(workItemPixelsPerSide * workItemPixelsPerSide);
```

The master process (as in Listing 5.38) prepares the work items in the array *w, declared in line 285, before starting to distribute them to the worker processes. Each worker process initially receives twice as many work items as the number of its host machine's available cores (lines 325-330). The rationale is to have load available so as to keep the threads busy while communications take place. Each result that is received by the master prompts the sending of more work items so as to keep the *inque of the corresponding worker full.

To be able to accomplish this task, each worker process starts its execution by sending to the master its host's available cores (line 370). These numbers are collected (line 308) and kept in the nodeCores array (line 313). Every result message that is delivered to the master, triggers the sending of more work items, so as *inque remains full (lines 325-330). In addition, the RESULTTAG-labeled message causes a call to the savePixels function, which lights up the resulting image pixels based on the worker results.

Once all the work items have been distributed (condition i != Xparts * Yparts fails in lines 306 and 325), the master starts listening for the last results from each worker process (the expected number is reflected in the workItemsAssignedToNode array elements) using the loop of lines 339-356. Once these are received, an ENDTAG-labeled message is sent (line 355) that will propagate to all the worker threads in the form of a NULL MandelWorkItem reference (line 402).

The `busyNodes` counter counts down the worker processes remaining with assigned work (line 353). Once this number reaches 0, the master process terminates the program by saving the resulting image (line 358), releasing memory (lines 360-363) and shutting down the MPI run-time.

```
261    if (rank == 0)    // master code
262    {
263        double upperCornerX, upperCornerY;
264        double lowerCornerX, lowerCornerY;
265        double partXSpan, partYSpan;
266        int Xparts, Yparts;
267        int imgX = 1024, imgY = 768;
268
269        upperCornerX = atof (argv[1]);
270        upperCornerY = atof (argv[2]);
271        lowerCornerX = atof (argv[3]);
272        lowerCornerY = atof (argv[4]);
273
274        // make sure that the image size is evenly divided in work ←
                items
275        Xparts = (int) ceil (imgX * 1.0 / workItemPixelsPerSide);
276        Yparts = (int) ceil (imgY * 1.0 / workItemPixelsPerSide);
277        imgX = Xparts * workItemPixelsPerSide;
278        imgY = Yparts * workItemPixelsPerSide;
279
280        partXSpan = (lowerCornerX − upperCornerX) / Xparts;
281        partYSpan = (upperCornerY − lowerCornerY) / Yparts;
282        QImage *img = new QImage (imgX, imgY, QImage::Format_RGB32);
283
284        // prepare the work items in individual structures
285        MandelWorkItem *w = new MandelWorkItem[Xparts * Yparts];
286        for (int i = 0; i < Xparts; i++)
287            for (int j = 0; j < Yparts; j++)
288            {
289                int idx = j * Xparts + i;
290
291                w[idx].upperX = upperCornerX + i * partXSpan;
292                w[idx].upperY = upperCornerY − j * partYSpan;
293                w[idx].lowerX = upperCornerX + (i + 1) * partXSpan;
294                w[idx].lowerY = upperCornerY − (j + 1) * partYSpan;
295
296                w[idx].imageX = i * workItemPixelsPerSide;
297                w[idx].imageY = j * workItemPixelsPerSide;
298                w[idx].pixelsX = workItemPixelsPerSide;
299                w[idx].pixelsY = workItemPixelsPerSide;
300            }
301
302        // now distribute the work item to the worker nodes
303        int *nodeCores = new int[N];
304        int *workItemsAssignedToNode = new int[N];
305        MandelResult *res = new MandelResult(0, 0);
306        for (int i = 0; i < Xparts * Yparts; i++)
```

```
307              {
308                  MPI_Recv (res->getResultAddress(), res->getResultSize(), ↵
                        MandelResult::type, MPI_ANY_SOURCE, MPI_ANY_TAG, ↵
                        MPI_COMM_WORLD, &status);
309                  int workerID = status.MPI_SOURCE;
310                  int tag = status.MPI_TAG;
311                  if(tag == CORESAVAILTAG)
312                  {
313                      nodeCores[workerID] = res->imgPart[0];
314                      workItemsAssignedToNode[workerID]=0;
315                  }
316                  else if (tag == RESULTTAG)
317                  {
318                      workItemsAssignedToNode[workerID]--;
319                      int idx = res->numItems;
320                      int imageX = res->imgPart[idx];  // extract location ↵
                            of image part
321                      int imageY = res->imgPart[idx+1];
322                      savePixels (img, res->imgPart, imageX, imageY, ↵
                            workItemPixelsPerSide, workItemPixelsPerSide);
323                  }
324
325                  while(workItemsAssignedToNode[workerID] != 2 * nodeCores[↵
                        workerID] && i != Xparts*Yparts)
326                  {
327                      MPI_Isend (&(w[i]), 1, MandelWorkItem::type, workerID,↵
                            WORKITEMTAG, MPI_COMM_WORLD, &request);
328                      i++;
329                      workItemsAssignedToNode[workerID]++;
330                  }
331                  i--;
332              }
333
334          // now send termination messages
335          int busyNodes=0;
336          for(int i=1;i<N;i++)
337              if(workItemsAssignedToNode[i]!=0) busyNodes++;
338
339          while(busyNodes != 0)
340          {
341              MPI_Recv (res->getResultAddress(),1,MandelResult::type, ↵
                    MPI_ANY_SOURCE, MPI_ANY_TAG, MPI_COMM_WORLD, &status);
342
343              int workerID = status.MPI_SOURCE;
344              int tag = status.MPI_TAG;
345
346              if (tag == RESULTTAG)
347              {
348                  int idx = res->numItems;
349                  int imageX = res->imgPart[idx];
350                  int imageY = res->imgPart[idx+1];
```

```
351            savePixels (img, res->imgPart, imageX, imageY, ↵
                   workItemPixelsPerSide, workItemPixelsPerSide);
352            workItemsAssignedToNode[workerID]--;
353            if(workItemsAssignedToNode[workerID]==0) busyNodes--;
354          }
355          MPI_Isend (NULL, 0, MandelWorkItem::type, workerID, ENDTAG↵
                 , MPI_COMM_WORLD, &request);
356        }
357
358        img->save ("mandel.png", "PNG", 0); // save the resulting ↵
                image
359
360        delete []w;
361        delete []nodeCores;
362        delete []workItemsAssignedToNode;
363        delete res;
364
365        end_time = MPI_Wtime ();
366        cout << "Total time : " << end_time - start_time << endl;
367      }
```

Each worker process starts by allocating the work items and result structure memory (lines 372, 373) and setting up the FIFO queues (lines 377, 378) that serve the threads. The threads are spawned with the loop of lines 381-385.

Once the threads are started, the main thread serves as the communication funnel between the worker threads and the master process via the loop of lines 391-436. The body of the loop is split into a sequence of two steps:

- Lines 394-410 are receiving work items from the master process and depositing them in *inque. If an ENDTAG-labelled message is received, as many as numCores NULL references are deposited to act as flags to the worker threads, and the endOfWork flag is set to avoid entering this step again.
- Lines 414-432 are sending back results if there are available items in *outque (condition in line 414). A MPI_Isent call is used to avoid the overhead of copying the message data to an MPI buffer.

The loop terminates only when all the results have been sent to the master process, indicated by having the numWorkerThreads counter become zero. The counter is decremented every time a thread deposits a NULL reference in the *outque, which indicates its termination (lines 417-420).

```
368      else     // worker code
369      {
370        MPI_Send (&numCores, 1, MPI_INT, 0, CORESAVAILTAG, ↵
               MPI_COMM_WORLD);    // publish available cores to master
371
372        MandelWorkItem *w = new MandelWorkItem[2*numCores];
373        MandelResult   *r = new MandelResult[2*numCores];
374        for(int i=0;i<2*numCores;i++)
375            r[i].init(0,0);
```

```
376
377        QueueMonitor<MandelWorkItem *> *inque = new QueueMonitor<↩
               MandelWorkItem *>(2*numCores, w);
378        QueueMonitor<MandelResult *> *outque = new QueueMonitor<↩
               MandelResult *>(2*numCores,r);
379
380        WorkerThread **thr = new WorkerThread*[numCores];
381        for(int i=0;i<numCores;i++)
382        {
383            thr[i] = new WorkerThread(i, inque, outque);
384            thr[i]->start();
385        }
386
387        // one loop for sending and recv messages
388        bool endOfWork=false;
389        int numWorkerThreads = numCores;
390        int assigned=0;
391        while (1)
392        {
393            // receiving part
394            if(!endOfWork && assigned != numCores )
395            {
396                MandelWorkItem *w = inque->reserve();
397                MPI_Recv (w, 1, MandelWorkItem::type, 0, MPI_ANY_TAG, ↩
                       MPI_COMM_WORLD, &status); // get a new work item
398                int tag = status.MPI_TAG;
399                if (tag == ENDTAG)
400                {
401                    for(int i=0;i<numCores;i++)
402                        inque->enque(NULL);
403                    endOfWork=true;
404                }
405                else
406                {
407                    inque->enque(w);
408                    assigned++;
409                }
410            }
411
412            // sending part
413            MandelResult *res;
414            if(outque->availItems() >0)
415            {
416                res = outque->deque();
417                if(res == NULL)
418                {
419                    numWorkerThreads--;
420                }
421                else
422                {
423                    MPI_Request r;
424                    MPI_Status s;
```

```
425
426              MPI_Isend (res->getResultAddress(), res->↵
                    getResultSize(), MandelResult::type, 0, ↵
                    RESULTTAG, MPI_COMM_WORLD, &r); // return the ↵
                    results
427              MPI_Wait(&r, &s);
428
429              outque->release(res);
430              assigned--;
431            }
432          }
433
434          if(!numWorkerThreads) // terminate the loop
435              break;
436        }
437
438        for(int i=0;i<numCores;i++)
439            thr[i]->wait();
440
441        // memory clean-up
442        for(int i=0;i<numCores;i++)
443            delete thr[i];
444        delete []thr;
445        delete inque;
446        delete outque;
447        delete []w;
448        delete []r;
449
450      }
451      MPI_Finalize ();
452      return 0;
453 }
```

This code can be easily modified to serve other scenarios. The core changes would mostly affect classes `MandelWorkItem`, `MandelResult`, and `MandelCompute` and the lines that modify or initialize their instances.

EXERCISES

1. Write a MPMD version of the "Hello World" program of Figure 5.2, in effect eliminating the `if/else` structure around which the program is built. You may use the C or C++ bindings.

2. Write a SPMD version of the two programs shown in Listing 5.5.

3. Modify the program shown in Listing 5.5 so that the master node prints a list of the process IDs for which the message has not been read yet. Your output should be similar to:

```
1  $ mpirun -np 1 master : -np 3 worker
2  Node 2 says Hi. Awaiting nodes : 1 3
3  Node 3 says Hi. Awaiting nodes : 1
4  Node 1 says Hi. Awaiting nodes :
```

4. Create a model of the characteristics of the communication link joining two processes running on two different machines, i.e., calculate the start-up latency and communication rate by implementing and testing a *ping-pong* benchmark program. A ping-pong program measures the time elapsed between sending a message, having it bounce at its destination, and receiving it back at its origin. By varying the message size, you can use statistical methods (least-squares) to estimate the start-up latency and rate as the intercept and slope, respectively, of the line fitted to the experimental data.

5. How would we need to modify the broadcasting program of Listing 5.9 if the source of the message were an arbitrary process and not the one with rank 0?

6. Assume that the execution platform of your program consists of four machines with identical architecture but different CPU clocks: one with 4GHz, one with 3 GHz, and two with 2 GHz. How should you split the matrix A used in the example of Section 5.11.1 in order to solve the matrix-vector product problem in the smallest possible time?

7. Write a program that performs gathering as efficiently as possible using point-to-point communications, i.e., the equivalent of MPI_Gather. What is the *time complexity* of your algorithm?

8. Write a program that performs scattering as efficiently as possible using point-to-point communications, i.e., the equivalent of MPI_Scatter. What is the *volume* of data collectively communicated if each process is to receive K number of items? Express this number as a function of K and the number of processes N.

9. The amount of data exchanged during every step of the butterfly pattern in Figure 5.9 doubles in relation to the previous step. If initially every process had data of size K bytes to exchange, what is the total time required for the operation to complete if we assume that each message exchange takes time $t_s + l \cdot V$, where t_s is the link's start-up latency, V is the volume of data to be sent, and l is the inverse of the communication speed?

10. An alternative parallel bucket sort algorithm would have the root process of a N-process run, scan the input data, and split them into N buckets before scattering the buckets to the corresponding processes. Implement this alternative design and compare its performance with the version presented in Section 5.11.5.

11. Write a function that could be used for providing multicasting capabilities to a program, i.e., to be able to send a message to a subset of the processes of a communicator. Use an appropriate collective operation for the task.

12. Write the equivalent of the ping-pong program using RMA functions and measure the communication speed achieved versus the size of the message used. Compare your results with the data rates accomplished with point-to-point communications.

13. Modify the program of Listing 5.7 so that the partitioning of the range depends on the relative speed of the participating nodes. One easy approach is to make the ranges proportional to the CPU operating frequency or the calculated

bogomips. Both numbers are available in the /proc/cpuinfo pseudo-file. The master can collect the numbers and reply back to the worker nodes with the calculated ranges. If we represent as m_i the i-node's bogomips, the percentage of the range α_i that should be assigned to node i can be calculated as $\alpha_i = \frac{m_i}{\sum_{\forall k} m_k}$

14. The butterfly communication scheme that is outlined in Section 5.11.4 is only one of the possible strategies for an all-to-all or all-reduce data exchange. A different approach would be mandated if the underlying communication infrastructure did not provide the required links, making the procedure inefficient. An example of such an architecture is the ring, where each node is directly connected to just two others.

    a. Write an MPI program that would implement an efficient all-to-all exchange of data on a ring of machines.

    b. How many steps would be required in comparison to a butterfly scheme if the number of nodes/processes were $N = 2^k$?

    c. If we assume that time taken to send V bytes over a communication link is given by $l \cdot V$, where l is the (inverse of the) link speed in $sec/byte$, how does your algorithm compare against the butterfly scheme in terms of overall communication time?

15. The case study on diffusion-limited aggregation in Section 5.20 decomposes the problem's data on a particle-wise basis. Explore the alternative of partitioning the 2D grid and assigning it to the processes involved. What are the benefits and drawbacks of this approach? Is the communication pattern involved different in this case? Does this approach produce similar results to the sequential program and alternative parallel programs?

16. Implement a 3D-space diffusion-limited aggregation simulation by extending the solutions provided in Section 5.20.

17. It is not unusual in NoWs setups to have machines with different capabilities. Create an MPI program that would have each process read from a file a number of integers that is proportional to its CPU speed as indicated by the operating frequency (its "clock"). Use appropriate *filetypes* and *views* to perform the data distribution in a cyclic-block manner.

18. The details of the trapezoidal rule for computing a function integral are discussed in Section 3.5.2. Implement an MPI-based version of the trapezoidal rule using (a) dynamic partitioning and (b) static partitioning. For part (a) you can base your solution on master-worker implementation of Section 5.22.1.

19. Use the master-worker code provided in Section 5.22 as a basis for the creation of a hierarchical master-worker configuration where nodes are organized in a three-level (or higher) tree instead of the two-level tree of the simple setup. The secondary master nodes of the middle tree layer(s) should be responsible for managing the load distribution in their subtrees, whereas the primary master at the root of the tree should be responsible for the overall workload distribution.

20. Modify the multithreaded master-worker code of Section 5.22.2 so that there are two separate threads in each worker process for communication: one for

receiving work items and one for sending back results. What are the benefits and drawbacks of this arrangement?

21. Conway's Game of Life is played on a rectangular grid of cells that may or may not contain an organism. The state of the cells is updated at each time step by applying the following set of rules:
    - Every organism with two or three neighbors survives.
    - Every organism with four or more neighbors dies from overpopulation.
    - Every organism with zero or one neighbors dies from isolation.
    - Every empty cell adjacent to three organisms gives birth to a new one.

    Create an MPI program that evolves a board of arbitrary size (dimensions could be specified at the command line) over several iterations. The board could be randomly generated or read from a file.

    Try applying the geometric decomposition pattern to partition the work among your processes. One example could be to evenly split the board row-wise. It is clear that each process can update its part of the board only by knowing the state of the bottom board row resident in the previous process and the state of the top board row resident in the next process (the boundary processes being an exception).

22. Radix sort is a linear complexity non-comparison-based sorting algorithm that is susceptible to concurrent execution. Radix sort sorts data by separating them into groups based on their digits (for integers) or characters (for strings). The data must be of fixed range, i.e., the number of bits or characters used must be known *a priori*.

    Radix sort comes in two forms: least-significant digit radix sort (LSD) or most-significant digit radix sort (MSD). The latter is suitable for parallel execution, as data that are partitioned in groups can be operated independently in subsequent phases of the algorithm. The MSD algorithm, which is very close to bucket-sort[19], can be implemented recursively as shown in the following pseudocode, for binary data. An extension for data with nonbinary digits (strings) is straightforward. The use of the auxiliary array B allows the sorting to be *stable*.

```
1   // Input: array A, with N elements, each D bits long.
2   // Output : A holds sorted data
3   radix_sort(A, N)
4       allocate memory B equal in size to A
5       tmp <- radix_aux(A, N, B, D-1)
6       if tmp <> A    // if sorted data end up in B array
7         copy B to A
8
9   // Auxiliary recursive function
10  // Use of temporary array B for a stable sort
```

---

[19]The major difference between radix sort and bucket sort is in how the keys are examined: piece-wise in radix sort and as a whole in bucket sort. In the latter, an arbitrary number of buckets can be prescribed.

```
11    // Returns location of sorted data
12    radix_aux( A, N, B, k)
13        if k = -1 Or N<2      // base case for termination
14            return A
15        else
16            let r be the number of items in A, with k-th bit set to 0
17            resetIdx <- 0
18            setIdx <- r
19            for i <- 0 to N-1    // separate data in two bins
20                if k-th bit of A[i] is set
21                    store A[i] in B[ setIdx ]
22                    setIdx <- setIdx + 1
23                else
24                    store A[i] in B[ resetIdx ]
25                    resetIdx <- resetIdx + 1
26
27            tmp1 <- radix_aux(B, r, A, k-1)          // sort bin with a 0 ↵
                    k-th bit, using the (k-1)-th bit
28            tmp2 <- radix_aux(B+r, N-r, A+r, k-1)  // sort bin with a 1 ↵
                    k-th bit, using the (k-1)-th bit
29            if tmp1 + r <> tmp2      // pointer comparison
30                if r > N - r      // make the smallest copy
31                    copy N-r elements from tmp2 to tmp1+r
32                    return tmp1
33                else
34                    copy r elements from tmp1 to tmp2-r
35                    return tmp2-r
36            else
37                return tmp1
```

Use divide-and-conquer decomposition as your decomposition pattern (see Section 2.3.2) to design and implement an MPI radix sort.

GPU programming

IN THIS CHAPTER YOU WILL

- Understand the memory hierarchy of GPUs and how the different memories can be utilized.
- Learn how computations are mapped to threads in Compute Unified Device Architecture (CUDA) using grids and blocks.
- Learn how to use streams and zero-copy memory to maximize the utilization of a GPU.
- Combine CUDA and MPI to handle big workloads over a cluster of GPU-equipped machines.
- Learn to use a step-by-step approach in the development of CUDA programs via the development of two case studies.

6.1 GPU PROGRAMMING

GPUs devote a big portion of their silicon real estate to compute logic, compared to conventional CPUs that devote large portions of it to on-chip cache memory. This results in having hundreds or thousands (!) of cores in contemporary GPUs, as shown in Section 1.3.2. In order to put all this computational power to use, we must create at least one separate thread for each core. Even more are needed so that computation can be overlapped with memory transfers. This obviously mandates a shift in the programming paradigm we employ. Going from a handful to thousands of threads requires a different way of partitioning and processing loads.

GPU program deployment has a characteristic that can be considered a major obstacle: GPU and host memories are typically disjoint, requiring explicit (or implicit, depending on the development platform) data transfer between the two. Only some low-cost, entry-level systems violate this rule by having a portion of the main memory allocated for display and GPU purposes at the expense of performance, since CPU and GPU compete for memory access.

The existing architectures are shown in Figure 6.1. Figure 6.1(a) represents a typical arrangement for discrete GPU solutions. AMD's Athlon 64 and later Intel's Nehalem architectures reduced the latency associated with main memory access by integrating the memory controller in the CPU die (as shown in Figure 6.1(b)). AMD's Accelerated Processor Unit (APU) chips integrate CPU and GPU in a single chip (as shown in Figure 6.1(c)). This is a breakthrough with great potential, especially with the introduction of the heterogeneous Unified Memory Access (hUMA) technology

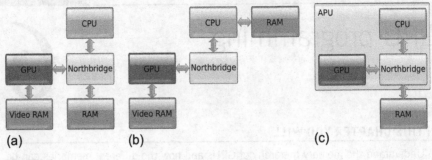

FIGURE 6.1

Existing architectures for CPU-GPU systems: (a) and (b) represent discrete GPU solutions, with a CPU-integrated memory controller in (b). Diagram (c) corresponds to integrated CPU-GPU solutions, such as the AMD's Accelerated Processing Unit (APU) chips.

that unifies the memory spaces of CPU and GPU and even maintains cache coherence between them. However, at present, the wafer real-estate compromises that these chips have to endure (sharing the same chip limits the amount of functionality that can be incorporated for both CPU and GPU alike), along with their coupling with slow memory subsystems, relegates them to low-cost market segments.

Having disjoint memories means that data must be explicitly transferred between the two whenever data need to be processed by the GPU or results collected by the CPU. Considering that memory access is a serious bottleneck in GPU utilization (despite phenomenal speeds like a maximum theoretical memory bandwidth of 336GB/s for Nvidia's GTX TITAN Black, and 320GB/s for AMD's Radeon R9 290X), communicating data over relatively slow peripheral buses like the PCIe[1] is a major problem. In subsequent sections we examine how this communication overhead can be reduced or "hidden" by overlapping it with computation.

A second characteristic of GPU computation is that GPU devices may not adhere to the same floating-point representation and accuracy standards as typical CPUs. This can lead to the accumulation of errors and the production of inaccurate results. Although this is a problem that has been addressed by the latest chip offerings by Nvidia and AMD, it is always recommended, as a precaution during development, to verify the results produced by a GPU program against the results produced by an equivalent CPU program. For example, CUDA code samples available with Nvidia's SDK typically follow this approach.

GPU programming has been advancing with leaps and bounds since the first early attempts. Current tools cover a wide range of capabilities as far as problem decomposition and expressing parallelism are concerned. On one side of the spectrum we have tools that require explicit problem decomposition, such as CUDA and

---

[1]PCIe 3.0 has theoretical speed of 8 GT/s (giga-transfers per second) per lane, which, over a typical 16-lane interface like the ones available in the majority of motherboards, translates to a maximum data rate of 16 GB/s.

OpenCL, and on the other extreme we have tools like OpenACC that let the compiler take care of all the data migration and thread spawning necessary to complete a task on a GPU.

Some of the most prominent GPU development platforms are as follows:

- **CUDA**: **C**ompute **U**nified **D**evice **A**rchitecture[2] was introduced by Nvidia in late 2006 as one of the first credible systems for GPU programming that broke free of the "code-it-as-graphics" approach used until then. CUDA provides two sets of APIs (a low, and a higher-level one), and it is available freely for Windows, Mac OS X, and Linux operating systems. Although it can be considered too verbose, for example requiring explicit memory transfers between the host and the GPU, it is the basis for the implementation of higher-level third-party APIs and libraries, as explained below. CUDA, as of Summer 2014 in its sixth incarnation, is specific to Nvidia hardware only.

- **OpenCL**: **Open** **C**omputing **L**anguage[3] is an open standard for writing programs that can execute across a variety of heterogeneous platforms that include GPUs, CPU, DSPs, or other processors. OpenCL is supported by both Nvidia and AMD. It is the primary development platform for AMD GPUs. OpenCL's programming model matches closely the one offered by CUDA.

- **OpenACC**: An open specification[4] for an API that allows the use of compiler directives (e.g., `#pragma acc`, in a similar fashion to OpenMP) to automatically map computations to GPUs or multicore chips according to a programmer's hints.

- **Thrust**: A C++ template library[5] that accelerates GPU software development by utilizing a set of container classes and a set of algorithms to automatically map computations to GPU threads. Thrust used to rely solely on a CUDA backend, but since version 1.6 it can target multiple device back-ends, including CPUs. Thrust has been incorporated in the CUDA SDK distribution since CUDA 4.1. It is covered in detail in Chapter 7.

- **ArrayFire**: A comprehensive GPU function library,[6] that covers mathematics, signal and image processing, statistics, and other scientific domains. ArrayFire functions operate on arrays of data in a similar fashion to Thrust. ArrayFire relies on a CUDA back end also. A `gfor` construct is provided that allows the parallel execution of a loop's iterations on the GPU.

- **C++ AMP**: C++ **A**ccelerated **M**assive **P**arallelism[7] is a Microsoft technology based on DirectX 11 that allows the transparent execution of C++ code on a CPU or a GPU based on a number of directives or language extensions that the programmer provides. C++ AMP extensions allow the description of parallelizable loops and multidimensional arrays that can be partitioned and

---

[2]https://developer.nvidia.com/category/zone/cuda-zone.
[3]http://www.khronos.org/opencl/.
[4]http://www.openacc-standard.org.
[5]http://code.google.com/p/thrust/.
[6]http://www.accelereyes.com/.
[7]http://msdn.microsoft.com/en-us/library/vstudio/hh265136.aspx.

transferred to a GPU for processing. The programming model is similar to the one employed by OpenMP.

In the following sections we explore CUDA. The Thrust platform which contributes in a big way towards the elimination of much of the logistical overhead (i.e., memory allocation and transfers) involved in GPU programming, is covered in Chapter 7. Appendix E addresses issues related to CUDA installation.

6.2 CUDA'S PROGRAMMING MODEL: THREADS, BLOCKS, AND GRIDS

The CUDA programming model follows the Globally Sequential Locally Parallel pattern (see Section 2.4). As GPUs are essentially coprocessors that can be used to accelerate parts of a program, a CUDA program executes as shown in Figure 6.2.

In order to properly utilize a GPU, the program must be decomposed into a large number of threads that can run concurrently. GPU schedulers can execute these threads with minimum switching overhead and under a variety of configurations based on the available device capabilities. However, there are two challenges that must be overcome:

1. How do we spawn the hundreds or thousands of threads required?
   CUDA's answer is to spawn all the threads as a group, running the same function with a set of parameters that apply to all.

CUDA Model of Execution

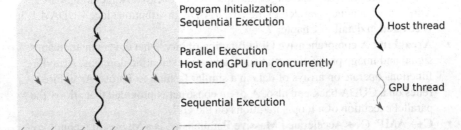

FIGURE 6.2

The GSLP CUDA execution model. The host machine may continue execution (default behavior) or may block, waiting for the completion of the GPU threads.

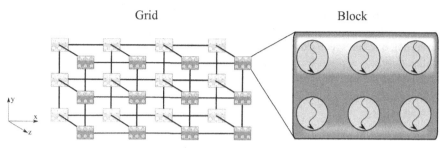

Grid   Block

FIGURE 6.3

An example of the grid/block hierarchy used to describe a set of threads that will be spawned by CUDA. The figure illustrates a 4x3x2 grid made by 3x2 blocks. The grid connections are there only for illustrative purposes.

2. How do we initialize the individual threads so that each one does a different part of the work?

CUDA solves this problem by organizing the threads in a 6D structure (lower dimensions are also possible)! Each thread is aware of its position in the overall structure via a set of intrinsic structure variables. With this information, a thread can map its position to the subset of data to which it is assigned.

Threads are organized in a hierarchy of two levels, as shown in Figure 6.3. At the lower level, threads are organized in *blocks* that can be of one, two or three dimensions. Blocks are then organized in *grids* of one, two, or three dimensions. The sizes of the blocks and grids are limited by the capabilities of the target device. The rationale behind this organization, which lies partly in hardware issues and partly in software engineering issues, is revealed in Sections 6.3 and 6.6.

Nvidia uses the *compute capability* specification to encode what each family/-generation of GPU chips is capable of. The part that is related to grid and block sizes is shown in Table 6.1. The compute capability of your GPU can be discovered by running the `deviceQuery` utility that comes with the CUDA SDK samples.

Table 6.1 Compute Capabilities and Associated Limits on Block and Grid sizes

Item	Compute Capability			
	1.x	**2.x**	**3.x**	**5.x**
Max. number of grid dimensions	2	3		
Grid maximum x-dimension	$2^{16} - 1$		$2^{31} - 1$	
Grid maximum y/z-dimension	$2^{16} - 1$			
Max. number of block dimensions	3			
Block max. x/y-dimension	512	1024		
Block max. z-dimension	64			
Max. threads per block	512	1024		
GPU example (GTX family chips)	8800	480	780	980

The programmer has to provide a function that will be run by all the threads in a grid. This function in CUDA terminology is called a *kernel*. During the invocation of the kernel, one can specify the thread hierarchy with a special *execution configuration* syntax ($<<<$ $>>>$). For example, running a kernel called foo() by a set of threads, like the one depicted in Figure 6.3, would require the following lines:

```
dim3 block(3,2);
dim3 grid(4,3,2);
foo<<<grid, block>>>();
```

The CUDA-supplied dim3 type represents an integer vector of three elements. If less than three components are specified, the rest are initialized by default to 1. In the special case where a 1D structure is desired, e.g., running a grid made up of five blocks, each consisting of 16 threads, the following shortcut is also possible:

```
foo<<<5, 16>>>();
```

Many different grid-block combinations are possible. Some examples are shown here:

```
dim3 b(3,3,3);
dim3 g(20,100);
foo<<<g, b>>>();      // Run a 20x100 grid made of 3x3x3 blocks
foo<<<10, b>>>();  // Run a 10-block grid, each block made by 3x3x3 ↩
    threads
foo<<<g, 256>>>(); // Run a 20x100 grid, made of 256 threads
foo<<<g, 2048>>>();// An invalid example: maximum block size is ↩
    1024 threads even for compute capability 5.x
foo<<<5, g>>>();      // Another invalid example, that specifies a ↩
    block size of 20x100=2000 threads
```

Listing 6.1 shows the CUDA equivalent of a "Hello World" program.

```
1   // File: hello.cu
2   #include <stdio.h>
3   #include <cuda.h>
4
5   __global__ void hello()
6   {
7       printf("Hello world\n");
8   }
9
10  int main()
11  {
12      hello<<<1,10>>>();
13      cudaDeviceSynchronize();
14      return 1;
15  }
```

LISTING 6.1

A "Hello World" CUDA program.

The program can be compiled and executed as follows (CUDA programs should be stored in files with a `.cu` extension):

```
$ nvcc -arch=sm_20 hello.cu -o hello
$ ./hello
```

and it will produce 10 lines of output. The "architecture" switch (`-arch=sm_20`) in the *Nvidia CUDA Compiler* (`nvcc`) driver command line above instructs the generation of GPU code for a device of compute capability 2.0. Compatibility with 2.0 and higher is a requirement for supporting `printf` output from code running on the device (line 7).

The key points of Listing 6.1 are the following:

- The kernel `hello()` is just like any other C function. The only difference is the decoration with the __global__ directive, which specifies that the `hello` function is supposed to be called from the host and run on the device. In devices of compute capability 3.5 and above, a __global__ function can be also called from the device.
- Kernels that are called from the host (i.e., __global__) are not supposed to return any value. They must be declared `void`. Any results that a kernel computes are stored in the device memory and must be explicitly transferred back to host memory, as discussed in Section 6.6.
- GPU execution is asynchronous (as implicitly indicated in Figure 6.2), i.e., the statement of line 12 specifies the execution configuration, but the time instance the threads will terminate (or even spawn) is undetermined. If the host requires that the GPU computation is done before proceeding (e.g., results are needed), an explicit *barrier* statement is needed (`cudaDeviceSynchronize` in line 13). If line 13 is commented out, there will be no output from the program. Can you guess why?

CUDA supports two more function specifiers: __device__ and __host__. A __device__ function can only be called from within a kernel, i.e., not from a host. A __host__ function can only run on the host. The __host__ is typically omitted unless used in combination with __device__ to indicate that the function can run on both the host and the device. This means that two binary executables must be generated: one for execution on the CPU and one for execution on the GPU. The CUDA toolkit conveniently packages both inside the same executable file.

Each of the CUDA threads is aware of its position in the grid/block hierarchy via the following intrinsic/built-in structures, all having 3D components x, y, and z:

- `blockDim`: Contains the size of each block, e.g., (B_x, B_y, B_z).
- `gridDim`: Contains the size of the grid, in blocks, e.g., (G_x, G_y, G_z).
- `threadIdx`: The (x, y, z) position of the thread within a block, with $x \in [0, B_x - 1]$, $y \in [0, B_y - 1]$, and $z \in [0, B_z - 1]$.
- `blockIdx`: The (b_x, b_y, b_z) position of a thread's block within the grid, with $b_x \in [0, G_x - 1]$, $b_y \in [0, G_y - 1]$, and $b_z \in [0, G_z - 1]$.

The purpose of making a thread aware of its position in the hierarchy is to allow it to identify its workload.

`threadIdx` is not unique among threads, since there could be two or more threads in different blocks with the same index. Deriving a unique scalar ID for each of the threads would require the use of all of the preceding information. Each thread can be considered an element of a 6D array with the following definition[8]:

```
Thread t[gridDim.z][gridDim.y][gridDim.x][blockDim.z][blockDim.y][↵
    blockDim.x];
```

Getting the offset of a particular thread from the beginning of the array would produce a unique scalar ID, as shown in Listing 6.2.

```
int myID = ( blockIdx.z * gridDim.x * gridDim.y +
             blockIdx.y * gridDim.x +
             blockIdx.x ) * blockDim.x * blockDim.y * blockDim.z +
             threadIdx.z *  blockDim.x * blockDim.y +
             threadIdx.y * blockDim.x +
             threadIdx.x;
```

LISTING 6.2

Calculation of a unique ID for a thread in a grid of blocks.

An alternative way for the calculation of a thread's global ID is to assume that each thread is an element of a 3D array with the following dimensions:

```
Thread t [ gridDim.z * blockDim.z ]
         [ gridDim.y * blockDim.y ]
         [ gridDim.x * blockDim.x ];
```

A thread's global coordinates would be:

```
// start of block + local component
int x = blockIdx.x * blockDim.x + threadIdx.x;
int y = blockIdx.y * blockDim.y + threadIdx.y;
int z = blockIdx.z * blockDim.z + threadIdx.z;
```

The following ID calculation, based on the above formulation, produces the same results as Listing 6.2:

```
int altMyID = threadIdx.x + blockIdx.x * blockDim.x +
              (blockIdx.y * blockDim.y + threadIdx.y) * gridDim.x * ↵
              blockDim.x+
              (blockIdx.z * blockDim.z + threadIdx.z) * gridDim.x * ↵
              blockDim.x * gridDim.y * blockDim.y;
```

---

[8]The index arrangements seems strange, with z components coming before the x ones. However, this is a definition compatible with the thread hierarchy depicted in Nvidia's CUDA C Programming Guide. Additionally, the mapping of the x, y, and z components of a thread's ID to a part of the data/workload is completely application-specific, i.e., alternative/different ID calculations are also possible.

The first three lines in Listing 6.2 relate to the inter-block offset (i.e., getting to the beginning of the block a thread belongs to) and the last three to the intra-block offset (i.e., the distance from the beginning of the block).

Fortunately, in most cases the layout of the threads uses a small subset of dimensions, allowing the simplification of this formula (treating the missing grid or block dimensions as equal to 1 and the corresponding coordinates as 0), or there is a direct association between the thread and data-to-be-processed layouts (e.g., processing points in a 3D lattice by an equal-size grid of threads), making the calculation of a scalar ID unnecessary.

Based on this discussion, we can modify the program of Listing 6.1 so that each thread prints its ID, as shown in Listing 6.3.

```
1   // File: hello2.cu
2   . . .
3   __global__ void hello()
4   {
5     int myID = ( blockIdx.z * gridDim.x * gridDim.y +
6                  blockIdx.y * gridDim.x +
7                  blockIdx.x ) * blockDim.x +
8                  threadIdx.x;
9
10    printf ("Hello world from %i\n", myID);
11  }
12  . . .
```

LISTING 6.3

A variation to the "Hello World" program of Listing 6.1. Only the changes are shown.

A question that normally arises from the examples of this section, is :"What happens if my device adheres to compute capability 1.x? Does that mean that I cannot use my GPU for running the CUDA programs of this book? Not for printing messages from the device, for sure! But this is a functionality that is desirable mainly for debugging purposes. GPUs in the context of high-performance computing are essentially coprocessors and are not meant to perform I/O of any kind.[9]

In the vast majority of scenarios, the host is responsible for I/O operations, passing the input and subsequently collecting the output data from the memory space of the GPU. Section 6.6 presents this process in detail as well as the memory hierarchy of CUDA devices. A clear understanding of the latter is essential for optimizing their operation.

---

[9]This excludes graphical output in visualization applications. However, these typically employ OpenGL for the task, not `printf`!

6.3 CUDA'S EXECUTION MODEL: STREAMING MULTIPROCESSORS AND WARPS

GPU cores are essentially vector processing units, capable of applying the same instruction on a large collection of operands. So, when a kernel is run on a GPU core, the same instruction sequence is *synchronously* executed by a large collection of processing units called *streaming processors*, or SPs. A group of SPs that execute under the control of a single control unit is called a *streaming multiprocessor*, or SM. A GPU can contain multiple SMs, each running each own kernel. Since each thread runs on its own SP, we will refer to SPs as cores (Nvidia documentation calls them CUDA cores), although a more purist approach would be to treat SMs as cores. Nvidia calls this execution model Single-Instruction, Multiple Threads (SIMT).

SIMT is analogous to SIMD. The only major difference is that in SIMT the size of the "vector" on which the processing elements operate is determined by the software, i.e., the block size.

The computational power of a GPU (and consequently, its target market) is largely determined, at least within the members of a family, by the number of SMs available. As an example, Table 6.2 lists a number of legacy, Fermi, Kepler, and Maxwell-class GPU offerings.

Threads are *scheduled* to run on an SM as a block. The threads in a block do not *run* concurrently, though. Instead they are executed in groups called *warps*. The size of a warp is hardware-specific. The current CUDA GPUs use a warp size of 32, but this could change in future GPU generations (the intrinsic integer variable warpSize can be used to query this number). At any time instance and based on the number of CUDA cores in an SM, we can have 32 threads active (one full active warp), 16 threads active (a half-warp active), or 8 threads active (a quarter-warp active). The benefit of interleaving the execution of warps (or their parts) is to hide the latency associated with memory access, which can be significantly high.

Threads in a block are split into warps according to their intra-block thread-ID, as calculated by the formula in Listing 6.2, if we set to zero the grid-related terms:

```
int myID = threadIdx.z * blockDim.x * blockDim.y +
           threadIdx.y * blockDim.x +
           threadIdx.x;
```

Table 6.2 A sample list of GPU chips and their SM capabilities

GPU	Cores	Cores/SM	SM	Compute Capab.
GTX 980	2048	128	16	5.2
GTX Titan	2688	192	14	3.5
GTX 780	2304	192	12	3.5
GTX 770	1536	192	8	3.0
GTX 760	1152	192	6	3.0
GTX 680	1536	192	8	3.0
GTX 670	1344	192	7	3.0
GTX 580	512	32	16	2.0

An SM can switch seamlessly between warps (or half- or quarter-warps) as each thread gets its own set of registers. Each thread actually gets its own private execution context that is maintained on-chip. This contradicts the arrangement used by multithreading on CPUs, where a very expensive context switch (involving the saving of CPU registers) accompanies thread switching.

Each SM can have multiple warp schedulers, e.g., in Kepler there are four. This means that up to four independent instruction sequences from four warps can be issued simultaneously. Additionally, each warp scheduler can issue up to two instructions as long as they are independent, i.e., the outcome of one does not depend on the outcome of the other. This is known as *instruction-level parallelism* (ILP). As an example, let's consider the following code:

```
a = a * b;
d = b + e;
```

These two statements can be executed concurrently, whereas the following example does not present such an opportunity due to the dependency between the two statements:

```
a = a * b;
d = a + e;   // needs the value of a
```

Once an SM completes the execution of all the threads in a block, it switches to a different block in the grid. In reality, each SM may have a large number of *resident blocks* and *resident warps*, i.e., executing concurrently. In compute capability 3.x devices, each SM[10] has 192 CUDA cores. So, how can we maximize the utilization of an SM if only 32 threads are active at any time? Obviously the answer is that we cannot, unless we have multiple warps running on the SM. Each SM of a compute capability 3.x device has four warp schedulers, which means it can direct four different instruction sequences. This would still leave $192 - 4 * 32 = 64$ cores unused. These are utilized by the SM for running more warps in case there is a stall.

In the Maxwell architecture, Nvidia has reduced the number of cores to 128 per SM, but they retain the four warp schedulers. Each scheduler is permanently assigned to a group of 32 cores, simplifying scheduling and improving efficiency, despite the overall reduction in cores.

The number of resident kernels, blocks, and warps depends on the memory requirements of a kernel and the limits imposed by the compute capability of a device. These limits are shown in Table 6.3.

As an example to the previous discussion, let's assume that we have a kernel that requires 48 registers per thread, and it is to be launched on a GTX 580 card, as a grid of 4x5x3 blocks, each 100 threads long. The registers demanded by each block are $100 * 48 = 4800$, which are below the 32k/SM available on this compute capability 2.0 card. The grid is made of $4 * 5 * 3 = 60$ blocks that need to be distributed to the 16 SMs of the card. Although Nvidia does not publish how the blocks are distributed to the SMs, we can safely assume that it should be a form of round-robin assignment.

---

[10]Nvidia is using the SMX acronym for SMs in Kepler, and the SMM acronym for SMs in the Maxwell architecture. For consistency, we keep using the SM term throughout this chapter.

Table 6.3 Compute Capabilities and Associated Limits on Kernel and Thread Scheduling

Item	Compute Capability					
	1.0, 1.1	1.2, 1.3	2.x	3.0	3.5	5.0
Concurrent kernels/device	1			16	32	
Max. resident blocks/SM	8			16		32
Max. resident warps/SM	24	32	48	64		
Max. resident threads/SM	768	1024	1536	2048		
32-bit registers/SM	8k	16k	32k	64k		
Max. registers/thread	128		63		255	

This means that there will be 12 SMs that will receive four blocks and six SMs that will receive three blocks. Obviously, this would be a source of inefficiency, since during the time the 12 SMs process the last of the four blocks they were assigned, the remaining four SMs are idle.

Additionally, each of the 100-thread blocks would be split into $\lceil \frac{100}{warpSize} \rceil = 4$ warps, assuming warpSize=32. The first three warps would have 32 threads and the last would have four threads! So, during the execution of the last warp of each block, $\frac{32-4}{32} = 87.5\%$ of the multiprocessors would be idle.

These issues indicate that kernel design and deployment are critical for extracting the maximum performance from a GPU. These issues are addressed in Section 6.7.

A programmer can safely ignore the mechanics of the thread scheduling since no control can be exercised over when or in what sequence the threads in a kernel invocation will run. Care should be given only to the case where multiple threads modify the same memory location. Operation atomicity should be maintained, but this is a concern shared by multicore CPU software as well.

There is however a significant reason why one needs to understand how threads and warps are executed, and that reason in *performance*. Threads in a warp may execute as one, but they operate on different data. So, what happens if the result of a conditional operation leads them to different paths? The answer is that all the divergent paths are evaluated (if threads branch into them) in sequence until the paths merge again. The threads that do not follow the path currently being executed are stalled. So, given the kernel in Listing 6.4, the execution of a warp would be as shown in Figure 6.4.

```
__global__ void foo()
{
  int ID = threadIdx.y * blockDim.x + threadIdx.x;
  if( ID % 2 == 0)
    {
      doSmt();
    }
  else
    {
```

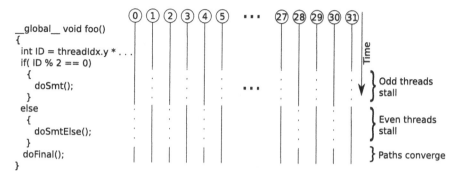

FIGURE 6.4

An illustration of the execution of the kernel in Listing 6.4 by a warp of threads. The dotted lines indicate a stall.

```
        doSmtElse();
    }
    doFinal();
}
```

LISTING 6.4

An example of a kernel that would slash the utilization of an SM in half by keeping half the threads in a warp stalled.

A solution to this problem is discussed in Section 6.7.2.

6.4 CUDA COMPILATION PROCESS

In this section we examine the process behind the compilation of a CUDA program into a form that can be deployed on a GPU. The nvcc compiler driver tool certainly makes the process transparent to the programmer, but in many cases intimate knowledge of this process can be beneficial and/or critical.

We begin by examining the various file formats that are handled or generated during the compilation process. A peculiarity of nvcc is that it will fail to process a file that does not have one of the recognized file prefixes:

- .cu: Source files for device and host functions. Since CUDA 5.0, multiple .cu files can be part of a project. Previously, all device code had to be placed in a single file.
- .cc, .cpp, .cxx: C++ source code.
- .c: C source code.
- .h, .cuh: Header files.
- .o (Linux), .obj (Windows): Object files. These are the products of the compilation process, and they serve as the input of the linking phase.
- .a (Linux) .lib (Windows): Static library files. During the linking phase, static libraries become part of the final binary executable file.

- .so: Shared object or dynamic library files. These are not embedded in the executable files.
- .gpu: Intermediate compilation file that contains only device source code.
- .cubin: CUDA binary file targeting a specific GPU. It should be stressed that Nvidia does not preserve binary compatibility across GPU families, since this would seriously hinder its ability to innovate and produce radical new designs.
- .ptx: A portable device assembly format. PTX code has to be compiled with a just-in-time (JIT) compiler before execution. PTX files are text files.

As can be deduced from the preceding list, a CUDA executable can exist in two forms: a binary one that can only target specific devices and an intermediate assembly one that can target any device by JIT compilation. In the latter case, the PTX Assembler (ptxas) performs the compilation during execution time, adding a start-up overhead, at least during the first invocation of a kernel.

A CUDA program can still target different devices by embedding multiple cubins into a single file (called a *fat binary*). The appropriate cubin is selected at run-time.

Figure 6.5 shows an abstracted overview of the compilation process with some of the steps removed. The actual steps are covered in (probably too much) detail in Nvidia's nvcc Reference Guide (file CUDA_Compiler_Driver_NVCC.pdf in ${CUDA}/doc/pdf[11]). Figure 6.5 conveys the essence of the process, and it is not a one-to-one accounting of every phase involved (Nvidia also declares that the process can be subject to change between SDK releases). An interested reader can observe this sequence in detail by calling the nvcc compiler driver with the -dryrun switch, forcing just the display but not the execution of the programs or tools involved and environmental parameters used, as shown in the following example:

```
$ nvcc —dryrun hello.cu
#$ _SPACE_=
#$ _CUDART_=cudart
#$ _HERE_=/opt/cuda/bin
#$ _THERE_=/opt/cuda/bin
#$ _TARGET_SIZE_=64
#$ TOP=/opt/cuda/bin/..
#$ LD_LIBRARY_PATH=/opt/cuda/bin/../lib:/opt/ati—stream—sdk/lib/x86_64↩
   :/opt/mpich2/lib:/usr/lib/fglrx:/opt/ati—stream—sdk/lib/x86_64:/↩
   opt/intel/Compiler/11.0/083/lib/intel64:/opt/cuda/lib64:/opt/cuda/↩
   lib:/opt/omnetpp/lib:/usr/l/checkout/gpuocelot/ocelot/build_local/↩
   lib
#$ PATH=/opt/cuda/bin/../open64/bin:/opt/cuda/bin/../nvvm:/opt/cuda/↩
   bin:/usr/local/sbin:/usr/local/bin:/usr/sbin:/usr/bin:/sbin:/bin:/↩
   usr/games:/opt/mpich2/bin:/opt/cuda/bin:/opt/ibm/systemsim—cell/↩
   bin:/opt/ibm/systemsim—cell/include/callthru/spu/:/opt/intel/↩
   Compiler/11.0/083/bin/intel64:/opt/omnetpp/bin:/usr/l/checkout/↩
   gpuocelot/ocelot/build_local/bin
```

---

[11]As a matter of convention, we refer to the location where the CUDA SDK and samples are installed as ${CUDA}. This is platform-specific, and it can even be manipulated by the user installing the SDK. If in doubt, finding the location of the nvcc tool will reveal this location, since nvcc is typically installed under ${CUDA}/bin.

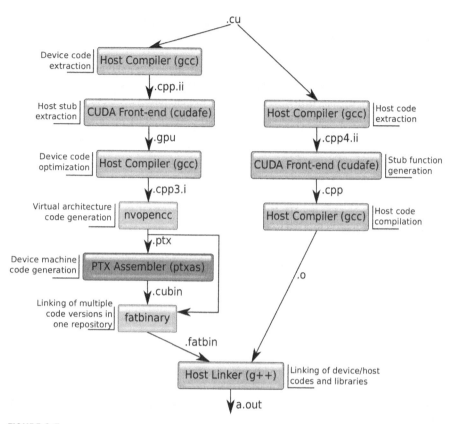

FIGURE 6.5

A high-level view of CUDA's compilation process. The two distinct paths operate on the device and host code, respectively, before the final linking phase that produces a single executable file. The stages are labeled with some of the most significant actions performed by them.

```
#$  INCLUDES="-I/opt/cuda/bin/../include"
#$  LIBRARIES=  "-L/opt/cuda/bin/../lib64" -lcudart
#$  CUDAFE_FLAGS=
#$  OPENCC_FLAGS=
#$  PTXAS_FLAGS=
#$  gcc -D__CUDA_ARCH__=100 -E -x c++    -DCUDA_FLOAT_MATH_FUNCTIONS -↵
      DCUDA_NO_SM_11_ATOMIC_INTRINSICS -DCUDA_NO_SM_12_ATOMIC_INTRINSICS↵
      -DCUDA_NO_SM_13_DOUBLE_INTRINSICS  -D__CUDACC__ -D__NVCC__   "-I/↵
      opt/cuda/bin/../include"   -include "cuda_runtime.h" -m64 -o "/tmp↵
      /tmpxft_00005553_00000000-6_hough.cpp1.ii" "hough.cu"
#$  cudafe . . .
```

The compilation process follows two distinct paths: one for the compilation of the device and one for the compilation of the host code. These are connected in more places than shown, as, for example, is the case of the generation of the stub host functions. These functions are called upon the invocation of a kernel by the host to set up and launch the respective device code.

As can be observed in Figure 6.5, CUDA can actually embed both cubin and PTX versions of the device code in the produced executable. This is actually the default behavior. The tricky part is that nvcc defaults to generating code that adheres to the compute capability 1.0 specification. This can be significantly suboptimal, given that a number of important operations, such as support of double precision floating-point arithmetic or a plethora of atomic operations, that are supported in hardware by more recent GPU incarnations (of higher compute capabilities) are forcefully performed by software in the code automatically generated.

nvcc accepts a number of parameters that control the code generation. We have already seen one used in the "Hello World" example of Section 6.2, to enable the use of printf from device code. The most significant of these are:

- -arch: Controls the "virtual" architecture that will be used for the generation of the PTX code, i.e., it controls the output of the nvopencc command. The possible values for this parameter are shown in the first column of Table 6.4.
- -code: Specifies the actual device that will be targeted by the cubin binary, i.e., it controls the output of the ptxas command. The possible values for this parameter are shown in the second column of Table 6.4.

As shown in Table 6.4, there is not an exact one-to-one correspondence between -arch and -code parameters. Although the first one enables the use of specific capabilities by the nvopencc compiler, the latter allows the compilation process to adapt to (optimize for) the peculiarities of a specific device and take this into account during the cubin generation.

The -arch parameter can take a single value, but the -code parameter can have a list of values, in which case a cubin is generated for each of the specified machines

Table 6.4 Possible values for the -arch and -code parameters of the nvcc command

Virtual Architecture (-arch)	Streaming Multiprocessing Code (-code)	Feature Enabled
compute_10	sm_10	Basic features
compute_11	sm_11	Global memory atomic operations
compute_12	sm_12	Shared memory atomic operations and vote instructions
compute_13	sm_13	Double precision floating-point support
compute_20	sm_20	Fermi support
	sm_21	SM structure changes (e.g., more cores)
compute_30	sm_30	Kepler support
compute_35	sm_35	Dynamic parallelism (enables recursion)
compute_50	sm_50	Maxwell support

and embedded in the fat binary. The list of values for the `-code` parameter can include a single virtual architecture, in which case the corresponding PTX code is also added to the fat binary. Obviously, the architecture targeted by `-code`, should never be below the compute capability of the virtual architecture specified. Otherwise, the compilation will fail.

Examples:

- `nvcc hello.cu -arch=compute_20 -code=sm_20,sm_30`: PTX generation phase involves compute capability 2.0 code. The fat binary incorporates two cubins, one for `sm_20` and one for `sm_30` (but no PTX).
- `nvcc hello.cu -arch=compute_20 -code=compute_20,sm_20,sm_30`: The same as the previous example with the addition of the PTX code in the fat binary.
- `nvcc hello.cu -arch=compute_20 -code=sm_10,sm_20`: Fails to compile.
- `nvcc hello.cu`: Shorthand for `nvcc hello.cu -arch=compute_10 -code=compute_10,sm_10`.
- `nvcc hello.cu -arch=sm_20`: Shorthand for `nvcc hello.cu -arch=compute_20 -code=compute_20,sm_20`.
- `nvcc hello.cu -arch=compute_20 -code=compute_20`: No cubin will be created, since the `ptxas` is not called. The fat binary will contain just the PTX code version.

On Linux platforms, `nvcc` defaults to using the GNU C/C++ compiler (`gcc`, or `g++`). On Windows it defaults to using the command-line version of the Visual Studio C/C++ compiler (`cl`). The compiler program should be in the executable path. Alternative compilers can be tested with the `-compiler-bindir` option.

6.5 PUTTING TOGETHER A CUDA PROJECT

The CUDA SDK provides a wealth of sample projects for someone to study CUDA and its application in a large array of domains.[12] Starting a new CUDA project under Linux or Mac OS X can be as easy as calling the CUDA C/C++ Project wizard of the NSight IDE (a derivative of the Eclipse IDE) provided with the SDK. Windows users can also use Microsoft Visual Studio or Microsoft Visual C++ Express Edition 2008, 2010, and 2012 for working with CUDA.

For Linux and Mac OS X platforms, there is also the possibility of working with a Makefile arrangement, an approach that makes it easier to integrate a multitude of tools (e.g., MPI or Qt) without the explicit support of an IDE. In this section we explore this option, since it also enables a closer understanding of the process of building a CUDA application.

---

[12] The sample projects location is OS, and installation-specific. Consult Nvidia's documentation and/or your site's administrator for this information.

The SDK provides a template project that can be used as a starting point for working with a Makefile. This is available under the 0_Simple/template location in samples. Unfortunately, trying to modify the template manually can be a source of frustration and mistakes.

For this reason we proceed to discuss how one can easily set up a Makefile from scratch for working with the CUDA Toolkit.

Since version 5.0, CUDA has supported the split of the device source code into multiple files. This is obviously beneficial for the structure and maintainability of a project, although certain limitations apply:

- Only devices of compute capability 2.0 and above can be targeted.
- No PTX version of the code can be embedded in the fat binary.
- Device code modules that are compiled separately must be compiled with the same parameters (-code) and must produce *relocatable device code* by specifying the nvcc's option -rdc=true. The combination of the -c (compile only) and -rdc=true switches can be shortened to -dc.

The process for *separate compilation* of device code modules is a bit different from the *whole-program* compilation explored in the previous section. An additional step that precedes the generation of the final executable has to be performed that merges together or links all the device code in a single fat binary. For this purpose, the nvlink tool is invoked prior to linking all the components together into the final executable. The modified process is shown in Figure 6.6.

Fortunately, most of the details are taken care of by nvcc with the use of appropriate parameters. Thankfully, Nvidia has made sure that many of nvcc's parameters match the ones that are typically used by the GNU C/C++ Compiler. These include -o for specifying the output destination file, -l for specifying libraries, -c for restricting the process to compilation but not linking, -O for optimization, -g for debugging information inclusion, -I for specifying include file directories, and -L for specifying library file directories.

As an example, let's consider a project made up of the following source code files:

- d.cuh: Header file for the device functions defined in a.cu and b.cu.
- a.cu: File containing a set of kernels.
- b.cu: File containing another set of kernels.
- hostFE.cu: File containing the host functions that call the kernels in a.cu and b.cu.
- main.cpp: C++ code that calls the front-end functions in hostFrondEnd.cu, using a Qt thread.

The compilation can be done with the following sequence of commands (include and library directories are obviously platform- and system-specific):

```
# Compile file a.cu. Compute capability 2.0 and above only support ↵
    separate compilation
nvcc —device-c —arch=sm_20 —o a.o a.cu
```

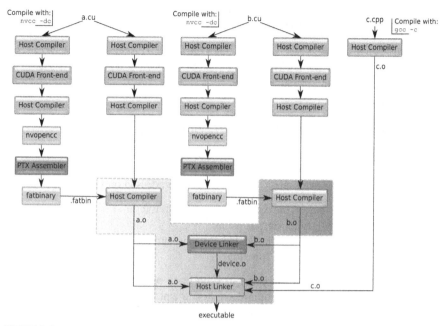

FIGURE 6.6

A high-level view of CUDA's separate compilation process. It is assumed that the project is made up of three source code files: two containing device code (a.cu and b.cu) and one containing host code only (c.cpp). The highlighted region contains the steps that differ from the whole-program compilation of Figure 6.5.

```
# Compile file b.cu
nvcc —device-c —arch=sm_20 —o b.o b.cu

# Compile front-end file hostFE.cu, that calls the kernels in a.cu and↩
    b.cu
nvcc —device-c —arch=sm_20 —o hostFE.o hostFE.cu

# Compile file main.cpp file, making use of Qt library
g++ —c main.cpp —I/usr/include/qt5/QtCore  —I/usr/include/qt5/QtGui —I↩
    /usr/include/qt5 —fPIC

# Link everything together. Notice the extra option for the Qt library↩
    files. Multiple lines are used to highlight the sets of different↩
    switches and options
nvcc —rdc=true —arch=sm_20    \\
    —L/usr/lib/x86_64-linux-gnu —lQt5Gui —lQt5Core —lpthread  \\
    main.o a.o b.o hostFE.o —o a.out
```

The creation of a makefile capable of utilizing CUDA and other tools in the same project is discussed in Appendix E.5.

6.6 MEMORY HIERARCHY

As discussed in Section 6.1, GPU memory is typically disjoint from the host's memory. So, passing chunks of data to a kernel in the form of a pointer to an array in the host's memory is not possible:

```
int *mydata = new int[N];
. . . // populating the array
foo<<<grid, block>>>(mydata, N);   // NOT POSSIBLE!
```

Instead, data have to be explicitly copied from the host to the device and back once the required processing has been completed. This entails the allocation of two regions of memory for every array that needs to be processed on the device:

1. One region on the host. This can be allocated with the new operator or the malloc and calloc functions, as usual.
2. One region on the device. This can be allocated and released with the cudaMalloc and cudaFree functions.[13]

In the listings that follow, in order to keep track of what kind of memory each pointer references, we prefix the pointers to host memory with h_ and the pointers to device memory with d_.

The transfer of data between the two memory spaces can be done with the cudaMemcpy function:

```
// Allocate memory on the device.
cudaError_t cudaMalloc ( void** devPtr,   // Host pointer address,
                                          // where the address of
                                          // the allocated device
                                          // memory will be stored
               size_t size )              // Size in bytes of the
                                          // requested memory block


// Frees memory on the device.
cudaError_t cudaFree ( void* devPtr );    // Parameter is the host
                                          // pointer address, returned
                                          // by cudaMalloc


// Copies data between host and device.
cudaError_t cudaMemcpy ( void* dst,       // Destination block address
               const void* src,           // Source block address
               size_t count,              // Size in bytes
               cudaMemcpyKind kind )      // Direction of copy.
```

cudaError_t is an enumerated type. If a CUDA function returns anything other than cudaSuccess (0), an error has occurred.

---

[13]The proper coupling of cudaMalloc with cudaFree calls cannot be stressed enough. Leaked device memory cannot be automatically recovered, given the absence of a full-blown operating system/garbage collector running on the device. The only remedy is a reboot!

The cudaMemcpyKind parameter of cudaMemcpy is also an enumerated type. The kind parameter can take one of the following values:

- cudaMemcpyHostToHost = 0, Host to Host
- cudaMemcpyHostToDevice = 1, Host to Device
- cudaMemcpyDeviceToHost = 2, Device to Host
- cudaMemcpyDeviceToDevice = 3, Device to Device (for multi-GPU configurations)
- cudaMemcpyDefault = 4, used when Unified Virtual Address space capability is available (see Section 6.7)

A simple data transfer example is shown in Listing 6.5 in the form of a vector addition program. The host is responsible for generating two random integer arrays that are passed to the device. Upon completion of the vector addition on the device, the result data are transferred back to the host.

```
1   // File: vectorAdd.cu
2   #include <stdio.h>
3   #include <stdlib.h>
4   #include <cuda.h>
5
6   static const int BLOCK_SIZE = 256;
7   static const int N = 2000;
8
9   #define CUDA_CHECK_RETURN(value) {                              \
10      cudaError_t _m_cudaStat = value;                            \
11      if (_m_cudaStat!= cudaSuccess) {                            \
12          fprintf(stderr, "Error %s at line %d in file %s\n", \
13                  cudaGetErrorString(_m_cudaStat),                \
14                  __LINE__, __FILE__);                            \
15          exit(1);                                                \
16      } }
17
18  // kernel that calculates only one element of the result
19  __global__ void vadd (int *a, int *b, int *c, int N)
20  {
21      int myID = blockIdx.x * blockDim.x + threadIdx.x;
22      if (myID < N)    // in case myID exceeds the array bounds
23          c[myID] = a[myID] + b[myID];
24  }
25
26  int main (void)
27  {
28      int *ha, *hb, *hc, *da, *db, *dc;    // host (h*) and device (d*) ↵
                pointers
29      int i;
30
31      // host memory allocation
32      ha = new int[N];
33      hb = new int[N];
34      hc = new int[N];
35
```

```
36    // device memory allocation
37    CUDA_CHECK_RETURN (cudaMalloc ((void **) &da, sizeof (int) * N));
38    CUDA_CHECK_RETURN (cudaMalloc ((void **) &db, sizeof (int) * N));
39    CUDA_CHECK_RETURN (cudaMalloc ((void **) &dc, sizeof (int) * N));
40
41    // arrays initialization
42    for (i = 0; i < N; i++)
43      {
44        ha[i] = rand () % 10000;
45        hb[i] = rand () % 10000;
46      }
47
48    // data transfer, host -> device
49    CUDA_CHECK_RETURN (cudaMemcpy (da, ha, sizeof (int) * N, ←
             cudaMemcpyHostToDevice ));
50    CUDA_CHECK_RETURN (cudaMemcpy (db, hb, sizeof (int) * N, ←
             cudaMemcpyHostToDevice ));
51
52    int grid = ceil (N * 1.0 / BLOCK_SIZE);
53    vadd <<< grid, BLOCK_SIZE >>> (da, db, dc, N);
54
55    CUDA_CHECK_RETURN (cudaDeviceSynchronize ());
56    // Wait for the GPU launched work to complete
57    CUDA_CHECK_RETURN (cudaGetLastError ());
58
59    // data transfer, device -> host
60    CUDA_CHECK_RETURN (cudaMemcpy (hc, dc, sizeof (int) * N, ←
             cudaMemcpyDeviceToHost ));
61
62    // sanity check
63    for (i = 0; i < N; i++)
64      {
65        if (hc[i]!= ha[i] + hb[i])
66          printf ("Error at index %i: %i VS %i\n", i, hc[i], ha[i] + hb[←
                 i]);
67      }
68
69    // memory release
70    CUDA_CHECK_RETURN (cudaFree ((void *) da));
71    CUDA_CHECK_RETURN (cudaFree ((void *) db));
72    CUDA_CHECK_RETURN (cudaFree ((void *) dc));
73    delete []ha;
74    delete []hb;
75    delete []hc;
76    CUDA_CHECK_RETURN (cudaDeviceReset ());
77
78    return 0;
79  }
```

LISTING 6.5

Adding two 2000-element vectors using CUDA.

One striking feature of this program is the use of the `CUDA_CHECK_RETURN` preprocessor macro, which is generated by the NSight IDE. Similar macros are employed by the CUDA SDK sample programs aiming to catch and report a CUDA call failure as early as possible. Once a CUDA function returns a non-zero value, the program is terminated after printing to the console the line and filename where the error occurred. However, these macros clearly obscure the program structure; for this reason we do not use them in the remaining sample programs of this chapter, although in practice you are advised to employ such measures.

Other key points of the preceding program are:

- The program manages six pointers, three pointing to host memory addresses and three pointing to device memory addresses. By convention and in order to easily identify them, host pointers are prefixed by h and device pointers by d.
- Data are copied from the host to the device prior to calling the kernel (lines 49, 50), and from the device to the host after the kernel completes (line 60). The device memory that holds our data is called *global memory*. The reservation of the required space in global memory is done in lines 37-39.
- Each CUDA thread calculates just a single element of the result matrix (line 23). This is not an advisable design in general, but it clearly illustrates that CUDA threads can be extremely lightweight.
- Each thread calculates its global position/ID in the grid (line 21) and uses it to index the parts of the input that it will operate upon.
- Each core proceeds with the calculation, only if its ID permits (line 22). This check is required when the workload is not evenly distributed between the thread blocks. In this case we have a grid of eight blocks (lines 52, 53), but in the last block of 256 threads we have an "assignment" for only $2000 - 7 * 256 = 208$ of them. An illustration of the grid/block arrangement and how they relate to the input arrays is shown in Figure 6.7.
- The `cudaGetLastError` function in line 57 is used to detect any errors that occurred during the execution of the kernel.

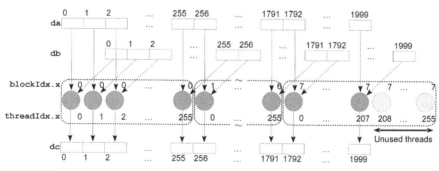

FIGURE 6.7

Illustration of the computation conducted by the vector addition code in Listing 6.5.

- The `cudaDeviceReset` call of line 76 destroys and cleans up all resources associated with the current device in the current process. This should be called only before program termination.
- Lines 63-67 check the results generated by the GPU against the ones calculated by the CPU for the same input. This validation step is required during the development phase in order to detect any anomalies introduced by erroneous algorithms/coding, rounding errors, or by the GPU's failure to conform to the IEEE Standard for Floating-Point Arithmetic (IEEE 754). Fortunately, compute capability 2.x and above devices comply to IEEE 754.[14] It is obvious that such checks should not be carried over to the production version of a software system.

GPUs follow a different paradigm from CPUs in the architectural design of their memory subsystem. In order for CPUs to operate at full speed, they need to have quick access to seemingly random data locations in main memory. Contemporary main memory technology (DDR3 RAM) is relatively slow, thus requiring the incorporation of big on-chip memory caches (where multiple levels of caches are a common feature).

On the other hand, GPUs, as part of their job to filter and transform huge amounts of graphical information, need to process big collections of contiguous data that are to be read at once, without requiring that they are kept on chip for subsequent operations. This means that GPUs benefit from big data buses and they can do with small or no on-chip cache memories. This picture has changed slightly over more recent GPU designs, with on-chip memories getting bigger and incorporating caches in order to more efficiently support generic computation.

The biggest discrepancy between CPU and GPU memory organizations lies in the fact that the GPU memory hierarchy is not transparent to the programmer. GPUs have faster on-chip memory, which occupies a separate address space than the off-chip one. CUDA programs can and should take advantage of this faster memory by moving frequently used data to it. CPU programs can be designed to exploit cache locality (e.g., by restricting the amount of data they work on at one time so that they all fit in the cache), but in the GPU world we have to explicitly manage data movement between the two types of memory.

Data movement between the host and the device can only involve what is identified as global memory. GPUs also employ other types of memory, most of them residing on-chip and in separate address spaces. These, along with their typical performance characteristics, are illustrated in Figure 6.8. Each of the memory types has a unique set of characteristics that make it suitable for particular tasks:

- **Local memory/registers**: Used for holding automatic variables.
- **Shared memory**: Fast on-chip RAM that is used for holding frequently used data. The shared on-chip memory can be used for data exchange between the cores of the same SM.

---

[14]A very useful discussion on the sensitive issue of IEEE 754 compliance is available at https://developer.nvidia.com/sites/default/files/akamai/cuda/files/NVIDIA-CUDA-Floating-Point.pdf.

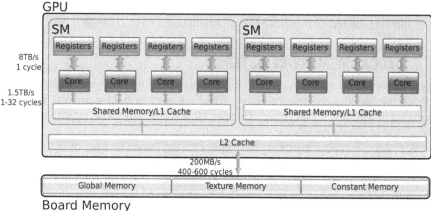

FIGURE 6.8

GPU memory hierarchy. Each bus is labeled with typical bandwidth and latency values.

- **Cache memory**: Cache memory is transparent to the programmer. In recent GPU generations (e.g., Fermi, Kepler), a fixed amount of fast on-chip RAM is divided between first-level cache (L1) and shared memory. The L2 cache is shared among the SMs.
- **Global memory**: Main part of the off-chip memory. High capacity, but relatively slow. The only part of the memory that is accessible to the host via the CUDA library functions.
- **Texture and surface memory**: Part of the off-chip memory. Its contents are handled by special hardware that permits the fast implementation of some filtering operations.
- **Constant memory**: Part of the off-chip memory. As its name suggests, it is read-only. However, it is cached on-chip, which means it can provide a performance boost.

Table 6.5 summarizes the different kinds of memories from the point of view of the lifetime and scope of the data residing in them.

In the following sections we discuss how these different memory types can be effectively incorporated in our kernel designs, with the ultimate goal of extracting

Table 6.5 Summary of the memory hierarchy characteristics

Type	Location	Access	Scope	Lifetime
Register	On-chip	R/W	Thread	Thread
Local	Off-chip	R/W	Thread	Thread
Shared	On-chip	R/W	Block	Block
Global	Off-chip	R/W	Grid	Controlled by host
Constant	Off-chip	R	Grid	Controlled by host
Texture	Off-chip	R	Grid	Controlled by host

more performance from a GPU. The optimization of their use is reserved for Section 6.7, allowing the reader to adsorb the information at a more controlled pace.

6.6.1 LOCAL MEMORY/REGISTERS

As discussed in Section 6.3, each multiprocessor gets a set of registers that are split among the resident executing threads. These are used to hold automatic variables declared in a kernel, speeding up operations that would otherwise require access to the global or shared memories.

A device's compute capability determines the maximum number of registers that can be used per thread. If this number is exceeded, local variables are allocated in the run-time stack, which resides in off-chip memory and it is thus slow to work with. This off-chip memory is frequently called *local memory*, but it is actually the global memory that it is used for this purpose. The "local" specifier just conveys the fact that whatever resides there is only accessible to a particular thread. Local memory locations can be cached by the L1 cache, so performance may not suffer much, but the outcome is application-specific.

The Nvidia compiler will automatically decide which variables will be allocated to registers and which will *spill over* to local memory. The nvcc compiler driver can be instructed to report the outcome of this allocation process with the -Xptxas -v or --ptxas-option=-v switches:

```
$ nvcc —Xptxas —v —arch=sm_20 warpFixMultiway.cu
ptxas info   : 0 bytes gmem, 14 bytes cmem[2]
ptxas info   : Compiling entry function '_Z3foov' for 'sm_20'
ptxas info   : Function properties for _Z3foov
    8 bytes stack frame, 0 bytes spill stores, 0 bytes spill loads
ptxas info   : Used 9 registers, 32 bytes cmem[0], 4 bytes cmem[16]
```

In this example, the generated code uses nine registers, and 0 bytes are spilled over to local memory.

The number of registers used per thread influences the maximum number of threads that can be resident at an SM. For example, assume that a kernel is using 48 registers and it is invoked as blocks of 256 threads, which means each block requires $48 \cdot 256 = 12,288$ registers. If the target GPU for running the kernel is a GTX 580, sporting 32k registers per SM, then each SM could have only two resident blocks (requiring $2 \cdot 12,288 = 24,576$ registers) as three would exceed the available register space ($3 \cdot 12,288 = 36,864 > 32,768$). This in turn means that each SM could have $2 \cdot 256 = 512$ resident threads running, which is well below the maximum limit of 1536 threads per SM. This undermines the GPU's capability to hide the latency of memory operations by running other ready warps.

In fact, Nvidia calls *occupancy* the ratio of resident warps over the maximum possible resident warps:

$$occupancy = \frac{resident\_warps}{maximum\_warps} \tag{6.1}$$

In our example, occupancy is equal to $\frac{2 \cdot \frac{256 \text{ threads}}{32 \text{ threads/warp}}}{48 \text{ warps}} = \frac{16}{48} = 33.3\%$. In general, an occupancy close to 1 is desirable, although other factors also influence the performance that can be "extracted" from a GPU. In order to raise the occupancy in our example, we could (a) reduce the number of required registers by the kernel, or (b) use a GPU with a bigger register file than GTX 580, such as GTX 680, a compute-capability 3.0 device. If the required registers per kernel fell to 40, then we could have three resident blocks (requiring a total of $3 \cdot 40 \cdot 256 = 30{,}720$ registers), resulting in an occupancy of $\frac{3 \cdot 8}{48} = 50\%$ because each block is made up of eight warps. If a GTX 680 were used, the resident blocks would go up to five, resulting in an occupancy of $\frac{5 \cdot 8}{64} = 63\%$.

Nvidia provides an occupancy calculator tool in the form of an Excel spreadsheet that allows the calculation of the occupancy, given the characteristics of the kernel and the target device. This tool provides not only single-point calculations (e.g., what is the current occupancy?), but it also provides guidance about how to modify the kernel and deployment characteristics by plotting the resulting effects on the occupancy.

6.6.2 SHARED MEMORY

Shared memory is a block of fast on-chip RAM that is shared among the cores of an SM. Each SM gets its own block of shared memory, which can be viewed as a user-managed L1 cache. In Fermi and Kepler architectures, shared memory and L1 cache are actually part of the same on-chip memory that can be programmatically partitioned in different ways. Currently, each SM in both architectures sports 64 KB RAM that can be partitioned as 16 KB/48 KB or 48 KB/16 KB to serve these two roles. Compute-Capability 3.x devices also have the option of a 32 KB/32 KB split. Compute-Capability 1.x devices come with only 16 KB shared memory and no L1 cache.

The recently introduced Compute Capability 5.2 Maxwell GPUs have 96KB of shared memory per SM, but each thread block can reserve up to 48KB only. The twist is that each of two concurrently running blocks could have its own dedicated 48KB chunk of shared memory.

A programmer can specify the *preferred* device-wide arrangement by calling the `cudaDeviceSetCacheConfig` function. A *preferred* kernel-specific arrangement can be also set with the `cudaFuncSetCacheConfig` function. Both of these functions set only a preference. The CUDA run-time will ultimately decide the appropriate configuration, given the shared memory requirements of a kernel.

Shared memory can be used in the following capacities:

- As a holding place for very frequently used data that would otherwise require global memory access
- As a fast *mirror* of data that reside in global memory, if they are to be accessed multiple times
- As a fast way for cores within an SM, to share data

So, how can we specify that the holding place of some data will be the shared memory of the SM and not the global memory of the device?

The answer is, via the __shared__ specifier. Shared memory can be statically or dynamically allocated. *Static allocation* can take place if the size of the required arrays is known at compile time. **Dynamic allocation** is needed if shared memory requirements can be only calculated at run-time, i.e., upon kernel invocation. To facilitate this mode of operation, the execution configuration has an alternative syntax, with a third parameter holding the size in bytes of the shared memory to be reserved.

For example, let's consider the problem of calculating the histogram of a collection of integers, i.e., counting the number of elements that belong to each one of a set of disjoint categories or bins/buckets. The histogram is a popular tool in image processing, so we will proceed to develop our example in this context.

If we were to calculate the histogram of a grayscale image consisting of N pixels, each taking up one byte in an array (in), the CPU code for performing this task could be in the form of the function shown in Listing 6.6.

```
1  // File: histogram/histogram.cu
2  . . .
3  void CPU_histogram (unsigned char *in, int N, int *h, int bins)
4  {
5    int i;
6    // initialize histogram counts
7    for (i = 0; i < bins; i++)
8      h[i] = 0;
9
10   // accummulate counts
11   for (i = 0; i < N; i++)
12     h[in[i]]++;
13 }
```

LISTING 6.6

CPU histogram calculation.

The bins-sized array h holds the result of the calculation. Obviously, the one byte per pixel restricts the number of categories: *bins* $\leq$ 256.

A multithreaded solution to this problem would require the partitioning of the image data into disjoint sets, the calculation of partial histograms by each thread, and finally, the consolidation of the partial histograms into the complete one.

The CUDA solution described here, follows the same guidelines, more or less, but with some key differences that go beyond the explicit data movement between the host and device memories:

- The data partitioning is *implicit*. All the spawned CUDA threads have access to all the image data but go through them using a different starting point and an appropriate stride that makes it possible to cover all the data while coalescing memory accesses (more on this topic in Section 6.7). This difference is highlighted in Figure 6.9.
- To speed up the update of the local counts, a "local" array is set up in shared memory. Because multiple threads may access its locations at any time, atomic addition operations have to be used for modifying its contents.

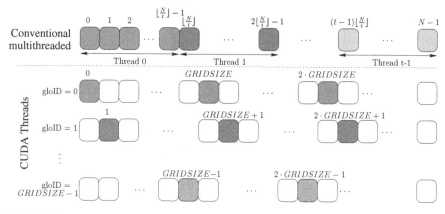

FIGURE 6.9

An illustrated comparison between the input data access patterns of a multithreaded CPU solution with *t* threads for histogram calculation and a CUDA solution. The symbols used here reference the variables of Listing 6.7.

- Because threads execute in blocks and each block executes warp by warp, explicit synchronization of the threads must take place between the discrete phases of the kernel, e.g., between initializing the shared-memory histogram array and starting to calculate the histogram, and so on.
- The global histogram array, i.e., the one that holds the final result, is also updated concurrently by multiple threads. Atomic addition operations have to be employed so that the results stay consistent.

If the number of bins are known *a priori*, we can allocate a fixed amount of local memory per block, as shown in Listing 6.7. The GPU_histogram_static kernel assumes that its execution configuration calls for a 1D grid of 1D blocks.

```
14   // File: histogram/histogram.cu
15   . . .
16   static const int BINS = 256;
17
18   __global__ void GPU_histogram_static (int *in, int N, int *h)
19   {
20     int gloID = blockIdx.x * blockDim.x + threadIdx.x;
21     int locID = threadIdx.x;
22     int GRIDSIZE = gridDim.x * blockDim.x;  // total number of threads
23     __shared__ int localH[BINS];            // shared allocation
24     int i;
25
26     // initialize the local, shared-memory bins
27     for (i = locID; i < BINS; i += blockDim.x)
28       localH[i] = 0;
29
30     // wait for all warps to complete the previous step
```

```
31      __syncthreads ();
32
33      // start processing the image data
34      for (i = gloID; i < N; i += GRIDSIZE)
35        {
36          int temp = in[i];
37          atomicAdd (localH + (temp & 0xFF), 1);
38          atomicAdd (localH + ((temp >> 8) & 0xFF), 1);
39          atomicAdd (localH + ((temp >> 16) & 0xFF), 1);
40          atomicAdd (localH + ((temp >> 24) & 0xFF), 1);
41        }
42
43      // wait for all warps to complete the local calculations, before ↵
            updating the global counts
44      __syncthreads ();
45
46      // use atomic operations to add the local findings to the global ↵
            memory bins
47      for (i = locID; i < BINS; i += blockDim.x)
48        atomicAdd (h + i, localH[i]);
49    }
```

LISTING 6.7

CUDA histogram calculation kernel using a static shared memory allocation.

The array declared as __shared__ in line 23 is shared between all the threads of a block. Although it is an automatic variable, it is not thread-specific. As such, all the threads in the block contribute to its initialization with the loop of lines 27, 28. Other key observations about the structure of GPU_histogram_static are:

- Each thread calculates its position in the block it belongs to (locID) and its position in the grid (gloID). The former is used as a starting point in the initialization of the localH array (line 27) and the updating of the h array in global memory (line 47). The gloID variable is used as a starting point in scanning the image data (line 34). The total number of threads (GRIDSIZE) is used as a stride.
- The image data are passed as individual pixels to the CPU_histogram function but as groups of four in GPU_histogram_static (in is passed as an array of int). The goal is to speed up or optimize the assessing of data from global memory.[15] Having lines 37-40 as the equivalent of the single statement in line 12 is effectively a partial unrolling of the loop. The bitwise shifts and ANDs of these lines isolate the individual pixel values, which are subsequently used as offsets to the base of the localH array.
- The peculiarities of CUDA's execution model mean that (a) the completion of phases must be followed by explicit synchronization (lines 31 and 44) to ensure

---

[15]The same could be done in the CPU code of Listing 6.6, but it was left on purpose in the simplest, most unoptimized form possible.

the validity of data, and (b) shared locations must be *atomically updated* (lines 37-40 and 48) to ensure *linearizability*.

The __syncthreads() function can be called inside a kernel to act as a barrier for all the threads in a *block*. The cudaDeviceSynchronize(), used in a previous section, is called by the host to wait for a *grid* of threads to complete.

The atomicAdd is an overloaded function that belongs to a set of atomic operations supported mostly by devices of compute capability 2.x and above. The int version shown here has analogous versions for unsigned int, long long int, and float operands:

```
int atomicAdd(int* address, // Location to modify
              int val);      // Value to add
```

If the number of categories is not known, the shared memory has to be allocated by the CUDA run-time based on the execution configuration parameters, as shown in Listing 6.8.

```
50  // File : histogram/histogram.cu
51  . . .
52  __global__ void GPU_histogram_dynamic (int *in, int N, int *h, int ↩
        bins)
53  {
54    int gloID = blockIdx.x * blockDim.x + threadIdx.x;
55    int locID = threadIdx.x;
56    extern __shared__ int localH[];
57    int GRIDSIZE = gridDim.x * blockDim.x;
58    int i;
59
60    // initialize the local bins
61    for (i = locID; i < bins; i += blockDim.x)
62      localH[i] = 0;
63
64    // wait for all warps to complete the previous step
65    __syncthreads ();
66
67    //start processing the image data
68    for (i = gloID; i < N; i += GRIDSIZE)
69      {
70        int temp = in[i];
71        atomicAdd (localH + (temp & 0xFF), 1);
72        atomicAdd (localH + ((temp >> 8) & 0xFF), 1);
73        atomicAdd (localH + ((temp >> 16) & 0xFF), 1);
74        atomicAdd (localH + ((temp >> 24) & 0xFF), 1);
75      }
76
77    // wait for all warps to complete the local calculations, before ↩
          updating the global counts
78    __syncthreads ();
79
80    // use atomic operations to add the local findings to the global ↩
          memory bins
```

```
81    for (i = locID; i < bins; i += blockDim.x)
82      atomicAdd (h + i, localH[i]);
83  }
```

LISTING 6.8

CUDA histogram calculation kernel, using **dynamic** shared memory allocation.

The only significant difference of kernel `GPU_histogram_dynamic` from `GPU_histogram_static` lies in the use of the `extern` keyword in line 56. The reservation of shared memory and the initialization of the `localH` pointer take place by the CUDA run-time, when the kernel is invoked in line 119. The change in the kernel signature was necessitated by the need to also pass the number of bins, which are in turn calculated (line 97) after an image is read (line 88):

```
84   // File: histogram/histogram.cu
85   . . .
86   int main (int argc, char **argv)
87   {
88     PGMImage inImg (argv[1]);
89
90     int *d_in, *h_in;
91     int *d_hist, *h_hist, *cpu_hist;
92     int i, N, bins;
93
94     h_in = (int *) inImg.pixels;
95     N = ceil ((inImg.x_dim * inImg.y_dim) / 4.0);
96
97     bins = inImg.num_colors + 1;
98     h_hist = (int *) malloc (bins * sizeof (int));
99     cpu_hist = (int *) malloc (bins * sizeof (int));
100
101    // CPU calculation used for testing
102    CPU_histogram (inImg.pixels, inImg.x_dim * inImg.y_dim, cpu_hist, ↩
         bins);
103
104    cudaMalloc ((void **) &d_in, sizeof (int) * N);
105    cudaMalloc ((void **) &d_hist, sizeof (int) * bins);
106    cudaMemcpy (d_in, h_in, sizeof (int) * N, cudaMemcpyHostToDevice);
107    cudaMemset (d_hist, 0, bins * sizeof (int));
108
109    GPU_histogram_static <<< 16, 256 >>> (d_in, N, d_hist);
110    cudaDeviceSynchronize ();      // Wait for the GPU launched work to ↩
         complete
111
112    cudaMemcpy (h_hist, d_hist, sizeof (int) * bins, ↩
         cudaMemcpyDeviceToHost);
113
114    for (i = 0; i < BINS; i++)
115      if (cpu_hist[i]!= h_hist[i])
116        printf ("Calculation mismatch (static) at: %i\n", i);
117
118    cudaMemset (d_hist, 0, bins * sizeof (int));
```

```
119    GPU_histogram_dynamic <<< 16, 256, bins * sizeof (int) >>> (d_in, N,↵
           d_hist, bins);
120    cudaDeviceSynchronize ();        // Wait for the GPU launched work to ↵
           complete
121
122    cudaMemcpy (h_hist, d_hist, sizeof (int) * bins, ↵
           cudaMemcpyDeviceToHost);
123
124    for (i = 0; i < BINS; i++)
125      if (cpu_hist[i]!= h_hist[i])
126        printf ("Calculation mismatch (dynamic) at: %i\n", i);
127
128    cudaFree ((void *) d_in);
129    cudaFree ((void *) d_hist);
130    free (h_hist);
131    free (cpu_hist);
132    cudaDeviceReset ();
133
134    return 0;
135  }
```

LISTING 6.9

main() function for the memory management and launch of the kernels in Listings 6.7 and 6.8.

The PGMImage class used in this code is available in the common directory, and it facilitates access to Portable Gray Map (PGM) formatted images. The class constructor allows the reading of a PGM image from a file, and public data members allow access to the image data, such as the dimensions (x_dim, y_dim), the number of gray values allowed (num_colors), and the actual pixels (*pixels).

The main function is responsible for the allocation of the host and device arrays, the movement of data between the host and device memories, and the initialization of the device histogram array (lines 107 and 118) via the cudaMemset function, which is modeled after the standard C library function memset:

```
cudaError_t cudaMemset (void *devPtr, // pointer to device memory
                        int value,    // value to set each byte
                        size_t count) // number of bytes
```

A question that arises is, *what if a kernel needs to dynamically allocate multiple arrays in shared memory?* The solution to this problem is awkward: The size of all the arrays need to be passed as a parameter to the execution configuration. Subsequently, this lump of shared memory needs to be divided manually between the arrays that use it, once the kernel starts executing.

As an example, let's consider a kernel that needs to set up up three dynamically allocated arrays in shared memory: int a[K], double b[L], and unsigned char c[M]. Then, the code snippet shown in Listing 6.10 would suffice.

```
1    __global__ void foo(int *arraySizes)
2    {
3        int K,L,M;
```

```
4      extern __shared__ int a[];
5      double *b;
6      unsigned int *c;
7
8      K = arraySizes[0];
9      L = arraySizes[1];
10     M = arraySizes[2];
11
12     b = (double *)(&a[K]);
13     c = (unsigned int *)(&b[L]);
14     . . .
15   }
16
17   int main (void)
18   {
19     int K=100, L=20, M=15;
20     int ha[3]={K,L,M};
21     int *da;
22
23     cudaMalloc ((void **) &da, sizeof (int) * 3);
24     cudaMemcpy(da, ha, sizeof (int) * 3, cudaMemcpyHostToDevice);
25     foo<<< 1, 256, K*sizeof(int) + L*sizeof(double) + L*sizeof(unsigned ↩
           int) >>>(da);
26     . . .
27   }
```

LISTING 6.10

An example of dynamically setting up multiple shared memory arrays.

The array sizes could be passed as parameters to the kernel (as is done here), or they could be calculated inside the kernel, making the passing of the array-Sizes parameter redundant. In both cases, the total of required shared memory must be reserved upon invoking the kernel (line 25 above). The array sizes can then be used inside the kernel to infer the beginning of each array (lines 12, 13). As an alternative, the arraySizes parameter could hold the starting offset in bytes of each array, allowing appropriate padding to be incorporated for aligned memory accesses. A third alternative would be to pass K, L, and M as individual parameters.

A feature of shared memory that is not utilized by our histogram example is its division into *banks*. The division is driven by the fact that shared memory has to be accessed simultaneously by multiple cores. As long as the threads in a warp access a different bank, access is instantaneous. If there is a conflict or collision, i.e., there is more than one thread trying to access the same bank, access will be serialized, forcing threads to stall. However, unlike access to global memory, access to shared memory does not cause the execution of another ready warp in order to hide the delay. Hence, shared memory bank collisions cause an SM to stall. Compute-capability 2.0 devices and above have 32 banks, whereas all earlier devices have 16 banks. Figure 6.10 illustrates the bank concept.

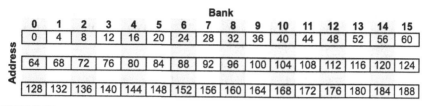

FIGURE 6.10

An illustration of how shared memory is divided into banks.

A modification of our histogram example that helps avoid bank conflicts is discussed in Section 6.7.3.

6.6.3 CONSTANT MEMORY

Constant memory may sound like a variation of ROM, but in reality it is just a portion of the off-chip device memory that is dedicated to holding constant data. Current specifications restrict constant memory to 64 KB. Constant memory offers two important characteristics: first, it is cached; second, it supports broadcasting a single value to all the threads of a warp. Nvidia GPUs provide 8 KB of cache memory per multiprocessor for the contents of the constant memory. These characteristics make constant memory a good candidate for placing frequently reused data that are not to be modified, saving in the process the precious little shared memory that is available.

Constant memory also serves to hold the function parameters that are passed to a kernel for devices of compute-capability 2.0 and above. Their total size is limited to 4 KB. For devices of compute-capability 1.x, function parameters are passed via shared memory and are limited to 256 bytes.

A variable can be allocated in constant memory via the __constant__ specifier.[16] For example:

```
__constant__ int ITERLIMIT=1000;
```

Since the introduction of the Fermi architecture, all Nvidia GPU offerings sport an L2 cache that handles all memory transactions, not just the ones involving constant memory. This makes the use of constant memory specifically, a less attractive prospect on newer machines. However, on legacy architectures (compute-capability 1.x devices) it is still a worthwhile consideration.

The only serious restriction involves the 64 KB size limit. If the data to be processed exceed this limit, one solution to making them available via the constant memory is to break them into "tiles," or blocks that satisfy the limit, and process

---

[16] ⊛ **Pitfall:** Variables that are allocated in constant memory should not be passed by reference from the host as parameters to a kernel. The compiler will not complain, but the kernel will fail when trying to access the variable.

them one after the other. The host has the capability to change the contents of constant memory (after all, it is only "viewed" as constant from the device) via the cudaMemcpyToSymbol template function:

```
template<class T > cudaError_t cudaMemcpyToSymbol (
        const T & symbol, // destination of copying operation
        const void *src,   // Source address
        size_t count,      // Number of bytes to copy
        size_t offset = 0,// Offset from start of symbol
        enum cudaMemcpyKind kind = cudaMemcpyHostToDevice );
```

As an example for the use of constant memory, let's explore the implementation of the *Hough transform*. The Hough transform is an image feature extraction technique that allows the detection of straight lines in an image. More elaborate shapes, both ones with analytical and ones with nonanalytical representations, can be also detected with the use of the generalized Hough transform proposed in 1981 by D. H. Ballard [6]. Our example focuses on the simple line-detecting version.

The linear Hough transform operates on black-and-white images that are typically the product of an edge-detection filter that helps eliminate from further consideration pixels that are not part of a line. The Hough transform is essentially a pixel voting system whereby each possible line in a discrete space is "voted for" by the pixels that can potentially belong to it. The lines that get the most votes are the ones that are detected. The theory behind it is explained here.

The (x, y) Cartesian coordinates of a point belonging to a straight line are bound by the following equation:

$$y = slope \cdot x + intercept$$

If r is the distance of the line from the origin and θ is the angle formed as illustrated in Figure 6.11, then (x, y) are connected via:

$$y = -\frac{cos(\theta)}{sin(\theta)}x + \frac{r}{sin(\theta)}$$

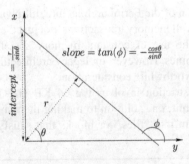

FIGURE 6.11

Describing a line in the 2D plane.

which can in turn be written as follows:

$$r = x \cdot cos(\theta) + y \cdot sin(\theta) \qquad (6.2)$$

During the application of the Hough transform, each lit pixel (x, y) of the examined image could be a part of a whole family of lines, as shown in Figure 6.12. By iterating over the possible angles θ, we can calculate the corresponding $r(\theta)$ via Equation 6.2. To make the calculation tractable, the possible angles are taken from a limited set (e.g., from 0 to 180 in one-degree increments). The final piece of the puzzle is the accumulator, a matrix of counters indexed by θ and $r(\theta)$, which are incremented when a pixel that "fits" the corresponding line is examined.

Obviously, a similar "quantization" process is applied for the calculated distances $r(\theta)$ so that the accumulator matrix can be accessed. The number of bins to be used for r, is dictated by the desired accuracy, but in our case it is actually restricted by the size of available shared memory, since maintaining a local accumulator per thread block would benefit the speed of the calculation.

A simple CPU implementation of the linear Hough transform is shown in Listing 6.11. A key observation for understanding the implementation(s) discussed in this section is that the axes origin is assumed to be on the image center, making the distance of the lines examined ranging between $[-rMax, rMax]$ (see Figure 6.12).

```
1   // File: hough/hough.cu
2   . . .
3   const int degreeInc = 2;
4   const int degreeBins = 90;
```

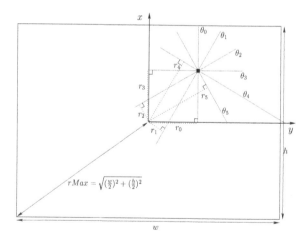

FIGURE 6.12

An example of six (θ_i, r_i) pairs of line parameters that would be associated with the pixel shown. The maximum possible line distance *rMax* for a *w* x *h* image is also shown, assuming the axes origin is on the image center.

```
5    const int rBins = 100;
6    const float radInc = degreeInc * M_PI / 180;
7    // *********************************************************************
8    void CPU_HoughTran (unsigned char *pic, int w, int h, int **acc)
9    {
10     float rMax = sqrt (1.0 * w * w + 1.0 * h * h) / 2;
11     *acc = new int[rBins * 180 / degreeInc];
12     memset (*acc, 0, sizeof (int) * rBins * 180 / degreeInc);
13     int xCent = w / 2;
14     int yCent = h / 2;
15     float rScale = 2 * rMax / rBins;
16
17     for (int i = 0; i < w; i++)
18       for (int j = 0; j < h; j++)
19         {
20           int idx = j * w + i;
21           if (pic[idx] > 0)
22             {
23               int xCoord = i - xCent;
24               int yCoord = yCent - j;   // y-coord has to be reversed
25               float theta = 0;          // actual angle
26               for (int tIdx = 0; tIdx < degreeBins; tIdx++)
27                 {
28                   float r = xCoord * cos (theta) + yCoord * sin (theta);
29                   int rIdx = (r + rMax) / rScale;
30                   (*acc)[rIdx * degreeBins + tIdx]++;
31                   theta += radInc;
32                 }
33             }
34         }
35   }
```

LISTING 6.11

A simple CPU implementation of the linear Hough transform.

As discussed previously, the two nested loops of lines 17 and 18 iterate over all the pixels of the examined image and update the accumulator matrix for any pixel found to be lit (condition of line 21). The (i, j) indices used to access a pixel's state are converted to appropriate (xCoord, yCoord) coordinates by lines 23 and 24 before the loop of lines 26-33 calculates and "quantizes" the (θ, r) values of the possible lines to produce the (tIdx, rIdx) indices for updating the accumulator matrix (line 30). Line 29 quantizes r, whereas θ escapes the need for a conversion by maintaining a separate variable for tIdx.

The expression for converting $r(\theta)$ into rIdx (line 29) incorporates an offset (+ rMax, as r could be negative and rIdx has to start from zero) and a scaling operation (divided by the full extent of the range 2 *rMax* and multiplied by rBins) so that the [−*rMax*, *rMax*] range is mapped to [0, *rBins*).

The GPU implementation shown in Listing 6.12 uses two arrays (d_Cos and d_Sin) allocated in constant memory for holding the precomputed values of the sine and cosine functions. Because only a small subset of angles are tested (degreeBins of them $\in [0, 180°]$ in increments of degreeInc), there is no need to calculate the cosine and sine terms of line 28 multiple times. The host calculates these values (lines 102-110) and transfers the results in the constant memory arrays (lines 116 and 117) via two cudaMemcpyToSymbol calls.

This approach utilizes both characteristics of constant memory, i.e., values are cached and broadcasted.

```
36   // File: hough/hough.cu
37   . . .
38   __constant__ float d_Cos[degreeBins];
39   __constant__ float d_Sin[degreeBins];
40
41   //*********************************************************************
42   // GPU kernel. One thread per image pixel is spawned.
43   // The accummulator memory needs to be allocated by the host in global↩
         memory
44   __global__ void GPU_HoughTran (unsigned char *pic, int w, int h, int *↩
         acc, float rMax, float rScale)
45   {
46     int i;
47     int gloID = blockIdx.x * blockDim.x + threadIdx.x;
48     if (gloID > w * h) return;        // in case of extra threads
49
50     int locID = threadIdx.x;
51     int xCent = w / 2;
52     int yCent = h / 2;
53
54     int xCoord = gloID % w - xCent;
55     int yCoord = yCent - gloID / w;
56
57     __shared__ int localAcc[degreeBins * rBins];  // each block is using↩
           a shared memory, local accummulator
58
59     // initialize the local, shared-memory accummulator matrix
60     for (i = locID; i < degreeBins * rBins; i += blockDim.x)
61       localAcc[i] = 0;
62
63     // wait for all warps to complete the previous step
64     __syncthreads ();
65
66
67     if (pic[gloID] > 0)
68       {
69         for (int tIdx = 0; tIdx < degreeBins; tIdx++)
70           {
71             float r = xCoord * d_Cos[tIdx] + yCoord * d_Sin[tIdx];
72             int rIdx = (r + rMax) / rScale;
73             atomicAdd (localAcc + (rIdx * degreeBins + tIdx), 1);
74           }
75       }
```

```
76
77    // wait for all warps to complete the local calculations, before ←↩
          updating the global counts
78    __syncthreads ();
79
80    // use atomic operations to add the local findings to the global ←↩
          memory accummulator
81    for (i = locID; i < degreeBins * rBins; i += blockDim.x)
82      atomicAdd (acc + i, localAcc[i]);
83  }
84
85
86  // ****************************************************************
87  int main (int argc, char **argv)
88  {
89    int i;
90
91    PGMImage inImg (argv[1]);
92
93    int *cpuht;
94    int w = inImg.x_dim;
95    int h = inImg.y_dim;
96
97    // CPU calculation
98    CPU_HoughTran (inImg.pixels, w, h, &cpuht);
99
100
101   // compute values to be stored in device constant memory
102   float *pcCos = (float *) malloc (sizeof (float) * degreeBins);
103   float *pcSin = (float *) malloc (sizeof (float) * degreeBins);
104   float rad = 0;
105   for (i = 0; i < degreeBins; i++)
106     {
107       pcCos[i] = cos (rad);
108       pcSin[i] = sin (rad);
109       rad += radInc;
110     }
111
112   float rMax = sqrt (1.0 * w * w + 1.0 * h * h) / 2;
113   float rScale = 2 * rMax / rBins;
114
115   // copy precomputed values to constant memory
116   cudaMemcpyToSymbol (d_Cos, pcCos, sizeof (float) * degreeBins);
117   cudaMemcpyToSymbol (d_Sin, pcSin, sizeof (float) * degreeBins);
118
119   // setup and copy data from host to device
120   unsigned char *d_in, *h_in;
121   int *d_hough, *h_hough;
122
123   h_in = inImg.pixels;
124
125   h_hough = (int *) malloc (degreeBins * rBins * sizeof (int));
```

```
126
127    cudaMalloc ((void **) &d_in, sizeof (unsigned char) * w * h);
128    cudaMalloc ((void **) &d_hough, sizeof (int) * degreeBins * rBins);
129    cudaMemcpy (d_in, h_in, sizeof (unsigned char) * w * h, ↵
               cudaMemcpyHostToDevice);
130    cudaMemset (d_hough, 0, sizeof (int) * degreeBins * rBins);
131
132    // execution configuration uses a 1-D grid of 1-D blocks, each made ↵
               of 256 threads
133    int blockNum = ceil (w * h / 256);
134    GPU_HoughTran <<< blockNum, 256 >>> (d_in, w, h, d_hough, rMax, ↵
               rScale);
135
136    cudaDeviceSynchronize ();      // Wait for the GPU launched work to ↵
               complete
137
138    // get results from device
139    cudaMemcpy (h_hough, d_hough, sizeof (int) * degreeBins * rBins, ↵
               cudaMemcpyDeviceToHost);
140
141    // compare CPU and GPU results
142    for (i = 0; i < degreeBins * rBins; i++)
143      {
144        if (cpuht[i]!= h_hough[i])
145          printf ("Calculation mismatch at: %i %i %i\n", i, cpuht[i], ↵
                 h_hough[i]);
146      }
147      . . .
148    }
```

LISTING 6.12

A GPU implementation of the linear Hough transform that uses constant memory.

The key points of Listing 6.12 are:

- The GPU_HoughTran kernel essentially encompasses the logic of the body of the two nested for loops of lines 17-34. It is operating on a single pixel that is indexed by the global ID (gloID) of each thread running it. A minimum of $w \times h$ threads are required. Because each block is set to 256 threads (lines 133 and 134), the size of the grid becomes $\lceil \frac{w \cdot h}{256} \rceil$ blocks. In the case that $w \cdot h$ is not a multiple of 256, extra threads without an assigned work item will be spawned; hence the need for the check of line 48.
- Each block of threads uses a shared memory accumulator matrix (declared in line 57) that is initialized by the loop of lines 60 and 61 in a staggered way, as described in detail in Section 6.7.3.
- The local accumulator matrix is added to the global one at the end of each block's execution (lines 81-82).
- The GPU-generated results are compared against the CPU ones with the loop of lines 142-146. This is a recommended approach during the development phases

of a CUDA program. Even if program correctness is not an issue (if only that were true!), hardware and software architectural differences between CPU and GPU can lead to discrepancies in the results. Detecting them and understanding their source is a very important step in producing reliable GPU software.

It should be stressed that it is unclear by how much our CUDA program could accelerate the Hough transform calculation; it all depends on the input data. A mostly empty image will result in the majority of threads exiting early. Our example primarily serves the purpose of showing how constant memory can be set up and utilized.

6.6.4 TEXTURE AND SURFACE MEMORY

Texture memory is accessed though two sets of special functions:

- **Texture Reference API** for compute-capability 1.x and 2.x devices
- **Texture Object API** for compute-capability 3.x devices

When a kernel calls one of these functions to read texture memory, it performs a *texture fetch*. A texture fetch is no ordinary memory read, though; it can perform filtering and/or translation of values by treating the texture residing in memory as the sampled/discrete representation of a 1D, 2D, or 3D function.

These special access functions are implemented in hardware, making them very fast and efficient to use. However, there are both size and representation limitations on the textures that can be stored in texture memory, making the use of texture memory rather limited in the GPGPU domain. For this reason we will not explore the topic further in this chapter.

6.7 OPTIMIZATION TECHNIQUES

CUDA is not known for its easy learning curve. However, it is not the language itself nor the thoroughly documented toolkit functions that make CUDA a challenge. This comes from the need to accommodate specific hardware traits in your programs if you are to extract the performance of which a GPU is capable. In the following paragraphs we discuss these essential techniques that span kernel structure and execution configuration design to asynchronous execution of device commands.

6.7.1 BLOCK AND GRID DESIGN

The optimization of the grid and block design depends on both the data layout of the problem and the hardware capabilities of the target device. In that regard, it is advisable to design an algorithm that adapts to the available CUDA hardware and dynamically deploys the threads as required to minimize the total execution time.

One of the aspects of the execution minimization problem is that the available computing hardware should be "occupied/busy" as much as possible. Two things must happen:

1. Enough work should be *assigned* to the CUDA cores (deployment/execution configuration phase).
2. The assigned work should allow *execution* with the minimum amount of stalling due to resource contention or slow memory access (execution phase).

Block and grid designs influence the first aspect; the second one is a multifaceted aspect of CUDA program design that is addressed in the sections that follow. In this section we discuss the sizes of the grid and block without regard to the dimensions used, i.e., as if they are both one dimensional. The reason is that the number of dimensions has no effect on the execution efficiency. The total number of threads per block and the total number of blocks in the grid do.

The first step in designing a host front-end function that adjusts the execution configuration to the capabilities of the target device is the discovery of said capabilities and primarily the number of available SMs. Central to querying the capabilities of a device is the cudaDeviceProp structure, which is populated by a call to the cudaGetDeviceProperties() function[17]:

```
cudaError_t cudaGetDeviceProperties(
            struct cudaDeviceProp *prop, // Pointer to structure for ↩
                storing info
            int device);                 // Integer identifying the ↩
                device to be querried. For systems with one GPU, 0 can↩
                be used.
```

Here is a small subset of the fields included in the cudaDeviceProp structure (the field names are self-explanatory):

```
struct cudaDeviceProp{
    char name[256]; // A string identifying the device
    int major;        // Compute capability major number
    int minor;        // Compute capability minor number
    int maxGridSize [3];
    int maxThreadsDim [3];
    int maxThreadsPerBlock;
    int maxThreadsPerMultiProcessor;
    int multiProcessorCount;
    int regsPerBlock; // Number of registers per block
    size_t sharedMemPerBlock;
    size_t totalGlobalMem;
    int warpSize;
    . . .
};
```

---

[17] The $CUDA/samples/1_Utilities/deviceQuery sample project provides a very good starting point for anyone trying to query the capabilities of a device.

The following is a generic approach that could be used for listing the names of the GPUs in a system equipped with multiple devices:

```
int deviceCount = 0;
cudaGetDeviceCount(&deviceCount);
if(deviceCount == 0)
    printf("No CUDA compatible GPU exists .\n");
else
{
    cudaDeviceProp pr;
    for(int i=0;i<deviceCount;i++)
    {
        cudaGetDeviceProperties(&pr, i);
        printf("Dev #%i is %s\n", i, pr.name);
    }
}
```

The `multiProcessorCount` field can be used to derive the minimum number of blocks a grid should be made of, if it is to use all the SMs in a GPU. Obviously we need at least as many blocks as the number of SMs. However, limiting this number to exactly the number of SMs may not be possible, depending on how many resources (e.g., registers and shared memory) each block will need to consume. A sound idea would be to have the block number be a multiple of the SMs, possibly giving a better balance of computational work assignments.

If the number of blocks cannot reach the number of SMs, another kernel could possibly run on the remaining SMs by scheduling it on a separate stream (see Section 6.7.7).

One of the myths surrounding kernel deployment optimization is that the best approach is the one maximizing occupancy (defined in Equation 6.1). This probably came to be, due to the importance Nvidia documentation gave to said subject. However, it has been proven that lower occupancy can lead to better performance [45].

A key point here is that there are cases in which lower occupancy and a smaller number of threads per block can provide better performance if the kernel is properly designed to take advantage of the more available resources per thread. Summarizing the general guidelines that one should follow:

- Do more parallel work per thread. Ideally, this work should be composed of items that can be executed concurrently by the warp schedulers.
- Use more registers per thread to avoid access to shared memory. This may mean that the number of threads has to be smaller than suggested here (e.g., 64).
- Threads per block should be a multiple of warp size to avoid wasting computing resources on underpopulated warps. An initial choice of between 128 and 256 threads is a good one for experimentation.
- The grid should be big enough to provide multiple (e.g., three or four) blocks per SM.

- Use big enough blocks to take advantage of multiple warp schedulers. Devices of Compute Capability 2.0 or newer, can run multiple warps at the same time, courtesy of having multiple warp schedulers per SM. In Compute Capability 3.0, 3.5 and 5.0 devices, we have four schedulers, which means we should have at least $4 \cdot$ *warpSize*-sized blocks.

The number of threads per block can be derived from the `warpSize`, the `maxThreadsPerBlock`, and the register and shared memory demands per thread of the kernel, given the `sharedMemPerBlock` and `regsPerBlock` fields of the `cudaDeviceProp` structure.

The following formula that incorporates this list of guidelines can be used to calculate an initial estimate for the the number of threads per block:

$$threadsPerBlock = min \begin{pmatrix} numWarpSchedulers \cdot warpSize, \\ \dfrac{regsPerBlock}{registersPerThread}, \\ \dfrac{sharedMem}{sharedPerThread}, \\ maxThreadsPerSM \end{pmatrix} \tag{6.3}$$

where the first line corresponds to our above suggestion of *numWarpSchedulers $\cdot$ warpSize* per block, the second line considers register restrictions, and the third line incorporates the limit imposed by shared memory consumption. The fourth line is there for completeness, as the first line should never exceed the target device's hardware limitation on the block size. We are assuming that these are given or supplied:

- `numberOfThreads`: The total number of threads that need to be executed.
- `sharedPerThread`: The total amount of shared memory needed by each thread (in bytes).
- `registersPerThread`: The total number of registers per thread needed. The output of `nvcc -Xptxas -v` can be used to get this information.

and the rest are retrieved by calling `cudaDeviceProperties()` on the target device.

The `threadsPerBlock` can be turned into a multiple of the `warpSize` via this simple calculation:

$$threadsPerBlock = warpSize \cdot \left\lceil \frac{threadsPerBlock}{warpSize} \right\rceil \tag{6.4}$$

Given the *threadsPerBlock*, we can then calculate the size of the grid:

$$totalBlocks = \left\lceil \frac{numberOfThreads}{threadsPerBlock} \right\rceil \tag{6.5}$$

Listing 6.13 shows a function that implements Equations 6.3-6.5 in an attempt to automate the process of execution configuration calculation. However, mixed results can be expected. The reason is that the optimum execution configuration is intimately interwoven with the structure of the kernel. Small changes to one can profoundly affect the other, leaving experimentation as the ultimate approach for optimization.

```
1   // File: executionConfHeur.cu
2   #define min(a,b) ((a<b) ? a: b)
3   #define max(a,b) ((a>b) ? a: b)
4   //------------------------------------------------------------
5   // In: numberOfThreads , registersPerThread , sharedPerThread
6   // Out: bestThreadsPerBlock , bestTotalBlocks
7   void calcExecConf (int numberOfThreads, int registersPerThread, int ←
        sharedPerThread, int &bestThreadsPerBlock, int &bestTotalBlocks)
8   {
9     cudaDeviceProp pr;
10    cudaGetDeviceProperties (&pr, 0);        // replace 0 with appropriate ←
          ID in case of a multi−GPU system
11
12    int maxRegs = pr.regsPerBlock;
13    int SM = pr.multiProcessorCount;
14    int warp = pr.warpSize;
15    int sharedMem = pr.sharedMemPerBlock;
16    int maxThreadsPerSM = pr.maxThreadsPerMultiProcessor;
17    int totalBlocks;
18    float imbalance, bestimbalance;
19    int threadsPerBlock;
20
21    int numWarpSchedulers;
22    switch (pr.major)
23      {
24      case 1:
25        numWarpSchedulers = 1;
26        break;
27      case 2:
28        numWarpSchedulers = 2;
29        break;
30      default:
31        numWarpSchedulers = 4;
32        break;
33      }
34
35    bestimbalance = SM;
36
37    // initially calculate the maximum possible threads per block. ←
          Incorporate limits imposed by:
38    // 1) SM hardware
39    threadsPerBlock = maxThreadsPerSM;
40    // 2) registers
41    threadsPerBlock = min(threadsPerBlock, maxRegs /registersPerThread);
42    // 3) shared memory size
43    threadsPerBlock = min(threadsPerBlock, sharedMem /sharedPerThread);
```

```
44
45    // make sure it is a multiple of warpSize
46    int tmp = threadsPerBlock / warp;
47    threadsPerBlock = tmp * warp;
48
49    for (; threadsPerBlock >= numWarpSchedulers * warp && bestimbalance↵
          != 0; threadsPerBlock -= warp)
50      {
51        totalBlocks = (int) ceil (1.0 * numberOfThreads / ↵
              threadsPerBlock);
52
53        if (totalBlocks % SM == 0)
54          imbalance = 0;
55        else
56          {
57            int blocksPerSM = totalBlocks / SM;   // some SMs get this ↵
                  number and others get +1 block
58            imbalance = (SM - (totalBlocks % SM)) / (blocksPerSM + 1.0);
59          }
60
61        if (bestimbalance >= imbalance)
62          {
63            bestimbalance = imbalance;
64            bestThreadsPerBlock = threadsPerBlock;
65            bestTotalBlocks = totalBlocks;
66          }
67      }
68    }
```

LISTING 6.13

A function for calculating the execution configuration of a kernel.

Lines 9-19 collect information about the target device and define the variables used in the subsequent calculations. As the number of warp schedulers per SM is not included in the `cudaDeviceProp` structure, we use the `switch` block of lines 22-33 and the Compute Capability major number to determine it.

Lines 39-43 use the second to fourth line of Equation 6.3 to get an upper bound on the number of threads per block that can be utilized. Lines 46, 47 then make sure that the number found is a multiple of the `warpSize`, before different block sizes (all multiples of the `warpSize`) are tested.

Function `calcExecConf()` couples the `threadsPerBlock` calculation to the number of blocks that will be distributed per SM (`blocksPerSM`). The rationale is that we should assign the same number of blocks to all SMs, to achieve a perfect balance of the workload. For this reason we use the loop of lines 49-67 to test a number of configurations before settling into the one that causes the least amount of "imbalance" in the load distribution, i.e., the one that gives to all SMs the same amount of work, if possible. The imbalance is defined by the formula:

$$imbalance = \begin{cases} 0 \text{ if } totalBlocks \text{ is a multiple of } SM \\ \dfrac{SM - (totalBlocks\%SM)}{blocksPerSM + 1} \text{ otherwise} \end{cases} \quad (6.6)$$

where $blockPerSM = \lfloor \frac{totalBlocks}{SM} \rfloor$ is the number of blocks all SMs get, with $totalBlocks\%SM$ of them getting one more. This means that $SM - (totalBlocks\%SM)$ multiprocessors remain idle for $\frac{1}{blocksPerSM+1}$ percent of the total execution time, assuming that all blocks have the same execution time. So the imbalance, as defined, translates to the accumulation of relative idle time of all SMs. Obviously, other metrics could be derived to quantify the imbalance caused by uneven workload distribution at the block or even individual thread level.

The loop of lines 49-67 ends either when the minimum $numWarpSchedulers \cdot warpSize$ is reached, or a configuration with 0 imbalance is found.

Odd inputs to the `calcExecConf()` function, such as a number of threads that is not a multiple of the `warpSize`, can produce suboptimal results. Instead of trying to derive a do-all function, we hope that this function will serve as a starting point to those writing their own derivatives.

With CUDA 6.5, Nvidia added a number of functions to the runtime API, for assisting programmers in the selection of the execution configuration. These are:

```
// Returns in *minGridSize and *blocksize suggested grid / block
// sizes, for achieving the best potential occupancy
template < class T > cudaError_t
cudaOccupancyMaxPotentialBlockSize (
        int *minGridSize,   // Smallest grid size for maximum
                            // occupancy (OUT)
        int *blockSize,     // Block size for maximum occupancy (OUT)
        T func,             // Kernel for which the calculation is
                            // done  (IN)
        size_t dynamicSMemSize, // Amount of memory (bytes) that is
                            // dynamically allocated in shared memory
                            // (IN)
        int blockSizeLimit); // Maximum block size allowed for func.
                            // Zero means no limit (IN)
//———————————————————————————————————————————————
// Variation of cudaOccupancyMaxPotentialBlockSize, for kernels that
// have different dynamic memory requirements, based on block size
template < typename UnaryFunction, class T > cudaError_t
cudaOccupancyMaxPotentialBlockSizeVariableSMem (
        int *minGridSize,   // Smallest grid size for maximum
                            // occupancy (OUT)
        int *blockSize,     // Block size for maximum occupancy (OUT)
        T func,             // Kernel for which the calculation is
                            // done  (IN)
        UnaryFunction blockSizeToDynamicSMemSize, // Unary function
                            // that gets the block size as input, and
                            // returns the shared memory requirements
                            // in bytes, as output (IN)
        int blockSizeLimit ); // Maximum block size allowed for func.
                            // Zero means no limit (IN)
```

The difference between these functions is that they apply to different types of kernels: `cudaOccupancyMaxPotentialBlockSize()` should be used when shared memory is statically allocated with a declaration such as:

```
__global__ myKernel(int *data, int N)
{
__shared__ int local[ 256 ];
 . . .
```

or the allocation is dynamic but with a *fixed size* per block.

If, on the other hand, the shared memory required depends on the size of the block, as in:

```
__global__ myKernel(int *data, int N)
{
  extern __shared__ int local[];
  . . .
}
. . .
int sharedReq = block * 10;
myKernel<<< grid, block, sharedRed * sizeof(int) >>>( d, N );
```

the `cudaOccupancyMaxPotentialBlockSizeVariableSMem()` function should be used instead.

In both cases, CUDA uses the device function information, the declared shared memory requirements and any limit on the block size, to return suggested grid and block sizes. The limit on the block size could be derived from the algorithm design, or it could be associated with the maximum number of threads we could run, i.e., the problem size.

For example, modifying the histogram calculating example of Section 6.6.2, to use the suggestions of `cudaOccupancyMaxPotentialBlockSize()` results in the following code:

```
1   // File: histogram_autoConf/histogram.cu
2   . . .
3   static const int BINS = 256;
4
5   // *****************************************************************
6   __global__ void GPU_histogram_static (int *in, int N, int *h)
7   {
8     __shared__ int localH[BINS];
9     . . .
10  }
11  // *****************************************************************
12  __global__ void GPU_histogram_dynamic (int *in, int N, int *h, int ↵
       bins)
13  {
14    extern __shared__ int localH[];
15    . . .
16  }
17
18  // *****************************************************************
19  int main (int argc, char **argv)
```

```
20  {
21     . . .
22     int blockSize, gridSize;
23     cudaOccupancyMaxPotentialBlockSize (&gridSize, &blockSize, (void *) ↵
           GPU_histogram_static, BINS * sizeof (int), N);
24     gridSize = ceil(1.0 * N / blockSize);
25
26     GPU_histogram_static <<< gridSize, blockSize >>> (d_in, N, d_hist);
27     . . .
28
29     cudaOccupancyMaxPotentialBlockSize (&gridSize, &blockSize, (void *) ↵
           GPU_histogram_dynamic, bins * sizeof (int), N);
30     gridSize = ceil(1.0 * N / blockSize);
31
32     GPU_histogram_dynamic <<< gridSize, blockSize, bins * sizeof (int) ↵
           >>> (d_in, N, d_hist, bins);
33     . . .
```

LISTING 6.14

CUDA execution configuration calculation, for the histogram kernels of Listings 6.7 and 6.8, using static and dynamic, fixed-per-block, shared memory allocation respectively. Only the modifications to the main() function of Listing 6.9 are shown.

A notable difference between the calcExecConf() function presented above, and cudaOccupancyMaxPotentialBlockSize(), is that the latter does not actually return a proper grid size (nor does the variable shared memory variant). Instead, it returns a grid size that would maximize occupancy, under the assumption that each thread will process multiple data items. For this reason, we have to calculate the proper grid size in lines 24 and 30.

Our next example, uses a shared memory allocation that depends on the block size. The kernel calculates the number of odd numbers in the input, by having each thread in a block keep a shared-memory counter. These counters are subsequently reduced to a single number per block, before being added to the global memory location holding the final result:

```
34  // File: odd.cu
35     . . .
36  __global__ void countOdds (int *d, int N, int *odds)
37  {
38     extern __shared__ int count[];
39
40     int myID = blockIdx.x * blockDim.x + threadIdx.x;
41     int localID = threadIdx.x;
42     count[localID] = 0;
43     if (myID < N)
44       count[localID] = (d[myID] % 2);
45     __syncthreads ();
46
47     // reduction phase: sum up the block
48     int step = 1;
```

```
49    while ((step < blockDim.x) && ((localID & step) == 0))
50      {
51        count[localID] += count[localID | step];
52        step *= 2;
53        __syncthreads ();
54      }
55
56    // add to global counter
57    if (localID == 0)
58      atomicAdd (odds, count[0]);
59  }
60
61  //————————————————————————————
62  int sharedSize (int b)
63  {
64    return b * sizeof (int);
65  }
66
67  //————————————————————————————
68
69  int main (int argc, char **argv)
70  {
71    int N = atoi (argv[1]);
72
73    int *ha, *hres, *da, *dres;    // host (h*) and device (d*) pointers
74
75    ha = new int[N];
76    hres = new int[1];
77
78    cudaMalloc ((void **) &da, sizeof (int) * N);
79    cudaMalloc ((void **) &dres, sizeof (int) * 1);
80
81    numberGen (N, MAXVALUE, ha);
82
83    cudaMemcpy (da, ha, sizeof (int) * N, cudaMemcpyHostToDevice);
84    cudaMemset (dres, 0, sizeof (int));
85
86    int blockSize, gridSize;
87    cudaOccupancyMaxPotentialBlockSizeVariableSMem (&gridSize, &
          blockSize, (void *) countOdds, sharedSize, N);
88
89    gridSize = ceil (1.0 * N / blockSize);
90    printf ("Grid: %i    Block: %i\n", gridSize, blockSize);
91    countOdds <<< gridSize, blockSize, blockSize * sizeof (int) >>> (da,
          N, dres);
92
93    cudaMemcpy (hres, dres, sizeof (int), cudaMemcpyDeviceToHost);
94
95    printf ("%i are odd\n", *hres);
96
97    cudaFree ((void *) da);
98    cudaFree ((void *) dres);
```

```
99    delete[]ha;
100   delete[]hres;
101   cudaDeviceReset ();
102
103   return 0;
104 }
```

LISTING 6.15

A CUDA program for counting the odd numbers in an input array. A shared memory counter with a size equal to the block size, constitutes a variable shared memory arrangement.

The kernel in lines 36-59 is relatively straightforward. Each thread uses its global ID to check if the corresponding array element is odd, and increment its own shared memory counter (line 44). Once all the threads in a block have completed this step (ensured via the __syncthreads() call in line 45), a reduction process begins, that consolidates all the partial counters into a single one, stored in count[0]. The first thread in the block can then add this value, using an atomic operation, to the global counter (line 58).

The execution configuration is calculated in 87, via the call to the cudaOccupancyMaxPotentialBlockSizeVariableSMem() function, as our kernel has variable shared memory requirements, i.e., the size of the count array is equal to the block size. In order to feed this information to the CUDA runtime, the sharedSize() (lines 62-65) is used to return for an input block size, the corresponding shared memory requirements in bytes. As in the previous example, once we have the suggested block size, we calculate the grid size in line 89.

In summary, this section provides an initial approach to solving the execution configuration problem, via a custom function and via the library functions provided by Nvidia for the same purpose. Neither is perfect. The best execution configuration can only be determined by experimentation, because performance depends on many factors, not just occupancy (e.g., register consumption). Thus it is imperative that the application be tested for various configurations and inputs. Nvidia's Visual Profiler is an indispensable tool in this quest (see Section 6.10).

6.7.2 KERNEL STRUCTURE

The structure of a kernel influences how efficiently an SM is utilized. A branching operation leads to the stalling of the threads that do not follow the particular branch, as illustrated in Figure 6.4. Listing 6.16 is a slight variation of the code in Listing 6.4, so that the work done by each thread depends explicitly on its ID:

```
__global__ void foo()
{
  int ID = threadIdx.y * blockDim.x + threadIdx.x;
  if( ID % 2 == 0)
    {
      doSmt( ID );
```

```
    }
  else
    {
        doSmtElse( ID );
    }
  doFinal( ID );
}
```

LISTING 6.16

An example of a kernel that causes half the threads in a warp to stall.

A way around the stalling problem would be to modify the condition so that all the threads in a warp follow the same execution path, but they diversify across warps or blocks. An alternative ID can be calculated for each thread (called ID-prime in the code samples that follow) that alternates between being universally even or universally odd for each warp. The new ID can be calculated from the formula:

$$ID' = (ID - warpSize \cdot \lceil \frac{warpID}{2} \rceil) \cdot 2 + (warpID\%2) \tag{6.7}$$

where *ID* is the original thread ID and *warpID* enumerates the warps using this formula: $warpID = \lfloor \frac{ID}{warpSize} \rfloor$. Equation 6.7 can be broken down and explained as follows:

- The last term, (*warpID%2*), forces all the threads in a warp to alternate between even or odd *ID'*s, matching the even or odd property of the *warpID*.
- The multiplier of the first term ($\cdot 2$) makes the threads form groups whose *ID'*s are different by 2 (effectively all the odd or all the even ones).
- The offset in the first term ($-warpSize \cdot \lceil \frac{warpID}{2} \rceil$) of the equation adjusts the beginning of each new even (odd) warp, so that it is warpSize-distant from the previous even (odd) warp.

Equation 6.7 can be easily calculated as:

```
int warpID = ID / warpSize;
int IDprime = (ID - (warpID + 1) / 2 * warpSize)*2 + (warpID % 2);
```

Or, by sacrificing a bit of portability by assuming a fix warp size of 32, we can efficiently implement the ceiling and floor functions of Equation 6.7 with bitwise operators, making the calculation much faster:

```
const int offPow=5;  // reflects a warp size of 32
. . .
int warpID = ID >> offPow;
int IDprime = ((ID - (((warpID + 1) >> 1) << offPow )) << 1)  + (↩
    warpID & 1);
```

The code in Listing 6.17 shows the complete modifications that result in a non-stalling kernel, despite the use of the if-else blocks.

```
1   // File : warpFix.cu
2   . . .
3   __global__ void foo ()
4   {
5     int ID = threadIdx.y * blockDim.x + threadIdx.x;
6     int warpID = ID >> offPow;
7     int IDprime = ((ID - (((warpID + 1) >> 1) << offPow )) << 1)  + (↩
         warpID & 1);
8
9     if( (warpID & 1) ==0 )  // modulo-2 condition
10    {
11      doSmt(IDprime);
12    }
13    else
14    {
15      doSmtElse(IDprime);
16    }
17    doFinal(IDprime);
18  }
```

LISTING 6.17

An example of a kernel that would not cause intra-warp branching while doing the same work as the one in Listing 6.16.

This solution works only if the block size is a multiple of 2 times the warp size, e.g., 64, 128, 192, and so on. If, for example, we have a block of size B with:

$$2 \cdot k \cdot warpSize \leq B \leq 2 \cdot (k + 1) \cdot warpSize$$

then the warps made of the threads with ID between $2 \cdot k \cdot warpSize - 1$ and $B - 1$ cannot use the program logic utilizing the IDprime.

What if the kernel involves a multiway decision? It is still possible to arrange threads in warps that follow the same path. Similar restrictions apply, i.e., if we have an N-way decision control structure (e.g., a switch statement with N outcomes), we can use the following ID calculation for blocks that are size-multiples of N*warpSize:

$$ID' = grpOff + (ID - grpOff - (warpID\%N) \cdot warpSize) \cdot N + (warpID\%N) \quad (6.8)$$

where:

$$grpOff = \lfloor \frac{warpID}{N} \rfloor \cdot warpSize \cdot N$$

Equation 6.8 can be broken down and explained as follows:

- *grpOff* represents the first thread ID of successive groups of $N \cdot warpSize$ threads. Beginning from this position, the second term in Equation 6.8 adjusts the ID's to the desired effect, i.e., making successive threads acquire ID's different by N.

- The multiplier of the second term ($\cdot N$) makes the threads form groups whose ID's are different by N. The terms that are subtracted from ID (i.e., $-grpOff - (warpID\%N) \cdot warpSize$) adjust ID' so that it begins from the $grpOff$ starting point.
- The last term, ($warpID\%N$), forces all the threads in a warp to get an ID' that leads them to the same path.

Listing 6.18 implements Equation 6.8 for a 3-way decision control structure.

```
1   // File: warpFixMultiway.cu
2   . . .
3   const int N = 3;
4
5   __global__ void foo ()
6   {
7     int ID = threadIdx.x;
8     int warpID = ID / warpSize;
9     int grpOff = (warpID / N) * warpSize * N;
10    int IDprime = grpOff + (ID - grpOff - (warpID % N) * warpSize) * N +↵
            (warpID % N);
11
12    printf ("Thread %i %i\n", ID, IDprime); // just for illustration ↵
            purposes
13
14    switch (warpID % N)
15      {
16      case 0:
17        doSmt (IDprime);
18        break;
19      case 1:
20        doSmtElse (IDprime);
21        break;
22      default:
23        doSmtElse2 (IDprime);
24      }
25    doFinal (IDprime);
26  }
```

LISTING 6.18

A solution to the stalling problem for a 3-way decision structure.

The ID, ID's pairs generated for a 192-thread block and $N = 3$ are shown in Table 6.6.

Obviously, kernel design also influences the block and grid arrangements, which are a concern at a different optimization "plane." These are discussed in the next section.

Table 6.6 Pairs of *ID* and *ID'* values for each of 6 warps running the program of Listing 6.18 for $N = 3$

Warp											
0		1		2		3		4		5	
ID	ID'	ID	ID'	ID	ID'	ID	ID'	ID	ID'	ID	ID'
0	0	32	1	64	2	96	96	128	97	160	98
1	3	33	4	65	5	97	99	129	100	161	101
2	6	34	7	66	8	98	102	130	103	162	104
3	9	35	10	67	11	99	105	131	106	163	107
4	12	36	13	68	14	100	108	132	109	164	110
5	15	37	16	69	17	101	111	133	112	165	113
6	18	38	19	70	20	102	114	134	115	166	116
7	21	39	22	71	23	103	117	135	118	167	119
8	24	40	25	72	26	104	120	136	121	168	122
9	27	41	28	73	29	105	123	137	124	169	125
10	30	42	31	74	32	106	126	138	127	170	128
11	33	43	34	75	35	107	129	139	130	171	131
12	36	44	37	76	38	108	132	140	133	172	134
13	39	45	40	77	41	109	135	141	136	173	137
14	42	46	43	78	44	110	138	142	139	174	140
15	45	47	46	79	47	111	141	143	142	175	143
16	48	48	49	80	50	112	144	144	145	176	146
17	51	49	52	81	53	113	147	145	148	177	149
18	54	50	55	82	56	114	150	146	151	178	152
19	57	51	58	83	59	115	153	147	154	179	155
20	60	52	61	84	62	116	156	148	157	180	158
21	63	53	64	85	65	117	159	149	160	181	161
22	66	54	67	86	68	118	162	150	163	182	164
23	69	55	70	87	71	119	165	151	166	183	167
24	72	56	73	88	74	120	168	152	169	184	170
25	75	57	76	89	77	121	171	153	172	185	173
26	78	58	79	90	80	122	174	154	175	186	176
27	81	59	82	91	83	123	177	155	178	187	179
28	84	60	85	92	86	124	180	156	181	188	182
29	87	61	88	93	89	125	183	157	184	189	185
30	90	62	91	94	92	126	186	158	187	190	188
31	93	63	94	95	95	127	189	159	190	191	191

6.7.3 SHARED MEMORY ACCESS

Concurrent access to shared memory can lead to performance deterioration if threads try to access the same memory bank. Figure 6.13 explores three different access patterns and their effect on bank conflicts.

We proceed to examine how a bank conflict-free design can be applied to the case of the histogram calculation example presented in Section 6.6.2.

The kernel design in Listing 6.7 does not consider the organization of shared memory into banks. In turn, this means it is open to bank conflicts, which can deteriorate performance by stalling whole warps. The random nature of the input data presents a challenge because we cannot predict which bank will be accessed by each thread at any time instance. The only way we can prevent conflicts from happening is to *force each thread to use a different bank*, which in turn means that we need a separate histogram count array *for every thread in the active warp*. This would raise the shared memory requirements by a `warpSize` factor! Depending on the number of our input image's maximum gray levels, we get the requirements listed in Table 6.7.

The memory requirement calculations in Table 6.7 are based on the formula:

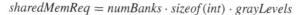

$$sharedMemReq = numBanks \cdot sizeof(int) \cdot grayLevels$$

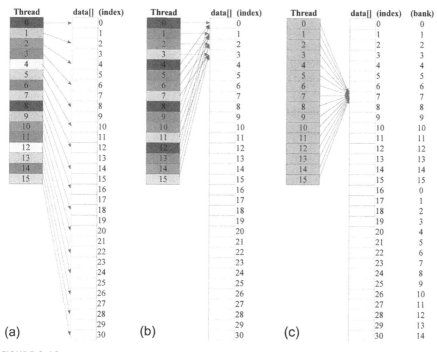

(a)   (b)   (c)

FIGURE 6.13

Three different shared memory access patterns and their effects on bank conflicts, assuming an organization with 16 banks. Threads are colored to reflect conflicts.
(a) Each thread accesses the `data[2*ID]` element, resulting in two way bank conflicts.
(b) Each thread accesses the `data[ID % 4]` element, resulting in four-way bank conflicts.
(c) All threads try to access element `data[7]`. The value is broadcast to all threads without stalling any of them.

Table 6.7 An estimation of the shared memory needed per SM, to provide conflict-free access during a histogram calculation of an image

Maximum gray levels	Compute Capability	Shared Memory Banks	Shared memory capacity	Memory requirements	Conflict-free Solution Feasible
16	1.x	16	16kB	1024	√
256				16384	√
512				32768	X
1024				65536	X
16	2.x, 3.x, 5.x	32	48kB	2048	√
256				32768	√
512				65536	X
1024				131072	X

A conflict-free solution mandates a staggered array allocation for each thread, in a manner similar to how input data are fetched from the global memory (see Figure 6.9), guaranteeing that each thread has exclusive use of one bank. This arrangement is shown in Figure 6.14.

The "trick" to restricting each thread to its own part of the localH array is to multiply the offset provided by a pixel's gray level by warpSize (or shift to the left by 5 bits for warpSize=32).

The resulting kernel is shown in Listing 6.19.

```
1   // File: histogram_noConflict/histogram_V1.cu
2   . . .
3   const int BINS4ALL = BINS * 32;
4
5   // *****************************************************************
6   __global__ void GPU_histogram_V1 (int *in, int N, int *h)
7   {
8      int gloID = blockIdx.x * blockDim.x + threadIdx.x;
9      int locID = threadIdx.x;
```

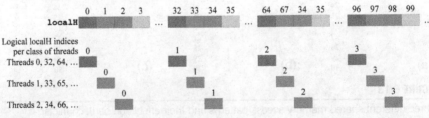

FIGURE 6.14

Assigning a different bank of shared memory to each thread in a warp by doing a staggered allocation of the local histogram array.

```
10    int GRIDSIZE = gridDim.x * blockDim.x;
11    __shared__ int localH[BINS4ALL];
12    int bankID = locID & 0x1F ; // Optimized version of locID % warpSize↩
         ;
13    int i;
14
15    // initialize the local , shared—memory bins
16    for (i = locID; i < BINS4ALL; i += blockDim.x)
17      localH[i] = 0;
18
19    // wait for all warps to complete the previous step
20    __syncthreads ();
21
22    //start processing the image data
23    for (i = gloID; i < N; i += GRIDSIZE)
24      {
25        int temp = in[i];
26        int v = temp & 0xFF;
27        localH[bankID + (v << 5) ]++;   // Optimized version of localH[↩
             bankID + v * warpSize]++
28        v = (temp >> 8) & 0xFF;
29        localH[bankID + (v << 5) ]++;
30        v = (temp >> 16) & 0xFF;
31        localH[bankID + (v << 5) ]++;
32        v = (temp >> 24) & 0xFF;
33        localH[bankID + (v << 5) ]++;
34      }
35
36    // wait for all warps to complete the local calculations , before ↩
         updating the global counts
37    __syncthreads ();
38
39    // use atomic operations to add the local findings to the global ↩
         memory bins
40    for (i = locID; i < BINS4ALL; i += blockDim.x)
41      atomicAdd (h + (i >> 5), localH[i]); // Optimized version of ↩
           atomicAdd (h + (i/warpSize), localH[i]);
42  }
```

LISTING 6.19

A conflict-free shared memory access histogram calculating kernel, with each thread in a warp using a private part of the localH array. The code assumes a fixed warp size of 32.

A side effect of eliminating the bank conflicts is that the atomicAdd operations become redundant (see lines 27, 29, 31, and 33 in Listing 6.19), providing an additional improvement to the overall execution speed.

A close examination of lines 25-33 in Listing 6.19 reveals that there are dependencies between successive lines, which prevents ILP. A simple solution is to rearrange the computations and introduce a few local variables.

Before we show the resulting kernel, we have to address one more issue: Recent Nvidia GPU architectures (e.g., all since Fermi) support the concurrent execution of multiple warps in an SM. This means that for these devices and for thread blocks that exceed the warpSize, the kernel in Listing 6.19 is wrong. The failure stems from the race conditions created between threads belonging to different warps through the sharing of the 32 local histograms. An easy fix is to limit the block size if the device has such capabilities, as shown in Listing 6.20.

```
1   // File: histogram_noConflict/histogram_V1.cu
2   . . .
3   int main (int argc, char **argv)
4   {
5   . . .
6     // examine the properties of the device
7     cudaDeviceProp deviceProp;
8     cudaGetDeviceProperties (&deviceProp, 0);
9
10    if (deviceProp.major >= 2)    // protect against SMs running ↩
            multiple warps concurrently
11        GPU_histogram_V1 <<< 16, 32 >>> (d_in, N, d_hist);
12    else
13        GPU_histogram_V1 <<< 16, 256 >>> (d_in, N, d_hist);
14    . . .
```

LISTING 6.20

Part of the main function that launches the kernel in Listing 6.19.

Of course, this raises the question of how efficient such an approach is, since a Fermi or Kepler GPU has 192 cores per SM, 160 of which would stay idle.

There are two solutions to this problem: (a) create as many local histograms as the number of threads in a block, or (b) use atomic operations. The first option requires a refactoring of the kernel, since 8-bit grayscale images demand $grayLevels \cdot sizeof(int) = 256 \cdot 4bytes = 1KB$ of shared memory. We can reduce the footprint per histogram if the maximum number of pixels examined per thread stays below 256. Then a single byte per counter can be used, reducing the memory per histogram to 256 bytes and bringing the maximum size of a block to $\frac{maximumSharedMem}{memPerHistogram} = \frac{48KB}{256B} = 192$ threads. Unfortunately, this solution eliminates the bank-conflict-free arrangement. The implementation of this alternative is shown in Listing 6.21.

```
1   // File: histogram_noConflict/histogram_V2.cu
2   . . .
3   const int BINS = 256;
4   const int BLOCKSIZE = 192;
5   const int MAXPIXELSPERTHREAD = 255; // to avoid overflowing a byte ↩
            counter
6   const int BINS4ALL = BINS * BLOCKSIZE;
7
```

```
8    // ****************************************************************
9    __global__ void GPU_histogram_V2 (int *in, int N, int *h)
10   {
11     int gloID = blockIdx.x * blockDim.x + threadIdx.x;
12     int locID = threadIdx.x;
13     int GRIDSIZE = gridDim.x * blockDim.x;
14     __shared__ unsigned char localH[BINS4ALL];
15     int bankID = locID;
16     int i;
17
18     // initialize the local, shared-memory bins
19     for (i = locID; i < BINS4ALL; i += blockDim.x)
20       localH[i] = 0;
21
22     // wait for all warps to complete the previous step
23     __syncthreads ();
24
25     // start processing the image data
26     unsigned char *mySharedBank = localH + bankID;
27     for (i = gloID; i < N; i += GRIDSIZE)
28         {
29           int temp = in[i];
30           int v = temp & 0xFF;
31           int v2 = (temp >> 8) & 0xFF;
32           int v3 = (temp >> 16) & 0xFF;
33           int v4 = (temp >> 24) & 0xFF;
34           mySharedBank[v * BLOCKSIZE]++;  // Optimized version of localH↵
                  [bankID + v * warpSize]++
35           mySharedBank[v2 * BLOCKSIZE]++;
36           mySharedBank[v3 * BLOCKSIZE]++;
37           mySharedBank[v4 * BLOCKSIZE]++;
38         }
39
40     // wait for all warps to complete the local calculations, before ↵
           updating the global counts
41     __syncthreads ();
42
43     // use atomic operations to add the local findings to the global ↵
           memory bins
44     for (i = locID; i < BINS4ALL; i += blockDim.x)
45       atomicAdd (h + (i/BLOCKSIZE), localH[i]);
46   }
47
48   // ****************************************************************
49   int main (int argc, char **argv)
50   {
51     . . .
52     // ensures that shared memory/L1 cache are split in 48KB/16KB ↵
           configuration
53     cudaDeviceSetCacheConfig( cudaFuncCachePreferShared );
54
55     int blocks = (int)ceil(N*4.0/(BLOCKSIZE * MAXPIXELSPERTHREAD));
```

```
56    GPU_histogram_V2 <<< blocks, BLOCKSIZE >>> (d_in, N, d_hist);
57    . . .
```

LISTING 6.21

A variation of the kernel in Listing 6.19 that avoids atomic operations by ensuring that each thread in a block has its own histogram. This kernel also caters for ILP by breaking interdependencies between successive statements.

The notable differences between Listings 6.21 and 6.19 are:

- The introduction of an ILP-friendly block in the for loop of lines 27-38.
- The dynamic calculation of the grid size based on the need to keep each thread doing no-more-than MAXPIXELSPERTHREAD pixel calculations (line 55).
- The individual elements of each histogram are BLOCKSIZE bytes apart, instead of warpSize positions.[18]

The second option, i.e., using atomic operations, is implemented in the kernel of Listing 6.22. The two notable changes relative to the original kernel of Listing 6.19 are the use of atomicAdd() in lines 29-32 (obviously) and the introduction of the if construct of line 21, which allows us to avoid using the costly atomic operations if the block size is not above the warpSize. In that case, we revert to the for loop of lines 35-46, which is identical to the one used in Listing 6.19. The mySharedBank pointer serves the elimination of the repeated calculation of localH+bankID, as done in lines 27, 29, 31, and 33 of Listing 6.19.

```
1  // File: histogram_noConflict/histogram_atomic.cu
2  . . .
3  __global__ void GPU_histogram_atomic (int *in, int N, int *h)
4  {
5    int gloID = blockIdx.x * blockDim.x + threadIdx.x;
6    int locID = threadIdx.x;
7    int GRIDSIZE = gridDim.x * blockDim.x;
8    __shared__ int localH[BINS4ALL];
9    int bankID = locID % warpSize;
10   int i;
11
12   // initialize the local, shared-memory bins
13   for (i = locID; i < BINS4ALL; i += blockDim.x)
14     localH[i] = 0;
15
16   // wait for all warps to complete the previous step
17   __syncthreads ();
18
```

[18]It is possible to maintain the conflict-free access to shared memory by using 128 threads per block and storing four histogram counters per int element of the localH array. This scheme is quite complex, requiring lengthy code modifications, without providing much benefit, due to the time-consuming bitwise manipulations required. For this reason, we do not elaborate more on it.

```
19      // start processing the image data
20      int *mySharedBank = localH + bankID;
21      if (blockDim.x > warpSize) // if the blocksize exceeds the warpSize,↵
            it is possible multiple warps run at the same time
22        for (i = gloID; i < N; i += GRIDSIZE)
23          {
24            int temp = in[i];
25            int v = temp & 0xFF;
26            int v2 = (temp >> 8) & 0xFF;
27            int v3 = (temp >> 16) & 0xFF;
28            int v4 = (temp >> 24) & 0xFF;
29            atomicAdd (mySharedBank + (v << 5), 1);
30            atomicAdd (mySharedBank + (v2 << 5), 1);
31            atomicAdd (mySharedBank + (v3 << 5), 1);
32            atomicAdd (mySharedBank + (v4 << 5), 1);
33          }
34      else
35        for (i = gloID; i < N; i += GRIDSIZE)
36          {
37            int temp = in[i];
38            int v = temp & 0xFF;
39            int v2 = (temp >> 8) & 0xFF;
40            int v3 = (temp >> 16) & 0xFF;
41            int v4 = (temp >> 24) & 0xFF;
42            mySharedBank[v << 5]++;   // Optimized version of localH[bankID↵
                + v * warpSize]++
43            mySharedBank[v2 << 5]++;
44            mySharedBank[v3 << 5]++;
45            mySharedBank[v4 << 5]++;
46          }
47
48      // wait for all warps to complete the local calculations, before ↵
            updating the global counts
49      __syncthreads ();
50
51      // use atomic operations to add the local findings to the global ↵
            memory bins
52      for (i = locID; i < BINS4ALL; i += blockDim.x)
53        atomicAdd (h + (i >> 5), localH[i]); // Optimized version of ↵
            atomicAdd (h + (i/warpSize), localH[i]);
54    }
```

LISTING 6.22

A variation of the kernel in Listing 6.19 that uses atomic operations to eliminate the race conditions caused by having multiple concurrently running warps access the shared memory partial histograms.

Which of the above versions is quicker depends, ultimately, on the characteristics of the target GPU architecture. For instance, atomic operations on shared memory have become cheaper and faster in recent GPUs. Table 6.8 summarizes the results

Table 6.8 Average and standard deviation of kernel execution times for different histogram-calculating kernels. Input data consisted of a 3264x2448, 8-bit, grayscale image. Reported times exclude the data transfer to/from the GPU

Kernel (Listing #)	Launch Conf. (Grid, Block)	Execution Time (msec)
GPU_histogram_V1 (6.19)	16, 32	8.0269 ± 0.0046
GPU_histogram_V2 (6.21)	164,192	8.6529 ± 0.0217
GPU_histogram_atomic (6.22)	16, 256	2.1918 ± 0.0086

of testing on a GTX 870M GPU, a compute-capability 3.0 device. The software environment involved CUDA 6.0 and GCC 4.8.2.

The results are only indicative, since we did not attempt to optimize the launch configurations. However, the differences in performance are so distinct that we can safely conclude that the version employing the atomic operations is the best for the given device.

6.7.4 GLOBAL MEMORY ACCESS

GPU memory subsystems are designed to perform transactions in large batches: 32, 64, or 128 bytes at a time. This allows GPUs to access memory at very high speeds, but with a catch: Any memory access operation can involve only a single such block of memory, starting at an address that is a multiple of this size. It is as though memory is segmented and we can access only one of these segments at any point in time.

When a warp executes an instruction involving access to global memory, the GPU *coalesces* or groups together the individual thread requests into operations involving these blocks. This creates two challenges:

1. Warp threads better access items within the same block of memory. Otherwise, they will be forced to execute in as many groups as the blocks being accessed.
2. Data should be arranged or aligned in memory so that if possible, they do not cross between two consecutive memory blocks. Also, in order to maximize the number of threads that can access items in a collection in a "coalesced" manner, that collection should begin at the starting point of a block.

Meeting the first challenge listed above may not be enough to guarantee fast access to memory. It all depends on the compute capability of the target device. Devices of compute capabilities 1.0 and 1.1 have several restrictions, one of which is that the threads must access the items in sequence. If, for example, they are trying to access the members of an int array d, the kth thread should access item d[k]. There are additional restrictions on the size of the items being accessed (e.g., 1, 4 or 8 bytes). The best source of information for this topic is Nvidia's "CUDA C Programming Guide". In this section we discuss the restrictions that apply to the more recent compute capability 2.x, 3.x and 5.x devices. In these devices, the existence of the L1 and L2 caches speeds up access and simplifies the rules involved.

The L1 cache is SM localized, since it is part of the shared memory, whereas L2 is GPU-wide.

The rules that apply for compute capability 2.x and higher devices, and in the context of a warp's execution are:

- If the data that the warp threads request exist in the L1 cache, then a 128-byte wide access operation is performed. The L1 cache is organized into 128-byte segments that map to global memory segments. Otherwise, data go through the L2 cache in 32-byte operations. This reduction in the cache-line size aims to improve the utilization of the L2 memory by avoiding over-fetching. Obviously, in the case of a cache hit, the access is performed at the speed of the corresponding cache. Otherwise, access is performed at the speed of global memory.
- Data may be accessed in any order within the range of a 32-byte (uncached or cached in L2) or 128-byte (cached in L1) block. This includes requests for the same memory location.
- If the collective size of the data exceeds the block size (e.g., when the size of each item is more than 4 bytes), the requests are split into separate 32-byte or 128-byte operations, again depending on cache residency.

Figure 6.15 illustrates the effects of coalesced memory access using a variety of scenarios.

Meeting the second challenge is a matter of properly aligning and/or padding data structures. To this end, the __align__ qualifier can be used so that the compiler can perform the alignment/padding automatically. The __align__ qualifier expects a parameter corresponding to the size in bytes of the memory reserved for the structure. An example is shown in Listing 6.23.

```
struct __align__(16) point{
    int x,y;
    unsigned char color[3];
};
. . .
point *d_p;
cudaMalloc ((void **) &d_p, sizeof (point) * DATASIZE);
```

LISTING 6.23

An example of a padded and aligned data structure. It occupies 16 bytes in memory, so when it is used in an array, all array elements start at an address that is a multiple of 16.

This example would reserve a global memory block similar to the one shown in Figure 6.16. The cudaMalloc function will return a block suitable for coalesced access.

Things get more "interesting" when a 2D array is to be used. For memory requests to be coalesced, we must have both a thread-block size and a matrix width, which are

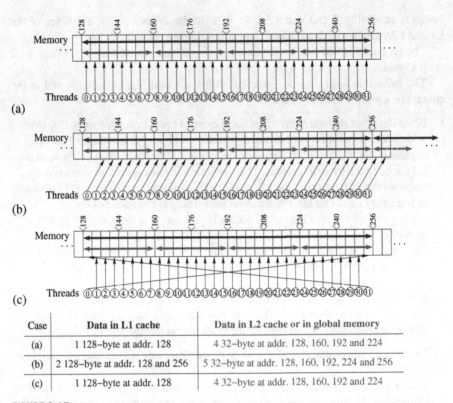

Case	Data in L1 cache	Data in L2 cache or in global memory
(a)	1 128-byte at addr. 128	4 32-byte at addr. 128, 160, 192 and 224
(b)	2 128-byte at addr. 128 and 256	5 32-byte at addr. 128, 160, 192, 224 and 256
(c)	1 128-byte at addr. 128	4 32-byte at addr. 128, 160, 192 and 224

FIGURE 6.15

An illustration of how different global memory access patterns are serviced according to cache residency for compute-capability 2.x and higher devices. It is assumed that each thread is trying to access a 4-byte data item.

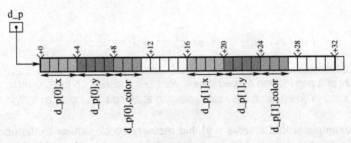

FIGURE 6.16

An illustration of the array produced as a result of the allocation of the "aligned" data structure of Listing 6.23.

a multiple of the warp size (or the half-warp size for the case of compute-capability 1.x devices). To ensure the second requirement, the cudaMallocPitch() function can be used:

```
cudaError_t cudaMallocPitch(
            void ** devPtr,    // Address of allocated memory (OUT)
            size_t * pitch,    // Actual size of row in bytes (OUT)
            size_t width,      // Requested table width in bytes (IN)
            size_t height);    // Requested table height in rows (IN)
```

The pitch parameter, which is returned upon a successful allocation, can be used for calculating the offset of individual matrix elements. If, for example, the following code segment is executed on the host:

```
int *d_matr, pitch;
cudaMallocPitch((void **)&d_matr, &pitch, 100, 100);
```

the total device memory allocated would be *pitch* · 100 bytes. A kernel trying to access d_p elements should receive as an additional parameter the pitch value and calculate the address of a matrix element (i, j) using one of the following two alternatives:

```
pitch /= sizeof(int); // works only if there is no remainder
. . .
int *p = d_matr + (j * pitch + i);

// Or without a division that changes the value of pitch:
int *p = (int *)((char *)d_matr + (j*pitch + i*sizeof(int)));
```

However, this is not the end of the story as far as coalesced access to data structures is concerned. There is nothing wrong with defining an *array of structures* (**AoS**) and passing it as a parameter to a kernel, until it is time to access its members. Alignment and padding may be fine, but when the following kernel is applied to an array of point structures, as the one defined in Listing 6.23:

```
// Eucledian distance calculation
__global__ void distance( point *data, float *dist, int N)
{
    int myID = blockIdx.x * blockDim.x + threadIdx.x; // assuming a 1-D↩
        grid of 1-D blocks
    if (myID >= N) return;
    dist[ myID ] = sqrt( data[myID].x * data[myID].x + data[myID].y * ↩
        data[myID].y );
}
```

upon accessing data[myID].x, the threads of a warp will cause the initiation of 16 successive global memory operations (assuming the thread has 32 warps) in devices of compute-capability 2.0 and above, since only two structures fit within a 32-byte block. The same goes for the y part of the formula.

An alternative (but counter-intuitive) solution to this problem is to organize the data as a *structure of arrays* (**SoA**), i.e., each of the structure components resides in

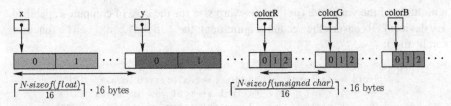

FIGURE 6.17

An illustration of the structure-of-arrays alternative of the array-of-structures option shown in Figure 6.16. Empty cells represent padding. The memory reserved for each array is also shown.

a separate array. The resulting kernel that truly provides coalesced memory access would be:

```
// Eucledian distance calculation for a Structure of Arrays
__global__ void distance2( float *x, float *y, unsigned char *colorR, ↵
    unsigned char *colorG, unsigned char *colorB, int N)
{
    int myID = blockIdx.x * blockDim.x + threadIdx.x; // assuming a 1-D↵
        grid of 1-D blocks
    if (myID >= N) return;
    dist[ myID ] = sqrt( x[myID] * x[myID] + y[myID] * y[myID] );
}
```

which would require just four global memory operations for accessing the x-component for the first time. The second access (as mandated by the x[myID] * x[myID] term) would utilize the L1 cache, or by a simple rewrite (using a temporary variable) it could be eliminated/replaced by a register access.

The resulting memory layout, which also has the side effect of utilizing approximately $\frac{16-11}{16} = 31\%$ less device memory because of the much-reduced demand for padding, is shown in Figure 6.17. Padding needs to be inserted only between the individual array memory spaces.

6.7.5 PAGE-LOCKED AND ZERO-COPY MEMORY

The term *page-locked* or *pinned* memory refers to host memory that cannot be swapped out as part of the regular virtual memory operations employed by most contemporary operating systems. Pinned memory is used to hold critical code and data that cannot be moved out of the main memory, such as the OS kernel. It is also needed for performing Direct Memory Access (DMA) transfers across the PCIe bus. When one uses regular memory for holding the host data, upon a request to transfer the data to the device, the Nvidia driver allocates paged-locked memory, copies the data to it, and, upon the completion of the transfer, frees up the pinned memory. This buffering overhead can be eliminated by using pinned memory for all data that are to be moved between the host and the device.

Pinned memory can be allocated with:

- `malloc()`, followed by a call to `mlock()`. Deallocation is done in the reverse order, i.e., calling `munlock()`, then `free()`.
- Or by calling the `cudaMallocHost()` function. Memory allocated in this fashion has to be deallocated with a call to `cudaFreeHost()`. Otherwise, the program may behave in an unpredictable manner:

```
cudaError_t cudaMallocHost(
                void ** ptr,    // Addr. of pointer to pinned
                                //   memory (IN/OUT)
                size_t size);   // Size in bytes of request (IN)

cudaError_t cudaFreeHost (void * ptr);
```

The only potential problem with pinned memory use is that if it is used in excess, it could lead to performance degradation due to the inability of the host to use virtual memory effectively.

The performance gain that page-locked memory can yield depends on the hardware platform and most importantly, on the size of the data involved. In the experiments reported by Cook in [18], there is virtually no gain for transfers below 32 KB, and the bus becomes saturated (i.e., reaches maximum throughput) when transfers go beyond 2 MB. For the plateaus Cook got beyond the 2 MB mark, the performance gain ranged between 10% and a massive 2.5x.

Zero-copy memory is a term used to convey that no explicit memory transfer between the host and the device needs to be initiated. Another, less fashionable term used for the same concept is *mapped memory*. Mapped memory is page-locked memory that can be mapped to the address space of the device. So, we have a memory region with two addresses: one for access from the host and one for access from the device. A transfer across the PCIe bus will be initiated by the CUDA run-time upon the first attempt to access a region of memory that is designated as mapped memory, stalling the active kernel while it is taking place.

This process may sound inefficient, but there is still justification for using mapped memory:

- It makes the program logic simpler because there is no need to separately allocate device memory and transfer the data from the host. This can be a viable option for early development phases that involve porting CPU code to CUDA. Devoting lengthy parts of the code for memory transfers may be a distraction that can be reserved for the later stages, when the core logic of the program behaves as expected.
- The CUDA run-time can automatically overlap kernel-originating memory transfers with *another* kernel execution. This can boost performance without the need for using streams.
- For low-end systems where the CPU and the GPU share the same physical RAM, no transfer ever takes place, making the use of mapped memory in such cases a no-brainer.

To set up a mapped memory region, we must call the `cudaHostAlloc()` function:

```
cudaError_t cudaHostAlloc(
        void ** pHost,        // Addr. of pointer to mapped
                              //   memory (IN/OUT)
        size_t size,          // Size in bytes of request (IN)
        unsigned int flags);  // Options for function (IN)
```

using the symbolic constant `cudaHostAllocMapped` for the `flags` parameter.

Because mapped memory is also page-locked memory, its release is done with the `cudaFreeHost()` function.

Mapped memory is referenced by two pointers: one on the host and one on the device. The device pointer, which is the one to be passed to a kernel, can be retrieved from the host pointer with the `cudaHostGetDevicePointer` function:

```
cudaError_t cudaHostGetDevicePointer(
        void ** pDevice,      // Address where the returned device
                              //    pointer is stored (IN/OUT)
        void * pHost,         // Address of host pointer (IN)
        unsigned int flags)   // Currently should be set to 0
```

So, we can have:

```
int *h_data, *d_data;
cudaHostAlloc((void **)&h_data, sizeof(int)* DATASIZE, ↩
    cudaHostAllocMapped);
cudaHostGetDevicePointer((void **)&d_data,(void *)h_data, 0);
doSmt<<< gridDim, blkDim >>>(d_data);
```

This sequence is unnecessary for 64-bit applications running under Windows or Linux and targeting devices of compute-capability 2.0 or above. In that case, a *unified virtual address* (UVA) space is formed, incorporating both device and host memory. Then the preceding sequence could be simplified, since the device pointer would be no different from the host pointer:

```
int *h_data;
cudaHostAlloc((void **)&h_data, sizeof(int)* DATASIZE, ↩
    cudaHostAllocMapped);
doSmt<<< gridDim, blkDim >>>(h_data);
```

UVA has significant implications for the performance of third-party devices and libraries because it can eliminate otherwise redundant data buffer copies (see Section 6.11). UVA simplifies the application code by delegating some of the work details to the libraries. For example, under UVA, `cudaMemcpy()` can be used just by specifying the source and destination pointers, without needing to explicitly specify the type of copy operation. So, the last line in the following sequence:

```
int *h_in;
int *h_out, *d_out;
. . .
cudaHostAlloc((void **)&h_in, sizeof(int)* DATAINSIZE, ↩
    cudaHostAllocMapped); // Allocate mapped memory
cudaMalloc((void **) &d_out, sizeof (int) * DATAOUTSIZE); ↩
                        // Allocate device memory
doSmt<<< gridDim, blkDim >>>(h_in, d_out);
```

```
cudaMemcpy(h_out, d_out, sizeof(int) * DATAOUTSIZE, ↩
    cudaMemcpyDeviceToHost);    // Device−to−host transfer
```

can be replaced with:

```
cudaMemcpy(h_out, d_out, sizeof(int)* DATAOUTSIZE, cudaMemcpyDefault);↩
    // ''Implied'' device−to−host transfer
```

making the use of the `cudaMemcpyDefault` flag exclusive, regardless of the "direction" of the copy. Note that as shown previously, we still have to "manually" get the output data from the device.

6.7.6 UNIFIED MEMORY

The separate memory spaces of host and device necessitate the explicit (or implicit via zero-copy memory) transfer of data between them so that a GPU can process the designated input and return the outcome of a computation. This results in a sequence of `cudaMemcpy()` operations, as shown in the examples of the previous sections. Unified Memory is a facility introduced in CUDA 6.0 that allows implicit transfers to take place both to and from the device, without the need for lengthy and error-prone `cudaMemcpy()` sequences.

Unified Memory introduces the concept of *managed memory*, which is essentially memory allocated on both host and device under the control of the device driver. The device driver ensures that the two memory ranges stay coherent, i.e., contain the same data, when they are being accessed by either CPU or GPU.

The *Unified Memory* term is justified by the fact that a program needs to maintain just a single pointer to the data, which is similar to the zero-copy memory described in Section 6.7.5. The difference is that for zero-copy memory, the transfer is triggered by access, i.e., during kernel execution, whereas in the Unified Memory case the transfer is initiated immediately before the launch and promptly after the termination of a kernel.

Unified Memory does not reduce the execution time of a program, since the transfers take place as in a typical CUDA program, albeit implicitly. In that regard, we can consider it an optimization technique only as far as the program structure is concerned.

Managed memory can be allocated in two ways:

- Dynamically, via a call to the `cudaMallocManaged()` function, which is just a variant of `cudaMalloc()`.
- Statically, by declaring a global variable as being __managed__.

In both cases, the resulting pointer/variable can be also accessed from the host, indicating the second host-side allocation. The key, however, is *when* this access is possible. The managed memory is "handed over" to the GPU for the duration of a kernel's execution. The host side of the memory is inaccessible while the kernel is being executed, actually generating a protection fault if access is attempted.[19]

---

[19]Fine-grained control can be exercised over access to managed memory via streams. For more information, please check Nvidia's documentation.

The syntax of `cudaMallocManaged()` is as follows:

```
template < class T > cudaError_t cudaMallocManaged (
        T **devPtr,    // Address for storing the memory pointer
                       // (IN/OUT)
        size_t size,   // Size in bytes of the required memory (IN)
        unsigned flags)// Creation flag, defaults to
                       // cudaMemAttachGlobal (IN)
```

The flag must be either `cudaMemAttachGlobal`, which means the allocated memory is accessible by all kernels (and locked when any is running), or `cudaMemAttach-Host`, which means that the memory is accessible only to kernels launched by the thread that allocates this block.

To show exactly how unified memory affects the source code, we contrast in Figure 6.18 two versions of the atomic-operations-based histogram calculation program that we covered in Section 6.7.3. Although the kernel is unchanged, the host code for preparing the input and collecting the output is significantly simplified. In fact, the host can use native functions (not CUDA library calls) to prepare the input and examine the output.

In the following discussion we comment only on the Unified Memory part of Figure 6.18. The differences start from the variable definitions of lines 6 and 7, since in Unified Memory there is no need for separate host and device allocations. The `cudaMallocManaged()` call of line 19 allocates space for the input on the host and the device, accessible by the single `in` pointer. The histogram array is statically allocated via the `__managed__`-decorated declaration in line 1. The host-side input is initialized by line 21; the device-side output is initialized by line 22. When `cudaMemset()` is applied to a managed memory pointer, it always affects the device-side memory region. The input data are implicitly transfered to the device upon the launch of the kernel in line 24.

In order to ensure that the kernel has terminated, before the managed memory regions can be accessed *an explicit synchronization call is required* via the `cudaDeviceSynchronize()` call of line 26. Finally, the managed memory is released by a `cudaFree()` call in line 28.

The code is undoubtedly shorter, but there are some shortcomings: In the explicit memory management version, the input is copied directly from the internal buffer of the `PGMImage`-type object `inImg` to the device memory (see lines 10 and 21 in the left pane of Figure 6.18). In the managed memory version, the input data have to be copied twice, the first time going from the `inImg`'s buffer to the host's portion of the managed memory (line 21 in the right pane of Figure 6.18).

This issue is not really a deal breaker, since it can actually be addressed by mixing unified and explicit memory management. A `cudaMemcpy()` call can be used instead of the `memcpy()` call in line 21, as shown here:

```
cudaMemcpy (in, inImg.pixels, sizeof(int)*N, cudaMemcpyHostToDevice);
```

What is important is that we understand the Unified Memory mechanism in order to avoid making choices that deteriorate performance.

Explicit memory Management	Unified Memory

```
1                                              __device__ __managed__ int hist[BINS];
2  int main (int argc, char **argv)            int main (int argc, char **argv)
3  {                                           {
4    PGMImage inImg (argv[1]);                   PGMImage inImg (argv[1]);
5
6    int *d_in, *h_in;                           int *in;
7    int *d_hist, *h_hist, *cpu_hist;            int *cpu_hist;
8    int i, N, bins;                             int i, N, bins;
9
10   h_in = (int *) inImg.pixels;
11   N = ceil ((inImg.x_dim * inImg.y_dim) / 4.0);   N = ceil ((inImg.x_dim * inImg.y_dim) / 4.0);
12
13   bins = inImg.num_colors + 1;                bins = inImg.num_colors + 1;
14   h_hist = (int *) malloc (bins * sizeof (int));
15   cpu_hist = (int *) malloc (bins * sizeof (int));   cpu_hist = (int *) malloc (bins * sizeof (int));
16
17   CPU_histogram (inImg.pixels, inImg.x_dim *      CPU_histogram (inImg.pixels, inImg.x_dim *
                   inImg.y_dim, cpu_hist, bins);                     inImg.y_dim, cpu_hist, bins);
18
19   cudaMalloc ((void **) &d_in, sizeof (int) * N);    cudaMallocManaged ((void **) &in, sizeof (int) * N);
20   cudaMalloc ((void **) &d_hist, sizeof (int) * bins);
21   cudaMemcpy (d_in, h_in, sizeof (int) * N,        memcpy (in, inImg.pixels, sizeof (int) * N);
               cudaMemcpyHostToDevice);
22   cudaMemset (d_hist, 0, bins * sizeof (int));     cudaMemset (hist, 0, bins * sizeof (int));
23
24   GPU_histogram_atomic <<< 16, 256 >>> (d_in, N, d_hist);   GPU_histogram_atomic <<< 16, 256 >>> (in, N, hist);
25
26   cudaMemcpy (h_hist, d_hist, sizeof (int) * bins,   cudaDeviceSynchronize (); // Wait for the GPU to finish
               cudaMemcpyDeviceToHost);
27
28   cudaFree ((void *) d_in);                        cudaFree ((void *) in);
29   cudaFree ((void *) d_hist);
30   free (h_hist);
31   free (cpu_hist);                                 free (cpu_hist);
```

FIGURE 6.18

Explicit memory management (left) and managed-memory-based (right) main functions for calculating the histogram of an image.

Although the Unified Memory facility is a device driver feature, Nvidia has chosen to make it available only to devices of compute-capability 3.0 and above. Because of this limitation, in addition to the fact that explicit transfers are more easy to micro-manage to the desired effect,[20] in the following sections we mostly use explicit memory transfers in the test cases we examine.

6.7.7 ASYNCHRONOUS EXECUTION AND STREAMS

As a general guideline, memory transfers between the host and the device should take place only when absolutely necessary. Contemporary GPUs are equipped with gigabytes of global memory that can be used to preserve intermediate data between the successive invocation of different kernels. The term *kernel fusion* is used to refer to the approach of replacing multiple kernel invocations by a single one in an attempt to minimize data transfer. Register file and shared memory restrictions may prevent one from creating a single kernel as a solution to a problem: It may not fit (see Section 6.7.1)! Factoring the algorithm in disjoint kernels is still doable and with small performance (if at all) penalties, as long as the problem data do not traverse the PCIe bus.

Alternatively, we could "hide" the cost of memory transfers by overlapping them with kernel execution. A *stream* is a sequence of commands (including device memory copies, memory setting, and kernel invocations) that are executed in order. A CUDA program can explicitly control device-level concurrency (for devices of compute capability 2.0 and above) by managing streams. Each stream will execute sequentially, but the commands from different streams (with commands possibly deposited from different host threads) can be issued concurrently. Thus, the relative execution order of commands residing in different streams is unknown. Execution is of course influenced by the availability (or not) of the resources needed; if we try to execute concurrently two kernels that, combined, require more than the total available device memory, the allocation directive for one of them will fail.

Streams are represented by the `cudaStream_t` type. There is a default stream (a.k.a. the `NULL` stream) associated with all the requests that have no stream reference attached. Using a stream involves the following steps:

1. **Creation**: A stream can be created by a call to the `cudaStreamCreate()` function:

   ```
   cudaError_t cudaStreamCreate(cudaStream_t * pStream); // Pointer to↩
       a new stream identifier
   ```

2. **Use**: A third version of the execution configuration syntax exists that can enqueue a kernel invocation in a chosen stream:

   ```
   kernelFunction <<< gridDim, blockDim, sharedMem, stream >>> ( ↩
       list_of_parameters );
   ```

---

[20] For example, in the block cipher encryption case study of Section 6.12.2, the input data are transfered in batches to the GPU and not in one go.

Additionally, there is a set of asynchronous (i.e., non-blocking) CUDA memory functions (all having the `Async` suffix) that accept an additional stream parameter so that they can be queued in a particular sequence. For example:

```
// Same as cudaMemcpy, with the addition of the cudaStream_t last ↵
    parameter. If the last parameter is ommitted, the command is ↵
    deposited in the default stream (stream 0)
cudaError_t cudaMemcpyAsync(void *dst,
                            const void *src,
                            size_t count,
                            enum cudaMemcpyKind kind,
                            cudaStream_t stream=0);

// Same as cudaMemSet, with the addition of the cudaStream_t last ↵
    parameter
cudaError_t cudaMemsetAsync(void *devPtr,
                            int value,
                            size_t count,
                            cudaStream_t stream=0);
```

3. **Destruction**: A stream can be destroyed via a call to the `cudaStreamDestroy()` function:

```
cudaError_t cudaStreamDestroy(cudaStream_t stream); // Stream ↵
    identifier
```

This is a blocking function that returns when all the pending commands in a stream are complete.

In the following example, two streams are used to coordinate two sequences involving a host-to-device data transfer, a kernel invocation, and a device-to-host results transfer:

```
1  // File: streamTest.cu
2  . . .
3  cudaStream_t str[2];
4  int *h_data[2], *d_data[2];
5  int i;
6
7  for(i=0;i<2;i++)
8  {
9    cudaStreamCreate(&(str[i]));
10   h_data[i] = (int *)malloc(sizeof(int) * DATASIZE);
11   cudaMalloc((void ** )&(d_data[i]), sizeof(int) * DATASIZE);
12
13   // initialize h_data[i]....
14
15   cudaMemcpyAsync(d_data[i], h_data[i], sizeof(int) * DATASIZE, ↵
         cudaMemcpyHostToDevice, str[i]);
16
17   doSmt <<< 10, 256, 0, str[i] >>> (d_data[i]);
18
19   cudaMemcpyAsync(h_data[i], d_data[i], sizeof(int) * DATASIZE, ↵
         cudaMemcpyDeviceToHost, str[i]);
```

```
20    }
21
22    cudaStreamDestroy(str[0]);
23    cudaStreamDestroy(str[1]);
24
25    for(i=0;i<2;i++)
26    {
27      free(h_data[i]);
28      cudaFree(d_data[i]);
29    }
```

The blocking calls of lines 22 and 23 ensure that by the time we get to free the allocated memory (loop of lines 25-29), all pending commands in our two streams have been completed.

There are two significant problems with the above listing. First, on devices that do support bi-directional transfers from and to the device, the host data must be on page-locked memory. This means that the copy of line 19 for str[0] and the copy of line 15 for str[1] could run concurrently for devices of compute capability 2.0 and above, only if h_data point to pinned memory. On the other hand, the two memory copy operations of line 15 (one for str[0] and one for str[1]) have to go in sequence regardless, because they require the use of the same communication medium.

The second problem is that page-locked host and device memory allocation are on a list of operations that block concurrency from taking place, at the time of their execution. The complete list includes:

- Page-locked host memory allocations
- Device memory allocation
- Device memory setting
- Any CUDA command that is added to the default stream
- Memory copy between two areas of the same device
- A change in the L1/shared memory configuration

To address these issues, we should modify the previous code as follows:

```
1   // File: streamTest2.cu
2   . . .
3     cudaStream_t str[2];
4     int *h_data[2], *d_data[2];
5     int i;
6
7     // Allocate memory first in both host and device
8     for(i=0;i<2;i++)
9     {
10      cudaMallocHost((void **) &(h_data[i]), sizeof(int) * DATASIZE);
11      cudaMalloc((void **) &(d_data[i]), sizeof(int) * DATASIZE);
12    }
13
14    // initialize h_data[i]....
15
16    // Now start populating the streams
```

```
17    for(i=0;i<2;i++)
18    {
19      cudaStreamCreate(&(str[i]));
20
21      cudaMemcpyAsync(d_data[i], h_data[i], sizeof(int) * DATASIZE, ↩
              cudaMemcpyHostToDevice, str[i]);
22
23      doSmt <<< 10, 256, 0, str[i] >>> (d_data[i]);
24
25      cudaMemcpyAsync(h_data[i], d_data[i], sizeof(int) * DATASIZE, ↩
              cudaMemcpyDeviceToHost, str[i]);
26    }
27
28    // Synchronization and clean-up
29    cudaStreamDestroy(str[0]);
30    cudaStreamDestroy(str[1]);
31
32    for(i=0;i<2;i++)
33    {
34      free(h_data[i]);
35      cudaFree(d_data[i]);
36    }
```

We have seen previously that one can use the cudaDeviceSynchronize() call to wait for the default stream queue to become empty. A number of CUDA functions and mechanisms are available to extend this functionality for explicitly or implicitly synchronizing streams. These functions, which are examined in the next section, allow us to establish coordination between different streams, or simply detect the completion of a command or set of commands.

6.7.7.1 Stream Synchronization: Events and Callbacks

The time instance a command (and everything preceding it in a stream) completes can be captured in the form of an **event**. CUDA uses the cudaEvent_t type for managing events. The available actions associated with cudaEvent_t instances are:

- Creation:
  ```
  cudaError_t cudaEventCreate (cudaEvent_t *event);
  ```
- Destruction:
  ```
  cudaError_t cudaEventDestroy (cudaEvent_t event);
  ```
- Recording the time an event takes place:
  ```
  cudaError_t cudaEventRecord(
                  cudaEvent_t event,      // Event identifier (IN)
                  cudaStream_t stream=0);// Stream identifier (IN)
  ```
  Essentially, this is a command enqueued in the specified stream.
- Finding the elapsed time between two events:
  ```
  cudaError_t cudaEventElapsedTime(
                  float *ms,              // Storage for elapsed time
                                          //   in msec units (OUT)
  ```

```
                    cudaEvent_t start,// Start event identifier (IN)
                    cudaEvent_t end); // End event identifier (IN)
```

cudaEventRecord and cudaEventElapsedTime can be used for instrumenting a CUDA program.

- Waiting for an event to occur:

```
cudaError_t cudaEventSynchronize (cudaEvent_t event);
```

This is a blocking call that can be used for explicit synchronization.

An example of how events can be used to instrument a CUDA program is provided in Listing 6.24, in the form of a program that measures the PCIe transfer speed as experienced through a series of cudaMemcpy calls.

```
1   // File: memcpyTest.cu
2   . . .
3   const int MAXDATASIZE = 1024 * 1024;
4
5   int main (int argc, char **argv)
6   {
7     int iter = atoi (argv[1]);
8     int step = atoi (argv[2]);
9     cudaStream_t str;
10    int *h_data, *d_data;
11    int i, dataSize;;
12    cudaEvent_t startT, endT;
13    float duration;
14
15    cudaMallocHost ((void **) &h_data, sizeof (int) * MAXDATASIZE);
16    cudaMalloc ((void **) &d_data, sizeof (int) * MAXDATASIZE);
17    for (i = 0; i < MAXDATASIZE; i++)
18      h_data[i] = i;
19
20    cudaEventCreate (&startT);
21    cudaEventCreate (&endT);
22
23    for (dataSize = 0; dataSize <= MAXDATASIZE; dataSize += step)
24      {
25        cudaEventRecord (startT, str);
26        for (i = 0; i < iter; i++)
27          {
28            cudaMemcpyAsync (d_data, h_data, sizeof (int) * dataSize, ↩
                  cudaMemcpyHostToDevice, str);
29          }
30        cudaEventRecord (endT, str);
31        cudaEventSynchronize (endT);
32        cudaEventElapsedTime (&duration, startT, endT);
33        printf ("%i %f\n", (int) (dataSize * sizeof (int)), duration / ↩
              iter);
34      }
35
36    cudaStreamDestroy (str);
```

```
37    cudaEventDestroy (startT);
38    cudaEventDestroy (endT);
39
40    cudaFreeHost (h_data);
41    cudaFree (d_data);
42    cudaDeviceReset ();
43    . . .
```

LISTING 6.24

An example of how a CUDA program can be instrumented with the use of events.

The program of Listing 6.24 performs a series of varying data size, memory copy operations from the host to the device. The program expects two command-line parameters (read at lines 7, 8) which are the number of iterations used for averaging the results for each data size and the step used to iterate from data size 0 to data size MAXDATASIZE. Lines 25 and 30 are the essential parts of the instrumentation, enclosing all the commands that are enqueued in the stream used. Line 31 waits for the endT event to occur, which effectively translates to the completion of a set of tests for a specific data size.

This code could be simplified a bit by using 0 in place of the str parameter (in lines 25, 28, and 30), forcing the use of the default stream.

Another mechanism pertaining to synchronization is the *callback*. A callback is a function that is called in response to the detection of an event. In terms of expressiveness, a callback is a much more generic, if expensive, mechanism than an event. A function that is to be called as a callback has to have the following signature:

```
void callback(cudaStream_t stream, // Stream calling the function (IN)
              cudaError_t status,   // Error condition (IN)
              void *userData);      // Pointer to arbitrary data (IN)
```

A function can be registered to be called when all the preceding commands have been completed in a stream by the cudaStreamAddCallback() function:

```
cudaError_t cudaStreamAddCallback(
            cudaStream_t stream,            // Stream that will trigger
                                            //    the function (IN)
            cudaStreamCallback_t callback,  // Pointer to callback
                                            //    function (IN)
            void *userData,                 // Data to be supplied to
                                            //    the callback (IN)
            unsigned int flags);            // Should be zero (reserved
                                            //    for future use)
```

A variation of Listing 6.24 using a callback function is shown in Listing 6.25.

```
1    // File: memcpyTestCallback.cu
2    . . .
3    const int MAXDATASIZE = 1024 * 1024;
4    //──────────────────────────────────────────────
5    void myCallBack (cudaStream_t stream, cudaError_t status, void *↵
         userData)
```

```
6    {
7      float *t = (float *) userData;
8      clock_t x = clock();
9      *t = x*1.0/CLOCKS_PER_SEC;
10   }
11   //————————————————————————————————————————
12   int main (int argc, char **argv)
13   {
14     int iter = atoi (argv[1]);
15     int step = atoi (argv[2]);
16     cudaStream_t str;
17     int *h_data, *d_data;
18     int i, dataSize;;
19
20     cudaStreamCreate(&str);
21     cudaMallocHost ((void **) &h_data, sizeof (int) * MAXDATASIZE);
22     cudaMalloc ((void **) &d_data, sizeof (int) * MAXDATASIZE);
23     for (i = 0; i < MAXDATASIZE; i++)
24       h_data[i] = i;
25
26     float t1, t2;
27     cudaStreamAddCallback (str, myCallBack, (void *) &t1, 0);
28     for (dataSize = 0; dataSize <= MAXDATASIZE; dataSize += step)
29       {
30         for (i = 0; i < iter; i++)
31           {
32             cudaMemcpyAsync (d_data, h_data, sizeof (int) * dataSize, ↩
                        cudaMemcpyHostToDevice, str);
33           }
34         cudaStreamAddCallback (str, myCallBack, (void *) &t2, 0);
35         cudaStreamSynchronize(str);
36         printf ("%i %f\n", (int) (dataSize * sizeof (int)), (t2 - t1) / ↩
                    iter);
37         t1 = t2;
38       }
39
40     cudaStreamDestroy (str);
41
42     cudaFreeHost (h_data);
43     cudaFree (d_data);
44     cudaDeviceReset ();
45   . . .
```

LISTING 6.25

A variation of Listing 6.24, illustrating the use of callback functions.

The myCallBack() function of lines 5-10 uses a pointer to float to return the time instance it is called. Two different pointers are specified as callback parameters in lines 27 and 34, allowing us to measure and output a time difference in line 36. Admittedly, the use of the clock() function in line 8 limits the accuracy of the results, but it should be stressed that callback functions are not allowed to use any

CUDA functions. Otherwise an error is produced. Fortunately, numerous alternative are available, but they are beyond the scope of this section.

6.8 DYNAMIC PARALLELISM

An unexpected limitation in the development of CUDA software had been the inability to write recursive functions. This had been a limitation in expressiveness more than anything else, as a large collection of algorithms can be naturally and compactly expressed using recursion. Examples include mergesort, quicksort, DFS graph traversal and others. Since the introduction of Compute Capability 2.0 devices, recursion is supported. However, as recursion can be removed with the integration of a stack, this has not been a really big issue.

Dynamic parallelism is a mechanism that is supported in devices of Compute Capability 3.5 and above, and it goes way beyond recursion, by enabling the launch of kernels from the device. This means that the divide-and-conquer decomposition pattern discussed in Section 2.3.2, can be conveniently implemented in CUDA, with a minimum of effort. A kernel can use the same syntax that the host is using, i.e., the triple angular brackets $<<<>>>$, to asynchronously launch other kernels.

A grid that is launched by a CUDA thread is considered a *child grid*. The grid of the launcher is called the *parent grid*. Child grids execute asynchronously, as if they were launched by the host. However, typical nesting rules apply, i.e., a parent grid is not considered finished, until all the child grids launched by its threads are also finished.

Device-launched kernels can be only monitored from threads belonging to the same block as the launcher thread. Streams and events can be used to synchronize and control dependencies between different launches, via a subset of the API that is available for the host. However, the launches cannot target another GPU device in a multi-GPU system. This is still host-only territory.

As far as memory management is concerned, a child grid launch can be passed references to global data, but not to shared memory, since shared memory is private to a specific SM. The same applies to local memory, as it is private to a thread.

As an example of dynamic parallelism, Listing 6.26 holds a CUDA implementation of the quicksort algorithm.

```
1   // File : quicksort_dynamic.cu
2   . . .
3   const int MAXRECURSIONDEPTH=16;
4
5   //*************************************************
6   void numberGen (int N, int max, int *store)
7   {
8     int i;
9     srand (time (0));
10    for (i = 0; i < N; i++)
11      store[i] = rand () % max;
12  }
```

```
13
14   //*************************************************
15   __device__ void swap (int *data, int x, int y)
16   {
17     int temp = data[x];
18     data[x] = data[y];
19     data[y] = temp;
20   }
21
22   //*************************************************
23   __device__ int partition (int *data, int N)
24   {
25     int i = 0, j = N;
26     int pivot = data[0];
27
28     do
29       {
30         do
31           {
32             i++;
33           }
34         while (pivot > data[i] && i < N);
35
36         do
37           {
38             j--;
39           }
40         while (pivot < data[j] && j > 0);
41         swap (data, i, j);
42       }
43     while (i < j);
44     // undo last swap
45     swap (data, i, j);
46
47     // fix the pivot element position
48     swap (data, 0, j);
49     return j;
50   }
51
52   //*************************************************
53   __device__ void insertionSort (int *data, int N)
54   {
55     int loc=1;
56     while(loc < N)
57       {
58         int temp = data[loc];
59         int i=loc-1;
60         while(i>=0 && data[i] > temp)
61           {
62             data[i+1]=data[i];
63             i--;
64           }
```

```
65        data[i+1] = temp;
66        loc++;
67      }
68    }
69
70    // **************************************************
71    __global__ void QSort (int *data, int N, int depth)
72    {
73      if(depth == MAXRECURSIONDEPTH)
74        {
75        insertionSort(data, N);
76        return;
77        }
78
79      if (N <= 1)
80        return;
81
82      // break the data into a left and right part
83      int pivotPos = partition (data, N);
84
85      cudaStream_t s0, s1;
86      // sort the left part if it exists
87      if (pivotPos > 0)
88        {
89          cudaStreamCreateWithFlags (&s0, cudaStreamNonBlocking);
90          QSort <<< 1, 1, 0, s0 >>> (data, pivotPos, depth+1);
91          cudaStreamDestroy (s0);
92        }
93
94      // sort the right part if it exists
95      if (pivotPos < N - 1)
96        {
97          cudaStreamCreateWithFlags (&s1, cudaStreamNonBlocking);
98          QSort <<< 1, 1, 0, s1 >>> (&(data[pivotPos + 1]), N - pivotPos ↩
                 - 1, depth+1);
99          cudaStreamDestroy (s1);
100       }
101   }
102
103   //────────────────────────────────────────────────────
104   int main (int argc, char *argv[])
105   {
106     if (argc == 1)
107       {
108         fprintf (stderr, "%s N\n", argv[0]);
109         exit (0);
110       }
111     int N = atoi (argv[1]);
112     int *data;
113     cudaMallocManaged ((void **) &data, N * sizeof (int));
114
115     numberGen (N, 1000, data);
```

```
116
117     QSort <<< 1, 1 >>> (data, N, 0);
118
119     cudaDeviceSynchronize ();
120
121     // clean-up allocated memory
122     cudaFree (data);
123     return 0;
124   }
```

LISTING 6.26

A CUDA implementation of quicksort that utilizes dynamic parallelism.

The majority of the code in Listing 6.26 is a straightforward implementation of the well-known sequential quicksort and insertion sort algorithms. For this reason we will not comment on the inner workings of the partition and insertionSort functions. The key points are as follows:

- The main function reads from the standard input the size N of the data array of integers to be sorted. It proceeds to allocate unified memory for this task (line 113), and initialize the data to random values (line 115).
- The host launches the QSort kernel with a grid of 1 block, with the block made-up of 1 thread. The concurrency is the outcome of asynchronously launching two more such grids in lines 90 and 98, after the data are partitioned using the partition __device__ function. The partition function (lines 23-50) returns the location in the sorted array of the element used to split the data in two (the pivot element), allowing QSort to decide whether the parts hold any data or not (condition checks in lines 87 and 95).
- The child grids are launched using two separate streams. Launching them into the default stream would force their sequential execution.
- The cudaStreamDestroy calls of lines 91 and 99 are non-blocking. The associated streams will be destroyed once the work items deposited in them are complete. Still, the parent grid cannot terminate before the child grids are complete.
- The recursion is limited by monitoring the depth of the child grids generated (line 73). The depth parameter is incremented whenever a child grid is launched. If it matches the threshold specified by the MAXRECURSIONDEPTH constant, we switch to the insertion sort algorithm (lines 53-68).

It should be noted that Listing 6.26 is just a demonstration of dynamic parallelism in action, and it is not meant to serve as a fast sorting implementation. After all, the design of quicksort is inherently unsuitable for GPU execution. Even if we were not launching 1-block grids of 1 thread, the unavoidable thread divergence would hinder any performance gains.

In order to compile the program of Listing 6.26, the following command in required:

```
$ nvcc quicksort_dynamic.cu —arch=compute_35 —code=sm_35 —rdc=true —o ↩
    quicksort_dynamic
```

A device of Compute Capability 3.5 or above is required for running the program.

6.9 DEBUGGING CUDA PROGRAMS

Nvidia provides two tools for debugging CUDA applications:

- The Parallel NSight Eclipse-based IDE (nsight) provides integrated GUI-based debugging for Linux and Mac OS X platforms. Under Windows, NSight integrates with Visual Studio.
- CUDA-GDB (cuda-gdb) is a command-line debugger based on GNU's debugger (gdb) and it is available for Linux and Mac OS X platforms. Putting aside the awkward interface, CUDA-GDB offers all the conveniences of a modern debugger, such as single-step execution, breakpoints in kernel code, inspection of individual threads, and so on. Additionally, because it shares the same commands with the GNU debugger, it can be used in tandem with front ends such as DDD, eliminating the need for someone to memorize its commands. For example:

```
$ ddd —debugger cuda—gdb myCudaProgram
```

Actually, in Linux and Mac OS X platforms, NSight is just a front end for CUDA-GDB.

Debugging CUDA programs suffers from a major drawback that stems from the peculiarity of using a display device for computations: It requires two GPUs, one for running the application under development and one for regular display. The former GPU may be hosted in the same machine or a remote one. Most users would find themselves under the second scenario, i.e., using a remote machine (e.g., a shared server) for debugging purposes. Those unfortunate enough to not have access to a second GPU will have to rely on printf() for probing the state of CUDA threads during execution.

In this section we explore how Parallel NSight can be used for remote debugging, following one of the most probable scenarios that one can encounter. A screenshot of the Eclipse-based Parallel NSight platform is shown in Figure 6.19.

A remote debugging session has to be initially configured by selecting the Run → Debug Remote Application... menu option. In response, the dialog box in Figure 6.20 will appear. The remote debugging is conducted by having the application run under the supervision of a cuda-gdbserver process. Unless the remote system is already running cuda-gdbserver, the first option should be selected in Figure 6.20.

The next dialog box, which is shown in Figure 6.21, controls how the remote system will get the application. Unless a common filesystem, e.g., an NFS volume, is being used, this has to be done by uploading the new binary. If the remote system is being used for the first time, pressing "Manage" allows the user to specify the connection details.

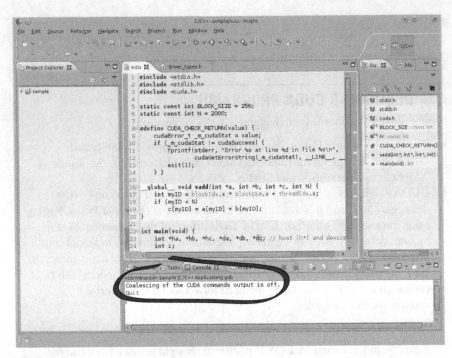

FIGURE 6.19

A screenshot of the Eclipse-based Parallel NSight platform running under Linux. The highlighted Console pane error message was generated by trying to debug the application locally, without a second GPU.

The connection details of all the remote systems used for debugging, are collectively managed by the dialog shown in Figure 6.22.

A new debugging session can commence by selecting the just created configuration from the "Run → Debug Configurations..." dialog window (see Figure 6.22).

Caution: It is a good idea to use the same CUDA SDK in both the local and remote hosts in order to avoid errors caused by missing libraries.

6.10 PROFILING CUDA PROGRAMS

Profilingal is an integral part of parallel program development, more so in the case of CUDA programs, where the idiosyncrasies of the underlying hardware deviate from what programmers think to be typical behavior. In the case of a sequential program, profiling can help us pinpoint the parts of the program that contribute the most to the execution time. In the case of a GPU program, profiling can help us understand the factors limiting or preventing the GPU from achieving its peak performance.

Nvidia provides profiling functionality via two tools:

- `nvprof` is a command-line-based utility for profiling CUDA programs. A number of switches enable control over the profiling process (e.g., what kind of

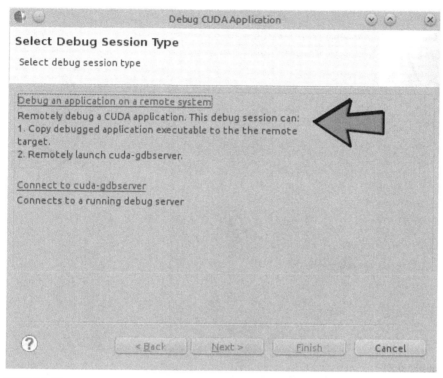

FIGURE 6.20

Parallel NSight dialog box for selecting the type of remote debug session.

metrics to collect). It is the tool of choice for profiling remote systems. In contrast with the debugging process, there is no mandate for using two GPUs, so profiling a remote system is just a choice.

- Nvidia Visual Profiler (nvvp) is a GUI-based tool for visualizing the execution timeline of a CUDA program. nvvp can provide a plethora of analyses, guiding the development of a CUDA program. nvvp can be also used for the visualization of data collected from nvprof.

The Visual Profiler can be used as a standalone tool or embedded within Parallel NSight. As a part of NSight, it can be used from within the IDE by switching to the Profile view. In this section we explore the capabilities of the Visual Profiler, the most relevant tool for the majority of users.

The starting point in profiling a program is to decide which are the parts to be examined. Profiling is a process that is characterized by the following:

1. The potential generation of huge amounts of visual data that increase monotonically as a function of the execution time. Extracting useful information from long runs can be very challenging. It is a better idea to focus on specific parts of the program.

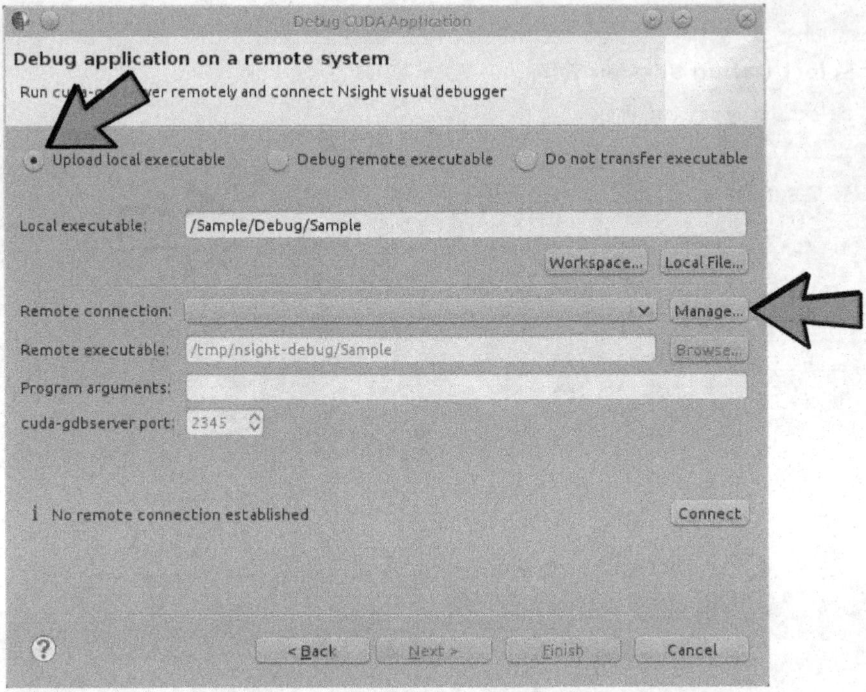

FIGURE 6.21

Parallel NSight dialog box for selecting how the application will reach the remote system (typically by uploading). By pressing "Manage" a user can specify the remote system connection parameters.

2. The profiler can influence the execution of the program by altering the timing of operations and the amount of I/O generated.
3. The profiler's results can be influenced by irregular operations timing. Because the profiler may need to run the program several times in order to collect reliable statistics, it is desirable, especially in the case of multi-threaded host programs that use different contexts/streams, to have a single CPU thread generate all the operations in the same sequence every time.

These problems can be minimized or eliminated by performing focused instead of whole-program profiling. In *focused profiling*, only parts of the program that are executed between calls to the `cudaProfilerStart()` and `cudaProfilerStop()` functions will be profiled, i.e., profiling is controlled programmatically from within the profiled program. The skeleton of a focused profiled program would be similar to:

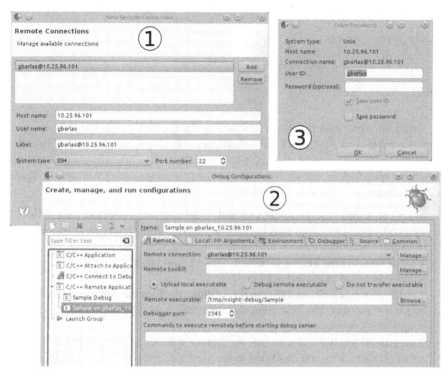

FIGURE 6.22

Parallel NSight dialogs for (1) managing remote connection information and (2) selecting the configuration for launching a new debugging session. The system may prompt the user for login credentials (3) depending on the selected connection protocol and system setup.

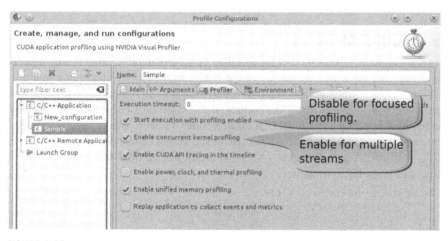

FIGURE 6.23

Parallel NSight dialog box for configuring the parameters of the profiler.

```
#include <cuda_profiler_api.h>  /* necessary include file */
. . .
cudaProfilerStart();

// calls to CPU and GPU routines

cudaProfilerStop();
. . .
```

Firing up a program in NSight and getting the profiler's report is pretty simple Run → Profile As... → Local C/C++ Application is all you need to select from the menu (this option is visible in the C/C++ view of the IDE). Only a handful of options need to be specified, as shown in the Profile Configurations dialog window of Figure 6.23. These are:

- **Start execution with profiling enabled**: If this option is selected, the profiler will collect data from the start till the end of execution. Otherwise, focused profiling is in effect.
- **Enable concurrent kernel profiling**: Should be selected only if multiple streams are used in the application.
- **Enable power, clock, and thermal profiling**: Enables the collection of these additional metrics. The collection also depends on whether the target GPU can supply this information.
- **Run guided analysis**: If selected, the profiler will run an analysis phase where a set of problem areas are identified in the program, and solutions are proposed. This option is not available from within NSight, but it is shown in Visual Profiler whenever a new session is created.

An example of the results of the guided analysis is shown in Figure 6.24. A detailed example of how the profiler can be used to guide our design decisions is provided in Section 6.12.

6.11 CUDA AND MPI

A GPU can be a formidable tool for speeding up a computation. So, it is only natural to expect that we could do more and we could go further by employing multiple GPUs. Nvidia's Scalable Link Interface (SLI) allows up to four GPUs[21] to be hosted inside the same chassis under the control of the same host (AMD's corresponding technology is called Crossfire). CUDA allows the transfer of data directly between the memories of SLI-connected GPUs. However, kernel launches can target only one GPU at a time. The cudaSetDevice() function can be used to specify the target device in multi-GPU systems:

```
cudaError_t cudaSetDevice (int device);  // a number between 0 and ↩
    the number_of_GPUs − 1
```

---

[21]Getting that many to work properly in one system is a big and expensive challenge because of power and thermal constraints.

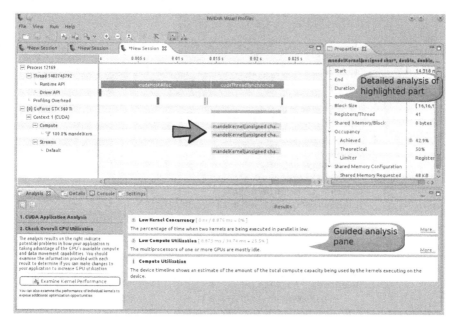

FIGURE 6.24

A sample screenshot of Nvidia's Visual Profiler in action.

How can we go beyond four GPUs? The solution is to employ MPI (see Chapter 5) to coordinate multiple hosts that in turn control one or more GPUs. MPI is designed to essentially transfer data between host buffers, making the transfer of data residing in GPU memory space a problem. There are two possible solutions, based on whether MPI is CUDA-aware or not:

1. **MPI is not CUDA-aware**: Data are explicitly transferred from the device to the host before making the desired MPI call. On the receiving side, these actions have to be repeated in reverse.
2. **MPI is CUDA-aware**: MPI can access device buffers directly, hence pointers to device memory can be used in MPI calls. An example of a CUDA-aware MPI implementation is OpenMPI.

To illustrate the differences between the two approaches, Listing 6.27 shows a modified version of a ping-pong program that is typically used to gauge the communication characteristics in MPI installations.

```
1  // File: ping_pong.cu
2  . . .
3    // allocate host and device memory in all hosts
4    char *d_data, *h_data;
5    cudaMalloc ((void **) &d_data, MAX_MESG);
```

```
6     h_data = (char *) malloc (MAX_MESG);
7
8     if (rank == 0)
9       {
10        for (int mesg_size = 0; mesg_size <= MAX_MESG; mesg_size += ↵
          1000)
11          {
12            start_time = MPI_Wtime ();
13            for (int i = 0; i < REP; i++)
14              {
15                // get data from device
16                cudaMemcpy (h_data, d_data, mesg_size, ↵
                    cudaMemcpyDeviceToHost);
17                // send it to other host
18                MPI_Send (h_data, mesg_size, MPI_CHAR, 1, tag, ↵
                    MPI_COMM_WORLD);
19                // wait to collect response
20                MPI_Recv (h_data, MAX_MESG, MPI_CHAR, 1, MPI_ANY_TAG, ↵
                    MPI_COMM_WORLD, &status);
21            // forward data to device
22                cudaMemcpy (d_data, h_data, mesg_size, ↵
                    cudaMemcpyHostToDevice);
23              }
24
25            end_time = MPI_Wtime ();
26            printf ("%i %lf\n", mesg_size, (end_time - start_time) / 2 /↵
              REP);
27          }
28
29        tag = END_TAG;
30        MPI_Send (h_data, 0, MPI_CHAR, 1, tag, MPI_COMM_WORLD);
31      }
32    else
33      {
34        while (1)
35          {
36            // get message
37            MPI_Recv (h_data, MAX_MESG, MPI_CHAR, 0, MPI_ANY_TAG, ↵
                MPI_COMM_WORLD, &status);
38            // filter -out end tag
39            if (status.MPI_TAG == END_TAG)
40              break;
41
42            // get size of message and sent it to the device
43            MPI_Get_count (&status, MPI_CHAR, &mesg_size);
44            cudaMemcpy (d_data, h_data, mesg_size, ↵
                cudaMemcpyHostToDevice);
45
46            // get response from the device
47            cudaMemcpy (h_data, d_data, mesg_size, ↵
                cudaMemcpyDeviceToHost);
48            // and send it back
```

```
49              MPI_Send (h_data, mesg_size, MPI_CHAR, 0, tag, ↩
                    MPI_COMM_WORLD);
50          }
51      }
52    . . .
```

LISTING 6.27

A variation of an MPI ping-pong program, where the source and destination buffers are in GPU memory without MPI being aware of it.

This above program can be compiled with a single command using the `nvcc` compiler driver just by including the MPI dynamic library (`-lmpi`) and specifying the location of the corresponding include files (`-I/usr/include/mpi`):

```
$ nvcc ping_pong.cu —lmpi —I/usr/include/mpi —o ping_pong
```

The explicit movement between host and device buffers is clear in lines 16, 22, 44, and 47. The program does not do anything useful; it is only meant to report the time it takes for the exchange to take place.

The second solution entails the use of 64-bit operating systems for the host and the use of 64-bit compilation mode for the device (affecting memory pointers) so that UVA can be enabled (a compute-capability 2.0 or above device is also necessary). UVA uses 64-bit addressing to unify the address space of the host along with the address spaces of any CUDA devices in the system. The value of a memory pointer can then be used to deduce exactly where the corresponding data reside (host or device and on which device). A CUDA-aware MPI implementation can then proceed to perform the transfer from the device to an MPI buffer, saving at least one memory copy on the sending and one memory copy on the receiving side.

The ping-pong implementation for a CUDA-aware MPI, is shown in Listing 6.28 (it can be compiled via an identical `nvcc` command-line as the program of Listing 6.27).

```
1   // File: ping_pong_CUDAaware.cu
2   . . .
3     char *d_data;
4     cudaMalloc ((void **) &d_data, MAX_MESG);
5
6     if (rank == 0)
7       {
8          for (int mesg_size = 0; mesg_size <= MAX_MESG; mesg_size += ↩
               1000)
9            {
10             start_time = MPI_Wtime ();
11             for (int i = 0; i < REP; i++)
12               {
13                  // send data to other host
```

```
14              MPI_Send (d_data, mesg_size, MPI_CHAR, 1, tag, ↩
                    MPI_COMM_WORLD);
15              // wait to collect response
16              MPI_Recv (d_data, MAX_MESG, MPI_CHAR, 1, MPI_ANY_TAG, ↩
                    MPI_COMM_WORLD, &status);
17          }
18
19          end_time = MPI_Wtime ();
20          printf ("%i %lf\n", mesg_size, (end_time - start_time) / 2 /↩
                REP);
21      }
22
23      tag = END_TAG;
24      MPI_Send (d_data, 0, MPI_CHAR, 1, tag, MPI_COMM_WORLD);
25  }
26  else
27  {
28      while (1)
29        {
30          // get message
31          MPI_Recv (d_data, MAX_MESG, MPI_CHAR, 0, MPI_ANY_TAG, ↩
                MPI_COMM_WORLD, &status);
32          // filter-out end tag
33          if (status.MPI_TAG == END_TAG)
34            break;
35
36          // get size of message and sent it to the device
37          MPI_Get_count (&status, MPI_CHAR, &mesg_size);
38
39          // send response back
40          MPI_Send (d_data, mesg_size, MPI_CHAR, 0, tag, ↩
                MPI_COMM_WORLD);
41        }
42  }
43
```

LISTING 6.28

A variation of a MPI ping-pong program for device data, where MPI is CUDA-aware and UVA is enabled.

Obviously, the second one is the method of choice, given the benefits of having a simpler program logic and streamlining any required memory copies. The striking difference between Listings 6.28 and 6.27 is the absence of a host buffer and the passing of device pointers directly to MPI_Send and MPI_Recv functions (lines 14, 16, 31, and 40).

The details of how a CUDA-aware MPI implementation will behave upon requested to operate on a device buffer, depend to a large degree on the compute capability of the device. Since 2010, Nvidia has introduced a set of technologies, collectively referred to as *GPUDirect*, that on devices of compute-capability 2.0 and above provide the following:

- **Faster communication with network and storage devices**: By using pinned memory, the CUDA driver and third-party device drivers can share a buffer, eliminating the need to make an extra copy of the data.
- **Peer-to-peer**[22] transfers between GPUs on the same PCIe bus, without going through the host's memory.
- **Peer-to-peer memory access**: A GPU can access the memory of another GPU using NUMA-style access. The difference between this and the previous item is in the volume of data involved: The previous item involves a `cudaMemcpy()` call.
- **Remote DMA (RDMA)**:
  A GPU buffer can be copied directly over a network to a remote GPU.

To clarify the difference between UVA and GPUDirect, UVA enables the simplification of the source code by allowing the value of a pointer to designate the memory space where the data reside. Library functions, both CUDA and third-party, can use this information to stage the appropriate memory copy operations in the background. GPUDirect, on the other hand, is a technology completely transparent to the application programmer (but not to the device driver or library developer) that enables fast access or communication of device data without the need for intermediate holding buffers.

The traffic generated by a plain-vanilla MPI implementation for a single send-receive pair of commands involving device buffers is illustrated and contrasted with the one generated by a CUDA-aware, RDMA-assisted MPI implementation in Figure 6.25. Because data to be transferred via DMA by a controller other than the CPU (e.g., PCIe south bridge, Ethernet controller, Infiniband, etc.) needs to reside on nonswappable, i.e., pinned memory, the operation in Figure 6.25(a) needs no less than six (!) memory copies before the data reach their destination. In Figure 6.25(b), RDMA bypasses all this overhead by allowing direct access to the source and destination buffers.

Even if we use a CUDA-**un**aware MPI implementation, if the host memory is pinned we can get away with only two memory copies, as shown in Figure 6.25(c), despite having to explicitly call `cudaMemcpy()`.

6.12 CASE STUDIES

In this section we explore the potential of CUDA with a number of easy-to-understand applications. The goal is to show how we can use CUDA to accelerate our computations while at the same time exercise the tools that are provided with the CUDA SDK.

In the code supplied in the following sections, we revert to the primitive but convenient CUDA error checking that a preprocessor macro can provide, as identified in Section 6.6. This is currently the safest bet for catching early errors occurring on

---

[22]"Peer" in this context refers to another GPU hosted on the same machine. No networking is involved.

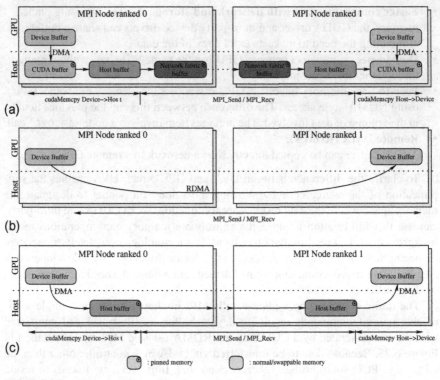

FIGURE 6.25

An illustration of the traffic generated for device-to-device communication by (a) a plain-vanilla MPI implementation, (b) a CUDA-aware MPI implementation using the GPUDirect RDMA mechanism, and (c) an MPI implementation taking advantage of pinned host memory. The network fabric buffer is a buffer used by a networking controller such as Ethernet or Infiniband.

the GPU. Although we purposefully omitted error checking in the previous sections, this was done for the sake of clarity and is obviously not recommended.

6.12.1 FRACTAL SET CALCULATION

In this section we explore the design of a solution to the Mandelbrot fractal generation problem. The particular application has been discussed extensively in this book (see Sections 3.8.2 and 5.22.1), so we will proceed directly with just a brief explanation.

The Mandelbrot set is a set of points $c = x + i \cdot y$ on the complex plane that produce a bounded sequence of numbers $z_0, z_1, z_2, \ldots$ when the recursive formula $z_{n+1} = z_n^2 + c$ with $z_0 = c$ is applied, i.e., $|z_n| = \sqrt{x_n^2 + y_n^2} < \infty \; \forall n$. In order to produce a graphical depiction of the Mandelbrot, we must apply the recursive formula on each point of the complex plane that corresponds to an image pixel until z_{n+1} diverges ($|z_n| > 2$) or n exceeds a preset threshold.

We explore and evaluate three possible design approaches that can be considered an evolution sequence:

1. Using one CUDA thread per pixel, with normal host and device memory allocations
2. Using one CUDA thread per pixel, with pitched device memory allocation and pinned host memory
3. Using one CUDA thread per block of pixels, with pitched device memory allocation and pinned host memory.

6.12.1.1 Version #1: One thread per pixel

The application of the recursive formula suggests an uneven computational cost for each point in the set, but an easy migration to a CUDA solution would be to just spawn a thread per point/pixel. This approach is shown in Listing 6.29.

```
1  // File: mandelCUDA_v1/kernel.cu
2  #include <QImage>
3  #include <QRgb>
4  . . .
5  static const int MAXITER = 255;
6
7  // ***********************************************************
8  // Checks to see how many iterations takes for (cx, cy) to diverge
9  __device__ int diverge (double cx, double cy)
10 {
11   int iter = 0;
12   double vx = cx, vy = cy, tx, ty;
13   while (iter < MAXITER && (vx * vx + vy * vy) < 4)
14     {
15       tx = vx * vx - vy * vy + cx;
16       ty = 2 * vx * vy + cy;
17       vx = tx;
18       vy = ty;
19       iter++;
20     }
21   return iter;
22 }
23
24 // ***********************************************************
25 // Each CUDA thread calculates the result for one point. The pitch ←
         parameter is identical to resX in this solution
26 __global__ void mandelKernel (unsigned char *d_res, double upperX, ←
         double upperY, double stepX, double stepY, int resX, int resY, int←
         pitch)
27 {
28   int myX, myY;
29   myX = blockIdx.x * blockDim.x + threadIdx.x;  // get the thread's ←
         grid coordinates
30   myY = blockIdx.y * blockDim.y + threadIdx.y;
31   if (myX >= resX || myY >= resY)
32     return;
```

```
33
34    double tempx, tempy;
35    tempx = upperX + myX * stepX;    // translate the thread's ID into a ←
          point in the complex plane
36    tempy = upperY - myY * stepY;
37    int color = diverge (tempx, tempy);
38    d_res[myY * pitch + myX] = color;
39  }
40
41  // *************************************************************
42  // Host front-end function that allocates the memory and launches the ←
        GPU kernel
43  void hostFE (double upperX, double upperY, double lowerX, double ←
        lowerY, QImage * img, int resX, int resY)
44  {
45    int blocksX, blocksY;
46    blocksX = (int) ceil (resX / 16);  // Rounds up the grid dimensions ←
          according to the block size
47    blocksY = (int) ceil (resY / 16);
48    dim3 block (16, 16);    // a block is made by 16x16 threads
49    dim3 grid (blocksX, blocksY);
50    int pitch;
51
52    unsigned char *h_res;
53    unsigned char *d_res;
54
55    pitch = resX;
56
57    // device and host memory allocation
58    CUDA_CHECK_RETURN (cudaMalloc ((void **) &d_res, resX * resY));
59    h_res = (unsigned char *) malloc (resY * pitch);
60
61    double stepX = (lowerX - upperX) / resX;  // x- and y-distance ←
          between neighboring points on the complex plane
62    double stepY = (upperY - lowerY) / resY;
63
64    // launch GPU kernel
65    mandelKernel <<< grid, block >>> (d_res, upperX, upperY, stepX, ←
          stepY, resX, resY, pitch);
66
67    // wait for GPU to finish
68    CUDA_CHECK_RETURN (cudaDeviceSynchronize ());  // wait for the ←
          computation to complete
69
70    // get the results
71    CUDA_CHECK_RETURN (cudaMemcpy (h_res, d_res, resY * pitch, ←
          cudaMemcpyDeviceToHost));
72
73    //copy results into QImage object
74    for (int j = 0; j < resY; j++)
75      for (int i = 0; i < resX; i++)
76        {
```

```
77          int color = h_res[j * pitch + i];
78          img->setPixel (i, j, qRgb (256 - color, 256 - color, 256 - ↩
               color));
79        }
80
81      // clean-up allocated memory
82      free (h_res);
83      CUDA_CHECK_RETURN (cudaFree (d_res));
84    }
```

LISTING 6.29

A CUDA thread-per-pixel solution for the calculation of the Mandelbrot set.

The code of Listing 6.29 consists of three functions:

- The hostFE() function (line 43) is called by the host's main() function to run the GPU code. It is responsible for allocating memory, spawning the CUDA threads, setting up the requested image (lines 74-79), and clearing-up memory. The execution configuration uses an ad hoc arrangement of 16x16-thread blocks, making up a 2D grid. The grid dimensions are calculated based on the image resolution (lines 46 and 47).
- The diverge() function (line 9) is identical to the one used in the examples of Chapters 3 and 5. It is just "decorated" by the __device__ qualifier, which means it is only callable from device code.
- The mandelKernel() function (line 26) first locates the position of a thread in the overall grid before mapping this position to the complex plane (lines 35 and 36) and calling diverge(). The number of iterations required before a point diverges (or MAXITER if it does not) is stored in a global array (line 38). Since these data are accessed only once, no provision for involving the shared memory is made. The mandelKernel() function signature is consistent across all three implementations.

Listing 6.30 shows a variation of hostFE() function using Unified Memory.

```
1    // File: mandelCUDA_v1_unified/kernel.cu
2    . . .
3    void hostFE (double upperX, double upperY, double lowerX, double ↩
         lowerY, QImage * img, int resX, int resY)
4    {
5      int blocksX, blocksY;
6      blocksX = (int) ceil (resX / 16);
7      blocksY = (int) ceil (resY / 16);
8      dim3 block (16, 16);
9      dim3 grid (blocksX, blocksY);
10     int pitch;
11
12     // single pointer to results array
13     unsigned char *res;
14
```

```
15   pitch = resX;
16
17   CUDA_CHECK_RETURN (cudaMallocManaged (( void **) &res, resX * resY));
18
19   double stepX = (lowerX - upperX) / resX;
20   double stepY = (upperY - lowerY) / resY;
21
22   // launch GPU kernel
23   mandelKernel <<< grid, block >>> (res, upperX, upperY, stepX, stepY, ↵
         resX, resY, pitch);
24
25   // wait for GPU to finish
26   CUDA_CHECK_RETURN (cudaDeviceSynchronize ());
27
28   //copy results into QImage object from host-side managed memory
29   for (int j = 0; j < resY; j++)
30     for (int i = 0; i < resX; i++)
31       {
32         int color = res[j * pitch + i];
33         img->setPixel (i, j, qRgb (256 - color, 256 - color, 256 - ↵
           color));
34       }
35
36   // clean-up allocated memory
37   CUDA_CHECK_RETURN (cudaFree (res));
38 }
```

LISTING 6.30

A Unified Memory variation of the code in Listing 6.29.

In the results reported in Section 6.12.1.4, we do not use the Unified Memory variant, since tests on a compute-capability 3.0 device have shown it to be slightly slower (3-4%) than the explicit memory management version.

6.12.1.2 Version #2: Pinned host and pitched device memory

There are two issues that can be improved in Listing 6.29 as per the techniques listed in Section 6.7: (a) we can use pinned host memory to improve the communication time over the PCIe interface between the host and the device, and (b) we can use pitched memory allocation on the device so that each image row occupies a multiple of 32 bytes of memory, allowing coalescing of memory accesses when line 38 in function mandelKernel() is executed.

These changes require only a small modification of the hostFE() function, as shown in Listing 6.31. The only lines that are different from Listing 6.29 are 18, 20 and 43, as a pitch variable was already used in Listing 6.29, but it was set to resX.

```
1   // File: mandelCUDA_v2/kernel.cu
2   . . .
3   //=============================================================
4   // Host front-end function that allocates the memory and launches the ↵
       GPU kernel
```

```
5   void hostFE (double upperX, double upperY, double lowerX, double ↵
        lowerY, QImage * img, int resX, int resY)
6   {
7     int blocksX, blocksY;
8     blocksX = (int) ceil (resX / 16.0);
9     blocksY = (int) ceil (resY / 16.0);
10    dim3 block (16, 16);
11    dim3 grid (blocksX, blocksY);
12    int pitch;
13
14    unsigned char *h_res;
15    unsigned char *d_res;
16
17    // make sure each row of the 2D array d_res, occupies a multiple of ↵
        32 bytes
18    CUDA_CHECK_RETURN (cudaMallocPitch ((void **) &d_res, (size_t *) & ↵
        pitch, resX, resY));
19    // allocate pinned host memory
20    CUDA_CHECK_RETURN (cudaHostAlloc (&h_res, resY * pitch, ↵
        cudaHostAllocMapped));
21
22    double stepX = (lowerX − upperX) / resX;
23    double stepY = (upperY − lowerY) / resY;
24
25    // launch GPU kernel
26    mandelKernel <<< grid, block >>> (d_res, upperX, upperY, stepX, ↵
        stepY, resX, resY, pitch);
27
28    // wait for GPU to finish
29    CUDA_CHECK_RETURN (cudaDeviceSynchronize ());
30
31    // get the results
32    CUDA_CHECK_RETURN (cudaMemcpy (h_res, d_res, resY * pitch, ↵
        cudaMemcpyDeviceToHost));
33
34    //copy results into QImage object
35    for (int j = 0; j < resY; j++)
36      for (int i = 0; i < resX; i++)
37        {
38          int color = h_res[j * pitch + i];
39          img−>setPixel (i, j, qRgb (256 − color, 256 − color, 256 − ↵
              color));
40        }
41
42    // clean−up allocated memory
43    CUDA_CHECK_RETURN (cudaFreeHost (h_res));
44    CUDA_CHECK_RETURN (cudaFree (d_res));
45  }
```

LISTING 6.31

A CUDA thread-per-pixel solution for the calculation of the Mandelbrot set using pinned host memory and pitched device memory allocation. Only the differences from Listing 6.29 are shown.

6.12.1.3 Version #3: Multiple pixels per thread

The use of one thread per pixel seems like overkill if we consider that a modest 1024x768 image results in 768 K threads, or 4 x 768 = 3072 blocks, given the grid-and-block arrangement used. These figures do not exceed the specifications of GPU capabilities, but they have a side effect: So many blocks cannot be resident on the device (e.g., for compute-capability 3.5 devices, the maximum number of resident blocks is 16 per SM), so the CUDA run-time has to distribute them as the SMs complete previously assigned blocks. This is a fact that we will consider again when we evaluate the performance of the three designs.

In order to process a block of points,[23] a nested for loop is set up inside mandelKernel(), as shown in Listing 6.32 (lines 14-27). The (myX, myY) pair that constitutes the ID of a thread is mapped to the upper left corner of the block to be processed. The size of the block is fixed, determined by the THR_BLK_X and THR_BLK_X constants defined in lines 2 and 3.

The only other modification that is required is the grid configuration calculations that take place in hostFE() in lines 35 and 36. Besides those two lines, hostFE() is identical to the function in Listing 6.31.

```
1    . . .
2    static const int THR_BLK_X = 4; // pixels per thread, x-axis
3    static const int THR_BLK_Y = 4; // pixels per thread, y-axis
4    static const int BLOCK_SIDE = 16;  // size of 2D block of threads
5    . . .
6    //=============================================================
7    __global__ void mandelKernel (unsigned char *d_res, double upperX, ↵
           double upperY, double stepX, double stepY, int resX, int resY, int↵
           pitch)
8    {
9      int myX, myY;
10     myX = (blockIdx.x * blockDim.x + threadIdx.x) * THR_BLK_X;
11     myY = (blockIdx.y * blockDim.y + threadIdx.y) * THR_BLK_Y;
12
13     int i, j;
14     for (i = myX; i < THR_BLK_X + myX; i++)
15       for (j = myY; j < THR_BLK_Y + myY; j++)
16         {
17           // check for "outside" pixels
18           if (i >= resX || j >= resY)
19             continue;
20
21           double tempx, tempy;
22           tempx = upperX + i * stepX;
23           tempy = upperY - j * stepY;
```

---

[23]This effectively corresponds to a 2D partitioning of the workload. A 1D partitioning is also possible, whereas a thread processes a vertical or horizontal line of points.

```
24
25            int color = diverge (tempx, tempy);
26            d_res[j * pitch + i] = color;
27          }
28    }
29
30    //=============================================================
31    // Host front-end function that allocates the memory and launches the ↩
           GPU kernel
32    void hostFE (double upperX, double upperY, double lowerX, double ↩
           lowerY, QImage * img, int resX, int resY)
33    {
34      int blocksX, blocksY;
35      blocksX = (int) ceil (resX * 1.0 / (BLOCK_SIDE * THR_BLK_X));
36      blocksY = (int) ceil (resY * 1.0 / (BLOCK_SIDE * THR_BLK_Y));
37      dim3 block (BLOCK_SIDE, BLOCK_SIDE);
38      dim3 grid (blocksX, blocksY);
39
40      int pitch;
41
42      unsigned char *h_res;
43      unsigned char *d_res;
44
45      CUDA_CHECK_RETURN (cudaMallocPitch ((void **) &d_res, (size_t *) & ↩
           pitch, resX, resY));
46      CUDA_CHECK_RETURN (cudaHostAlloc (&h_res, resY * pitch, ↩
           cudaHostAllocMapped));
47
48      double stepX = (lowerX - upperX) / resX;
49      double stepY = (upperY - lowerY) / resY;
50
51      // launch GPU kernel
52      mandelKernel <<< grid, block >>> (d_res, upperX, upperY, stepX, ↩
           stepY, resX, resY, pitch);
53
54      // wait for GPU to finish
55      CUDA_CHECK_RETURN (cudaDeviceSynchronize ());
56
57      // get the results
58      CUDA_CHECK_RETURN (cudaMemcpy (h_res, d_res, resY * pitch, ↩
           cudaMemcpyDeviceToHost));
59
60      //copy results into QImage object
61      for (int j = 0; j < resY; j++)
62        for (int i = 0; i < resX; i++)
63          {
64            int color = h_res[j * pitch + i];
65            img->setPixel (i, j, qRgb (256 - color, 256 - color, 256 - ↩
               color));
66          }
67
68      // clean-up allocated memory
```

```
69    CUDA_CHECK_RETURN (cudaFreeHost (h_res));
70    CUDA_CHECK_RETURN (cudaFree (d_res));
71  }
```

LISTING 6.32

A CUDA thread-per-block-of-pixels solution for the calculation of the Mandelbrot set. Only the differences from Listing 6.29 are shown.

6.12.1.4 Evaluation

A convenient way to evaluate the performance of a CUDA program is to use the Nvidia Visual Profiler. As shown in Figure 6.23, the profiler times all CUDA calls and reports detailed information about the performance of a kernel and the utilization of the GPU. Figure 6.23 actually shows the timing of an execution of our first solution. There is just one problem: The duration of the program is too small to allow concrete conclusions to be reached about which is performing best and under which conditions.

The only way around this problem is to benchmark each program under a variety of inputs and configurations. Admittedly, the evaluation performed here is not as thorough as it should be for a production situation, but it does depict the correct strategy to deal with this problem.

The main() function shown in Listing 6.33 is common for all three solutions because it is only responsible for I/O operations and calling the front-end function hostFE() in kernel.cu. As can be observed, the project uses Qt for image I/O. The details of how this can be accomplished in terms of properly compiling and linking the code are in Section E.5.

```
1   // File: mandelCUDA_v[123]/main.cpp
2   #include <QImage>
3   #include <QRgb>
4   #include <QTime>
5   . . .
6   int main (int argc, char *argv[])
7   {
8     double upperCornerX, upperCornerY;
9     double lowerCornerX, lowerCornerY;
10
11    upperCornerX = atof (argv[1]);
12    upperCornerY = atof (argv[2]);
13    lowerCornerX = atof (argv[3]);
14    lowerCornerY = atof (argv[4]);
15
16    // support for timing the operation
17    int iterations = 1;
18    if (argc > 5)
19      iterations = atoi(argv[5]);
20
21    int imgX = 1024, imgY = 768;
22    QImage *img = new QImage (imgX, imgY, QImage::Format_RGB32);
```

```
23
24    QTime t;
25    t.start();
26
27    int i = iterations;
28    while (i--)
29      hostFE (upperCornerX, upperCornerY, lowerCornerX, lowerCornerY, ↵
                img, imgX, imgY);
30
31    cout << "Time (ms) per iteration " << t.elapsed()*1.0/iterations << ↵
            endl;
32
33    img->save ("mandel.png", "PNG", 0);
34    return 0;
35  }
```

LISTING 6.33

The `main()` function of the CUDA programs for the calculation of the Mandelbrot set.

The program is called by supplying the upper-left and lower-right corner coordinates of the complex plane to be investigated as command-line parameters. For example:

```
$ ./mandelCUDA -.75 0.131 -.74 0.121
```

In order to support accurate evaluation of the three solutions, the call to `hostFE()` in line 29 is inside a while loop that can be optionally (if there is a fifth argument in the command line, as per the condition in line 18) run more than one time. The `QTime` class is used for conveniently timing the execution of the GPU on the host side: Line 25 starts the timer, and the `elapsed()` method that is called in line 31 returns the time passed in msec.

The following settings were used for testing:

- Two regions of the plane were calculated:
  - One covering the whole Mandelbrot set, between corners $(-1.5, 1.25)$ and $(1, -1.25)$, identified as "Low detail."
  - One covering a small portion of the set, between corners $(-.75, 0.131)$ and $(-.74, 0.121)$, identified as "High detail." The first takes less time to calculate but features very diverse computing requirements per point/pixel; the second takes more computational time, but the differences in the number of iterations between points are less extreme.
- A total of 1000 iterations were performed for each test, i.e., `hostFE()` was called 1000 times.
- For the third solution we used two configurations: one with a 2x2 block of points per thread and one with an 8x8 block per thread.

The results are shown in Figure 6.26.

The third approach is the one with the worst results, a fact that is easy to explain: Assigning multiple points per thread has the undesirable effect of increasing

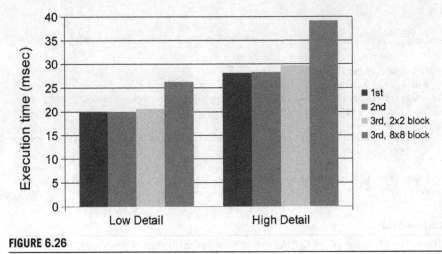

FIGURE 6.26

Average duration of GPU execution for the three Mandelbrot set calculation approaches on a GTX 560 Ti GPU.

the circumstances in which warp threads diverge in their execution, leading to underutilization of the SMs. When an 8x8 block of points/pixels is assigned per thread, we end up with 8 x 6 = 48 blocks, which can be evenly distributed among the 8 SMs of the GTX 560 Ti GPU used in our tests. However, warp threads stall even more.

What is unexpected, though, is that the first, unoptimized approach is superior to the one utilizing pinned host memory and pitched device memory allocation. The profiler hints to the reasons behind this seemingly baffling situation: The cudaMallocPitch() call is more expensive than the plain cudaMalloc() one. Something similar can be expected for the host memory allocation. The small amount of data that move through the PCIe and the small duration of the kernel execution relative to the memory allocation, as shown in Figure 6.27, do not allow the benefits of improved memory management to materialize.

The results demonstrate just how challenging CUDA program optimization can be: Something that works for one situation does not work for another. Proper testing of design alternatives is the recommended strategy.

6.12.2 BLOCK CIPHER ENCRYPTION

In this section we explore the use of CUDA and MPI for the encryption of large volumes of data on a cluster of GPU nodes using the AES algorithm.

The Advanced Encryption Standard (AES) was established in 2001 by the U.S. National Institute of Standards and Technology (NIST) as the successor to the Data Encryption Standard (DES) for the encryption of digital information. Encryption is the process of encoding data in a way that prevents unauthorized users from accessing that data. Encryption algorithms are also known as *ciphers*. The original

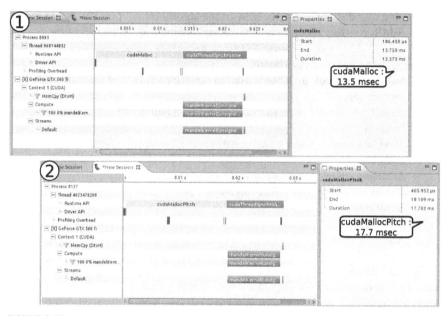

FIGURE 6.27

Nvidia Visual Profiler screenshots for (1) the first Mandelbrot set calculator and (2) the second Mandelbrot set calculator. The device memory allocation calls are highlighted.

data are called *plaintext*, and the encrypted output of a cipher is called *ciphertext*. Data can be restored to their original form by the reverse process, which is known as *decryption*.

Encryption and decryption typically need one or more keys, e.g., a passphrase or a number, that are used in the transformation from plaintext to ciphertext and back. AES is a symmetric-key cipher, i.e., it uses the same key for both processes. Obviously, the key should be kept secret because it enables the decryption to take place.

AES (also known as the Rijndael cipher) is a block cipher, which means that it operates on blocks of plaintext that are 16 bytes long. The data to be encrypted have to be broken up into 16-byte-long pieces before having AES operate independently on each piece. The key is a number that can be 128, 192 or 256 bits long. Each 16-byte block is treated as though arranged in a 4x4 matrix, and it is subjected to multiple rounds of repetitive manipulations. The number of rounds depends on the length of the encryption key, i.e., we have 10 rounds for a 128-bit key, 12 for a 192-bit key, and 14 for a 256-bit key. The 16-byte block is called the *state* of the cipher.

Each AES encryption round is a sequence of the following operations:

- **KeyExpansion**: The encryption key is expanded, i.e., a bigger key is created, so that individual, disjoint parts of it can be used in the subsequent rounds.

- The first round is applied to the state of the algorithm:
  - **AddRoundKey**: Each byte of the state is combined with a part of the expanded key using bitwise XOR.
- The second to next-to-last rounds:
  - **SubBytes**: A look-up table is used to replace each byte of the state with another value.
  - **ShiftRows**: Each row of the state is shifted a number of steps based on its location.
  - **MixColumns**: A linear transformation step that operates on the state's columns.
  - **AddRoundKey**: Same as above.
- Final round (missing a MixColumns step):
  - **SubBytes**
  - **ShiftRows**
  - **AddRoundKey**

Figure 6.28 displays how the four operations that constitute AES operate on the state. AES is covered thoroughly in a large number of online and printed documentation (Wikipedia's article at http://en.wikipedia.org/wiki/Advanced_Encryption_Standard is quite informative). In this section we focus only on the aspects that are relevant to the GPU deployment of the algorithm.

The AES operations can be sped up considerably by using look-up tables to perform them. The following are snippets of the AES reference implementation (http://embeddedsw.net/zip/Rijndael_Original.zip, last accessed in September 2014) that shows how this is accomplished in C code. The KeyExpansion phase is implemented by function:

```
int rijndaelSetupEncrypt(
        unsigned long *rk,          // expanded key (OUT)
        const unsigned char *key,   // original encryption key (IN)
        int keybits);               // size of original key (IN)
```

which is called once, before the encryption phase. The rounds of AddRoundKey, SybBytes, ShiftRows, etc. for each group of 16 bytes, are performed by function:

```
void rijndaelEncrypt(
        const unsigned long *rk,     // pointer to the expanded key (IN)
        int nrounds,                 // number of rounds to perform (IN)
        const unsigned char plaintext[16], // original "state"    (IN)
        unsigned char ciphertext[16]);  // final "state" storage (OUT)
```

A short sample of the AES reference implementation is shown in Listing 6.34.

```
1  // File: AES_MPI/Rijndael_Original/rijndael.c
2  typedef unsigned long u32;
3  typedef unsigned char u8;
4
```

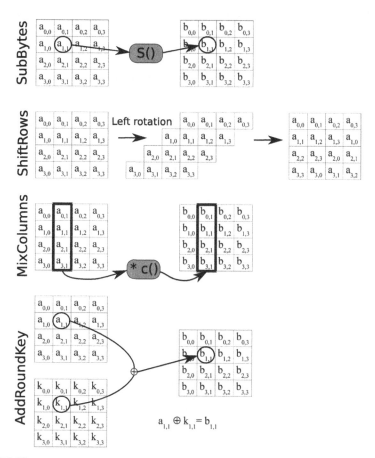

FIGURE 6.28

A demonstration of how the four elementary operations of AES modify the state of the algorithm. S() is a substitution function; c() is a polynomial that is multiplied by each column of the state to produce a new column.

```
 5    static const u32 Te0[256] =
 6    {
 7      0xc66363a5U, 0xf87c7c84U, 0xee777799U, 0xf67b7b8dU, . . .};
 8
 9    static const u32 Te1[256] =
10    {
11      0xa5c66363U, 0x84f87c7cU, 0x99ee7777U, 0x8df67b7bU, . . .};
12
13    static const u32 Te2[256] =
14    {
15      0x63a5c663U, 0x7c84f87cU, 0x7799ee77U, 0x7b8df67bU, . . .};
16
17    static const u32 Te3[256] =
```

```
18  {
19      0x6363a5c6U, 0x7c7c84f8U, 0x777799eeU, 0x7b7b8df6U, . . .};
20
21  static const u32 Te4[256] =
22  {
23      0x63636363U, 0x7c7c7c7cU, 0x77777777U, 0x7b7b7b7bU, . . .};
24
25  . . .
26
27  #define GETU32(plaintext) (((u32)(plaintext)[0] << 24) ^ \
28                          ((u32)(plaintext)[1] << 16) ^ \
29                          ((u32)(plaintext)[2] <<  8) ^ \
30                          ((u32)(plaintext)[3]))
31
32  #define PUTU32(ciphertext, st) { (ciphertext)[0] = (u8)((st) >> 24); \
33                          (ciphertext)[1] = (u8)((st) >> 16); \
34                          (ciphertext)[2] = (u8)((st) >>  8); \
35                          (ciphertext)[3] = (u8)(st); }
36  . . .
37  void rijndaelEncrypt(const u32 *rk, int nrounds, const u8 plaintext↩
        [16], u8 ciphertext[16])
38  {
39      u32 s0, s1, s2, s3, t0, t1, t2, t3;
40      . . .
41      /*
42       * map byte array block to cipher state
43       * and add initial round key:
44       */
45      s0 = GETU32(plaintext     ) ^ rk[0];
46      s1 = GETU32(plaintext +  4) ^ rk[1];
47      s2 = GETU32(plaintext +  8) ^ rk[2];
48      s3 = GETU32(plaintext + 12) ^ rk[3];
49
50  #ifdef FULL_UNROLL
51      /* round 1: */
52      t0 = Te0[s0 >> 24] ^ Te1[(s1 >> 16) & 0xff] ^ Te2[(s2 >>  8) & 0↩
        xff] ^ Te3[s3 & 0xff] ^ rk[ 4];
53      t1 = Te0[s1 >> 24] ^ Te1[(s2 >> 16) & 0xff] ^ Te2[(s3 >>  8) & 0↩
        xff] ^ Te3[s0 & 0xff] ^ rk[ 5];
54      t2 = Te0[s2 >> 24] ^ Te1[(s3 >> 16) & 0xff] ^ Te2[(s0 >>  8) & 0↩
        xff] ^ Te3[s1 & 0xff] ^ rk[ 6];
55      t3 = Te0[s3 >> 24] ^ Te1[(s0 >> 16) & 0xff] ^ Te2[(s1 >>  8) & 0↩
        xff] ^ Te3[s2 & 0xff] ^ rk[ 7];
56      /* round 2: */
57      s0 = Te0[t0 >> 24] ^ Te1[(t1 >> 16) & 0xff] ^ Te2[(t2 >>  8) & 0↩
        xff] ^ Te3[t3 & 0xff] ^ rk[ 8];
58      s1 = Te0[t1 >> 24] ^ Te1[(t2 >> 16) & 0xff] ^ Te2[(t3 >>  8) & 0↩
        xff] ^ Te3[t0 & 0xff] ^ rk[ 9];
59      s2 = Te0[t2 >> 24] ^ Te1[(t3 >> 16) & 0xff] ^ Te2[(t0 >>  8) & 0↩
        xff] ^ Te3[t1 & 0xff] ^ rk[10];
60      s3 = Te0[t3 >> 24] ^ Te1[(t0 >> 16) & 0xff] ^ Te2[(t1 >>  8) & 0↩
        xff] ^ Te3[t2 & 0xff] ^ rk[11];
```

```
61     /* round 3: */
62     t0 = Te0[s0 >> 24] ^ Te1[(s1 >> 16) & 0xff] ^ Te2[(s2 >>  8) & 0↩
            xff] ^ Te3[s3 & 0xff] ^ rk[12];
63     t1 = Te0[s1 >> 24] ^ Te1[(s2 >> 16) & 0xff] ^ Te2[(s3 >>  8) & 0↩
            xff] ^ Te3[s0 & 0xff] ^ rk[13];
64     t2 = Te0[s2 >> 24] ^ Te1[(s3 >> 16) & 0xff] ^ Te2[(s0 >>  8) & 0↩
            xff] ^ Te3[s1 & 0xff] ^ rk[14];
65     t3 = Te0[s3 >> 24] ^ Te1[(s0 >> 16) & 0xff] ^ Te2[(s1 >>  8) & 0↩
            xff] ^ Te3[s2 & 0xff] ^ rk[15];
66     /* round 4: */
67     . . .
68     s0 =
69       (Te4[(t0 >> 24)      ] & 0xff000000) ^
70       (Te4[(t1 >> 16) & 0xff] & 0x00ff0000) ^
71       (Te4[(t2 >>  8) & 0xff] & 0x0000ff00) ^
72       (Te4[(t3      ) & 0xff] & 0x000000ff) ^
73       rk[0];
74     PUTU32(ciphertext      , s0);
75     s1 =
76       (Te4[(t1 >> 24)      ] & 0xff000000) ^
77       (Te4[(t2 >> 16) & 0xff] & 0x00ff0000) ^
78       (Te4[(t3 >>  8) & 0xff] & 0x0000ff00) ^
79       (Te4[(t0      ) & 0xff] & 0x000000ff) ^
80       rk[1];
81     PUTU32(ciphertext +  4, s1);
82     . . .
83  }
```

LISTING 6.34

A sample of the AES reference implementation.

This snippet exposes the key features of the reference implementation code that we can use to create an efficient CUDA derivative:

- The state of the algorithm (the 16 bytes) is read in four variables s0, s1, s2, and s3 (lines 45-48). The state is updated by exchanging these values between the s? and t? variables, as shown in lines 52-65.
- The four operations that constitute each round of AES are performed via five lookup tables Te0[] to Te4[], each made up of 256 32-bit unsigned integers (lines 5-23). The decoding process employs five tables also (not shown above) of the same size as the ones used in encoding.
- The GETU32 and PUTU32 macros ensure that the data are treated as though they were processed in a big-indian architecture.

The sample encrypt.c file from the AES reference implementation reveals the sequence that should be followed for the encryption of a set of data (see Listing 6.35).

```
84  // File: AES_MPI/Rijndael_Original/encrypt.c
85  . . .
86  int main(int argc, char **argv)
87  {
88    unsigned long rk[RKLENGTH(KEYBITS)];    // expanded key
89    unsigned char key[KEYLENGTH(KEYBITS)]; // encryption key
90    int i;
91    int nrounds;
92    . . .
93    nrounds = rijndaelSetupEncrypt(rk, key, 256);  // key expansion
94    while (!feof(stdin)) // while there are more input data
95    {
96      // read a 16-byte block
97      unsigned char plaintext[16];
98      unsigned char ciphertext[16];
99      int j;
100     for (j = 0; j < sizeof(plaintext); j++)
101     {
102       int c = getchar();
103       if (c == EOF)
104         break;
105       plaintext[j] = c;
106     }
107     if (j == 0)
108       break;
109     for (; j < sizeof(plaintext); j++)  // replace any missing data ←
            with spaces
110       plaintext[j] = ' ';
111
112     rijndaelEncrypt(rk, nrounds, plaintext, ciphertext); // encrypt ←
            plaintext block
113
114     if (fwrite(ciphertext, sizeof(ciphertext), 1, output)!= 1)
115     {
116       fclose(output);
117       fputs("File write error", stderr);
118       return 1;
119     }
120   }
121   fclose(output);
122 }
```

LISTING 6.35

Part of a main() function that highlights the sequence of calls required for encrypting a set of data using the AES reference implementation.

In the following paragraphs we describe two standalone and one cluster-based AES implementations. The compilation of the sources can be done via the provided Makefile in the AES_MPI directory. The details of how the Makefile is put together can be found in Appendix E.5. In addition, a short description of the files used in the following sections and the dependencies between them are shown in Figure 6.31.

6.12.2.1 Version #1: The case of a standalone GPU machine

Our ultimate goal is the development of a solution capable of utilizing a cluster of GPUs for AES encryption. This can be a tall order, however, because the detection of bugs can become a daunting task. For this reason, we set as our first stepping stone the development of a standalone GPU solution. A working CUDA program subsequently allows us to narrow down any required debugging efforts on the MPI side only.

The characteristics identified in the previous section allow us to develop a CUDA solution that minimizes access to global memory for the input and output data and maximizes the memory subsystem throughput by using cached constant memory and registers.

The primary components of the kernel solution, as shown in Listing 6.36, are:

- Constant memory is utilized for holding the tables that are used for speeding up the encoding and encoding processes. The total constant memory requirements sum up to a little over 10 KB, if one factors in the 10 1 KB tables and the memory where the expanded encryption or decryption key is stored (array defined in line 20). However, during encryption, only half of this is necessary, making the 8 KB constant memory cache more than sufficient.
- The automatic variables used in `rijndaelGPUEncrypt()` need only a small number of registers per thread. The `nvcc` compiler driver automatically places the s? and t? variables on registers, as the output in Figure 6.29 reveals.
- The signature of the `rijndaelGPUEncrypt()` kernel is substantially different from the one used by the `rijndaelEncrypt()` reference function, although they both operate on a single 16-byte block. The reasons are:
  - In order to avoid the overhead of allocating a separate memory region for the output data, the input data are just overwritten upon the completion of the encryption/decryption.
  - The type of the input array is changed from `unsigned char` to `unsigned int` in order to reduce the global memory access overhead by performing

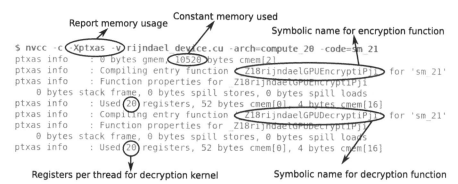

FIGURE 6.29

Compiler report for the device memory allocation related to the AES encryption and decryption kernel functions.

one 32-bit instead of four 8-bit accesses. Especially for the latter part, the GETU32 and PUTU32 macros are replaced by the RESHUFFLE macro (defined in line 22) that is functionally identical but operating on a 32-bit integer variable instead of a four-element array of characters.

- The expanded or rounds key is stored in constant memory so it can be reused through a series of kernel invocations. The d_rk array defined in line 20 is used to hold the rounds key. This array should be initialized by the host prior to calling the encryption/decryption kernels.
- Finally, as the kernel is executed by a bunch of threads operating collectively on multiple 16-byte blocks, the size of the input array in bytes is also supplied in the form of the N parameter (line 28).

- The only major addition to the rijndaelGPUEncrypt() kernel compared to the original rijndaelEncrypt() function, is the code calculating the location of the data that a thread should operate upon in lines 34-39. The thread ID calculation assumes a configuration of a 1D grid of 1D blocks. Once the grid-wide thread ID is established in line 34, a simple multiplication by 4 (the number of 32-bit integers per block) produces the data array offset to be used for input/output.

```
1   // File: AES_MPI/rijndael_device.cu
2   . . .
3   __constant__ u32 Te0[256] = {
4     0xc66363a5U, 0xf87c7c84U, 0xee777799U, 0xf67b7b8dU, . . .};
5
6   __constant__ u32 Te1[256] = {
7     0xa5c66363U, 0x84f87c7cU, 0x99ee7777U, 0x8df67b7bU, . . .};
8
9   __constant__ u32 Te2[256] = {
10    0x63a5c663U, 0x7c84f87cU, 0x7799ee77U, 0x7b8df67bU, . . .};
11
12  __constant__ u32 Te3[256] = {
13    0x6363a5c6U, 0x7c7c84f8U, 0x777799eeU, 0x7b7b8df6U, . . .};
14
15  __constant__ u32 Te4[256] = {
16    0x63636363U, 0x7c7c7c7cU, 0x77777777U, 0x7b7b7b7bU, . . .};
17
18  . . .
19
20  __constant__ u32 d_rk[RKLENGTH (256)];  // allocate the maximum ↵
          possible needed space for the expanded key
21
22  #define RESHUFFLE(i) (((i & 0xFF) << 24) | \
23                        ((i & 0xFF00) << 8) | \
24                        ((i & 0xFF0000) >> 8) | \
25                        ((i & 0xFF000000) >> 24 ))
26
27  // ================================================================
```

```
28   __global__ void rijndaelGPUEncrypt (int nrounds, u32 * data, int N)
29   {
30     u32 s0, s1, s2, s3, t0, t1, t2, t3;
31     const u32 *rk = d_rk;              // to avoid changing d_rk in the code
32     u32 aux;
33
34     int myID = blockIdx.x * blockDim.x + threadIdx.x;
35     // check if there is a block to process
36     if (myID >= (N >> 4))
37       return;
38
39     int myDataIdx = myID << 2;      // *4 to offset 16 bytes
40
41 #ifndef FULL_UNROLL
42     int r;
43 #endif /* ?FULL_UNROLL */
44     /*
45      * map byte array block to cipher state
46      * and add initial round key:
47      */
48     aux = data[myDataIdx];   s0 = RESHUFFLE(aux) ^ rk[0];
49     aux = data[myDataIdx+1]; s1 = RESHUFFLE(aux) ^ rk[1];
50     aux = data[myDataIdx+2]; s2 = RESHUFFLE(aux) ^ rk[2];
51     aux = data[myDataIdx+3]; s3 = RESHUFFLE(aux) ^ rk[3];
52
53 #ifdef FULL_UNROLL
54     /* round 1: */
55     t0 = Te0[s0 >> 24] ^ Te1[(s1 >> 16) & 0xff] ^ Te2[(s2 >> 8) & 0xff] ←
          ^ Te3[s3 & 0xff] ^ rk[4];
56     t1 = Te0[s1 >> 24] ^ Te1[(s2 >> 16) & 0xff] ^ Te2[(s3 >> 8) & 0xff] ←
          ^ Te3[s0 & 0xff] ^ rk[5];
57     t2 = Te0[s2 >> 24] ^ Te1[(s3 >> 16) & 0xff] ^ Te2[(s0 >> 8) & 0xff] ←
          ^ Te3[s1 & 0xff] ^ rk[6];
58     t3 = Te0[s3 >> 24] ^ Te1[(s0 >> 16) & 0xff] ^ Te2[(s1 >> 8) & 0xff] ←
          ^ Te3[s2 & 0xff] ^ rk[7];
59     /* round 2: */
60     . . .
61     s0 = (Te4[(t0 >> 24)] & 0xff000000) ^ (Te4[(t1 >> 16) & 0xff] & 0←
          x00ff0000) ^ (Te4[(t2 >> 8) & 0xff] & 0x0000ff00) ^ (Te4[(t3) & ←
          0xff] & 0x000000ff) ^ rk[0];
62     data[myDataIdx] = RESHUFFLE(s0);
63
64     s1 = (Te4[(t1 >> 24)] & 0xff000000) ^ (Te4[(t2 >> 16) & 0xff] & 0←
          x00ff0000) ^ (Te4[(t3 >> 8) & 0xff] & 0x0000ff00) ^ (Te4[(t0) & ←
          0xff] & 0x000000ff) ^ rk[1];
65     data[myDataIdx + 1] = RESHUFFLE(s1);
66
67     s2 = (Te4[(t2 >> 24)] & 0xff000000) ^ (Te4[(t3 >> 16) & 0xff] & 0←
          x00ff0000) ^ (Te4[(t0 >> 8) & 0xff] & 0x0000ff00) ^ (Te4[(t1) & ←
          0xff] & 0x000000ff) ^ rk[2];
68     data[myDataIdx + 2] = RESHUFFLE(s2);
69
```

```
70    s3 = (Te4[(t3 >> 24)] & 0xff000000) ^ (Te4[(t0 >> 16) & 0xff] & 0↵
          x00ff0000) ^ (Te4[(t1 >> 8) & 0xff] & 0x0000ff00) ^ (Te4[(t2) & ↵
          0xff] & 0x000000ff) ^ rk[3];
71    data[myDataIdx + 3] = RESHUFFLE(s3);
72  }
```

LISTING 6.36

Major parts of the AES encryption CUDA implementation. Only the changes affecting the
reference implementation code are shown. The parts related to decryption are omitted for
brevity.

The key expansion is a procedure that needs to be done only once for the
encryption/decryption, regardless of the number of 16-byte groups that need to be
processed. For this reason, the key is expanded by the host and stored in constant
memory for all subsequent kernel launches. The main() function, as shown in Listing
6.37, computes the expanded key, calculates the size of the input data (lines 111-113),
reads the input data in a single call (line 117), calls a host function that serves as a
front end for the kernel invocations (line 121), and saves the ciphertext data (line 126)
after releasing any memory reserved on the device (line 123).

Reading the whole file in one go is a controversial step; the operating system
can do this faster than in multiple steps, but on the other hand we cannot overlap
host I/O with GPU computation, making the overall program duration potentially
longer. At the end, this was chosen so a proper evaluation of the different design
approaches could be conducted on the basis of how much time was spend on the
actual computation, without contamination from the I/O overhead.

```
73  // File: AES_MPI/aesCUDA.cu
74  . . .
75
76  static const int keybits = 256;
77
78  // ===============================================================
79  int main (int argc, char *argv[])
80  {
81    int lSize = 0;
82    FILE *f, *f2;
83    unsigned char *iobuf;
84
85    if (argc < 4)
86      {
87        fprintf (stderr, "Usage: %s inputfile outputfile threadsPerBlock↵
              \n", argv[0]);
88        exit (1);
89      }
90
91    // encryption key
92    unsigned char key[32] = { 1, 2, 3, 4, 5, 6, 7, 8, 9, 10, 11, 12, 13,↵
              14, 15, 16, 17, 18, 19, 20, 21, 22, 23, 24, 25, 26, 27, 28, 29,↵
              30, 31, 32 };
```

```
93    u32 rk[RKLENGTH (keybits)];
94    // expanded key preparation
95    int nrounds = rijndaelSetupEncrypt (rk, key, keybits);
96
97    if ((f = fopen (argv[1], "r")) == NULL)
98      {
99        fprintf (stderr, "Can't open %s\n", argv[1]);
100       exit (EXIT_FAILURE);
101     }
102
103   if ((f2 = fopen (argv[2], "w")) == NULL)
104     {
105       fprintf (stderr, "Can't open %s\n", argv[2]);
106       exit (EXIT_FAILURE);
107     }
108
109   int thrPerBlock = atoi (argv[3]);
110
111   fseek (f, 0, SEEK_END); // calculate size of required buffer
112   lSize = ftell (f);
113   rewind (f);
114
115   iobuf = new unsigned char[lSize];
116   assert (iobuf!= 0);
117   fread (iobuf, 1, lSize, f);
118   fclose (f);
119
120   // encrypt a lSize-long block located at iobuf
121   rijndaelEncryptFE (rk, keybits, iobuf, iobuf, lSize, thrPerBlock);
122
123   rijndaelShutdown ();    // release device memory
124
125   // save ciphertext
126   fwrite(iobuf, 1, lSize, f2);
127   fclose(f2);
128
129   delete[]iobuf;    // release host memory
130   return 0;
131 }
```

LISTING 6.37

The main() function used in the CUDA implementation of the AES encryption.

The rijndaelEncryptFE() front-end function, as shown in Listing 6.38, is responsible for:

- Allocating device memory: The allocation is done when the function is called for the first time (lines 163, 164). The amount of device memory allocated is fixed, determined by the DEVICEMEMSIZE constant.
- Copying the rounds key to constant memory (line 168).

- Copying data to global memory (line 179) and back (line 189): The input data are split into `DEVICEMEMSIZE`-sized subblocks and transferred to the device.
- Calculating the grid configuration (line 182) based on the specified threads-per-block value and the number of data blocks to be encrypted (line 175). The total number of grid threads per iteration of the line 172 for loop coincides with the number of data blocks.

```
132  // File: AES_MPI/rijndael_host.cu
133  . . .
134  // Host-side copies of the arrays used in key expansion.
135  // Identifiers are the same as in the AES_MPI/rijndael_device.cu file,←
           but there is no naming conflict as the arrays are declared as ←
           static
136  static const u32 Te4[256] =
137  {
138    0x63636363U, 0x7c7c7c7cU, 0x77777777U, 0x7b7b7b7bU, . . .};
139
140  static const u32 Td0[256] =
141  {
142    0x51f4a750U, 0x7e416553U, 0x1a17a4c3U, 0x3a275e96U, . . .};
143
144  . . .
145  //============================================================
146  // Expands the encryption key and returns the number of rounds for the←
           given key size
147  int rijndaelSetupEncrypt(u32 *rk, const u8 *key, int keybits)
148  {
149    // This function in not shown here as it is identical to the one ←
           provided by the reference implementation
150    . . .
151  }
152  //============================================================
153
154  const int DEVICEMEMSIZE=(1<<24); // 16 MB
155  u32 *d_buffer=NULL;
156  extern __constant__ u32 d_rk[RKLENGTH(256)];  // externally defined ←
           symbol, allocated in device constant memory
157  //============================================================
158  // Host FE function responsible for calling the device
159  // Setups the grid of blocks and calls the kernel
160  // N is the size of the plaintext in bytes and it should be a multiple←
           of 16
161  void rijndaelEncryptFE(const u32 *rk, int keybits, unsigned char *←
           plaintext, unsigned char *ciphertext, int N, int thrPerBlock=256)
162  {
163    if(d_buffer == NULL)
164      CUDA_CHECK_RETURN(cudaMalloc((void **)&d_buffer, DEVICEMEMSIZE←
               ));
165
166    int nrounds = NROUNDS(keybits);
167
```

```
168        CUDA_CHECK_RETURN(cudaMemcpyToSymbol (d_rk[0], (void *)rk, ↩
               RKLENGTH(keybits)*sizeof(u32)));
169
170        // data to be encrypted are broken-up into DEVICEMEMSIZE chunks ↩
               and send to the device
171        int dataPos;
172        for(dataPos=0; dataPos<N; dataPos += DEVICEMEMSIZE)
173        {
174            int toSend = (N - dataPos < DEVICEMEMSIZE) ? N-dataPos: ↩
                   DEVICEMEMSIZE;  // how much data to send to the device
175            int numDataBlocks = (int)ceil(toSend /16.0);
176            toSend = numDataBlocks * 16;
177
178            // copy data to device
179            CUDA_CHECK_RETURN(cudaMemcpy(d_buffer, plaintext + dataPos, ↩
                   toSend, cudaMemcpyHostToDevice));
180
181            // grid calculation
182            int grid = ceil(numDataBlocks *1.0/ thrPerBlock);
183
184            rijndaelGPUEncrypt<<< grid, thrPerBlock >>>(nrounds, d_buffer,↩
                   toSend);
185
186            // wait for encryption to complete
187            CUDA_CHECK_RETURN(cudaDeviceSynchronize());
188            // retrieve encpted data
189            CUDA_CHECK_RETURN(cudaMemcpy(ciphertext + dataPos, d_buffer, ↩
                   toSend, cudaMemcpyDeviceToHost));
190        }
191    }
192
193    // ============================================================
194    // Called to clean-up memory allocation on the device
195    void rijndaelShutdown()
196    {
197        if(d_buffer!= NULL)
198            CUDA_CHECK_RETURN(cudaFree((void *)d_buffer));
199        d_buffer = NULL;
200        CUDA_CHECK_RETURN (cudaDeviceReset ());
201    }
```

LISTING 6.38

Host code for launching the AES encryption kernel. The nearly identical decryption-related parts are not shown.

The `rijndaelShutdown()` function releases the device memory, and so it should be called after the encryption/decryption completes.

The program receives as command-line parameters the filenames of the input and output data as well as the number of threads per block to be used in the kernel execution configuration. For example:

```
$ ./aesCUDA in.data out.data 256
```

This allows us to easily experiment with alternative configurations without the need to recompile the code.

6.12.2.2 Version #2: Overlapping GPU communication and computation

The application at hand is one requiring the transfer of massive amounts of data across the PCIe bus. A design strategy that can effectively "hide" the communication overhead is the use of streams (see Section 6.7.7), at least as long as the target device supports concurrent kernel and memory copy executions.

The introduction of streams into the CUDA code presented in the previous section, requires only small modifications to the host front-end functions rijndael-lEncryptFE() and rijndaelDecryptFE(). The rijndaelShutdown() is also affected, but it is only of minor concern since it merely cleans up the allocated memory and destroys the stream objects.

The modifications that need to be carried out are shown in Listing 6.39.

```
1   // File: AES_MPI/rijndael_host_streams.cu
2   . . .
3   static cudaStream_t str[2];
4
5   //==============================================================
6   void rijndaelEncryptFE (const u32 * rk, int keybits, unsigned char *↩
        plaintext, unsigned char *ciphertext, int N, int thrPerBlock = ↩
        256)
7   {
8     if (d_buffer[0] == NULL)
9       {
10        CUDA_CHECK_RETURN (cudaMalloc ((void **) &(d_buffer[0]), ↩
              DEVICEMEMSIZE));
11        CUDA_CHECK_RETURN (cudaMalloc ((void **) &(d_buffer[1]), ↩
              DEVICEMEMSIZE));
12        CUDA_CHECK_RETURN (cudaStreamCreate (&(str[0])));
13        CUDA_CHECK_RETURN (cudaStreamCreate (&(str[1])));
14      }
15
16    int nrounds = NROUNDS (keybits);
17
18    CUDA_CHECK_RETURN (cudaMemcpyToSymbol (d_rk[0], (void *) rk, ↩
          RKLENGTH (keybits) * sizeof (u32)));
19
20    // data to be encrypted are broken-up into DEVICEMEMSIZE chunks and ↩
          send to the device
21    int dataPos;
22    int whichStream = 1;
23    for (dataPos = 0; dataPos < N; dataPos += DEVICEMEMSIZE)
24      {
25        int toSend = (N - dataPos < DEVICEMEMSIZE) ? N - dataPos: ↩
              DEVICEMEMSIZE; // how much data to send to the device
26        int numDataBlocks = (int) ceil (toSend / 16.0);
```

```
27        toSend = numDataBlocks * 16;
28
29        whichStream =!whichStream;
30
31        // copy data to device
32        CUDA_CHECK_RETURN (cudaMemcpyAsync (d_buffer[whichStream], ↵
              plaintext + dataPos, toSend, cudaMemcpyHostToDevice));
33
34        // grid calculation
35        int grid = ceil (numDataBlocks * 1.0 / thrPerBlock);
36
37        rijndaelGPUEncrypt <<< grid, thrPerBlock, 0, str[whichStream] ↵
              >>> (nrounds, d_buffer[whichStream], toSend);
38
39        // retrieve encpyted data
40        CUDA_CHECK_RETURN (cudaMemcpyAsync (ciphertext + dataPos, ↵
              d_buffer[whichStream], toSend, cudaMemcpyDeviceToHost));
41      }
42    // wait for encyption to complete
43    CUDA_CHECK_RETURN (cudaStreamSynchronize (str[0]));
44    CUDA_CHECK_RETURN (cudaStreamSynchronize (str[1]));
45  }
46
47  //============================================================
48  // Called to clean-up memory allocation on the device
49  void rijndaelShutdown ()
50  {
51    if (d_buffer[0]!= NULL)
52      {
53        CUDA_CHECK_RETURN (cudaFree ((void *) d_buffer[0]));
54        CUDA_CHECK_RETURN (cudaFree ((void *) d_buffer[1]));
55        CUDA_CHECK_RETURN (cudaStreamDestroy (str[0]));
56        CUDA_CHECK_RETURN (cudaStreamDestroy (str[1]));
57      }
58    d_buffer[0] = NULL;
59    CUDA_CHECK_RETURN (cudaDeviceReset ());
60  }
```

LISTING 6.39

Host code for launching the AES encryption kernel using streams. Only the changes from Listing 6.38 are shown. The function names remain the same, allowing the compilation of the new program without mandating any modifications to the other source code files in the project.

The differences can be boiled down to the allocation of two separate device buffers and the construction of two streams that are fed alternating pieces of the data to be processed. The whichStream variable is used to change the target stream in every iteration of the for loop of lines 23-41. In order to utilize the two stream objects that are created in lines 12 and 13, the cudaMemcpy() calls are replaced with cudaMemcpyAsync() calls and the kernel invocation of line 37 carries a fourth parameter that references the target stream. The synchronization is performed only once for each stream, past the end of the for loop in lines 43 and 44.

6.12.2.3 Version #3: Using a cluster of GPU machines

Having a working CUDA program from the previous sections tremendously simplifies the task of moving to a cluster solution. The design of the cluster implementation in this section follows the master-worker paradigm: Extending the data break-up practiced in both `rijndaelEncryptFE()` functions above, a master process breaks up the input data into fixed-sized chunks and distributes them on a first-come, first-served basis to the worker nodes. The workers return the ciphertext before getting one more piece of the plaintext, and so on. until all the data are encrypted.

This technique provides an easy path to load balancing; however, internode communication can no longer overlap with computation. Nevertheless, we proceed with this approach, more as a teaching aid for the techniques involved and less as a performance improvement. This approach is convenient, but it has been shown to be inferior to more elaborate partitioning attempts [11]. This issue is addressed in more detail in Chapter 8.

The only change that needs to be carried out in the code of the previous section is in the `main()` function so that communication between nodes can be orchestrated. The new main function is shown in Listing 6.40.

The protocol used for the communication between the master and worker nodes is shown in the form of a UML sequence diagram in Figure 6.30. The protocol involves the exchange of three types of messages, as identified by their tag[24]:

- `TAG_DATA`: The message carries data to be processed (coming from the master) or data that have been processed already (coming from a worker). A `TAG_DATA` message is always preceded by one of the other types of messages.
- `TAG_RES`: A "result" message sent by a worker that acts as a prologue to a `TAG_DATA` message. This message carries the offset in the output data array, where the processed data are to be deposited.
- `TAG_WORK`: A "work item" message that is sent by the master to a worker. This message carries the offset/position in the input array of the data to be processed that are subsequently sent in a `TAG_DATA` message.

The conversation between the master and a worker is triggered by the latter. A worker announces its availability by sending a `TAG_RES` message with a negative data offset (line 104). The master will then respond by sending a block of input data to the worker (lines 69, 70). When the worker receives a work item, it calls the `rijndaelEncryptFE()` function (line 111) after determining the exact size of the data to be processed (line 110). This function in turn sets up and carries through a sequence of kernel invocations in order to encrypt all the input data.

---

[24]A protocol can be established that uses only two types of messages for the exchange. The key is making the messages that carry the data offset redundant. This would also reduce the overall message count by a factor of 2. This can be accomplished by having the master process maintain a record of what piece of the data has been assigned to each worker. This modification is left as an exercise.

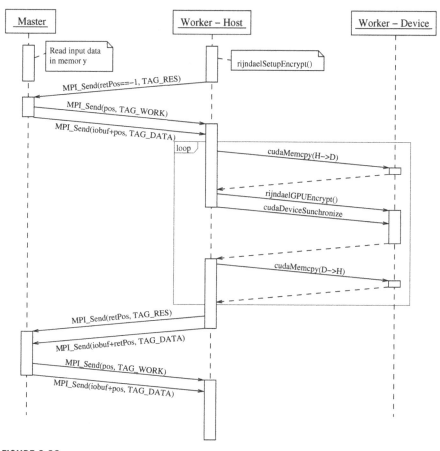

FIGURE 6.30

UML sequence diagram of the master-worker exchanges in the MPI-based AES implementation of Listing 6.40.

Once rijndaelEncryptFE() returns, the worker sends a TAG_RES followed by a TAG_DATA messages (line 112, 113) and awaits its next assignment (line 116).

Once all the data have been assigned by the master (end of while loop of lines 60-73), the master sends a TAG_WORK message to each worker with a negative data offset (lines 77-86) as soon as the workers report back with the results of their last assignment (lines 80-82). The negative data offset acts as a flag to the end of the computation (line 106).

```
1   // File: AES_MPI/main.cpp
2   . . .
3   #define TAG_RES   0
4   #define TAG_WORK  1
5   #define TAG_DATA  2
6
7   static const int keybits = 256;
```

```
8
9   //==========================================================
10  int main (int argc, char *argv[])
11  {
12    int rank;
13    unsigned char *iobuf;
14
15    int lSize = 0;
16    FILE *f;
17
18    int comm_size = 0;
19    MPI_Status status;
20    MPI_Init (&argc, &argv);
21    MPI_Comm_rank (MPI_COMM_WORLD, &rank);
22    MPI_Comm_size (MPI_COMM_WORLD, &comm_size);
23    MPI_Request req;
24    MPI_Status stat;
25
26    if (argc < 5)
27      {
28        if (rank == 0)
29          fprintf (stderr, "Usage: %s inputfile outputfile workItemSize ↵
                threadsPerBlock\n", argv[0]);
30
31        exit (1);
32      }
33
34    //encryption key
35    unsigned char key[32] = { 1, 2, 3, 4, 5, 6, 7, 8, 9, 10, 11, 12, 13,↵
                14, 15, 16, 17, 18, 19, 20, 21, 22, 23, 24, 25, 26, 27, 28, 29,↵
                30, 31, 32 };
36    u32 rk[RKLENGTH (keybits)];
37    rijndaelSetupEncrypt (rk, key, keybits);
38
39    if (rank == 0)
40      {
41        if ((f = fopen (argv[1], "r")) == NULL)
42          {
43            fprintf (stderr, "Can't open %s\n", argv[1]);
44            exit (EXIT_FAILURE);
45          }
46
47        int workItemSize = atoi (argv[3]);
48
49        fseek (f, 0, SEEK_END);
50        lSize = ftell (f);
51        rewind (f);
52
53        iobuf = new unsigned char[lSize];
54        assert (iobuf!= NULL);
55        fread (iobuf, 1, lSize, f);
56        fclose (f);
```

```
57
58        // master main loop
59        int pos = 0;
60        while (pos < lSize)
61          {
62            int retPos;
63            MPI_Recv (&retPos, 1, MPI_INT, MPI_ANY_SOURCE, TAG_RES, ↩
                   MPI_COMM_WORLD, &stat);
64            if (retPos >= 0)       // if not the first dummy worker call
65              MPI_Recv (iobuf + retPos, workItemSize, MPI_UNSIGNED_CHAR, ↩
                     stat.MPI_SOURCE, TAG_DATA, MPI_COMM_WORLD, &stat);
66
67            // assign next work item
68            int actualSize = (workItemSize < lSize - pos) ? workItemSize↩
                   : (lSize - pos);
69            MPI_Send (&pos, 1, MPI_INT, stat.MPI_SOURCE, TAG_WORK, ↩
                   MPI_COMM_WORLD);
70            MPI_Send (iobuf + pos, workItemSize, MPI_UNSIGNED_CHAR, stat↩
                   .MPI_SOURCE, TAG_DATA, MPI_COMM_WORLD);
71
72            pos += actualSize;
73          }
74
75        // wait for last results
76        pos = -1;
77        for (int i = 1; i < comm_size; i++)
78          {
79            int retPos;
80            MPI_Recv (&retPos, 1, MPI_INT, MPI_ANY_SOURCE, TAG_RES, ↩
                   MPI_COMM_WORLD, &stat);
81            if (retPos >= 0)        // if not the first dummy worker call
82              MPI_Recv (iobuf + retPos, workItemSize, MPI_UNSIGNED_CHAR, ↩
                     stat.MPI_SOURCE, TAG_DATA, MPI_COMM_WORLD, &stat);
83
84            // indicate end of operations
85            MPI_Send (&pos, 1, MPI_INT, stat.MPI_SOURCE, TAG_WORK, ↩
                   MPI_COMM_WORLD);
86          }
87
88      FILE *fout;
89      if ((fout = fopen (argv[2], "w")) == NULL)
90        {
91          fprintf (stderr, "Can't open %s\n", argv[2]);
92          exit (EXIT_FAILURE);
93        }
94      fwrite(iobuf, 1, lSize, fout);
95      fclose (fout);
96    }
97  else                            // GPU worker
98    {
99      int workItemSize = atoi (argv[3]);
100     int thrPerBlock = atoi (argv[4]);
```

```
101        int pos = -1;
102        iobuf = new unsigned char[workItemSize];
103
104        MPI_Send (&pos, 1, MPI_INT, 0, TAG_RES, MPI_COMM_WORLD);
105        MPI_Recv (&pos, 1, MPI_INT, 0, TAG_WORK, MPI_COMM_WORLD, &stat);
106        while (pos >= 0)
107          {
108            MPI_Recv (iobuf, workItemSize, MPI_UNSIGNED_CHAR, 0, ↵
                     TAG_DATA, MPI_COMM_WORLD, &stat);
109            int actualSize;
110            MPI_Get_count(&stat, MPI_UNSIGNED_CHAR, &actualSize);
111            rijndaelEncryptFE (rk, keybits, iobuf, iobuf, actualSize, ↵
                     thrPerBlock);
112            MPI_Send (&pos, 1, MPI_INT, 0, TAG_RES, MPI_COMM_WORLD);
113            MPI_Send (iobuf, actualSize, MPI_UNSIGNED_CHAR, 0, TAG_DATA,↵
                     MPI_COMM_WORLD);
114
115            // get next work item start
116            MPI_Recv (&pos, 1, MPI_INT, 0, TAG_WORK, MPI_COMM_WORLD, &↵
                     stat);
117          }
118        rijndaelShutdown ();
119      }
120
121    MPI_Finalize ();
122
123    delete [] iobuf;
124    return 0;
125  }
```

LISTING 6.40

Main function for handling the interaction between nodes in an MPI cluster implementation of the AES encription/decryption. Time-measurement related code is omitted for brevity.

The program receives as command-line parameters the filenames of the input and output data, the work item size (i.e., the size of the parts communicated to the workers, and the number of threads per block to be used in the kernel execution configuration. An example run with three GPU worker nodes would be:

```
$ mpirun -np 4 ./aesMPI in.data out.data 1000000 256
```

Again, the goal is to easily experiment with alternative configurations without the need to recompile the code.

In order to accommodate both GPU and CPU worker nodes without complicated initialization procedures and extensive code modifications, we resorted to creating a version of the program in Listing 6.40 for CPU worker nodes only and using a MPMD launch configuration. The only modification that needs to be carried out is in the else block of lines 97-119. The resulting code is shown in Listing 6.41, constructed so that it utilizes the AES reference implementation function rijndaelEncrypt(), which has been renamed for clarity to rijndaelCPUEncrypt().

```
126   // File : AES_MPI / mainCPUWorker . cpp
127   . . .
128   else                           // CPU worker
129     {
130       int workItemSize = atoi (argv[3]);
131       int thrPerBlock = atoi (argv[4]);
132       int pos = −1;
133       workItemSize = (workItemSize / 16 + 1) * 16;        // making sure ↵
                enough space for zero−padding is available
134
135       iobuf = new unsigned char[workItemSize];
136       int nrounds = NROUNDS (keybits);
137
138       // report for duty!
139       MPI_Send (&pos, 1, MPI_INT, 0, TAG_RES, MPI_COMM_WORLD);
140       // get 1st assigned block location
141       MPI_Recv (&pos, 1, MPI_INT, 0, TAG_WORK, MPI_COMM_WORLD, &stat);
142       while (pos >= 0)
143         {
144           MPI_Recv (iobuf, workItemSize, MPI_UNSIGNED_CHAR, 0, ↵
                  TAG_DATA, MPI_COMM_WORLD, &stat);
145           int actualSize;
146           MPI_Get_count (&stat, MPI_UNSIGNED_CHAR, &actualSize);
147
148           // Padding is added at the end of the array, to produce an ↵
                  integer
149           // number of 16−byte blocks
150           int paddedSize = ceil (actualSize / 16.0) * 16;
151           for (int k = actualSize; k < paddedSize; k++)
152             iobuf[k] = ' ';
153
154           // Assigned data block is processed in 16−byte blocks at a ↵
                  time
155           int dataPos;
156           for (dataPos = 0; dataPos < actualSize; dataPos += 16)
157             {
158               // encrypt 16−byte block
159               rijndaelCPUEncrypt (rk, nrounds, iobuf + dataPos, iobuf ↵
                      + dataPos);
160             }
161
162           // Return results, and their location in the overall ↵
                  ciphertext
163           MPI_Send (&pos, 1, MPI_INT, 0, TAG_RES, MPI_COMM_WORLD);
164           MPI_Send (iobuf, actualSize, MPI_UNSIGNED_CHAR, 0, TAG_DATA, ↵
                  MPI_COMM_WORLD);
165
166           // get next work item start
167           MPI_Recv (&pos, 1, MPI_INT, 0, TAG_WORK, MPI_COMM_WORLD, &↵
                  stat);
168         }
169     }
```

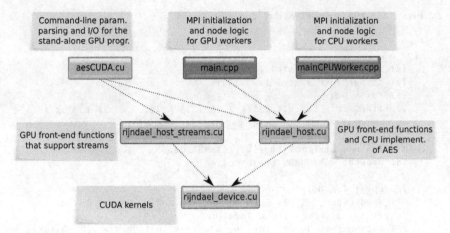

FIGURE 6.31

Dependencies between the files that make up the AES implementations described in Section 6.12.2. A different subset of these files is used to generate each of the examined programs.

```
170
171     MPI_Finalize ();
172
173     delete[] iobuf;
174     return 0;
175  }
```

LISTING 6.41

Part of the main() function that targets AES encryption on CPU worker nodes. The remaining code is identical to the one shown in Listing 6.40.

In summary, the files used in our three AES encryption implementations and their dependencies are shown in Figure 6.31.

As stated, Listings 6.40 and 6.41 are used to generate two executables, one targeting GPU and one targeting CPU workers respectively. These are jointly used to be able to support the deployment of the program over a network of mixed capability nodes. Figure 6.32 shows a mixed cluster of machines example, that we will use to illustrate how MPMD program deployment can be performed. An appfile (application file) detailing the destination of each executable and the number of processes spawned in each machine is all that is needed, as shown in Listing 6.42.

```
−host achilleas −np 2 aesMPI in512.dat ciphertext.dat 16777216 512
−host achilleas −np 3 aesMPICPUWorker in512.dat ciphertext.dat ↵
      16777216 512
−host perseas −np 1 aesMPI in512.dat ciphertext.dat 16777216 512
```

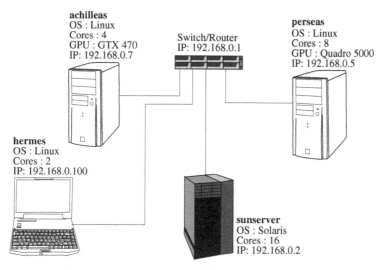

FIGURE 6.32

Intranet example used for explaining the MPMD deployment of an MPI program that utilizes GPU-equipped, multicore nodes.

```
—host perseas —np 7 aesMPICPUWorker in512.dat ciphertext.dat 16777216 ↵
    512
```

LISTING 6.42

Appfile for spawning 13 MPI processes, one master, two GPU workers, and 10 CPU workers on the two desktops of the intranet in Figure 6.32.

These lines need to be stored in an application file (e.g., `encryptionMPMD.conf`) and used in the following fashion[25]:

```
$ mpirun —app encryptionMPMD.conf
```

MPI numbers the spawned processes in the order in which they are listed in the appfile. So, the appfile in Listing 6.42 produces the processes shown in Table 6.9. The four-core `achilleas` is scheduled to run 5 MPI processes, since the master process is mostly idle in terms of CPU time, dedicated to exchanging messages with the workers.

6.12.2.4 Evaluation
Compared to the previous case study, AES encryption has the additional characteristic of putting a big emphasis on I/O. In this section we explore not only the issue of GPU

---

[25]MPI requires that the node from which the launch is done is included in the execution. If the user is using hermes for launching the program, the above appfile will fail. A remote launch is possible via an ssh session running on achilleas.

Table 6.9 MPI processes generated in response to the appfile of Listing 6.42

Appfile Line	MPI Processes Generated
`-host achilleas -np 2 aesMPI ...`	0: master 1: GPU worker
`-host achilleas -np 3 aesMPICPUWorker ...`	2-4: CPU workers
`-host perseas -np 1 aesMPI ...`	5: GPU worker
`-host perseas -np 7 aesMPICPUWorker ...`	6-11: CPU workers

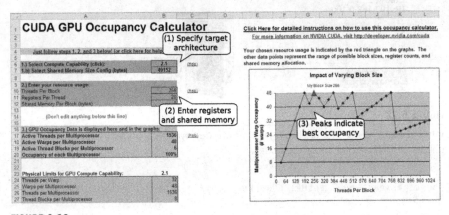

FIGURE 6.33

Occupancy calculation for the `rijndaelGPUEncrypt()` kernels.

code optimization but also the issue of overall efficiency, especially in comparison with a CPU implementation. To produce a quantitative answer to this question, the code presented in the previous sections is structured so that file I/O is completely decoupled from the encryption process. The same approach is used in order to measure the CPU execution time.

The test platforms used were a first-generation i7 950 processor, clocked at 3.07 GHz with 8 GB of DDR2 RAM, and a GTX 470 GPU card, clocked at 1260 MHz and having 1280 MB of DDR5 RAM. A PCIe 2.0 interface provided the interconnect between the GPU and its host. As shown in Figure 6.29, the `rijndaelGPUEncrypt()` and `rijndaelGPUDecrypt()` kernels use 20 registers. The CUDA occupancy calculator for a compute-capability 2.0/2.1 device reveals the optimum settings for the number of threads per block (see Figure 6.33) as being 192, 256, 384, 512, or 768.

In our tests we chose to vary the number of threads between 64, 128, 256, and 512 so as to explore the effect of this parameter on the performance. Additionally, the size of the data blocks that are processed per grid was set to 1 MB, 16 MB, or 32 MB in order to support streaming. Two files of randomly generated data, one 128

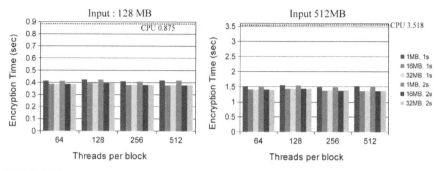

FIGURE 6.34

Average AES encryption times on a i7 950 and a GTX 470. Bars are colored according to the data-block-size per grid (1 MB, 16 MB, or 32 MB) and the number of streams used (1 or 2).

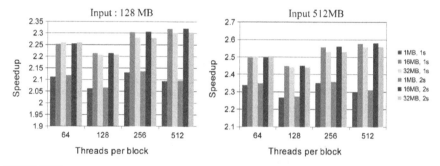

FIGURE 6.35

Speed-up of the AES GPU-based encryption over the CPU-based one.

MB and one 512 MB, were used for timing the execution. These were produced by utilizing the dd command and the /dev/urandom Linux device:

```
$ dd if=/dev/urandom of=in128.dat bs=1M count=128
```

The correctness of the GPU code was tested by decrypting the data and checking them against the original input.

The average encryption-only execution times (averaged over 100 runs) are shown in Figure 6.34. All code was compiled with a GCC 4.4.7 compiler, and optimization was turned on for the CPU program (using switch -O2).

Because the times are difficult to quantify in relative terms, Figure 6.35 shows the corresponding speed-up achieved.

The results suggest that the best configuration consists of processing the data in batches of 16 MB by grids of 512-thread blocks. Additionally, Figures 6.34 and 6.35 reveal a surprising fact: Streaming has no tangible benefit on performance! The GTX 470 GPU used in our tests had only one copy engine, i.e., although it can overlap

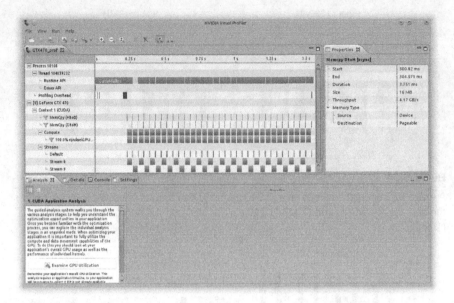

FIGURE 6.36

A screenshot of Nvidia's Visual Profiler displaying the data captured during a profiling session of the AES encryption using two streams.

kernel execution and data movement, it can move data in only one direction at a time. Additionally, the data communication is a comparatively small fraction of the overall execution time, as shown in the Visual Profiler snapshot in Figure 6.36.

Although the roughly 2.5x speedup offered by the CUDA solution is not negligible, one could argue that we were using only one of the available CPU cores. A multithreaded version of the CPU version would most certainly be faster than the GPU one without even considering using the AES-NI instruction set introduced in more recent Intel and AMD CPU offerings. The AES-NI set provides hardware support for the AES standard, speeding up the encryption/decryption process by as much as sixfold [22].

However, the proper point of view is that a GPU is just another computational resource at our disposal, one that should be used in tandem and not in isolation with whatever is available in a system. In that respect, the MPI version of the AES encoder that tries to integrate all available computational resources is a step in the right direction.

The performance potential of the cluster solution was tested on the same single-machine environment used for generating the results of the GPU-only solutions (the explanation for not testing on an actual cluster is given shortly). The outcome, averaged over 100 runs, is shown in Figure 6.37. As can be observed, performance is only marginally better than the standalone GPU solution, and this is only feasible if

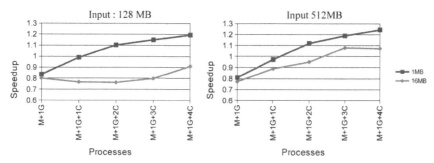

FIGURE 6.37

Speed-up offered by the AES MPI implementation over the standalone GPU implementation when the input data are distributed as 1 MB and 16 MB work items. The x-axis labels indicate the composition of the processes taking part in the computation, namely, M for master, G for GPU worker, and C for CPU worker.

the size of the work item is relatively small compared to the size of the overall load (1 MB in our tests), to allow load balancing to take place.

A seemingly odd observation in Figure 6.37 is that the MPI implementation is inferior to the standalone GPU one when identical hardware resources are involved, i.e., when only one GPU worker is used. The reason for this behavior comes down to the way MPI programs are made up: as message exchanging processes. In the MPI implementation, the host-device-host overhead is augmented with the master-worker exchange costs, bogging down the execution.

Only when multiple CPU workers are involved and the grain of the work item is fine enough to allow them to get an appropriate slice of the workload does the MPI solution start to offer a small advantage. Clearly, the increased communication overhead, even for processes sharing memory (!), evaporates any potential performance gains from adding more computational resources. This is the reason that in the absence of a very fast communication medium such as Infiniband, we chose not to test over a cluster.

EXERCISES

1. An array of type `float` elements is to be processed in a one-element-per-thread fashion by a GPU. Suggest an execution configuration for the following scenarios:
   a. The array is 1D and of size N. The target GPU has 8 SMs, each with 16 SPs.
   b. The array is 2D and of size NxN. The target GPU has 5 SMs, each with 48 SPs.

   For each of these scenarios calculate the minimum size that N should satisfy to make the GPU computation a desirable alternative to CPU computation.

2. A reduction is an operation frequently encountered in a many algorithms: summing up the elements of an array, finding the minimum, maximum, etc. One possible solution to a CUDA kernel that calculates the sum of an array would be:

```
__global__ void sum(float *in, float *out)
{
    __shared__ float localStore[];   // to speedup data access

    int globalID = threadIdx.x + blockIdx.x * blockDim.x;
    int localID = threadIdx.x;

    localStore[localID] = in[globalID];   // copy to shared memory
    for(int i=1; i< blockDim.x ; i*=2)
        {
            if(localID % (2*i) == 0)
                localStore[localID] += localStore[localID + i];
            __syncthreads ();
        }
    if(localID == 0)
        out[blockIdx.x] = localStore[0];
}
```

This solution needs to be called multiple times, each time reducing the size of the data by the number of threads in a block. Data at each kernel launch should be multiples of the block size.

Analyze this code in relation to the following criteria and how they reflect on the execution speed: thread divergence, memory coalescing, use of SPs within a warp. Suggest modifications that would improve the performance.

3. The reduction operation discussed in the previous exercise is a special case of the "scan" or prefix-sum operation that can be applied to the elements of a vector or list. In general, the operator applied can be any of summation, subtraction, minimum, maximum, and so on. Implement a CUDA kernel capable of performing a prefix-sum operation. The "Prefix-Sums and Their Applications" paper, by Guy Blelloch, available at http://www.cs.cmu.edu/~guyb/papers/Ble93.pdf, is a wonderful resource for learning more on the topic.

4. Create CUDA implementations of the gsl_stats_mean() and gsl_stats_variance() functions offered by the GNU Scientific Library that produce the mean and variance statistics of an array of type double data. Their signatures are:

```
double gsl_stats_mean (const double DATA[], // Pointer to input ↩
    data
                        size_t STRIDE,       // Step used to read ↩
                            the input. Normally this should be set ↩
                            to 1.
                        size_t N);           // Size of DATA array
double gsl_stats_variance (const double DATA[], // Same as above.
                            size_t STRIDE ,
                            size_t N);
```

Assuming that the STRIDE is 1, create a memory access pattern that utilizes coalescing. Suggest ways to deal with the problem if the stride is not 1.

5. Design and implement a CUDA program for calculating the histogram of a 24-bit color image. In this case, three separate histograms will be produced, one for each color component of the image.

6. Create a variation of the program in Listing 6.24 to discover and plot the memory copy speed for host-to-device and device-to-host operations and for all the available types of host memory allocations: pageable, pinned, and mapped. To test the last type of allocation, you will have to call a kernel that will try to access the memory, triggering the transfer. Compare your results with the ones returned by the `$CUDA/samples/1_Utilities/bandwidthTest` sample program.

7. The Mandelbrot set calculators of Section 6.12.1 are limited to a maximum of 255 iterations per pixel. However, the beauty of the Mandelbrot set is revealed for thousands or millions of iterations. Modify one or more of the solutions of Section 6.12.1 so that up to $2^{16} - 1$ iterations can be performed for each pixel. Profile your program and analyze its performance. What is the grid/block arrangement that yields the best performance?

8. The standalone CUDA AES implementations of Section 6.12.2 suffer from a dominating data-transfer overhead that exceeds the computational cost of the encryption/decryption. Which of the following modifications (if any) will offer the biggest performance improvement?

   a. *Use pinned host memory*: Are there any concerns about the use of pinned memory for holding the whole of the data to be processed?

   b. *Move the tables from constant to shared memory*: The constant memory cache is faster than global memory, but it is still slower than shared memory. Will the speed improvement offset the need to copy the tables to constant memory for every block of threads?

   c. *Process multiple 16-byte blocks per thread*: Turning `rijndaelGPUEncrypt()` into a `__device__` function and introducing another `__global__` function as a front end to it, to be called by `rijndaelEncryptFE()`, should require the smallest possible effort.

   Modify the source code of the Version #2 program in order to introduce your chosen changes, and measure the performance improvement obtained.

9. The MPI cluster AES implementation of Section 6.12.2 does not provide overlapping of communication and computation. This issue could be addressed if a new "work item" were downloaded by the worker nodes while the GPU was processing an already downloaded part. Modify the MPI solution to provide this functionality. Do you expect any problems with the load balancing of the modified solution?

10. Modify the MPI cluster AES implementations of Section 6.12.2 so that only two types of messages are needed for data exchange, instead of the current three. How can this be combined with the modification of the previous exercise?

11. The whole point of the multicore "adventure" is to accelerate our programs. This should be our sole focus, beyond any mis- or preconceptions. The evaluation of the different AES parallel implementations conducted in Section 6.12.2.4 considered only the encryption process, disregarding any I/O costs incurred. Perform your own experiment whereby the overall execution time and not just the encryption time is considered. Make sure that the file cache provided by the operating system is not utilized by:

    * Either calling the following from the command line (root permissions are required):

        ```
        $ sync ; echo 3 > /proc/sys/vm/drop_caches
        ```

    * Or calling the `posix_fadvice()` function from within your program prior to any I/O:

        ```
        #include <unistd.h>
        #include <fcntl.h>
        int main(int argc, char *argv[]) {
          int fd;
          fd = open(argv[1], O_RDONLY); // Open the file holding the ↩
              input data
          fdatasync(fd);
          posix_fadvise(fd, 0,0,POSIX_FADV_DONTNEED); // clear cache
          close(fd);
          ...
        }
        ```

    Analyze your findings.

The Thrust template library

7

IN THIS CHAPTER YOU WILL

- Learn how to accelerate the development and ease the maintenance of GPU/multicore programs by using the Thrust library.
- Learn the datatypes used in Thrust and how to employ them to represent your problem data.
- Learn the algorithms implemented in Thrust and how to use them as building blocks in your own programs.

7.1 INTRODUCTION

Thrust is a C++ template library, both implementing and facilitating the implementation of parallel algorithms. Thrust's syntax resembles the Standard Template Library (STL), making it easy for seasoned C++ programmers to transition to parallel programming without going through the process of mastering complex tools like CUDA. This chapter assumes that the reader possesses at least some basic knowledge of STL template classes.

Originally, Thrust was introduced as a CUDA front end, a library to simplify GPU programming. However, since version 1.6, Thrust includes support for CUDA, OpenMP, Intel Thread Building Blocks (TBB), and standard C++ as device back ends. This means that a simple switch (programmatic or compiler command line) can make the same Thrust-based source code run using any of the listed back ends, utilizing Nvidia GPUs or multicore CPUs in the process. So, although we frequently refer to Thrust in the context of GPUs and CUDA in this chapter, it is without question that Thrust can be used for harnessing the power of multicore CPUs as well.

Thrust provides the means for a developer to describe the computations that need to take place at a very high level, in the form of operations to be applied to a data collection. Thrust takes care of the "ugly" details of partitioning the data, deploying them, spawning the processes/kernels that perform the computation, and collecting the results. Thrust will try to do all these tasks in a near-optimal manner, but it can be easily deduced, given the complexity of these tasks, that it trades off performance for ease of use. For example, when using the CUDA back end, Thrust will try to maximize occupancy, although it has been reported many times in the literature that higher occupancy can lead to lower performance [45]. The exact extend of the trade-off depends on the application being developed. Thankfully, Thrust maintains full interoperability with the back ends it employs, allowing the programmer to shift between Thrust and CUDA or Thrust and OpenMP at will. It is even possible to switch between back ends within the same program.

This flexibility elevates Thrust to one of the prime tools for parallel development. A possible development plan could involve these steps:

1. Using Thrust to quickly prototype an application, regardless of the computing capabilities of the development platform.
2. Profiling the application and identifying the "hot spots" that dominate the execution time.
3. Refining the code that runs inefficiently by using CUDA or other techniques that allow platform awareness to translate to more efficient execution (e.g., explicit use of shared memory, etc.).

Thrust's use of templates means that (a) the provided algorithms are generic, applicable to any user-defined datatype, and (b) there is no need for a binary component that must be installed for the library to function. To start using Thrust, one has to just include the Thrust files in a project and point the compiler to the appropriate include directories.

Thrust is an Open Source Software (OSS) project released under the Apache License v2.0. Although it is not affiliated with Nvidia, its popularity has literally "thrust" it into Nvidia's toolkit. Programmers who download the latest CUDA SDK also get a version (probably not the most recent) of the Thrust library. Anyone interested in having the latest release can separately download and install Thrust from http://thrust.github.io/. At the time of this writing, the CUDA SDK 6.5.14 incorporates the latest 1.7 version of Thrust. A number of the features discussed in this chapter require Thrust 1.6 or newer.

Thrust, being an OSS endeavor, suffers from lack of proper documentation. Fortunately, a large collection of samples is available for study at https://github.com/thrust/thrust/tree/master/examples. Additionally, Thrust's header files typically contain, in the form of comments, a healthy set of samples that can be used as starting points for programmers to come to grips with the Thrust template classes.

7.2 FIRST STEPS IN THRUST

A simple program in Thrust that just allows you to check the version available in your disposal is the following:

```
1  // File : hello.cu
2  #include <iostream>
3  #include <thrust/version.h>
4
5  using namespace std;
6
7  int main()
8  {
9    cout << "Hello World from Thrust v " << THRUST_MAJOR_VERSION << "." ↩
          << THRUST_MINOR_VERSION << endl;
10   return 0;
11 }
```

The program compiles and runs with the commands:

```
$ nvcc hello.cu —o hello
$ ./hello
```

The program displays the major and minor version numbers of the Thrust library that is accessible by default with the CUDA SDK.[1]

The example in Listing 7.1 performs something at least remotely useful by computing the average of an array of integers.

```
1   // File : sum.cu
2   #include <stdlib.h>
3   #include <time.h>
4   #include <iostream>
5   #include <thrust/device_vector.h>
6   #include <thrust/host_vector.h>
7   #include <thrust/reduce.h>
8
9   using namespace std;
10
11  int main (int argc, char **argv)
12  {
13    srand (time (NULL));
14    int N = atoi (argv[1]);
15    thrust::host_vector < int >h_d (N);
16    for (int i = 0; i < N; i++)
17      h_d[i] = rand () % 10000;   // limit the range to [0, 9999]
18
19    thrust::device_vector < int >d_d (N);
20    d_d = h_d;   // host -> device transfer
21
22    cout << "Average computed on CPU :" << thrust::reduce (h_d.begin (),↩
           h_d.end ()) * 1.0 / N << endl;
23
24    cout << "Average computed on GPU :" << thrust::reduce (d_d.begin (),↩
           d_d.end ()) * 1.0 / N << endl;
25
26    return 0;
27  }
```

LISTING 7.1

A Thrust program that calculates the average of an array of random integers. The array size is passed as a command-line parameter.

---

[1] You can access a more recent or different version of Thrust by, either, pointing the nvcc compiler driver to the appropriate directory (assuming that Thrust is installed in your home directory):

```
$ nvcc hello.cu -o hello -I ~/thrust
```

Or, by replacing the contents of the SDK's include/thrust directory with the desired library.

Listing 7.1 reveals many of the strengths and idiosyncrasies of working with Thrust. Lines 5-7 show that one has to individually include all the header files corresponding to the required functionality.

All the classes and functions that make up Thrust belong to the thrust namespace. As a matter of caution, one should avoid introducing a "using namespace thrust" statement in a program, to prevent conflicts with STL, since many of the classes and functions provided by Thrust have matching names to their STL counterparts.

Data in Thrust are stored in two types of vectors, which are functionally equivalent to the STL vector template class:

- host_vector<>: For data residing in host memory
- device_vector<>: For data residing in device memory

The novelty about using these vector types is that data transfer between the host and the device. or vice versa, is implemented by overloading the assignment operator, as shown in line 20.

Thrust functions operate on vector ranges, which are defined using iterators following the STL's legacy. Thrust functions, such as the reduction used in lines 22 and 24, automatically call the appropriate code (host or device) based on the type of vector/iterator passed to them. Additionally, the decision on which code to use is done at compile time, avoiding any execution overheads. This is known as *static dispatching*. The only restriction is that when multiple iterators are used (as in multiple vectors), they should all reside in the same memory space (all in host or all in device). Otherwise the compiler will produce an error message. This obviously excludes the functions that copy data between the memory spaces.

Another example that showcases the extremely expressive power of Thrust is shown in Listing 7.2.

```
1   // File : min.cu
2   #include <iostream>
3   #include <thrust/device_vector.h>
4   #include <thrust/sequence.h>
5   #include <thrust/extrema.h>
6
7   #include <stdlib.h>
8   #include <time.h>
9
10  using namespace std;
11  //****************************************************
12  struct functor
13  {
14    __host__ __device__
15    float operator()(const float &x) const{
16      return x*x;    // just a simple example function
17    }
18  };
```

```
19   // ****************************************************
20   int main(int argc, char **argv)
21   {
22     float st, end;
23     st = atof(argv[1]);
24     end = atof(argv[2]);
25     int dataPoints = atoi(argv[3]);
26     float step= (end-st)/dataPoints;
27
28     thrust::device_vector<float> d_x(dataPoints);
29     thrust::device_vector<float> d_y(dataPoints);
30     thrust::sequence(d_x.begin(), d_x.end(), st, step);  // fill-up ↵
            array with sequence
31
32     functor f;
33     thrust::transform(d_x.begin(), d_x.end(), d_y.begin(), f);  // ↵
            calculate function for all values in d_x
34
35     int idx = thrust::min_element(d_y.begin(), d_y.end()) - d_y.begin()↵
            ;
36     cout << "Function minimum over ["<< st <<"," << end << "] occurs at ↵
            " << d_x[idx] << endl;
37
38     return 0;
39   }
```

LISTING 7.2

A Thrust program that calculates the point in a range that produces the smallest value of a function. The range limits and the number of samples taken within the range are passed as command-line parameters.

A key component of Listing 7.2 is the use of a **functor**. A functor or "**function object**", is the C++ equivalent of a C function pointer. The added benefit that a functor offers over a simple function pointer is that it can have a state, i.e., it can be initialized to perform in a customized fashion that is independent of the parameters on which it operates. Because a functor is just a normal C++ object, it can carry a battery of data members that allow this customization.

In simple terms, a functor is just an *instance of a class or structure* that overloads the () operator. Such a structure is provided in lines 12-18 of Listing 7.2. Because the operator() method should be callable from both device and host code (based on the type of iterator provided to Thrust functions), it has to be decorated by both __host__ and __device__ specifiers. In our example, the function computed is $y = x^2$, but we could have used any unary function in Listing 7.2.

The thrust::sequence function in line 30 initializes a device vector (d_x) to the values $st, st + step, st + 2 \cdot step$, etc. The resulting vector is then "transformed" in line 33 by applying the f functor (defined in line 32) on all the vector elements (range d_x.begin() to d_x.end()-1 inclusive) and storing the results in the d_y device vector. The `thrust::transform` function (called an *algorithm* in Thrust jargon) supports either unary or binary functors only.

It should be noted that the preparation of the input array `d_x` is not done by the host but rather by the device. In fact, the only data exchange between the host and the device takes place in lines 35 and 36. In line 35 an iterator to the minimum element of device vector `d_y` is found by the call to function `thrust::min_element`. By subtracting the beginning of `d_y`, the offset to the `d_x` value that produced the minimum is found and output by direct access to the corresponding device vector element (line 36).

Thrust provides direct access to device data, but this is a capability that should be used sparingly, since it always results in a call to `cudaMemcpy()`.

7.3 WORKING WITH THRUST DATATYPES

The Thrust vector classes provide the same functionality as the STL `vector` template class. This means that we can use the `[]` operator for accessing individual vector elements:

```
int N=100;
thrust::device_vector<int> d_x(N); // allocate a 100-element vector on↵
    the device
d_x[0] = 1;
d_x[1] = 2;
```

Vectors can be resized:

```
d_x.resize(1000);
```

Vectors can queried:

```
cout << "New device vector size : " << d_x.size() << endl;
```

Vectors can be copied in a variety of ways:

```
#include <thrust/copy.h>
. . .
thrust::host_vector<float> h_x(N);
thrust::copy(d_x.begin()+10, d_x.begin()+20, h_x.begin()); // copies ↵
    10 elements to the beginning of h_x, starting from the 11-th ↵
    element of d_x. If N<10, only the first N of the 10 elements are ↵
    copied to h_x.
```

Vectors can be inserted into other vectors (the difference with `thrust::copy` is that the target vector gets "enlarged"):

```
thrust::host_vector < int >h_data (10, 0);        // all set to 0
thrust::host_vector < int >h_add (10);
```

```
h_data.insert (h_data.begin (), h_add.begin (), h_add.end ()); // ↩
    h_data is now 20 elements long
```

Vectors can have part of their content eliminated:

```
// erase all elements from the 13th till the end
h_data.erase(h_data.begin()+12, h_data.end());
```

And they can be initialized by the `thrust:sequence` and `thrust:fill` functions:

```
#include <thrust/fill.h>
#include <thrust/sequence.h>
. . .
thrust::fill(d_x.begin(), d_x.begin()+10, 100);   // fills the first ↩
    10 elements of d_x with 100. d_x[10] is exluded.
thrust::sequence(d_x.begin()+10, d_x.begin()+20); // fills the next 10↩
    elements of d_x with the sequence 0, 1, 2, ... The initial and ↩
    step values can be also specified. d_x[20] is excluded.
```

Thrust provides full interoperability with CUDA, which means that device data can be allocated, manipulated, and passed to kernels or Thrust functions seamlessly. This way, a programmer can always use the best tool for the job at hand.

The only modifications required, stem from the need to use an "augmented" data representation in Thrust: a "raw" pointer to an array just does not suffice for Thrust because it prohibits static dispatching. Data must be encapsulated in a vector template class or referenced by a special type of pointer such as the `thrust::device_ptr` template class. This unavoidably sets the stage for explicit typecasting.

In order to use memory allocated by `cudaMalloc` in Thrust, the corresponding pointer must be "wrapped" using the procedure exemplified by Listing 7.3.

```
1   // File : datatype.cu
2   #include <thrust/device_ptr.h>
3   #include <thrust/reduce.h>
4   #include <thrust/functional.h>
5   ...
6     int *d_data;
7     int *h_data;
8
9     h_data = new int[N];
10    cudaMalloc(&d_data, N*sizeof(int));
11    ... // populate h_data
12
13    cudaMemcpy(d_data, h_data, sizeof(int)*N, cudaMemcpyHostToDevice);
14
15    thrust::device_ptr<int> thr_d (d_data);
16
17    int sum = thrust::reduce(thr_d, thr_d + N, 0, thrust::plus<int>());
18
19    thrust::device_vector<int> d_vec(thr_d, thr_d + N);
20
```

```
21    int sum2 = thrust::reduce(d_vec.begin(), d_vec.end());
22
23    cout << "Sum is " << sum2 << endl;
24    ...
```

LISTING 7.3

Casting a raw pointer to a `thrust::device_ptr` datatype so that memory allocated by `cudaMalloc` can be used in Thrust algorithms.

The `thrust::device_ptr<int>` type variable defined in line 15 behaves as an iterator, as shown in line 17. If we prefer to use the Thrust vector types, a conversion is also possible with the constructor called in line 19.

Moving in the opposite direction, i.e., using Thrust to allocate memory and subsequently passing it to a CUDA kernel, can be accomplished by the `thrust::raw_pointer_cast`, as shown in Listing 7.4.

```
1    ...
2    using namespace std;
3
4    const int BLOCKSIZE = 256;
5    // ***********************************************
6    __global__ void foo(int *data, int N)
7    {
8       int gID = blockDim.x * blockIdx.x + threadIdx.x;
9       if(gID < N)
10         data[gID] *= 2;
11   }
12   // ***********************************************
13   int main (int argc, char **argv)
14   {
15      int N = atoi (argv[1]);
16
17      //--------------------------------------------
18      // way #1
19      thrust::host_vector<int> h_vec(N);
20      thrust::device_vector<int> d_vec(N);
21
22      for (int i = 0; i < N; i++)
23        h_vec[i] = rand () % 10000;
24
25      for(int i=0;i<min(10, N);i++)
26        cout << h_vec[i] << " ";
27      cout << endl;
28
29      d_vec = h_vec;
30
31      thrust::device_ptr<int> d_ptr = d_vec.data();
32
33      int *d_data = thrust::raw_pointer_cast(d_ptr);
```

```
34
35     dim3 block(BLOCKSIZE);
36     dim3 grid( (N + BLOCKSIZE−1)/BLOCKSIZE ); // equivalent to ceil(1.0*↩
         N/BLOCKSIZE)
37
38     foo<<<grid, block>>>(d_data, N);
39
40     h_vec = d_vec;
41
42     for(int i=0;i<min(10, N);i++)
43       cout << h_vec[i] << " ";
44     cout << endl;
45
46     //————————————————————————————————
47     // way #2
48     thrust::device_ptr<int> d_ptr2 = thrust::device_malloc<int>(N);
49     thrust::copy( h_vec.begin(), h_vec.end(), d_ptr2);
50
51 // Allowed but very inefficient
52 //     for (int i = 0; i < N; i++)
53 //       d_ptr2[i] = rand () % 10000;
54
55     int *d_data2 = thrust::raw_pointer_cast(d_ptr2);
56
57     foo<<<grid, block>>>(d_data2, N);
58
59     thrust::copy( d_ptr2, d_ptr2 + N, h_vec.begin());
60     thrust::device_free(d_ptr2);
61     ...
```

LISTING 7.4

Example showing how data allocated by Thrust can be passed to a CUDA kernel.

In the first part of Listing 7.4 (lines 19-44), memory is allocated and communicated via thrust vectors. Line 31 extracts a pointer to the data of the device vector used and wraps it inside a device_ptr<int> class instance. This can be subsequently cast to a raw pointer in line 33.

In the second part of Listing 7.4 (lines 48-60), memory is allocated with the Thrust equivalent of the malloc() function, thrust::device_malloc<>(), which in turn necessitates the need to explicitly free memory with the thrust::device_free() function (line 60). Data can still be transferred between Thrust vectors and the allocated memory blocks via the thrust::copy algorithm (lines 49, 59).

7.4 THRUST ALGORITHMS

Thrust provides efficient implementations for a number of important algorithms that can be used as building blocks to problem solutions. These including sorting, scanning, subset selection, and reduction implementations. Not only does Thrust boost programmer productivity and program readability and maintenance, but it can also boost performance because it can adjust the execution configuration to the available GPU capabilities and resources.

These algorithms fall into five categories:

- Transformations
- Sorting and searching
- Reductions
- Scans/prefix-sums
- Data management/manipulation

Some of these algorithms were introduced in the previous sections in an informal manner. In the sections that follow we examine each category of algorithm and provide a number of examples on their use.

7.4.1 TRANSFORMATIONS

Transformations operate on an input sequence by applying a supplied operation on each element. Contrary to a reduction, the produced output is equal in size (in terms of granularity) to the input. The following is a list of Thrust transformations that we got a glimpse of in the previous introductory examples:

- `thrust::fill`: Fills the elements of a vector with a specific value.
- `thrust::copy`: Copies a sub vector to another location (actually a data management algorithm; see Section 7.4.5).
- `thrust::sequence`: Initializes the elements of a vector to a sequence specified by an initial value and an optional step.
- `thrust::transform`: Generic form of transformation. Applies a user- (or Thrust-) supplied operation on every element of a vector.

As shown in Listing 7.2, `thrust::transform` requires the use of a named (i.e., accessible through a variable) or unnamed functor that will be used to process the elements of a vector(s). As an example, let's consider the calculation of the AXPY operation (short for A*X plus Y), which is a basic linear algebra vector operation:

$$\vec{z} = a \cdot \vec{x} + \vec{y}$$

An implementation of the double-precision AXPY (DAXPY) vector operation is shown in Listing 7.5.

```
1  // File : daxpy.cu
2  #include <iostream>
3  #include <thrust/host_vector.h>
4  #include <thrust/device_vector.h>
5  #include <thrust/transform.h>
6  #include <thrust/sequence.h>
7  #include <thrust/fill.h>
8
9  using namespace std;
```

```
10   // **************************************************************
11   // Helper template function
12   template < typename t >
13   void print (char c, thrust::host_vector < t > &v)
14   {
15     cout << "Version " << c << " : ";
16     thrust::copy (v.begin (), v.end (),
17                   ostream_iterator < t > (cout, ", "));
18     cout << endl;
19   }
20   // **************************************************************
21   struct saxpy
22   {
23     double a;
24     saxpy ():a (1.0)  {};
25     saxpy (double i):a (i)  {};
26
27     __host__ __device__
28     double operator () (double &x, double &y)  {
29       return a * x + y;
30     }
31   };
32   // **************************************************************
33   int main ()
34   {
35     thrust::device_vector < double >d_x (100);
36     thrust::device_vector < double >d_y (100);
37     thrust::device_vector < double >d_res (100);
38     thrust::sequence (d_x.begin (), d_x.end (), 0.0, .1);
39     thrust::fill (d_y.begin (), d_y.end (), 0.5);
40
41     saxpy funct;
42     funct.a = 1.2;
43
44     thrust::transform (d_x.begin (), d_x.end (),
45                        d_y.begin (),
46                        d_res.begin (),
47                        funct);
48   //** alternative call using an unnamed functor
49   // thrust::transform(d_x.begin (), d_x.end (), d_y.begin (), d_res.begin ↩
         (), saxpy(1.2));
50
51     thrust::host_vector < double >h_res (d_res);
52     print < double >('A', h_res);
53
54     return 0;
55   }
```

LISTING 7.5

Using thrust::transform to perform the DAXPY vector operation.

The template helper function of lines 12-19, copies the host_vector of type t elements to the standard output stream using the ",⎵" string as a separator. Line 16 is a convenient alternative to an explicit for loop.

Listing 7.5 shows the use of both a named and an unnamed functor, the latter as part of the commented-out line 49. The unfamiliar notation used (saxpy(1.2)) returns a reference (i.e., a constant pointer) to an instance of class saxpy allocated as a temporary object,[2] in contrast with the more identifiable new saxpy(1.2), which would return a pointer to an object allocated in the heap.

The thrust::transform algorithm can operate on one or two vectors, storing the result in a third one. Because the second vector and the one that will hold the result must be at least equal in size to the first one, we can omit the iterators pointing to their end. Appropriate overloaded template functions support this functionality, as we can observe by inspecting the contents of the thrust/transform.h header file:

```
template<typename InputIterator,
         typename OutputIterator,
         typename UnaryFunction>
OutputIterator transform(InputIterator first, InputIterator last,
                         OutputIterator result,
                         UnaryFunction op);


template<typename InputIterator1,
         typename InputIterator2,
         typename OutputIterator,
         typename BinaryFunction>
OutputIterator transform(InputIterator1 first1, InputIterator1 last1,
                         InputIterator2 first2,
                         OutputIterator result,
                         BinaryFunction op);
```

A work-around for supporting functors with a longer argument list is possible through the zip_iterator (see Section 7.5).

The operator() method of line 28 has to be decorated with both __host__ and __device__ directives so that the CUDA compiler driver can generate code that can be applied to elements of both host_vector and device_vector containers.

Thrust provides a number of built-in functors, that are available in the thrust/functional.h header file. These include the following that correspond to basic arithmetic operators:

- thrust::plus
- thrust::minus
- thrust::negate
- thrust::modulus
- thrust::divides
- thrust::multiplies

---

[2]Temporary entities get out of scope, i.e., they get destroyed, when the expression that uses them completes execution.

The DAXPY example of Listing 7.5 can be also performed with the built-in functors as well, as shown in Listing 7.6.

```
1   // File : daxpy_builtin.cpp
2   ...
3   #include <thrust/functional.h>
4   ...
5   int main ()
6   {
7     ...
8     thrust::fill (d_y.begin (), d_y.end (), 0.5);
9
10    thrust::transform (d_x.begin (), d_x.end (),
11                       thrust::constant_iterator<double >(1.2),
12                       d_res.begin (), thrust::multiplies<double >());
13    thrust::transform (d_res.begin (), d_res.end (),
14                       d_y.begin(), d_res.begin (),
15                       thrust::plus<double >());
16
17    thrust::host_vector < double >h_res (d_res);
18    ...
```

LISTING 7.6

Using `thrust::transform` and the built-in functors to perform the DAXPY vector operation. Only the changes relative to Listing 7.5 are shown.

Line 11 in Listing 7.6 introduces the `thrust::constant_iterator` template class, instances of which can be used in Thrust algorithms in the place of vector iterators when a constant value needs to be used.

Line 13 in Listing 7.6 reveals that it is possible to store the output of a transformation back into the input vector container. In a situation where *in-place* storage of the transformation results is desirable, the `thrust::for_each` algorithm can be also used, as shown in Listing 7.7.

```
1   // File : daxpy_foreach.cpp
2   #include <thrust/for_each.h>
3   ...
4   // unary functor supported only
5   struct atx
6   {
7     double a;
8     atx ():a (1.0)  {};
9     atx (double i):a (i)  {};
10
11    __host__ __device__
12      void operator () (double &x)  {
13      x *= a;
14    }
15  };
16
17  // ************************************************************
```

```
18   int main ()
19   {
20     ...
21     atx funct;
22     funct.a = 1.2;
23
24     thrust::for_each (d_x.begin (), d_x.end (), funct);
25     thrust::transform(d_x.begin(), d_x.end(),
26                       d_y.begin(), d_res.begin(),
27                       thrust::plus<double >());
28
29     thrust::host_vector < double >h_res (d_res);
30     ...
```

LISTING 7.7

A variation of Listing 7.5 that employs thrust::for_each.

The major difference of the thrust::for_each algorithm over the thrust::transform, is that only unary functors can be utilized. If the operator() function returns anything, it is ignored by thrust::for_each.

7.4.2 SORTING AND SEARCHING

Thrust provides efficient GPU implementations of two stable sorting algorithms: mergesort and radix sort. The choice of algorithm depends on the type of input data : radix sort is used for primitive data types (e.g. int, char, float, etc.) while mergesort is employed for anything else.

The collection of sorting and searching tools includes:

- thrust::sort.
- thrust::sort_by_key: Sorts two sequences in tandem, one serving as the "values" and one as the "keys."
- thrust::is_sorted: Returns true if the input vector is sorted. This is a reduction operation (see Section 7.4.3).
- thrust::is_sorted_until: Returns an iterator to the last position (exclusive) that the input vector is sorted.
- thrust::lower_bound: Searches an ordered sequence to find the first position where, if an item were inserted, it would not violate the ordering of the sequence.
- thrust::upper_bound: Searches an ordered sequence to find the last position where, if an item were inserted, it would not violate the ordering of the sequence.
- thrust::binary_search: Returns true of false based on whether an item can be found in an ordered sequence.
- thrust::equal_range: A combination of thrust::lower_bound, and thrust::upper_bound in that it returns a pair of iterators delimiting a range of elements matching a supplied one.

These searching algorithms have both scalar and vector implementations in the sense that multiple items can be searched for in an input sequence. A demonstration of these algorithms is given in the form of Listing 7.8.

```
1   // File : sort_example.cu
2   ...
3   #include <thrust/binary_search.h>
4   #include <thrust/sort.h>
5
6   using namespace std;
7
8   //***********************************************************
9   template < typename T> void print (char *s, thrust::host_vector < T > ↵
        &v )
10  {
11    cout << s ;
12    thrust::copy (v.begin (), v.end (), ostream_iterator < T > (cout, " ↵
        "));
13    cout << endl;
14  }
15
16  //***********************************************************
17
18  int main ()
19  {
20    int salary[] = { 1000, 2000, 1001, 2000, 3000, 5000 };
21    int numItems = sizeof (salary) / sizeof (int);
22    thrust::host_vector < int >h_salary (salary, salary + numItems);
23    int SSN[] = { 212, 122, 34, 456, 890, 102 };
24    thrust::host_vector < int >h_SSN (SSN, SSN + numItems);
25
26    thrust::device_vector < int >d_salary (h_salary);
27    thrust::device_vector < int >d_SSN (h_SSN);
28
29    //─────────────────────────
30    // Example − thrust::sort_by_key
31    thrust::sort_by_key (d_salary.begin (), d_salary.end (), d_SSN.begin↵
        ());
32    h_salary = d_salary;
33    h_SSN = d_SSN;
34    print("Keys : ", h_salary);
35    print("Values : ", h_SSN);
36    //Output is:
37    // Keys : 1000 1001 2000 2000 3000 5000
38    // Values : 212 34 122 456 890 102
39
40    //─────────────────────────
41    // Example − thrust::is_sorted
```

```cpp
42    cout << thrust::is_sorted (h_salary.begin (), h_salary.end ()) << ↩
          endl;
43    //Output is:
44    // 1
45
46    //──────────────────────────────
47    // Searching on the device : SCALAR VERSIONS
48    thrust::device_vector < int >::iterator i = thrust::lower_bound (↩
          d_salary.begin (), d_salary.end (), 1500);
49    cout << "Found at index " << i - d_salary.begin () << " Value " << *↩
          i << endl;
50    //Output is:
51    // Found at index 2 Value 2000
52
53    i = thrust::upper_bound (d_salary.begin (), d_salary.end (), 2500);
54    cout << "Found at index " << i - d_salary.begin () << " Value " << *↩
          i << endl;
55    //Output is:
56    // Found at index 4 Value 3000
57
58    thrust::pair < thrust::device_vector < int >::iterator, thrust::↩
          device_vector < int >::iterator > p;
59    p = thrust::equal_range (d_salary.begin (), d_salary.end (), 2000);
60    cout << "Range equal to item is between indices " << p.first - ↩
          d_salary.begin () << " " << p.second - d_salary.begin () <<endl;
61    //Output is:
62    // Range equal to item is between indices 2 4
63
64    p = thrust::equal_range (d_salary.begin (), d_salary.end (), 2222);
65    cout << "Range equal to item is between indices " << p.first - ↩
          d_salary.begin () << " " << p.second - d_salary.begin () <<endl;
66    //Output is:
67    // Range equal to item is between indices 4 4
68
69    cout << thrust::binary_search (d_salary.begin (), d_salary.end (), ↩
          1500) << endl;
70    //Output is:
71    // 0
72
73    //──────────────────────────────
74    // Searching on the host
75    thrust::host_vector < int >::iterator j = thrust::lower_bound (↩
          h_salary.begin (), h_salary.end (), 2000);
76    cout << j - h_salary.begin () << " " << *j << endl;
77    //Output is:
78    // 2 2000
79
80    //──────────────────────────────
81    // Searching on the device : VECTOR VERSIONS
82    thrust::device_vector<int> itemsToLook(10);
83    thrust::sequence(itemsToLook.begin(), itemsToLook.end(), 0, 500);
84    thrust::device_vector<int> results;
```

```
85    thrust::host_vector<int> h_r;
86    results.resize(itemsToLook.size());
87    h_r = itemsToLook;
88    print("Searching for : ", h_r);
89    // Output is:
90    // Searching for : 0 500 1000 1500 2000 2500 3000 3500 4000 4500
91
92    thrust::lower_bound (d_salary.begin (), d_salary.end (), itemsToLook↩
          .begin(), itemsToLook.end(), results.begin());
93    h_r = results;
94    print("Lower bounds : ", h_r);
95    // Output is:
96    // Lower bounds : 0 0 0 2 2 4 4 5 5 5
97
98    thrust::upper_bound (d_salary.begin (), d_salary.end (), itemsToLook↩
          .begin(), itemsToLook.end(), results.begin());
99    h_r = results;
100   print("Upper bounds : ", h_r);
101   // Output is:
102   // Upper bounds : 0 0 1 2 4 4 5 5 5 5
103
104   thrust::binary_search (d_salary.begin (), d_salary.end (), ↩
          itemsToLook.begin(), itemsToLook.end(), results.begin());
105   h_r = results;
106   print("Binary search results : ", h_r);
107   // Output is:
108   // Binary search results : 0 0 1 0 1 0 1 0 0 00
109
110   return 0;
111   }
```

LISTING 7.8

Sample code illustrating how the searching and sorting capabilities of Thrust can be invoked.

This code is more or less self-explanatory. There are just two fine details we must observe: First, the result of searching through a vector is expressed in the form of an iterator, as shown in lines 48, 53, and 75. Second, `thrust::equal_range` returns an instance of the `thrust::pair` template class. The two individual items that make up the pair can be accessed via the `first` and `second` data members (see line 65).

A more meaningful example that uses the sorting and searching capabilities of Thrust to calculate the histogram of an input sequence is given in Listing 7.9. Given that CUDA requires jumping through a number of hoops to achieve good performance in the calculation of a histogram (see Section 5.6.2), the following program is a much shorter and easier-to-maintain implementation, albeit sub-optimal (given that the CUDA version does not have to sort as a preprocessing step).

```
1   // File : histogram .cu
2   ...
3   #include <thrust/transform.h>
4   #include <thrust/sort.h>
5   #include <thrust/binary_search.h>
6   #include <thrust/iterator/counting_iterator.h>
7   ...
8   template < typename T > void print (char *s, thrust::host_vector < T >↩
        &v)
9   {
10    cout << s << ":";
11    thrust::copy (v.begin (), v.end (), ostream_iterator < T > (cout, " ↩
        "));
12    cout << endl;
13  }
14
15  // ********************************************************
16  template < typename T > void histogram (thrust::device_vector < T > &↩
        data, thrust::device_vector < int >&hist)
17  {
18    // start by sorting the data
19    thrust::sort (data.begin (), data.end ());
20
21    // the data range is now known, allowing the proper sizing of the ↩
        histogram vector
22    T min = data[0];
23    T max = data[data.size () − 1];
24    T range = max − min + 1;
25    hist.resize (range);
26
27    thrust::device_vector < int >aux;
28    aux.push_back (0);
29    aux.resize (hist.size () + 1);
30
31    // a counting_iterator is used to generate all the numbers in the ↩
        range [min, max]
32    thrust::counting_iterator < int >search (min);
33
34    // the vector version of upper_bound calculates for each item in the↩
        range, the index of the smallest item bigger than it
35    thrust::upper_bound (data.begin (), data.end (), search, search + ↩
        range, aux.begin () + 1);
36
37    // a simple subtraction produces the size of each group of identical↩
        items, i.e. the histogram
38    thrust::transform (aux.begin () + 1, aux.end (), aux.begin (), hist.↩
        begin (), thrust::minus < T > ());
39  }
40
41  // ********************************************************
42  int main (int argc, char **argv)
43  {
```

```
44      int N = atoi (argv[1]);
45      thrust::host_vector < int >h_x (N);1
46      thrust::host_vector < int >h_hist;
47      thrust::device_vector < int >d_x;
48      thrust::device_vector < int >d_hist;
49
50      srand (time (0));
51      for (int i = 0; i < N; i++)
52        h_x[i] = rand () % 20;
53
54      d_x = h_x;
55
56      histogram (d_x, d_hist);
57      h_hist = d_hist;
58      print ("Hist ", h_hist);
59
60      return 0;
61    }
```

LISTING 7.9

Histogram calculation using `thrust::sort` and `thrust::upper_bound`.

The inner workings of the `histogram()` function of Listing 7.9 are traced via a numerical example in Figure 7.1. Once identical values are clustered following the sorting of line 19, the `thrust::upper_bound` algorithm essentially produces, for every possible value in the input data range (generated by the `counting_iterator` of line 32), the array index that follows the group of items matching that value. Another interpretation of the results produced by line 35 is that they represent

Statement	Input	Value
	data	0 7 5 3 3 7 7 0 2 8 6 8 5
	hist	\<empty vector\>
	Output	**Value**
`thrust::sort (data.begin (), data.end ());`	data	0 0 2 3 3 5 5 6 7 7 7 8 8
`T min = data[0];`	min	0
`T max = data[data.size () - 1];`	max	8
`T range = max - min + 1;`	range	9
`hist.resize (range);`	hist	0 0 0 0 0 0 0 0 0
`thrust::device_vector < int >aux;`	aux	\<empty vector\>
`aux.push_back (0);`	aux	0
`aux.resize (hist.size () + 1);`	aux	0 0 0 0 0 0 0 0 0 0
`thrust::counting_iterator < int >search (min);`	search	0 1 2 ... (not an actual vector)
`thrust::upper_bound (data.begin (), data.e...`	aux	0 2 2 3 5 5 7 8 11 13
`thrust::transform (aux.begin () + 1, aux.e...`	hist	2 0 1 2 0 2 1 3 2

FIGURE 7.1

An example illustrating how the `histogram()` function of Listing 7.9 calculates the histogram of integer data.

the prefix sum of the histogram array. As such, the transformation of line 38 uses subtraction of neighboring values to yield the histogram array.

7.4.3 REDUCTIONS

A reduction algorithm extracts a single value from an input sequence by applying a binary operation. A summation is a simple example of a reduction. And it can be performed with the generic `thrust::reduce` algorithm:

```
#include <thrust/reduce.h>
...
  thrust::device_vector<double> d_x;
  ...
  double total = thrust::reduce(d_x.begin(), d_x.end(), 0.0L, thrust::↵
      plus<double >());
  double total = thrust::reduce(d_x.begin(), d_x.end(), 0.0L);
  double total = thrust::reduce(d_x.begin(), d_x.end());
...
```

All three of these statements are equivalent because the initial reduction result value (the third parameter) and the reduction functor (the fourth parameter) default to zero and `thrust::plus<>()`, respectively.

Thrust provides a large collection of additional reduction algorithms as shown in the following list:

- `thrust::min_element`: Returns the smallest from a sequence.
- `thrust::max_element`: Returns the largest from a sequence.
- `thrust::is_sorted`: Returns true if the sequence is sorted.
- `thrust::inner_product`: Calculates the inner product of two vectors. In its generic form, this algorithm can be supplied custom "multiplication" (transformation) and custom "addition" (reduction) functors.
- `thrust::count`: Counts the elements matching a given value.
- `thrust::count_if`: Returns the count of elements that satisfy a predicate functor, i.e., a functor with an `operator()` member function that returns a boolean.
- `thrust::reduce_by_key`: Performs a reduction operation on (key, value) pairs. For each group of consecutive pairs with identical keys, the reduction is done on the corresponding values.

Kernel fusion, i.e., the replacement of multiple kernel invocations by a single one (see Section 5.7.7), is a device optimization technique that aims to eliminate redundant data transfers over the PCIe bus. Kernel fusion is relevant to Thrust also, and in that spirit Thrust designers have provided a fusion of transformation and reduction operations in the form of the `thrust::transform_reduce` and `thrust::inner_product` algorithms. Their difference is that the former applies to a single vector, while the latter applies to two.

The `thrust::inner_product` and `thrust::reduce_by_key` algorithms can be used to calculate the sparse histogram of an array of values, i.e., a histogram in which the counts of only encountered values are calculated. The process involves the sorting of the input array so that groups of identical values are formed. Subsequently, groups of identical values are reduced to produce partial sums (the histogram counts), as shown in Listing 7.10.

```
1   // File : histogram_sparse.cu
2   ...
3   #include <thrust/reduce.h>
4   #include <thrust/inner_product.h>
5   #include <thrust/iterator/constant_iterator.h>
6   ...
7   template < typename T >
8   void histogram_sparse (thrust::device_vector < T > &data,
9                          thrust::device_vector < T > &value,
10                         thrust::device_vector < int >&count)
11  {
12    thrust::sort (data.begin (), data.end ());
13
14    // calculate how many different values exist in the vector
15    // by comparing successive values in the sorted data.
16    // For every different pair of keys (i.e. a change from one set to ↩
           the next)
17    // a value of 1 is produced and summed up
18    int numBins = thrust::inner_product (data.begin (), data.end () − 1,
19                                         data.begin () + 1,
20                                         0,
21                                         thrust::plus < int >(),
22                                         thrust::not_equal_to < T > ());
23
24    // output vectors are resized to fit the results
25    value.resize (numBins);
26    count.resize (numBins);
27
28    // the groups of identical keys, get their values (1) summed up
29    // producing as a result a count
30    thrust::reduce_by_key (data.begin (), data.end (),
31                           thrust::constant_iterator < int >(1),
32                           value.begin (),
33                           count.begin ());
34  }
35
36  // ***********************************************************
37  int main (int argc, char **argv)
38  {
39    int N = atoi (argv[1]);
40    thrust::host_vector < int >h_x (N);
41    thrust::host_vector < int >h_value;
42    thrust::host_vector < int >h_count;
43    thrust::device_vector < int >d_x;
44    thrust::device_vector < int >d_value;
45    thrust::device_vector < int >d_count;
46
```

```
47    srand (time (0));
48    for (int i = 0; i < N; i++)
49      h_x[i] = rand () % 10000;
50
51    d_x = h_x;
52
53    histogram_sparse (d_x, d_value, d_count);
54    h_value = d_value;
55    h_count = d_count;
56    print ("Values ", h_value);
57    print ("Counts ", h_count);
58
59    return 0;
60  }
```

LISTING 7.10

Sparse histogram calculation using `thrust::reduce_by_key` and `thrust::inner_product`. Code shared with Listing 7.9 is not shown.

The key points of the `histogram_sparse()` function are:

1. The number of "bins," i.e., distinct values that are encountered in the input data, needs to be determined in order to resize the output vectors. This is the task accomplished by line 18, whereas successive data items are compared (the transformation step of `thrust::inner_product`, via functor `thrust::not_equal_to`) against each other. Unequal pairs contribute by +1 to the overall sum produced by the reduction step, afforded by functor `thrust::plus`. Parameter 0 of line 20 is just the initial value for the reduction.
2. Once the number of bins is found, the sorted input data, treated as keys, are paired with a "value" vector implicitly generated by the anonymous `thrust::constant_iterator` of line 31. The `thrust::reduce_by_key` algorithm thus counts the cardinality of each group of "keys," effectively producing the desired histogram.

This process is illustrated via a numerical example in Figure 7.2.

In terms of outright performance, Listing 7.10 is expected to perform more slowly than the corresponding CUDA solution that does not have to sort the values first. However, it clearly illustrates the conceptual shift required for efficient use of Thrust to solve problems: One has to think in terms of vector/array manipulations.

7.4.4 SCANS/PREFIX SUMS

Reduction operations are a special form of prefix sums, also known as scans. Despite the "sum" part of the name, prefix sums can be defined for arbitrary operators. The formal definition of a prefix-sum operation calls for the application of a *binary associative* operator $\oplus$ (i.e., one that satisfies $(a \oplus b) \oplus c = a \oplus (b \oplus c)$) on an

Input	Value
data	0 7 5 3 3 7 7 0 2 8 6 8 5
value	\<empty vector\>
count	\<empty vector\>

Statement	Output	Value
`thrust::sort (data.begin (), data.end ());`	data	0 0 2 3 3 5 5 6 7 7 7 8 8
`int numBins = thrust::inner_product (d...`	numBins	7
`value.resize (numBins);`	value	0 0 0 0 0 0 0
`count.resize (numBins);`	count	0 0 0 0 0 0 0
`thrust::reduce_by_key (data.begin (), d...`	value	0 2 3 5 6 7 8
	count	2 1 2 2 1 3 2

FIGURE 7.2

An example illustrating how the `histogram_sparse()` function of Listing 7.10 calculates the histogram of integer data.

ordered set of n elements $[a_0, a_1, \ldots, a_{n-1}]$ so that the following set is produced: $[a_0, (a_0 \oplus a_1), \ldots, (a_0 \oplus a_1 \oplus \cdots \oplus a_{n-1})]$.

The output of a scan operation is a vector, in contrast to a reduction operation, where only a single element of that vector is of interest and thus computed.

Scans are a building block of many parallel algorithms. Some of the applications include:

- Radix sort
- Polynomial evaluation
- Recurrence evaluation

Thrust provides a small collection of algorithms for computing prefix sums. These include:

- `thrust::inclusive_scan`: The result associated with an input element includes the contribution of that element. The default binary operation is summation.
- `thrust::exclusive_scan`: The result associated with an input element excludes the contribution of that element. So, the output sequence is $[I, a_0, (a_0 \oplus a_1), \ldots, (a_0 \oplus a_1 \oplus \cdots \oplus a_{n-2})]$, where I is the identity value for $\oplus$ (e.g., 0 for summation).
- `thrust::transform_inclusive_scan`.
- `thrust::transform_exclusive_scan`: Same as above, with the addition of having a unary functor operate on the input vector elements before the scan.

The following short program illustrates the results produced by these algorithms:

```
// File : scan_example.cu
...
#include <thrust/scan.h>
...
// ***********************************************************
```

```
int main ()
{
  int data[] = { 10, 1, 34, 7, 8, 10, 17 };
  int numItems = sizeof(data)/sizeof(int);
  thrust::host_vector < int >h_data (data, data + numItems);
  thrust::host_vector < int >h_r;

  thrust::device_vector < int >d_data(h_data);
  thrust::device_vector < int >d_r(numItems);

  thrust::inclusive_scan(d_data.begin (), d_data.end (), d_r.begin());
  h_r = d_r;
  print("Inclusive scan : ", h_r);
  // Output is:
  // Inclusive scan : 10 11 45 52 60 70 87

  thrust::exclusive_scan(d_data.begin (), d_data.end (), d_r.begin());
  h_r = d_r;
  print("Exclusive scan : ", h_r);
  // Output is:
  // Exclusive scan : 0 10 11 45 52 60 70

  thrust::inclusive_scan(d_data.begin (), d_data.end (), d_r.begin(), ↵
      thrust::multiplies<int >());
  h_r = d_r;
  print("Inclusive scan product : ", h_r);
  // Output is:
  // Inclusive scan product : 10 10 340 2380 19040 190400 3236800

  return 0;
}
```

A more meaningful example of the scan algorithm comes in the form of solving the DNA sequence alignment problem, as described in Section 7.7.2.

7.4.5 DATA MANAGEMENT AND MANIPULATION

Thrust provides ways to manipulate the elements of a vector by allowing selective copying, replacement, removal, or partitioning. The supplied algorithms are:

- thrust::copy: Copies one vector to another.
- thrust::remove: Removes all elements that match a supplied value.
- thrust::replace: Replaces with a new value all elements that match a supplied value.
- thrust::remove_copy: Removal takes place during copying to another vector.
- thrust::replace_copy: Replacement takes place during copying to another vector.

- `thrust::unique`: From each group of identical, consecutive elements, all but the first one are removed.
- `thrust::unique_copy`: During copying to another vector, only the first element of each group of identical consecutive elements is copied.
- `thrust::unique_by_key`: Applies the same operation as `thrust::unique` but for two vectors, one serving as the keys and one as the values. The keys vector is the one where groups are identified.
- `thrust::unique_by_key_copy`: Same as the previous one, but the data are copied to two other vectors.
- `thrust::partition`: Reorders the elements of a sequence according to the value of a predicate functor. All the elements for which `true` is returned are placed before the ones for which `false` is returned. Relative order is not preserved among the elements of each group. This is equivalent to the partition function used by quicksort.
- `thrust::partition_copy`: Same as the previous one, but the reordered sequence is stored in another vector.

These are augmented by versions that perform the filtering action (replacement, removal, etc.) not if a specific value is matched but if a predicate functor returns true. These include the algorithms `thrust::copy_if`, `thrust::remove_if`, `thrust::replace_if`, `thrust::replace_copy_if`, `thrust::remove_if`, and `thrust::remove_copy_if`.

The algorithms that modify the length of the vector or produce as output a new vector with different size, return an iterator that points to the end of the new vector. Any data beyond that point should be ignored.

The following sample program shows how the above algorithms work as well as the difference between the two groups of algorithms:

```
1  // File : data_manage_example.cu
2  ...
3  #include <thrust/copy.h>
4  #include <thrust/replace.h>
5  #include <thrust/remove.h>
6  #include <thrust/unique.h>
7  #include <thrust/partition.h>
8  ...
9
10 struct evenFunct
11 {
12   __host__ __device__
13   bool operator()(int i)  {
14     return i%2==0;    }
15 };
16 // *********************************************************
17 struct pivotFunct
18 {
19   int pivot;
20   pivotFunct(int p) : pivot(p){}
```

```
21
22      __host__ __device__
23        bool operator()(int i)   {
24          return i<pivot;    }
25    };
26    // ************************************************************
27    int main ()
28    {
29      int aux[] = { 5, 1, 3, 3, 2, 4, 2, 7, 6, 7 };
30      char aux2[] = { 'A', 'B', 'C', 'D', 'E', 'F', 'G', 'H', 'I', 'J'};
31      int numItems = sizeof(aux)/sizeof(int);
32      thrust::host_vector < int >h_keys (aux, aux + numItems);
33      thrust::host_vector < char >h_values(aux2, aux2 + numItems);
34
35      thrust::host_vector<int> dest_keys(numItems);
36      thrust::host_vector<char> dest_values(numItems);
37
38      thrust::host_vector<int >::iterator newEnd = thrust::copy_if(h_keys.↩
            begin(), h_keys.end(), dest_keys.begin(), evenFunct());
39      dest_keys.resize( newEnd − dest_keys.begin());
40      print("copy_if : ", dest_keys);
41      // Output is:
42      // copy_if : 2 4 2 6
43
44      dest_keys.resize(numItems);
45      newEnd = thrust::remove_copy(h_keys.begin(), h_keys.end(), dest_keys↩
            .begin(), 3);
46      dest_keys.resize( newEnd − dest_keys.begin());
47      print("remove_copy : ", dest_keys);
48      // Output is:
49      // remove_copy : 5 1 2 4 2 7 6 7
50
51      dest_keys.resize(numItems);
52      newEnd = thrust::unique_copy(h_keys.begin(), h_keys.end(), dest_keys↩
            .begin());
53      dest_keys.resize( newEnd − dest_keys.begin());
54      print("unique_copy : ", dest_keys);
55      // Output is:
56      // unique_copy : 5 1 3 2 4 2 7 6 7
57
58      thrust::pair<thrust::host_vector<int >::iterator,
59                  thrust::host_vector<char >::iterator> endsPair =
60                  thrust::unique_by_key_copy(h_keys.begin(), h_keys.end()↩
                        , h_values.begin(), dest_keys.begin(), dest_values.↩
                        begin());
61      dest_keys.resize(endsPair.first − dest_keys.begin());
62      dest_values.resize(endsPair.second − dest_values.begin());
63      print("unique_by_key_copy (keys)  : ", dest_keys);
64      print("unique_by_key_copy (values): ", dest_values);
65      // Output is:
66      // unique_by_key_copy (keys)  : 5 1 3 2 4 2 7 6 7
67      // unique_by_key_copy (values): A B C E F G H I J
```

```
68
69    thrust::sort(h_keys.begin(), h_keys.end());
70    dest_keys.resize(numItems);
71    newEnd = thrust::unique_copy(h_keys.begin(), h_keys.end(), dest_keys↵
          .begin());
72    dest_keys.resize( newEnd - dest_keys.begin());
73    print("unique_copy for sorted : ", dest_keys);
74    // Output is:
75    // unique_copy for sorted : 1 2 3 4 5 6 7
76
77    thrust::replace_if(h_keys.begin(), h_keys.end(), evenFunct(), 0);
78    print("replace_if : ", h_keys);
79    // Output is:
80    // replace_if : 1 0 0 3 3 0 5 0 7 7
81
82    thrust::partition(h_keys.begin(), h_keys.end(), pivotFunct( h_keys↵
          [0] ));
83    print("partition : ", h_keys);
84    // Output is:
85    // partition : 0 0 0 0 1 3 3 5 7 7
86
87    return 0;
88  }
```

There are several key points related to the steps shown above:

- When the output of an algorithm is destined for another container/vector, that vector should be large enough to accommodate the data, i.e., it must be properly sized *a priori* (see lines 35, 36, 44, 51).
- To avoid problems, the iterator returned by the size-modifying algorithms such as `thrust::remove` should be used to resize the affected vectors (see lines 39, 46, 53, 61, 62, and 72).
- The `thrust::*_by_key*` family of algorithms that modify the size of their input vectors return a pair of iterators in the form of a `thrust::pair<>` instance (see line 58).

7.5 FANCY ITERATORS

The term *fancy* is used in Thrust to characterize special-purpose iterators that are used either to generate data without having to occupy memory or to combine vectors in an effort to adhere to the structure-of-arrays design principle discussed in Section 5.7.4. We have already seen the `thrust::constant_iterator` in action in Listing 7.6 and the `thrust::counting_iterator` in Listing 7.9.

The list of fancy iterators includes:

- `thrust::constant_iterator`: Returns the same constant value.
- `thrust::counting_iterator`: Returns a sequence of increasing values. The user can specify the starting value, but the increment step is fixed to 1.

- thrust::transform_iterator: Returns a sequence produced by applying a transformation to the elements of another vector/fancy iterator. It provides a convenient way to combine multiple transformations in one statement, serving the principle of *kernel fusion*.
- thrust::permutation_iterator: Returns a subset of a sequence with its elements retrieved at a user-specified/arbitrary order. It uses two vectors: one serves as a data source and the other as a index map/data selector. The index map vector allows us to use a subset of a data vector as input to an algorithm, while at the same time controlling the order in which the data will be used.
- thrust::zip_iterator: Allows the combination of two or more data sequences into a sequence of tuples. In doing so, it allows us to emulate a array-of-structures while storing the data in a structure-of-arrays manner. It also enables us to have functors with arbitrary parameter lists, since the majority of the algorithms allow only unary or binary functors.

Most of these iterators were used in examples in the previous sections. We will proceed to explore the use of the thrust::zip_iterator to solve the following problem: Given a set of points in 3D space, find the one that is most distant from the origin, i.e., from point (0,0,0).

The first issue that needs to be addressed is that of data representation. Having a structure and a functor such as:

```
struct Point3D {
  float x, y, z;
};

struct distanceSqrFunct {
  __host__ __device__
  float operator ()(Point3D &p) {
    return p.x*p.x + p.y*p.y + p.z*p.z;
  }
};
```

may be convenient, but this solution suffers from two major drawbacks: First, it is counter-efficient for device execution (see memory coalescing in Section 5.7.4). Second, using a thrust::transform_reduce algorithm on an array of such points would produce the maximum distance but not the coordinates or index of the corresponding point.

On the other hand, using three different arrays to represent the problem data raises the obstacle that only unary and binary functors are supported by Thrust algorithms, that is, until the thrust::zip_iterator steps into the picture. Before we delve into the solution to this problem, let's, see how the zip iterator can be used. Zip iterators are created with the assistance of the thrust::make_zip_iterator() function, which in turn requires the use of the thrust::make_tuple() function to "glue" together individual arrays into a logical tuple. For example:

```
typedef thrust::device_vector<int >::iterator DVIint;  // typedef can
                                          // shorten the necessary code
```

```
typedef thrust::device_vector<float>::iterator DVIfloat;

// tuple instances with 3 elements each
thrust::tuple < DVIint, DVIint, DVIfloat> aTuple, anotherTuple;

// given the above declarations, in the statement below, x and y must
// be device vectors of int and alpha must be a device vector of float
aTuple = thrust::make_tuple (x.begin(), y.begin(), alpha.begin());

anotherTuple =thrust::make_tuple (x.begin()+10,
                                  y.begin()+10,
                                  alpha.begin()+10);
```

To access individual elements of a tuple in a functor, the following syntax is required:

```
template < typename Tuple >
__host__ __device__
float operator() (Tuple t)
  {
    int x = thrust::get < 0 > (t);   // get the first component
    int y = thrust::get < 1 > (t);   // get the second comp.
    float alpha = thrust::get < 2 > (t);   // etc.
    return alpha * x  + y ;
  }
```

Given a starting tuple, a zip iterator can be used to synchronously and incrementally access the elements of the individual arrays:

```
typedef thrust::tuple < DVIint, DVIint, DVIfloat> tupleDef;
thrust::zip_iterator< tupleDef > ziter;
ziter = thrust::make_zip_iterator(aTuple);

// output the x component of the first tuple
cout << thrust::get < 0 > (ziter[0]) << endl;

// output the y component of the sixth tuple
cout << thrust::get < 1 > (ziter[5]) << endl;
```

Having covered the basic syntax of the Thrust tuple class and the zip iterator, we can proceed to solve the posed problem as shown in Listing 7.11.

```
1   // File : max3d.cu
2   ...
3   #include <thrust/iterator/zip_iterator.h>
4   #include <thrust/iterator/counting_iterator.h>
5   #include <thrust/transform.h>
6   #include <thrust/reduce.h>
7   #include <thrust/random.h>
8   #include <thrust/tuple.h>
9   #include <math.h>
10
11  using namespace std;
```

```
12
13    // Calculate the square of the distance
14    struct distSqrFunct
15    {
16      template < typename Tuple >
17      __host__ __device__
18      float operator () (Tuple t)
19      {
20        int x = thrust::get < 0 > (t);
21        int y = thrust::get < 1 > (t);
22        int z = thrust::get < 2 > (t);
23        return x * x + y * y + z * z;
24      }
25    };
26
27    // ****************************************************
28    struct maxFunct
29    {
30      thrust::device_ptr < int >dis;
31      maxFunct (thrust::device_ptr < int >d):dis (d)   {}
32
33      __host__ __device__
34      int operator () (int idx1, int idx2)
35      {
36        if (dis[idx1] > dis[idx2])
37          return idx1;
38        return idx2;
39      }
40    };
41
42    // ****************************************************
43    int main (int argc, char **argv)
44    {
45      // initialize the RNG
46      thrust::default_random_engine rng (time(0));
47      thrust::uniform_int_distribution<int> uniDistr(-10000,10000);
48
49      int N = atoi (argv[1]);
50
51      // generate the data on the host and move them to the device
52      thrust::device_vector < int >x (N);
53      thrust::device_vector < int >y (N);
54      thrust::device_vector < int >z (N);
55      thrust::device_vector < int >dis (N);
56      thrust::host_vector<int> aux(N);
57      for (int i = 0; i < x.size (); i++) aux[i] = uniDistr(rng);
58      x = aux;
59      for (int i = 0; i < x.size (); i++) aux[i] = uniDistr(rng);
60      y = aux;
61      for (int i = 0; i < x.size (); i++) aux[i] = uniDistr(rng);
62      z = aux;
63
```

```
64    // "zip" together the 3 arrays into one
65    // typedefs make the code easier to read
66    typedef thrust::device_vector < int >::iterator DVIint;
67    typedef thrust::tuple < DVIint, DVIint, DVIint > tTuple;
68    tTuple a = thrust::make_tuple (x.begin (), y.begin (), z.begin ());
69    tTuple b = thrust::make_tuple (x.end (), y.end (), z.end ());
70
71    // calculate the distance for each point
72    thrust::transform (thrust::make_zip_iterator (a),
73                       thrust::make_zip_iterator (b),
74                       dis.begin (),
75                       distSqrFunct ());
76
77    // initialize the functor that will find the maximum distance, so ↩
         that it has access to the distance data
78    maxFunct f (dis.data());
79
80    // reduce the index of the most distant point
81    int furthest = thrust::reduce (thrust::counting_iterator < int >(0),
82                                   thrust::counting_iterator < int >(N),
83                                   0,
84                                   f);
85
86    float maxDist = dis[furthest]; // get max distance^2 from the device ↩
         memory
87    cout << "The most distant point is the " << furthest << "-th one, ↩
         with a distance of " << sqrt(maxDist) << endl;
88
89    return 0;
90  }
```

LISTING 7.11

Using the `thrust::zip_iterator` to find the coordinates of a point in 3D space that is the most distant from the origin.

Aside from the part of the program concerned with data generation (lines 57-62) that utilizes the Thrust random-number generation capabilities (for more details on this topic, see Section 7.7.1), the rest of the program involves two steps: the transformation to compute the distances for all the points (lines 72-75) and the reduction to find the point furthest from the origin (lines 81-84).

The details of the solution of Listing 7.11 are:

- In order to allow for device memory coalescing, the coordinates of the data points are held in separate arrays (defined in lines 52-54). The number of points is controlled by command-line input (line 49).
- The data are randomly generated on the host (lines 57, 59, 61) and then transferred as a single step to the device (lines 58, 60, 62), thus avoiding

extraordinary PCIe traffic. To clarify this point, it is possible that the data were generated as follows:

```
for (int i = 0; i < x.size (); i++) {
  x[i] = uniDistr(rng);
  y[i] = uniDistr(rng);
  z[i] = uniDistr(rng);
}
```

But this would result in a separate PCIe transfer (cudaMemcpy operation) for each array element!

- The square of the distance of each point[3] is calculated by the distSqrFunct functor of lines 14-25. The zip iterators created in lines 72 and 73, based on the tuples representing the collective beginning and the collective end of the arrays (lines 68, 69), permit Thrust to process each point with a unary functor.
- The reduction process involves a bit of a hack, given that the desired output is an index, but the data on which the reduction must be performed are the distances. The solution is to provide the functor access to the distances by passing its constructor a pointer to the device memory holding them (line 78). Once the memory location of the distances is known, the pair of indices that are passed to the functor during the reduction can be used to fetch and compare the corresponding distances (line 36).

  It should be stressed that passing a reference to the actual device_vector object, as in:

```
struct maxFunct
{
  thrust::device_vector < int > *dis;
    maxFunct (thrust::device_vector< int > *d) : dis(d)  {}

  __host__ __device__
  int operator() (int idx1, int idx2)
  {
    if ((*dis)[idx1] > (*dis)[idx2])
      return idx1;
    return idx2;
  }
};
...
  maxFunct f (&dis);
...
```

is both a logical and a syntax error and it will result in an admittedly cryptic and far-from-user-friendly long list of compilation error messages. The essence is that while the dis.data() call returns a device memory pointer as the one required to perform the reduction, the dis device_vector *object itself is an entity living in host memory.*

---

[3] The calculation of the square root has no significance in finding the greatest distance; thus it constitutes a run-time cost that can be avoided.

- The reduction requires a list of the point indices. Instead of having an extra vector occupying memory and taking up time to allocate and populate, it suffices to have a pair of `thrust::counting_iterators` denoting the first (line 81) and (beyond) last (line 82) index to use. The zero index (line 83) serves as our initial reduction value.
- Finally, the greatest distance, as represented by `dis[furthest]`, cannot be output to the console directly. Instead, a memory copy from the device to the host must be initiated (line 86) before this action can take place.

7.6 SWITCHING DEVICE BACK ENDS

Thrust was originally designed to be a CUDA front end, i.e., the ultimate compilation of the provided algorithms was relegated to a CUDA compiler driver back end. However, the latest incarnations of Thrust go beyond CUDA and GPUs by allowing the use of other back ends for compilation.

As of Thrust version 1.7, these so-called *device back ends* are:

- CUDA compiler driver (default)
- OpenMP compiler
- Intel Thread Building Blocks (TBB) templates
- Standard C++ compiler

The choice of device back end is controlled by the `THRUST_DEVICE_SYSTEM` symbolic name.[4] For example, if we were to compile the histogram program of Section 7.4.2 with the standard C++ compiler, the following line would be required:

```
nvcc histogram.cu —DTHRUST_DEVICE_SYSTEM=THRUST_DEVICE_SYSTEM_CPP —o ↩
    histogram_stdc
```

The use of the alternative device back ends may require additional compiler switches, such as library/include file locations, extra libraries to link against, or other compiler directives (these are compiler and system environment dependent). Table7.1

Table 7.1 Thrust device back ends and their associated compiler switches. GCC is assumed to be the compiler used by `nvcc`

Device Back End	THRUST_DEVICE_SYSTEM Value	Other Compiler Switches
CUDA	THRUST_DEVICE_SYSTEM_CUDA	N/A
OpenMP	THRUST_DEVICE_SYSTEM_OMP	`-Xcompiler -fopenmp -lgomp`
TBB	THRUST_DEVICE_SYSTEM_TBB	`-ltbb`
C++	THRUST_DEVICE_SYSTEM_CPP	N/A

---

[4]Older Thrust versions use the `THRUST_DEVICE_BACKEND` name.

lists the value required for THRUST_DEVICE_SYSTEM and any additional compiler switches for each of the available back ends.

So, compiling the histogram program for execution using OpenMP or TBB, we would need the commands:

```
#OpenMP
nvcc histogram.cu —DTHRUST_DEVICE_SYSTEM=THRUST_DEVICE_SYSTEM_OMP —↩
    Xcompiler —fopenmp —lgomp —o histogram_omp

#TBB
nvcc histogram.cu —DTHRUST_DEVICE_SYSTEM=THRUST_DEVICE_SYSTEM_TBB —↩
    ltbb —o histogram_tbb
```

The difference in performance is immediately apparent between the different back ends. For instance, calculating the histogram of 10^6 values on a system equipped with a third-generation i7 3770K processor clocked at 4.2 GHz and a GTX 560 Ti GPU card clocked at 1645 MHz produced the following execution times:[5]

```
$ time ./histogram_cuda 1000000
Hist :49807 49892 50238 49656 49800 50030 50082 49965 49980 50090 ↩
      49935 50216 50044 50281 49981 49958 49728 50018 49966 50333

real    0m0.093s
user    0m0.054s
sys     0m0.038s
$ time ./histogram_tbb 1000000
Hist :49694 49679 49666 49871 49834 50203 49821 50404 50226 49989 ↩
      49748 50034 50044 50163 50081 50482 50224 50150 49875 49812

real    0m0.283s
user    0m1.127s
sys     0m0.027s
$ time ./histogram_omp 1000000
Hist :50189 49743 49984 50194 50092 49908 50034 49940 50175 50109 ↩
      49953 50182 49665 50040 49376 50430 50047 50204 49880 49855

real    0m1.186s
user    0m2.608s
sys     0m0.016s
$ time ./histogram_stdc 1000000
Hist :50234 50109 49930 49957 50073 49909 49717 50268 49573 50064 ↩
      50412 50036 49988 50056 50079 49705 50061 49896 49928 50005

real    0m0.338s
user    0m0.334s
sys     0m0.004s
```

These times are not indicative of how well a particular back end will perform under any and all circumstances (especially given the very small execution time that would exaggerate any difference in back-end initialization time). Compiler choice (e.g., gcc versus icc) and program design can have a big influence on the outcome.

---

[5]Sample outputs are different because each run uses randomly generated data.

7.7 CASE STUDIES

7.7.1 MONTE CARLO INTEGRATION

Monte Carlo integration is an approximation technique for calculating definite integrals. It is typically used for higher-dimensional integrals, where an analytical solution is impossible.

If we pick N random points x_i with $i \in [0, N - 1]$, uniformly distributed in a n-dimensional space $V \in \Re^n$, then the integral of a function f over V can be approximated by:

$$I = \int_V f dx = V\bar{f} \pm V\sqrt{\frac{\overline{f^2} - \bar{f}^2}{N - 1}} \tag{7.1}$$

where the overline represents arithmetic mean over the N points, i.e., $\bar{f} = \frac{1}{N}\sum_{i=0}^{N-1} f(x_i)$, and the $\pm$ part of the equation represents an error estimate based on the unbiased standard deviation of f.

The error decreases at a rate of $\frac{1}{N}$, which means that the larger the set of points, the better the accuracy of the result.

If the volume V cannot be calculated, we can select a space W such that $V \subseteq W$ and proceed to sample W. Then:

$$I = \int_V f dx = W\bar{g} \tag{7.2}$$

where the function g is defined as:

$$g(x) = \begin{cases} f(x), & \text{if } x \in V \\ 0, & \text{if } x \notin V \end{cases} \tag{7.3}$$

For example, let's apply a Monte Carlo approach to the calculation of π. Approximating π can be accomplished by finding the integral:

$$I = \int_0^1 \sqrt{1 - x^2} dx \tag{7.4}$$

The function, in this case, is the equation of the unit circle ($x^2 + y^2 = 1$), and so the integral should be equal to a quarter of the unit circle's area: $\frac{\pi}{4}$.

The pseudocode for a program calculating π in this fashion, given the number of sample points N,[6] is shown in Listing 7.12.

```
int inside=0;
for(int i=0;i<N;i++)   {
   double x, y, distance;
   x = rand();     // generate an x and y coordinates in the
   y = rand();     // [0,1]x[0,1] part of the plane
   distance = x*x + y*y;
```

---

[6]A nice GIF animation that shows the influence of N on the calculation accuracy can be found at http://en.wikipedia.org/wiki/File:Pi_30K.gif.

```
        if( distance <= 1 )  inside++; // check if it is inside the ↩
            circle
    }
    double PI = 4.0 * inside /  N;
```

LISTING 7.12

Pseudocode of a Monte Carlo-based calculation of π.

A critical component of Monte Carlo methods is the random-number generator (RNG). Most computational methods rely on pseudo-random generators (PRNG), i.e., algorithms that produce seemingly random sequences based on an initial "seed" value. The sequence is deterministic, however, since as the same seed will always produce the same sequence.

The approach used by Thrust for random-number generation differs from the one provided by standard-C and the pair of srand(), rand() functions. Thrust provides a number of PRNG engines that are used as the back end to other algorithms that adapt the generated numbers to a specific range or distribution (e.g., uniform, normal, etc.). For example, the default PRNG engine can be used to generate custom distribution numbers as follows:

```
thrust::default_random_engine rng(seed);  // provide seed in case ↩
    results need to be reproducible

// generates floating point numbers using a uniform distribution in ↩
    the [a,b] interval
thrust::uniform_real_distribution<double> uniDistr(a,b);
double aNum = uniDistr(rng);

// generates integer numbers using a uniform distribution in the [a,b]↩
    interval
thrust::uniform_int_distribution<long> uniDistrInt(a,b);
long anotherNum =  uniDistrInt(rng);

// generates floating point numbers using a normal distribution with ↩
    mean a and standard deviation b
thrust::random::normal_distribution<float> normalDistr(a, b);
float thirdNum = normalDistr(rng);
```

In order to speed up the calculation of the integral, the random-number generation process should run in parallel as well. To avoid having identical sequences that could taint the results, each point should be generated by a RNG initialized with a different seed. However, this still cannot guarantee that the same subset of a RNG's sequence will not be used.

A better alternative would be to partition a sequence among the threads invoked by Thrust, effectively eliminating the possibility of pseudo-random number reuse. This is a possibility afforded by the discard method of the PRNG provided by Thrust, which allows us to skip over a set of numbers in the sequence, as shown in the implementation of Listing 7.13 (line 27).

```
1    \\ File : pi.cu
2    #include <thrust/device_vector.h>
3    #include <thrust/host_vector.h>
4    #include <thrust/transform_reduce.h>
5    #include <thrust/random.h>
6    #include <thrust/functional.h>
7
8    #include <iostream>
9    #include <iomanip>
10
11   using namespace std;
12
13   //**********************************************************
14   struct MonteCarloPi
15   {
16     int seed;
17     int pointsPerThread;
18
19     MonteCarloPi(int s, int p) : seed(s), pointsPerThread(p){}
20
21     __host__ __device__
22     long operator()(int segment)
23     {
24       double x, y, distance;
25       long inside=0;
26       thrust::default_random_engine rng(seed);
27       rng.discard(segment * 2 * pointsPerThread);  // skip the parts of ↵
             the sequence that belongs to previous threads
28
29       thrust::uniform_real_distribution<double> uniDistr(0,1);
30
31       for(int i=0;i<pointsPerThread;i++)
32       {
33         x = uniDistr(rng);    // generate (x,y) coordinates in the
34         y = uniDistr(rng);    // [0,1]x[0,1] part of the plane
35         distance = x*x + y*y;
36         inside += ( distance <= 1 ); // optimized check
37       }
38       return inside;
39     }
40   };
41
42   //**********************************************************
43   int main (int argc, char **argv)
44   {
45     int N = atoi (argv[1]); // total points to examine
46     int M = atoi (argv[2]); // points per thread
47
48     N = (N+M-1)/M * M; // make sure N is a multiple of M
49
50     long total = thrust::transform_reduce(
51                       thrust::counting_iterator<int>(0),
```

```
52              thrust::counting_iterator<int>(N/M),
53              MonteCarloPi(0, M),  // transformation functor
54              0,                   // reduction initial value
55              thrust::plus<int>());// reduction functor
56    cout << setprecision(15);
57    cout << 1.0L * total / N * 4.0L << endl;
58    return 0;
59  }
```

LISTING 7.13

Thrust implementation of the Monte Carlo π calculation.

As indicated by Equation 7.1, Monte Carlo methods produce more accurate results the more random points are used in the calculation. Although CUDA allows for millions of threads to be generated, it is also true that increasing the arithmetic density of our kernels (the functors in Thrust) improves the execution efficiency. There is no obstacle against using each functor invocation for calculating the contribution of multiple points in our integral. Hence, the unary functor in lines 31-37 generates and checks a number of pointsPerThread points.

The total number of points N, as well as the M (or pointsPerThread) parameter, are controlled by user input (lines 45, 46). The thrust::counting_iterator parameters of line 50 generate $[0, \dots, N/M)$ transformation functor invocations, each with its own unique segment number referring to a distinct part of the PRNG sequence. Once the transformation is complete, a simple summation produces the total number out of the N points examined that fell within the unit circle.

Having both N and M available as inputs enables us to finely control the execution configuration that will be used. This is essential for successfully using a CPU device back end, which is not as efficient as a GPU in the generation and management of thousands of threads.

7.7.2 DNA SEQUENCE ALIGNMENT

DNA is composed of a sequence of organic molecules called *nucleotides* represented by the letters G, A, T, and C, from the initials of their names. Thus a DNA sequence can be effectively represented as a string of these four letters. In bioinformatics, comparing two (or more) DNA sequences allows us to identify regions of similarity between them that could indicate ancestral relationships, mutations, functional similarities, or the like. The comparison is performed by attempting an optimum alignment, i.e., a relative placement between the two sequences that maximizes the pairs of nucleotides that match. The alignment can involve the introduction of gaps in the sequences, since DNA sequencing technologies are known to produce such inconsistencies (gaps) in their output.

Many possible alignments are typically possible. To compute the best one, we have to come up with an objective function, i.e., a way to measure the quality of the resulting match. The Smith-Waterman algorithm[7] can be used to find the best alignment by applying the following conventions. A weight/score is assigned to each of the formed pairs of nucleotides: $+w$ if they are identical, $-y$ if there is a mismatch or a gap. The score of a particular alignment is the sum of the individual scores.

Assuming that we have two sequences, S and T, of length N and M, respectively, we can calculate the best score H that can be achieved for two prefixes/substrings $S[1, ..., i]$ and $T[1, ..., j]$, with $i \in [1, N]$ and $j \in [1, M]$ as follows:

$$H(j,i) = max \begin{cases} H(j-1,i) - y, & \text{if we insert a gap in } S \\ H(j-1,i-1) + w, & \text{if } S[i] = T[j] \\ H(j,i-1) - y, & \text{if we insert a gap in } T \end{cases} \qquad (7.5)$$

When we are not using any letters from one of the two sequences to calculate H, the score is set to zero:

$$H(j,0) = H(0,i) = 0 \text{ for } \forall i,j \qquad (7.6)$$

The recursive computation described by Equation 7.5 can be efficiently performed using dynamic programming. We simply have to allocate a $(M+1)x(N+1)$ matrix H and initialize its first row and column to zero (corresponding to the base cases of Equation 7.6). Then the computation can be done row by row or column by column, so that the previous values required at every step have been calculated. The best score will be deposited at the $H[M][N]$ location. An illustration of the calculation is shown in Figure 7.3.

The example in Figure 7.3 seems to indicate that the calculation has to be performed sequentially. However, because the `max` operator used in Equation 7.5 is

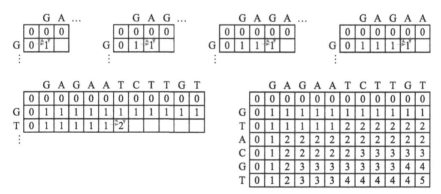

FIGURE 7.3

An example illustrating how the best alignment score of DNA sequences GAGAATCTTGTA and GTACGT can be calculated in a row-by-row fashion, starting from the top-left corner. The arrows show the dependencies between matrix cells, as mandated by Equation 7.5.

---

[7] See http://en.wikipedia.org/wiki/Smith-Waterman_algorithm, last accessed Feb. 2014.

	G	A	G	A	A	T	C	T	T	G	T
	0	0	0	0	0	0	0	0	0	0	0	0
G	0	1	1	1	1	1	1	1	1	1	1	1
T	0	1	1	1	1	1	2	2	2	2	2	2
A	0	1	2	2	2	2	2	2	2	2	2	2
C	0	1	2	2	2	2	2	3	3	3	3	3
G	0											
T	0											

```
Previous row :  0   1   2   2   2   2   2   3   3   3   3   3
Transformation: 0   1   2   3   2   2   2   3   3   3   4   3
        Scan :  0   1   2   3   3   3   3   3   3   3   4   4
```

FIGURE 7.4

The calculation of the shaded fifth row of the *H* matrix used in Figure 7.3 with a two-step process involving a transformation and a scan. The arrows show the data dependencies and the bold text highlights the cells affected by the second step.

associative and commutative, we can perform the calculation of each row *j* in two parallelizable steps:

1. Use a transformation algorithm to calculate temporary values for the current row, using the previous row, according to:

$$H_{temp}(j,i) = max \begin{Bmatrix} H(j-1,i) - y \\ H(j-1,i-1) \end{Bmatrix} \tag{7.7}$$

2. Use a scan algorithm to calculate the final values according to:

$$H(j,i) = max \begin{Bmatrix} H_{temp}(j,i) \\ H_{temp}(j,i-1) - y \end{Bmatrix} \tag{7.8}$$

An example of the successful application of this idea is shown in Figure 7.4, where the calculation of a row of the *H* matrix used in Figure 7.3 is performed.

The row-by-row (or column-by-column) calculation means that if we are only interested in the best score, we need to allocate only two rows (columns). This is the approach followed in Listing 7.14, where it is also assumed that $w = 1$ and $y = 0$, i.e., no penalty is accumulated for inserting gaps.

```
1   \\ File : dna.cu
2   ...
3   #include <thrust/transform.h>
4   #include <thrust/scan.h>
5   #include <thrust/fill.h>
6   #include <thrust/iterator/counting_iterator.h>
7   #include <thrust/functional.h>
8
```

```
9   using namespace std;
10
11  struct Phase1_funct
12  {
13    thrust::device_ptr < char >S;
14    char T; // T single character used here
15    thrust::device_ptr < int >prev;
16
17    Phase1_funct (thrust::device_ptr < char >s, char t, thrust::↵
          device_ptr < int >p):S (s), T (t), prev (p) {}
18
19    // just finds the maximum that can be obtained from
20    // the two cells from the previous iteration
21    __host__ __device__ int operator () (int &j) const
22    {
23      int max = prev[j];
24
25      int tmp = prev[j - 1];
26
27      if (S[j - 1] == T)
28        tmp++;
29      if (max < tmp)
30        max = tmp;
31
32      return max;
33    }
34  };
35  // ***********************************************************
36
37  int main ()
38  {
39    char *S = "GAATTCAGTTA";        // sample data
40    char *T = "GGATCGA";
41    int N = strlen (S);
42    int M = strlen (T);
43
44    // allocate and initialize the equivalent of 2 N+1-length vectors
45    // [0] is used to hold at the end of each iteration, the last ↵
          computed
46    // row of the matrix
47    thrust::device_vector < int >H[2];
48    H[0].resize (N + 1);
49    H[1].resize (N + 1);
50    thrust::fill (H[0].begin (), H[0].end (), 0);
51
52    // transfer the big DNA strand to the device
53    thrust::device_vector < char >d_S (N);
54    thrust::copy (S, S + N, d_S.begin ());
55
56    thrust::counting_iterator < int >c0 (1);
57    thrust::counting_iterator < int >c1 (N + 1);
58
```

```
59    // calculate the rows, one-by-one
60    for (int j = 0; j < M; j++)
61      {
62        char oneOfT = T[j];
63        // first phase using the previous row in the matrix
64        thrust::transform (c0, c1, H[1].begin () + 1, Phase1_funct (d_S.↩
                 data (), oneOfT, H[0].data ()));
65
66        // second phase using the current row in the matrix
67        thrust::inclusive_scan (H[1].begin () + 1, H[1].end (), H[0].↩
                 begin () + 1, thrust::maximum < int >());
68      }
69
70    cout << "Best matching score is " << H[0][N] << endl;
71    return 0;
72  }
```

LISTING 7.14

Thrust implementation of the Smith-Waterman DNA sequence alignment algorithm.

This program uses three device vectors to facilitate the calculation of the optimum score: two vectors representing successive H matrix rows, and one for holding one of the DNA sequences (d_S). The H[0] vector is used to hold the outcome of the last calculation (or the very first row used, initialized to zero in line 50), whereas the H[1] vector is used to hold the intermediate result of the transformation step in line 64.

The Thrust implementation of Equation 7.8 hinges on having the functor employed for the task (defined in lines 11-34) satisfy the following conditions:

- The functor that produces each element of the H[1] vector must be aware of the element's position i in the vector/matrix row in order to be able to locate the two corresponding elements in the previous vector H[0][i] and H[0][i-1].
- The functor should be also aware of the DNA sequence labeling the columns of the matrix and the element of the second DNA sequence that labels the row (see the illustration in Figure 7.4).

All the necessary data, including the previous vector H[0], are passed to the constructor of the functor (line 64). The position information is passed by applying the transformation on an integer sequence representing the range of indices $[0, N]$. The range limits are represented by the two counting_iterator objects c0 and c1, defined in lines 56 and 57.

Finally, the second step of the calculation, as expressed by Equation 7.8, is performed by the inclusive_scan algorithm in line 67. Using the H[1] vector as input and the H[0] vector as output allows us to perform the calculation row by row while minimizing the device memory requirements.

However, if the actual optimum alignment is required, the whole of matrix H must be kept in memory. The optimum alignment (or at least one of them, since multiple ones are typically possible) can be calculated by tracing back the steps

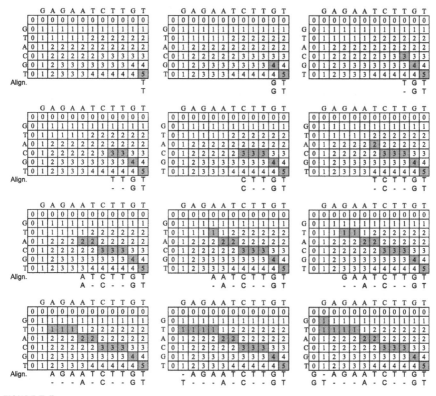

FIGURE 7.5

The calculation is based on the dark gray/blue-shaded cells, progressing from the top-left to the bottom-right state. Below each state, the alignment as calculated at that point, is shown.

taken whenever Equation 7.5 was applied, starting from the $H[M][N]$ element of the matrix all the way to the top row or left column. Figure 7.5 shows how the optimum alignment can be extracted for the example of Figure 7.3.

In this section we do not address the issue of getting the alignment. However, Listing 7.15 shows how the whole matrix can be obtained by *fusing* the two phases of row calculation via the `thrust::transform_inclusive_scan` algorithm (see lines 63-66).

```
1   \\ File : dna_fusion.cu
2   ...
3   #include <thrust/transform_scan.h>
4   #include <thrust/sequence.h>
5   #include <thrust/fill.h>
6   #include <thrust/iterator/counting_iterator.h>
7   #include <thrust/functional.h>
8
9   using namespace std;
10
```

```
11   // ************************************************************
12   template < typename D >
13   struct Pass1_funct
14   {
15     thrust::device_ptr < char >S;
16     char T;                          // T single character used here
17     thrust::device_ptr< D >prev;
18
19       Pass1_funct (thrust::device_ptr < char >s, char t, thrust::↵
             device_ptr < D >p):S (s), T (t), prev (p) {}
20
21     // just finds the maximum that can be obtained from
22     // the two cells from the previous iteration
23     __host__ __device__ D operator () (const D & j) const
24     {
25       D max = prev[j];
26       // optimized check that avoids path divergence
27       D tmp = prev[j − 1] + (S[j − 1] == T);
28
29       if (max < tmp)  max = tmp;
30
31       return max;
32     }
33   };
34   // ************************************************************
35
36   int main ()
37   {
38     char *S = "GAATTCAGTTA"; // sample data
39     char *T = "GGATCGA";
40     int N = strlen (S);
41     int M = strlen (T);
42
43     // allocate and initialize the equivalent of a (M+1)x(N+1) matrix
44     thrust::device_vector < int >H[M + 1];
45     thrust::device_vector < int >aux;
46     for (int i = 0; i < M + 1; i++)
47       H[i].resize (N + 1);
48
49     thrust::fill (H[0].begin (), H[0].end (), 0);
50     for (int j = 1; j < M + 1; j++)
51       H[j][0] = 0;
52
53     // transfer to the device the big DNA strand
54     thrust::device_vector < char >d_S (N);
55     thrust::copy (S, S + N, d_S.begin ());
56
57     thrust::counting_iterator < int >c (1);
58
59     // fill −in the DP table , row−by−row
60     for (int j = 1; j < M + 1; j++)
61       {
```

```
62          char oneOfT = T[j - 1];
63          thrust::transform_inclusive_scan (c, c + N,
64                                       H[j].begin () + 1,
65                                       Pass1_funct <int >(d_S.data (),  ↩
                                            oneOfT, H[j - 1].data ()),
66                                       thrust::maximum < int >());
67      }
68
69      cout << "Best matching score is " << H[M][N] << endl;
70      return 0;
71 }
```

LISTING 7.15

Thrust implementation of the Smith-Waterman DNA sequence alignment algorithm that employs kernel fusion in the form of a combined transform-and-scan algorithm.

While following the same guidelines for the construction of the unary functor performing the transformation step (structure `Pass1_funct`, defined in lines 12-33), as set out in the preceding paragraphs, the major difference of Listing 7.15 is in the use of a template syntax for `Pass1_funct`. This is mandated by the Thrust library for employing the `thrust::transform_inclusive_scan` algorithm, although the same was not a requirement for using the `Pass1_funct` functor of Listing 7.14 with `thrust::transform`. Missing this detail would result in a large collection of unintelligible compilation error messages.

Another minor change relates to the logic of the unary functor's `operator()` method: By turning the block of lines 25-28 in Listing 7.14 into the statement of line 27 in Listing 7.15, we can avoid path divergence, which is a performance-sapping problem for GPU execution (see Section 5.7.2).

EXERCISES

1. Develop a Thrust program for calculating the inner product of two vectors by using the `thrust::transform` algorithm and an appropriate functor.
2. Calculate the inner product of two vectors by using the `thrust::inner_product` algorithm. Compare the performance of this version with the performance of a CUDA-based solution.
3. Use Thrust algorithms to find the absolute maximum of an array of values.
4. Write a Thrust program for calculating the sum of two matrices.
5. Write a Thrust program for calculating the definite integral of a function $f(x)$ over a range $[a, b]$ using the trapezoidal rule. Consider a solution that avoids the need to create a vector for all the x-values for which a trapezoid is calculated. The details of the trapezoidal rule can be found in Section 3.5.2.

6. Use Thrust to calculate the mean and variance of a data set X of cardinality N. For convenience, the corresponding formulas are:

$$E[X] = \frac{\sum_{i=0}^{N-1} x_i}{N} \tag{7.9}$$

$$\sigma^2 = E[X^2] - (E[X])^2 \tag{7.10}$$

7. Measure the performance of the `thrust::sort` algorithm in Thrust by sorting varying volumes of data. Compare the achieved times with the STL version running on the host. For this purpose, create a big array (make sure it is not too big to fit in the GPU's memory) and populate it with random data.

8. Measure the performance hit that an array-of-structures design approach will have in device-based sorting of 10^8 randomly generated instances of the following structure:

```
struct TestStr {
    int key;
    float value;

    __host__ __device__
    bool operator <(const TestStr &o) const
    {
        return this.key < o.key;
    }
};
```

To measure the performance deterioration, you will have to implement and time a structure-of-arrays alternative.

9. Create a Thrust program for computing the Mandelbrot set. Section 4.22.1 covers the mathematical details of how the set is calculated.

10. A problem related to the furthest-distance point solved in Section 7.5 is the problem of finding the pair of points that are the furthest apart from each other. Create a brute-force solution to this problem, i.e., by examining all pairs of points, using Thrust. Consider the case where the number of points is too big to allow storage of all the calculated distances. You should avoid duplicate calculations, since the distance from point A to B is the same as the distance from B to A.

11. The all-pairs-shortest-paths graph problem can be solved by the dynamic programming algorithm of Floyd and Warshall. Assuming that the graph is described by a $V{\times}V$ adjacency matrix, where V is the number of vertices, then the pseudocode of the following algorithm shows how the solution is obtained in V stages, where each stage involves the update of the distance matrix via the involvement of an intermediate vertex:

```
// initialization phase
Allocate a VxV distance matrix, and set all elements to infinity
for each vertex v
    distance[v][v] <- 0
```

```
for each edge (u,v)
    distance[u][v] <- adj(u,v)  // the weight of the edge (u,v)

// computation phase
for k from 1 to V    // for each k intermediate vertex
    for i from 1 to V  // reconsider each pair of vertices
        for j from 1 to V
            if distance[i][j] > distance[i][k] + distance[k][j]
                distance[i][j] <- distance[i][k] + distance[k][j]
            end if
return distance
```

Create a Thrust program that could perform the *V* individual stages of the algorithm in parallel, i.e., parallelize the two inner loops of the algorithm.

Load balancing

IN THIS CHAPTER YOU WILL

- Learn how to use static and/or dynamic load balancing for improving the execution time of parallel/multicore programs.

- Understand the trade-off between extra coordination cost and reduced execution time that different load-balancing techniques offer.

- Apply divisible load theory techniques to optimally partition the workload to the nodes of a parallel/multicore platform.

- Learn how load balancing can be used to split up workload between heterogeneous computing nodes.

8.1 INTRODUCTION

The idea behind load balancing is to shift workload to computational resources that are underutilized, with the ultimate goal of reducing the overall execution time. A great deal of research has been devoted to the topic, and this trend contines with grid computing and distributed computation. In the realm of multicore computing, though, the notion of load balancing may seem alien. A typical multicore system consists of identical cores that communicate using a shared memory space. The same holds true for GPUs as well. So, an even partitioning of the load among available cores should suffice to produce a minimum execution time.

However, this argument is easily countered by the fact that we can have a collection of work items, each with different or unknown computation requirements. In that case, an even or equal partitioning would not be feasible. To top this, a typical multicore system can employ heterogeneous cores, as shown in Figure 8.1, even without going outside the boundaries of a single system.

If a distributed memory system is employed as an execution platform, communication overheads can become a serious performance concern. In all, properly partitioning the workload is paramount to maximizing performance. Toward this goal, we must take into consideration as many of the platform (e.g., computational speed) and problem characteristics (e.g., cost of data transmission) as possible. In the following section we examine both dynamic and static approaches to load balancing. Although our coverage is not complete, it is wide enough to allow the reader to make informed decisions about the best design approach for a given problem.

Dynamic load balancing refers to a large collection of algorithms that perform or modify load assignments online, i.e., during the execution of a program.

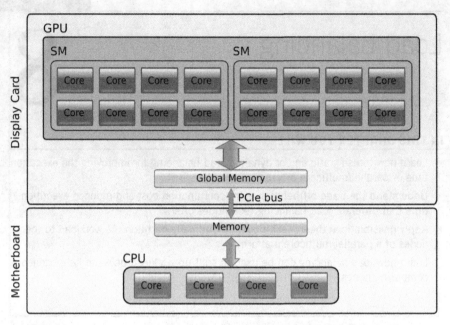

FIGURE 8.1

An example of a single-system heterogeneous computing platform.

Static load balancing, on the other hand, refers to algorithms that assign workload offline, i.e., either, before the beginning or at the very start of the execution.

Dynamic load balancing is characterized by the ability to adapt to changes to the execution platform (e.g., nodes going offline, communication links becoming congested, etc.) but at the expense of additional coordination overhead. Static load balancing can provide a near-optimum solution to the load-partitioning problem, the trade-offs being the inability to adjust to run-time changes and the need to establish intimate knowledge about the performance characteristics of the individual components making up the execution platform.

An example of dynamic load balancing was presented in the master-worker MPI-based implementation of Section 5.22. In this chapter, we present a comprehensive view of load balancing, including recent advances in the area of static load balancing.

A particular contribution of this chapter is that CPU-GPU hybrid execution is explicitly tackled.

8.2 DYNAMIC LOAD BALANCING: THE LINDA LEGACY

Linda is a coordination language that was originally introduced in the mid-1980s [4] as an alternative to message passing and/or shared memory operations that are the primary tools for synchronizing shared-nothing and shared-memory systems, respectively.

Linda creators boast that the language offers orthogonality to computation, completely decoupling the computational nodes in both the spatial and temporal domains. This means that we can have distributed nodes running programs written in different languages and on top of diverse platforms that can coordinate asynchronously. This is accomplished via the use of an entity called *tuplespace*. A tuplespace is a repository of a collection of ordered sequences of data objects called *tuples*. As long as the tuplespace remains operational, nodes can come and go from the computation, thus providing a degree of fault tolerance and adaptability.[1] Linda's tuplespace supports the following basic operations that can be invoked by any process participating in the computation:

- in: Gets/extracts a tuple from tuplespace.
- rd: Reads a tuple but without removing it.
- out: Writes a tuple into tuplespace.
- eval: Creates a new process to evaluate a tuple. The result of the computation is written into tuplespace.

The in operation specifies the tuple to be retrieved using a form of associative memory, whereas some of the fields in the tuple are specified and others are left as wildcards. This form of tuple is called an *antituple*, or template. An illustration of the interaction of two processes via a tuplespace is shown in Figure 8.2. Upon the successful execution of the in operation in 8.2, variables x and y are set to 3 and 7 respectively. If multiple tuples match the antituple, a randomly chosen one can be returned.

Over the years, more operations have been added to various Linda implementations to enable faster tuplespace manipulation (such as extracting the "smallest" from a collection of tuples) or nonblocking variants of rd (rdp) and in (inp). Additionally,

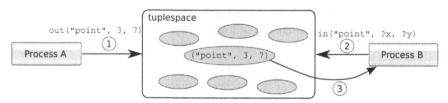

FIGURE 8.2

An example of an interaction of two processes via out (step 1) and in (step 2) tuplespace operations. The ? prefix represents wildcard components that will be bound once a matching tuple is found (step 3).

---

[1] The tuplespace itself is a liability in terms of both fault tolerance and scalability. However, the idea of a distributed tuplespace has been explored in the literature.

the tuplespace has been implemented as a single repository or as a distributed one, in order to facilitate better scaling [46].

In the context of multicore programming, Linda might seem overkill, given that shared memory allows for substantially faster operations. However, when we considers scaling beyond the boundaries of a single system, Linda can be a viable alternative for coordination and implicit load balancing. Linda does not impose any restrictions on how the tuples are exchanged between the nodes of the system. In fact, MPI can be used quite effectively to that effect!

8.3 STATIC LOAD BALANCING: THE DIVISIBLE LOAD THEORY APPROACH

Dynamic load balancing works reasonably well and (given the right circumstances) it can be the only possible way to accelerate a program using heterogeneous computational resources. There is just one chink in its armor: It requires extensive communication. Communication is a performance drain that needs to be avoided as much as possible.

This performance drain can be minimized if we know *a priori*, i.e., before the execution or at least before the distribution of the workload, what each of our nodes needs to do. This is the definition of static load balancing. Of course, short of consulting an oracle, obtaining this knowledge is not a trivial proposition.

The perfect load partitioning can be elusive, but we can still approximate it by a systematic study of the problem at hand.

Divisible load theory[2] (DLT) is a systematic approach to model and solve partitioning and operation-sequencing problems for parallel computation and/or data distribution problems in general. Using DLT to load-balance a parallel computation hinges on the following conditions:

- The computational load (typically associated with the input data) can be arbitrarily divided and assigned to the nodes of the parallel platform.
- There are no interdependencies between the disjoint parts assigned to the computational nodes.

These conditions may seem severe, but they are actually honored, to a large extent, by a big collection of problems that include, among others, low-level image processing [13, 43], query processing [13], linear algebra operations (e.g., matrix-vector multiplication) [20], DNA sequencing, distributed Video-on-Demand [14, 41], image registration [9] and video transcoding [10, 32]. In addition, when the first condition is not met, we can still use DLT to derive an approximate solution that can be subsequently adapted to the peculiarities of the problem [12].

---

[2]Literature also refers to this methodology as Divisible Load Scheduling or DLS.

The application of DLT typically involves the following steps:

- **Modeling costs**: Creating mathematical cost models for each component of a parallel program's execution, including both communication[3] and computation phases.
- **Communication configuration**: Specifying how the load/data reach the compute nodes and whether communication and computation can overlap. This is obviously meaningful in the context of distributed-memory programming. Oddly, this also applies for execution on heterogeneous platforms that combine CPU and GPU resources, since the device's memory is disjoint from the host's memory.
- **Analysis**: Combining the models and the communication setup to predict how the computation load should be partitioned and distributed in order to minimize the overall execution time.

It all comes down to determining the *part_i* percentages of the computational load that will be assigned to each of the $i \in [0, N - 1]$ nodes of a parallel platform. The parts should be disjoint and sum up to 100%, i.e.:

$$\sum_{i=0}^{N-1} part_i = 1 \tag{8.1}$$

Equation 8.1 is known as the *normalization equation*.

When communications are involved, it is quite usual that (a) the load/input data are distributed, and (b) the output is collected by a central/master node. If the distribution of the load is done in sequence, i.e., each part is communicated sequentially one after the other, we also have to determine the *optimum distribution/collection sequence* in terms of the overall execution time. This communication configuration is also known as single-port (**1-port**) versus the alternative, where all parts are communicated concurrently (**N-port**), in which case the order is irrelevant.

8.3.1 MODELING COSTS

The problem at hand is how to model the time spent on the individual parts or phases of a parallel program as a function of the problem size. This is similar to the way the time and space complexities of algorithms are derived, with one paramount difference: The outcome serves to predict the actual execution time and is not for counting the times a basic operation is performed.

The costs models should be preferably linear or affine (i.e., linear with an additional constant overhead). The authors in [15] have shown that divisible loads cannot benefit from parallel execution unless the cost is linearly or close-to linearly dependent on the size of the data. The reason is that there is a very significant cost

---

[3]Communication cost can be ignored for shared memory machines. However, shared memory platforms typically involve homogeneous/identical computing nodes, a scenario that makes static load balancing a piece of cake: Just break up the load in to equal pieces.

left-over for the "merging" of the partial results produced by the parallel execution. For example, if for M inputs we have to perform M^2 operations to calculate the result, splitting the input into N equal pieces and processing them in parallel would result in performing a total of $N\left(\frac{M}{N}\right)^2 = \frac{M^2}{N}$ operations. The resulting deficit of $M^2(1 - \frac{1}{N})$ operations has to be carried-out sequentially, which for a large N translates to effectively doing everything sequentially. Of course, this simplistic argument extends to pretty much any workload that is to be executed in parallel.

The counter argument is that we should devise a data partitioning and distribution method, that allows each node to perform $\frac{M^2}{N}$ operations, which means that each node may be receiving more that $\frac{M}{N}$ items. In fact, there have been several publications that show that it is possible to apply DLT for non-linear cost models[26], or even for costs which are approximated by arbitrary continuous functions [27]. The only real shortcoming for non-linear cost models, is that they result in complex equations that cannot yield closed-form solutions. Instead, approximations [39] or other heuristic techniques [27] can be employed for solving them.

Before we can show an example of how such models are derived, we need to clarify how the volume or size of a computation can be quantified. In the vast majority of cases, this size is intimately connected to the size of the input data. This is not entirely unambiguous, though: Do we measure the size in number of data items, or in bytes? This is not a trivial question; a data representation change, e.g., from int to long, will double the size in bytes, even if the number of items is unchanged.

The answer to this dilemma is simple: Because we need to use *compatible* cost models for both the communication and the computation phases and because communication cost is typically expressed as a function of data volume, e.g., bytes, we will also express the computational cost as a function of data volume.

As an example, let's consider the problem of sharpening an image by performing convolution with a *kernel* (a term used to refer to an odd-sized square constant matrix). An illustration of the process is shown in Figure 8.3. (Image convolution is discussed in detail in Section 2.2.)

The convolution process takes place in the image's luminance plane in order to avoid unwanted chromatic alternations by the sharpen filter. The process is summarized in Listing 7.1.

```
1   // File : sharpen_sequential/sharper.cpp
2   ...
3   // arrays holding the color components
4   R = new int[X * Y];
5   G = new int[X * Y];
6   B = new int[X * Y];
7   L = new float[X * Y];
8   a = new float[X * Y];
9   b = new float[X * Y];
10
11  // main body : RGB -> LAB conversion
12  for (j = 0; j < Y; j++)
13      for (i = 0; i < X; i++)
```

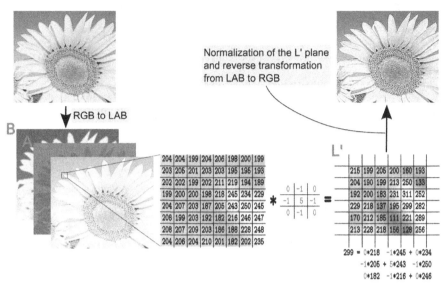

FIGURE 8.3

An illustration of the application of a 3x3 convolution kernel for sharpening an image. The calculation for one of the pixels of the "sharpened" luminance plane is shown in detail. A normalization of the new L' plane is required, since the convolution can result in luminance values that are outside the nominal range $[0, 2^n - 1]$, where n is the bits per color component.

```
14          {
15              loc = j * X + i;
16              RGB2LAB (R[loc], G[loc], B[loc], L[loc], a[loc], b[loc]);
17          }
18
19      // convolution
20      for (j = 0; j < Y; j++)
21          for (i = 0; i < X; i++)
22          {
23              double temp;
24              temp = 5.0 * pixel_L (i, j);
25              temp -= (pixel_L (i - 1, j) + pixel_L (i + 1, j) + pixel_L (i,↩
                    j - 1) + pixel_L (i, j + 1));
26
27              loc = j * X + i;
28              new_L[loc] = round (temp);
29              if (new_L[loc] <= 0)  new_L[loc] = 0;
30          }
31
32
33      // LAB -> RGB inverse color conversion
34      for (j = 0; j < Y; j++)
```

```
35    for (i = 0; i < X; i++)
36      {
37        loc = j * X + i;
38        LAB2RGB (new_L[loc], a[loc], b[loc], R[loc], G[loc], B[loc]);
39
40            // Fix conversion under-/over-flow which is
41            // just a shortcut replacing proper normalization.
42            // "max_value" represents the maximum value of a
43            // color component
44            if (R[loc] < 0)
45              R[loc] = 0;
46            else if (R[loc] > max_value)
47              R[loc] = max_value;
48            if (G[loc] < 0)
49              G[loc] = 0;
50            else if (G[loc] > max_value)
51              G[loc] = max_value;
52            if (B[loc] < 0)
53              B[loc] = 0;
54            else if (B[loc] > max_value)
55              B[loc] = max_value;
56      }
57    ...
```

LISTING 8.1

Sequential code for applying a sharpen convolution kernel to an image of resolution $X * Y$.

The time complexity of the code fragment in Listing 8.1 is clearly a linear function of the number of pixels involved, i.e., $\in \Theta(X \cdot Y)$. A simple timing test also exposes this relationship: Measuring the execution time of this program for different-size (pixel-wise) input images produces the scatter plot of Figure 8.4.

Figure 8.4 leaves little doubt of the linear relationship between pixel count and execution time. If we were to express the relationship between execution time and picture size in terms of bytes (i.e., how many bytes it takes to represent the input image), we could modify the regression equation shown in Figure 8.4 as:

$$t_{comp} = \frac{4.892 \cdot 10^{-07}}{3} L - 0.00033 \approx 1.631 \cdot 10^{-07} L \tag{8.2}$$

where $L = 3X \cdot Y$ is the size of the input, with each pixel being represented by 3 bytes, one per color component.

We should expect to get this linear behavior (bar any discrepancies caused by CPU caches) for *sequential* execution on any contemporary CPU, although the slope of the line would be different. In general, we should expect to get:

$$t_{comp} = p \cdot L \tag{8.3}$$

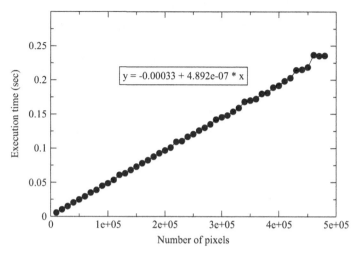

FIGURE 8.4

Execution time of the sharpen convolution in Listing 8.1 on a 4.2 GHz i7 3770K CPU versus the input image size. Times are averaged over 100 runs. The regression line coefficients are shown in the inset.

where p is a node-specific constant that could be regarded as being inversely proportional to the speed of a node. Table 8.1 summarizes the symbols used in this chapter and their semantics.

Thus, if we were to assign $0 \leq part_i \leq 1$ of an image to a node P_i, we would expect the computation to last for:

$$t^{(i)}_{comp} = p_i \cdot part_i \cdot L \tag{8.4}$$

We could argue that the model of Equation 8.4 is lacking. What about the cost of allocating all those big arrays that hold the color components? We can augment our model to accommodate any residual costs e_i that are *independent of the input*:

$$t^{(i)}_{comp} = p_i(part_i \cdot L + e_i) \tag{8.5}$$

The overhead e_i is assumed to be node-specific for extra flexibility.

Sending $part_iL$ volume of data to a remote node and then collecting the outcome of the computation could entail some significant communication cost. Communication cost is generally not application-specific in the sense that what matters is the communicated volume and not the semantics of what is communicated. Thus, a communication cost model needs to be derived only once for a particular installation, as long as the hardware and software communication stack (including any OS and user-space libraries) remain unchanged.

Communication cost can be measured with the assistance of a "ping-pong" program that measures the time elapsed between sending a message, having it bounce at its destination, and receiving it back at its origin. By varying the message size, one

Table 8.1 Symbol table. Examples of typical units are shown

Symbol	Description	Unit
a	Constant ≥ 1 used in the data distribution cost model. It is greater than 1 when used to account for the extra data that need to be communicated to a node in order to eliminate data interdependencies.	N/A
b	The constant overhead associated with load distribution.	Byte
b_i	A node-specific constant overhead associated with load distribution.	Byte
c	Constant ≥ 1 used in the result collection cost model, which is analogous to a.	N/A
d	The constant overhead associated with result collection.	Byte
e_i	A load-independent computational overhead at node P_i.	Byte
L	The load that has to be processed/volume of input data.	Byte
l	Inversely proportional to the speed of the communication links in a homogeneous network.	sec/B
l_i	Inversely proportional to the speed of the link connecting P_i and its load originating node.	sec/B
p	Inversely proportional to the processing speed of a processor in a homogeneous platform.	sec/B
p_i	Inversely proportional to the speed of P_i.	sec/B
$part_i$	Part of the load L assigned to P_i, hence $0 \leq part_i \leq 1$. P_i's total load assignment is $part_i L + e_i$.	N/A

can estimate the transmission rate l[4] as the regression line intercept[5]:

$$t_{comm} = l \cdot V \tag{8.6}$$

where V is the volume of data communicated.

Equation 8.6 requires a number of refinements before it is suitable for describing the communication costs in our example. First, it falls short of describing the distribution cost. As shown in Figure 8.5, because the calculation of each new luminance value of a pixel requires four more surrounding pixels, processing $part_i L$ input requires the presence in node P_i of extra data. Depending on the application, these extra data could be a percent $a - 1$ of the actual data to be processed, or they could be a fixed overhead. In the first case, we only need to multiply $part_i L$

---

[4]l is actually the inverse of the communication speed as it is expressed in time/volume units, e.g., sec/byte.
[5]The exact shape of the curve one gets from such an experiment, depends heavily on the MPI implementation, the hardware testbed, and the range of message sizes tested. For example, in the measurements reported in [38], bandwidth rose and fell with increasing message sizes. Amazingly, Rabenseifner et al. report cases where inter-node communications beat intra-socket ones! Fortunately, for an application where the message sizes are not too diverse, we can get a piece-wise linear curve, making the use of a constant l a good approximation.

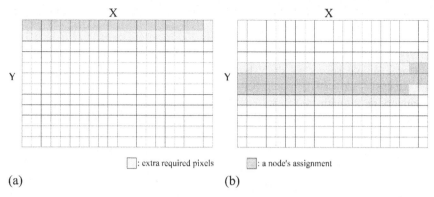

: extra required pixels **: a node's assignment**

(a) (b)

FIGURE 8.5

Two examples of pixel regions that could be assigned to a remote node for processing. (a) involves a boundary row of pixels; (b) is a more generic case. The highlighted regions surrounding the assigned pixels are also required for a convolution with a 3x3 kernel.

by a a to find the distribution communication demands: $t_{comm} = l \cdot a \cdot part_i L$. In the latter case, we could incorporate the extra cost into an additional constant b: $t_{comm} = l(part_i L + b)$.

Our image-sharpening example does not seem to fit either of the two cases, since the extra data are neither constant (in Figure 8.5(a), only an extra row is required, whereas in Figure 8.5(b), two are needed instead) nor proportional to the $part_i L$.

A simple solution can be given to this problem if we assume that all the nodes will require two extra rows of pixels, thus having $b = 2 \cdot 3 \cdot X$ (each row has X pixels, each with 3 color components). We can also be more specific if we assume that $b_0 = b_{N-1} = 3 \cdot X$ and $b_j = 2 \cdot 3 \cdot X$ for $\forall j \neq 0, N-1$, if P_0 gets the top and P_{N-1} the bottom rows.

The alternative (i.e., using a) is also possible if we expect to get more or less equal, row-wise partitioning of the data among our N compute nodes. Then each would process approximately $\frac{Y}{N}$ rows while requiring two extra rows of pixels. Based on this assumption we could have $a = 1 + \frac{2}{\frac{Y}{N}} = 1 + \frac{2N}{Y}$. In the next section we will use b to refine our communication cost model for the image-sharpening example.

In general, we will employ the following data distribution cost model[6]:

$$t_{distr}^{(i)} = l_i(a \cdot part_i \cdot L + b) \tag{8.7}$$

where l_i is the inverse of the communication speed of the link connecting the master node and node P_i.

---

[6]An alternative formulation would be $t_{distr} = l \cdot a \cdot part_i \cdot L + b$, which b is expressed in time units instead of data volume units. However, these are not two different models but rather variations of the same one. The added benefit of Equation 8.7 is that it is more convenient for the analysis step shown in Section 8.3.3.

The same treatment should be extended to the data collection cost, although the constants need not be the same:

$$t_{coll}^{(i)} = l_i(c \cdot part_i \cdot L + d) \tag{8.8}$$

This example serves to show both the kind of cost models we can use in DLT analysis[7] as well as the process through which they can be derived, i.e., benchmarking. Equations 8.5, 8.7, and 8.8 constitute generic costs models that can be customized to reflect specific scenarios. In the following section we show how these models can provide us with both optimization guidelines and an extraordinary insight into the performance behavior of parallel platforms, as they can yield closed-form solutions to the partitioning and distribution problems.

An alternative to establishing the cost models off-line (before parallel execution), is to derive them during runtime. For example, it is possible that the execution cost varies wildly based on the quality of the input data and not just their volume (e.g., video transcoding cost may depend on the genre of the input movie, e.g., adventure, animation, romance, etc., and not just the resolution and frame rate [10]). Such a scenario would make predetermined model parameters inaccurate, and these would in turn compromise the efficiency of the partitioning.

Run-time model calculation could involve the separation of the execution into two phases (three or more phases may be used to hide the delay between measuring the initial performance and calculating the model parameters and resulting partitioning by the master): an initial benchmarking phase that serves to calculate the cost models, and a second processing phase where the remaining workload is partitioned appropriately [10, 27].

8.3.2 COMMUNICATION CONFIGURATION

Equations 8.5, 8.7, and 8.8 constitute generic enough models to capture the computation and communication cost of many applications. Before we can use them to solve the partitioning problem, we must determine the communication setup of the application. We have to answer three questions:

1. How many compute nodes can receive load and return results simultaneously? Possible answers are one (*1-port*) or all (*N-port*). Using a single-port configuration is not really a hardware limitation but rather a software design feature. Contemporary networking hardware and software stacks allow the buffering and sending of messages to multiple destinations concurrently. However, if this is done via time-division multiplexing, communication costs become larger as the capacity of the communication medium has to be shared. In general, an evaluation of possible design approaches should be carried out. Figure 8.6 shows the test results of measuring communication speed on an intranet of Linux-running machines connected with 1 Gbps Ethernet.

---

[7]Quadratic and other generally nonlinear models can be also employed [26]. The trade-off is a harder-to-perform analysis.

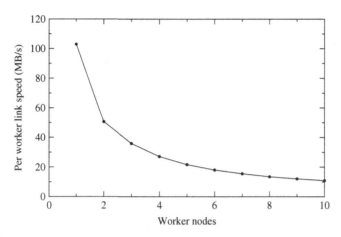

FIGURE 8.6

Average communication speed per node for a *N*-port setup, for an intranet of PC workstations connected over 1 Gbps Ethernet.

The measurements were conducted over 100 runs with a message size of 10^7 bytes sent via MPI_Isend calls. A modified "ping-pong" program was used to measure the times.

2. Is it possible to start the computation prior to the completion of the transfer of the load assigned to a node? If the answer is negative, we have *block-type* tasks; if it is positive, we have *stream-type* tasks. The decision between the two options depends on the software architecture and the nature of the input data. Stream-type computation is generally more complex to setup and run correctly, as one has to ensure that the part(s) of the input data required for processing are available at the proper time.

3. In how many phases is the distribution and/or collection taking place? In the simplest of cases, we have only one phase, but we can also employ multiple ones, especially when block-type computations are involved, in order to minimize the time before the computations can commence. The former case is called *single-installment*, whereas the latter is called *multiple-installment* distribution. Multiple installment distribution can be considered a form of "streaming", as it allows the computation to start before all the assigned data become available at a node. Installments may be fixed to an a priori specified size (e.g., the data is split into k equal pieces [35]), or they could be determined based on the optimization of an objective function [9].

Multiple installment strategies are also referred to in the literature, as "multi-round" strategies. In [47] the authors show that the multiple installment problem, is in its general form, NP-hard (via reduction from 2-Partition). Fortunately, problem specific conditions (e.g., when no result collection is required) , or model simplifications

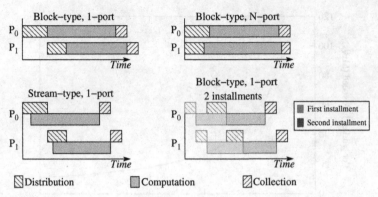

FIGURE 8.7

Gantt charts of four samples from the plethora of possible communication configurations. The graphs are not supposed to be comparable as far as their duration is concerned. Also the optimality of the sequences is not considered here.

(e.g., assuming homogeneous communication links) allows us to solve this problem, either, in closed-form, or using some other exact (e.g., linear programming) or approximation technique.

Figure 8.7 shows contrasting examples of a subset of the possible arrangements. The one to be selected for the final analysis step depends on the software architecture and the application at hand. For example, stream-type tasks could be used for our image-sharpening example: Assuming a row-wise distribution of an image, the arrival of three rows is sufficient for the start of the computation if a 3x3 kernel is used. The problem is writing a program that can figure out when rows become "locally" available, i.e., ready for processing.

We might be tempted to conclude that there are only eight[8] possible configurations that need to be examined. However, when multiple installments are used, the number of installments becomes a factor.[9] And the questions do not stop there: Are all the installments identical? Does the first need to carry additional data or not? Is the collection also performed in multiple installments? Are all nodes available from the beginning of the execution, or might they become available some time later? Is the master node participating in the processing of the load? If it does, does it have a coprocessor that handles all the communications (i.e., equipped with a communication front end) while is is processing, or does it have to wait until all data are sent out to the workers before it can process its share of the load?

---

[8] Each of the three questions posed earlier has two possible answers, for a total of 2^3 combinations.
[9] Another dilemma pops up: How many installments are optimal?

These questions clearly illustrate that there are many possibilities, well beyond the product of the three binary alternatives listed previously. A clear understanding of the parallel platform and the desired software design is critical for setting the proper specification in this step.

8.3.3 **ANALYSIS**

Equations 8.5, 8.7, and 8.8 constitute generic enough models to capture the computation and communication cost of many applications. The problem is that these equations cannot be solved for all possible communication configurations in their generic form; they need to be simplified.

The procedure used for the analysis is more or less the same regardless of the communication configuration:

1. Establish a relation between $part_i$s and $part_0$.
2. Use the normalization Equation 8.1 to derive a closed-form solution to $part_0$.
3. Use the solution to $part_0$ to calculate the other $part_i$s and the overall execution time.[10]

In this section we analyze two cases:

- **N-port, block-type, single-installment**: This is a commonly used communication configuration. It is precisely the setup used by a master node that makes `MPI_Isend()` calls to distribute the input data to the workers of a distributed-memory parallel machine.
- **One-port, block-type, single-installment**: We derive the solution for the kernel convolution (e.g., image-sharpening) example used in this section. For single-port setups, the optimum sequence has to be also established. This is a more intricate procedure for which our simple example is well suited to show how it can be performed.

In both cases we assume that the parallel platform is made up of a master and worker nodes arranged in a single-level tree, with the master at the root, as shown in Figure 8.8. We also assume that the master is participating in the computation and it is equipped with a communication front end, allowing it to compute while communicating with the workers.

---

[10]*Insight*: The normalization equation and the relationships that connect $part_i$s with $part_0$ or other $part_j$s form a sparse system of N linear equations. This sequence of steps uses the peculiarities of our settings to avoid a typical linear-algebra solution to the system (e.g., using Gauss-Jordan elimination) while also providing the formulas that allow further study of the parallel platform.

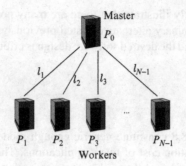

FIGURE 8.8

The target platform for our DLT analysis is composed of N nodes, arranged in a single-level tree. P_0 is assumed to serve as the master.

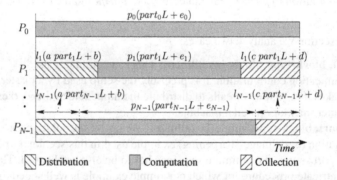

FIGURE 8.9

Optimum configuration for the case of N-port communications and block-type computation.

8.3.3.1 N-Port, Block-Type, Single-Installment Solution

Our goal is to minimize the overall execution time. It is obvious that the only arrangement capable of achieving this is the one shown in Figure 8.9. It is easy to prove that any other configuration that allows nodes to terminate at different times is liable to further reduction in execution time by taking load from the nodes that finish last and assigning it to the nodes that finish first. So, the only optimum configuration is the one where all nodes finish at the same time.

Because the collective duration of all the operations at nodes P_i and P_j for $i,j \in [0, N-1]$ must be equal, we have:

$$t_{distr}^{(i)} + t_{comp}^{(i)} + t_{coll}^{(i)} = t_{distr}^{(j)} + t_{comp}^{(j)} + t_{coll}^{(j)} = t_{comp}^{(0)} \Rightarrow$$

$$l_i(a\, part_i L + b) + p_i(part_i L + e_i) + l_i(c\, part_i L + d) =$$

$$l_j(a\, part_j L + b) + p_j(part_j L + e_j) + l_j(c\, part_j L + d) =$$

$$p_0(part_0 L + e_0) \qquad (8.9)$$

which can be rewritten as:

$$part_i L(l_i(a + c) + p_i) + l_i(b + d) + p_i e_i = p_0(part_0 L + e_0) \Rightarrow$$

$$part_i = part_0 \frac{p_0}{l_i(a + c) + p_i} + \frac{p_0 e_0 - p_i e_i - l_i(b + d)}{L(l_i(a + c) + p_i)} \qquad (8.10)$$

By replacing the $part_j$ components of the normalization equation with Equation 8.10, we get:

$$\sum_{j=0}^{N-1} part_j = 1 \Rightarrow$$

$$part_0 \left(1 + \sum_{j=1}^{N-1} \frac{p_0}{l_j(a + c) + p_j} \right) + \sum_{j=1}^{N-1} \frac{p_0 e_0 - p_j e_j - l_j(b + d)}{L(l_j(a + c) + p_j)} = 1 \Rightarrow$$

$$part_0 = \frac{1 + L^{-1} \sum_{j=1}^{N-1} \frac{p_j e_j - p_0 e_0 + l_j(b+d)}{l_j(a+c)+p_j}}{p_0 \sum_{j=0}^{N-1} \left(l_j(a + c) + p_j \right)^{-1}} \qquad (8.11)$$

where, in the denominator, 1 is absorbed in the summation, with the assumption that $l_0 = 0$ (obviously there is no communication cost from P_0 to P_0).

Equations 8.11 and 8.10 allow the calculation of the optimum partitioning and the overall execution duration in linear time $\Theta(N)$. We can also consider that the whole system is behaving as a single equivalent node with characteristics $p_{equiv} = p_0 part_0$ and $e_{equiv} = \frac{e_0}{part_0}$.

Both equations allow the production of negative results for $part_i$s. Such an outcome would signify that the corresponding node(s) is too slow to be assigned any load (the problem could also be with the node's link). This brings up another facet of the load-balancing problem that we did not mention before: *Finding the optimum set of nodes* on which to run the program. The beauty of Equations 8.11 and 8.10 is that they are cheap enough to evaluate multiple times; as many times as would be required by a heuristic or even an exhaustive/brute-force algorithm (for small N) in order to determine this set. We leave the design of such algorithms as an exercise.

If the master node were to not participate in the processing of the workload (i.e., $part_0 = 0$), we would have, for $\forall i \neq j$ and $i, j \neq 0$:

$$t_{total} = l_i(a\, part_i L + b) + p_i(part_i L + e_i) + l_i(c\, part_i L + d) =$$

$$l_j(a\, part_j L + b) + p_j(part_j L + e_j) + l_j(c\, part_j L + d) \Rightarrow$$

$$part_i = part_j \frac{l_j(a + c) + p_j}{l_i(a + c) + p_i} + \frac{p_j e_j - p_i e_i + (l_j - l_i)(b + d)}{L(l_i(a + c) + p_i)} \qquad (8.12)$$

which produces for $part_1$ via the normalization equation:

$$\sum_{j=0}^{N-1} part_j = 1 \Rightarrow part_1 = \frac{1 + L^{-1} \sum_{j=2}^{N-1} \frac{p_j e_j - p_1 e_1 + (l_j - l_1)(b+d)}{l_j(a+c)+p_j}}{(l_1(a+c)+p_1)\sum_{j=1}^{N-1}\left(l_j(a+c)+p_j\right)^{-1}} \tag{8.13}$$

8.3.3.2 One-Port, Block-Type, Single-Installment Solution

The generic cost models of Equations 8.5, 8.7, and 8.8 can be adapted for our kernel convolution example by setting $a = 1$, $c = 1$, $d = 0$, and $e_i = 0$[11] as per the discussion in Section 8.3.1. If we also assume homogeneous communication links $l_i \equiv l$, our models are simplified to:

$$t_{comp}^{(i)} = p_i part_i \cdot L \tag{8.14}$$

$$t_{distr}^{(i)} = l(part_i \cdot L + b_i) \tag{8.15}$$

$$t_{coll}^{(i)} = lpart_i \cdot L \tag{8.16}$$

There is a small change in Equation 8.15 relevant to Equation 8.7 in that a node-specific b_i constant is used. In normal circumstances, making the cost models more complex than necessary would be ill-advised, since doing so can make our work much more challenging. The reason for this change will become apparent later.

The issue with one-port communication is that the optimum distribution and collection sequences have to be established. For a platform with N workers, the possible configurations are $(N!)^2$, since each of the distribution and collection sequences can be done in $N!$ different ways.

We consider the problem in its simplest possible form when only two nodes are involved. In the following discussion and until explicitly mentioned otherwise, we purposefully ignore the contribution of the master node, since it does not participate in the distribution/collection sequence.

For two workers there are only four possible configurations, as shown in Figure 8.10. This setting is much easier to tackle than a generic N-node platform, and it can provide us with useful insights about the optimum sequence.

The overall duration of each configuration can be found by calculating $part_1$ from the system of equations produced by combining the normalization Equation 8.1 and one of:

$$p_1 part_1 L = l(part_2 L + b_2) + p_2 part_2 L + l\, part_2 L \text{ for conf. \#1} \tag{8.17}$$

---

[11] Despite the extra memory allocation overhead, we can assume that the allocation takes place during the initialization of our program, prior to the distribution of the input data. Hence our computational cost adheres to the model we derived from test data in Equation 8.2.

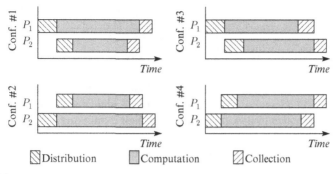

FIGURE 8.10

The four possible distribution/collection sequences for the case of two nodes sharing a load *L*.

$$p_2part_2L = l(part_1L + b_1) + p_1part_1L + l\,part_1L \text{ for conf. \#2} \qquad (8.18)$$

$$p_1part_1L + lpart_1L = l(part_2L + b_2) + p_2part_2L \text{ for conf. \#3} \qquad (8.19)$$

$$p_2part_2L + lpart_2L = l(part_1L + b_1) + p_1part_1L \text{ for conf. \#4} \qquad (8.20)$$

These (and following) equations can be derived directly from the Gantt charts in Figure 8.10. Subsequently, we can calculate the overall execution times (the actual solutions are not shown due to their length):

$$t_{\#1} = l(part_1L + b_1) + p_1part_1L + lpart_1L \qquad (8.21)$$

$$t_{\#2} = l((1 - part_1)L + b_2) + p_2(1 - part_1)L + l(1 - part_1)L \qquad (8.22)$$

$$t_{\#3} = l(part_1L + b_1) + p_1part_1L + l\,L \qquad (8.23)$$

$$t_{\#4} = l((1 - part_1)L + b_2) + p_2(1 - part_1)L + l\,L \qquad (8.24)$$

Calculating the differences in overall execution times yields[12]:

$$t_{\#3} - t_{\#1} = -\frac{l^2\,(L + b_2)}{p_1 + p_2 + 2\,l} < 0 \qquad (8.25)$$

$$t_{\#4} - t_{\#2} = -\frac{l^2\,(L + b_1)}{p_1 + p_2 + 2\,l} < 0 \qquad (8.26)$$

---

[12] A computer algebra system such as Maxima (http://maxima.sourceforge.net) can produce the desired results quickly and in an error-free manner.

$$t_{\#3} - t_{\#4} = -\frac{l\,(b_2 p_2 - b_1 p_1 + b_2\,l - b_1\,l)}{p_1 + p_2 + 2\,l} \tag{8.27}$$

The sign of the first two differences is clearly negative, which means that the optimum configuration can be either #3 or #4. If the two nodes are sorted in ascending order of their $b_i(p_i + l)$ property, then Equation 8.27 becomes negative and configuration #3 is the optimum one. For two identical b_i constants, we only need to sort the nodes in descending order of their computing power as expressed by p_is.

We could speculate at this point that the same should be true for an arbitrary number of nodes. We proceed to prove that this is true in a proper mathematical fashion. The impatient reader may chose to skip the lemmas and theorem that follow and see the net outcome in the form of Equation 8.39.

We can summarize out findings so far with the following lemma:

Lemma 8.3.1. *Given two nodes P_1 and P_2 that are to perform kernel convolution, the minimum execution time is achieved using a configuration where the nodes receive their input and send back the results in ascending order of their $b_i(p_i + l)$ property.*

Proof. The proof is given in the form of the Equations 8.25, 8.26, and 8.27. □

For the discussion that follows, we assume that $b_2(p_2 + l) \geq b_1(p_1 + l)$, making configuration #3 the optimum one.

The overall execution time for configuration #3 can be found to be:

$$t_{\#3} = \frac{p_1 p_2 L + 2\,l\,p_2 L + 2\,l\,p_1 L + 3\,l^2 L + b_1 p_2 l + l\,b_2 p_1 + l\,b_1 p_1 + b_2 l^2 + 2\,b_1 l^2}{p_1 + p_2 + 2\,l} \tag{8.28}$$

which can be rewritten in the following form:

$$t_{\#3} = l(L + b_1 + b_2) + \frac{p_1\,p_2\,L - l^2\,L - b_2\,l\,p_2 - b_2\,l^2}{(p_1 + p_2 + 2\,l)\,L}L + l\,L \tag{8.29}$$

Equation 8.29 expresses the total time as the time it would take a node *equivalent* (a.k.a. aggregate) to the two original ones to process the input at the same time while incurring the exact same communication overhead:

$$t_{distr}^{(equiv)} = l(L + b_1 + b_2) \tag{8.30}$$

$$t_{coll}^{(equiv)} = l\,L \tag{8.31}$$

$$t_{comp}^{(equiv)} = L\frac{p_1 p_2 L - l^2 L - l\,b_2 p_2 - b_2 l^2}{(p_1 + p_2 + 2\,l)\,L} \tag{8.32}$$

We could describe the equivalent node as having $p_{equiv} = \frac{p_1 p_2 L - l^2 L - l\,b_2 p_2 - b_2 l^2}{(p_1 + p_2 + 2\,l)L}$ and $b_{equiv} = b_1 + b_2$ (this is where the switch from b to b_i in Equation 8.15 comes in handy).

The equivalent node also has the following property:

$b_2(p_2 + l) - b_{equiv}(p_{equiv} + l) =$

$$\frac{(p_2 + l)\,(L(b_2(p_2 + l) - b_1(p_1 + l)) + b_2 l(b_1 + b_2))}{(p_1 + p_2 + 2\,l)\,L} > 0 \quad (8.33)$$

The outcome of Equation 8.33 is positive, since by definition we have $b_2(p_2 + l) \geq b_1(p_1 + l)$.

We have just added one more component in our mathematical arsenal that will assist us in proving how to optimize N nodes.

Lemma 8.3.2. *Given two nodes P_1 and P_2, assumed without loss of generality to have $b_1(p_1 + l) \leq b_2(p_2 + l)$, that are to perform kernel convolution on L data in an optimum configuration, they collectively behave as an equivalent node P_{equiv} that incurs the same communication costs and sports properties $p_{equiv} = \frac{p_1 p_2 L - l^2 L - l\,b_2 p_2 - b_2 l^2}{(p_1 + p_2 + 2\,l)L}$ and $b_{equiv} = b_1 + b_2$, such that $b_{equiv}(p_{equiv} + l) \leq b_2(p_2 + l)$.*

Proof. The proof is given in the form of Equations 8.29 and 8.33. □

The process of replacing a pair of nodes with an equivalent one can be applied iteratively when an arbitrary number of nodes exist. We can assume without loss of generality that after sorting the nodes in ascending order of their $b_i(p_i + l)$ property, we get the sequence P_1, P_2, P_3, etc. (after all, it is just a labeling issue). Then we can replace the pair of P_1, P_2 with their equivalent $P_{equiv}^{(1,2)}$, then the pair of $P_{equiv}^{(1,2)}$, P_3 with their equivalent $P_{equiv}^{(1,2,3)}$, and so on. Configuration #3 will remain the optimum in every case as the new equivalent nodes preserve the sorting order according to Lemma 8.3.2.

This constitutes the basis of our proof for the optimum sequence theorem.

Theorem 8.3.3. *Given a single-level tree of N worker nodes and a load L that is big enough to guarantee the usage of all the nodes (more on this later) the optimum sequence for load distribution and result collection in one-port, block-type computation of kernel convolution is produced by sorting the nodes in nondecreasing order of the quantity $b_i(p_i + l)$.*

Proof. We will prove this theorem by induction. We have already proven the theorem for $N = 2$ via Lemma 8.3.1. We will assume that it is true for k nodes and show that it holds for $k + 1$. We can assume without loss of generality that after sorting the k nodes in ascending order of their $b_i(p_i + l)$ property, we get the sequence P_1, P_2, ..., P_k. The first k nodes can be replaced by their equivalent P_{equiv}, for which we have two possibilities: (a) $b_{equiv}(p_{equiv} + l) < b_{k+1}(p_{k+1} + l)$ or (b) $b_{equiv}(p_{equiv} + l) \geq b_{k+1}(p_{k+1} + l)$.

In case (a), configuration #3 is optimum for the pair of P_{equiv}, P_{k+1} and we either have $b_k(p_k + l) \leq b_{k+1}(p_{k+1} + l)$, which satisfies the theorem, or $b_k(p_k + l) > b_{k+1}(p_{k+1} + l)$. If the latter is true, we can switch the order of P_k and P_{k+1} in the distribution and collection sequence and reduce the overall execution time of the part of the load that is assigned to them. As depicted in Figure 8.11, rearranging the P_k and P_{k+1} nodes (going from the state shown in Figure 8.11(a) to the state in Figure 8.11(b)), communication times are unchanged ($t_2 - t_1$ for distribution and $t_4 - t_3$ for

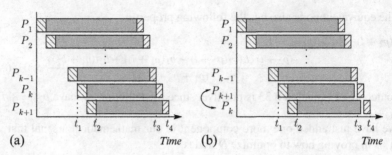

FIGURE 8.11

Switching the order of nodes P_k and P_{k+1} in the distribution and collection sequences reduces their computation time while keeping their communication time unchanged, if $b_k(p_k + l) > b_{k+1}(p_{k+1} + l)$.

collection), but changing the configuration of the pair from what is effectively #4 to #3 reduces the pair's computation time. This means that an overall redistribution of the load is possible, which will reduce the overall execution time.

This can continue until we find a node P_X that satisfies $b_X(p_X + l) \leq b_{k+1}(p_{k+1} + l)$, or P_{k+1} becomes the first node in the sequence, which proves the theorem.

In case (b), configuration #4 is optimum and thus P_{k+1} should precede P_{equiv} in the sequence. If $b_{k+1}(p_{k+1} + l) \leq b_1(p_1 + l)$, the theorem is satisfied. Otherwise, we can follow the same process as before but in reverse, e.g., swapping P_{k+1} and P_1 if $b_1(p_1 + l) > b_{k+1}(p_{k+1} + l)$, etc. The swapping of nodes in the sequence can stop only when the order speculated by the theorem holds, which completes the proof. $\square$

Theorem 8.3.3 allows us to derive a solution beyond the two-nodes case. For every pair of successive nodes P_i and P_{i+1} in the distribution/collection sequence, the following should hold:

$$t_{comp}^{(i)} + t_{coll}^{(i)} = t_{distr}^{(i+1)} + t_{comp}^{(i+1)} \Rightarrow$$

$$p_i part_i L + l\, part_i L = l(part_{i+1}L + b_{i+1}) + p_{i+1}part_{i+1}L \Rightarrow$$

$$part_{i+1} = part_i \frac{p_i + l}{p_{i+1} + l} - \frac{lb_{i+1}}{L(p_{i+1} + l)} \tag{8.34}$$

Now that we have figured out the optimum sequence of the workers, we can also consider the role of the master node. If P_0 is participating in the computation, then Equation 8.34 holds for $i \in [1, N - 2]$, and we also have the following relation between P_0 and P_1:

$$t_{comp}^{(0)} = t_{distr}^{(1)} + t_{comp}^{(1)} + \sum_{j=1}^{N-1} t_{coll}^{(j)} \Rightarrow$$

$$p_0 part_0 L = l(part_1 L + b_1) + p_1 part_1 L + l\, L(1 - part_0) \Rightarrow$$

$$part_0 L(p_0 + l) = part_1 L(p_1 + l) + l(b_1 + L) \Rightarrow$$

$$part_1 = part_0 \frac{p_0 + l}{p_1 + l} - \frac{lb_1}{L(p_1 + l)} - \frac{l}{p_1 + l} \tag{8.35}$$

Equation 8.35 allows us to express the other $part_i$s as a function of $part_0$:

$$part_2 = part_1 \frac{p_1 + l}{p_2 + l} - \frac{lb_2}{L(p_2 + l)} =$$

$$\left(part_0 \frac{p_0 + l}{p_1 + l} - \frac{l(b_1 + L)}{L(p_1 + l)} \right) \frac{p_1 + l}{p_2 + l} - \frac{lb_2}{L(p_2 + l)} =$$

$$part_0 \frac{p_0 + l}{p_2 + l} - \frac{lb_1}{L(p_2 + l)} - \frac{lb_2}{L(p_2 + l)} - \frac{l}{p_2 + l} \quad (8.36)$$

$$part_3 = part_2 \frac{p_2 + l}{p_3 + l} - \frac{lb_3}{L(p_3 + l)} =$$

$$\left(part_0 \frac{p_0 + l}{p_2 + l} - \frac{l(b_1 + L)}{L(p_2 + l)} - \frac{lb_2}{L(p_2 + l)} \right) \frac{p_2 + l}{p_3 + l} - \frac{lb_3}{L(p_3 + l)} =$$

$$part_0 \frac{p_0 + l}{p_3 + l} - \frac{l(b_1 + L)}{L(p_3 + l)} - \frac{lb_2}{L(p_3 + l)} - \frac{lb_3}{L(p_3 + l)} =$$

$$part_0 \frac{p_0 + l}{p_3 + l} - \frac{lb_1}{L(p_3 + l)} - \frac{lb_2}{L(p_3 + l)} - \frac{lb_3}{L(p_3 + l)} - \frac{l}{(p_3 + l)} =$$

$$part_0 \frac{p_0 + l}{p_3 + l} - \frac{l}{L(p_3 + l)} \sum_{j=1}^{3} b_j - \frac{l}{p_3 + l} \quad (8.37)$$

or in general:

$$part_k = part_0 \frac{p_0 + l}{p_k + l} - \frac{l}{L(p_k + l)} \sum_{j=1}^{k} b_j - \frac{l}{p_k + l} \quad (8.38)$$

The normalization equation can then provide us with the answer for $part_0$:

$$\sum_{k=0}^{N-1} part_k = 1 \Rightarrow$$

$$part_0 \sum_{k=0}^{N-1} \frac{p_0 + l}{p_k + l} - \sum_{k=1}^{N-1} \left(\frac{l}{L(p_k + l)} \sum_{j=1}^{k} b_j \right) - \sum_{k=1}^{N-1} \frac{l}{p_k + l} = 1 \Rightarrow$$

$$part_0 = \frac{1 + \sum_{k=1}^{N-1} \left(\frac{l}{L(p_k + l)} \sum_{j=1}^{k} b_j \right) + \sum_{k=1}^{N-1} \frac{l}{p_k + l}}{(p_0 + l) \sum_{k=0}^{N-1} (p_k + l)^{-1}} \quad (8.39)$$

Equation 8.39 allows the calculation of $part_0$ and the overall execution time (equal to $p_0 part_0 L$) in linear time complexity $\Theta(N)$.

As an example of the application of our analysis, we consider an instance of the kernel convolution problem with the following characteristics:

- A parallel platform made up of four nodes with $p_0 = 1.631 \cdot 10^{-07}$, $p_1 = 2 \cdot (1.631 \cdot 10^{-07})$, $p_2 = 3 \cdot (1.631 \cdot 10^{-07})$, and $p_3 = 4 \cdot (1.631 \cdot 10^{-07})$, all in sec/B. P_0 is considered the master node holding the input data. The parameters are derived from the result reported in Equation 8.2 in order to represent a heterogeneous machine.

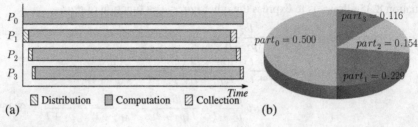

FIGURE 8.12

(a) Gantt chart for a four-node heterogeneous platform example that performs kernel image convolution, as predicted by DLT-based analysis. (b) Pie chart of the percentages $part_i$.

- An input image of UHD resolution, i.e., 3840x2160 pixels, with 24 bits color accuracy. This translates to $L = 3840 * 2160 * 3B = 23.73MB$.
- A network with 102.98 MB/sec speed, or $l = 9.26 \cdot 10^{-9} sec/B$.
- The cost model is completed with $b_1 = b_2 = 2 \cdot 3 \cdot 2160B$ and $b_3 = 3 \cdot 2160B$, given the length of the image row.

Figure 8.12 illustrates the results produced by Equations 8.39 and 8.38. It is obvious that in real life these results can only be expected in the most ideal of situations. The side effects of additional workloads, network activity, CPU cache utilization, and other factors will invariably cause deviations from this ideal scenario.

This weakness does not diminish the usefulness of DLT as a modeling and load-balancing tool. The beauty of these equations is that they can be quickly evaluated to either guide partitioning decisions or even allow performance estimation at an abstract level.

8.3.4 SUMMARY - SHORT LITERATURE REVIEW

The three-stage process outlined above, can provide elegant closed-form solutions, that can guide the design of both parallel software and hardware. It is not uncommon in DLT literature to encounter optimal arrangement theorems, where the authors derive the optimal hardware configuration in regards to the examined application or setting [39, 42]. These typically come in the form of how to pair communication and computation resources.

However, this three-stage process is not rigid. It is possible that the outcome of the modeling and communication configuration phases, does not allow the derivation of analytical solutions. In such cases, researchers have resorted to linear programming [9, 21], genetic algorithms[8] or other heuristics[28] in order to get the desired partitioning and operations schedules.

Figure 8.13 puts into perspective some of the recent publications in the DLT domain, relative to the design choices outlined above.

Recent research efforts have focused, apart from the ever growing set of applications targeted, in the following key areas:

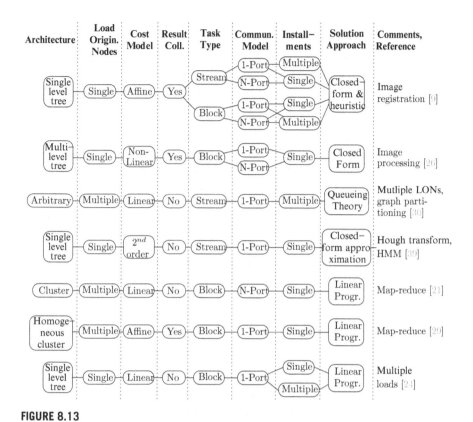

FIGURE 8.13

Samples of DLT bibliography, in reference to key problem modeling factors.

1. **Non-linear cost functions** : a number of applications, including classical problems such as e.g., matrix multiplication, or sorting, do not conform to a linear or an affine cost model. Expanding the DLT framework to cover these cases can significantly enhance the impact of the methodology.
2. **Multiple load-originating nodes** : a typical characteristic in networking, but also in parallel file systems, is that data may reside in disjoint nodes. Taking into account this platform characteristic, changes significantly how load distribution should be conducted, which is a very significant performance parameter.
3. **Processing of multiple loads** : computation clouds and high performance computing facilities employ job queues in order to perform long-term scheduling. Processing multiple loads is a different problem than processing a single one, needing to take into consideration among other things, resource consumption and node release times, i.e., when machines become free to process something new.

Beaumont et al. have shown in [15] that non-linear cost functions present a problem for parallel execution, especially in the context of a map-reduce pattern. The reduction phase which is typically less amenable to parallelization than mapping, can negate any gains that the parallel execution of the mapping phase may yield. Beaumont et al. show that problems can be overcome by replicating data, e.g., sending "augmented" data sets to the compute nodes. This effectively shifts the burden from computation to communication.

One of the first break-throughs came from Hung and Robertazzi [26], who were able to use quadratic and power-of-x computational cost models for multi- and single-level trees respectively. In a more recent publication, Suresh et al. [39] were able to prove an "optimal sequencing"[13] and an "optimal arrangement"[14] theorems, for partitioning a second-order cost workload, on a single level tree. Suresh et al. used a 1-port configuration and stream-type tasks to derive closed-form approximations under certain problem assumptions.

Ilic and Sousa propose in [27] a two-phase scheduling algorithm consisting of an initial benchmarking phase called "initialization phase", that serves to calculate the cost models, and a second processing phase, called the "iterative phase". During the initialization phase the load is equally partitioned among the available machines. Upon termination, the measured execution times are used to establish cost models that are applied and refined during subsequent executions (iterative phase). A major novelty of their work is the use of continuous generic cost functions, that combine both communication and computation costs.

In [30] the authors study two scheduling strategies that partition the graph representing the network joining sources (a.k.a. Load Originating Nodes or LONs) and sinks (workers) into disjoint sub-graphs. A limitation of the proposed strategies is that each of the sources carries a separate, disjoint queue of individual loads. This hinders their application in the case of parallel file systems, or in cases where the sources share a load. The same limitation applies to the work presented in [44], where the authors suggest three resource-aware scheduling schemes that implicitly use multiple installments to process the loads present at the sources, under deadline considerations. The size of the installments is dictated by the buffer space available in the workers at any given time.

Multiple LONs have been also examined in the context of map-reduce computations. Gu et al. in [21] use linear programming to calculate how the input data resident at multiple LONs, should be partitioned among "mapper" nodes (i.e., nodes that perform the mapping phase). Berlinska and Drozdowski in [29], use a homogeneous computation with varying communication costs model, to propose two heuristic methods for the load partitioning in a map-reduce context, but without using multiple LONs. The set of timing constraints produced, involving both the mapping and the reduction phases, are solved with a linear programming solver.

---

[13]"Sequencing" translates to the order in which nodes receive load.
[14]"Arrangement" translates to how nodes and communication links should pair with each-other, as in during hardware setup.

The processing of multiple loads that are enqueued at a single LON, is the subject of the work by Hu and Veeravalli in [24]. Hu and Veeravalli propose a static and a dynamic scheduling strategies, that differ in how the release of a node from a previous assignment is detected. In the static strategy, the release times are assumed to be known a priori, while in the dynamic strategy the workers signal the LON upon finishing their work. The dynamic strategy resorts to multiple installments to be able to incorporate newly released nodes into the working set for a job.

Hu and Veeravalli have also worked on the joined scheduling of divisible and indivisible (i.e., sequential) loads on clusters [25] by proposing a heuristic algorithm called Hybrid Load Scheduling (HMS). HMS tries to fill-in the "gaps" (i.e., time periods of idleness) left-over from the computation of the indivisible tasks that are scheduled first, with divisible loads.

8.4 DLTLIB: A LIBRARY FOR PARTITIONING WORKLOADS

A large number of application scenarios have been studied over the years under the prism of DLT. In the previous sections we explored two relatively straightforward cases that illustrate the analysis approach and challenges involved. In this section we present a software library that can assist in the application of the work that has been done over the years, without the need for a programmer to implement the "scary-looking" equations.

Our DLTlib library incorporates only a subset of the published results, but because it is released under the GNU GPL V3 Open Source Software License, it can serve as a starting point for anyone willing to experiment and/or augment it.

DLTlib operations depend on two classes/structures : `Node`, which represents a computing node and contains as data members all the needed node-specific information, and class `Network`, which is supposed to be a container of `Node` instances. The `Network` class provides all the methods that calculate the partitioning of a load based on the problem circumstances. Node instances are connected with a parent-child relationship to form a multilevel tree, although most of the supplied methods can operate on single-level trees only.

Appendix F contains detailed information about the functionality provided by DLTlib. In this section we describe the basic steps needed for incorporating it in a project, which include the following:

1. Declare an instance of the `Network` class.
2. Add to the `Network` instance all the compute nodes that make up the parallel machine. These nodes are assumed to be organized in a tree. The first node to be inserted should be the root of the tree. The insertion requires the specification of the node-specific attributes, i.e., p_i, l_i, and e_i.
3. Call a `Network` method to solve the partitioning problem. Any application-specific parameters (e.g., L, a,b, etc.) are passed at this point to the library.
4. Iterate over the `Network`'s collection of `Node` structures to query about their assigned part.

As an example, let's use the problem of image registration, i.e., finding among a pool of images the one that best suits a target image (this is a common problem in medical informatics). This is an application that can be parallelized by following the map-reduce pattern (see Section 2.4.4), whereas the "mapping" step involves the calculation of comparison metrics between the target and each pool image. The reduction step involves the selection of the best image. We will ignore the reduction step in our partitioning, because it is typically substantially smaller in cost than the mapping step.

We assume that the problem attributes are:

- A pool of 1000 images, each 1 MB in size, and a target image of the same size.
- Three CPU nodes, each node capable of comparing two images in $p_{cpu} = 0.02sec/image$. One of them serves as the host.
- A GPU capable of comparing two images in $p_{gpu} = 0.005sec/image$.
- All nodes are connected with a network capable of 100 MB/sec transfer rates, or $l = 0.01sec/image$.[15]

In Listing 8.2, we implement the sequence of steps shown above to solve the image registration example.

```
1   // File : DLTlib/DLTdemo.cpp
2   ...
3   //————————————————————————————————————————————————
4   // DLTlib specific definitions that need to be used by the library.
5   // Control of the seed allows manipulation of the output of any
6   // pseudo—random generated structures in case repetitive tests
7   // are needed.
8   long global_random_seed;
9
10  #include "dltlib.cpp"
11  //————————————————————————————————————————————————
12
13  int main ()
14  {
15      double p_cpu = 0.01;
16      double p_gpu = 0.005;
17      double l = 0.01;
18      long int L = 1000;
19      int M = 2;                  // number of installments
20
21      // STEP 1
22      Network platform;      // object representing parallel platform
23
24      // STEP 2
25      // insert one-by-one the nodes that make up the machine
26      // LON stands for Load Originating Node. It can be considered to be
```

---

[15]The units used here are different than the ones used in earlier examples. However, they are still "time/data volume" units. As long as they are consistent across all the constants employed, no problem exists.

```
27  // equivalent to the file server as it does not participate in the ←
        computation
28  platform.InsertNode ((char *) "LON", p_cpu, 0, (char *) NULL, 1, ←
        true );
29  platform.InsertNode ((char *) "GPU", p_gpu, 0, (char *) "LON", 1, ←
        true );
30  platform.InsertNode ((char *) "CPU0", p_cpu, 0, (char *) "LON", 1, ←
        true );
31  platform.InsertNode ((char *) "CPU1", p_cpu, 0, (char *) "LON", 1, ←
        true );
32  platform.InsertNode ((char *) "CPU2", p_cpu, 0, (char *) "LON", 1, ←
        true );
33
34  // STEP 3
35  // Solve the partitioning problem for 1−port, block−type computation←
        and M installments
36  double execTime = platform.SolveImageQuery_NInst (L, 1, 0, M);
37
38  // print out the results, if the solution is valid
39  if (platform.valid == 1)
40    {
41      cout << "Predicted execution time: " << execTime << endl;
42
43      // STEP 4
44      // Compute nodes are stored in a public linked−list that allows
45      // rearrangement to the order of distribution and collection
46      cout << "Solution in terms of load percent :\n";
47      Node *h = platform.head;
48      while (h != NULL)
49        {
50          // For a single installment case, the following statement ←
                should be used
51          //cout << h−>name << " " << h−>part << endl;
52
53          cout << h−>name;
54          for (int i = 0; i < M; i++)
55            cout << "\t" << h−>mi_part[i];        // array mi_part holds←
                    the parts for each installment
56          cout << endl;
57          h = h−>next_n;
58        }
59
60      cout << "Solution in terms of images :\n";
61      h = platform.head;
62      while (h != NULL)
63        {
64          cout << h−>name;
65          for (int i = 0; i < M; i++)
66            cout << "\t" << h−>mi_part[i] * L;
67          cout << endl;
68          h = h−>next_n;
69        }
```

```
70        }
71    else
72        cout << "Solution could not be found\n";
73    return 0;
74 }
```

LISTING 8.2

A demonstration of DLTlib in action.

DLTlib depends on the GNU Linear Programming Toolkit for compilation. Hence it needs access to the corresponding header file (glpk.h) and shared library (libglpk.so). The following command line would suffice for compiling and linking our sample program:

```
$ g++ DLTdemo.cpp -lstdc++ -lglpk -o DLTdemo
```

The output generated is shown in Listing 8.3.

```
$ ./DLTdemo
Predicted execution time: 10.1106
Solution in terms of load percent :
LON     0          0
GPU     0.635698            0
CPU0    0.172554            0.028259
CPU1    0.0928417           0.0141295
CPU2    0.0494532           0.00706475
Solution in terms of images :
LON     0       0
GPU     635.698 0
CPU0    172.554 28.259
CPU1    92.8417 14.1295
CPU2    49.4532 7.06475
```

LISTING 8.3

Output of the program in Listing 8.2.

As a final word, DLTlib has evolved over a span of many years. It has been used as a research tool and a validation platform by the author. Although much effort has been devoted in making it bug-free, we cannot provide guarantees for its correctness or appropriateness for any software project. We hope that its release under the GNU GPL V3 software license will spur its growth with the assistance of the community.

8.5 CASE STUDIES

8.5.1 HYBRID COMPUTATION OF A MANDELBROT SET "MOVIE": A CASE STUDY IN DYNAMIC LOAD BALANCING

In this section we show how dynamic load balancing can be used to speed up the calculation of the Mandelbrot set in the context of heterogeneous or hybrid computational resources (combining GPU and CPU computation). The details of the

Mandelbrot set are covered in Section 3.8.2. Since large portions of the code used in this project have appeared before (see Chapters 3 and 6), in the paragraphs that follow we mainly focus on the problem of how the computation can be efficiently partitioned in order to achieve the minimum possible execution time. Nonessential information, such as how the pixels are pseudo-colored, etc., is not covered, to avoid over-bloating this section.

In contrast with the case studies of previous chapters that employed the particular fractal, in this one we consider the problem of generating an animation, i.e., a sequence of images, of the Mandelbrot fractal as we pan and zoom between two regions of the complex plane, as shown in Figure 8.14.

Given the coordinates of the first (A,B) and last (C,D) images in the sequence, the coordinates of the intermediate frames are linearly interpolated. So, for the $j-th$ frame in a N-frame sequence, with $j \in [0, N-1]$, the upper and lower corner points are calculated as:

$$U(j) = A + j \cdot \frac{C-A}{N-1} \qquad (8.40)$$

$$L(j) = B + j \cdot \frac{D-B}{N-1} \qquad (8.41)$$

The same methodology is applied for figuring out the maximum number of iterations to be performed.[16]

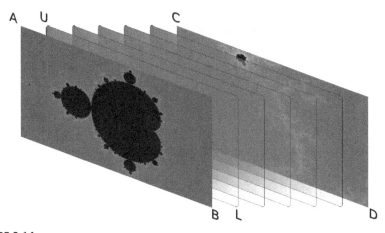

FIGURE 8.14

The corners of the two end frames *A*, *B*, *C*, and *D* are used to interpolate the corner coordinates *U* and *L* of each intermediate frame.

---

[16]In the actual implementation in Listing 8.4, a slightly bigger denominator is used (i.e., N) to avoid round-off errors that can prohibit the rendering of the last image in the sequence by making corners U and L cross.

The calculation still relies on the direct application of the recurrence formula of Equation 3.1 for every pixel of the target image(s).

Bringing out the detail of the fractal requires the increase of the maximum number of iterations, way beyond the 255 limit employed in Listing 6.31. This, however, introduces a new problem for GPU deployment: High variability in the number of iterations needed for convergence in neighboring pixels leads to CUDA thread divergence (i.e., some threads finish earlier than others), effectively diminishing the utilization of the GPU's SMs.

To address this deficiency, we evaluate how appropriate a region is for GPU processing by calculating the number of iterations needed to process its four corners. If their variation (as measured by the difference between the maximum and minimum number of iterations) is too big, the region is broken into four equal pieces that are in turn examined individually. A region is considered suitable for GPU processing if the following criterion is satisfied:

$$maxIter - minIter < diffThres \cdot maxIter \tag{8.42}$$

where $maxIter = max_{\forall i}(cornerIter[i])$ and $minIter_{\forall i} = min(cornerIter[i])$ for $i \in [0, 3]$, and $diffThres < 1$ is an ad hoc specified fixed threshold.

This subdivision process is repeated until the condition 8.42 is met or until a region's pixel count falls below a fixed threshold *pixelSizeThresh*. Through experimentation, we found that $diffThres = 0.5$ and $pixelSizeThresh = 32768$ are reasonably good choices, at least for the test platform and setup reported here.

In the listings that follow, each frame or image to be calculated is represented by an instance of the MandelFrame class shown in Listing 8.4.

```
1    // File : mandelbrot_hybrid / mandelframe .h
2    ...
3    class MandelFrame
4    {
5    public:
6        int MAXITER;
7        double upperX, upperY;          // complex plane corners
8        double lowerX, lowerY;
9        double stepX, stepY;
10       int pixelsX, pixelsY;           // image resolution
11       QImage *img;                    // object holding pixel values
12       char fname[MAXFNAME+1];         // filename used for storage
13       QAtomicInt remainingRegions;    // atomic counter for regions
14                                       // left to be computed
15       MandelFrame(double, double, double, double, int, int, char*, int);
16       void regionSplit();
17       void regionComplete();
18    };
```

LISTING 8.4

Class used to represent an image.

Each of the subregions that make up a frame is represented by an instance of the
MandelRegion class, as shown in Listing 8.5.

```
19  // File : mandelbrot_hybrid / mandelregion .h
20  ...
21  class MandelRegion
22  {
23  private :
24    int diverge (double cx, double cy); // calculates the number
25                                         // of iterations for a pixel
26    double upperX, upperY;  // complex plane coordinates of region
27    double lowerX, lowerY;
28    int imageX, imageY;      // location in target image
29    int pixelsX, pixelsY;    // and pixel dimensions
30    int cornersIter[4];      // iterations for the four corners
31    MandelFrame *ownerFrame;
32    static QRgb *colormap;  // used for pseudocoloring the pixels
33    static double diffThresh; // thresholds that trigger calculation
34    static int pixelSizeThresh;
35
36  public :
37    MandelRegion (double, double, double, double, int, int, int, int, ↵
          MandelFrame *);
38    void compute (bool onGPU);       // calculates a region's pixels
39    void examine (WorkQueue &, bool onGPU);  // evaluate the GPU
40                                             // suitability of a region,
41                                             // possibly computing it
42    bool operator < (const MandelRegion & a);
43    static void initColorMapAndThrer (int, double, int);
44  };
```

LISTING 8.5

Class used to represent a part of an image.

Each MandelFrame is originally made up of just one MandelRegion that is
inserted in an instance of the WorkQueue class, which is shown in Listing 8.6.

```
45  // File : mandelbrot_hybrid / workqueue .h
46  ...
47  class WorkQueue
48  {
49  private :
50    QMutex l;    // lock ensuring thread safety
51    deque<MandelRegion *> queue; // container
52
53  public :
54    void append(MandelRegion *);
55    MandelRegion* extract ();
56    int size ();
57  };
```

LISTING 8.6

Thread-safe, FIFO queue class for managing regions to be computed.

Each worker thread (represented by an instance of the `CalcThr` class) extracts a `MandelRegion` object from the work queue and proceeds to either process it or subdivide it and place the pieces back in the queue. Once all the pieces of a frame have been calculated, the frame is saved to the filesystem in the form of a PNG image.

The main part of the program is shown in Listing 8.7.

```
58  // File : mandelbrot_hybrid/main.cpp
59  ...
60
61  // ************************************************************
62  // Generic worker-thread front-end
63  class CalcThr:public QThread
64  {
65  private:
66    WorkQueue * que;
67    bool isGPU;
68
69  public:
70      CalcThr (WorkQueue * q, bool gpu):que (q), isGPU (gpu)
71    {
72    }
73    void run ();
74  };
75
76  void CalcThr::run ()
77  {
78    MandelRegion *t;
79    while ((t = que->extract ()) != NULL)
80      {
81        t->examine (*que, isGPU);
82        delete t;
83      }
84  }
85
86  // ************************************************************
87  //   Expects an input file with the following data:
88  //   numframes resolutionX resolutionY imageFilePrefix
89  //   upperX upperY lowerX lowerY maxIterations  ; for first frame
90  //   upperX upperY lowerX lowerY maxIterations  ; for last frame
91  //
92  // Command-line param.:   spec_file numThr GPUenable diffT pixelT
93  //          spec_file : file holding the parameters mentioned above
94  //          numThr : number of threads (optional, defaults to the
95  //                   number of cores)
96  //          GPUenable : 0/1, 1 (default) enables the GPU code (opt.)
97  //          diffT pixelT : optional thresholds for frame
98  //                          partitioning heuristics
99  int main (int argc, char *argv[])
100 {
101   int numframes, resolutionX, resolutionY;
102   char imageFilePrefix[MAXFNAME - 8];
```

```
103    double upperCornerX[2], upperCornerY[2], lowerCornerX[2], ↵
           lowerCornerY[2];
104    int maxIterations[2];
105    double diffT = 0.5;
106    int pixT = 32768;
107
108    if (argc < 2)
109      {
110        cerr << "Usage : " << argv[0] << "spec_file numThr GPUenable\n";
111        exit (1);
112      }
113
114    int numThreads = sysconf (_SC_NPROCESSORS_ONLN);
115    if (argc > 2)
116      numThreads = atoi (argv[2]);
117
118    bool enableGPU = true;
119    if (argc > 3)
120      enableGPU = (bool) atoi (argv[3]);
121
122    if (argc > 4)
123      diffT = atof (argv[4]);
124
125    if (argc > 5)
126      pixT = atoi (argv[5]);
127
128    ifstream fin (argv[1]);
129    fin >> numframes >> resolutionX >> resolutionY;
130    fin >> imageFilePrefix;
131    fin >> upperCornerX[0] >> upperCornerY[0] >> lowerCornerX[0] >> ↵
           lowerCornerY[0] >> maxIterations[0];
132    fin >> upperCornerX[1] >> upperCornerY[1] >> lowerCornerX[1] >> ↵
           lowerCornerY[1] >> maxIterations[1];
133    fin.close ();
134
135    // generate the pseudocolor map to be used for all frames
136    int MAXMAXITER = max (maxIterations[0], maxIterations[1]);
137    MandelRegion::initColorMapAndThrer (MAXMAXITER, diffT, pixT);
138
139    WorkQueue workQ;
140
141    // generate the needed frame objects and the corresponding regions
142    MandelFrame **fr = new MandelFrame *[numframes];
143    double uX = upperCornerX[0], uY = upperCornerY[0];
144    double lX = lowerCornerX[0], lY = lowerCornerY[0];
145    int iter = maxIterations[0];
146    double sx1, sx2, sy1, sy2;
147    int iterInc;
148
149    // steps sx1 and sx2 are a little bit smaller to avoid round-off
150    // errors causing the last image to not render
151    sx1 = (upperCornerX[1] - upperCornerX[0]) / numframes;
```

```
152   sx2 = (lowerCornerX[1] − lowerCornerX[0]) / numframes;
153   sy1 = (upperCornerY[1] − upperCornerY[0]) / numframes;
154   sy2 = (lowerCornerY[1] − lowerCornerY[0]) / numframes;
155   iterInc = (maxIterations[1] − maxIterations[0]) * 1.0 / numframes;
156   char fname[MAXFNAME];
157   for (int i = 0; i < numframes; i++)
158     {
159       sprintf (fname, "%s%04i.png", imageFilePrefix, i);
160       fr[i] = new MandelFrame (uX, uY, lX, lY, resolutionX, ←
               resolutionY, fname, iter);
161       workQ.append (new MandelRegion (uX, uY, lX, lY, 0, 0, ←
               resolutionX, resolutionY, fr[i]));
162       uX += sx1;
163       uY += sy1;
164       lX += sx2;
165       lY += sy2;
166       iter += iterInc;
167     }


170   // generate the threads that will process the workload
171   CalcThr **thr = new CalcThr *[numThreads];
172   thr[0] = new CalcThr (&workQ, enableGPU);
173   for (int i = 1; i < numThreads; i++)
174     {
175       thr[i] = new CalcThr (&workQ, false);
176       thr[i]->start ();
177     }

179   // use the main thread to run one of the workers
180   if (enableGPU)
181     {
182       CUDAmemSetup (resolutionX, resolutionY);
183       thr[0]->run ();
184       CUDAmemCleanup ();
185     }
186   else
187     thr[0]->run ();

189   for (int i = 1; i < numThreads; i++)
190     thr[i]->wait ();

192   return 0;
193 }
```

LISTING 8.7

Main part of the hybrid, Mandelbrot-animation calculation program.

The main program reads the input parameters from the command line and the associated file (lines 108-133), generates the MandelFrame instances that correspond to the frames that need to be calculated (lines 142-167), and spawns the worker threads that will process the workload (lines 171-177).

Once the setup is complete, the master thread proceeds to serve as a worker (there is no reason why it should be idle for the duration of the computation) by calling the run() method of a CalcThr instance (lines 180-187). If GPU computation is enabled, the master thread allocates the device memory required (line 182) prior to the run().

Each thread, as mentioned previously, extracts a MandelRegion object from the work queue (line 79) and assesses what should be done next by calling the MandelRegion::examine() method, shown in lines 241-306 of Listing 8.8. The size and statements' length of this method might look intimidating, but the actual logic is very simple: Lines 246-269 calculate (if not previously done during the evaluation of the 'parent' region) the number of iterations required for the four corners of the region to diverge (or not) and evaluate the condition described by Equation 8.42 in line 272.

If the condition is satisfied, the pixels of the regions are calculated by calling the MandelRegion::compute() method. Otherwise, the region is split into four equally-sized subregions (lines 279-305), which are appended into the work queue. The information for the four corners of the parent-region is preserved in the new MandelRegion instances via lines 291, 294, 297, and 300.

The MandelRegion::compute() method (lines 196-237) performs the calculation on either the GPU (lines 205-220) or the CPU (lines 224-236), according to a thread-supplied parameter (onGPU).

```
194   // File : mandelbrot_hybrid/mandelregion.cpp
195   ...
196   void MandelRegion::compute (bool onGPU)
197   {
198     double stepX = ownerFrame->stepX;
199     double stepY = ownerFrame->stepY;
200     QImage *img = ownerFrame->img;
201     int MAXGRAY = ownerFrame->MAXITER;
202
203     if (onGPU)
204       {
205         unsigned int *h_res;
206         int pitch;
207
208         hostFE (upperX, upperY, lowerX, lowerY, pixelsX, pixelsY, &h_res←
                  , &pitch, MAXGRAY);
209         pitch /= sizeof (int);
210
211         //copy results into QImage object
212         for (int i = 0; i < pixelsX; i++)
213           for (int j = 0; j < pixelsY; j++)
214             {
215               int color = h_res[j * pitch + i];
216               if (color == MAXGRAY)
217                 img->setPixel (imageX + i, imageY + j, qRgb (0, 0, 0));
218               else
219                 img->setPixel (imageX + i, imageY + j, colormap[color]);
220             }
```

```
221     }
222     else                          // CPU execution
223     {
224       for (int i = 0; i < pixelsX; i++)
225         for (int j = 0; j < pixelsY; j++)
226         {
227           double tempx, tempy;
228           tempx = upperX + i * stepX;
229           tempy = upperY - j * stepY;
230           int color = diverge (tempx, tempy);
231           if (color == MAXGRAY)
232             img->setPixel (imageX + i, imageY + j, qRgb (0, 0, 0));
233           else
234             img->setPixel (imageX + i, imageY + j, colormap[color]);
235         }
236     }
237 }
238
239 //─────────────────────────────────────────────
240 // if the region is small enough, process it, or split it in 4 regions
241 void MandelRegion::examine (WorkQueue & q, bool onGPU = false)
242 {
243   int minIter = INT_MAX, maxIter = 0;
244
245   // evaluate the corners first
246   for (int i = 0; i < 4; i++)
247   {
248     if (cornersIter[i] == UNKNOWN)
249     {
250       switch (i)
251       {
252       case (UPPER_RIGHT):
253         cornersIter[i] = diverge (lowerX, upperY);
254         break;
255       case (UPPER_LEFT):
256         cornersIter[i] = diverge (upperX, upperY);
257         break;
258       case (LOWER_RIGHT):
259         cornersIter[i] = diverge (lowerX, lowerY);
260         break;
261       default:                      // LOWER_LEFT
262         cornersIter[i] = diverge (upperX, lowerY);
263       }
264     }
265     if (minIter > cornersIter[i])
266       minIter = cornersIter[i];
267     else if (maxIter < cornersIter[i])
268       maxIter = cornersIter[i];
269   }
270
271   // either compute the pixels or break the region in 4 pieces
```

```
272    if (maxIter − minIter < diffThresh * maxIter || pixelsX * pixelsY < ↵
           pixelSizeThresh)
273    {
274      compute (onGPU);
275      ownerFrame−>regionComplete ();
276    }
277  else
278    {
279      double midDiagX1, midDiagY1;        // data for new subregions
280      double midDiagX2, midDiagY2;
281      int subimageX, subimageY;
282      subimageX = pixelsX / 2;  // concern the upper left quad.
283      subimageY = pixelsY / 2;
284      midDiagX1 = upperX + (subimageX − 1) * ownerFrame−>stepX;
285      midDiagY1 = upperY − (subimageY − 1) * ownerFrame−>stepY;
286      midDiagX2 = midDiagX1 + ownerFrame−>stepX;
287      midDiagY2 = midDiagY1 − ownerFrame−>stepY;
288
289      MandelRegion *sub[4];
290      sub[UPPER_LEFT] = new MandelRegion (upperX, upperY, midDiagX1, ↵
             midDiagY1, imageX, imageY, subimageX, subimageY, ownerFrame)↵
             ;
291      sub[UPPER_LEFT]−>cornersIter[UPPER_LEFT] = cornersIter[↵
             UPPER_LEFT];
292
293      sub[UPPER_RIGHT] = new MandelRegion (midDiagX2, upperY, lowerX, ↵
             midDiagY1, imageX + subimageX, imageY, pixelsX − subimageX, ↵
             subimageY, ownerFrame);
294      sub[UPPER_RIGHT]−>cornersIter[UPPER_RIGHT] = cornersIter[↵
             UPPER_RIGHT];
295
296      sub[LOWER_LEFT] = new MandelRegion (upperX, midDiagY2, midDiagX1↵
             , lowerY, imageX, imageY + subimageY, subimageX, pixelsY − ↵
             subimageY, ownerFrame);
297      sub[LOWER_LEFT]−>cornersIter[LOWER_LEFT] = cornersIter[↵
             LOWER_LEFT];
298
299      sub[LOWER_RIGHT] = new MandelRegion (midDiagX2, midDiagY2, ↵
             lowerX, lowerY, imageX + subimageX, imageY + subimageY, ↵
             pixelsX − subimageX, pixelsY − subimageY, ownerFrame);
300      sub[LOWER_RIGHT]−>cornersIter[LOWER_RIGHT] = cornersIter[↵
             LOWER_RIGHT];
301
302      for (int i = 0; i < 4; i++)
303          q.append (sub[i]);
304      ownerFrame−>regionSplit ();
305    }
306  }
307  ...
```

LISTING 8.8

The core part of the MandelRegion class, responsible for carrying out the computations.

The CPU code is a straightforward nested loop, iterating over all the possible pixels of a region in sequence. The GPU code, administered by the hostFE() function shown in Listing 8.9, is nearly identical to the code shown in Listing 6.29.

The single most significant difference between the two programs is in *device memory management*: Whereas in Listing 6.29, a single allocation and deallocation are required for the one-time kernel launch, in this section multiple kernel invocations have to be carried out. Multiple allocations/deallocations would severely penalize performance in this case. For this reason, the maximum amount of global device memory that could be ever needed is allocated *a priori* (function CUDAmem-Setup(), lines 358-363). Based on the width (resX) of the region to be processed by hostFE(), the memory pitch (ptc) is calculated on the fly (lines 375-377) in order to keep memory accesses coalesced.

```
308   // File : mandelbrot_hybrid/kernel.cu
309   ...
310   static const int BLOCK_SIDE = 16;        // size of 2D block of threads
311
312   // *********************************************************
313   __device__ int diverge (double cx, double cy, int MAXITER)
314   {
315     int iter = 0;
316     double vx = cx, vy = cy, tx, ty;
317     while (iter < MAXITER && (vx * vx + vy * vy) < 4)
318       {
319         tx = vx * vx - vy * vy + cx;
320         ty = 2 * vx * vy + cy;
321         vx = tx;
322         vy = ty;
323         iter++;
324       }
325     return iter;
326   }
327
328   // *********************************************************
329   __global__ void mandelKernel (unsigned *d_res, double upperX, double ↩
         upperY, double stepX, double stepY, int resX, int resY, int pitch,↩
         int MAXITER)
330   {
331     int myX, myY;
332     myX = blockIdx.x * blockDim.x + threadIdx.x;
333     myY = blockIdx.y * blockDim.y + threadIdx.y;
334     if (myX >= resX || myY >= resY)
335       return;
336
337     double tempx, tempy;
338     tempx = upperX + myX * stepX;
339     tempy = upperY - myY * stepY;
340     int color = diverge (tempx, tempy, MAXITER);
```

```
341     d_res[myY * pitch/sizeof(int) + myX] = color;
342   }
343
344   //**********************************************************
345   int maxResX = 0;
346   int maxResY = 0;
347   int pitch = 0;
348   unsigned int *h_res;
349   unsigned int *d_res;
350   //**********************************************************
351   extern "C" void CUDAmemCleanup ()
352   {
353     CUDA_CHECK_RETURN (cudaFreeHost (h_res));
354     CUDA_CHECK_RETURN (cudaFree (d_res));
355   }
356
357   //**********************************************************
358   extern "C" unsigned int *CUDAmemSetup (int maxResX, int maxResY)
359   {
360     CUDA_CHECK_RETURN (cudaMallocPitch ((void **) &d_res, (size_t *) & ↩
            pitch, maxResX * sizeof (unsigned), maxResY));
361     CUDA_CHECK_RETURN (cudaHostAlloc (&h_res, maxResY * pitch, ↩
            cudaHostAllocMapped ));
362     return h_res;
363   }
364
365   //**********************************************************
366   // Host front-end function that allocates the memory and launches the ↩
         GPU kernel
367   extern "C" void hostFE (double upperX, double upperY, double lowerX, ↩
         double lowerY, int resX, int resY, unsigned int **pixels, int *↩
         currpitch, int MAXITER)
368   {
369     int blocksX, blocksY;
370     blocksX = (int) ceil (resX * 1.0/ BLOCK_SIDE);
371     blocksY = (int) ceil (resY * 1.0/ BLOCK_SIDE);
372     dim3 block (BLOCK_SIDE, BLOCK_SIDE);
373     dim3 grid (blocksX, blocksY);
374
375     int ptc = 32;
376     while (ptc < resX * sizeof (unsigned))
377       ptc += 32;
378
379     double stepX = (lowerX - upperX) / resX;
380     double stepY = (upperY - lowerY) / resY;
381
382     // launch GPU kernel
383     mandelKernel <<< grid, block >>> (d_res, upperX, upperY, stepX, ↩
            stepY, resX, resY, ptc, MAXITER);
384
385     // get the results
```

```
386    CUDA_CHECK_RETURN (cudaMemcpy (h_res, d_res, resY * ptc, ↩
           cudaMemcpyDeviceToHost ));
387    *pixels = h_res;
388    *currpitch = ptc;
389    }
```

LISTING 8.9

Kernel and front-end functions used for carrying out the GPU computations.

Our program was tested on a Linux platform, equipped with a third-generation i7 3770 processor overclocked at 4.2 GHz, 32 GB of DDR3 RAM, and a GTX 560 Ti GPU card clocked at 1645 MHz and having 1 GB of DDR5 RAM. Figure 8.15 illustrates the average timing results over 10 runs for the generation of 100 frames at HD resolution (1920x1080). The starting frame was set to a maximum iteration limit of 100, and the ending frame was set to a maximum iteration limit of 10,000.

Figure 8.15 clearly illustrates the superior computation capability of the GPU (even a very modest one as the GTX 560 Ti chip), since the GPU achieves a 2.5x reduction in execution time over a fully utilized quad-core hyperthreaded CPU. But then again, such a result was probably expected.

The real finding of this experiment is that even with such a performance disparity, the *CPU can assist the GPU* processing the workload: A 24% decrease in execution time is nontrivial. Hence, a hybrid design should be pursued whenever possible.

In conclusion, the preceding configuration for the hybrid computation of the Mandelbrot set is one of many possible designs. For example, the task queue/tuple space can be active and not passive, i.e., it could detect/pick the tasks appropriate

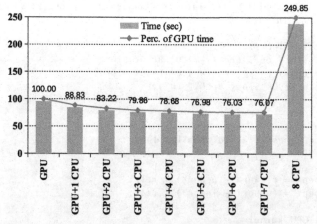

FIGURE 8.15

Average execution time (bars) for the calculation of a 100-frame full-HD resolution sequence for a variety of thread configurations. The line and number labels represent the time as a percentage of the execution time achieved by the GPU alone.

for a type of machine and "push" them along, in contrast to the "pull" setup described above. Although our design is not a tuplespace approach, it does illustrate the potential of this paradigm, and it can hopefully spark ideas about improved hybrid/heterogeneous computation designs.

Additionally, several improvement could be incorporated into this initial approach. For example, preallocation and explicit memory management of the `MandelRegion` objects would eliminate much of the host-memory allocation overhead. However, this and others potential improvements go beyond the scope of the application at hand, which was meant as a concept illustration tool.

8.5.2 DISTRIBUTED BLOCK CIPHER ENCRYPTION: A CASE STUDY IN STATIC LOAD BALANCING

The problem of encrypting large volumes of data on a cluster of GPU nodes using the AES algorithm has been explored in Section 6.12.2. In that case study, a dynamic load-balancing approach that involved a handshake between the master and worker nodes was utilized, but with only mediocre results. In this section we extend this work by balancing the load statically. The analysis is generic enough to apply to any block cipher and not just AES.

In Section 4.21 we examined the problem of statically partitioning a 2^{56}-sized key space in a quest to decrypt a DES-encrypted ciphertext. The DES, brute-force cracking case study featured a partitioning scheme that assigned equal parts of the key space to every compute node, regardless of their relative power. This is an obvious shortcoming that can compromise performance.

Here we tackle the balancing problem by using divisible load analysis. The first step, as mentioned in Section 8.3, is to establish the cost model parameters that relate input size and execution time. This comes down to encrypting plaintexts of varying sizes and determining the corresponding execution time. The results averaged over 100 runs are shown in Figure 8.16.[17] It is clear that a linear or affine model is not a good fit to the entirety of either the CPU or the GPU curves. What is intriguing is that the GPU is way slower than the CPU for small to medium-sized messages, compromised by the need to transfer the data over the PCI Express bus. It is not until 16 MB inputs are used that the GPU starts to offer a tangible advantage.

The curves can be considered piecewise linear as for the range of $[2, 256]MB$ for the CPU and $[16, 256]MB$ for the GPU, a line is a reasonable approximation, with:

$$t_{CPU} = 6.504 \cdot 10^{-9} \frac{sec}{Byte} L + 0.00269 sec \tag{8.43}$$

and

$$t_{GPU} = 2.4779 \cdot 10^{-9} \frac{sec}{Byte} L + 0.0480 sec \tag{8.44}$$

---

[17]The execution platform, both hardware- and software-wise, is identical to the one used in Section 6.12.2.

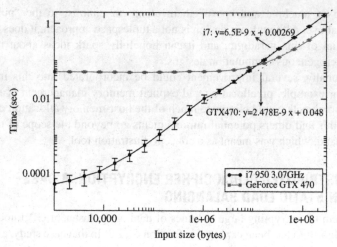

FIGURE 8.16

Log-log graph of the average execution time on a CPU core and a GPU versus the plaintext size. Message sizes range from 2^{10} to 2^{28} *bytes* in exponential steps. Error bars correspond to the standard deviation for the associated set of experiments.

where L is the plaintext size.

These ranges are suitable for our analysis, since we will be breaking up the input into larger chunks than the ones used in Section 6.12.2. Furthermore, these line equations suit the computation model of Equation 8.5, i.e., $t_{comp} = p_i(part_iL + e_i)$, if we use:

$$p_{CPU} = 6.504 \cdot 10^{-9} \frac{s}{B} \text{ and } e_{CPU} = \frac{00269s}{6.504 \cdot 10^{-9}s/B} = 413260B \qquad (8.45)$$

$$p_{GPU} = 2.4779 \cdot 10^{-9} \frac{s}{B} \text{ and } e_{GPU} = \frac{0480s}{2.4779 \cdot 10^{-9}s/B} = 19376844B \qquad (8.46)$$

A similar procedure (via a ping-pong program; see Exercise 4 in Chapter 5) can produce the communication model parameters. For MPI processes running on the same i7 950 host, we get a least-squares line: $y = 1.244 \cdot 10^{-10} \cdot x + 9.217 \cdot 10^{-7}$. This line equation translates to the following communication parameters: $l = 1.244 \cdot 10^{-10}s/B$ and $b = d = 7409B$.

If one-port, single-installment distribution and block-type computation were chosen (e.g., by using MPI_Ssend calls for distributing the workload), and since b and d are small enough to be ignored, the problem setting would fit the "image processing" class of problems that have known DLT solutions, as identified in Appendix F.1.3. In that case, we could use the methods described in Appendix F as part of the DLTlib to calculate the partitioning.

In this section we follow an alternative route by using parallel I/O operations for all workers, making the communication configuration a N-port, single-installment, block-type computation one. The program in the case study of Section 6.12.2 reads the whole input file in the local memory of the master node before distributing the pieces to the workers on a first-come, first-served basis. In this section we calculate the single-piece-per-worker part of the input using DLT analysis and communicate to the workers only the start index and length of their assignment, i.e., only a description of which part of the input they are supposed to process. Each worker then proceeds to perform I/O in parallel. The cost of communicating the assignment descriptions is insignificant relevant to the massive I/O costs incurred, and for this reason it can be safely ignored.

As the I/O for both the distribution and collection phases is done in parallel, we can apply the analysis of Section 8.3.3.1 and Equations 8.12 and 8.13. The reasoning is that the bulk of the communications concerns I/O operations done in parallel and thus the sequence of events matches the one shown in Figure 8.17. Adapting Equations 8.12 and 8.13 to our particular problem means setting the parameters as follows: $a = 1, c = 1, l_i = l$. Also given that there is no master node as far as the I/O is concerned, so that node 0 in our setting is the equivalent of worker 1 in Equations 8.12 and 8.13, we can simplify them to:

$$(8.12) \Rightarrow part_i = part_0 \frac{2 \cdot l + p_0}{2 \cdot l + p_i} + \frac{p_0 e_0 - p_i e_i}{L(2 \cdot l + p_i)} \tag{8.47}$$

and

$$(8.13) \Rightarrow part_0 = \frac{1 + \sum_{j=1}^{N-1} \frac{p_j e_j - p_0 e_0}{L(2 \cdot l + p_j)}}{(2 \cdot l + p_0) \sum_{j=0}^{N-1} \left(2 \cdot l + p_j\right)^{-1}} \tag{8.48}$$

It should be noted that l, as measured by the ping-pong process *on the same host*, corresponds essentially to a memory-to-memory copy. This is sufficient for

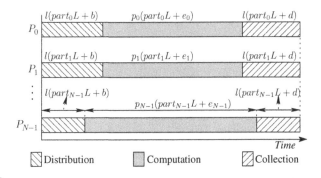

FIGURE 8.17

An illustration of the optimum N-port, single-installment, block-type computation configuration for block-cipher encryption.

our testing/benchmarking purposes, since the operating system disk cache typically ends up holding the entire input file. As a result, repeated tests with the same input read only from memory and not from the hard drive. Special management of the disk cache (e.g., clearing it prior to every single test) should be conducted if the "communication" parameters are supposed to reflect real-life scenarios.

The implementation of Equations 8.47 and 8.48 is given in Listing 8.10.

```cpp
// File : AES_MPI_nodatacopy/partition.cpp
...
// **********************************************************************
// Returns the predicted execution time
// and the calculated parts in array part[]
double nPortPartition(double *p, double *e, long L, double l, double b↩
    , double d, double *part, int N)
{
    // temporary arrays for speeding-up the calculation
    double lacp[N];
    double sumTerms[N];

    lacp[0]=1.0/p[0];
    for(int i=1;i<N;i++)
        lacp[i] = 1.0/(l*2+p[i]);

    // sumTerms[0] is not utilized
    for(int i=1;i<N;i++)
        sumTerms[i] = (p[0]*e[0] - p[i]*e[i]-l*(b+d)) * lacp[i] / L;

    // calculate the nominator and denominator for finding part_0
    double nomin=1, denom=0;
    for(int i=1;i<N;i++)
    {
        nomin -= sumTerms[i];
        denom += lacp[i];
    }
    denom*=p[0];
    denom++;

    part[0] = nomin/denom;

    // calculate the other parts now
    for(int i=1;i<N;i++)
        part[i] = part[0] * p[0]*lacp[i] + sumTerms[i];

    // sanity check - always a good idea!
    double sum=0;
    for(int i=0;i<N;i++)
        sum += part[i];
    assert(fabs(sum -1)<0.001);

    // return the exec. time
    return l*(2*part[0] + b+d) + p[0]*(part[0]*L+e[0]);
}
```

```
45   // ****************************************************************
46   // returns the assigned load in array assign[], that are multiples of ↵
         quantum (assuming L is also a multiple of quantum)
47   void quantize(double *part, long L, int quantum, int N, long *assign)
48   {
49       int totAssigned=0;
50       for(int i=1;i<N;i++)
51       {
52         // truncate the parts assigned to all workers but node 0
53         assign[i] = ((long)floor(part[i]*L/quantum))*quantum;
54         totAssigned += assign[i];    // accummulate
55       }
56       // node 0 gets everything else
57       assign[0] = L - totAssigned;
58   }
```

LISTING 8.10

Code implementing the DLT partitioning Equations 8.47 and 8.48.

The function `nPortPartition()` is called by node 0 (it would be superficial to call it the master node), followed by a call to function `quantize()` so that the parts to be assigned are integer multiples of the load "quantum," which in our case is a 16-byte-long block (AES processes data in 16-byte blocks).

Before the optimum partitioning can be calculated, node 0 collects from every other node their respective p and e parameters. In our code, these parameters are hardcoded in the source code targeting the different types of nodes: There is a dedicated source code file for GPU and CPU nodes. There are many alternatives to having fixed, *a priori* determined computing parameters:

- p and e can be derived online by, for example, having each node calculate them based on the outcome of processing a small part of the data.
- Interpolation or extrapolation could be used to estimate p and e based on the parameters of a prototypical node. For example, if $p_{10\ SM} = 1$ for a GPU having 10 SMs, another GPU of the same architecture (e.g., Kepler) and clock frequency, with 20 SMs, could be estimated as having $p_{20\ SM} = 0.5$ (i.e., twice as fast).
- A database could be used to hold the past performance of each node and use these figures to estimate p and e.

The `quantize()` function in lines 47-58 truncates the load assigned to all worker nodes indexed between 1 and $N - 1$, leaving the rest of the load to be assigned to node 0, assuming that node 0 is a GPU. This is not the optimum procedure for this task. More elaborate algorithms are described in [12] and implemented in DLTlib.

A large portion of the source code is shared with the project of Section 6.12.2. The only difference, apart from the addition of the partitioning functions described above, is the `main` function structure as shown in Listing 8.11.

```
59   // File : AES_MPI_nodatacopy/main.cpp
60   // Assumes that the encryption will take place on GPU nodes
61   ...
62   #include "rijndael.h"
63   #include "partition.cpp"
64
65   using namespace std;
66
67   #define TAG_MODEL 0
68   #define TAG_WORK 1
69
70   const double modelParams[]={2.477876056907E-009, 19376843.5401888}; //←
         p_i and e_i
71   const double l= 1.2441013041013E-010;  // speed for a single transfer
72   const double b= 7408.7996426914;
73   const double d= 7408.7996426914;
74
75   static const int keybits = 256;
76
77   //*********************************************************************
78   int main (int argc, char *argv[])
79   {
80     int rank;
81     unsigned char *iobuf;
82
83     int lSize = 0;
84     FILE *f;
85
86     int comm_size = 0;
87     MPI_Status status;
88     MPI_Init (&argc, &argv);
89     MPI_Comm_rank (MPI_COMM_WORLD, &rank);
90     MPI_Comm_size (MPI_COMM_WORLD, &comm_size);
91     MPI_Request req;
92     MPI_Status stat;
93
94
95     if (argc < 4)
96       {
97         if (rank == 0)
98           fprintf (stderr, "Usage : %s inputfile outputfile ←
                 threadsPerBlock\n", argv[0]);
99
100        exit (1);
101      }
102
103    //encryption key
104    unsigned char key[32] = { 1, 2, 3, 4, 5, 6, 7, 8, 9, 10, 11, 12, 13,←
             14, 15, 16, 17, 18, 19, 20, 21, 22, 23, 24, 25, 26, 27, 28, 29,←
             30, 31, 32 };
105    u32 rk[RKLENGTH (keybits)];
106    rijndaelSetupEncrypt (rk, key, keybits);
```

```
107
108    // node 0 is reserved for the GPU
109    if (rank == 0)
110      {
111        if ((f = fopen (argv[1], "r")) == NULL)
112          {
113              fprintf (stderr, "Can't open %s\n", argv[1]);
114              exit (EXIT_FAILURE);
115          }
116
117        fseek (f, 0, SEEK_END);
118        lSize = ftell (f);
119        rewind (f);
120
121        // allocate the arrays needed for calculating the partitioning
122        double *p=new double[comm_size];
123        double *e=new double[comm_size];
124        double *part=new double[comm_size];
125        long *assignment = new long[comm_size];
126        long *offset = new long[comm_size];
127        long *indLenPairs = new long[comm_size*2];
128        MPI_Request *rq = new  MPI_Request[comm_size];
129
130        // get the characteristics of each node
131        p[0] = modelParams[0];
132        e[0] = modelParams[1];
133        double temp[2];
134        for(int i=1;i<comm_size;i++)
135          {
136              MPI_Recv (temp, 2, MPI_DOUBLE, MPI_ANY_SOURCE, TAG_MODEL, ←
                      MPI_COMM_WORLD, &stat);
137              int idx = stat.MPI_SOURCE;
138              p[idx] = temp[0];
139              e[idx] = temp[1];
140          }
141        // calculate the assignment. Communication speed is divided ←
                between the N−1 workers
142        double predTime = nPortPartition(p, e, lSize, l*(comm_size−1), b←
                , d, part, comm_size);
143
144        quantize(part, lSize, 16, comm_size, assignment);
145
146        // calculate the start_offset, length of the assignment parts
147        long pos = 0;
148        for(int i=0;i<comm_size;i++)
149          {
150              indLenPairs[2*i] = pos;
151              indLenPairs[2*i+1] = assignment[i];
152              pos +=assignment[i];
153          }
154
155        // communicate the assigned plaintext start_off, length pairs
```

```
156        for(int i=1;i<comm_size;i++)
157            MPI_Isend (indLenPairs +2*i, 2, MPI_LONG, i, TAG_WORK, ↵
                   MPI_COMM_WORLD, &req);
158
159
160        iobuf = new unsigned char[assignment[0]];
161        assert (iobuf != NULL);
162        fread (iobuf, 1, assignment[0], f);
163        fclose (f);
164
165        // process part0 of the input on the GPU
166        int thrPerBlock = atoi (argv[3]);
167        rijndaelEncryptFE (rk, keybits, iobuf, iobuf, assignment[0], ↵
                   thrPerBlock);
168
169        rijndaelShutdown ();
170
171        FILE *fout;
172        if ((fout = fopen (argv[2], "w")) == NULL)
173          {
174            fprintf (stderr, "Can't open %s\n", argv[2]);
175            exit (EXIT_FAILURE);
176          }
177        fwrite(iobuf, 1, assignment[0], fout);
178        fclose (fout);
179
180        MPI_Barrier(MPI_COMM_WORLD);
181
182        delete[] p;
183        delete[] e;
184        delete[] part;
185        delete[] assignment;
186        delete[] offset;
187        delete[] rq;
188        delete[] indLenPairs;
189      }
190    else                            // GPU worker
191      {
192        long indLenPairs[2];
193
194        // send model parameters
195        MPI_Send ((void*)modelParams, 2, MPI_DOUBLE, 0, TAG_MODEL, ↵
                   MPI_COMM_WORLD);
196
197        // get size of assignment and allocate appropriate buffer
198        MPI_Recv (indLenPairs, 2, MPI_LONG, 0, TAG_WORK, MPI_COMM_WORLD,↵
                   &stat);
199
200        long jobSize = indLenPairs[1];
201        iobuf = new unsigned char[jobSize];
202        FILE *f;
203        if ((f = fopen (argv[1], "r")) == NULL)
```

```
204        {
205            fprintf (stderr, "Can't open %s\n", argv[1]);
206            exit (EXIT_FAILURE);
207        }
208      fseek(f, indLenPairs[0], SEEK_SET);
209      fread(iobuf, 1, indLenPairs[1], f);
210      fclose (f);
211
212      int thrPerBlock = atoi (argv[3]);
213
214      rijndaelEncryptFE (rk, keybits, iobuf, iobuf, jobSize, ↩
             thrPerBlock);
215      rijndaelShutdown ();
216
217      FILE *fout;
218      if ((fout = fopen (argv[2], "w")) == NULL)
219        {
220            fprintf (stderr, "Can't open %s\n", argv[2]);
221            exit (EXIT_FAILURE);
222        }
223      fseek(f, indLenPairs[0], SEEK_SET);
224      fwrite(iobuf, 1, jobSize, fout);
225      fclose (fout);
226
227      MPI_Barrier(MPI_COMM_WORLD);
228    }
229  ...
```

LISTING 8.11

Main module, holding the logic to be executed by GPU nodes.

We have already outlined the steps involved in the execution of this program. The following list contains the main points of Listing 8.11 in more detail:

- Node 0 is using the loop of lines 134-140 to collect the p and e parameters of all nodes and populate the p[] and e[] arrays defined in lines 122,123.
- The p and e parameters of each node are held in the modelParams array, defined in line 70. The array is convenient for allowing easy communication of said parameters in lines 195 (sender) and 136 (receiver).
- Node 0 calculates the parts that should be assigned to each node (lines 142-144) and then converts these figures to (start-index, length) integer pairs that identify which part of the input data each node will process (lines 147-153).
- The (start-index, length) pairs are stored in the same array (indLenPairs) in consecutive positions (lines 150,151) for easy communication to the worker nodes (lines 156,157).
- The communication of the (start-index, length) pairs could be also done by a MPI_Scatter call. The MPI_Isend calls in line 157 allow node 0 to proceed to the actual input processing sooner.

- The input processing takes place on the GPU via a call to the front-end function `rijndaelEncryptFE()`.
- Once a node has the details of its assignment (past line 198 for nodes other than 0), it allocates the necessary memory (lines 160 and 201) and reads the input data (lines 162 and 209).
- The input data buffer is also used to hold the ciphertext result, which is stored in the proper location of the output file (lines 177 for node 0 and 223, 224 for all the others).

A file similar to the one shown in Listing 8.11, targeting CPU execution is also supplied in the project directory (`AES_MPI_nodatacopy/mainCPUWorker.cpp`). Its only differences are the values of the *p* and *e* constants as defined in line 70 and the use of a plain `for` loop to go over the assigned part of the input in 16-byte blocks.

The actual code, part of which is shown in Listing 8.11, contains statements for measuring the execution time. These lines are not shown for brevity.

The program can be executed by utilizing an application file so that the GPU can be reserved by a single process, avoiding unnecessary resource contentions. For example, if we were to run four processes on a host, one utilizing the GPU, we would create an application file similar to:

```
# GPU node 0
-host 127.0.0.1 -np 1 aesMPI in512 cipher 256

# 3 more CPU nodes
-host 127.0.0.1 -np 3 aesMPICPUWorker in512 cipher 256
```

and execute the program by calling:

```
$ mpirun --app applFile
```

The expected command-line parameters are the input filename, the output filename, and the number of threads per block, the latter being essential for the GPU node only.

Figure 8.18 compares the averaged-over-100-runs performance results of the parallel I/O design, with DLT-based partitioning outlined in this section, against the dynamic load-balancing design of Section 6.12.2 running on the same hardware, i.e., a i7 950 processor clocked at 3.07 GHz with 8 GB of DDR2 RAM and a GTX 470 GPU card clocked at 1260 MHz and having 1280 MB of DDR5 RAM.

Two observations can be made on the static load-balancing curve of Figure 8.18: First, the addition of CPU workers beyond the first one does not contribute to the reduction of the execution time. Actually (although practically invisible on the figure itself), the average for one GPU and three CPU workers is slightly higher than the one for one GPU and two CPU workers (4.71s vs. 4.69s). Second, the variability of the execution times increases as the number of nodes increases, as indicated by the standard deviation bars.

Both of these observations can be attributed to a single cause: MPI process start-up delays. Process spawning is a much more expensive operation than the creation of a thread. Because the processes that make up the application start at different times

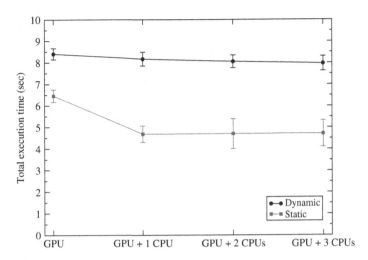

FIGURE 8.18

Average total execution times and corresponding standard deviation for dynamic and static load balancing to encrypt 512 MB of data.

(something we do not account for in our analysis), the overall execution duration can vary wildly, causing the evaporation of any performance gains the exact partitioning would afford.

The results do not constitute a good basis for comparing the static and dynamic load-balancing strategies, given the different approaches in I/O management, in the sense that they do not allow generic conclusions to be drawn. However, they do show that static load-balancing performs well while minimizing communication overheads. It is quite possible to mix the two strategies by, for example, adapting performance metrics between execution rounds.

Ideally, a software engineer should evaluate the circumstances of the execution platform, e.g., machine load and resource availability (such as memory) variations in a multiuser environment, network traffic, etc., and the application requirements to establish the best strategy for minimizing the execution time.

EXERCISES

1. Design a brute-force/exhaustive algorithm for determining the optimum subset of N nodes/processors in the case of static load balancing. What is the complexity of your algorithm?
2. Design a greedy algorithm for determining the optimum subset of N nodes/processors in the case of static load balancing. Will you always get the same solution as the one provided by an exhaustive algorithm?
3. The closed-form solutions in Section 8.3.3.1 for the N-port communication setup are based on the assumption that the master participates in the processing

of the load. Derive the equations that would govern the solution if the master abstained from this task, facilitating only I/O functionality instead.

4. Write a program that calculates $part_0$ from Equations 8.11 and 8.39 in a linear number of steps.

5. Solve the example at the end of Section 8.3.3.2 by reversing the computing power of the nodes: $p_0 = 3 \cdot 1.631 \cdot 10^{-07}$, $p_1 = 3 \cdot (1.631 \cdot 10^{-07})$, $p_2 = 2 \cdot (1.631 \cdot 10^{-07})$, and $p_3 = (1.631 \cdot 10^{-07})$.

6. An alternative to having the master node distribute the load is to have all the nodes access a network filesystem and retrieve the data from there. What kind of communication configuration would correspond to such an arrangement? Calculate the partitioning that would be produced in this case for the same problem setting as the previous question.

7. The partitioning performed using DLT in the kernel convolution example returns the percentage of the input bytes that should be assigned to each node. How can we convert this number to pixels? One may argue that we should instead use image rows. How can we convert the result of our analysis to rows?

8. Use the `tiobench` utility available at http://sourceforge.net/projects/tiobench/ to measure the performance you can get by concurrent access to a network filesystem (e.g., a NFS volume). Calculate the collective throughput of the server versus the number of threads used.

9. One way to improve the distribution cost of input data is to compress them. What kind of compression algorithms could be used in this case? How could we adapt the cost models to reflect this change?

10. Use the DLTlib library to calculate the optimum partitioning for a "query processing" application, where the communication cost is independent of the workload, consisting of a query during distribution and the result during the collection. You can assume that $b = d = 1$, the workload consists of $L = 10^6$ items, and the parallel platform is made of 10 compute nodes connected in a single level tree, with $p_i = (i + 1) \cdot 0.01 sec/item$ $\forall i \in [0, 9]$ and $l = 0.001 sec/item$.
What would happen if the communication were 10 times slower?

11. Derive the equivalent of Equations 8.47 and 8.48 for arbitrary a and c, and implement them as part of a partitioning function.

12. The DLT examples presented in Sections 8.3.3.1 and 8.3.3.2, do not address an aspect of the problem which is significant : what is the optimum subset of nodes to use to process a load? Implement the heuristic algorithm you came up with in Exercise 2, to derive such a set.
Hint: nodes that should not be part of this set, get a negative load assignment $part_i$.

Compiling Qt programs

A.1 USING AN IDE

Using an Integrated Development Environment (IDE) is the best choice for beginning to explore Qt's functionality. Qt can be easily integrated with Eclipse or Microsoft's Visual Studio. One can also use the Qt Creator IDE supplied by Digia, which is a lightweight alternative to the aforementioned IDEs. The IDEs take care of the library dependencies and include directory locations that are needed for compiling a Qt program.

For experimenting with Qt threads, only a console application project needs to be created. The three initial steps for Qt Creator are shown in Figure A.1.

A.2 THE qmake UTILITY

The qmake utility (supplied as part of the Qt tool chain) solves the problem of tracking dependencies across different platforms. A short project description (in the form of a text file with a .pro extension) is all that is needed. For example, let's assume that a project consists of the following files:

```
main.cpp
client.cpp
calc.h
```

Then the .pro file (e.g., myapp.pro) has to contain the following self-explanatory directives:

```
CONFIG += qt
HEADERS += calc.h
SOURCES += main.cpp
SOURCES += client.cpp
TARGET = myapp
```

Running the qmake command:

```
$ qmake myapp.pro
```

will produce the Makefile necessary for compiling the source files and linking them with the required libraries (Qt). Running the qmake utility is necessary only when the set of files making up the project is modified (added to or removed from). Once qmake is run, every subsequent compilation of the project requires only an execution of the make utility.

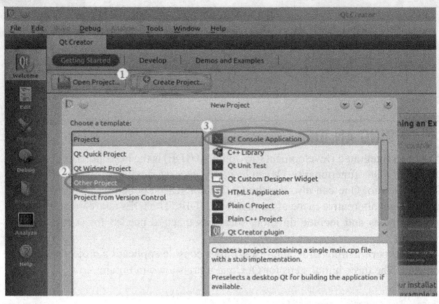

FIGURE A.1

Three initial steps for creating a console application in Qt Creator.

Note that Qt also provides a command-line utility called `qtpromaker` for automatically generating a project file. All one has to do is run `qtpromaker` inside the source code directory of a project. Subsequently, `qmake` can be used according to the previously described steps.

Running MPI programs: preparatory and configuration steps

B

B.1 PREPARATORY STEPS

The problem with having a Network of Workstations (*NoW*) as a parallel platform is that each of the workstations must provide a mechanism for remotely starting a process. The usual way of doing this is, either through Remote Shell (RSH), or through Secure Shell (SSH). The former is obsolete because it is highly insecure (passwords are communicated in plaintext form).

SSH would normally require an interactive login process to take place on each of the workstations in order for a MPI program to execute! This lengthy and tedious procedure can be avoided by having an authentication agent perform the login transaction on our behalf. The following steps achieve this goal:

1. Create an authentication key, i.e., a number that will uniquely identify your user account:

   ```
   $ ssh—keygen —t dsa
   ```

   You will be prompt for a pass phrase that controls access to your keys. This does not have to be the same as your user account password. The `ssh-keygen` command generates two files holding a public and a secret key, respectively (the $\sim$ sign represents your home directory):

   ```
   ~/.ssh/id_dsa
   ~/.ssh/id_dsa.pub
   ```

2. Copy the public key `~/.ssh/id_dsa.pub` file:

   ```
   $ cp ~/.ssh/id_dsa.pub ~/.ssh/authorized_keys2
   ```

3. Make sure that the copied file has the correct permissions:

   ```
   $ chmod go—rwx ~/.ssh/authorized_keys2
   ```

4. Steps 1-3 have to be done only once (unless you forget the pass phrase!). Before each MPI session, you need to start the agent program:

   ```
   $ ssh—agent bash
   ```

or

```
$ ssh-agent $SHELL
```

5. Handing over the keys to the agent is done via the command:

```
$ ssh-add
```

Now you are almost ready to run your first parallel program. Using a Network of Workstations as a parallel platform entails one more step, outlined in the next section.

B.2 COMPUTING NODES DISCOVERY FOR MPI PROGRAM DEPLOYMENT

Deploying an MPI program over a NoWs requires a list of the corresponding IP addresses or DNS names. For the lucky few who have access to dedicated clusters or supercomputing facilities, the problem of node availability is largely solved and governed by the policies of their institution. However, when a generic intranet with dynamic-IP machines is utilized, the list of machines might have to be compiled again every time prior to the launch of a program. This section describes the steps that can be used for the generation of this list.

B.2.1 HOST DISCOVERY WITH THE nmap UTILITY

The **Network Map**per (nmap) program is a security scanner developed to discover hosts and the services they support on a computer network. It has been primarily used for vulnerability detection, and as such it has been used by both system administrators (for securing systems) and hackers (for breaking in). For this reason, the use of nmap over an intranet may be monitored and/or controlled. It is a good idea to discuss your planned fair use of nmap with your site sysadmin before attempting the commands and scripts that are described here.

For the problem at hand, nmap will be used to detect the hosts available in a user-supplied range of IPs and enumerate the open ports on these machines. The latter is needed for safe identification of the machines that run sshd, since the OS detection supported by nmap is not always accurate. Additionally, for security reasons many operating systems spoof their replies to the calls nmap uses to deduce their identities.

If we assume that the machines that will be used to run our MPI program lie in the IP ranges of 10.25.32.* and 10.25.34.*, then the following sequence will produce a list of machine that are candidates for deployment:

```
$ nmap -oG hosts 10.25.32.* 10.25.34.*
$ grep ssh hosts | gawk -F " " '{print $2}' > hostsWithSSH
```

The -oG switch of the first line is used to save the output of nmap to a file (hosts is specified) in a text format that can be filtered with the grep utility. The next command line does just that, i.e., it filters the output for lines containing `ssh`. These are in turn passed to the `gawk` utility for extracting their second column, which contains the IP of the corresponding host.

The hosts can be subsequently verified, i.e., the user credentials are appropriate for logging on, via the following line, which attempts to run an `echo` command in each of them:

```
$ for f in `cat hostsWithSSH`; do ssh $f echo $f; done
```

This line should be attempted only after the SSH agent has started, as shown in Section B.1.

B.2.2 AUTOMATIC GENERATION OF A HOSTFILE

A MPI hostfile can potentially hold the number of processes each of the hosts can support. An obvious reason for doing this is to maximize the hosts' utilization, since the number of cores can be incorporated into MPI's deployment process.

The following script combines the steps explained in the previous section and the information available in the `/proc` pseudo-filesystem of Linux to automatically generate an appropriate hostfile:

```
1  #!/bin/bash
2  # File: hostBuild.sh
3
4  tmpFile=/tmp/hosts_`whoami`
5  tmpFile2=/tmp/hosts2_`whoami`
6
7  # Discover all the hosts matching the supplied IP pattern(s)
8  nmap -oG ${tmpFile} $* >/dev/null
9
10 # Get the IP of the localhost. It has to participate in the launch
11 ifconfig | head -n 2 | tail -n 1 | gawk -F "addr:" '{print $2}' | gawk↩
       '{print $1}' > ${tmpFile2}
12
13 # Filter out the hosts not supporting SSH
14 grep ssh ${tmpFile} | gawk -F " " '{print $2}' >> ${tmpFile2}
15
16 # Remove -if it exists- a duplicate entry for localhost
17 uniq ${tmpFile2} ${tmpFile}
18
19 # Get the cores for each host in the temporary file
20 for h in `cat ${tmpFile}`
21 do
22     res=`ssh -o ConnectTimeout=5 -o BatchMode=yes -o ↩
           StrictHostKeyChecking=no $h cat /proc/cpuinfo | grep processor↩
           | wc | gawk '{print $1}'`
23
24     # Output the IP only if there is a valid response from the ↩
           previous command
```

```
25        if [ "${res:-0}" -ne 0 ]
26           then
27              echo "$h slots= ${res}"
28        fi
29   done
```

The lines that constitute something new in the preceding script are the following:

- Line 11: Inserts the IP of the host running the script to the hostfile.
- Line 17: Uses the uniq utility to remove any duplicate entries from the hostfile. This involves only the localhost.
- Lines 20-29: The loop iterates over all entries in the temporary hostfile and outputs the ones that respond to the command issued via ssh in line 22.
- Line 22: Runs the ssh command noninteractively (-o BatchMode=yes) with a maximum waiting period of 5 seconds (-o ConnectTimeout=5) and without performing strict key checking (-o StrictHostKeyChecking=no). Each host is required to run the cat /proc/cpuinfo | grep processor | wc | gawk '{print $1}' pipeline, which, if successful, returns the number of cores as recognized by the operating system. Note that there is no distinction between hyperthreaded cores and those that are not hyperthreaded.

The script can be simply used in the fashion shown in the following example, i.e., by providing a space-separated list of IP patterns and redirecting the output to a file:

```
$ bash hostBuild.sh 10.25.32.* 10.25.34.*  > myHosts
```

Time measurement

C.1 INTRODUCTION

High-resolution measurement of time is a critical capability for calculating performance and keeping track of events in your system, e.g., for debugging purposes. After all, the bottom line is how much time we can gain by introducing threads, GPU computation and the like in an application.

Time measurement can be identified as absolute or relative. The concept of absolute or universal time dates back to Isaac Newton, and many will argue that in the post-general-relativity era there is no such thing as absolute time! In our context, absolute time has no place either, since we are concerned with time spans, as in relative time.

A common pattern that is used in all the sections that follow is that of subtracting timestamps. The time functions that are provided by the various libraries typically measure time from a fixed point, e.g., the beginning of program execution, the boot-up time of the system, or the distance to a fixed point in time (usually 00:00 Jan 1, 1970).

It should be noted that *system clocks can be modified by time adjustments performed by the operating system.* Many systems run daemons that periodically synchronize the system time with Internet time servers via the NTP protocol. Real-time clock adjustments are typically done once on a daily basis, but they can produce wild time differences, e.g., very big or even negative ones! In such an event, the results should be discarded as bogus and the experiment repeated.

C.2 POSIX HIGH-RESOLUTION TIMING

POSIX (Portable Operating System Interface for UniX) is an IEEE standard that defines a set of APIs. POSIX was designed to provide cross-platform compatibility at the source-code level. Programs written to use POSIX functions can be recompiled and executed in any system offering POSIX compatibility.

POSIX defines a set of functions for high-resolution timing:

```
int clock_getres(clockid_t clk_id, struct timespec *res);  // returns ↩
    the clock resolution of the specified clock

int clock_gettime(clockid_t clk_id, struct timespec *tp);  // return ↩
    the time according to the specified clock
```

The functions are defined in header file `time.h`, and the `-lrt` switch has to be used during the linking process of a program.

Both functions return 0 for success and -1 for failure, and they operate on a pair of parameters of these types:

- `clockid_t`: An integer identifying the clock to be queried. A number of clocks can be supported, either systemwide or process, or even thread-specific. The most important ones, represented by symbolic constants, are:
  - `CLOCK_REALTIME`: Systemwide real-time clock.
  - `CLOCK_MONOTONIC`: Represents time since an unspecified starting point.
  - `CLOCK_PROCESS_CPUTIME_ID`: Process-specific timer.
- `struct timespec`: Contains two integer fields representing seconds and a fraction of a second, the second field in nanosecond units:

```
struct timespec {
    time_t   tv_sec;        /* seconds */
    long     tv_nsec;       /* nanoseconds */
};
```

So, given an instance of `ts` of `struct timespec`, the time is `ts.tv_sec + ts.tv_nsec/1000000000.0`.

Equipped with these functions, we can write a set of functions for conveniently measuring the time instance of events from a specified moment in time. The time can be expressed in nanoseconds as an integer or in seconds as a floating-point quantity, as shown in Listing C.1.

```
1   // File: clock_example.cpp
2   . . .
3   #include <time.h>
4
5   long time0_nsec = 0;
6
7   double time0_sec = 0;
8
9   // ************************************************
10  double hrclock_sec ()
11  {
12    timespec ts;
13    clock_gettime (CLOCK_REALTIME, &ts);
14    double aux = ts.tv_sec + ts.tv_nsec / 1000000000.0;
15    return aux — time0_sec;
16  }
17
18  // ************************************************
19
20  long hrclock_nsec ()
```

```
21  {
22    timespec ts;
23    clock_gettime (CLOCK_REALTIME, &ts);
24    long aux = ts.tv_sec * 1000000000 + ts.tv_nsec;
25    return aux - time0_nsec;
26  }
27
28  // ************************************************
29
30  int main ()
31  {
32    time0_nsec = hrclock_nsec ();
33
34    time0_sec = hrclock_sec ();
35    sleep (1);
36    cout << hrclock_nsec () << endl;
37    cout << hrclock_sec () << endl;
38    return 0;
39  };
```

LISTING C.1

An example of how the POSIX high-resolution timing functions can be utilized to measure execution times. The hrclock_sec (hrclock_nsec) function returns the time since the time0_sec (time0_nsec) variable was initialized in seconds (nanoseconds).

C.3 TIMING IN QT

Qt provides a convenient class for timing events: QTime. The most useful methods supported are:

```
void QTime::start();    // Set the time in the QTime object to the ←
    current time.
int QTime::elapsed (); // Returns the number of milliseconds passed ←
    since the previous call to start() of restart().
int QTime::restart (); // Set the time in the QTime object to the ←
    current time, and returns the elapsed time in milliseconds since ←
    the previous call to start() of restart().
```

Using QTime for timing purposes is straightforward, as the following example shows:

```
...
QTime t;
t.start();

do_something();

printf("Time elapsed %i (ms)\n", t.elapsed());
```

C.4 TIMING IN OPENMP

OpenMP provides a timing function in the form of

```
double omp_get_wtime ( void );
```

that returns the time elapsed from "some time in the past".

The resolution of the timer used is reported by:

```
double omp_get_wtick ( void );
```

The duration of a portion of a program can be estimated by subtracting two readings of the omp get wtime() function, as in the example shown below:

```
double timeStart, timeEnd;
timeStart = mpi_get_wtime();
. . . // do something
timeEnd = mpi_get_wtime();
cout << "Total time spent: " << timeEnd - timeStart << endl;
```

C.5 TIMING IN MPI

In terms of timing, MPI provides two functions: MPI_Wtime (wall time) and MPI_Wticks. The first reads the system clock; the second returns the clock's resolution in seconds per tick. Their syntax is the following:

```
double MPI_Wtime( void );
double MPI_Wtick( void );
```

MPI_Wtime returns the time since an unspecified time in the past. Therefore, a single returned value has no meaning, but by subtracting two readings of the function, we can measure a time span.

```
double timeStart, timeEnd;
timeStart = MPI_Wtime();
. . . // do something
timeEnd = MPI_Wtime();
cout << "Total time spent: " << timeEnd - timeStart << endl;
```

C.6 TIMING IN CUDA

Timing in CUDA is inherently tied to the use of events and streams, as explained in Section 6.7.7.1. CUDA kernel launches are asynchronous, i.e., the host returns immediately without waiting for the GPU to complete its assignment. The host can measure the timing of events on the GPU by inserting cudaEvent_t objects in streams.

An example of how events can be used to instrument a CUDA program is provided in Listing C.2.

```
1   . . .
2   cudaStream_t str;
3   cudaEvent_t startT, endT;
4   float duration;
5
6   // initialize two events
7   cudaEventCreate (&startT);
8   cudaEventCreate (&endT);
9
10  // enclose kernel launch between startT and endT events
11  cudaEventRecord (startT, str);
12  doSmt<<< grid, block, 0, str>>>(...);   // launch request has to be ←
        placed in a stream
13  cudaEventRecord (endT, str);
14
15  // wait for endT event to take place
16  cudaEventSynchronize (endT);
17
18  // calculate elapsed time
19  cudaEventElapsedTime (&duration, startT, endT);
20  printf("Kernel executed for %f\n", duration);
21
22  // clean-up allocated objects and reset device
23  cudaStreamDestroy (str);
24  cudaEventDestroy (startT);
25  cudaEventDestroy (endT);
26  cudaDeviceReset ();
27  . . .
```

LISTING C.2

An example of how a CUDA program can be instrumented with the use of events.

It should be noted that cudaEventRecord() in lines 11 and 13 (and subsequently the kernel launch of line 12) can be performed without an explicit stream parameter str. In that case, the cudaEventSynchronize() call of line 16 will return when all the preceding operations in the CUDA context have been completed. These may include operations created by different host threads.

Boost.MPI

D.1 MAPPING FROM MPI C TO BOOST.MPI

Table D.1 lists the most commonly used MPI functions and constants and their respective Boost.MPI counterparts. Only a subset of MPI functions is available through the Boost.MPI classes, but a program is allowed to have a mix of Boost.MPI methods and MPI C calls.

Table D.1 MPI functions and constants and their Boost.MPI counterparts

MPI	Boost.MPI
Various Functions	
MPI_Abort	environment::abort
MPI_Comm_size	communicator::size
MPI_Comm_rank	communicator::rank
MPI_Finalize	Called by environment destructor
MPI_Init	Called by environment constructor
Point-to-Point Communications	
MPI_Bsend	N/A
MPI_Buffer_attach	N/A
MPI_Buffer_detach	N/A
MPI_Get_count	status::count
MPI_Ibsend	N/A
MPI_Iprobe	communicator::iprobe
MPI_Irsend	N/A
MPI_Isend	communicator::isend
MPI_Issend	N/A
MPI_Irecv	communicator::irecv
MPI_Probe	communicator::probe
MPI_Recv	communicator::recv
MPI_Rsend	N/A

Continued

Table D.1 MPI functions and constants and their Boost.MPI counterparts
Continued

MPI_Send	communicator::send
MPI_Ssend	N/A
MPI_Test	request::test
MPI_Testall	test_all
MPI_Testany	test_any
MPI_Wait	request::wait
MPI_Waitall	wait_all
MPI_Waitany	wait_any

Constants

MPI_ANY_SOURCE	any_source
MPI_ANY_TAG	any_tag

Collective Communications

MPI_Allgather	all_gather
MPI_Allgatherv	N/A
MPI_Allreduce	all_reduce
MPI_Alltoall	all_to_all
MPI_Alltoallv	N/A
MPI_Barrier	communicator::barrier
MPI_Bcast	broadcast
MPI_Gather	gather
MPI_Gatherv	N/A
MPI_Reduce	reduce
MPI_Scan	scan
MPI_Scatter	scatter
MPI_Scatterv	N/A

Setting up CUDA

E.1 INSTALLATION

CUDA SDK installation is typically a trouble-free experience. Nvidia has shifted in recent SDK releases to a single archive approach: You just have to download a single file from https://developer.nvidia.com/cuda-downloads and either run it (if you select the executable one), or feed it to your system software administration tool in the case of Linux or Mac OS X (if you select the deb/rpm/pkg one). The single archive contains the Nvidia tool chain in addition to reference and tutorial documentation, and sample programs.

Nvidia's site is the ultimate source of information for proper installation steps. In this section we highlight some of the pitfalls that can plague someone making their first steps into the CUDA world:

- Always install the Nvidia display driver that accompanies the CUDA release you select to install, or a newer one. Failure to do so may cause your CUDA programs, or even the samples that come with the toolkit, to fail to run, even if they manage to compile without a problem.
- In multiuser systems such as Linux, a CUDA sample programs installation on a system-wide location (e.g., /opt or /usr) will create problems for users who try to compile or modify these programs due to permission limitations. In that case, we have to copy the entire samples directory to our home directory to perform any of these actions.

E.2 ISSUES WITH GCC

The Nvidia Cuda Compiler driver has been known to have incompatibility problems with newer GCC versions. The remedy to obtain a properly working tool chain is to install an older GCC version. In the case of the Ubuntu Linux distribution, the following commands will accomplish just that (for this particular example, version 4.4 was chosen, but the ultimate choice depends on the CUDA SDK installed and the particular Linux distribution):

```
$ sudo update-alternatives --install /usr/bin/gcc gcc /usr/bin/gcc-4.4↩
    50
$ sudo update-alternatives --config gcc
```

The response to the last command is the following prompt that allows the switch to the alternate C compiler:

Selection	Path	Priority	Status
0	/usr/bin/g++-4.7	50	auto mode
1	/usr/bin/g++-4.4	10	manual mode
* 2	/usr/bin/g++-4.7	50	manual mode

```
Press enter to keep the current choice[*], or type selection number:
```

The same sequence should be repeated separately for the C++ compiler:

```
$ sudo update-alternatives --install /usr/bin/g++ g++ /usr/bin/g++-4.4↩
    50
$ sudo update-alternatives --config g++
```

As mentioned, this is a CUDA SDK version-specific issue, so your mileage may vary. For example, CUDA 6.5.14 is able to work properly with GCC 4.8.2, successfully compiling all Nvidia-supplied CUDA sample projects.

E.3 RUNNING CUDA WITHOUT AN Nvidia GPU

CUDA is available in all the GPUs that Nvidia has been producing for some time. However, there is still a big market share of machines that are equipped with AMD's, GPUs or Intel's graphics solutions, neither of which are capable of running CUDA programs. Fortunately, there are two solutions:

1. Emulate a CUDA GPU on the CPU by compiling CUDA programs with the `-deviceemu` switch. Example:

```
$ nvcc -deviceemu hello.cu -o hello
$ ./hello
```

The problem with this approach is that the `-deviceemu` switch has been deprecated. The last CUDA release supporting it is 2.3. Although we can still download and use this version, it requires an old GCC compiler (version 4.3), which is no longer available as an option in the majority of the contemporary Linux distributions. Additionally, recent CUDA releases have a wealth of additional features that make the use of CUDA 2.3 a viable option only if we fail to use the alternative given next.

2. Use the **Ocelot**[1] framework. Ocelot is a dynamic compilation framework (i.e., code is compiled at run-time) providing various back-end targets for CUDA programs. Ocelot allows CUDA programs to be executed on both AMD GPUs and x86-CPUs. Employing Ocelot requires a number of additional steps during compilation. Here is an example for a CUDA program called `hello.cu`. The first step involves the compilation of the device code into PTX format:

```
$ nvcc -arch=sm_20 -cuda hello.cu -o hello.cu.cpp
```

---

[1] http://code.google.com/p/gpuocelot/, last visited in July 2013.

The `hello.cu.cpp` file that is produced contains the device PTX code in the form of an array of bytes. The next step compiles the intermediate source code into an object file:

```
$ g++ -o hello.cu.o -c -Wall -g hello.cu.cpp
```

The last step links the object file (or files, for larger projects) with the Ocelot shared library, along with a number of libraries required by Ocelot (GLU, GLEW, and glut) into the final executable file:

```
$ g++ -o hello hello.cu.o -lglut -locelot -lGLEW -lGLU -L/usr/l/↵
    checkout/gpuocelot/ocelot/build_local/lib/
```

In this code, the `-L` switch points to the location where the Ocelot library is installed.

The only concern with using Ocelot for running CUDA programs is that certain attributes of the virtual platform may not match what is normally expected from a physical GPU, making code that adapts to GPU characteristics (such as the number of SMs) likely to fail or to perform in unexpected ways. For example, `warpSize` is set equal to the block size.

E.4 RUNNING CUDA ON OPTIMUS-EQUIPPED LAPTOPS

Nvidia Optimus is an energy-saving technology that automatically performs GPU switching, i.e., switching between two graphics adapters, based on the workload generated by client applications. The two adapters are typically an Intel CPU-integrated unit that draws minimum power but has low performance and an Nvidia GPU that offers higher performance at the expense of more power consumption.

On Linux, the switch between the two GPUs is not seamless; instead it requires a third party software called Bumblebee.[2] Distribution-specific installation instructions are provided at http://bumblebee-project.org/install.html. In Ubuntu, Bumblebee can be installed with the following commands that ensure the respective repository is added to the system prior to the installation procedure:

```
$ sudo add-apt-repository ppa:bumblebee/stable
$ sudo apt-get update
$ sudo apt-get install bumblebee bumblebee-nvidia virtualgl
```

A program that requires the use of the Nvidia GPU for *graphical display* should be invoked, as the following example illustrates:

```
$ optirun glxspheres64
Polygons in scene: 62464
Visual ID of window: 0x20
Context is Direct
OpenGL Renderer: GeForce GTX 870M/PCIe/SSE2
```

---

[2] http://bumblebee-project.org.

```
322.733922 frames/sec — 360.171056 Mpixels/sec
325.732381 frames/sec — 363.517338 Mpixels/sec
322.636157 frames/sec — 360.061951 Mpixels/sec
```

where the `optirun` command is the GPU switcher provided by Bumblebee, and `glxspheres64` is a program used to test graphics performance in OpenGL.

The use of `optirun` is not required if the CUDA program does not utilize screen graphics capabilities.

E.5 COMBINING CUDA WITH THIRD-PARTY LIBRARIES

Nvidia offers Parallel NSight as the primary IDE for CUDA development on all supported platforms. However, Parallel NSight does not accommodate easy integration into a project of other tools such as Qt's toolchain. Although the sequence of commands is straighforward, making NSight or Qt's `qmake` generate this sequence is a challenge. For this reason we present a makefile that can perform this task while at the same time being easy to modify and adapt.

The key points are:

- Have all `.cu` files *compiled* separately by `nvcc`. The compilation has to generate relocatable device code (`-device-c`).
- Have all the `.c`/`.cpp` files that do not contain device code *compiled* separately by `gcc`/`g++`.
- Have all the object files `.o` *linked* by `nvcc`. The linking has to generate relocatable device code (`-rdc=true`).

During compilation, all the necessary include file directories should be supplied. Similarly, during the linking process, all the library directories and dynamic/static libraries needed, must be specified.

We use the fractal generation test case of Section 5.12.1 as an example. That particular project is made up of the following files:

- `kernel.cu`: Contains device code for calculating the Mandelbrot fractal set. It also contains a host front-end function for launching the kernel, copying the results from the device to the host, and using them to color the pixels of a `QImage` object. Hence it needs to include Qt header files.
- `kernel.h`: Header file containing the declaration of the host function that launches the GPU kernel. Needed by `main.cpp`.
- `main.cpp`: Program entry point responsible for parsing user input, calling the host front-end function in `kernel.cu`, and saving the output with the assistance of Qt.

Given the above, the following makefile can be used to compile and link the project:

```
NVCC = nvcc
CC = g++
```

```
CUDA_COMPILE_FLAGS = --device-c -arch=compute_20 -code=sm_21
CUDA_LINK_FLAGS = -rdc=true -arch=compute_20 -code=sm_21

QT_COMPILE_FLAGS = -I/usr/include/qt5/QtCore  -I/usr/include/qt5/QtGui↩
    -I/usr/include/qt5
QT_LINK_FLAGS = -L/usr/lib/x86_64-linux-gnu -lQtGui -lQtCore -lpthread

mandelbrotCUDA: main.o kernel.o
        ${NVCC} ${CUDA_LINK_FLAGS} ${QT_LINK_FLAGS} $^ -o $@

main.o: main.cpp kernel.h
        ${CC} ${QT_COMPILE_FLAGS} -c main.cpp

kernel.o: kernel.cu kernel.h
        ${NVCC} ${CUDA_COMPILE_FLAGS} ${QT_COMPILE_FLAGS} -c kernel.cu

clean:
        rm *.o
```

In the above, the automatic variable $@ represents the target, i.e., mandel-brotCUDA for that particular rule, and $^ represents all the dependencies listed.

A similar procedure can be applied for integrating MPI and CUDA, or any possible combination of tools. As an example, let's consider the makefile used in the MPI-CUDA implementation of the AES block cipher described in Section 5.12.2. This makefile describes the creation of three targets, two standalone GPU implementations, aesCUDA and aesCUDAStreams, and the MPI-enhanced version aesMPI:

```
NVCC = nvcc
CC = g++
CUDA_LINK_FLAGS = -rdc=true -arch=compute_20 -code=sm_21
CUDA_COMPILE_FLAGS = -g --device-c -arch=compute_20 -code=sm_21
CC_COMPILE_FLAGS = -g -I/usr/include/openmpi
CC_LINK_FLAGS = -lm -lstdc++ -lmpi -L/usr/lib -lpthread -lmpi_cxx

all: aesMPI aesCUDA aesCUDAStreams

aesMPI: main.o rijndael_host.o rijndael_device.o
    ${NVCC} ${CUDA_LINK_FLAGS} ${CC_LINK_FLAGS} $^ -o $@

main.o: main.cpp rijndael.h
    ${CC} ${CC_COMPILE_FLAGS} -c main.cpp

rijndael_host.o: rijndael_host.cu rijndael.h rijndael_device.h
    ${NVCC} ${CUDA_COMPILE_FLAGS} ${CC_COMPILE_FLAGS} -c rijndael_host↩
        .cu

rijndael_device.o: rijndael_device.cu rijndael.h rijndael_device.h
    ${NVCC} ${CUDA_COMPILE_FLAGS} ${CC_COMPILE_FLAGS} -c ↩
        rijndael_device.cu
```

```
aesCUDA: aesCUDA.o rijndael_host.o rijndael_device.o
    ${NVCC} ${CUDA_LINK_FLAGS} ${CC_LINK_FLAGS} $^ -o $@

aesCUDA.o: aesCUDA.cu rijndael.h
    ${NVCC} ${CUDA_COMPILE_FLAGS} ${CC_COMPILE_FLAGS} -c aesCUDA.cu

aesCUDAStreams: aesCUDA.o rijndael_host_streams.o rijndael_device.o
    ${NVCC} ${CUDA_LINK_FLAGS} ${CC_LINK_FLAGS} $^ -o $@

rijndael_host_streams.o: rijndael_host_streams.cu rijndael.h ↩
    rijndael_device.h
    ${NVCC} ${CUDA_COMPILE_FLAGS} ${CC_COMPILE_FLAGS} -c ↩
        rijndael_host_streams.cu

clean:
    rm *.o
```

An issue that can be encountered is that the third-party libraries to be linked with your project require the generation of "position-independent code." This can be accomplished by the use of the -fPIC or -fPIE compiler flags. These flags cannot be passed directly to nvcc, but they have to "pass through" to the GCC compiler. The appropriate nvcc flag to achieve this is: -Xcompiler '-fPIC'.

DLTlib

F

F.1 DLTlib FUNCTIONS

The library does break good software engineering practices by making a number of data members public. The reason for this violation is just convenience, given the primary use of the library as a research tool.

The mathematical underpinnings of the library have been published in [19] and [12]. These publications contain a far more extended analysis than the one allowed by a reference appendix.

The library provides methods for solving the partitioning and optimum node subset problems for three categories of problems:

- **Query processing**: Class of problems whereby the communication cost does not depend on the workload. Conceptually, it is similar to running a query on the records of a database. The overall execution time depends on the size of the tables, but the communication involves only a query statement and a result set.
- **Image processing**: Class of problems whereby the communication is linearly dependent on the size of the workload. Low-level image filtering is a characteristic example.
- **Image registration (aka image query)**: A mix of the previous two cases whereby the distribution cost depends on the workload, but the collection cost does not. Distribution cost entails the communication of the images against which a comparison is made, whereas the collection cost only accounts for the indices (and possibly comparison metrics) of the best matches.

The library is built around two classes: Node and Network. Tables F.1 and F.2 list the most significant data components of Node and Network, respectively. The notations used in these tables refer to the cost models of Section 7.4.1, i.e., Equations 7.5, 7.7, and 7.8, that we also list here for convenience:

$$t_{comp}^{(i)} = p_i(part_i \cdot L + e_i)$$

$$t_{distr}^{(i)} = l_i(a \cdot part_i \cdot L + b)$$

$$t_{coll}^{(i)} = l_i(c \cdot part_i \cdot L + d)$$

Table F.1 Short reference of structure `Node`. Fields are listed in alphabetical order

Field	Type	Description
child	Node *[]	Array of pointers to children nodes
collection_order	int	Used in the one-port image query to encode the suggested collection order
degree	int	The number of children of this Node
e0	double	The constant part of the computation
L	double	The load assigned to *tree* rooted at this node
Lint	long	The "quantized" load assigned to this node (not to subtree)
l2par	double	Link to parent, i.e., l_i
mi_part	double[]	Array of parts, one for each installment
name	char[]	Identifier used for this node
next_n	Node *	Pointer to the next Node structure in a linked list
parent	Node *	Pointer to the parent Node
part	double	The part of the computation assigned to a Node, in the case of one installment only
power	double	Corresponds to p_i
through	char	A value of 1 indicates that the Node is not participating in the computation (e.g., too slow), instead sending all its received load to its children

Table F.2 Short reference of data members of class `Network`

Field	Type	Description
head	Node *	Points to the first in a linked-list of Node instances. Can be used to traverse the list and examine a solution.
valid	char	Set to 1 by the methods to indicate if a solution to a partitioning problem is feasible and correct. It should be checked immediately after a partitioning is attempted.
clipping	char	Set by Quantify method to 1 if the set of current nodes has redundant items, i.e., a subset should be used.

The following subsections summarize the most important methods offered by the `Network` class, categorized by the target partitioning problem they address.

F.1.1 CLASS Network: GENERIC METHODS

```
// Removes Nodes with no assigned load from a Network
void ClipIdleNodes();

// Generates a random tree according to the given parameters
void GenerateRandomTree(
            bool ImageOrQuery,  // 0: query, 1: image proc.
            int N,              // number of nodes
```

```
          float min_p,          // minimum p_i
          float max_p,          // maximum p_i
          float min_l,          // minimum l_i
          float max_l,          // maximum l_i
          float min_e,          // minimum e_i
          float max_e,          // maximum e_i
          bool fultree=false ,// If true, the interal nodes will
                              // be filled-up with children, up
                              // to the maximum degree specified
                              // by the MAX_NODE_DEGREE constant
          bool all_fe=false );// All nodes have comm. front-end?

// Inserts a Node in a Network and returns a reference to it
Node* InsertNode(char *c,          // Name of node
              double speed,        // p_i
              double e,            // e_i
              char *parent,        // Name of parent
              double link2parent,// l_i
              bool fe = false ,    // Comm. front-end equipped?
              bool thru = false );// Is it a "conductor" node? I.e.
                                  // does it participate in the
                                  // computation?

// Overloaded version of the previous method. A reference to the  <-
    parent Node is passed instead of its name
Node* InsertNode(char *c,
              double speed,
              double e,
              Node *parent,
              double link2parent,
              bool fe = false ,
              bool thru = false );

// Prints to standard output a description of the Node objects managed<->
    by a Network
void PrintNet(void);

// Prints the assigned parts to a Network's nodes
void PrintSolution(bool quantized = 0); // If set to true, the Lint  <-
    field is used

// Rounds the assigned loads, to integer quantities. It returns the  <-
    estimated execution time
double Quantify( bool ImageOrQuery, // 0: query, 1: image processing
              double ab,           // contains the 'a' parameter for
                                  // image, or 'b' otherwise
              double cd);          // contains the 'c' parameter for
                                  // image, or 'd' otherwise

// Generates a random tree by reusing the existing nodes of a Network.<->
    Parameters are identical to the GenerateRandomTree method
void ReUseRandomTree(
```

```
                   bool ImageOrQuery,
                   float min_p,
                   float max_p,
                   float min_l,
                   float max_l,
                   float min_e,
                   float max_e,
                   bool full_tree = false ,
                   bool all_fe = false );
```

F.1.2 **CLASS** Network: **QUERY PROCESSING**

The term *query processing* refers to a scenario in which the communication costs are independent from the workload that is to be partitioned. In other words, we have $a = c = 0$ in Equations 7.7 and 7.8. The following methods assume the use of one-port communications and a single installment load distribution, but they can solve the problem for arbitrary trees of Node instances.

```
// Uses a greedy algorithm to find the best subset from the available ←
      nodes, that can process a workload. The algorithm adds nodes one—←
      by—one, as long as the execution time decreases.
void GreedyQuery(Network &s, // Reference to the best performing
                             // subset of nodes (OUT)
              long L,        // Workload
              double b,      // Comm. model parameters
              double d);     //


// Similar to GreedyQuery, with the exception that the algorithm ←
      starts from the complete machine and attempts to remove leaf nodes←
      one—by—one, as long as the execution time decreases.
void GreedyQueryRev(
              Network &s, // Reference to the best performing
                          // subset of nodes (OUT)
              long L,     // Workload
              double b,   // Comm. model parameters
              double d);  //


// Implements an exhaustive algorithm for finding the optimum node ←
      subset. It can be very time—consuming
void OptimumQuery(
              Network &s, // Reference to the optimum performing
                          // subset of nodes (OUT)
              long L,     // Workload
              double b,   // Comm. model parameters
              double d);  //


// Determines the execution time for a load that has been partitioned ←
      already, not necessarily using DLT
double SimulateQuery(
              double b,            // Comm. model parameters
              double d,            //
              bool output = 1); // By default results are also
```

```
                                    // dumped to standard output

// Applies the DLT formulas for calculating the optimum assignement to↩
    a given set of nodes. Calculated parts are stored in the "part" ↩
    field of each Node structure
void SolveQuery( long L,          // Workload
                double b,         // Comm. model parameters
                double d,         //
                bool plain = 0);  // Should be set to 0 or omitted


// Similar to the GreedyQuery method, but specifically addressing ↩
    homogeneous parallel platforms, p_i=p, l_i=l
void UniformQueryGreedy(
                Network &s,// Reference to the best performing
                           // subset of nodes (OUT)
                long L,    // Workload
                double b,  // Comm. model parameters
                double d); //
```

F.1.3 CLASS Network: IMAGE PROCESSING

The term *image processing* refers to a scenario in which the communication costs are linearly dependent from the workload that is to be partitioned. In other words, we have $b = d = 0$ in Equations 7.7 and 7.8. Additionally, it is assumed that the communication media are uniform, i.e., $l_i \equiv l$, at least as far as the children of each individual node are concerned.

The following methods assume the use of one-port communications and a single installment load distribution, but they can solve the problem for arbitrary trees of Node instances.

```
// Uses a greedy algorithm to find the best subset from the available ↩
    nodes, that can process a workload. The algorithm adds nodes one-↩
    by-one, as long as the execution time decreases.
void GreedyImage(Network &s, // Reference to the best performing
                             // subset of nodes (OUT)
                long L,      // Workload
                double a,    // Comm. model parameters
                double c);


// Uses a greedy algorithm to find the best subset from the available ↩
    nodes, that can process a workload. The algorithm starts from the ↩
    complete machine and attempts to remove leaf nodes one-by-one, as ↩
    long as the execution time decreases.
void GreedyImageRev(
                Network &s,  // Reference to the best performing
                             // subset of nodes (OUT)
                long L,      // Workload
                double a,    // Comm. model parameters
                double c);
```

```
// Implements an exhaustive algorithm for finding the optimum node ↩
    subset. It can be very time-consuming
void OptimumImage(
                Network &s, // Reference to the optimum performing
                            // subset of nodes (OUT)
                long L,     // Workload
                double a,   // Comm. model parameters
                double c);

// Determines the execution time for a load that has been partitioned ↩
    already, not necessarily using DLT
double SimulateImage(
                double a,           // Comm. model parameters
                double c,           // //
                bool output = 1); // By default results are also
                                    // dumped to standard output

// Applies the DLT formulas for calculating the optimum assignement to↩
    a given set of nodes. Calculated parts are stored in the "part" ↩
    field of each Node structure
void SolveImage( long L,         // Workload
                double a,         // Comm. model parameters
                double c,         // //
                bool plain = 0);// Should be set to 0 or omitted


void UniformQueryGreedy(
                Network &s, // Reference to the best performing
                            // subset of nodes (OUT)
                long L,     // Workload
                double b,   // Comm. model parameters
                double d); // //

// Similar to the GreedyImage method, but specifically addressing ↩
    homogeneous parallel platforms, p_i=p, l_i=l
void UniformImageGreedy(
                Network &s, // Reference to the best performing
                            // subset of nodes (OUT)
                long L,     // Workload
                double a,   // Comm. model parameters
                double c); // //
```

F.1.4 CLASS Network: IMAGE REGISTRATION

In this case, which is also known as image query, the distribution cost depends on the workload, but the collection cost does not. The following methods cover almost all possible communication setups, but they can solve the problem for single-level node trees only. By default, all methods assume single installment distribution using one-port communications and block-type computation. The naming convention used for methods covering other scenarios is to add one or more of the following extensions:

- NInst: Using $M \geq 2$ installments
- NPort: N-port communication
- ST: Stream-type computation

A major difference between the following methods and the ones listed in Sections F.1.2 and F.1.3 is that these can cater for multiple executions, where the workload is distributed during the first execution and possibly rebalanced during subsequent ones. The key idea is that each time a new image is to be compared against a pool of images, the latter do not have to be communicated again to the compute nodes. The term used here is *embedding*, i.e., making the previously used images a part of the local or resident workload. The resident load is represented by the e_i parameter of the Node objects (field e0).

```
// Makes workload L, part of the resident load
void ImageQueryEmbed(long L);

// Makes workload L that was distributed over M installments , part of ↩
    the resident load
void ImageQueryEmbed_Ninst(
                long L,   // Workload
                int M);   // Number of installments


// Estimates and returns the execution time, for arbitrarily ↩
    partitioned loads
double SimulateImageQuery_Nport(
                long L,                   // Workload
                long b,                   // Comm. model parameters
                double d,                 //
                bool isstream = false);   // Set to true for
                                          // stream-type computation

// Estimates and returns the execution time, for arbitrarily ↩
    partitioned loads
double SimulateImageQuery_ST(
                long L,   // Workload
                long b,   // Comm. model parameters
                double d);//

// Estimates and returns the execution time, for arbitrarily ↩
    partitioned loads
double SimulateImageQuery(
                long L,   // Workload
                long b,   // Comm. model parameters
                double d); //
```

```
// Solves the partitioning problem, for multiple installments and N-
//    port. Returns the execution time.
double SolveImageQuery_NInst_NPort(
               long L,     // Workload
               long b,     // Comm. model parameters
               double d,   //
               int M);     // Number of installments
```

```
// Solves the partitioning problem for multiple installments optimally
//    , and returns the execution time. Distribution and collection
//    sequences are found via exhaustive search. L and b parameters may
//    be modified in the case of stream-type computation for proper
//    timing. Works for single installment as well.
double SolveImageQuery_NInst_Optimum(
               long &L,                 // Workload (IN/OUT)
               long &b,                 // Comm. model parameters
                                        // (IN/OUT)
               double d,                //
               int M,                   // Number of installments
               bool blocktype = true,   // Selects between
                                        // block and stream type
               double *worstp = NULL);  // Execution time of worst
                                        // possible sequences. Just
                                        // for comparison (OUT)
```

```
// Solves the partitioning problem for multiple installments and
//    returns the execution time. Distribution and collection sequences
//    are heuristically found. L and b parameters may be modified for
//    timing purposes, if the nodes hold no resident load.
double SolveImageQuery_NInst_ST(
               long &L,    // Workload (IN/OUT)
               long &b,    // Comm. model parameters (IN/OUT)
               double d,   //
               int M);     // Number of installments
```

```
// Solves the partitioning problem for multiple installments and
//    returns the execution time. Distribution and collection sequences
//    are heuristically found.
double SolveImageQuery_NInst(
               long L,     // Workload
               long b,     // Comm. model parameters
               double d,   //
               int M);     // Number of installments
```

```
// Solves the partitioning problem for a single installment, stream-
//    type computation, and returns the execution time.
double SolveImageQuery_NPort_ST(
               long &L,    // Workload(IN/OUT)
               long b,     // Comm. model parameters
               double d);  //
```

```
// Solves the partitioning problem for a single installment, N-port ←
    communications, and returns the execution time. L is passed by ←
    reference to allow resident load rebalancing
double SolveImageQuery_NPort(
                long &L,   // Workload(IN/OUT)
                long b,    // Comm. model parameters
                double d); //


// Solves the partitioning problem for a single installment, 1-port ←
    communications, and returns the execution time. L is passed by ←
    reference to allow resident load rebalancing
double SolveImageQuery(
                long &L,                 // Workload (IN/OUT)
                long b,                  // Comm. model parameters
                double d,                //
                bool blocktype = true,   // Selects block (default) or
                                         // stream-type computation
                bool firstcall = false,  // Set to true to indicate
                                         // the first image query run
                bool equalLoad = true);  // If true, causes the load
                                         // to be equally partitioned.
                                         // This is reserved for runs
                                         // following the first one.


// Simplified version of method SolveImageQuery, for homogeneous ←
    platforms
double SolveImageQueryHomogeneous(
                long &L,        // Workload (IN/OUT)
                long b,         // Comm. model parameters
                double d,       //
                bool firstcall);// If true, causes the load to be
                                // equally partitioned. This is
                                // reserved for runs following the
                                // first one.
```

F.2 DLTLIB FILES

Table F.3 contains a list of the files that make up the library. These can reside either within the directory of the project that uses them or at a systemwide centralized location (e.g., /usr/include and /usr/lib) for all users to access.

Table F.3 A list of the files that make up the DLTlib library

File	Description
dltlib.cpp	Contains the source code of all the required methods. This is the only file that needs to be included if the library is compiled as part of another source code file.
dltlib.h	Only file that needs to be included if dltlib.cpp is compiled separately.
node_que.cpp	Contains a Queue class definition that is used for Node management.
random.c	Contains a number of pseudo-random number-generation functions. The file is included directly in dltlib.cpp
random.h	Header file for random.c. This file needs to be included only if a program needs to directly use the supplied functions.

Glossary

activation frame A memory block reserved in the run-time stack that serves for storing function parameters and the return address upon calling a function.

activation record see activation frame.

communicator A group of processes in MPI. Processes inside a communicator are sequentially indexed starting from 0. The default communicator that incorporates all processes is `MPI_COMM_WORLD`.

functor A C++ function object, i.e., an instance of a class that overloads `operator()`, the "function call" operator.

iteration space dependency graph A graph used to visualize the iterations performed by a loop or a set of nested loops, and the data dependencies between them. The nodes in this graph represent iterations and the edges represent flow of data.

kernel fusion The action of combining two or more CUDA kernels into one so that memory access and transfer overheads are eliminated.

managed memory Term used to describe two memory regions, one on the CPU/host and one on the GPU/device, that are maintained so that they stay coherent (i.e., holding the same data) by the device driver.

Message-Passing Interface A standard specification for a library aimed at writing portable programs for distributed memory platforms.

MPI See Message-Passing Interface.

MPMD See Multiple-Program, Multiple-Data.

Multiple-Program, Multiple-Data A software construction paradigm for distributed-memory machines, where each node runs a different program while also operating on different data.

NoW Network of Workstations, a term loosely used to describe an intranet of computers running parallel software.

occupancy The ratio of resident warps in a GPU over the maximum possible resident warps.

SIMD See Single-Instruction Multiple Data.

SIMT See Single Instruction Multiple Threads.

Single Instruction Multiple Threads Nvidia's GPU execution model, where multiple threads operating on different data are executing synchronously the same instruction sequence.

Single-Instruction Multiple Data One of the categories of Flynn's computer taxonomy, where multiple processing elements operate on multiple data, following the same instruction sequence.

Single-Program, Multiple-Data A software construction paradigm for distributed-memory machines where the same program runs on all the nodes but it operates on different data.

SM See Streaming Multiprocessor.

SP See Streaming Processor.

SPMD See Single-Program, Multiple Data.

Streaming Multiprocessor A group of CUDA cores that execute under the control of a single control unit, i.e., all running the same instruction at any time instance.

Streaming Processor Also referred to as CUDA core.

warp A set of CUDA threads that run on a SM as a unit, i.e., executing synchronously the same instruction.

Bibliography

[1] IBM's Elastic Storage, http://www-03.ibm.com/systems/platformcomputing/products/gpfs/. Last accessed September 2014.

[2] Parallel Virtual File System v2, http://www.pvfs.org/. Last accessed September 2014.

[3] *Writing reentrant and threadsafe code*, IBM Knowledge Center, http://www-01.ibm.com/support/knowledgecenter/ssw_aix_71/com.ibm.aix.genprogc/writing_reentrant_thread_safe_code.htm?cp=ssw_aix_71%2F12-3-12-18. Last accessed September 2014.

[4] Sudhir Ahuja, Nicholas Carriero, and David Gelernter. Linda and friends. *IEEE Computer*, 19(8):26–34, August 1986.

[5] Randy Allen and Ken Kennedy. *Optimizing Compilers for Modern Architectures: A Dependence-based Approach*. Number 978-1558602861. Morgan Kaufmann, 1 edition, 2001.

[6] D. H. Ballard. Generalizing the Hough transform to detect arbitrary shapes. *Pattern Recognition*, 13(2):111–122, 1981.

[7] Savina Bansal, Padam Kumar, and Kuldip Singh. An improved duplication strategy for scheduling precedence constrained graphs in multiprocessor systems. *IEEE Trans. on Parallel & Distributed Systems*, 14(6):533–544, June 2003.

[8] G. D. Barlas and Khaled El-Fakih. A GA-based Movie-on-Demand platform using multiple distributed servers. *Multimedia Tools and Applications*, 40(3):361–383, December 2008.

[9] Gerassimos Barlas. An analytical approach to optimizing parallel image registration/retrieval. *IEEE Trans. on Parallel & Distributed Systems*, 21(8):1074–1088, August 2010.

[10] Gerassimos Barlas. Cluster-based optimized parallel video transcoding. *Parallel Computing*, 38(4-5):226–244, April-May 2012.

[11] Gerassimos Barlas, Ahmed Hassan, and Yasser Al Jundi. An analytical approach to the design of parallel block cipher encryption/decryption: A CPU/GPU case study. In *Proc. of PDP 2011*, pages 247–251, Ayia Napa, Cyprus, February. 9-11, 2011.

[12] Gerassimos Barlas and Bharadwaj Veeravalli. Quantized load distribution for tree and bus connected processors. *Parallel Computing*, 30(7):841–865, July 2004.

[13] Gerassimos D. Barlas. Collection-aware optimum sequencing of operations and closed-form solutions for the distribution of a divisible load on arbitrary processor trees. *IEEE Trans. on Parallel & Distributed Systems*, 9(5):429–441, May 1998.

[14] Gerassimos D. Barlas and Bharadwaj Veeravalli. Optimized distributed delivery of continuous-media documents over unreliable communication links. *IEEE Trans. on Parallel & Distributed Systems*, 16(10), October 2005.

[15] Olivier Beaumont, Hubert Larcheveque, and Loris Marchal. Non linear divisible loads: There is no free lunch. In *2013 IEEE 27th International Symposium on Parallel & Distributed Processing*, pages 863–873, 2013.

[16] Rohit Chandra, Leo Dagum, David Kohr, Dror Maydan, Jeff McDonald, and Ramesh Menon. *Parallel Programming in OpenMP*. Number 1-55860-671-8. Morgan Kaufmann, 2001.

[17] Martin J. Chorley and David W. Walker. Performance analysis of a hybrid MPI/OpenMP application on multi-core clusters. *Journal of Computational Science*, 1(3):168–174, 2010.

[18] Shane Cook. *CUDA Programming: A Developer's Guide to Parallel Computing with GPUs*. ISBN-13: 978-0124159334. Morgan Kaufmann, 2012.

[19] Ian Foster. *Designing and Building Parallel Programs: Concepts and Tools for Parallel Software Engineering*. Addison-Wesley, 1995. ISBN 978-0201575941. Available at www.mcs.anl.gov/dbpp/. Last accessed October 2012.

[20] D. Ghose and H. J. Kim. Load partitioning and trade-off study for large matrix-vector computations in multicast bus networks with communication delays. *Journal of Parallel and Distributed Computing*, 55(1):32–59, 1998.

[21] Tao Gu, Qun Liao, Yulu Yang, and Tao Li. Scheduling divisible loads from multiple input sources in mapreduce. In *IEEE 16th International Conference on Computational Science and Engineering*, pages 1263–1270, 2013.

[22] Tom's Hardware Guide. AES-NI performance analyzed, limited to 32nm Core i5 CPUs. www.tomshardware.com/reviews/clarkdale-aes-ni-encryption,2538-5.html, February 2010. Last accessed September 2014.

[23] Maurice Herlihy and Nir Shavit. *The Art of Multiprocessor Programming*. ISBN-13: 978-0123973375. Morgan Kaufmann, 2012.

[24] Menglan Hu and Bharadwaj Veeravalli. Requirement-aware strategies with arbitrary processor release times for scheduling multiple divisible loads. *IEEE Trans. on Parallel & Distributed Systems*, 22(10):1967–1704, October 2011.

[25] Menglan Hu and Bharadwaj Veeravalli. Scheduling hybrid divisible and indivisible loads on clusters. In *17th IEEE International Conference on Networks (ICON)*, pages 141–146, December 2011.

[26] Jui Tsun Hung and Thomas G. Robertazzi. Scheduling nonlinear computational loads. *IEEE Transactions on Aerospace and Electronic Systems*, 44(3):1169 – 1182, July 2008.

[27] Aleksandar Ilic and Leonel Sousa. On realistic divisible load scheduling in highly heterogeneous distributed systems. In *20th Euromicro International Conference on Parallel, Distributed and Network-based Processing*, pages 426–433, 2012.

[28] J. Berlinska and M. Drozdowski. Heuristics for multi-round divisible loads scheduling with limited memory. *Parallel Computing*, 36(4):199–211, 2010.

[29] J. Berlinska and M. Drozdowski. Scheduling divisible mapreduce computations. *Journal of Parallel and Distributed Computing*, 71(3):450–459, March 2011.

[30] Jingxi Jia, Bharadwaj Veeravalli, and Jon Weissman. Scheduling multi-source divisible loads on arbitrary networks. *IEEE Trans. on Parallel & Distributed Systems*, 21(4):521–531, April 2010.

[31] George Kyriazis. Heterogeneous System Architecture: A technical review. http://amd-dev.wpengine.netdna-cdn.com/wordpress/media/2012/10/hsa10.pdf. Last accessed September 2014.

[32] Ping Li, Bharadwaj Veeravalli, and Ashraf A. Kassim. Design and implementation of parallel video encoding strategies using divisible load analysis. *IEEE Trans. on Circuits and Systems for Video Technology*, 15(9):1098–1112, September 2005.

[33] Timothy G. Mattson, Beverly A. Sanders, and Berna Massingill. *Patterns for Parallel Programming*. ISBN 0-321-22811-1. Addison-Wesley, 2005.

[34] Paul E. McKenney. Memory barriers: a hardware view for software hackers, April 2009. http://www.rdrop.com/users/paulmck/scalability/paper/whymb.2009.04.05a.pdf. Last accessed Aug. 2014.

[35] M. Drozdowski and M. Lawenda. Multi-installment divisible load processing in heterogeneous distributed systems. *Concurrency and Computation: Practice and Experience*, 19(17):2237–2253, December 2007.

[36] J. Montagnat, H. Duque1, J.M. Pierson, V. Breton, L. Brunie, and I. E. Magnin. Medical image content-based queries using the grid. In *Proc. of HealthGrid 03*, 2003.

[37] OpenMP ARB. *OpenMP Application Program Interface Version 4.0*, http://www.openmp.org/mp-documents/OpenMP4.0.0.pdf, July 2013. Last accessed September 2014.

[38] Rolf Rabenseifner, Georg Hager, and Gabriele Jost. Hybrid MPI/OpenMP parallel programming on clusters of multi-core SMP nodes. In *17th Euromicro Int. Conf. on Parallel, Distributed and Network-based Processing*, pages 427–436, February 2009.

[39] S. Suresh, Cui Run Hyoung Joong Kim, Thomas G. Robertazzi, and Young-Il Kim. Scheduling second-order computational load in master-slave paradigm. *IEEE Trans. on Aerospace and Electronic Systems*, 48(1):780–793, January 2012.

[40] Herb Sutter. Eliminate false sharing, May 2009. Dr. Dobb's Journal, http://www.drdobbs.com/parallel/eliminate-false-sharing/217500206. Last accessed September 2014.

[41] Bharadwaj Veeravalli and Gerassimos Barlas. *Distributed Multimedia Retrieval Strategies for Large Scale Networked Systems*. Springer, 2006. ISBN 0-387-28873-2.

[42] Bharadwaj Veeravalli, D. Ghose, V. Mani, and T.G. Robertazzi. *Scheduling Divisible Loads in Parallel and Distributed Systems*. IEEE Computer Society Press, Los Alamitos, California, 1996.

[43] Bharadwaj Veeravalli, Li Xiaolin, and Ko Chi Chung. Efficient partitioning and scheduling of computer vision and image processing data on bus networks using divisible load analysis. *Image and Vision Computing*, 18(11):919–938, 1999.

[44] Sivakumar Viswanathan, Bharadwaj Veeravalli, and Thomas G. Robertazzi. Resource-aware distributed scheduling strategies for large-scale computational cluster/grid systems. *IEEE Trans. on Parallel & Distributed Systems*, 18(10):1450–1461, October 2007.

[45] Vasily Volkov. Better performance at lower occupancy. http://www.cs.berkeley.edu/~volkov/volkov10-GTC.pdf, September 2010. Presentation at GTC 2010. Last accessed September 2014.

[46] George Wells. Coordination languages: Back to the future with Linda. In *Proc. of WCAT'05*, pages 87–98, 2005.

[47] Yang Yang, Henri Casanova, Maciej Drozdowski, Marcin Lawenda, and Arnaud Legrand. On the complexity of multi-round divisible load scheduling. Technical Report 6096, INRIA, January 2007.

[48] Jerry Zhao and Jelena Pjesivac-Grbovic. Mapreduce: The programming model and practice, 2009. http://research.google.com/archive/papers/mapreduce-sigmetrics09-tutorial.pdf. Last accessed September 2014.

Index

Note: Page numbers followed by *f* indicate figures, *t* indicate tables and *np* indicate footnote.

Printed in the United States
By Bookmasters